THE
BLACK CANARY
BIRD OF PREY

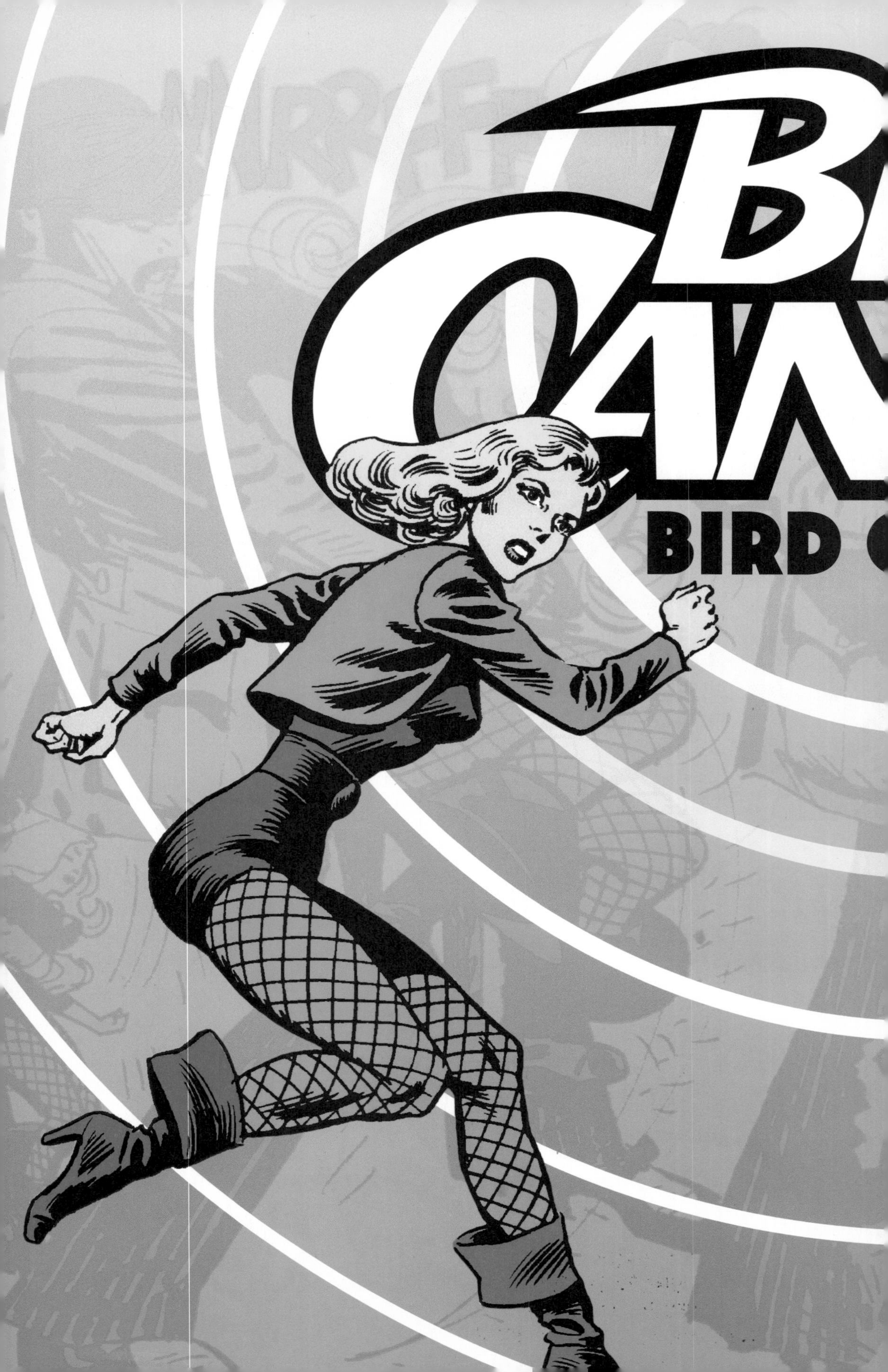
BIRD

THE ACK ARY PREY

writers **ROBERT KANIGHER** **GARDNER FOX** **DENNIS O'NEIL**

artists **CARMINE INFANTINO** **MURPHY ANDERSON** **ALEX TOTH**
JOE GIELLA **FRANK GIACOIA** **BERNARD SACHS**

collection cover artist **CARMINE INFANTINO**

SHELDON MAYER
JULIUS SCHWARTZ
MORT WEISINGER
MIKE SEKOWSKY
JOE ORLANDO Editors – Original Series
E. NELSON BRIDWELL
MARK HANERFELD Assistant Editors – Original Series
REZA LOKMAN Editor – Collected Edition
STEVE COOK Design Director – Books
MEGEN BELLERSEN Publication Design
TOM VALENTE Publication Production

MARIE JAVINS Editor-in-Chief, DC Comics

DANIEL CHERRY III Senior VP – General Manager
JIM LEE Publisher & Chief Creative Officer
DON FALLETTI VP – Manufacturing Operations & Workflow Management
LAWRENCE GANEM VP – Talent Services
ALISON GILL Senior VP – Manufacturing & Operations
NICK J. NAPOLITANO VP – Manufacturing Administration & Design
NANCY SPEARS VP – Revenue
MICHELE R. WELLS VP & Executive Editor, Young Reader

THE BLACK CANARY: BIRD OF PREY

DC Comics, 2900 West Alameda Ave., Burbank, CA 91505
Printed by LSC Communications, Owensville, MO, USA. 1/29/21. First Printing.
ISBN: 978-1-77950-908-6

Library of Congress Cataloging-in-Publication Data is available.

PEFC Certified
This product is from sustainably managed forests and controlled sources
PEFC
PEFC/29-31-337
www.pefc.org

TABLE OF CONTENTS

*Stories in parentheses were
originally untitled.

DC strives to be as thorough as possible in
its efforts to determine creators' identities
from all available sources. This process is not
perfect, and as a result, some attributions
may be incomplete or wrongly assigned.

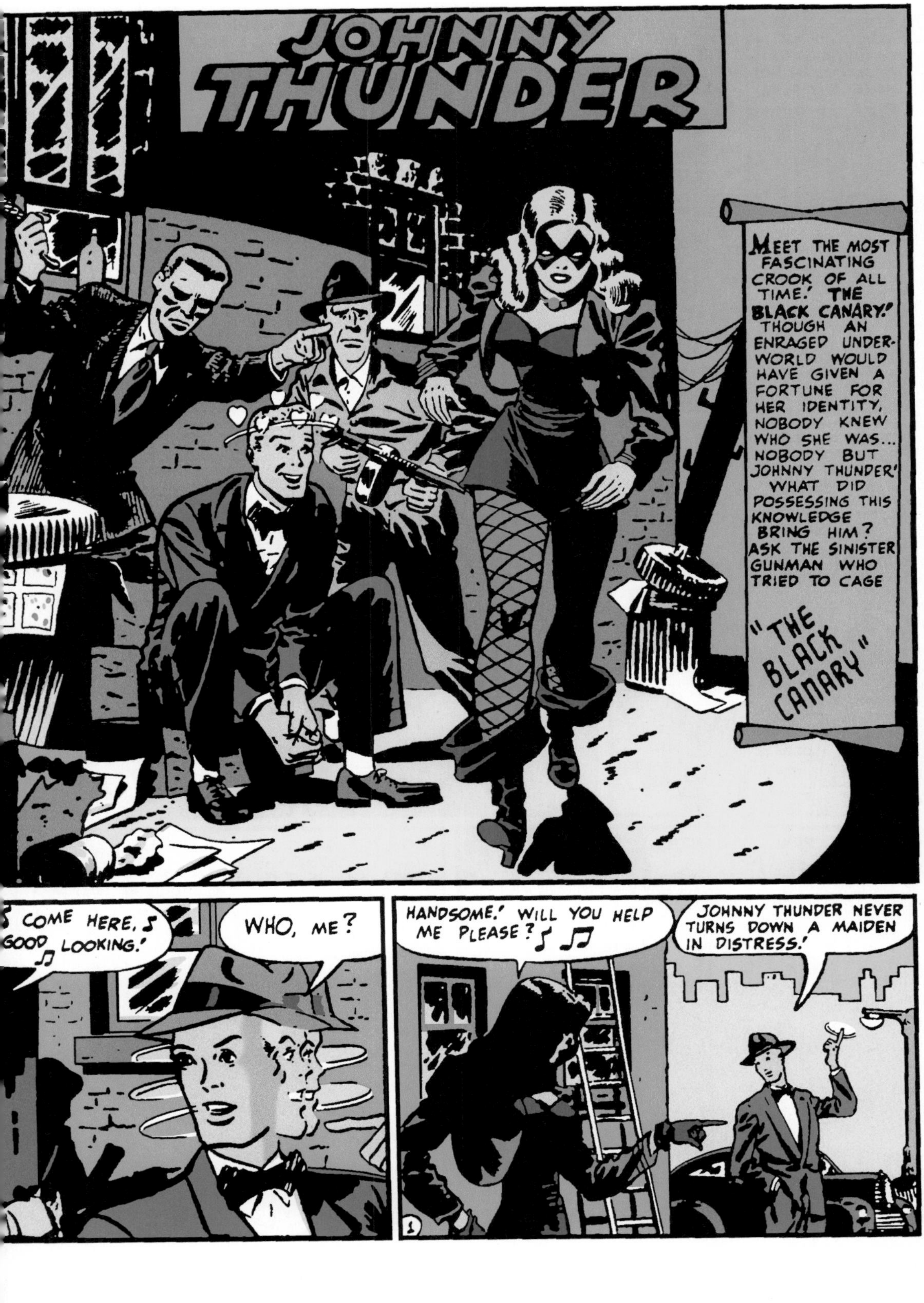
JOHNNY THUNDER
MEET THE MOST FASCINATING CROOK OF ALL TIME.' THE BLACK CANARY.' THOUGH AN ENRAGED UNDER-WORLD WOULD HAVE GIVEN A FORTUNE FOR HER IDENTITY, NOBODY KNEW WHO SHE WAS... NOBODY BUT JOHNNY THUNDER' WHAT DID POSSESSING THIS KNOWLEDGE BRING HIM? ASK THE SINISTER GUNMAN WHO TRIED TO CAGE
"THE BLACK CANARY"
COME HERE, GOOD LOOKING.'
WHO, ME?
HANDSOME.' WILL YOU HELP ME PLEASE?
JOHNNY THUNDER NEVER TURNS DOWN A MAIDEN IN DISTRESS.'

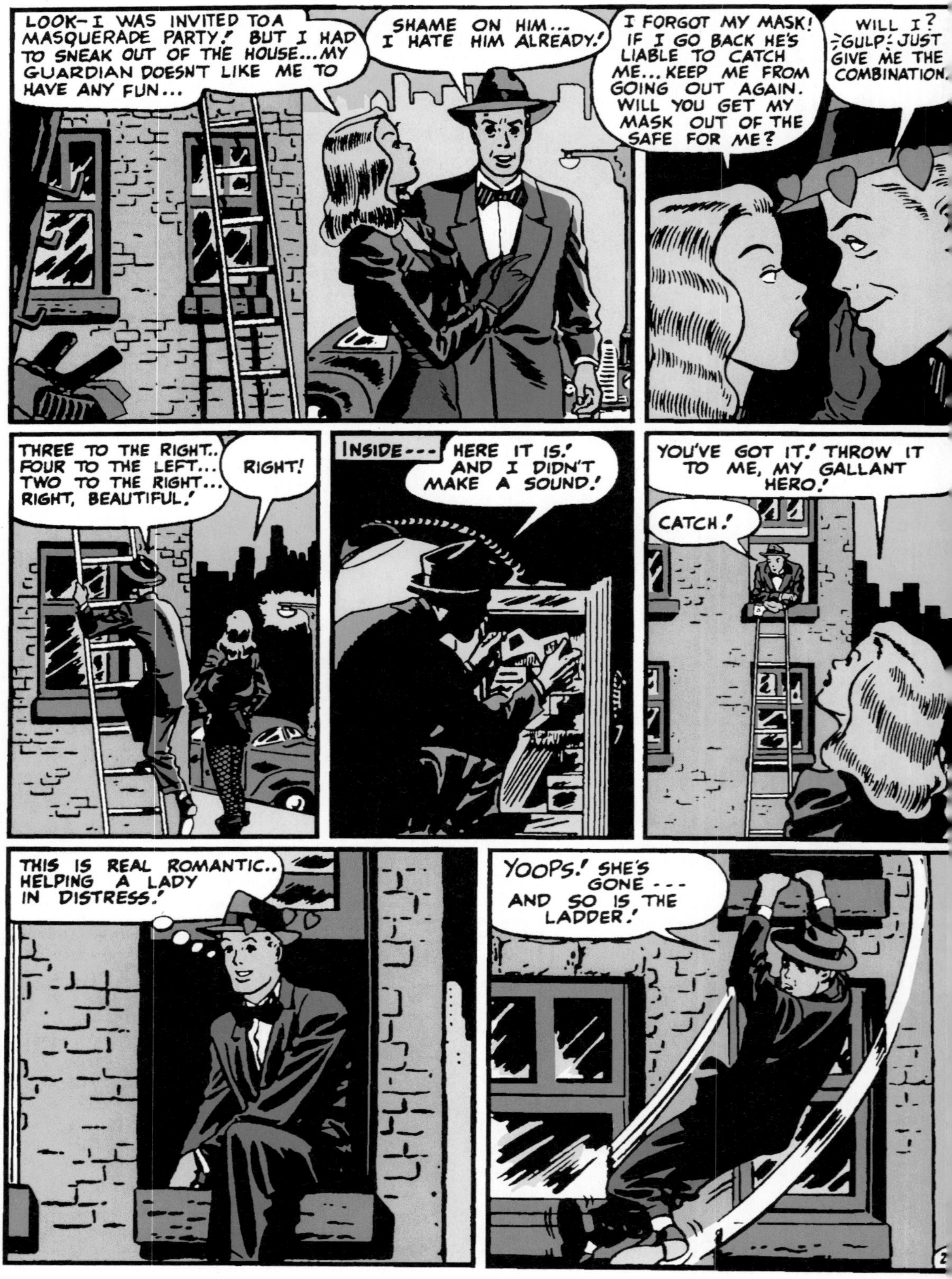
LOOK– I WAS INVITED TO A MASQUERADE PARTY! BUT I HAD TO SNEAK OUT OF THE HOUSE... MY GUARDIAN DOESN'T LIKE ME TO HAVE ANY FUN...
SHAME ON HIM... I HATE HIM ALREADY!
I FORGOT MY MASK! IF I GO BACK HE'S LIABLE TO CATCH ME... KEEP ME FROM GOING OUT AGAIN. WILL YOU GET MY MASK OUT OF THE SAFE FOR ME?
WILL I? –GULP!– JUST GIVE ME THE COMBINATION.
THREE TO THE RIGHT.. FOUR TO THE LEFT... TWO TO THE RIGHT... RIGHT, BEAUTIFUL!
RIGHT!
INSIDE---
HERE IT IS! AND I DIDN'T MAKE A SOUND!
YOU'VE GOT IT! THROW IT TO ME, MY GALLANT HERO!
CATCH!
THIS IS REAL ROMANTIC.. HELPING A LADY IN DISTRESS!
YOOPS! SHE'S GONE --- AND SO IS THE LADDER!

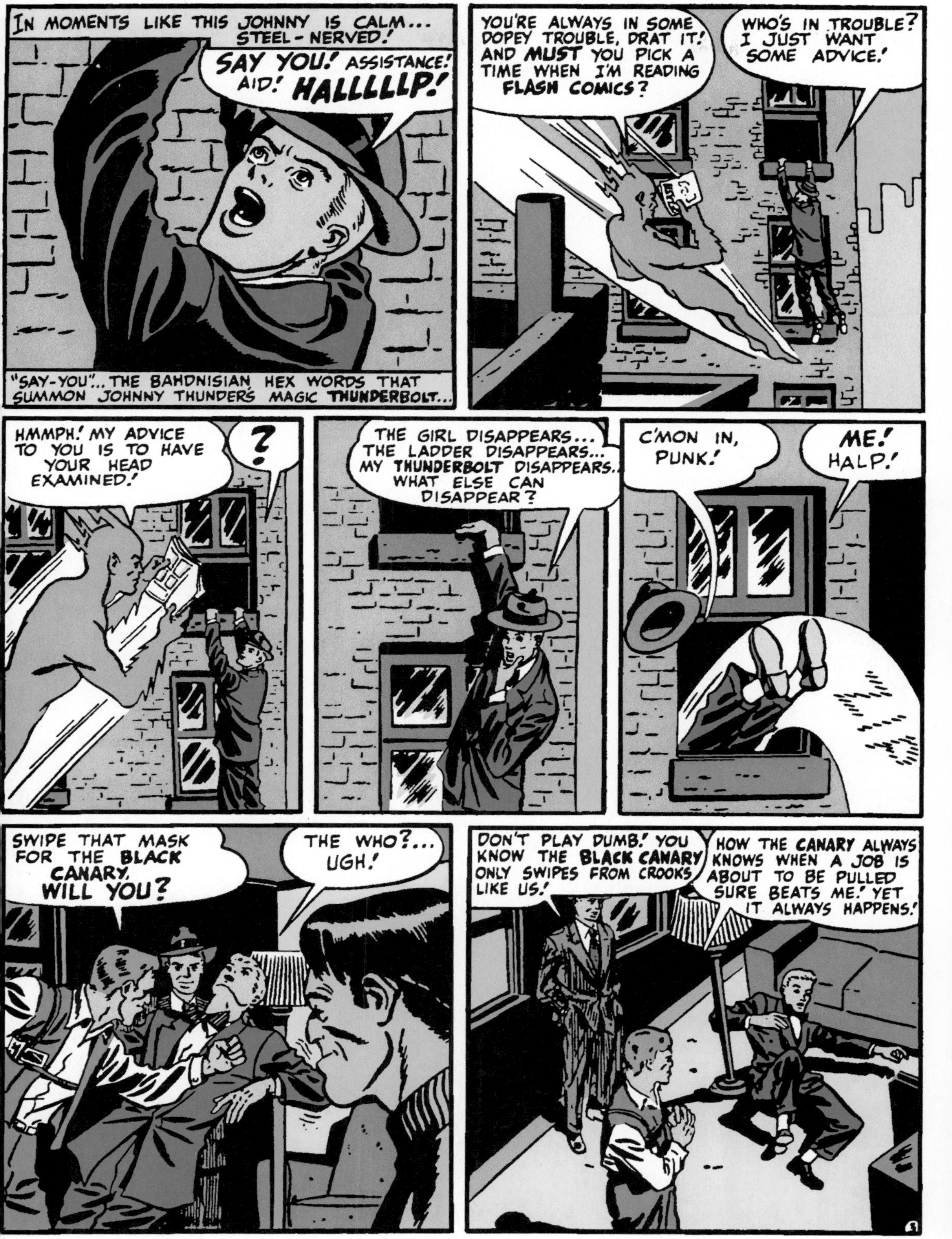
IN MOMENTS LIKE THIS JOHNNY IS CALM... STEEL-NERVED!
SAY YOU! ASSISTANCE! AID! HALLLLLP!
"SAY-YOU"... THE BAHDNISIAN HEX WORDS THAT SUMMON JOHNNY THUNDER'S MAGIC THUNDERBOLT...
YOU'RE ALWAYS IN SOME DOPEY TROUBLE, DRAT IT! AND MUST YOU PICK A TIME WHEN I'M READING FLASH COMICS?
WHO'S IN TROUBLE? I JUST WANT SOME ADVICE!
HMMPH! MY ADVICE TO YOU IS TO HAVE YOUR HEAD EXAMINED!
?
THE GIRL DISAPPEARS... THE LADDER DISAPPEARS... MY THUNDERBOLT DISAPPEARS.. WHAT ELSE CAN DISAPPEAR?
C'MON IN, PUNK!
ME! HALP!
SWIPE THAT MASK FOR THE BLACK CANARY, WILL YOU?
THE WHO?... UGH!
DON'T PLAY DUMB! YOU KNOW THE BLACK CANARY ONLY SWIPES FROM CROOKS LIKE US!
HOW THE CANARY ALWAYS KNOWS WHEN A JOB IS ABOUT TO BE PULLED SURE BEATS ME! YET IT ALWAYS HAPPENS!

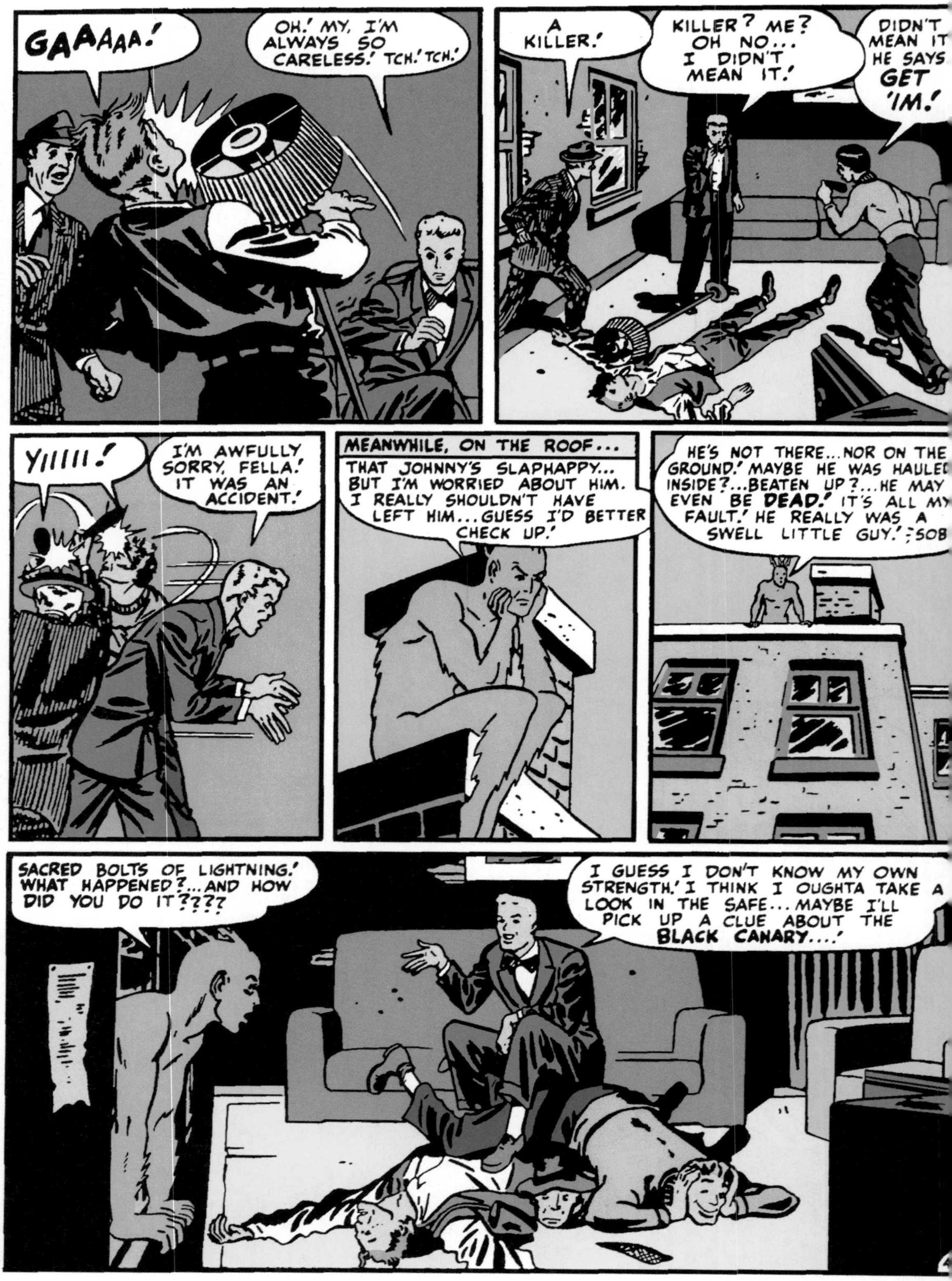
GAAAAA!
OH! MY, I'M ALWAYS SO CARELESS! TCH! TCH!
A KILLER!
KILLER? ME? OH NO... I DIDN'T MEAN IT!
DIDN'T MEAN IT HE SAYS GET 'IM!
YIIIII!
I'M AWFULLY SORRY, FELLA! IT WAS AN ACCIDENT!
MEANWHILE, ON THE ROOF...
THAT JOHNNY'S SLAPHAPPY... BUT I'M WORRIED ABOUT HIM. I REALLY SHOULDN'T HAVE LEFT HIM... GUESS I'D BETTER CHECK UP!
HE'S NOT THERE...NOR ON THE GROUND! MAYBE HE WAS HAULEI INSIDE?...BEATEN UP?...HE MAY EVEN BE DEAD! IT'S ALL MY FAULT! HE REALLY WAS A SWELL LITTLE GUY! SOB
SACRED BOLTS OF LIGHTNING! WHAT HAPPENED?...AND HOW DID YOU DO IT????
I GUESS I DON'T KNOW MY OWN STRENGTH! I THINK I OUGHTA TAKE A LOOK IN THE SAFE... MAYBE I'LL PICK UP A CLUE ABOUT THE BLACK CANARY...!

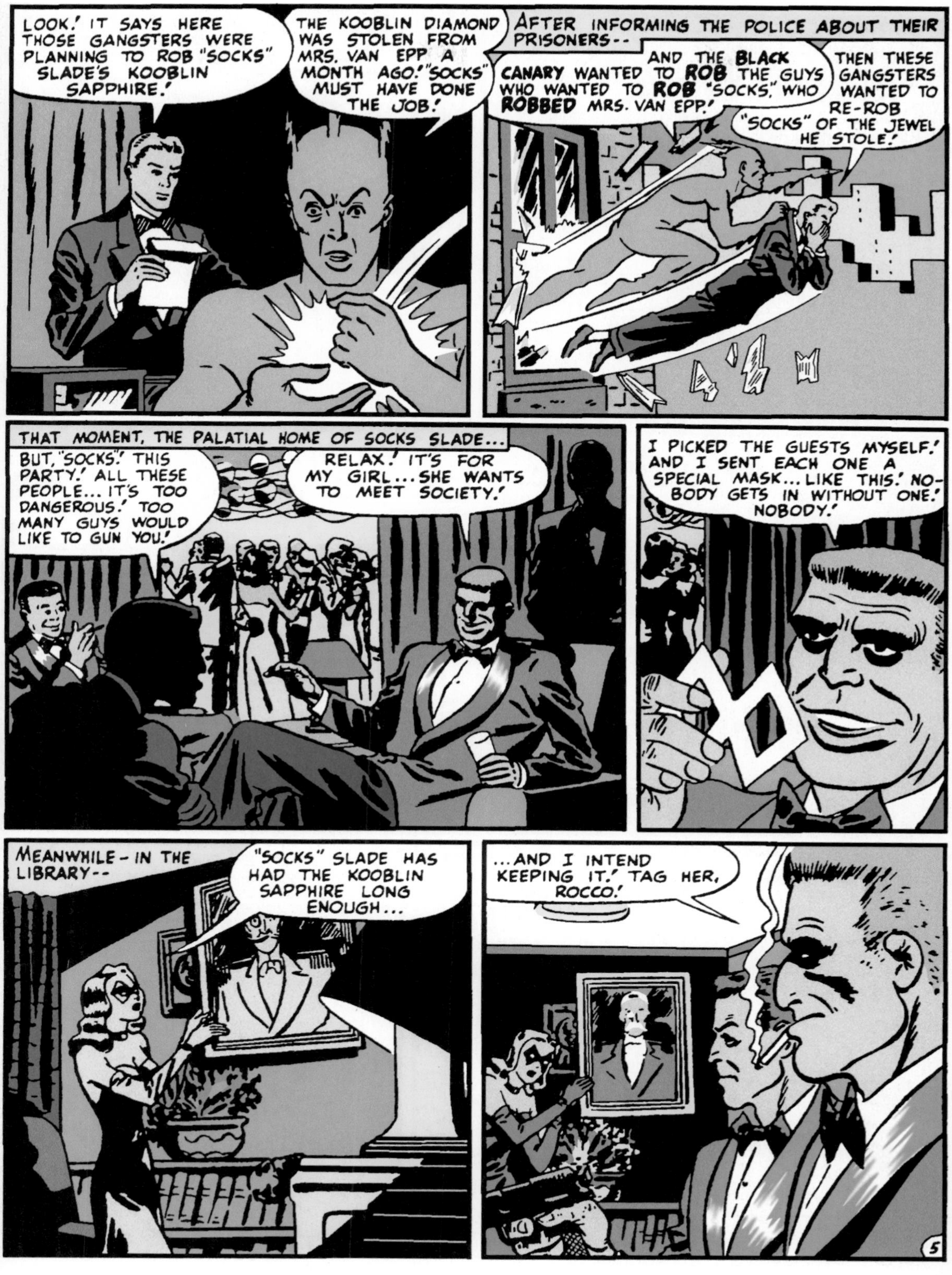
LOOK! IT SAYS HERE THOSE GANGSTERS WERE PLANNING TO ROB "SOCKS" SLADE'S KOOBLIN SAPPHIRE!
THE KOOBLIN DIAMOND WAS STOLEN FROM MRS. VAN EPP A MONTH AGO! "SOCKS" MUST HAVE DONE THE JOB!
AFTER INFORMING THE POLICE ABOUT THEIR PRISONERS--
THEN THESE GANGSTERS WANTED TO RE-ROB "SOCKS" OF THE JEWEL HE STOLE!
AND THE BLACK CANARY WANTED TO ROB THE GUYS WHO WANTED TO ROB "SOCKS," WHO ROBBED MRS. VAN EPP!
THAT MOMENT, THE PALATIAL HOME OF SOCKS SLADE...
BUT, "SOCKS"! THIS PARTY! ALL THESE PEOPLE... IT'S TOO DANGEROUS! TOO MANY GUYS WOULD LIKE TO GUN YOU!
RELAX! IT'S FOR MY GIRL... SHE WANTS TO MEET SOCIETY!
I PICKED THE GUESTS MYSELF! AND I SENT EACH ONE A SPECIAL MASK... LIKE THIS! NO-BODY GETS IN WITHOUT ONE! NOBODY!
MEANWHILE - IN THE LIBRARY--
"SOCKS" SLADE HAS HAD THE KOOBLIN SAPPHIRE LONG ENOUGH...
...AND I INTEND KEEPING IT! TAG HER, ROCCO!
5

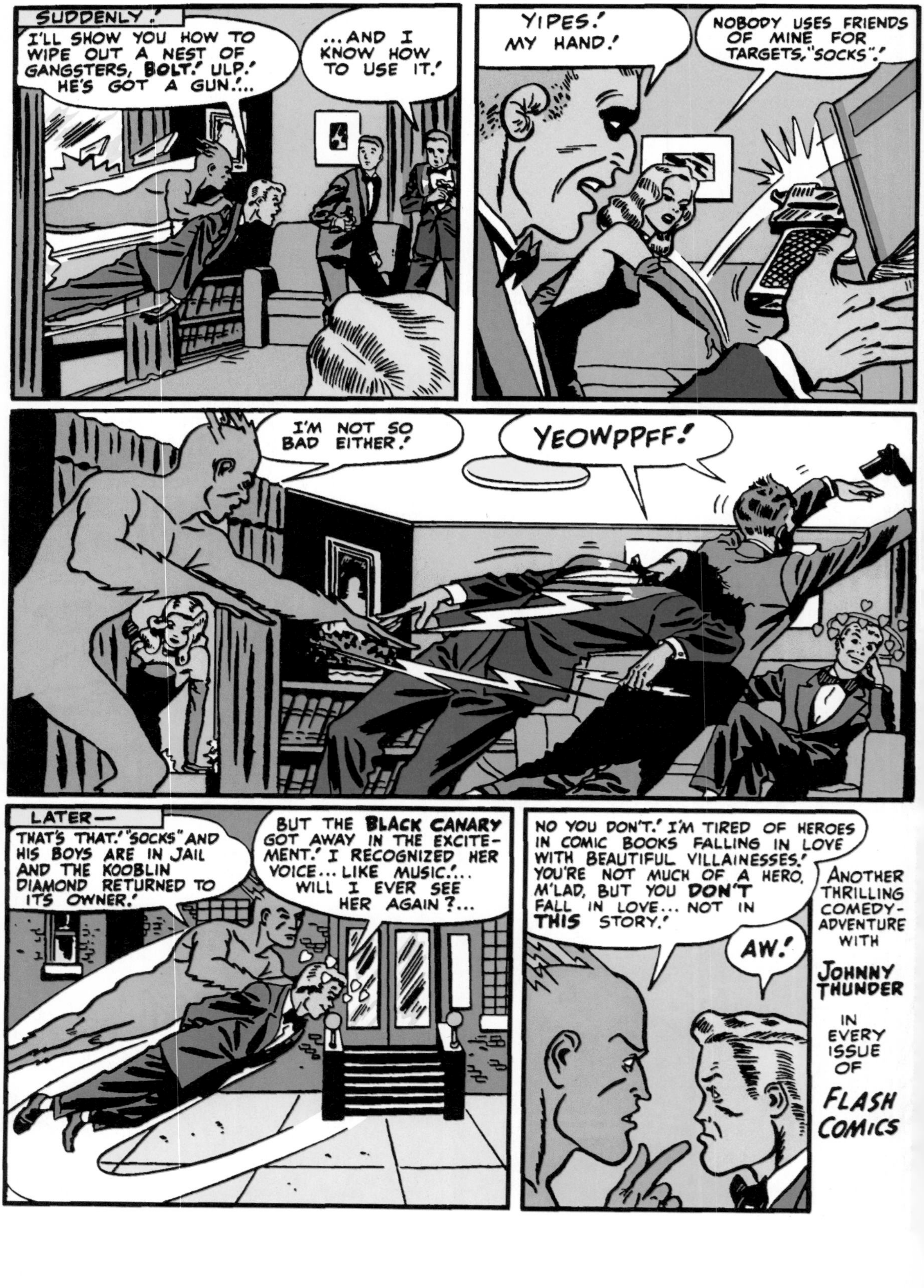
SUDDENLY!
I'LL SHOW YOU HOW TO WIPE OUT A NEST OF GANGSTERS, BOLT! ULP! HE'S GOT A GUN!...
...AND I KNOW HOW TO USE IT!
YIPES! MY HAND!
NOBODY USES FRIENDS OF MINE FOR TARGETS, "SOCKS"!
I'M NOT SO BAD EITHER!
YEOWPPFF!
LATER—
THAT'S THAT! "SOCKS" AND HIS BOYS ARE IN JAIL AND THE KOOBLIN DIAMOND RETURNED TO ITS OWNER!
BUT THE BLACK CANARY GOT AWAY IN THE EXCITEMENT! I RECOGNIZED HER VOICE... LIKE MUSIC!... WILL I EVER SEE HER AGAIN?...
NO YOU DON'T! I'M TIRED OF HEROES IN COMIC BOOKS FALLING IN LOVE WITH BEAUTIFUL VILLAINESSES! YOU'RE NOT MUCH OF A HERO, M'LAD, BUT YOU DON'T FALL IN LOVE... NOT IN THIS STORY!
AW!
ANOTHER THRILLING COMEDY-ADVENTURE WITH JOHNNY THUNDER IN EVERY ISSUE OF FLASH COMICS

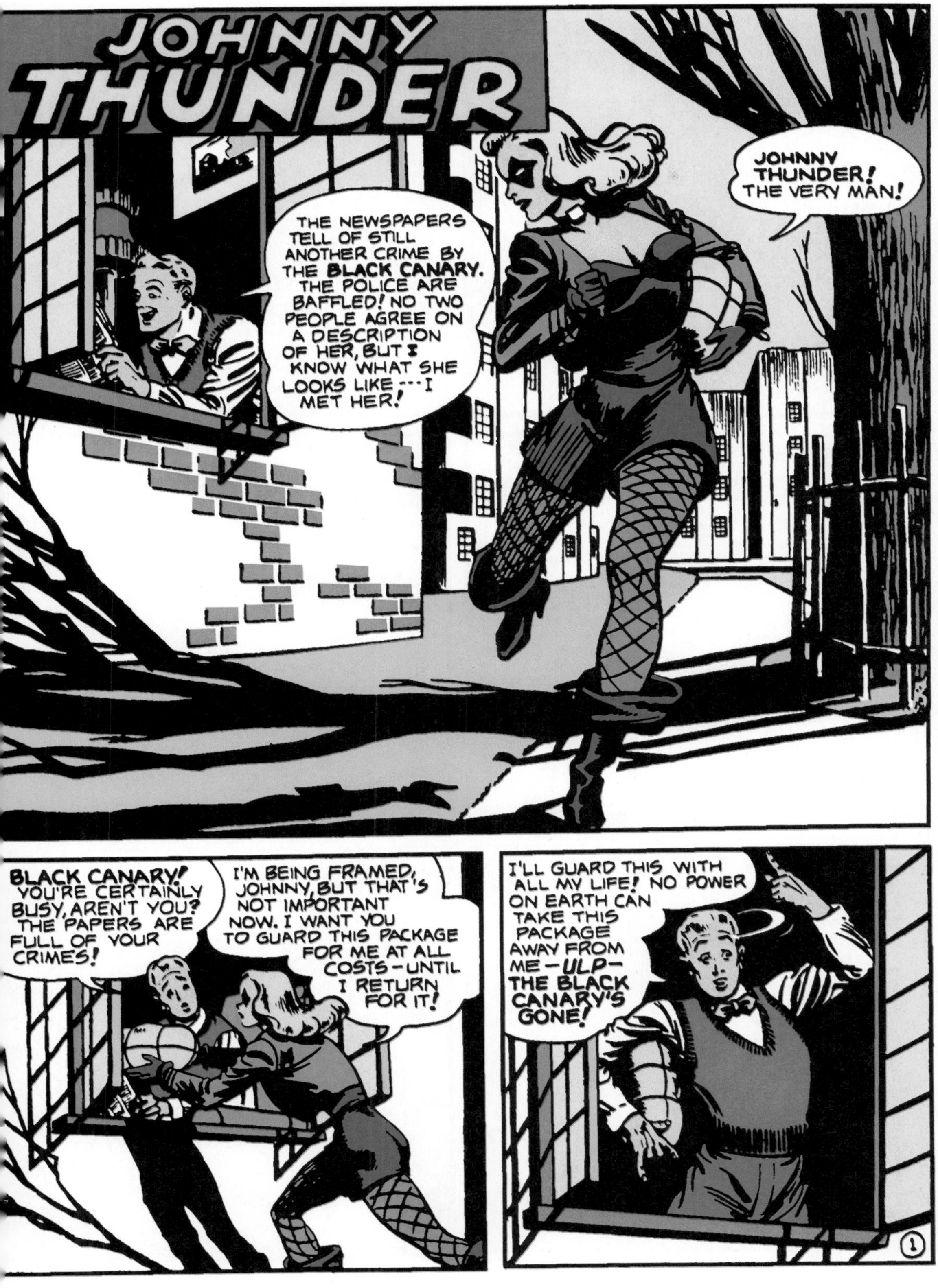
JOHNNY THUNDER
THE NEWSPAPERS TELL OF STILL ANOTHER CRIME BY THE BLACK CANARY. THE POLICE ARE BAFFLED! NO TWO PEOPLE AGREE ON A DESCRIPTION OF HER, BUT I KNOW WHAT SHE LOOKS LIKE --- I MET HER!
JOHNNY THUNDER! THE VERY MAN!
BLACK CANARY! YOU'RE CERTAINLY BUSY, AREN'T YOU? THE PAPERS ARE FULL OF YOUR CRIMES!
I'M BEING FRAMED, JOHNNY, BUT THAT'S NOT IMPORTANT NOW. I WANT YOU TO GUARD THIS PACKAGE FOR ME AT ALL COSTS—UNTIL I RETURN FOR IT!
I'LL GUARD THIS WITH ALL MY LIFE! NO POWER ON EARTH CAN TAKE THIS PACKAGE AWAY FROM ME—ULP—THE BLACK CANARY'S GONE!
1

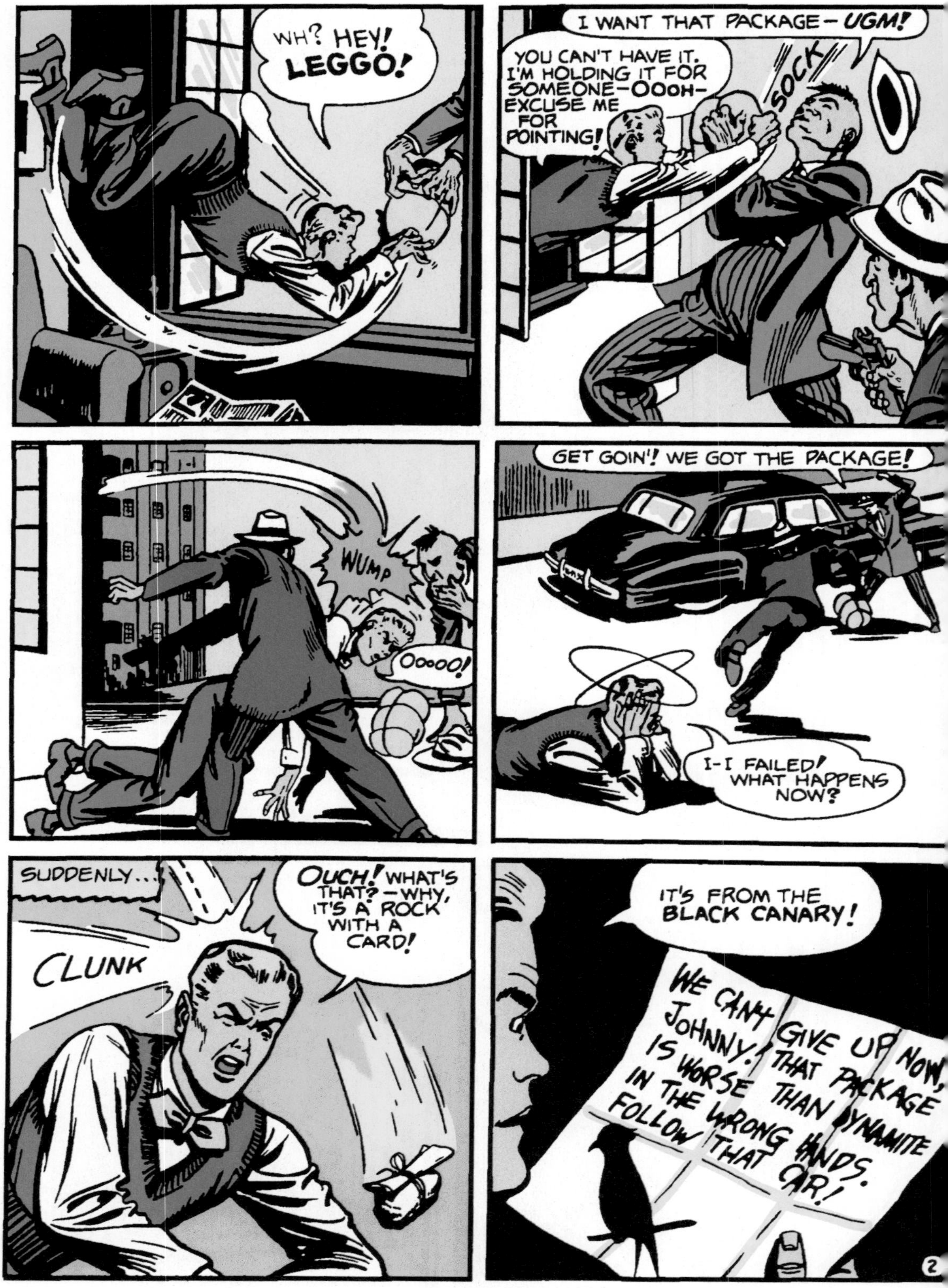
WH? HEY! LEGGO!
I WANT THAT PACKAGE—UGM!
YOU CAN'T HAVE IT. I'M HOLDING IT FOR SOMEONE—OOOH—EXCUSE ME FOR POINTING!
SOCK
WUMP
OOOOO!
GET GOIN'! WE GOT THE PACKAGE!
I-I FAILED! WHAT HAPPENS NOW?
SUDDENLY...
OUCH! WHAT'S THAT?—WHY, IT'S A ROCK WITH A CARD!
CLUNK
IT'S FROM THE BLACK CANARY!
WE CAN'T GIVE UP NOW, JOHNNY! THAT PACKAGE IS WORSE THAN DYNAMITE IN THE WRONG HANDS. FOLLOW THAT CAR!
2

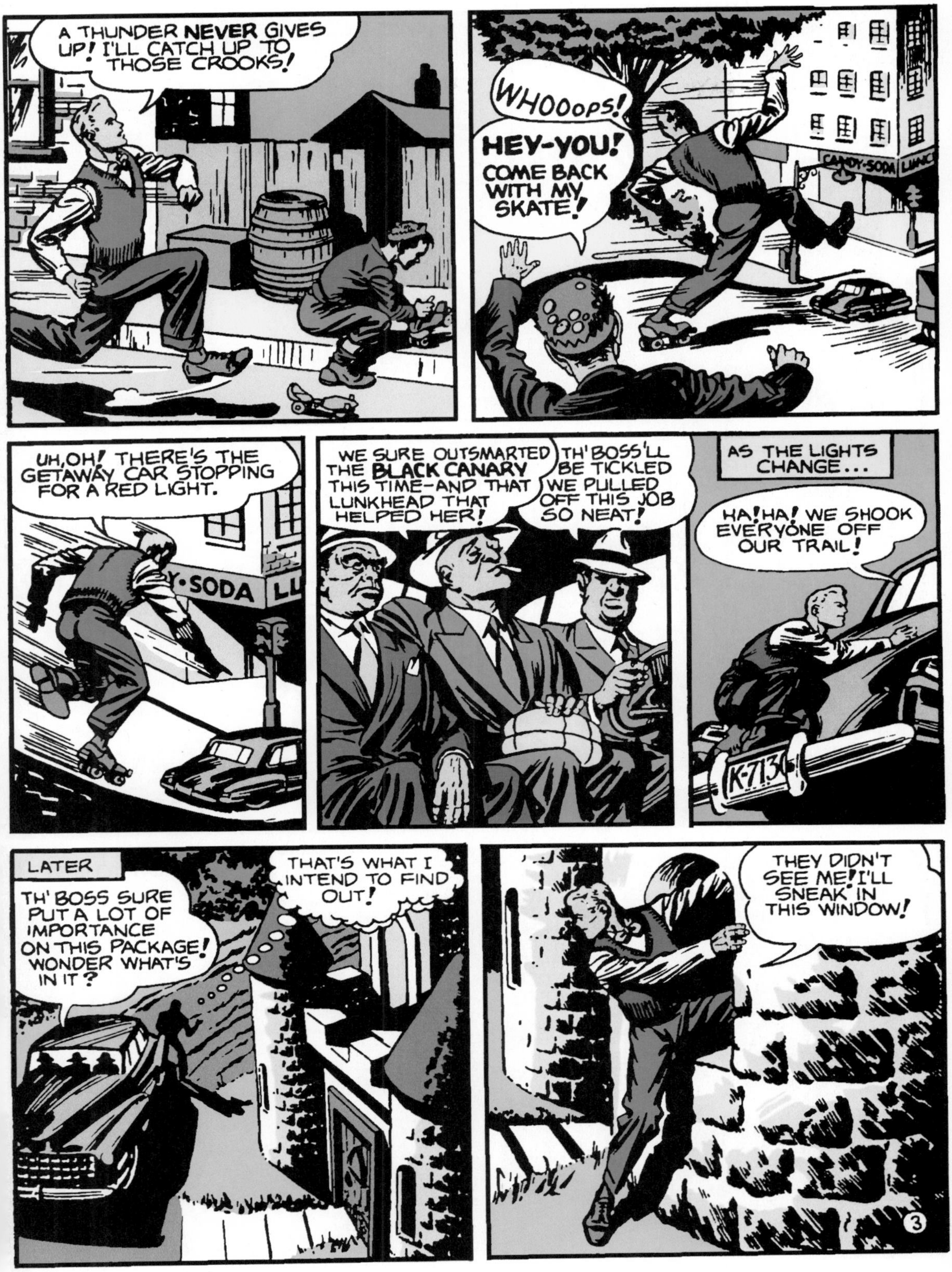
A THUNDER **NEVER** GIVES UP! I'LL CATCH UP TO THOSE CROOKS!
WHOOops!
HEY-YOU! COME BACK WITH MY SKATE!
CANDY-SODA
UH,OH! THERE'S THE GETAWAY CAR STOPPING FOR A RED LIGHT.
WE SURE OUTSMARTED THE **BLACK CANARY** THIS TIME-AND THAT LUNKHEAD THAT HELPED HER!
TH' BOSS'LL BE TICKLED WE PULLED OFF THIS JOB SO NEAT!
AS THE LIGHTS CHANGE...
HA! HA! WE SHOOK EVERYONE OFF OUR TRAIL!
K-7130
LATER
TH' BOSS SURE PUT A LOT OF IMPORTANCE ON THIS PACKAGE! WONDER WHAT'S IN IT?
THAT'S WHAT I INTEND TO FIND OUT!
THEY DIDN'T SEE ME! I'LL SNEAK IN THIS WINDOW!
3

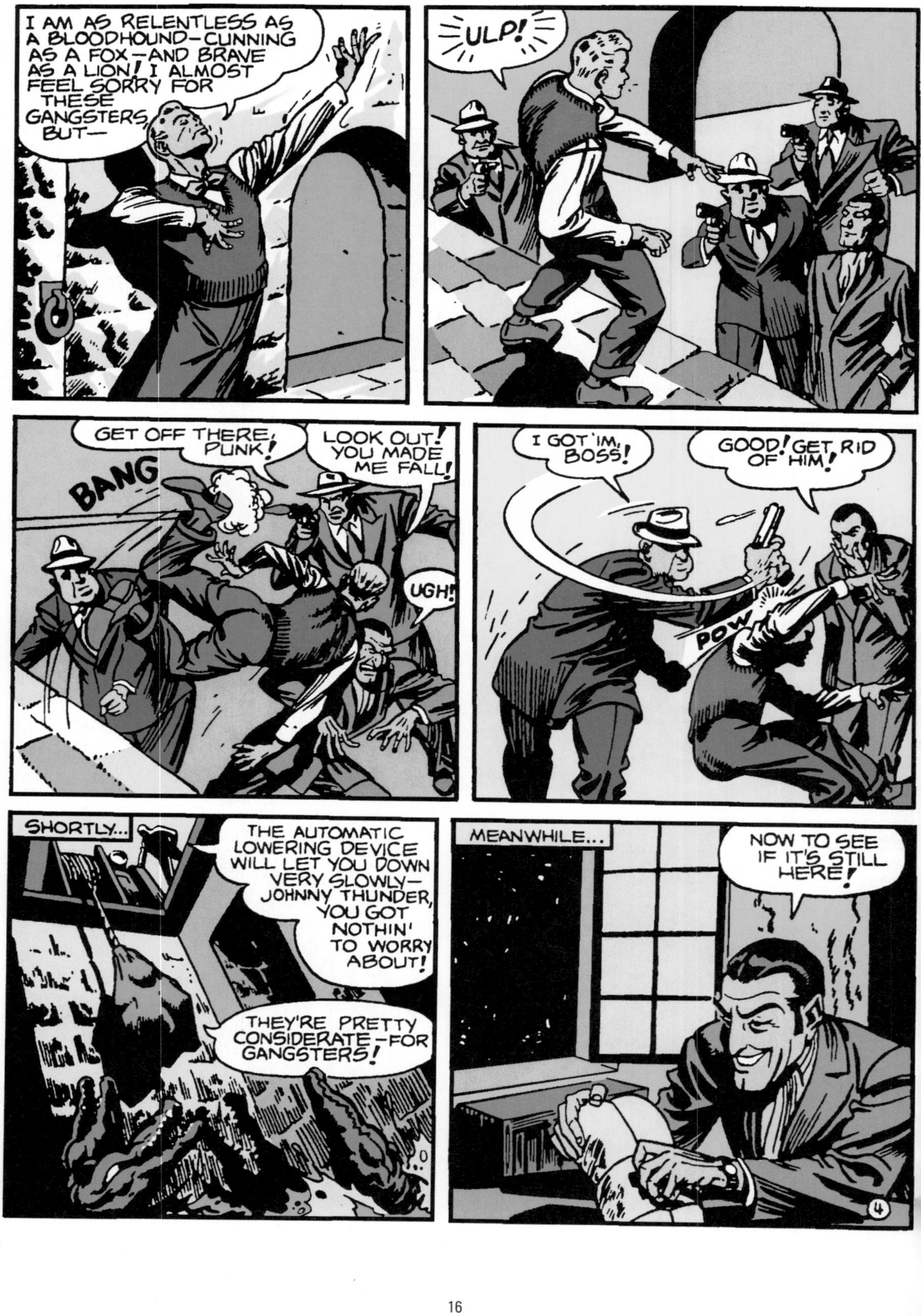
I AM AS RELENTLESS AS A BLOODHOUND—CUNNING AS A FOX—AND BRAVE AS A LION! I ALMOST FEEL SORRY FOR THESE GANGSTERS BUT—
ULP!
GET OFF THERE, PUNK!
BANG
LOOK OUT! YOU MADE ME FALL!
UGH!
I GOT 'IM, BOSS!
GOOD! GET RID OF HIM!
POW
SHORTLY...
THE AUTOMATIC LOWERING DEVICE WILL LET YOU DOWN VERY SLOWLY—JOHNNY THUNDER, YOU GOT NOTHIN' TO WORRY ABOUT!
THEY'RE PRETTY CONSIDERATE—FOR GANGSTERS!
MEANWHILE...
NOW TO SEE IF IT'S STILL HERE!
4

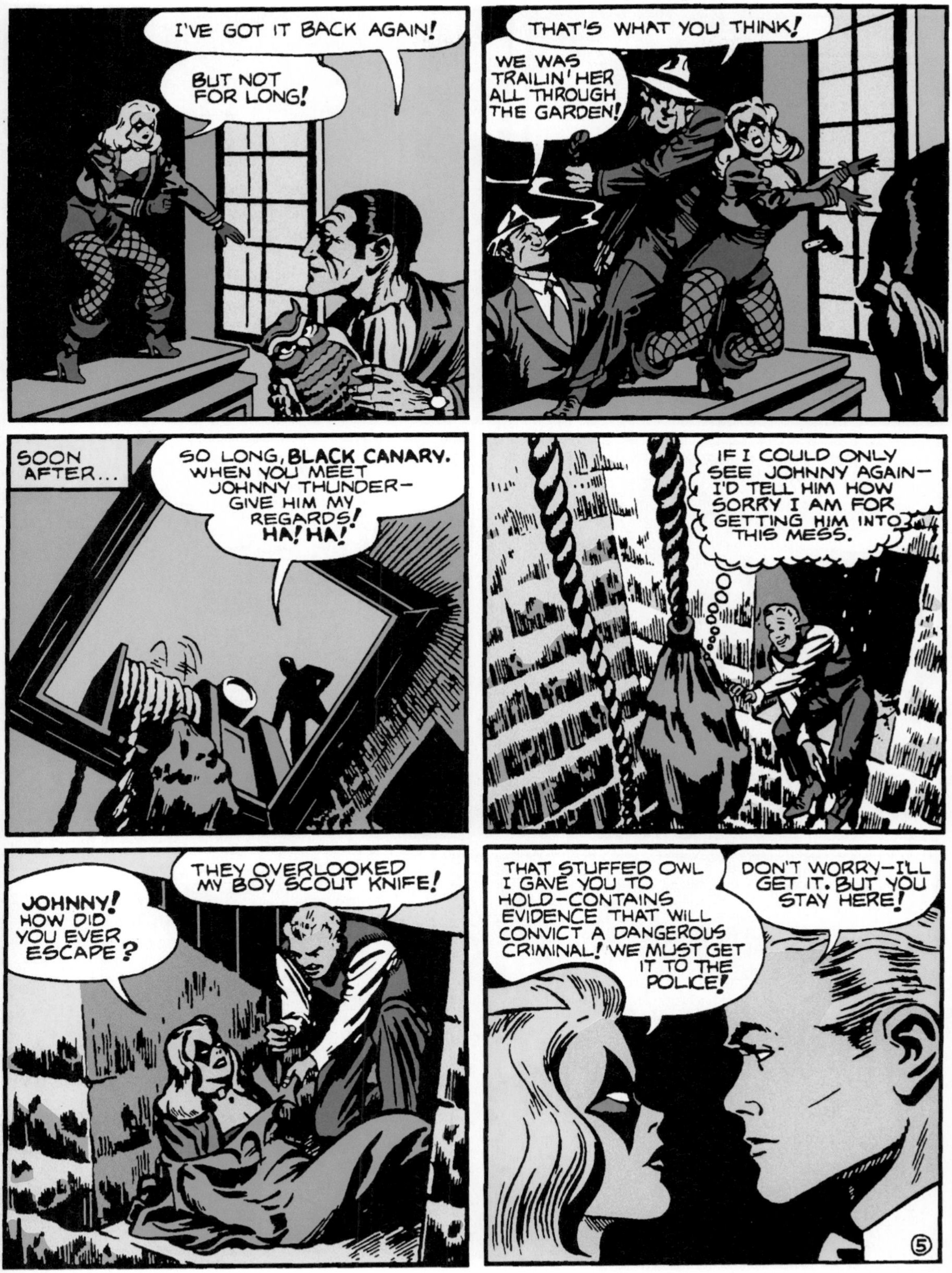
I'VE GOT IT BACK AGAIN!
BUT NOT FOR LONG!
THAT'S WHAT YOU THINK!
WE WAS TRAILIN' HER ALL THROUGH THE GARDEN!
SOON AFTER...
SO LONG, BLACK CANARY. WHEN YOU MEET JOHNNY THUNDER— GIVE HIM MY REGARDS! HA! HA!
IF I COULD ONLY SEE JOHNNY AGAIN— I'D TELL HIM HOW SORRY I AM FOR GETTING HIM INTO THIS MESS.
JOHNNY! HOW DID YOU EVER ESCAPE?
THEY OVERLOOKED MY BOY SCOUT KNIFE!
THAT STUFFED OWL I GAVE YOU TO HOLD—CONTAINS EVIDENCE THAT WILL CONVICT A DANGEROUS CRIMINAL! WE MUST GET IT TO THE POLICE!
DON'T WORRY—I'LL GET IT. BUT YOU STAY HERE!
5

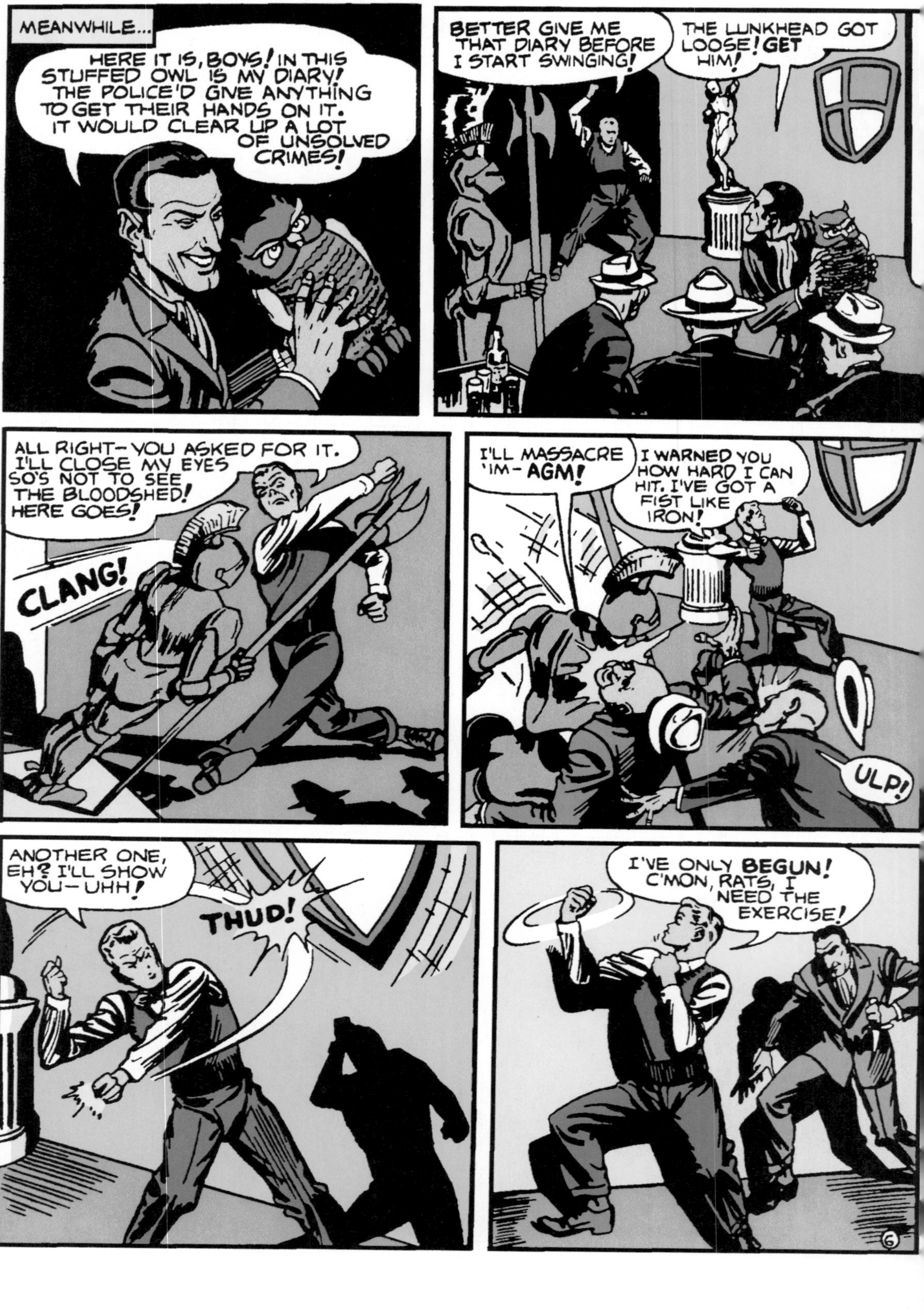
MEANWHILE...
HERE IT IS, BOYS! IN THIS STUFFED OWL IS MY DIARY! THE POLICE'D GIVE ANYTHING TO GET THEIR HANDS ON IT. IT WOULD CLEAR UP A LOT OF UNSOLVED CRIMES!
BETTER GIVE ME THAT DIARY BEFORE I START SWINGING!
THE LUNKHEAD GOT LOOSE! GET HIM!
ALL RIGHT- YOU ASKED FOR IT. I'LL CLOSE MY EYES SO'S NOT TO SEE THE BLOODSHED! HERE GOES!
CLANG!
I'LL MASSACRE 'IM- AGM!
I WARNED YOU HOW HARD I CAN HIT. I'VE GOT A FIST LIKE IRON!
ULP!
ANOTHER ONE, EH? I'LL SHOW YOU- UHH!
THUD!
I'VE ONLY BEGUN! C'MON, RATS, I NEED THE EXERCISE!
6

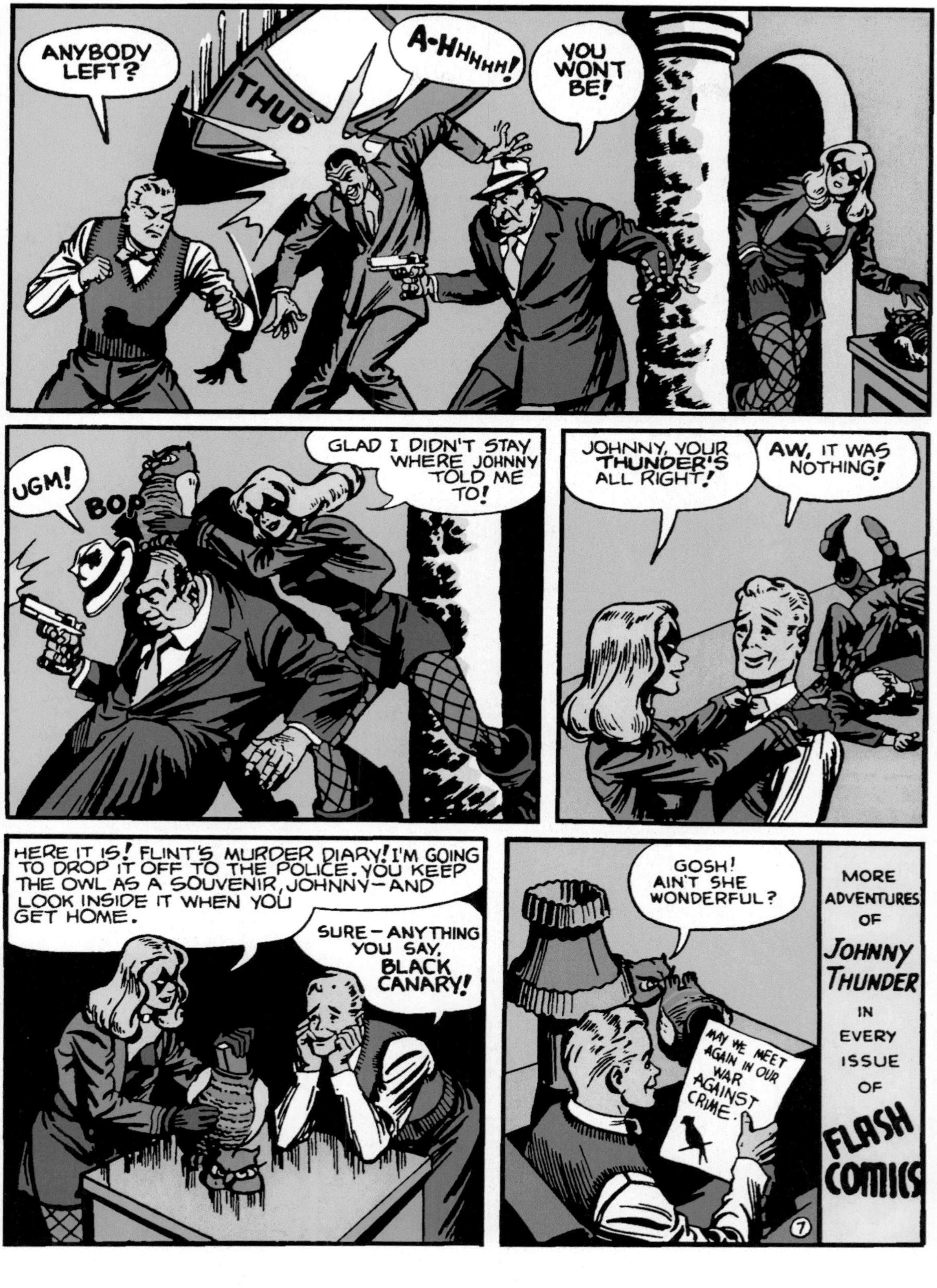
ANYBODY LEFT?
THUD
A-HHHHH!
YOU WON'T BE!
UGM!
BOP
GLAD I DIDN'T STAY WHERE JOHNNY TOLD ME TO!
JOHNNY, YOUR THUNDER'S ALL RIGHT!
AW, IT WAS NOTHING!
HERE IT IS! FLINT'S MURDER DIARY! I'M GOING TO DROP IT OFF TO THE POLICE. YOU KEEP THE OWL AS A SOUVENIR, JOHNNY—AND LOOK INSIDE IT WHEN YOU GET HOME.
SURE—ANYTHING YOU SAY, BLACK CANARY!
GOSH! AIN'T SHE WONDERFUL?
MAY WE MEET AGAIN IN OUR WAR AGAINST CRIME.
7
MORE ADVENTURES OF JOHNNY THUNDER IN EVERY ISSUE OF FLASH COMICS

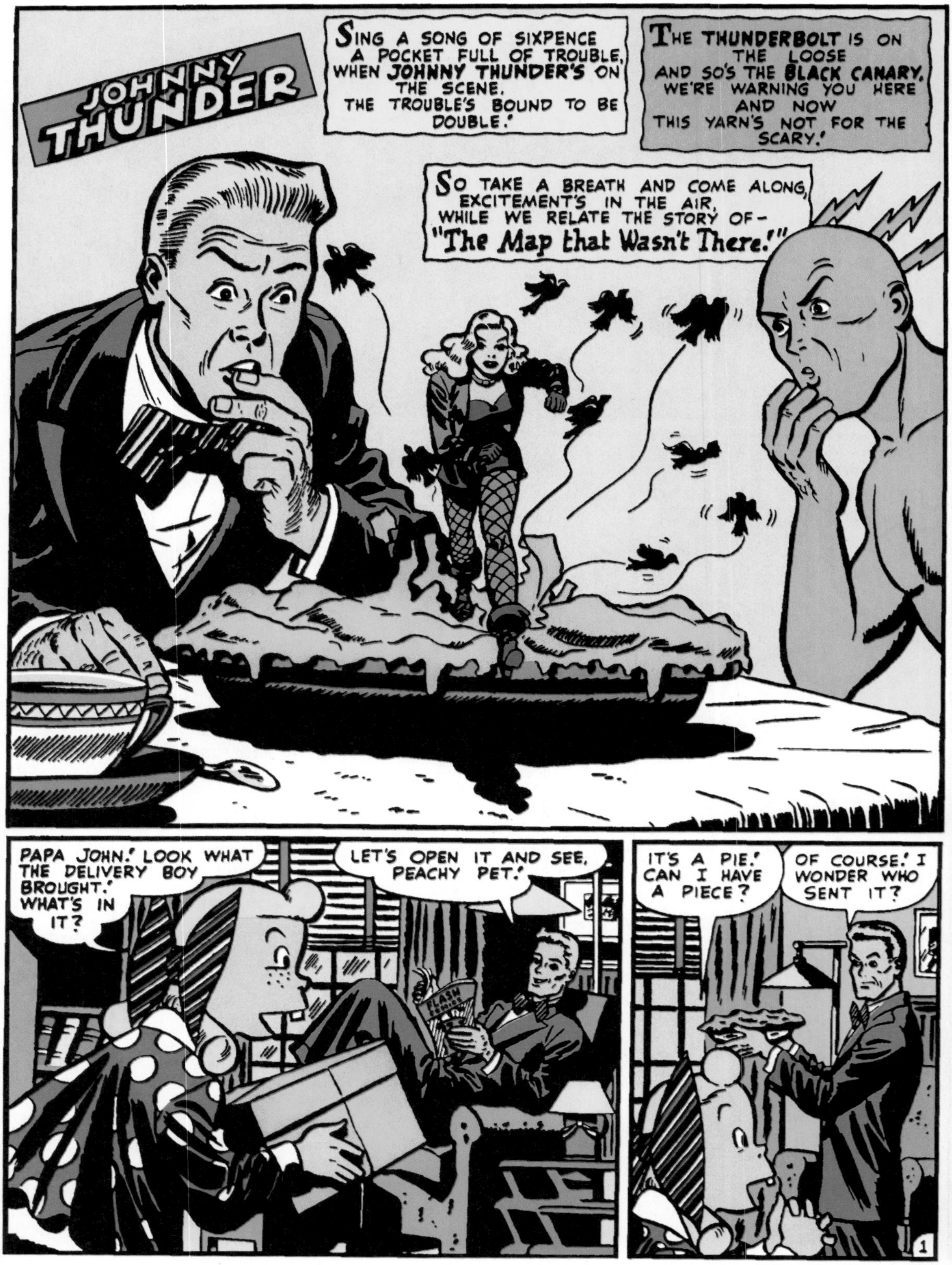
JOHNNY THUNDER
SING A SONG OF SIXPENCE A POCKET FULL OF TROUBLE, WHEN JOHNNY THUNDER'S ON THE SCENE, THE TROUBLE'S BOUND TO BE DOUBLE!
THE THUNDERBOLT IS ON THE LOOSE AND SO'S THE BLACK CANARY, WE'RE WARNING YOU HERE AND NOW THIS YARN'S NOT FOR THE SCARY!
SO TAKE A BREATH AND COME ALONG, EXCITEMENT'S IN THE AIR, WHILE WE RELATE THE STORY OF– "The Map that Wasn't There!"
PAPA JOHN! LOOK WHAT THE DELIVERY BOY BROUGHT! WHAT'S IN IT?
LET'S OPEN IT AND SEE, PEACHY PET!
FLASH COMICS
IT'S A PIE! CAN I HAVE A PIECE?
OF COURSE! I WONDER WHO SENT IT?
1

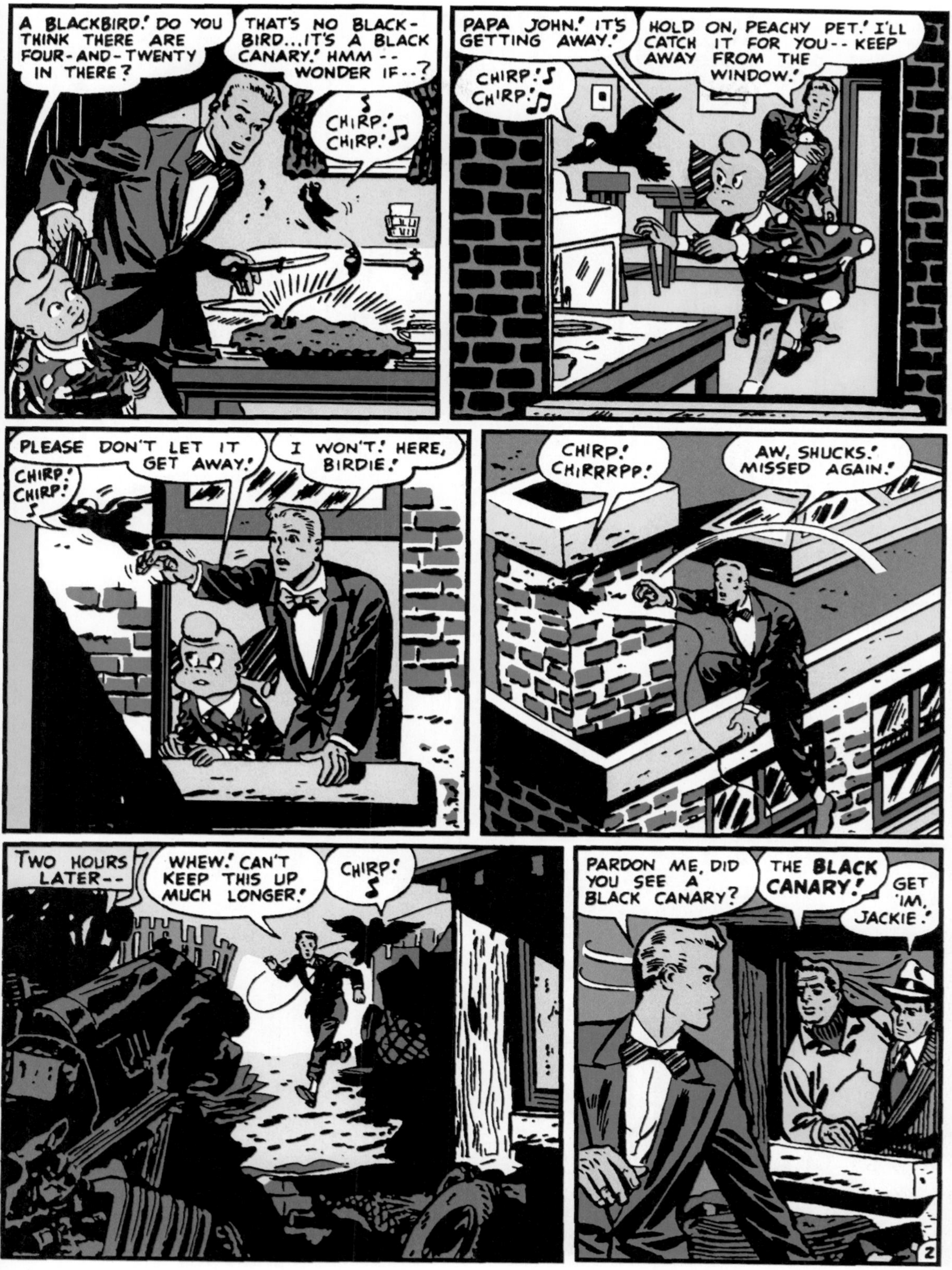
A BLACKBIRD! DO YOU THINK THERE ARE FOUR-AND-TWENTY IN THERE?
THAT'S NO BLACK-BIRD...IT'S A BLACK CANARY! HMM -- WONDER IF--?
CHIRP! CHIRP!
PAPA JOHN! IT'S GETTING AWAY!
HOLD ON, PEACHY PET! I'LL CATCH IT FOR YOU-- KEEP AWAY FROM THE WINDOW!
CHIRP! CHIRP!
PLEASE DON'T LET IT GET AWAY!
I WON'T! HERE, BIRDIE!
CHIRP! CHIRP!
CHIRP! CHIRRRPP!
AW, SHUCKS! MISSED AGAIN!
TWO HOURS LATER--
WHEW! CAN'T KEEP THIS UP MUCH LONGER!
CHIRP!
PARDON ME, DID YOU SEE A BLACK CANARY?
THE **BLACK CANARY**!
GET 'IM, JACKIE!
2

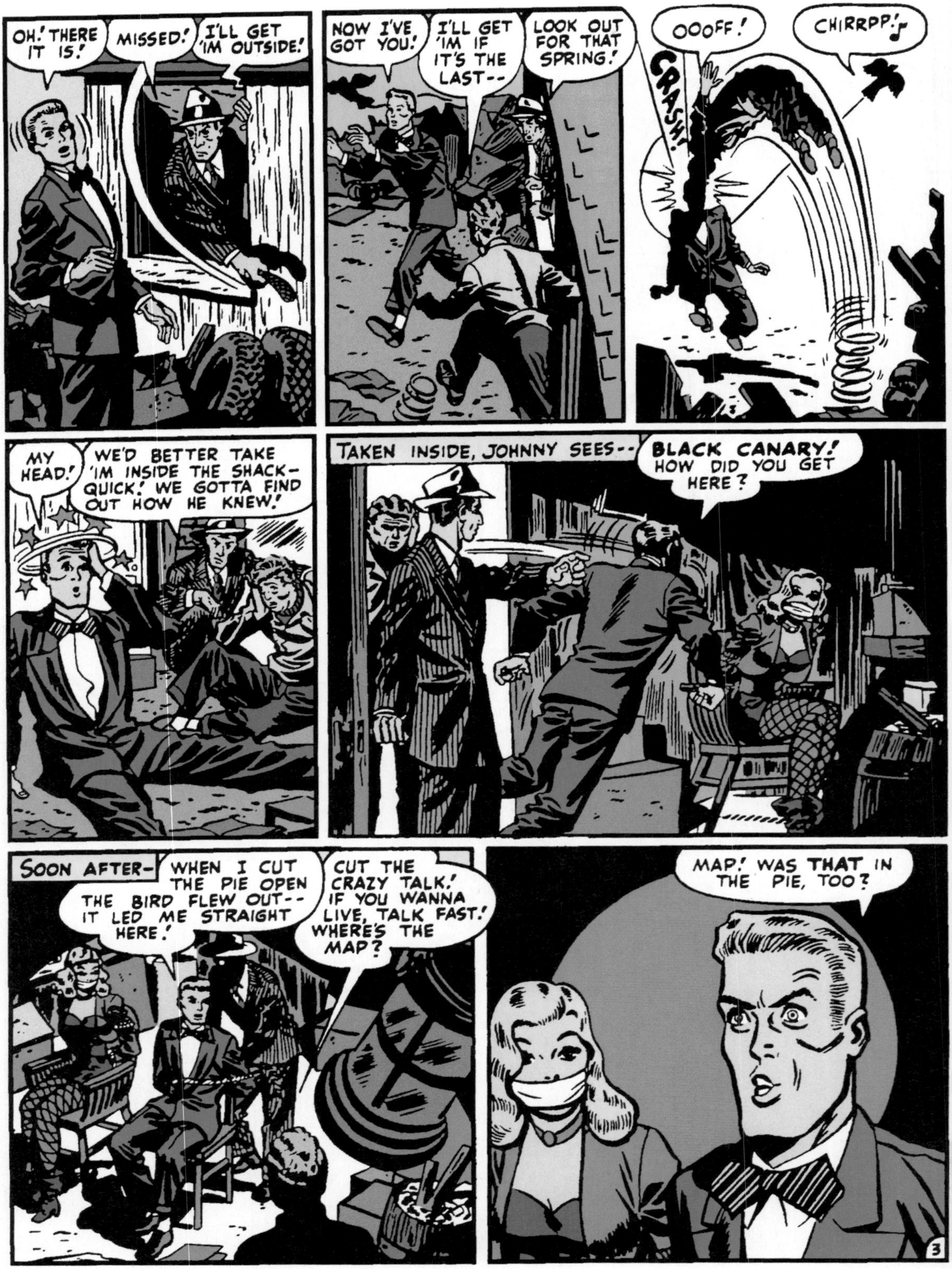
OH! THERE IT IS!
MISSED!
I'LL GET 'IM OUTSIDE!
NOW I'VE GOT YOU!
I'LL GET 'IM IF IT'S THE LAST--
LOOK OUT FOR THAT SPRING!
OOOFF!
CRASH!
CHIRRPP!
MY HEAD!
WE'D BETTER TAKE 'IM INSIDE THE SHACK-QUICK! WE GOTTA FIND OUT HOW HE KNEW!
TAKEN INSIDE, JOHNNY SEES--
BLACK CANARY! HOW DID YOU GET HERE?
SOON AFTER-
WHEN I CUT THE PIE OPEN THE BIRD FLEW OUT-- IT LED ME STRAIGHT HERE!
CUT THE CRAZY TALK! IF YOU WANNA LIVE, TALK FAST! WHERE'S THE MAP?
MAP! WAS THAT IN THE PIE, TOO?
3

SO THAT'S IT! THAT'S WHY THE **BLACK CANARY** RAN INTO THAT BAKERY WHEN WE WERE FOLLOWING HER! SHE STUCK THE MAP INTO THE PIE!

DID I SAY SOMETHING WRONG?

HEY! CUT THAT OUT! IT TICKLES!

WE'LL GET THIS GUY'S ADDRESS FROM HIS WALLET. THEN HOP OVER THERE FAST AND GET RID OF HIM AND HIS GIRL FRIEND AT THE SAME TIME!

SOON AFTER—

THIS CAGE, LEFT OVER BY A CIRCUS, IS THE BEST WE COULD DO FER YOU ON SUCH A SHORT NOTICE, CANARY! GET IN!

I DON'T UNDERSTAND ABOUT THE BIRD!

IT'S ESPECIALLY TRAINED! I THOUGHT WHEN YOU SAW IT YOU'D KNOW WHO THE PIE CAME FROM, JOHNNY, AND HOLD ON TO IT!

WHAT'S THIS ABOUT A MAP?

THESE NICE BOYS STOLE SOME CHARITY FUNDS AND CACHED THE LOOT! I'M PRETTY HARD-BOILED BUT I DON'T GO FOR THAT! I GOT THEIR MAP AND STUCK IT IN THE PIE-- THE REST YOU KNOW!

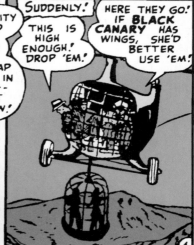

SUDDENLY!

THIS IS HIGH ENOUGH! DROP 'EM!

HERE THEY GO! IF **BLACK CANARY** HAS WINGS, SHE'D BETTER USE 'EM!

4

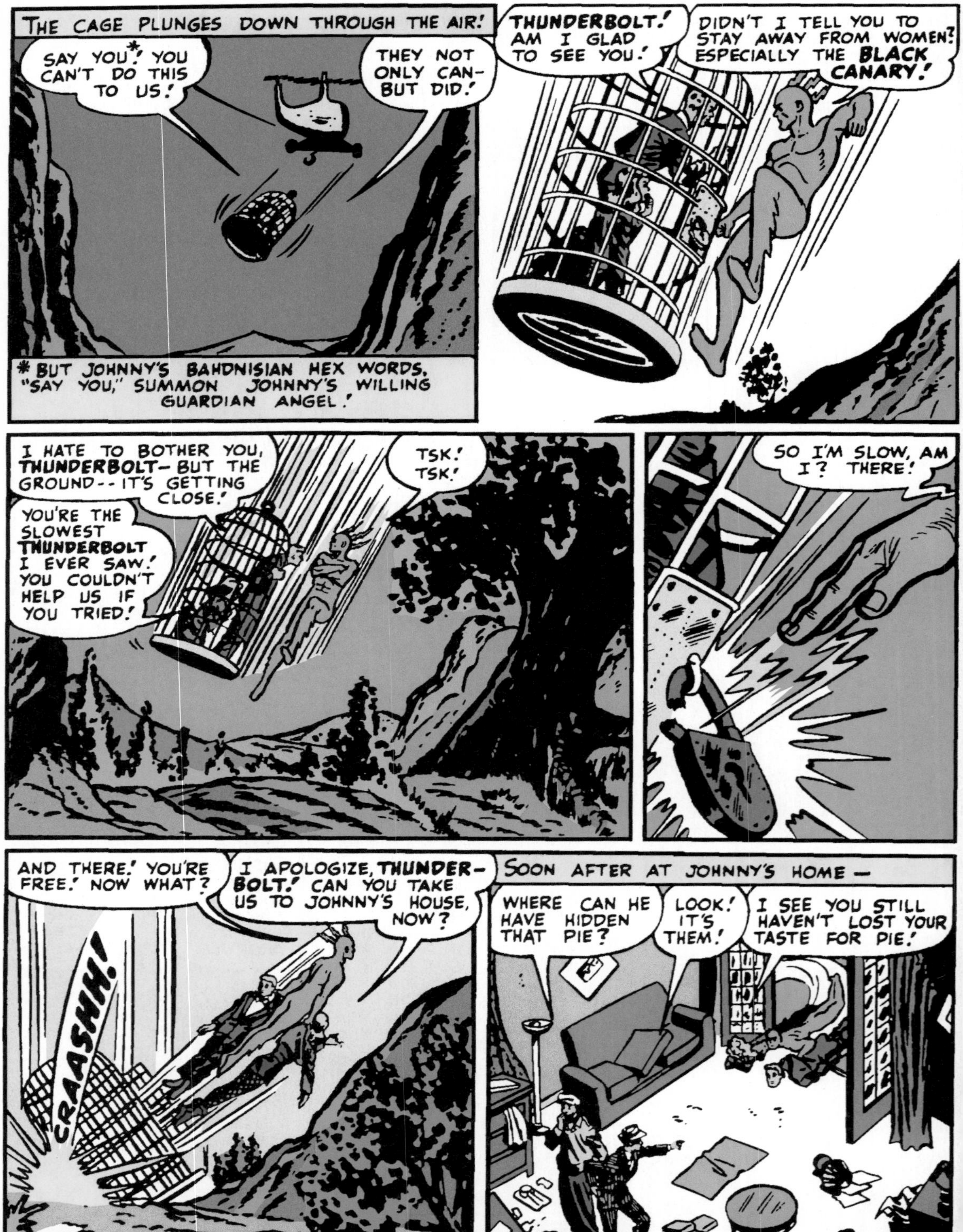
THE CAGE PLUNGES DOWN THROUGH THE AIR!
SAY YOU*! YOU CAN'T DO THIS TO US!
THEY NOT ONLY CAN-BUT DID!
*BUT JOHNNY'S BAHDNISIAN HEX WORDS, "SAY YOU," SUMMON JOHNNY'S WILLING GUARDIAN ANGEL!
THUNDERBOLT! AM I GLAD TO SEE YOU!
DIDN'T I TELL YOU TO STAY AWAY FROM WOMEN? ESPECIALLY THE BLACK CANARY!
I HATE TO BOTHER YOU, THUNDERBOLT- BUT THE GROUND-- IT'S GETTING CLOSE!
TSK! TSK!
YOU'RE THE SLOWEST THUNDERBOLT I EVER SAW! YOU COULDN'T HELP US IF YOU TRIED!
SO I'M SLOW, AM I? THERE!
AND THERE! YOU'RE FREE! NOW WHAT?
I APOLOGIZE, THUNDERBOLT! CAN YOU TAKE US TO JOHNNY'S HOUSE, NOW?
CRAASHH!
SOON AFTER AT JOHNNY'S HOME —
WHERE CAN HE HAVE HIDDEN THAT PIE?
LOOK! IT'S THEM!
I SEE YOU STILL HAVEN'T LOST YOUR TASTE FOR PIE!
5

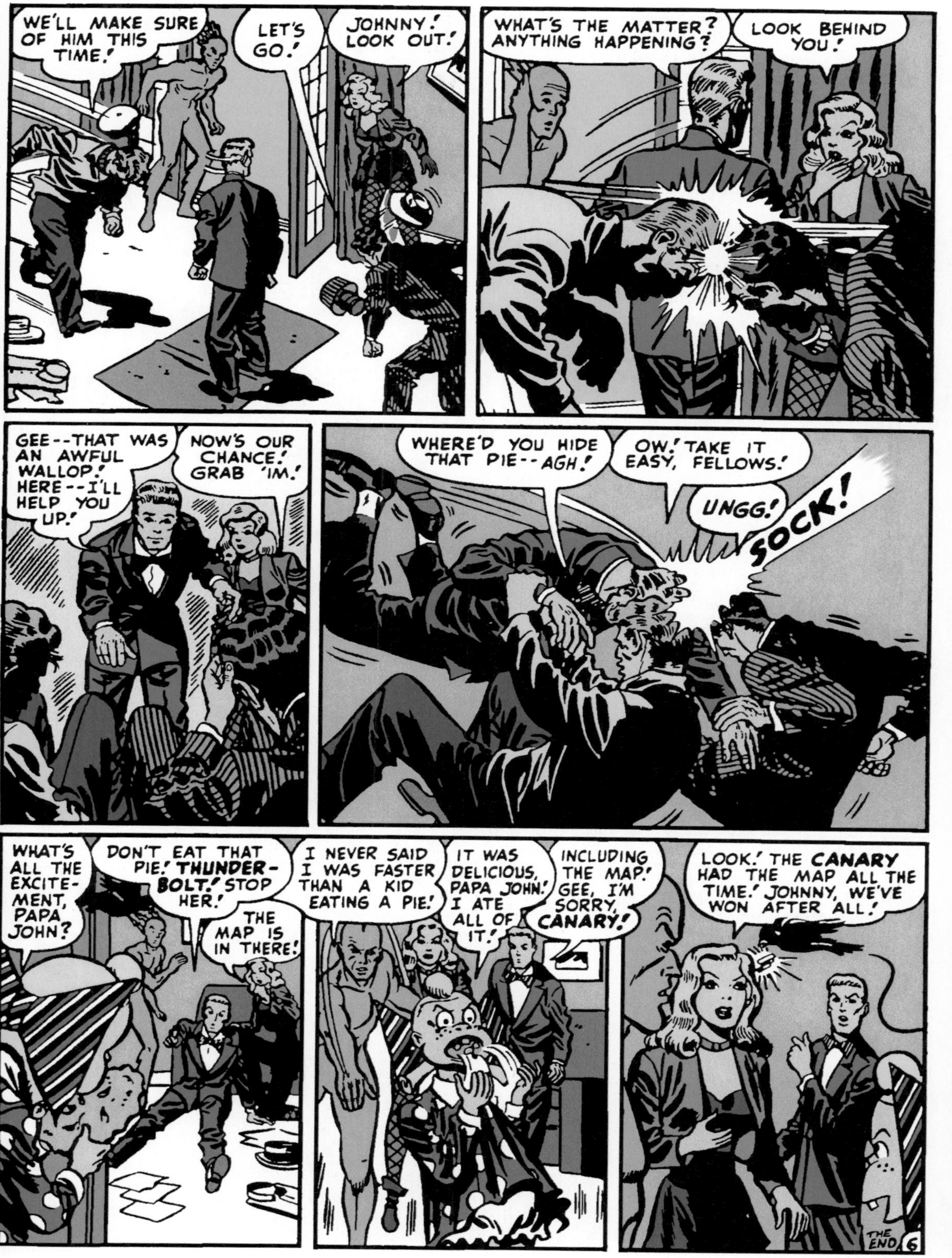
WE'LL MAKE SURE OF HIM THIS TIME!
LET'S GO!
JOHNNY! LOOK OUT!
WHAT'S THE MATTER? ANYTHING HAPPENING?
LOOK BEHIND YOU!
GEE--THAT WAS AN AWFUL WALLOP! HERE--I'LL HELP YOU UP!
NOW'S OUR CHANCE! GRAB 'IM!
WHERE'D YOU HIDE THAT PIE--AGH!
OW! TAKE IT EASY, FELLOWS!
UNGG!
SOCK!
WHAT'S ALL THE EXCITEMENT, PAPA JOHN?
DON'T EAT THAT PIE! THUNDERBOLT! STOP HER!
THE MAP IS IN THERE!
I NEVER SAID I WAS FASTER THAN A KID EATING A PIE!
IT WAS DELICIOUS, PAPA JOHN! I ATE ALL OF IT!
INCLUDING THE MAP! GEE, I'M SORRY, CANARY!
LOOK! THE CANARY HAD THE MAP ALL THE TIME! JOHNNY, WE'VE WON AFTER ALL!
THE END
6

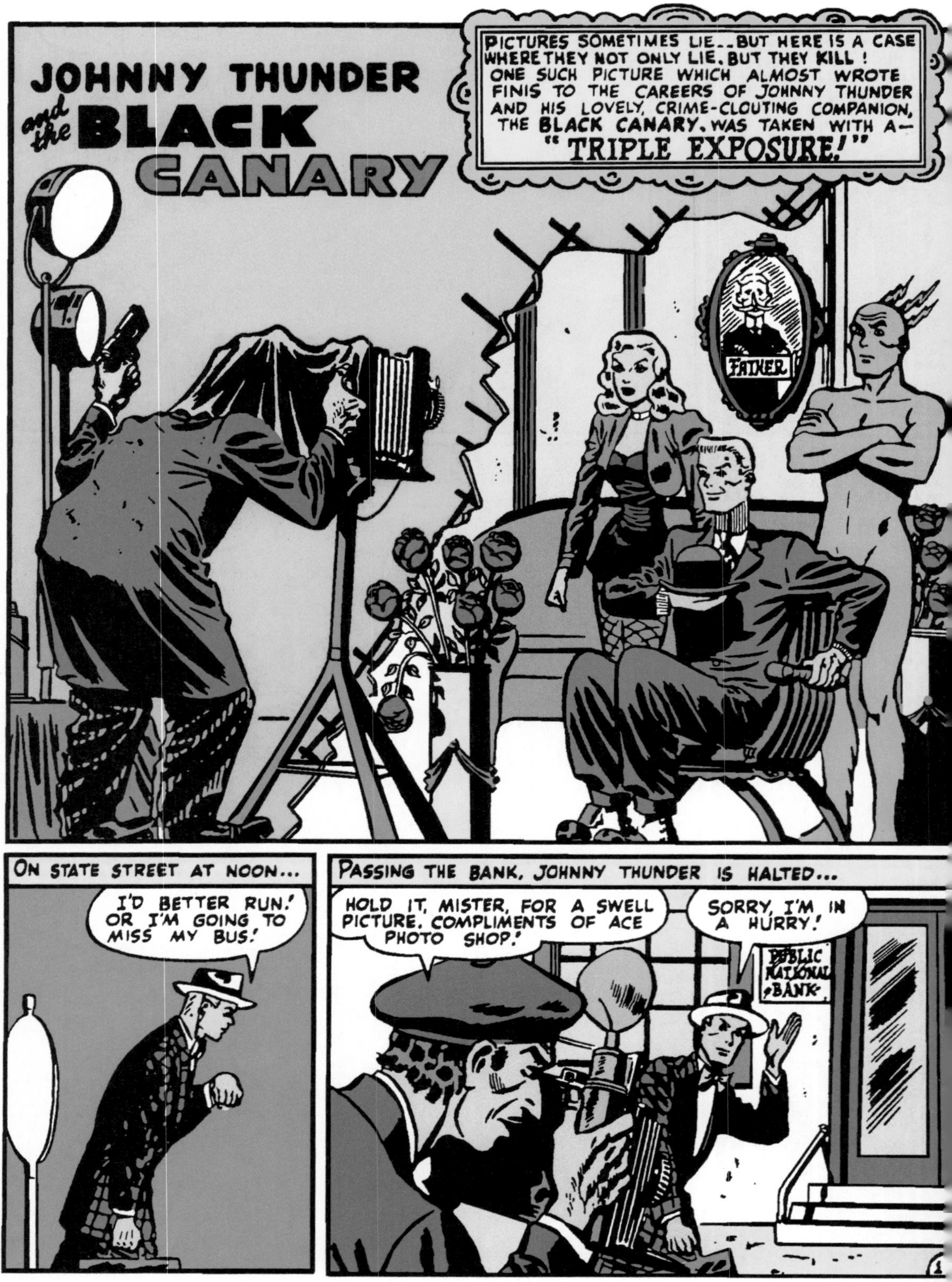
JOHNNY THUNDER and the BLACK CANARY
PICTURES SOMETIMES LIE.. BUT HERE IS A CASE WHERE THEY NOT ONLY LIE, BUT THEY KILL! ONE SUCH PICTURE WHICH ALMOST WROTE FINIS TO THE CAREERS OF JOHNNY THUNDER AND HIS LOVELY, CRIME-CLOUTING COMPANION, THE BLACK CANARY, WAS TAKEN WITH A— "TRIPLE EXPOSURE!"
FATHER
ON STATE STREET AT NOON...
I'D BETTER RUN! OR I'M GOING TO MISS MY BUS!
PASSING THE BANK, JOHNNY THUNDER IS HALTED...
HOLD IT, MISTER, FOR A SWELL PICTURE, COMPLIMENTS OF ACE PHOTO SHOP!
SORRY, I'M IN A HURRY!
PUBLIC NATIONAL BANK
1

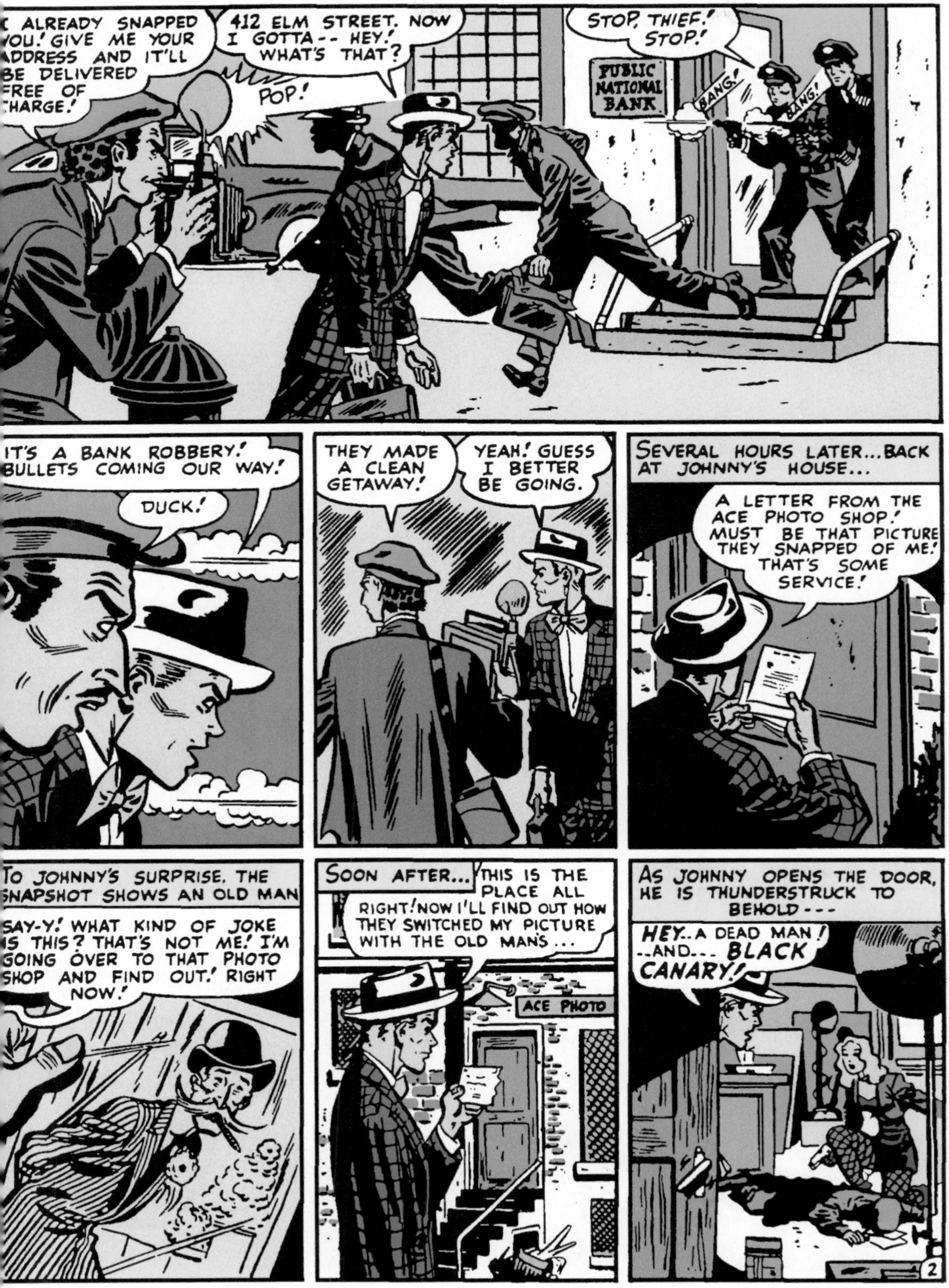
I ALREADY SNAPPED YOU! GIVE ME YOUR ADDRESS AND IT'LL BE DELIVERED FREE OF CHARGE!
412 ELM STREET. NOW I GOTTA-- HEY! WHAT'S THAT?
POP!
STOP, THIEF! STOP!
PUBLIC NATIONAL BANK
BANG!
BANG!
IT'S A BANK ROBBERY! BULLETS COMING OUR WAY!
DUCK!
THEY MADE A CLEAN GETAWAY!
YEAH! GUESS I BETTER BE GOING.
SEVERAL HOURS LATER... BACK AT JOHNNY'S HOUSE...
A LETTER FROM THE ACE PHOTO SHOP! MUST BE THAT PICTURE THEY SNAPPED OF ME! THAT'S SOME SERVICE!
TO JOHNNY'S SURPRISE, THE SNAPSHOT SHOWS AN OLD MAN
SAY-Y! WHAT KIND OF JOKE IS THIS? THAT'S NOT ME! I'M GOING OVER TO THAT PHOTO SHOP AND FIND OUT! RIGHT NOW!
SOON AFTER...
THIS IS THE PLACE ALL RIGHT! NOW I'LL FIND OUT HOW THEY SWITCHED MY PICTURE WITH THE OLD MAN'S...
ACE PHOTO
AS JOHNNY OPENS THE DOOR, HE IS THUNDERSTRUCK TO BEHOLD---
HEY.. A DEAD MAN! ..AND... BLACK CANARY!
2

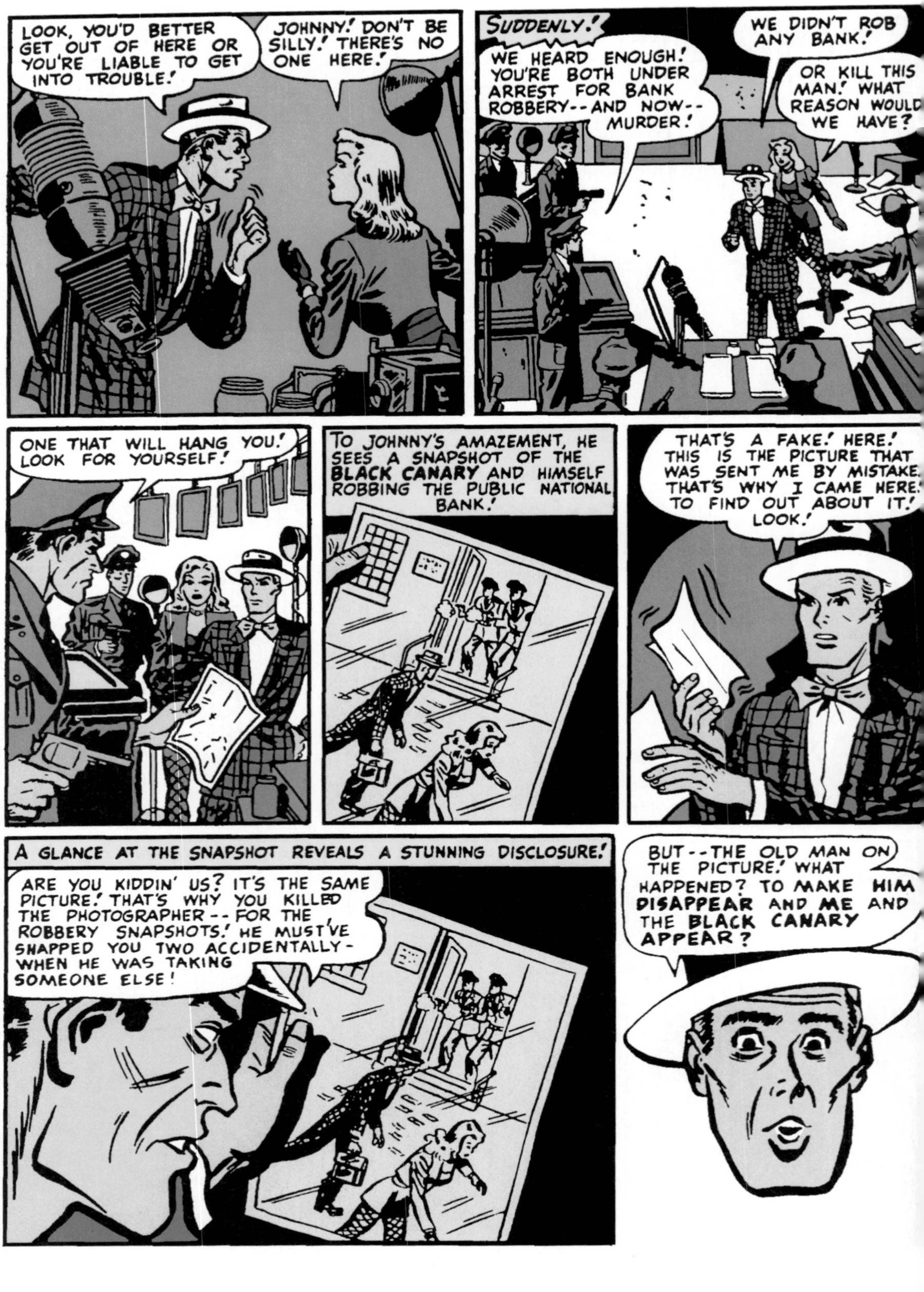
LOOK, YOU'D BETTER GET OUT OF HERE OR YOU'RE LIABLE TO GET INTO TROUBLE!
JOHNNY! DON'T BE SILLY! THERE'S NO ONE HERE!
SUDDENLY!
WE HEARD ENOUGH! YOU'RE BOTH UNDER ARREST FOR BANK ROBBERY--AND NOW--MURDER!
WE DIDN'T ROB ANY BANK!
OR KILL THIS MAN! WHAT REASON WOULD WE HAVE?
ONE THAT WILL HANG YOU! LOOK FOR YOURSELF!
TO JOHNNY'S AMAZEMENT, HE SEES A SNAPSHOT OF THE BLACK CANARY AND HIMSELF ROBBING THE PUBLIC NATIONAL BANK!
THAT'S A FAKE! HERE! THIS IS THE PICTURE THAT WAS SENT ME BY MISTAKE. THAT'S WHY I CAME HERE: TO FIND OUT ABOUT IT! LOOK!
A GLANCE AT THE SNAPSHOT REVEALS A STUNNING DISCLOSURE!
ARE YOU KIDDIN' US? IT'S THE SAME PICTURE! THAT'S WHY YOU KILLED THE PHOTOGRAPHER--FOR THE ROBBERY SNAPSHOTS! HE MUST'VE SNAPPED YOU TWO ACCIDENTALLY-WHEN HE WAS TAKING SOMEONE ELSE!
BUT--THE OLD MAN ON THE PICTURE! WHAT HAPPENED? TO MAKE HIM DISAPPEAR AND ME AND THE BLACK CANARY APPEAR?

As the two are taken to the police station...

OKAY, COPPERS, REACH!

IT'S ALL RIGHT, **BLACK CANARY!** YOU DIDN'T THINK WE'D LET 'EM TAKE YOU? AFTER THAT NIFTY BANK JOB YOU PULLED FOR US!

They are hurried into the gangsters' car..

BANKO JIM! YOU SICCED THE POLICE ON **US** TO THROW THEM OFF **YOUR** TRAIL!

SURE! THE PHOTOGRAPHER SNAPPED JOHNNY AND ACCIDENTALLY GOT **US** TOO IN THE **BACKGROUND**, WHILE WE WERE ROBBING THE BANK! WE BLANKED OURSELVES OUT — AND SUPERIMPOSED A PICTURE OF **YOU** ON IT!

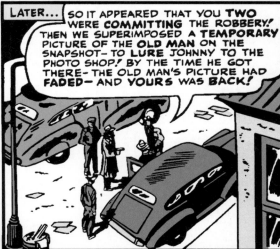

LATER...

SO IT APPEARED THAT YOU **TWO** WERE **COMMITTING THE ROBBERY!** THEN WE SUPERIMPOSED A **TEMPORARY** PICTURE OF THE **OLD MAN** ON THE SNAPSHOT— TO **LURE** JOHNNY TO THE PHOTO SHOP! BY THE TIME HE GOT THERE— THE OLD MAN'S PICTURE HAD **FADED**— AND **YOURS** WAS **BACK!**

Suddenly—

JOE! LOOK OUT— UHHHH!

COME ON, JOHNNY, RUN! NOW'S OUR CHANCE!

SO THAT'S IT! (PANT-) THEY PUT THE PICTURE OF THE OLD MAN ON TOP OF MINE-- (PANT-) MINE WAS LEFT ON TOP OF THE——

SAVE YOUR BREATH! HEAD FOR THE GAS TANK!

YEOW! THAT BULLET CAME CLOSE! HURRY!

BANG!

4

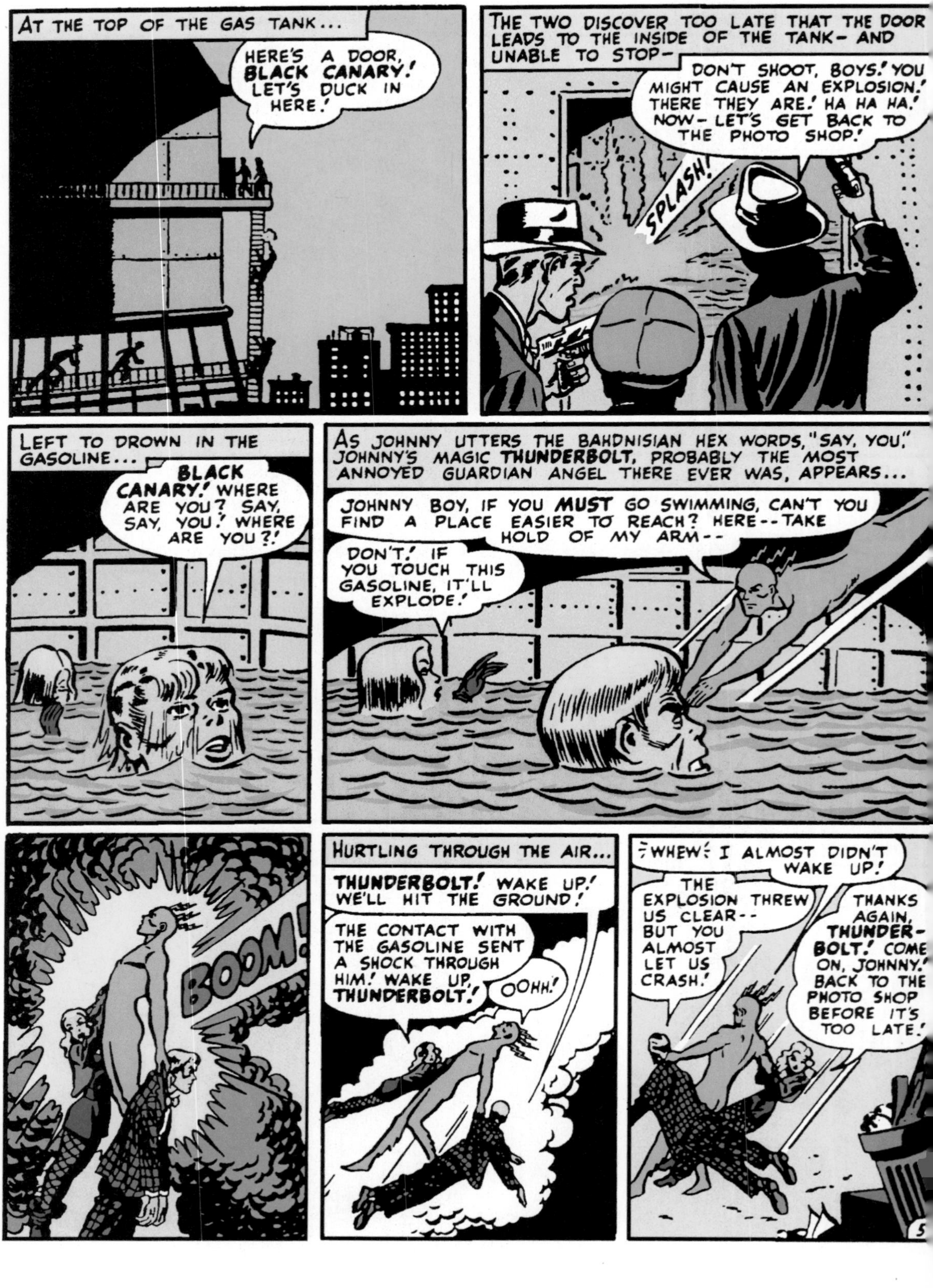

AT THE TOP OF THE GAS TANK...
HERE'S A DOOR, BLACK CANARY! LET'S DUCK IN HERE!
THE TWO DISCOVER TOO LATE THAT THE DOOR LEADS TO THE INSIDE OF THE TANK- AND UNABLE TO STOP-
DON'T SHOOT, BOYS! YOU MIGHT CAUSE AN EXPLOSION! THERE THEY ARE! HA HA HA! NOW- LET'S GET BACK TO THE PHOTO SHOP!
SPLASH!
LEFT TO DROWN IN THE GASOLINE...
BLACK CANARY! WHERE ARE YOU? SAY, SAY, YOU! WHERE ARE YOU?!
AS JOHNNY UTTERS THE BAHDNISIAN HEX WORDS, "SAY, YOU," JOHNNY'S MAGIC THUNDERBOLT, PROBABLY THE MOST ANNOYED GUARDIAN ANGEL THERE EVER WAS, APPEARS...
JOHNNY BOY, IF YOU MUST GO SWIMMING, CAN'T YOU FIND A PLACE EASIER TO REACH? HERE--TAKE HOLD OF MY ARM--
DON'T! IF YOU TOUCH THIS GASOLINE, IT'LL EXPLODE!
BOOM!
HURTLING THROUGH THE AIR...
THUNDERBOLT! WAKE UP! WE'LL HIT THE GROUND!
THE CONTACT WITH THE GASOLINE SENT A SHOCK THROUGH HIM! WAKE UP, THUNDERBOLT!
OOHH!
WHEW! I ALMOST DIDN'T WAKE UP!
THE EXPLOSION THREW US CLEAR-- BUT YOU ALMOST LET US CRASH!
THANKS AGAIN, THUNDERBOLT! COME ON, JOHNNY! BACK TO THE PHOTO SHOP BEFORE IT'S TOO LATE!
5

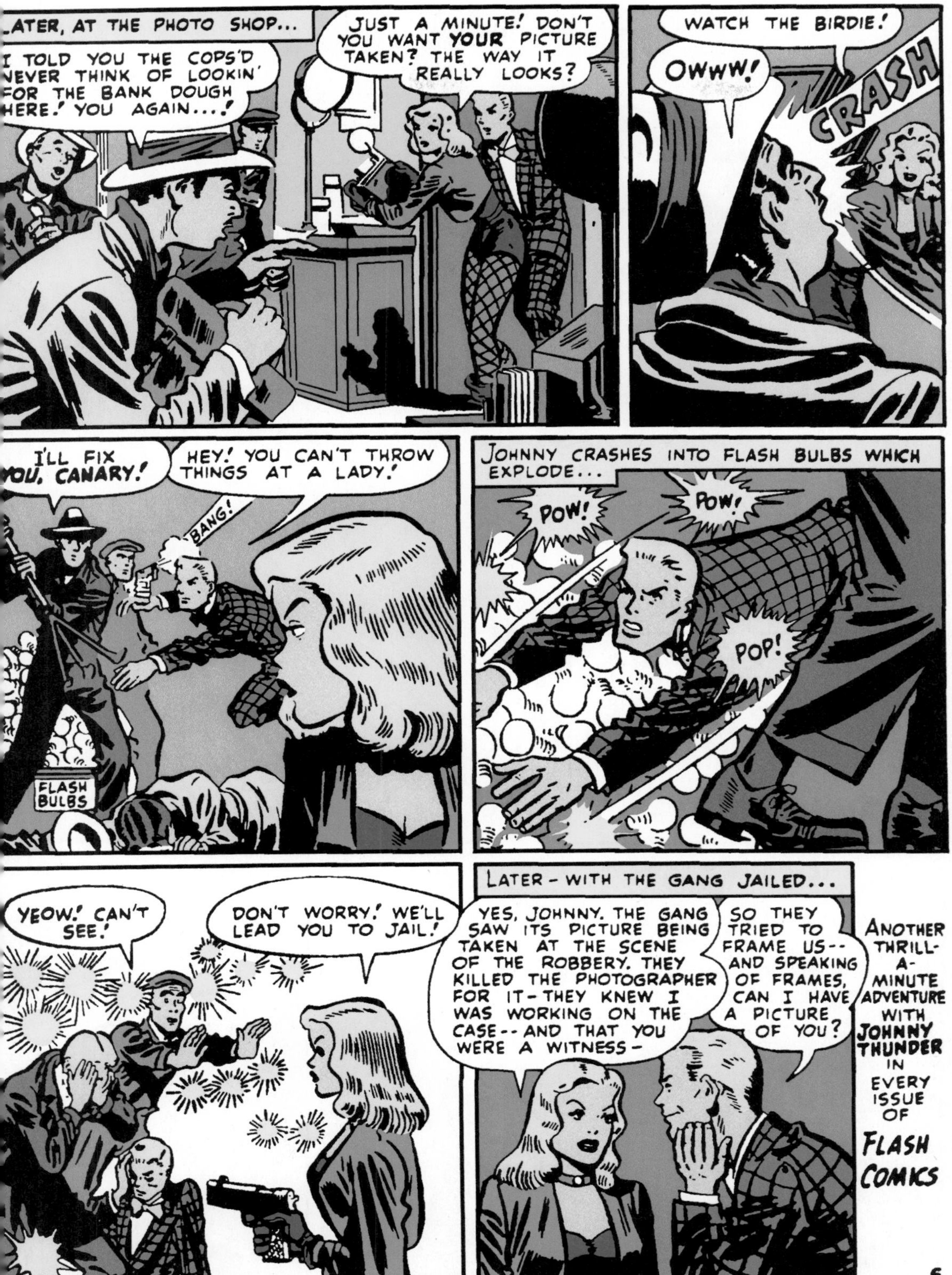
LATER, AT THE PHOTO SHOP...
I TOLD YOU THE COPS'D NEVER THINK OF LOOKIN' FOR THE BANK DOUGH HERE! YOU AGAIN...!
JUST A MINUTE! DON'T YOU WANT YOUR PICTURE TAKEN? THE WAY IT REALLY LOOKS?
WATCH THE BIRDIE!
OWWW!
CRASH
I'LL FIX YOU, CANARY!
HEY! YOU CAN'T THROW THINGS AT A LADY!
BANG!
FLASH BULBS
JOHNNY CRASHES INTO FLASH BULBS WHICH EXPLODE...
POW!
POW!
POP!
YEOW! CAN'T SEE!
DON'T WORRY! WE'LL LEAD YOU TO JAIL!
LATER - WITH THE GANG JAILED...
YES, JOHNNY. THE GANG SAW ITS PICTURE BEING TAKEN AT THE SCENE OF THE ROBBERY. THEY KILLED THE PHOTOGRAPHER FOR IT - THEY KNEW I WAS WORKING ON THE CASE -- AND THAT YOU WERE A WITNESS -
SO THEY TRIED TO FRAME US -- AND SPEAKING OF FRAMES, CAN I HAVE A PICTURE OF YOU?
ANOTHER THRILL-A-MINUTE ADVENTURE WITH JOHNNY THUNDER IN EVERY ISSUE OF FLASH COMICS
6

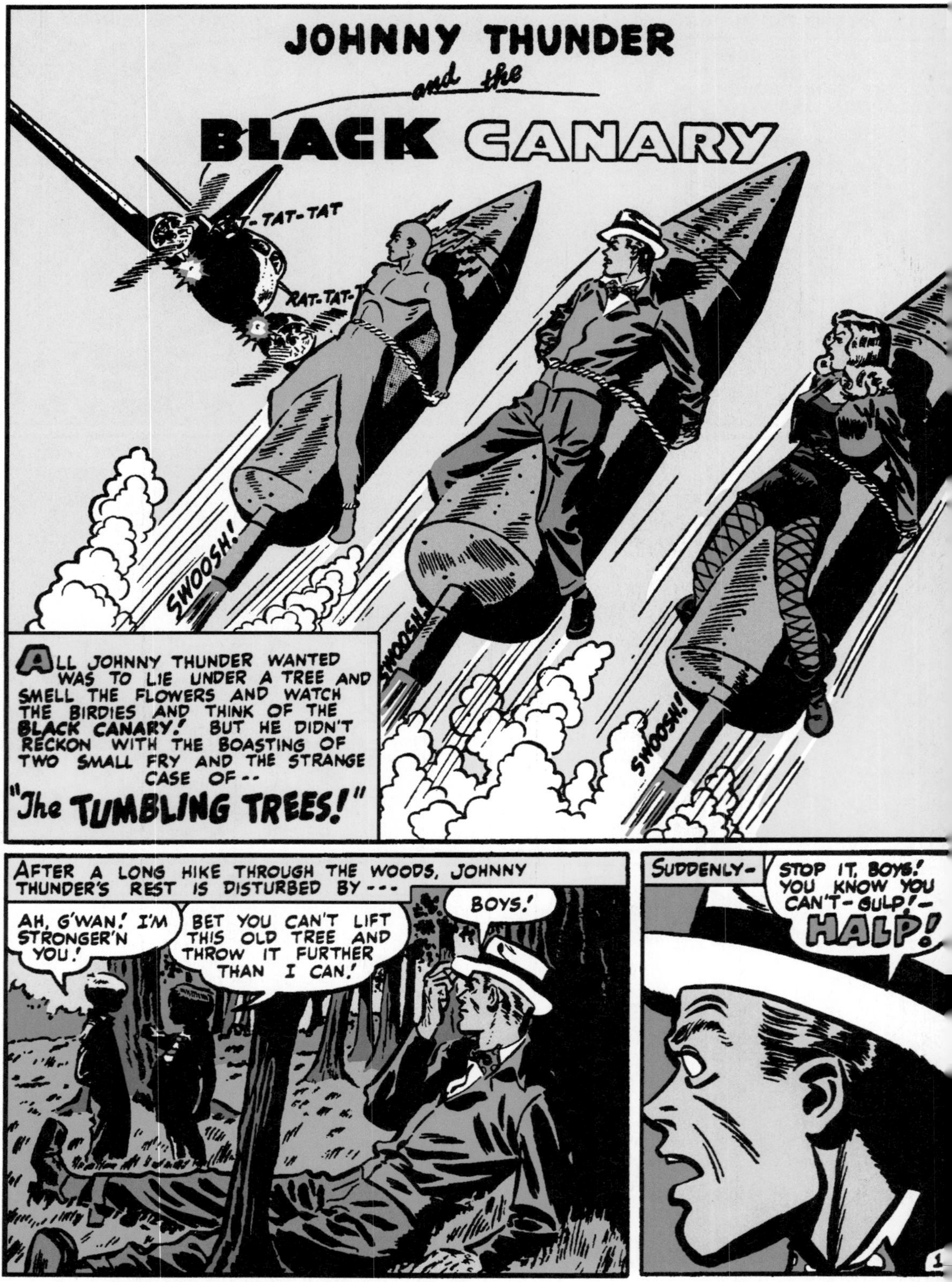
JOHNNY THUNDER
and the
BLACK CANARY
TAT-TAT-TAT
RAT-TAT-T
SWOOSH!
SWOOSH!
SWOOSH!
ALL JOHNNY THUNDER WANTED WAS TO LIE UNDER A TREE AND SMELL THE FLOWERS AND WATCH THE BIRDIES AND THINK OF THE BLACK CANARY! BUT HE DIDN'T RECKON WITH THE BOASTING OF TWO SMALL FRY AND THE STRANGE CASE OF --
"The TUMBLING TREES!"
AFTER A LONG HIKE THROUGH THE WOODS, JOHNNY THUNDER'S REST IS DISTURBED BY ---
AH, G'WAN! I'M STRONGER'N YOU!
BET YOU CAN'T LIFT THIS OLD TREE AND THROW IT FURTHER THAN I CAN!
BOYS!
SUDDENLY-
STOP IT, BOYS! YOU KNOW YOU CAN'T-GULP!- HALP!
1

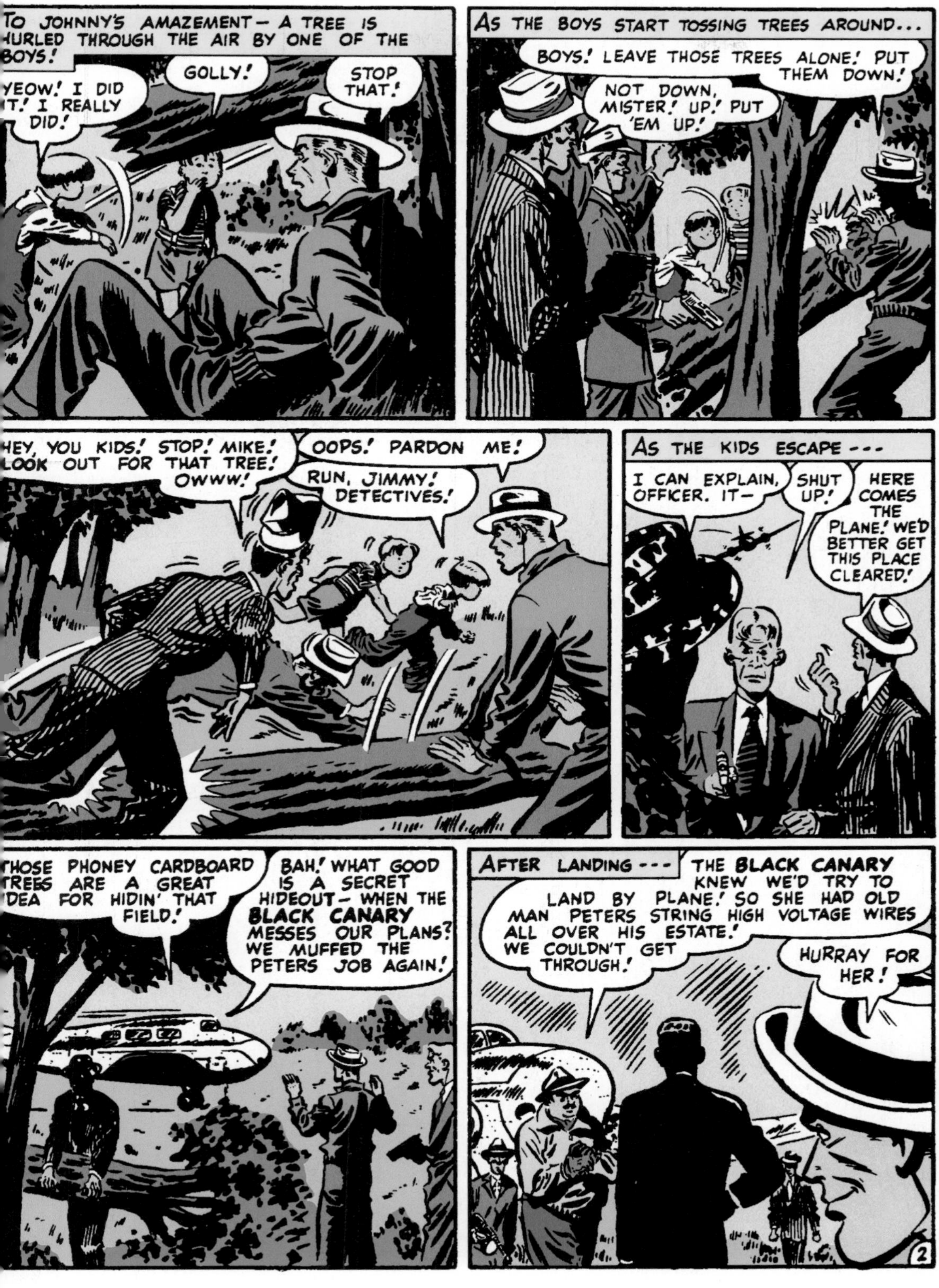
TO JOHNNY'S AMAZEMENT — A TREE IS HURLED THROUGH THE AIR BY ONE OF THE BOYS!
YEOW! I DID IT! I REALLY DID!
GOLLY!
STOP THAT!
AS THE BOYS START TOSSING TREES AROUND...
BOYS! LEAVE THOSE TREES ALONE! PUT THEM DOWN!
NOT DOWN, MISTER! UP! PUT 'EM UP!
HEY, YOU KIDS! STOP! MIKE! LOOK OUT FOR THAT TREE! OWWW!
OOPS! PARDON ME!
RUN, JIMMY! DETECTIVES!
AS THE KIDS ESCAPE ---
I CAN EXPLAIN, OFFICER. IT—
SHUT UP!
HERE COMES THE PLANE! WE'D BETTER GET THIS PLACE CLEARED!
THOSE PHONEY CARDBOARD TREES ARE A GREAT IDEA FOR HIDIN' THAT FIELD!
BAH! WHAT GOOD IS A SECRET HIDEOUT— WHEN THE BLACK CANARY MESSES OUR PLANS? WE MUFFED THE PETERS JOB AGAIN!
AFTER LANDING ---
THE BLACK CANARY KNEW WE'D TRY TO LAND BY PLANE! SO SHE HAD OLD MAN PETERS STRING HIGH VOLTAGE WIRES ALL OVER HIS ESTATE! WE COULDN'T GET THROUGH!
HURRAY FOR HER!
2

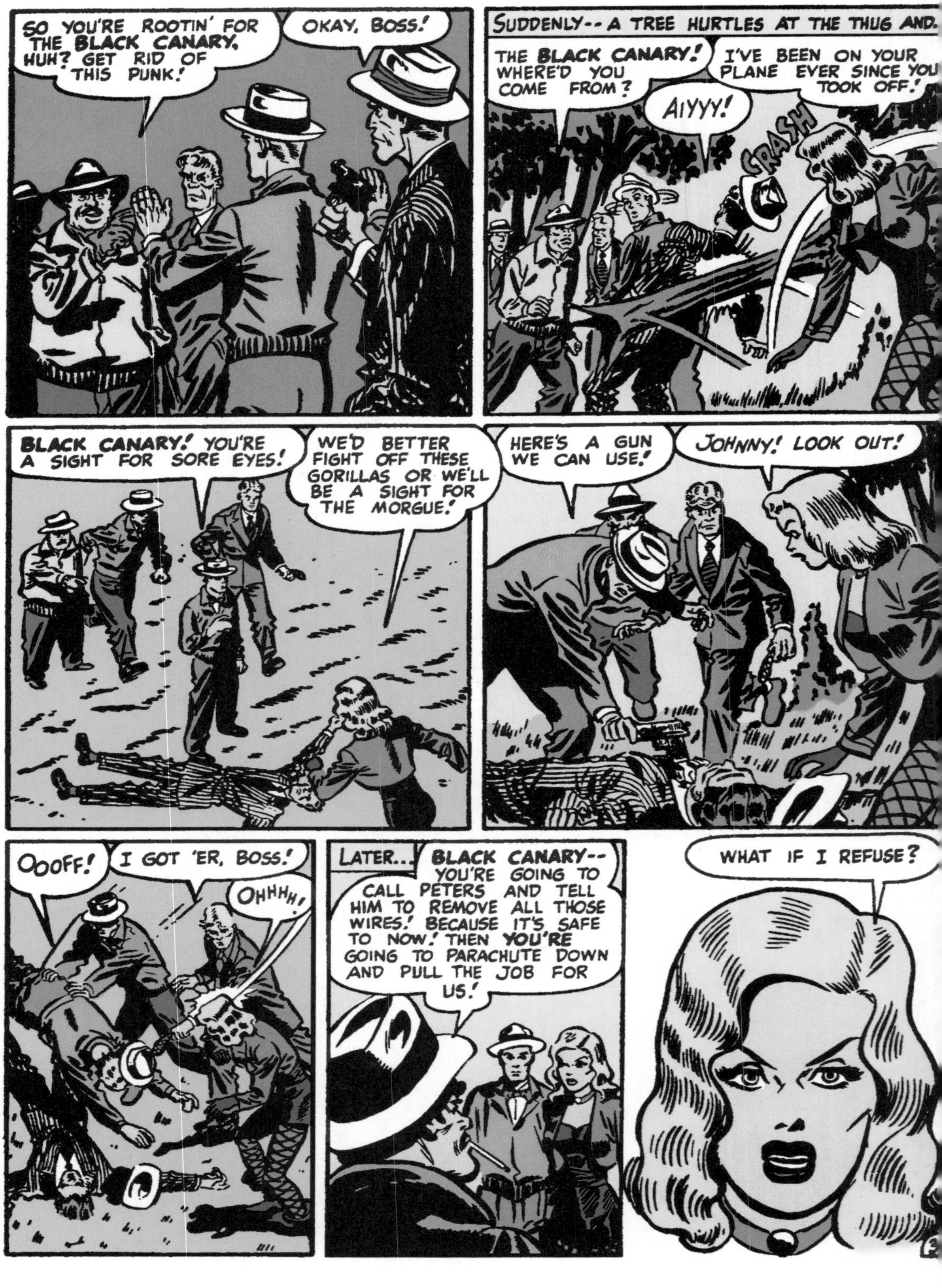
SO YOU'RE ROOTIN' FOR THE BLACK CANARY, HUH? GET RID OF THIS PUNK!
OKAY, BOSS!
SUDDENLY-- A TREE HURTLES AT THE THUG AND...
THE BLACK CANARY! WHERE'D YOU COME FROM?
I'VE BEEN ON YOUR PLANE EVER SINCE YOU TOOK OFF!
AIYYY!
CRASH
BLACK CANARY! YOU'RE A SIGHT FOR SORE EYES!
WE'D BETTER FIGHT OFF THESE GORILLAS OR WE'LL BE A SIGHT FOR THE MORGUE!
HERE'S A GUN WE CAN USE!
JOHNNY! LOOK OUT!
OOOFF!
I GOT 'ER, BOSS!
OHHHH!
LATER...
BLACK CANARY-- YOU'RE GOING TO CALL PETERS AND TELL HIM TO REMOVE ALL THOSE WIRES! BECAUSE IT'S SAFE TO NOW! THEN YOU'RE GOING TO PARACHUTE DOWN AND PULL THE JOB FOR US!
WHAT IF I REFUSE?

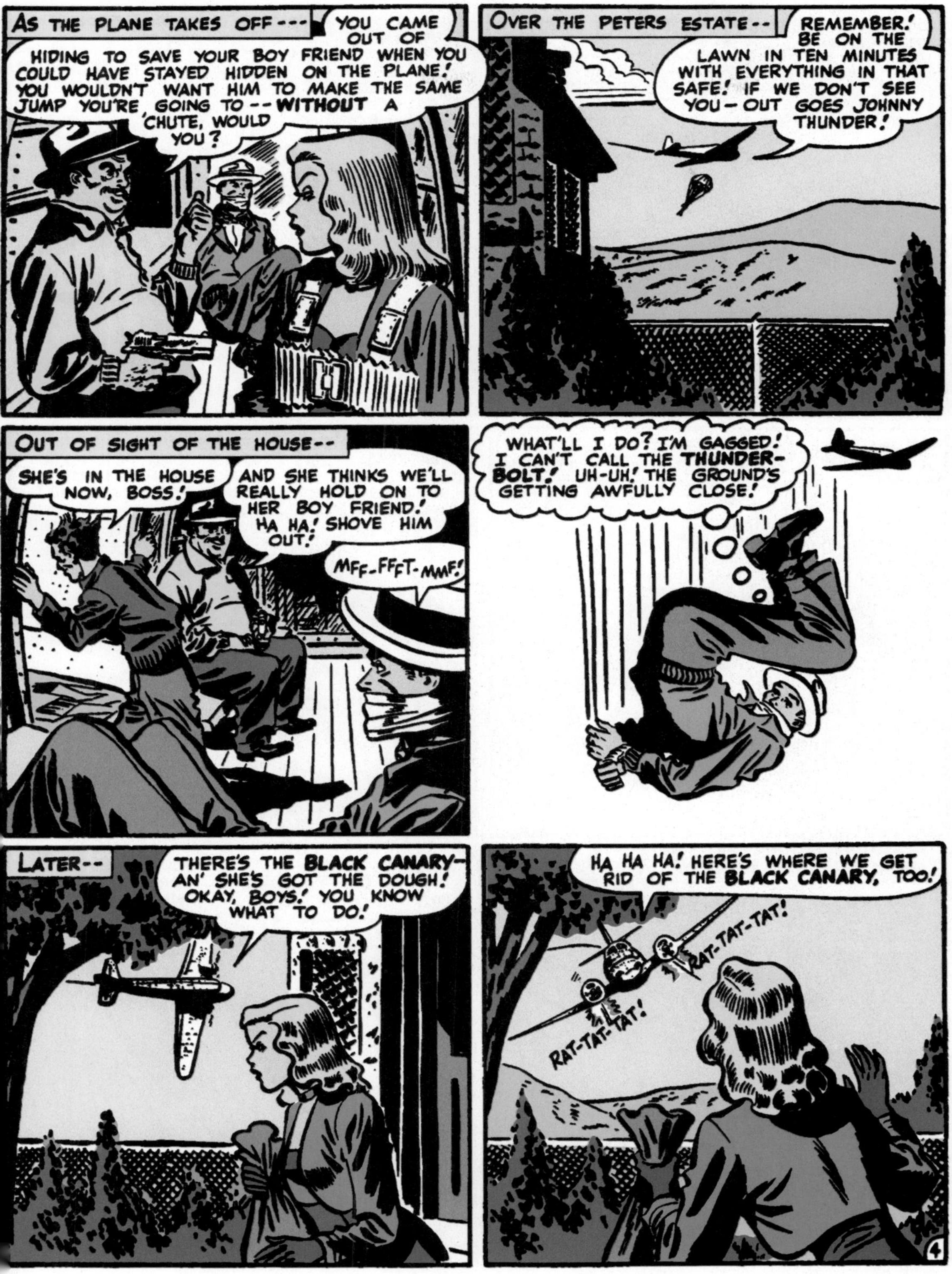
AS THE PLANE TAKES OFF---
YOU CAME OUT OF HIDING TO SAVE YOUR BOY FRIEND WHEN YOU COULD HAVE STAYED HIDDEN ON THE PLANE! YOU WOULDN'T WANT HIM TO MAKE THE SAME JUMP YOU'RE GOING TO -- WITHOUT A 'CHUTE, WOULD YOU?
OVER THE PETERS ESTATE--
REMEMBER! BE ON THE LAWN IN TEN MINUTES WITH EVERYTHING IN THAT SAFE! IF WE DON'T SEE YOU - OUT GOES JOHNNY THUNDER!
OUT OF SIGHT OF THE HOUSE--
SHE'S IN THE HOUSE NOW, BOSS!
AND SHE THINKS WE'LL REALLY HOLD ON TO HER BOY FRIEND! HA HA! SHOVE HIM OUT!
MFF-FFFT-MMF!
WHAT'LL I DO? I'M GAGGED! I CAN'T CALL THE THUNDER-BOLT! UH-UH! THE GROUND'S GETTING AWFULLY CLOSE!
LATER--
THERE'S THE BLACK CANARY-- AN' SHE'S GOT THE DOUGH! OKAY, BOYS! YOU KNOW WHAT TO DO!
HA HA HA! HERE'S WHERE WE GET RID OF THE BLACK CANARY, TOO!
RAT-TAT-TAT!
RAT-TAT-TAT!
4

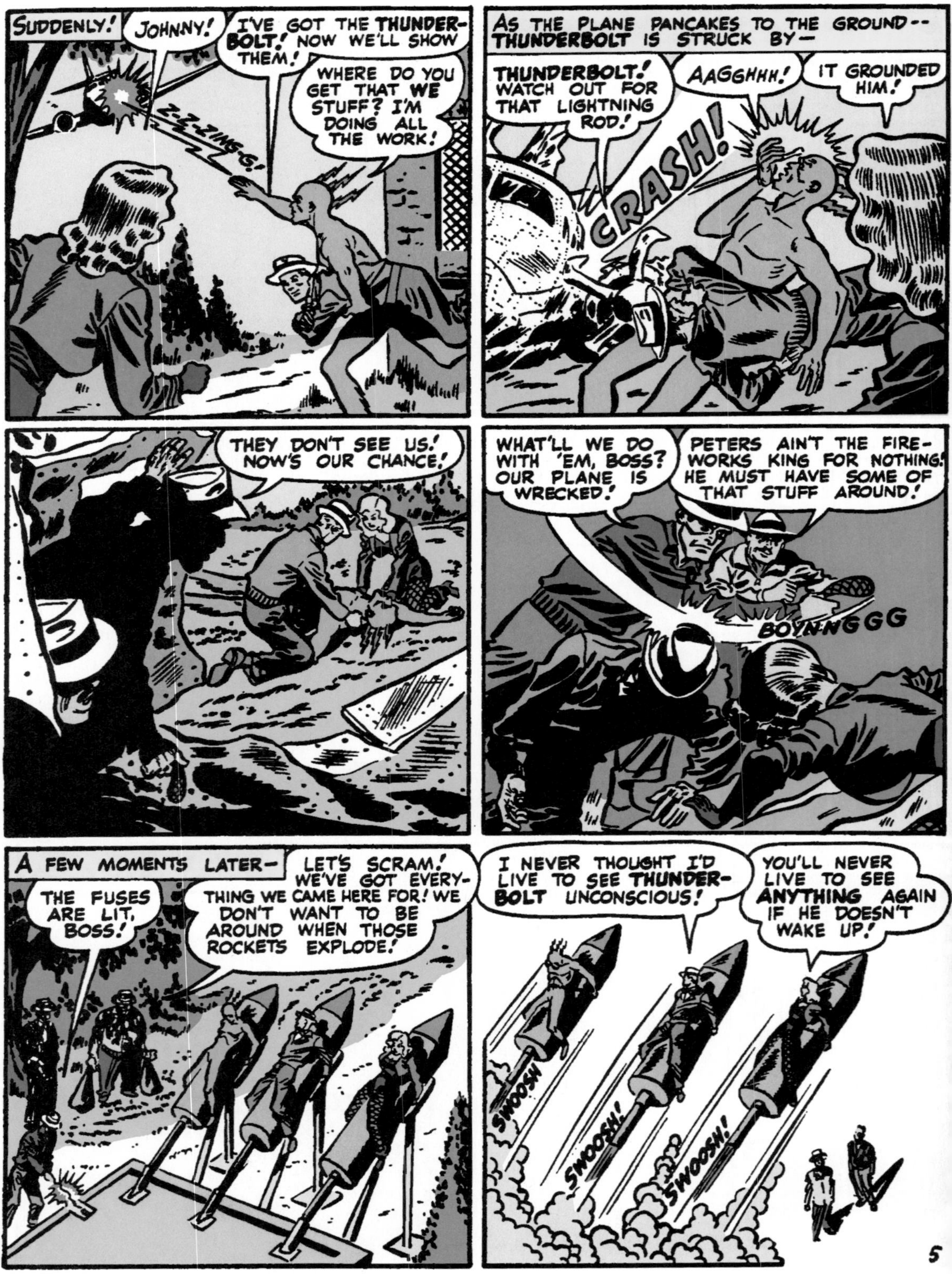
SUDDENLY!
JOHNNY!
I'VE GOT THE THUNDERBOLT! NOW WE'LL SHOW THEM!
WHERE DO YOU GET THAT WE STUFF? I'M DOING ALL THE WORK!
Z-Z-ZING-G-G!
AS THE PLANE PANCAKES TO THE GROUND-- THUNDERBOLT IS STRUCK BY--
THUNDERBOLT! WATCH OUT FOR THAT LIGHTNING ROD!
AAGGHHH!
IT GROUNDED HIM!
CRASH!
THEY DON'T SEE US! NOW'S OUR CHANCE!
WHAT'LL WE DO WITH 'EM, BOSS? OUR PLANE IS WRECKED!
PETERS AIN'T THE FIREWORKS KING FOR NOTHING! HE MUST HAVE SOME OF THAT STUFF AROUND!
BOYNNGGG
A FEW MOMENTS LATER--
THE FUSES ARE LIT, BOSS!
LET'S SCRAM! WE'VE GOT EVERYTHING WE CAME HERE FOR! WE DON'T WANT TO BE AROUND WHEN THOSE ROCKETS EXPLODE!
I NEVER THOUGHT I'D LIVE TO SEE THUNDERBOLT UNCONSCIOUS!
YOU'LL NEVER LIVE TO SEE ANYTHING AGAIN IF HE DOESN'T WAKE UP!
SWOOSH
SWOOSH!
SWOOSH!
5

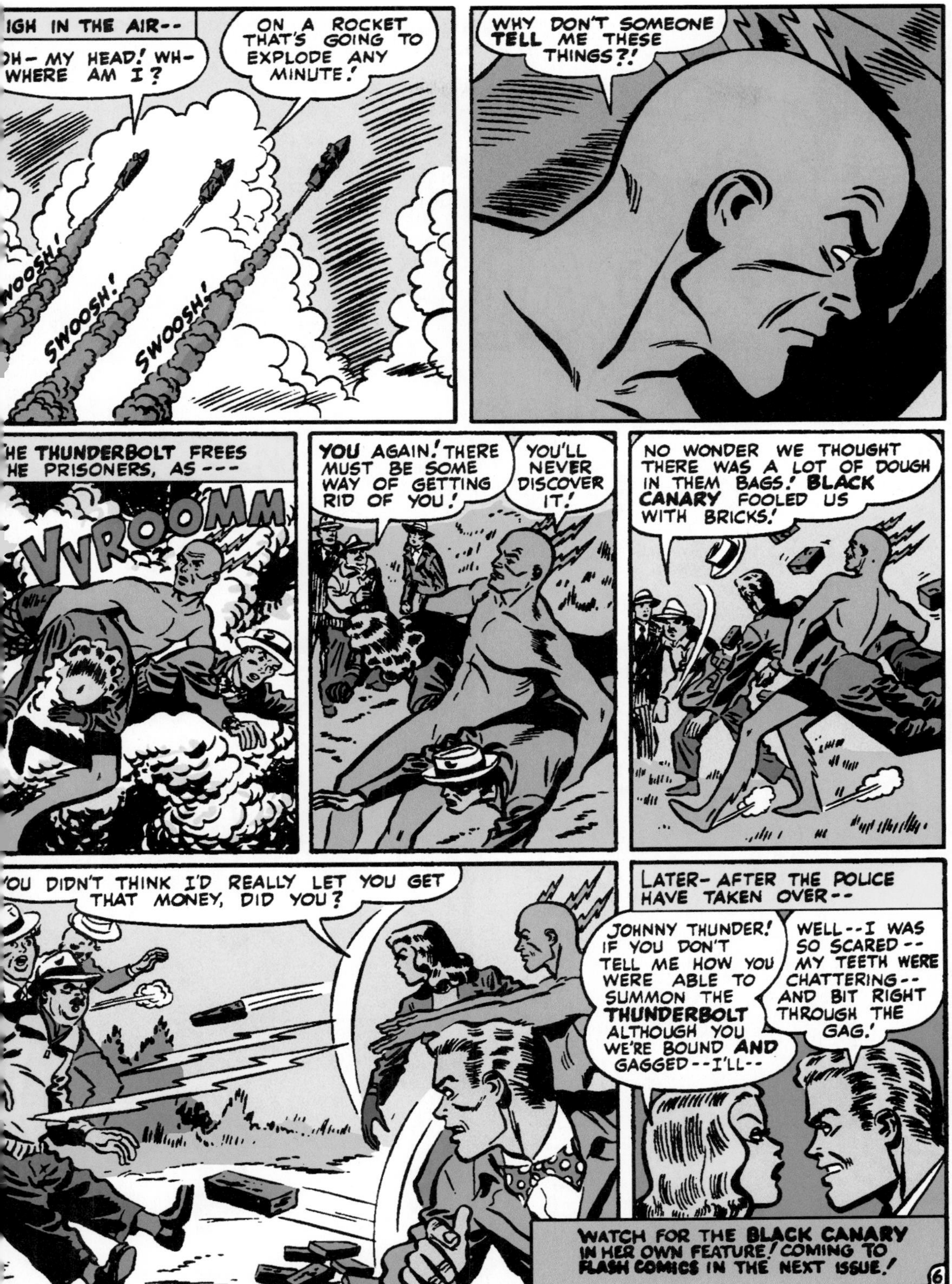
IGH IN THE AIR--
OH- MY HEAD! WH- WHERE AM I?
ON A ROCKET THAT'S GOING TO EXPLODE ANY MINUTE!
WOOSH!
SWOOSH!
SWOOSH!
WHY DON'T SOMEONE TELL ME THESE THINGS?!
HE THUNDERBOLT FREES HE PRISONERS, AS---
VVROOMM
YOU AGAIN! THERE MUST BE SOME WAY OF GETTING RID OF YOU!
YOU'LL NEVER DISCOVER IT!
NO WONDER WE THOUGHT THERE WAS A LOT OF DOUGH IN THEM BAGS! BLACK CANARY FOOLED US WITH BRICKS!
YOU DIDN'T THINK I'D REALLY LET YOU GET THAT MONEY, DID YOU?
LATER- AFTER THE POLICE HAVE TAKEN OVER--
JOHNNY THUNDER! IF YOU DON'T TELL ME HOW YOU WERE ABLE TO SUMMON THE THUNDERBOLT ALTHOUGH YOU WE'RE BOUND AND GAGGED--I'LL--
WELL--I WAS SO SCARED-- MY TEETH WERE CHATTERING-- AND BIT RIGHT THROUGH THE GAG!
WATCH FOR THE BLACK CANARY IN HER OWN FEATURE! COMING TO FLASH COMICS IN THE NEXT ISSUE!
6

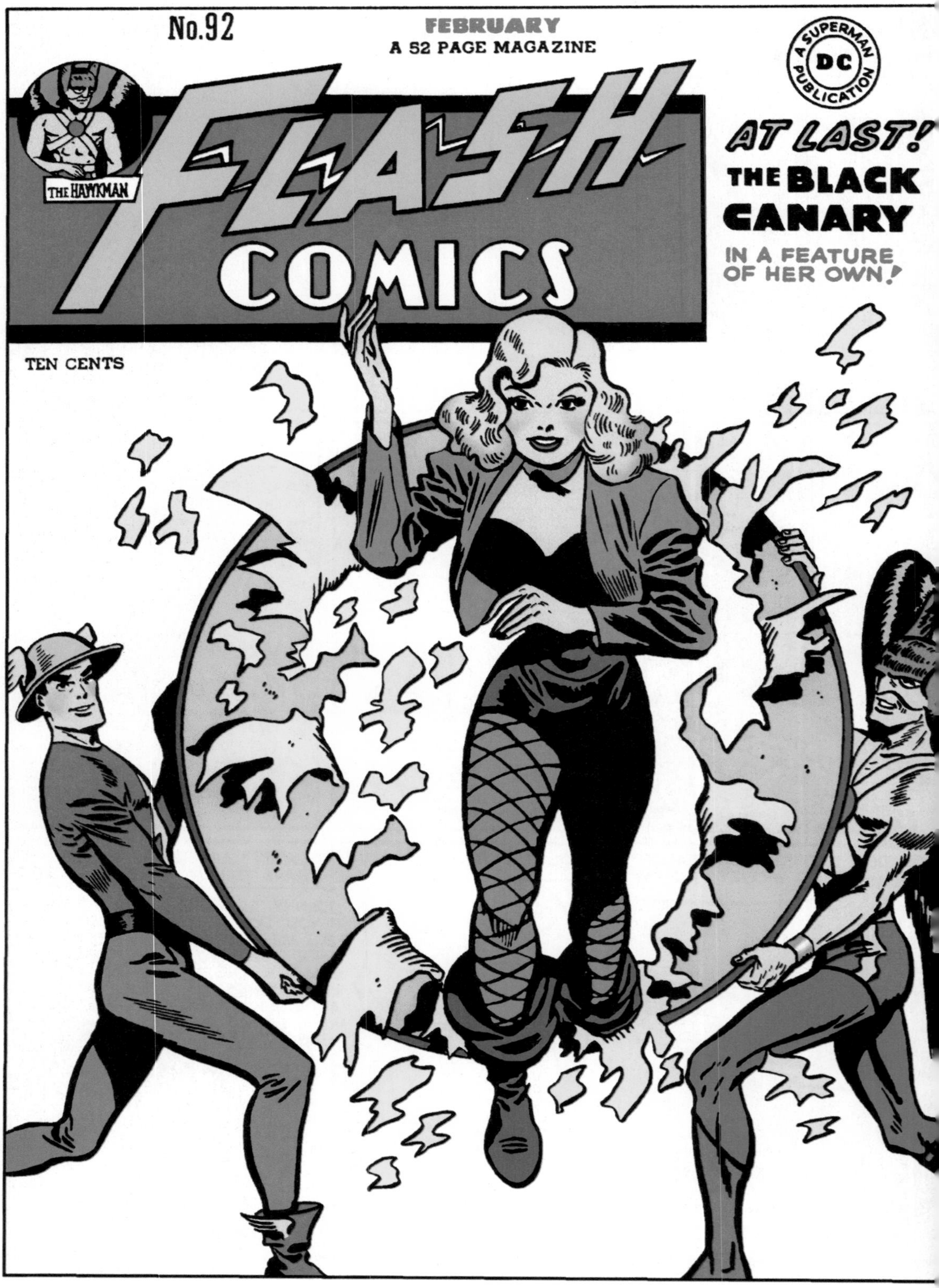
No.92
FEBRUARY
A 52 PAGE MAGAZINE
A SUPERMAN DC PUBLICATION
THE HAWKMAN
FLASH COMICS
AT LAST!
THE BLACK CANARY
IN A FEATURE OF HER OWN!
TEN CENTS

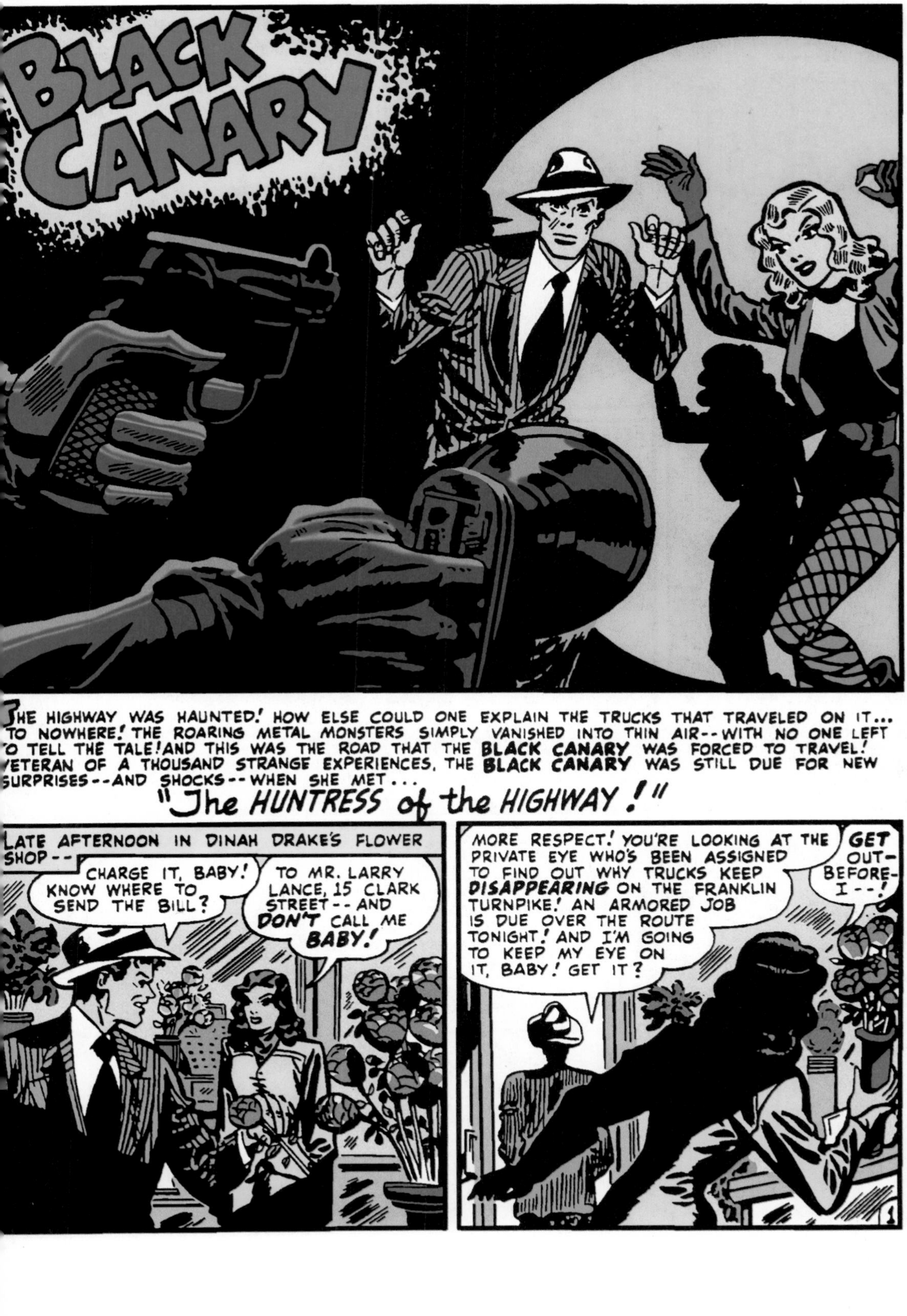
BLACK CANARY
THE HIGHWAY WAS HAUNTED! HOW ELSE COULD ONE EXPLAIN THE TRUCKS THAT TRAVELED ON IT... TO NOWHERE! THE ROARING METAL MONSTERS SIMPLY VANISHED INTO THIN AIR--WITH NO ONE LEFT TO TELL THE TALE! AND THIS WAS THE ROAD THAT THE BLACK CANARY WAS FORCED TO TRAVEL! VETERAN OF A THOUSAND STRANGE EXPERIENCES, THE BLACK CANARY WAS STILL DUE FOR NEW SURPRISES--AND SHOCKS--WHEN SHE MET...
"The HUNTRESS of the HIGHWAY!"
LATE AFTERNOON IN DINAH DRAKE'S FLOWER SHOP--
CHARGE IT, BABY! KNOW WHERE TO SEND THE BILL?
TO MR. LARRY LANCE, 15 CLARK STREET--AND DON'T CALL ME BABY!
MORE RESPECT! YOU'RE LOOKING AT THE PRIVATE EYE WHO'S BEEN ASSIGNED TO FIND OUT WHY TRUCKS KEEP DISAPPEARING ON THE FRANKLIN TURNPIKE! AN ARMORED JOB IS DUE OVER THE ROUTE TONIGHT! AND I'M GOING TO KEEP MY EYE ON IT, BABY! GET IT?
GET OUT--BEFORE I--!
1

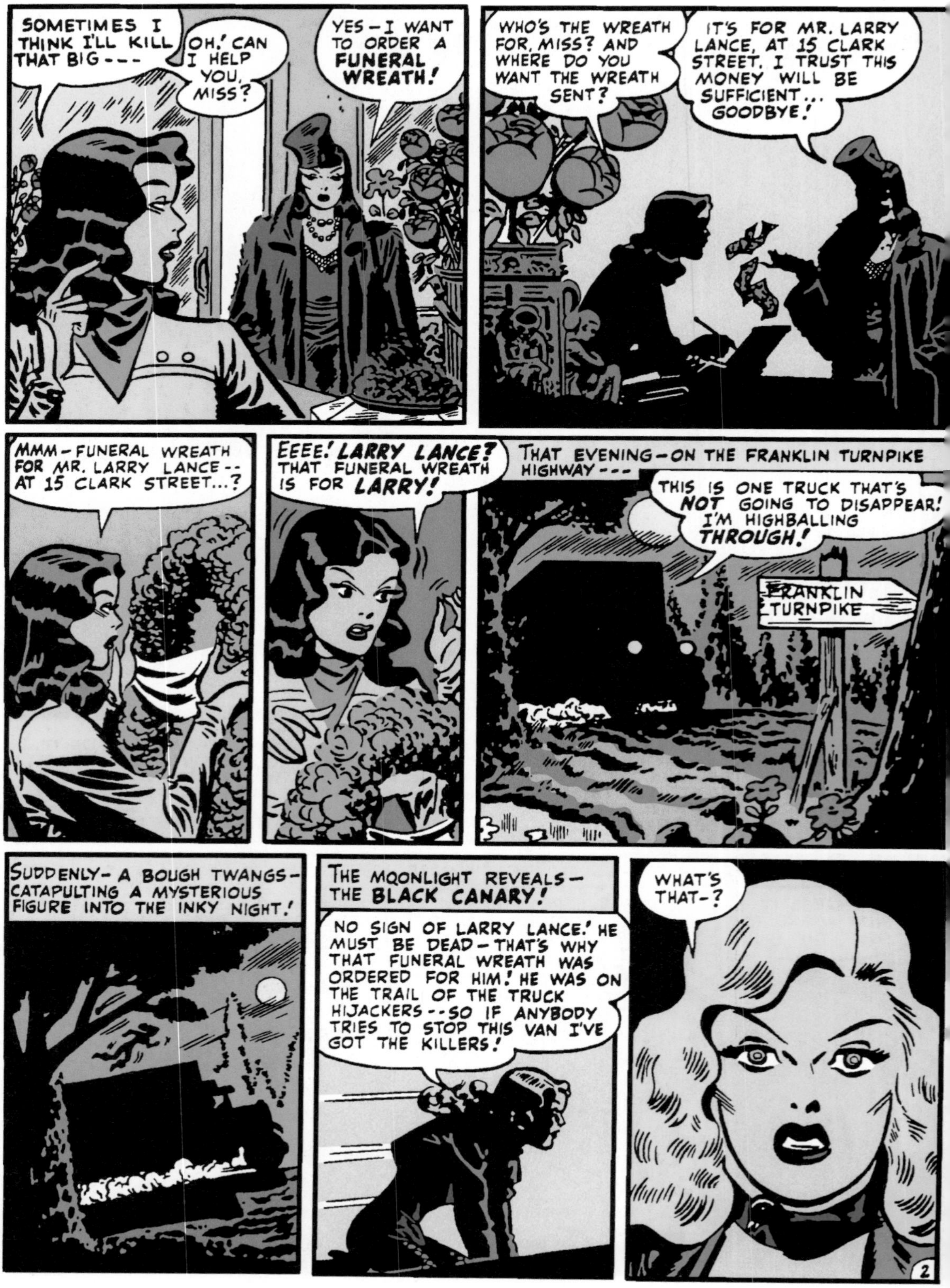
SOMETIMES I THINK I'LL KILL THAT BIG---
OH! CAN I HELP YOU, MISS?
YES-I WANT TO ORDER A FUNERAL WREATH!
WHO'S THE WREATH FOR, MISS? AND WHERE DO YOU WANT THE WREATH SENT?
IT'S FOR MR. LARRY LANCE, AT 15 CLARK STREET. I TRUST THIS MONEY WILL BE SUFFICIENT... GOODBYE!
MMM-FUNERAL WREATH FOR MR. LARRY LANCE--AT 15 CLARK STREET...?
EEEE! LARRY LANCE? THAT FUNERAL WREATH IS FOR LARRY!
THAT EVENING-ON THE FRANKLIN TURNPIKE HIGHWAY---
THIS IS ONE TRUCK THAT'S NOT GOING TO DISAPPEAR! I'M HIGHBALLING THROUGH!
FRANKLIN TURNPIKE
SUDDENLY-A BOUGH TWANGS-CATAPULTING A MYSTERIOUS FIGURE INTO THE INKY NIGHT!
THE MOONLIGHT REVEALS-THE BLACK CANARY!
NO SIGN OF LARRY LANCE! HE MUST BE DEAD-THAT'S WHY THAT FUNERAL WREATH WAS ORDERED FOR HIM! HE WAS ON THE TRAIL OF THE TRUCK HIJACKERS--SO IF ANYBODY TRIES TO STOP THIS VAN I'VE GOT THE KILLERS!
WHAT'S THAT-?
2

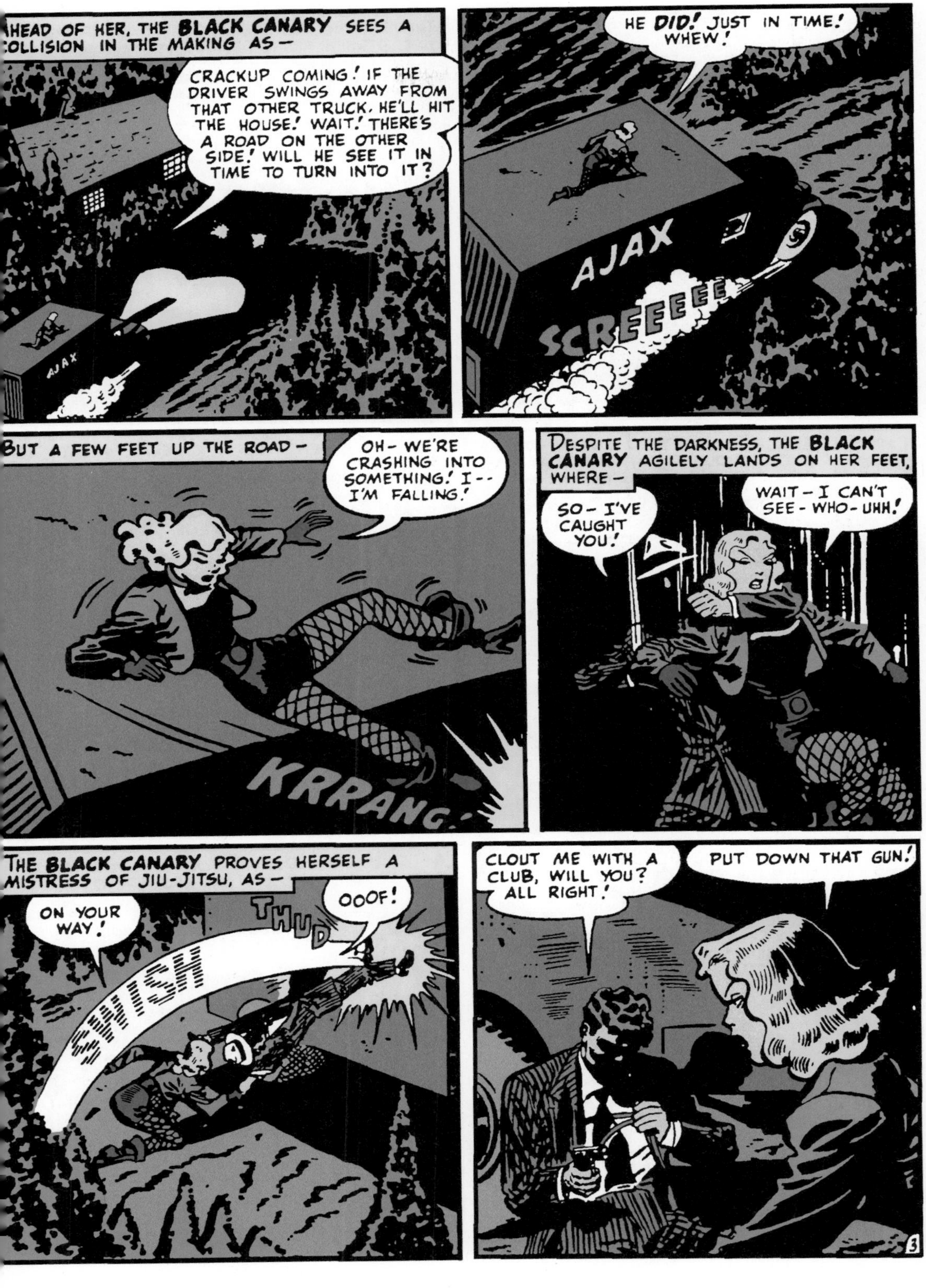

AHEAD OF HER, THE BLACK CANARY SEES A COLLISION IN THE MAKING AS —
CRACKUP COMING! IF THE DRIVER SWINGS AWAY FROM THAT OTHER TRUCK, HE'LL HIT THE HOUSE! WAIT! THERE'S A ROAD ON THE OTHER SIDE! WILL HE SEE IT IN TIME TO TURN INTO IT?
AJAX
HE DID! JUST IN TIME! WHEW!
AJAX
SCREEEEEE
BUT A FEW FEET UP THE ROAD —
OH- WE'RE CRASHING INTO SOMETHING! I-- I'M FALLING!
KRRANG!
DESPITE THE DARKNESS, THE BLACK CANARY AGILELY LANDS ON HER FEET, WHERE —
SO- I'VE CAUGHT YOU!
WAIT - I CAN'T SEE - WHO- UHH!
THE BLACK CANARY PROVES HERSELF A MISTRESS OF JIU-JITSU, AS —
ON YOUR WAY!
OOOF!
THUD
SWISH
CLOUT ME WITH A CLUB, WILL YOU? ALL RIGHT!
PUT DOWN THAT GUN!
3

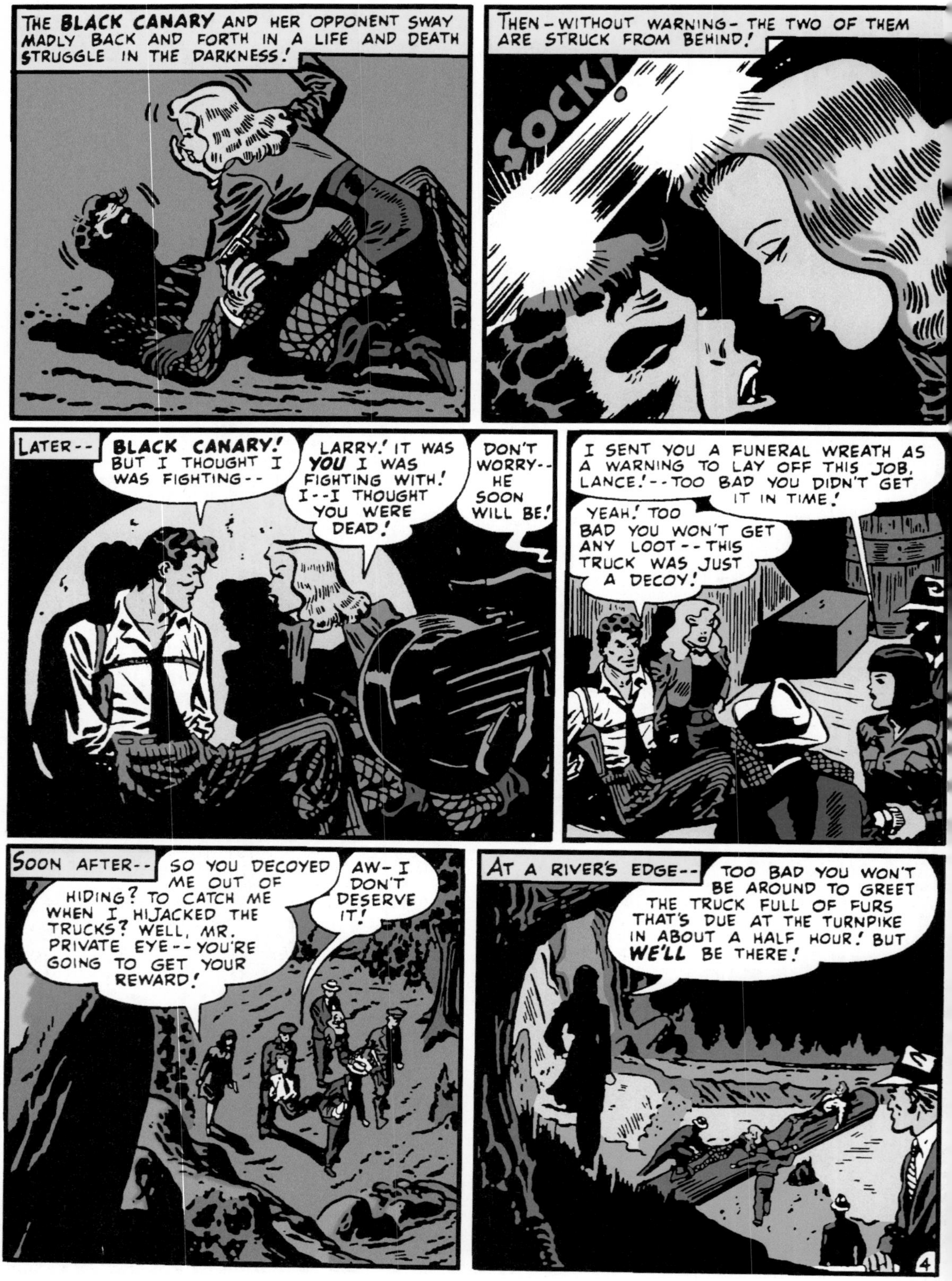

THE BLACK CANARY AND HER OPPONENT SWAY MADLY BACK AND FORTH IN A LIFE AND DEATH STRUGGLE IN THE DARKNESS!
THEN - WITHOUT WARNING - THE TWO OF THEM ARE STRUCK FROM BEHIND!
SOCK!
LATER--
BLACK CANARY! BUT I THOUGHT I WAS FIGHTING--
LARRY! IT WAS YOU I WAS FIGHTING WITH! I--I THOUGHT YOU WERE DEAD!
DON'T WORRY-- HE SOON WILL BE!
I SENT YOU A FUNERAL WREATH AS A WARNING TO LAY OFF THIS JOB, LANCE!--TOO BAD YOU DIDN'T GET IT IN TIME!
YEAH! TOO BAD YOU WON'T GET ANY LOOT--THIS TRUCK WAS JUST A DECOY!
SOON AFTER--
SO YOU DECOYED ME OUT OF HIDING? TO CATCH ME WHEN I HIJACKED THE TRUCKS? WELL, MR. PRIVATE EYE--YOU'RE GOING TO GET YOUR REWARD!
AW- I DON'T DESERVE IT!
AT A RIVER'S EDGE--
TOO BAD YOU WON'T BE AROUND TO GREET THE TRUCK FULL OF FURS THAT'S DUE AT THE TURNPIKE IN ABOUT A HALF HOUR! BUT WE'LL BE THERE!
4

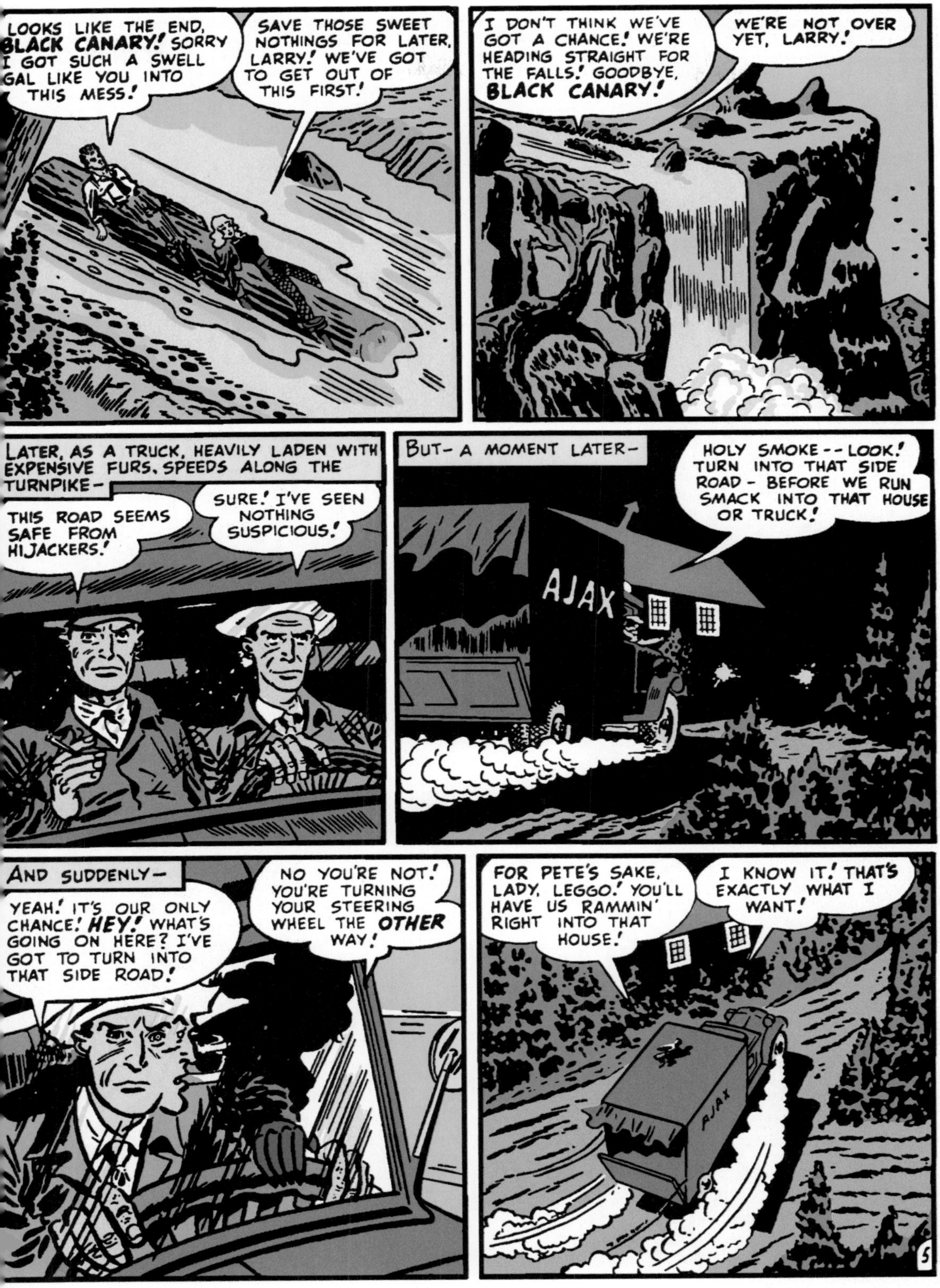
LOOKS LIKE THE END, BLACK CANARY! SORRY I GOT SUCH A SWELL GAL LIKE YOU INTO THIS MESS!
SAVE THOSE SWEET NOTHINGS FOR LATER, LARRY! WE'VE GOT TO GET OUT OF THIS FIRST!
I DON'T THINK WE'VE GOT A CHANCE! WE'RE HEADING STRAIGHT FOR THE FALLS! GOODBYE, BLACK CANARY!
WE'RE NOT OVER YET, LARRY!
LATER, AS A TRUCK, HEAVILY LADEN WITH EXPENSIVE FURS, SPEEDS ALONG THE TURNPIKE—
THIS ROAD SEEMS SAFE FROM HIJACKERS!
SURE! I'VE SEEN NOTHING SUSPICIOUS!
BUT— A MOMENT LATER—
HOLY SMOKE--LOOK! TURN INTO THAT SIDE ROAD - BEFORE WE RUN SMACK INTO THAT HOUSE OR TRUCK!
AJAX
AND SUDDENLY—
YEAH! IT'S OUR ONLY CHANCE! HEY! WHAT'S GOING ON HERE? I'VE GOT TO TURN INTO THAT SIDE ROAD!
NO YOU'RE NOT! YOU'RE TURNING YOUR STEERING WHEEL THE OTHER WAY!
FOR PETE'S SAKE, LADY, LEGGO! YOU'LL HAVE US RAMMIN' RIGHT INTO THAT HOUSE!
I KNOW IT! THAT'S EXACTLY WHAT I WANT!
AJAX
5

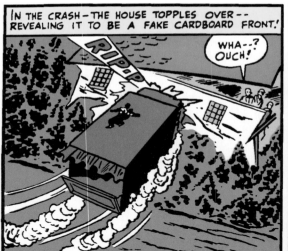

IN THE CRASH--THE HOUSE TOPPLES OVER-- REVEALING IT TO BE A FAKE CARDBOARD FRONT.

WHA--? OUCH!

LET'S BLOW-- UGH! LARRY LANCE! HOW'D YOU ESCAPE?

IT'S SIMPLE! I'M A FRIEND OF THE BLACK CANARY!

SO IT'S MR. PRIVATE EYE AGAIN!

NO--YOU DON'T!

BLACK CANARY!

SWISH

I SEE YOU'VE PUT THE BOYS TO SLEEP!

♪ YEOW!--I'M SURE GLAD THAT I'M ON YOUR SIDE, BLACK CANARY!

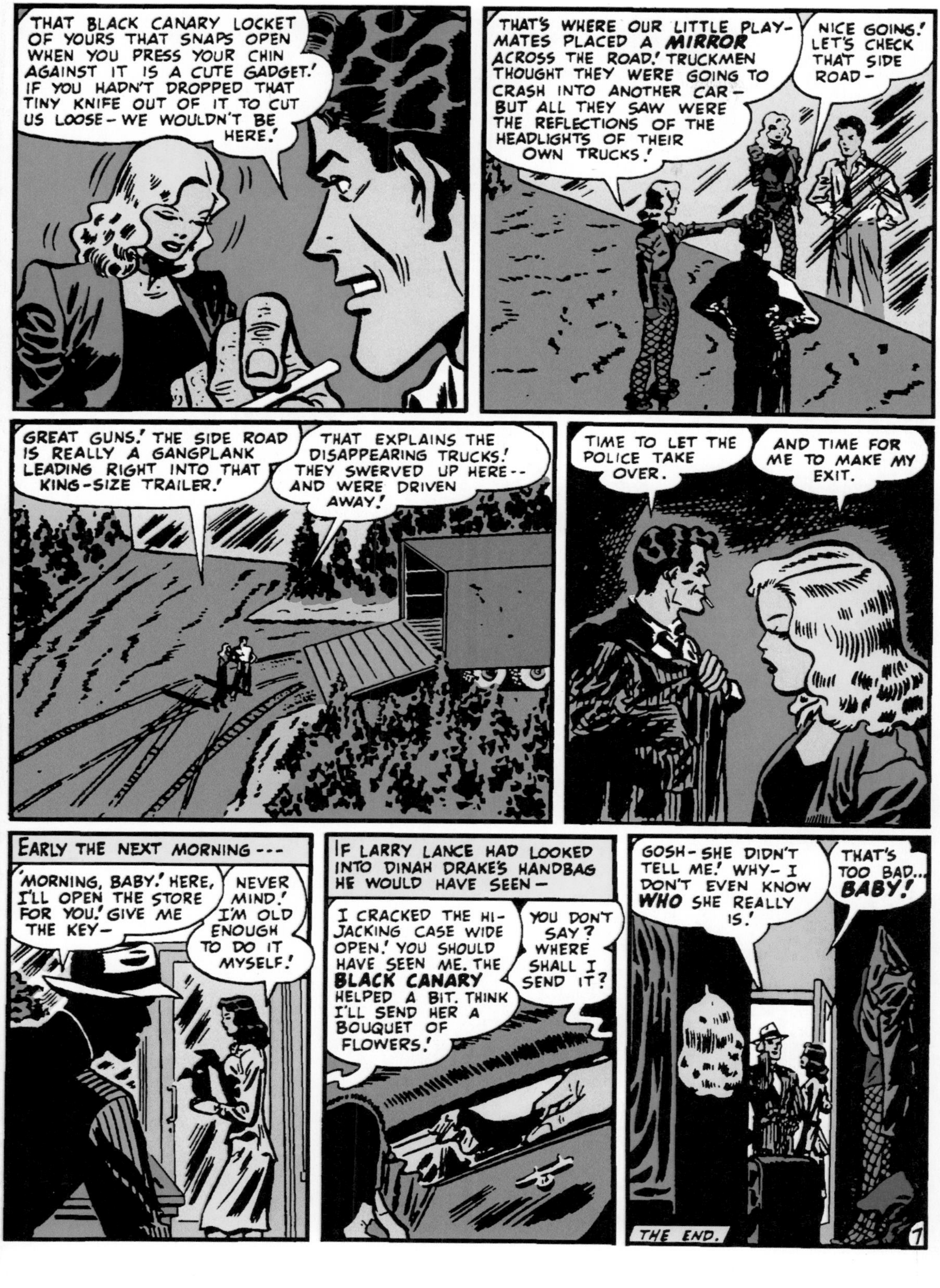
THAT BLACK CANARY LOCKET OF YOURS THAT SNAPS OPEN WHEN YOU PRESS YOUR CHIN AGAINST IT IS A CUTE GADGET! IF YOU HADN'T DROPPED THAT TINY KNIFE OUT OF IT TO CUT US LOOSE - WE WOULDN'T BE HERE!
THAT'S WHERE OUR LITTLE PLAY-MATES PLACED A MIRROR ACROSS THE ROAD! TRUCKMEN THOUGHT THEY WERE GOING TO CRASH INTO ANOTHER CAR - BUT ALL THEY SAW WERE THE REFLECTIONS OF THE HEADLIGHTS OF THEIR OWN TRUCKS!
NICE GOING! LET'S CHECK THAT SIDE ROAD -
GREAT GUNS! THE SIDE ROAD IS REALLY A GANGPLANK LEADING RIGHT INTO THAT KING-SIZE TRAILER!
THAT EXPLAINS THE DISAPPEARING TRUCKS! THEY SWERVED UP HERE -- AND WERE DRIVEN AWAY!
TIME TO LET THE POLICE TAKE OVER.
AND TIME FOR ME TO MAKE MY EXIT.
EARLY THE NEXT MORNING ---
'MORNING, BABY! HERE, I'LL OPEN THE STORE FOR YOU! GIVE ME THE KEY -
NEVER MIND! I'M OLD ENOUGH TO DO IT MYSELF!
IF LARRY LANCE HAD LOOKED INTO DINAH DRAKE'S HANDBAG HE WOULD HAVE SEEN -
I CRACKED THE HI-JACKING CASE WIDE OPEN! YOU SHOULD HAVE SEEN ME. THE BLACK CANARY HELPED A BIT. THINK I'LL SEND HER A BOUQUET OF FLOWERS!
YOU DON'T SAY? WHERE SHALL I SEND IT?
GOSH - SHE DIDN'T TELL ME! WHY - I DON'T EVEN KNOW WHO SHE REALLY IS!
THAT'S TOO BAD... BABY!
THE END.
7

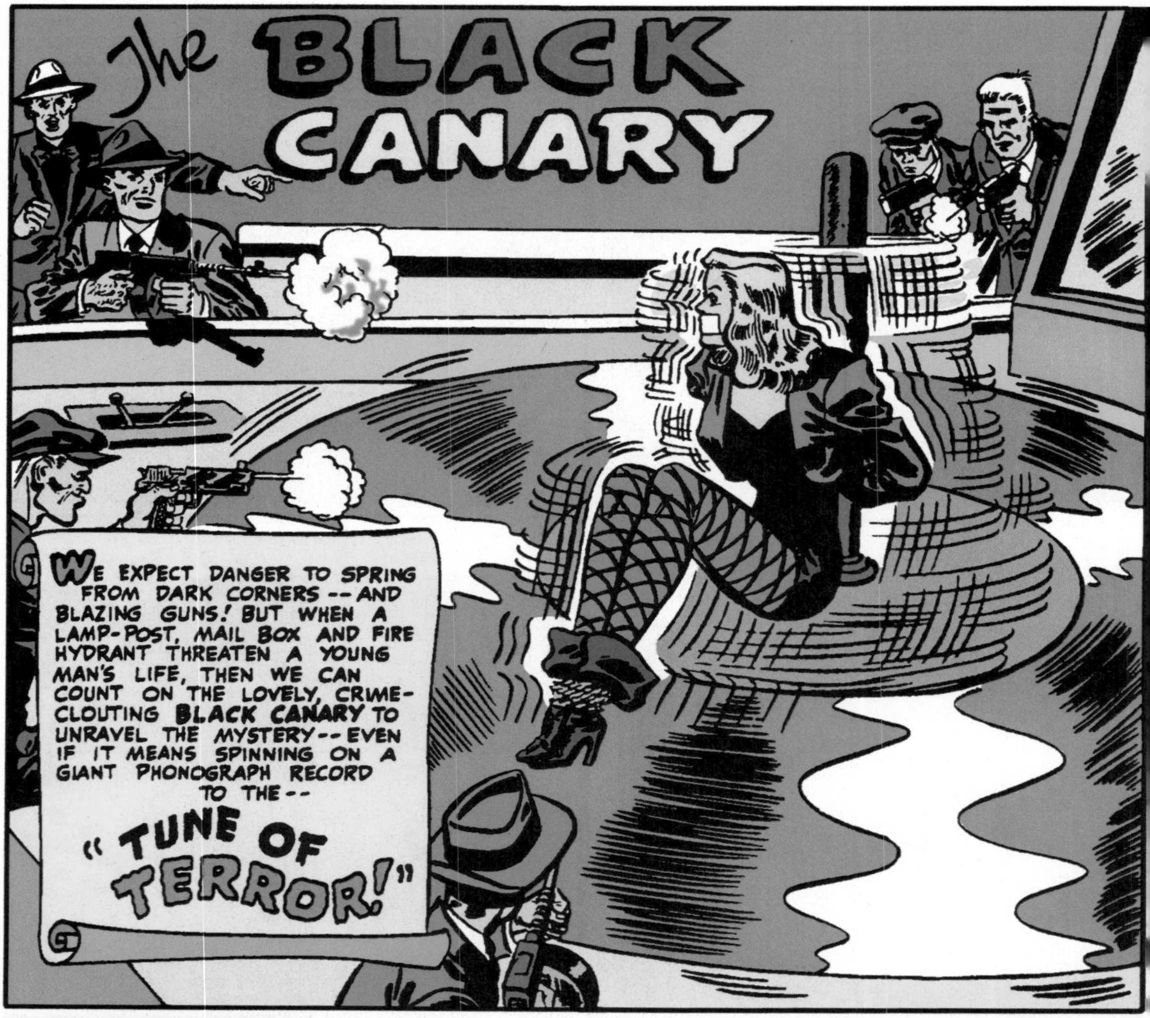
The BLACK CANARY
WE EXPECT DANGER TO SPRING FROM DARK CORNERS -- AND BLAZING GUNS! BUT WHEN A LAMP-POST, MAIL BOX AND FIRE HYDRANT THREATEN A YOUNG MAN'S LIFE, THEN WE CAN COUNT ON THE LOVELY, CRIME-CLOUTING BLACK CANARY TO UNRAVEL THE MYSTERY -- EVEN IF IT MEANS SPINNING ON A GIANT PHONOGRAPH RECORD TO THE --
"TUNE OF TERROR!"

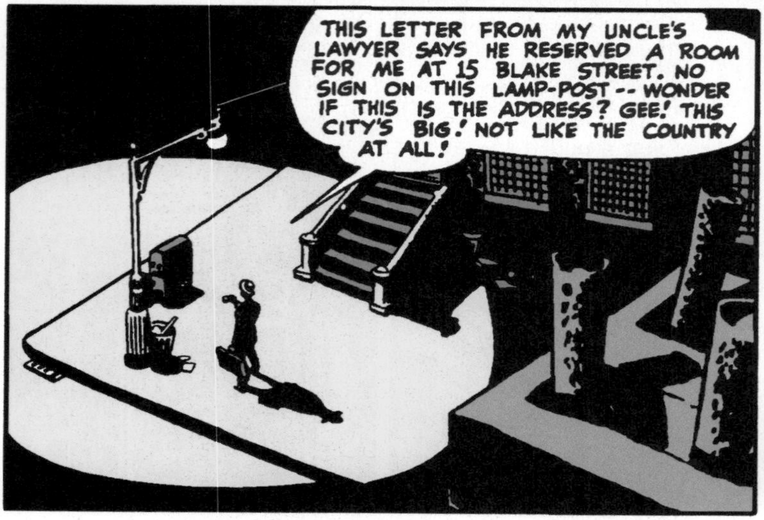
THIS LETTER FROM MY UNCLE'S LAWYER SAYS HE RESERVED A ROOM FOR ME AT 15 BLAKE STREET. NO SIGN ON THIS LAMP-POST -- WONDER IF THIS IS THE ADDRESS? GEE! THIS CITY'S BIG! NOT LIKE THE COUNTRY AT ALL!

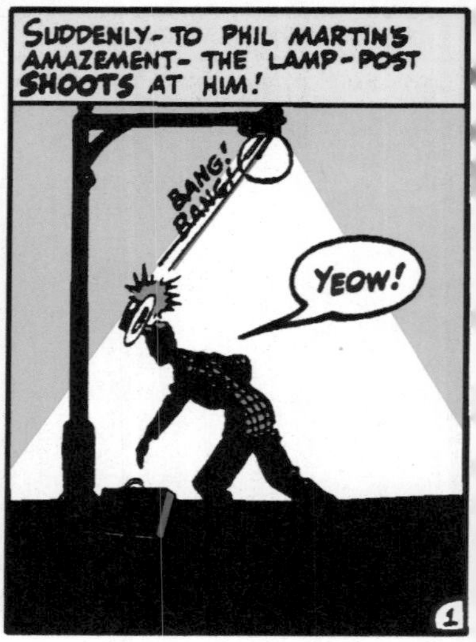
SUDDENLY - TO PHIL MARTIN'S AMAZEMENT - THE LAMP-POST SHOOTS AT HIM!
BANG! BANG!
YEOW!
1

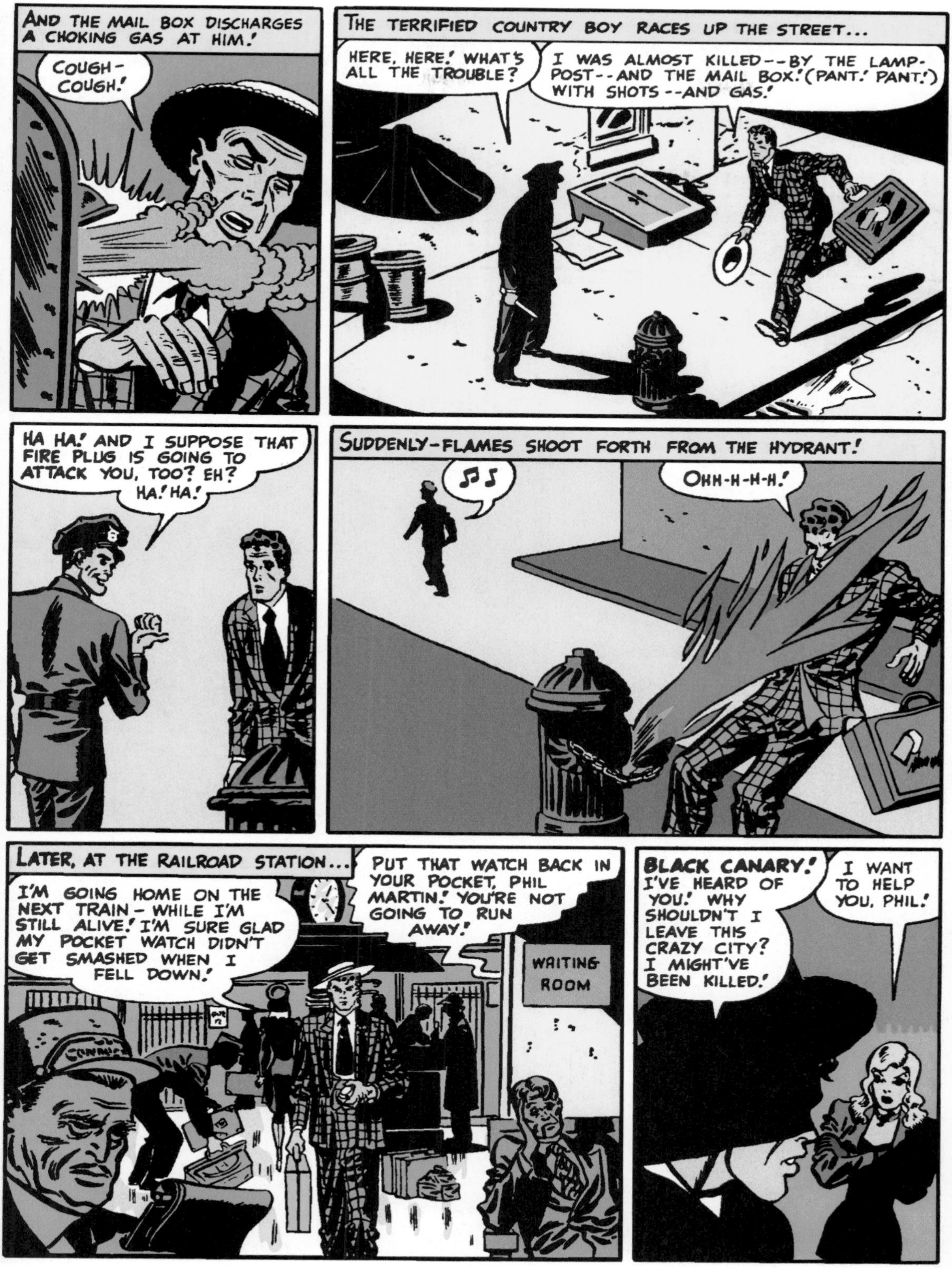
AND THE MAIL BOX DISCHARGES A CHOKING GAS AT HIM!
COUGH-COUGH!
THE TERRIFIED COUNTRY BOY RACES UP THE STREET...
HERE, HERE! WHAT'S ALL THE TROUBLE?
I WAS ALMOST KILLED--BY THE LAMP-POST--AND THE MAIL BOX! (PANT! PANT!) WITH SHOTS--AND GAS!
HA HA! AND I SUPPOSE THAT FIRE PLUG IS GOING TO ATTACK YOU, TOO? EH? HA! HA!
SUDDENLY-FLAMES SHOOT FORTH FROM THE HYDRANT!
OHH-H-H-H!
LATER, AT THE RAILROAD STATION...
I'M GOING HOME ON THE NEXT TRAIN - WHILE I'M STILL ALIVE! I'M SURE GLAD MY POCKET WATCH DIDN'T GET SMASHED WHEN I FELL DOWN!
PUT THAT WATCH BACK IN YOUR POCKET, PHIL MARTIN! YOU'RE NOT GOING TO RUN AWAY!
WAITING ROOM
BLACK CANARY! I'VE HEARD OF YOU! WHY SHOULDN'T I LEAVE THIS CRAZY CITY? I MIGHT'VE BEEN KILLED!
I WANT TO HELP YOU, PHIL!

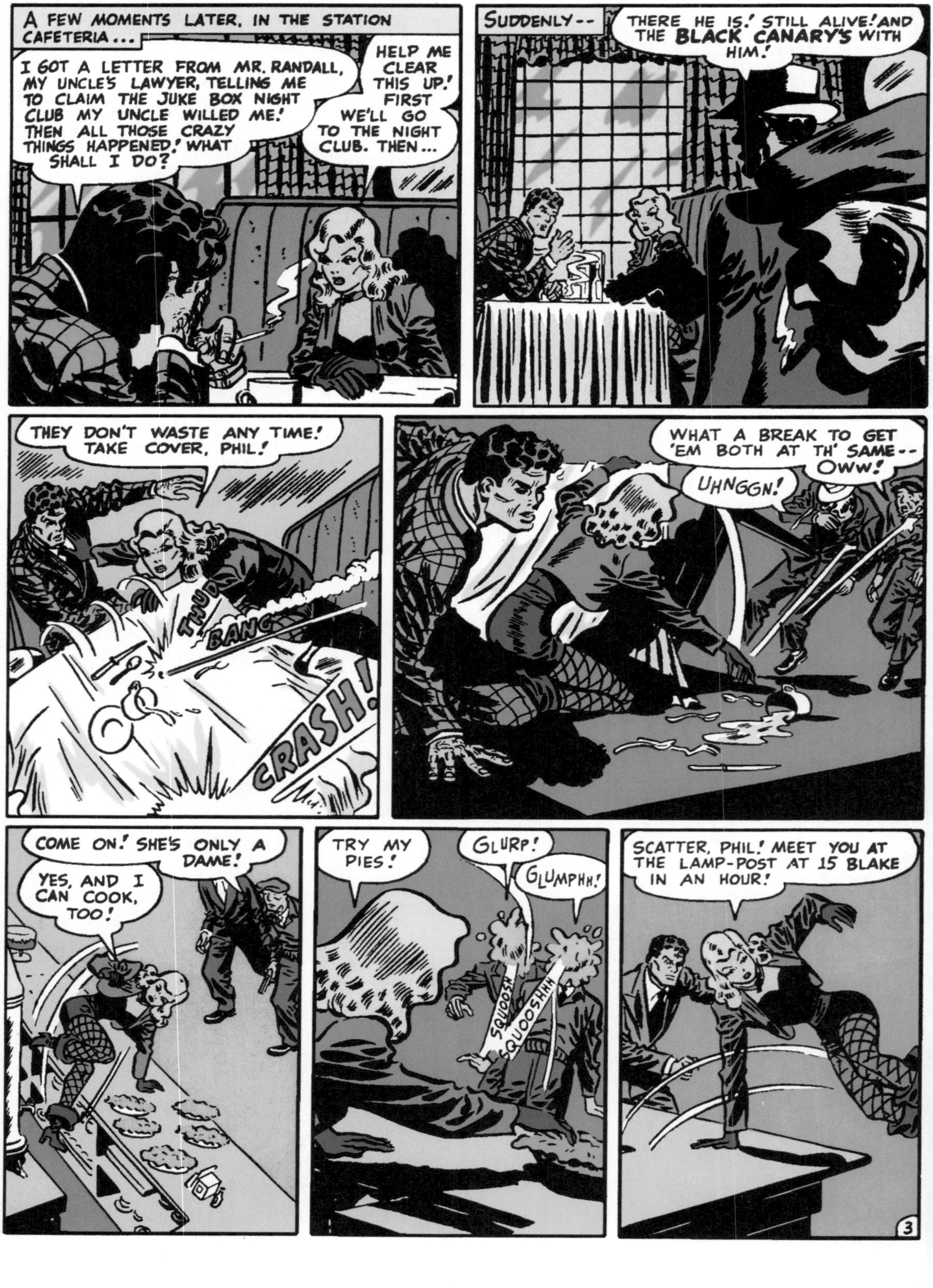

A FEW MOMENTS LATER, IN THE STATION CAFETERIA...
I GOT A LETTER FROM MR. RANDALL, MY UNCLE'S LAWYER, TELLING ME TO CLAIM THE JUKE BOX NIGHT CLUB MY UNCLE WILLED ME! THEN ALL THOSE CRAZY THINGS HAPPENED! WHAT SHALL I DO?
HELP ME CLEAR THIS UP! FIRST WE'LL GO TO THE NIGHT CLUB. THEN...
SUDDENLY--
THERE HE IS! STILL ALIVE! AND THE BLACK CANARY'S WITH HIM!
THEY DON'T WASTE ANY TIME! TAKE COVER, PHIL!
THUD
BANG
CRASH!
WHAT A BREAK TO GET 'EM BOTH AT TH' SAME-- OWW!
UHNGGN!
COME ON! SHE'S ONLY A DAME!
YES, AND I CAN COOK, TOO!
TRY MY PIES!
GLURP!
GLUMPHH!
SQUOOSH
SQUOOSHHH
SCATTER, PHIL! MEET YOU AT THE LAMP-POST AT 15 BLAKE IN AN HOUR!
3

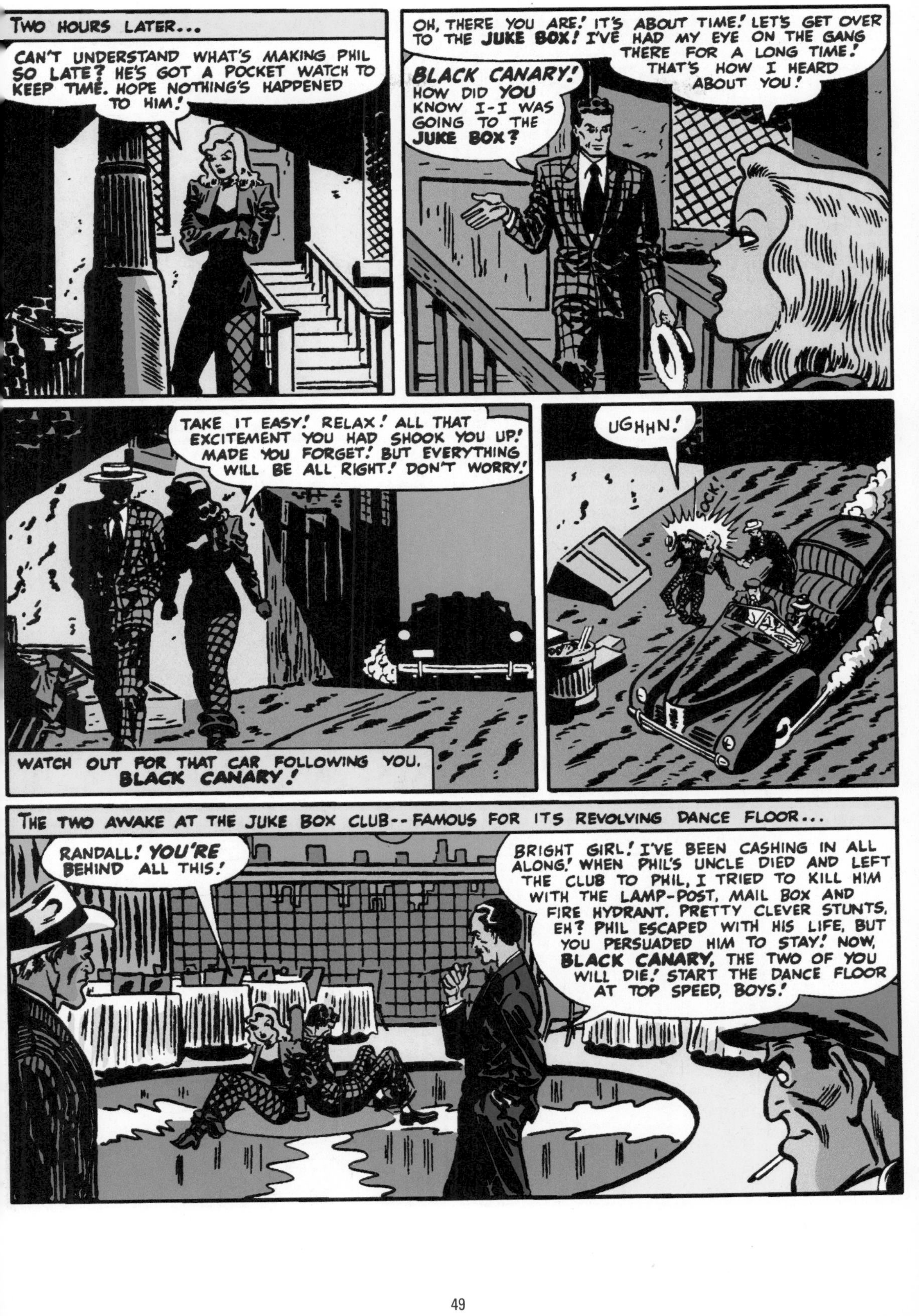

TWO HOURS LATER...
CAN'T UNDERSTAND WHAT'S MAKING PHIL SO LATE? HE'S GOT A POCKET WATCH TO KEEP TIME. HOPE NOTHING'S HAPPENED TO HIM!
BLACK CANARY! HOW DID YOU KNOW I-I WAS GOING TO THE JUKE BOX?
OH, THERE YOU ARE! IT'S ABOUT TIME! LET'S GET OVER TO THE JUKE BOX! I'VE HAD MY EYE ON THE GANG THERE FOR A LONG TIME! THAT'S HOW I HEARD ABOUT YOU!
TAKE IT EASY! RELAX! ALL THAT EXCITEMENT YOU HAD SHOOK YOU UP! MADE YOU FORGET! BUT EVERYTHING WILL BE ALL RIGHT! DON'T WORRY!
WATCH OUT FOR THAT CAR FOLLOWING YOU, BLACK CANARY!
UGHHN!
THE TWO AWAKE AT THE JUKE BOX CLUB--FAMOUS FOR ITS REVOLVING DANCE FLOOR...
RANDALL! YOU'RE BEHIND ALL THIS!
BRIGHT GIRL! I'VE BEEN CASHING IN ALL ALONG! WHEN PHIL'S UNCLE DIED AND LEFT THE CLUB TO PHIL, I TRIED TO KILL HIM WITH THE LAMP-POST, MAIL BOX AND FIRE HYDRANT. PRETTY CLEVER STUNTS, EH? PHIL ESCAPED WITH HIS LIFE, BUT YOU PERSUADED HIM TO STAY! NOW, BLACK CANARY, THE TWO OF YOU WILL DIE! START THE DANCE FLOOR AT TOP SPEED, BOYS!

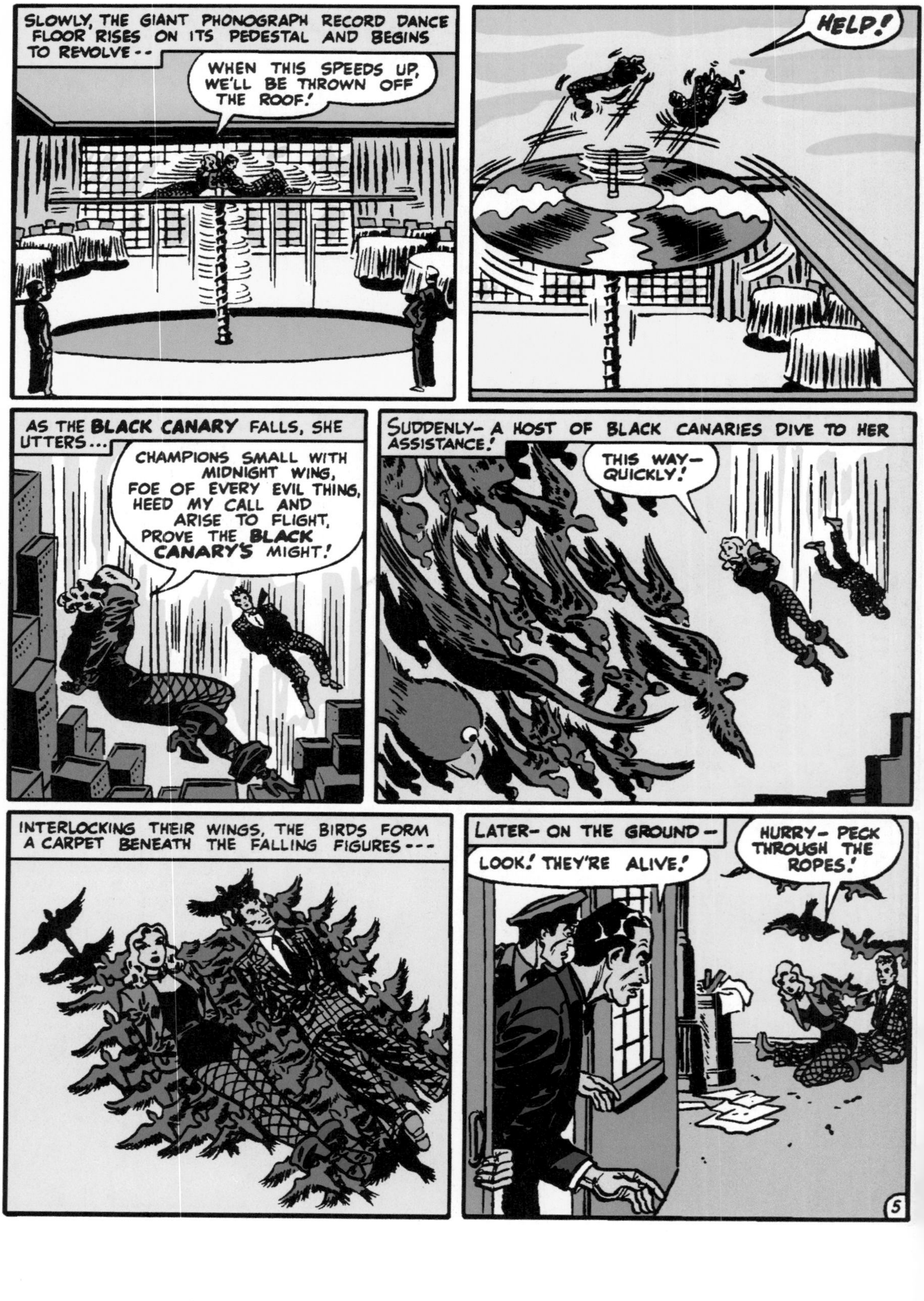
SLOWLY, THE GIANT PHONOGRAPH RECORD DANCE FLOOR RISES ON ITS PEDESTAL AND BEGINS TO REVOLVE--
WHEN THIS SPEEDS UP, WE'LL BE THROWN OFF THE ROOF!
HELP!
AS THE BLACK CANARY FALLS, SHE UTTERS...
CHAMPIONS SMALL WITH MIDNIGHT WING, FOE OF EVERY EVIL THING, HEED MY CALL AND ARISE TO FLIGHT, PROVE THE BLACK CANARY'S MIGHT!
SUDDENLY- A HOST OF BLACK CANARIES DIVE TO HER ASSISTANCE!
THIS WAY- QUICKLY!
INTERLOCKING THEIR WINGS, THE BIRDS FORM A CARPET BENEATH THE FALLING FIGURES---
LATER- ON THE GROUND-
LOOK! THEY'RE ALIVE!
HURRY- PECK THROUGH THE ROPES!
5

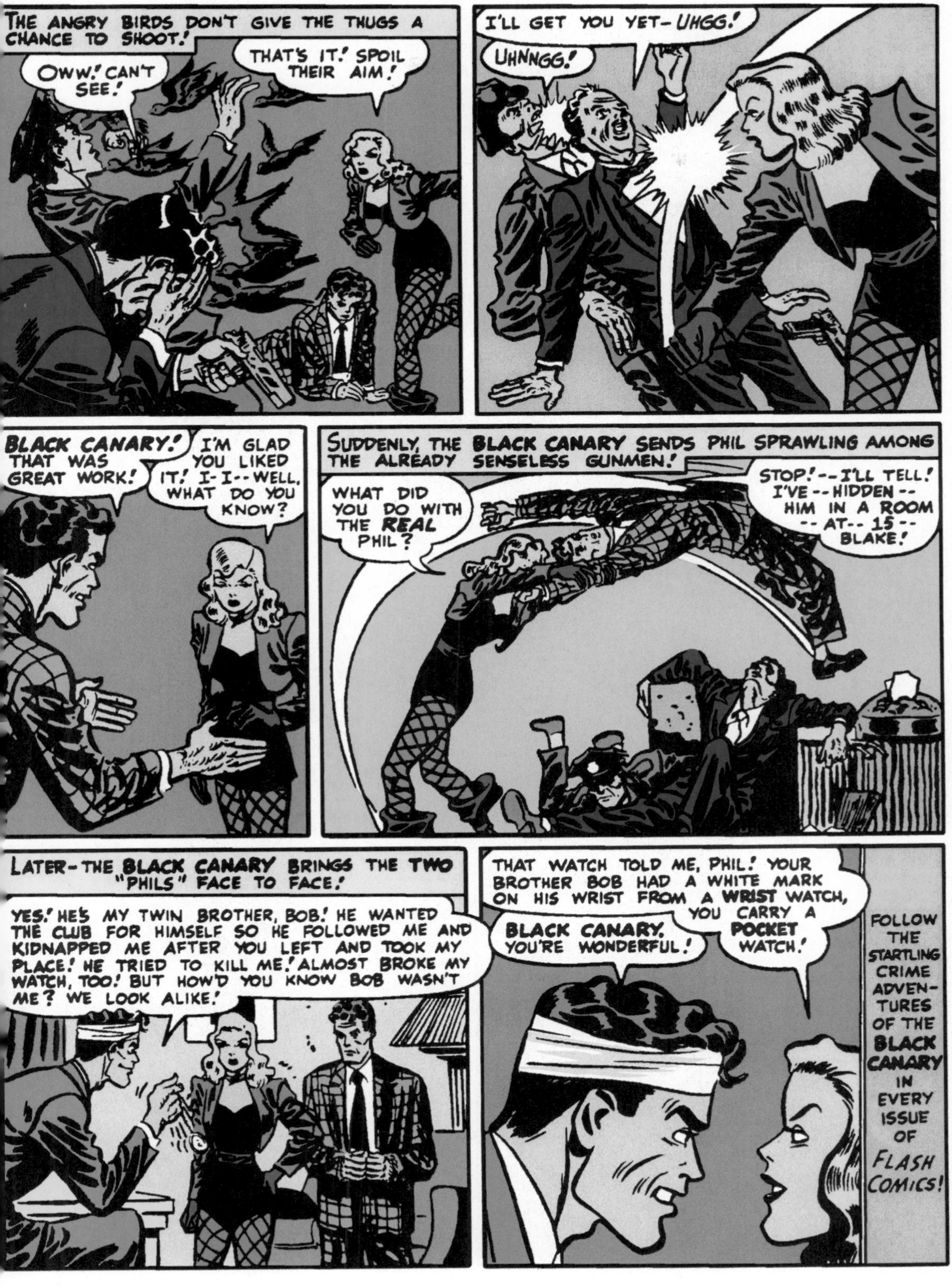

THE ANGRY BIRDS DON'T GIVE THE THUGS A CHANCE TO SHOOT!
OWW! CAN'T SEE!
THAT'S IT! SPOIL THEIR AIM!
I'LL GET YOU YET- UHGG!
UHNNGG!
BLACK CANARY! THAT WAS GREAT WORK!
I'M GLAD YOU LIKED IT! I- I--WELL, WHAT DO YOU KNOW?
SUDDENLY, THE BLACK CANARY SENDS PHIL SPRAWLING AMONG THE ALREADY SENSELESS GUNMEN!
WHAT DID YOU DO WITH THE REAL PHIL?
STOP!--I'LL TELL! I'VE--HIDDEN--HIM IN A ROOM --AT-- 15 -- BLAKE!
LATER-THE BLACK CANARY BRINGS THE TWO "PHILS" FACE TO FACE!
YES! HE'S MY TWIN BROTHER, BOB! HE WANTED THE CLUB FOR HIMSELF SO HE FOLLOWED ME AND KIDNAPPED ME AFTER YOU LEFT AND TOOK MY PLACE! HE TRIED TO KILL ME! ALMOST BROKE MY WATCH, TOO! BUT HOW'D YOU KNOW BOB WASN'T ME? WE LOOK ALIKE!
THAT WATCH TOLD ME, PHIL! YOUR BROTHER BOB HAD A WHITE MARK ON HIS WRIST FROM A WRIST WATCH, YOU CARRY A POCKET WATCH!
BLACK CANARY, YOU'RE WONDERFUL!
FOLLOW THE STARTLING CRIME ADVENTURES OF THE BLACK CANARY IN EVERY ISSUE OF FLASH COMICS!

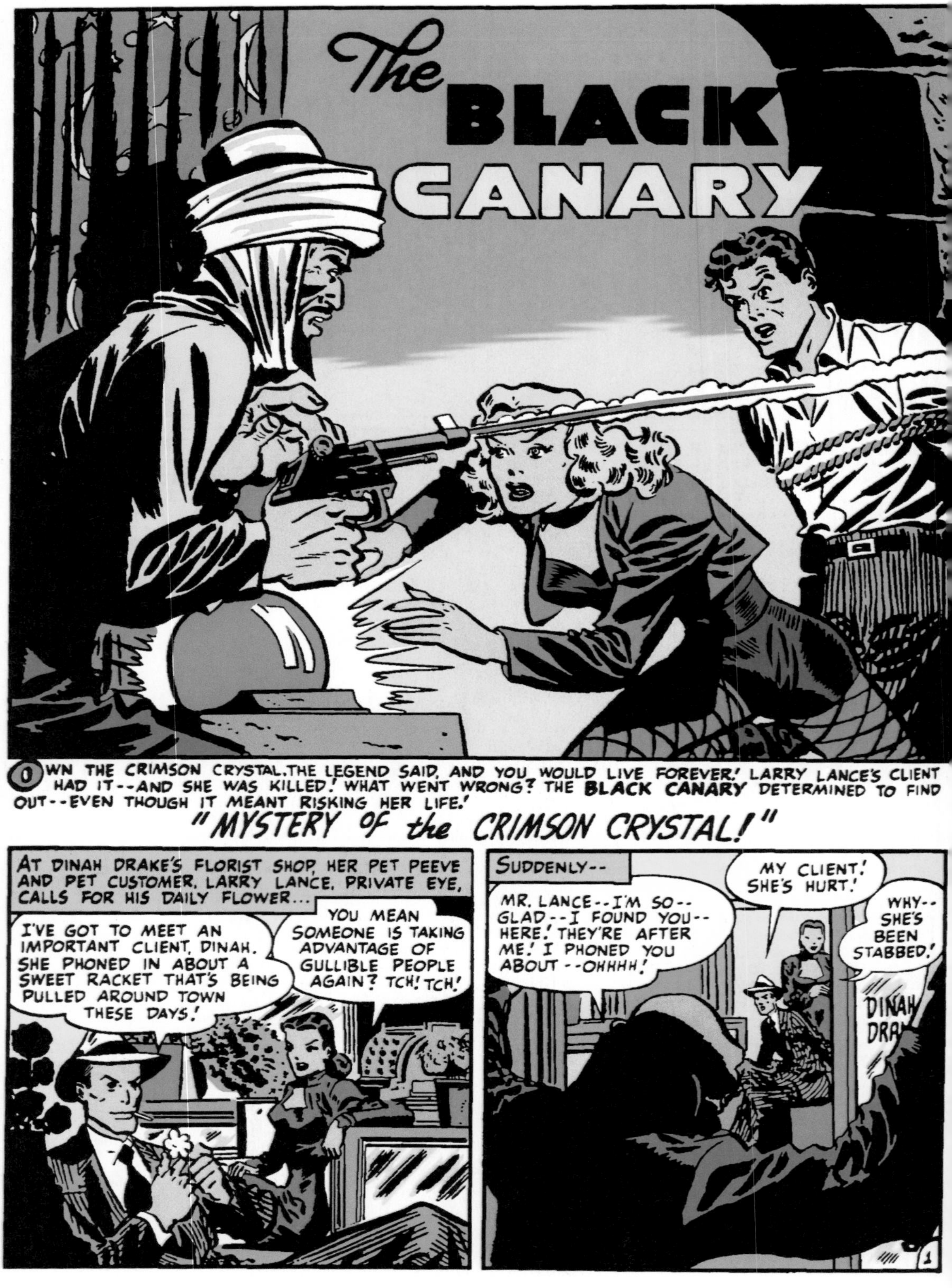
The BLACK CANARY
OWN THE CRIMSON CRYSTAL, THE LEGEND SAID, AND YOU WOULD LIVE FOREVER! LARRY LANCE'S CLIENT HAD IT--AND SHE WAS KILLED! WHAT WENT WRONG? THE BLACK CANARY DETERMINED TO FIND OUT--EVEN THOUGH IT MEANT RISKING HER LIFE!
"MYSTERY OF the CRIMSON CRYSTAL!"
AT DINAH DRAKE'S FLORIST SHOP, HER PET PEEVE AND PET CUSTOMER, LARRY LANCE, PRIVATE EYE, CALLS FOR HIS DAILY FLOWER...
I'VE GOT TO MEET AN IMPORTANT CLIENT, DINAH. SHE PHONED IN ABOUT A SWEET RACKET THAT'S BEING PULLED AROUND TOWN THESE DAYS!
YOU MEAN SOMEONE IS TAKING ADVANTAGE OF GULLIBLE PEOPLE AGAIN? TCH! TCH!
SUDDENLY--
MR. LANCE--I'M SO--GLAD--I FOUND YOU--HERE! THEY'RE AFTER ME! I PHONED YOU ABOUT--OHHHH!
MY CLIENT! SHE'S HURT!
WHY--SHE'S BEEN STABBED!
1

SHE'S DEAD! SAY, WHO ARE YOU?

SHUT UP! AND HAND OVER THE CRIMSON CRYSTAL! UNLESS YOU WANT WHAT SHE GOT!

MEANWHILE, DINAH DRAKE, IN THE BACK ROOM, FEVERISHLY CHANGES TO THE COSTUME OF THE **BLACK CANARY**...

THEY'RE AWFULLY QUIET IN THERE ALL OF A SUDDEN! HOPE LARRY CAN HOLD THEM OFF!

A MOMENT LATER...

GONE! THOSE WOMEN MUST HAVE TAKEN LARRY AND LEFT THE BODY! SHE WAS TRYING TO TELL US SOMETHING! POOR WOMAN! I'LL SEE IF SHE HAS ANY IDENTIFICATION ON HER!

AS THE **BLACK CANARY** UNCLENCHES THE DEAD WOMAN'S FIST, SHE FINDS --

LOOK AT THE SIZE OF THIS CRIMSON CRYSTAL! MUST BE PRICELESS! THAT'S PROBABLY WHAT SHE WAS KILLED FOR ---

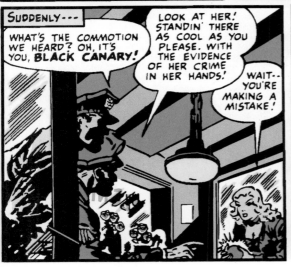

SUDDENLY ---

WHAT'S THE COMMOTION WE HEARD? OH, IT'S YOU, **BLACK CANARY**!

LOOK AT HER! STANDIN' THERE AS COOL AS YOU PLEASE. WITH THE EVIDENCE OF HER CRIME IN HER HANDS!

WAIT-- YOU'RE MAKING A MISTAKE!

YOU'RE THE ONE WHO'S MADE THE MISTAKE, **BLACK CANARY**! ONE THAT'LL COST YOU YOUR LIFE! GRAB HER!

RIGHT!

I WON'T ARGUE!

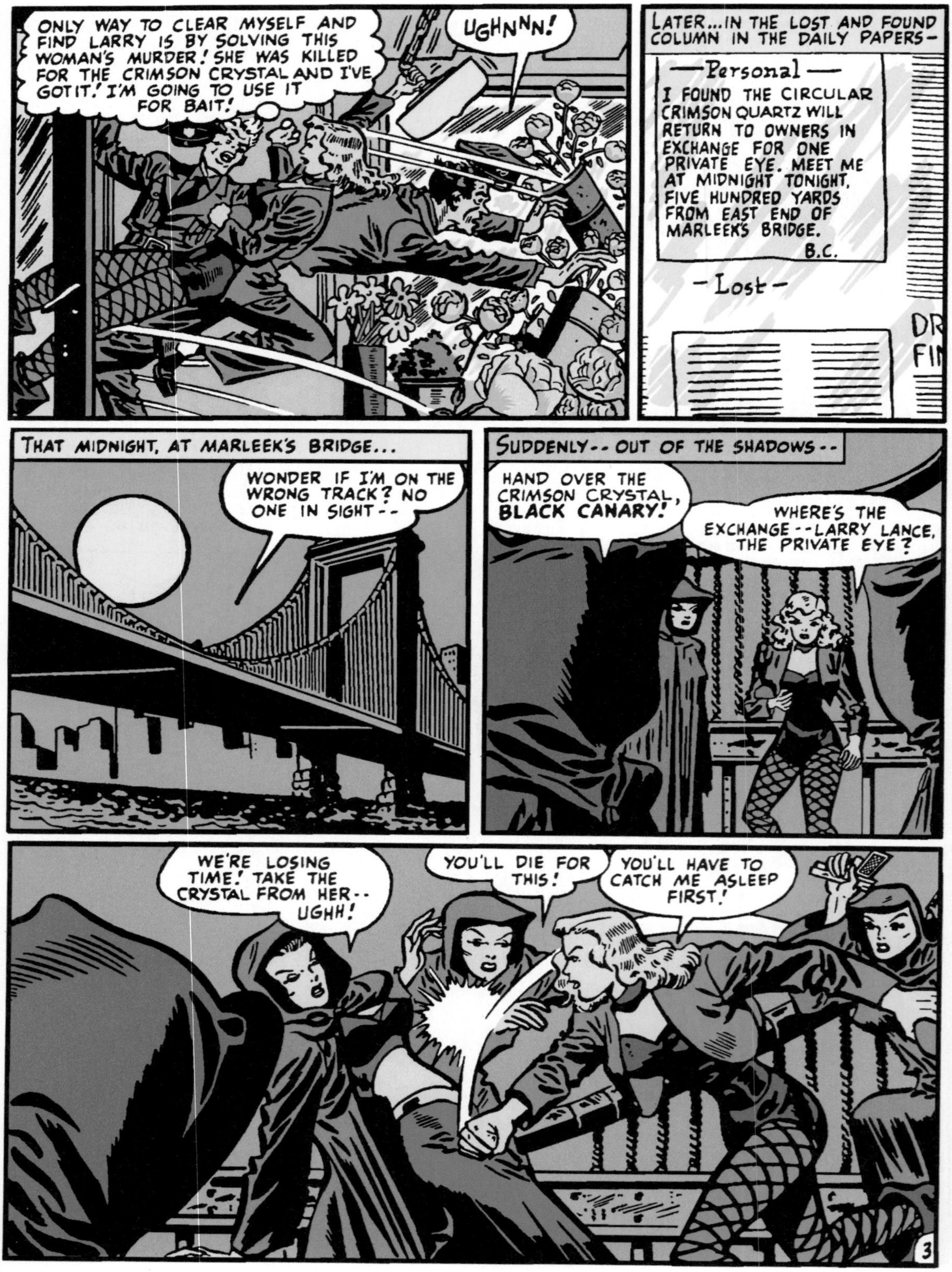
ONLY WAY TO CLEAR MYSELF AND FIND LARRY IS BY SOLVING THIS WOMAN'S MURDER! SHE WAS KILLED FOR THE CRIMSON CRYSTAL AND I'VE GOT IT! I'M GOING TO USE IT FOR BAIT!
UGHNNN!
LATER...IN THE LOST AND FOUND COLUMN IN THE DAILY PAPERS–
—Personal—
I FOUND THE CIRCULAR CRIMSON QUARTZ WILL RETURN TO OWNERS IN EXCHANGE FOR ONE PRIVATE EYE. MEET ME AT MIDNIGHT TONIGHT, FIVE HUNDRED YARDS FROM EAST END OF MARLEEK'S BRIDGE.
B.C.
–Lost–
THAT MIDNIGHT, AT MARLEEK'S BRIDGE...
WONDER IF I'M ON THE WRONG TRACK? NO ONE IN SIGHT--
SUDDENLY-- OUT OF THE SHADOWS--
HAND OVER THE CRIMSON CRYSTAL, BLACK CANARY!
WHERE'S THE EXCHANGE--LARRY LANCE, THE PRIVATE EYE?
WE'RE LOSING TIME! TAKE THE CRYSTAL FROM HER-- UGHH!
YOU'LL DIE FOR THIS!
YOU'LL HAVE TO CATCH ME ASLEEP FIRST!
3

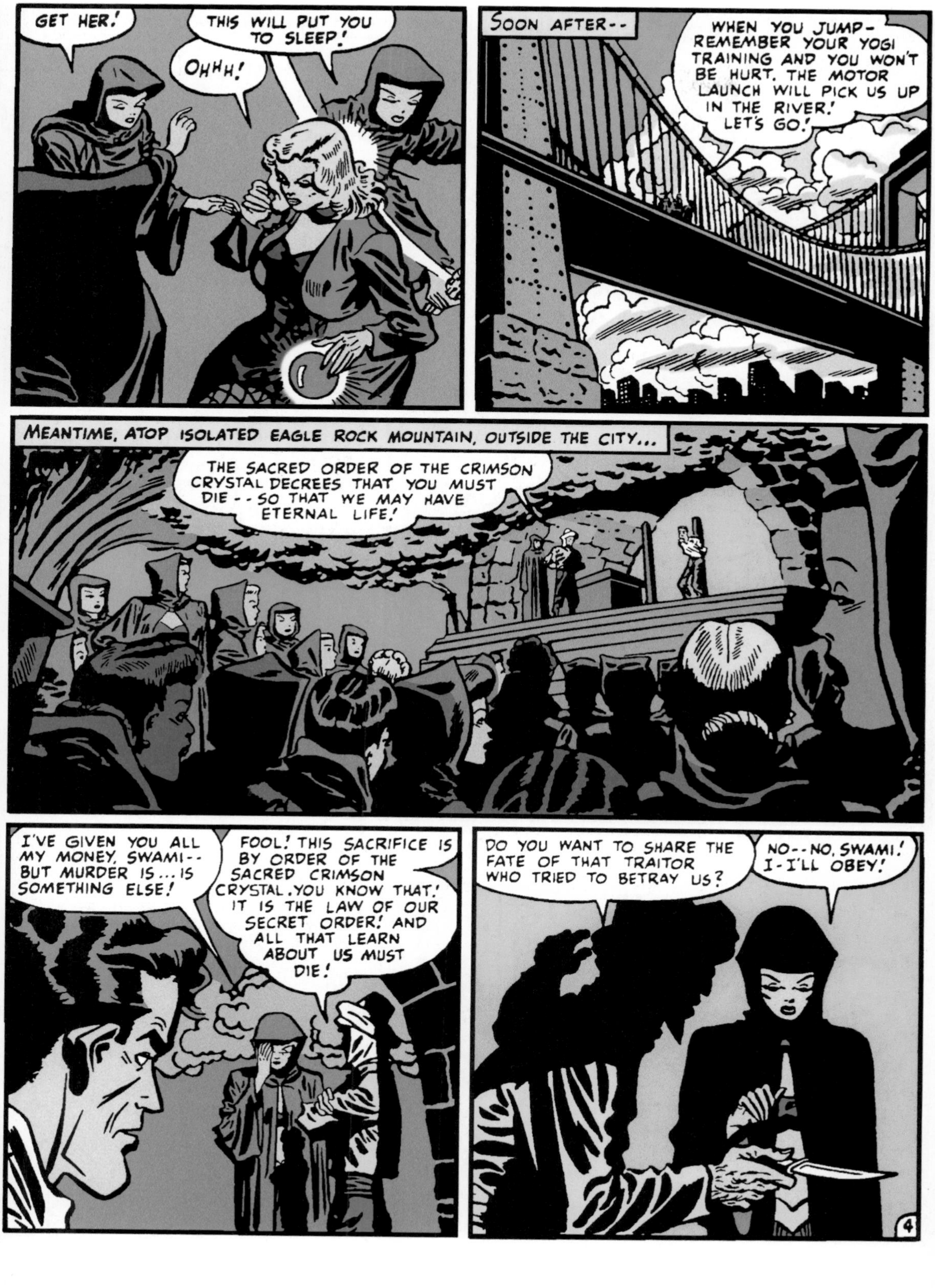
GET HER!
THIS WILL PUT YOU TO SLEEP!
OHHH!
SOON AFTER--
WHEN YOU JUMP-REMEMBER YOUR YOGI TRAINING AND YOU WON'T BE HURT. THE MOTOR LAUNCH WILL PICK US UP IN THE RIVER! LET'S GO!
MEANTIME, ATOP ISOLATED EAGLE ROCK MOUNTAIN, OUTSIDE THE CITY...
THE SACRED ORDER OF THE CRIMSON CRYSTAL DECREES THAT YOU MUST DIE--SO THAT WE MAY HAVE ETERNAL LIFE!
I'VE GIVEN YOU ALL MY MONEY, SWAMI--BUT MURDER IS...IS SOMETHING ELSE!
FOOL! THIS SACRIFICE IS BY ORDER OF THE SACRED CRIMSON CRYSTAL. YOU KNOW THAT! IT IS THE LAW OF OUR SECRET ORDER! AND ALL THAT LEARN ABOUT US MUST DIE!
DO YOU WANT TO SHARE THE FATE OF THAT TRAITOR WHO TRIED TO BETRAY US?
NO--NO, SWAMI! I-I'LL OBEY!
4

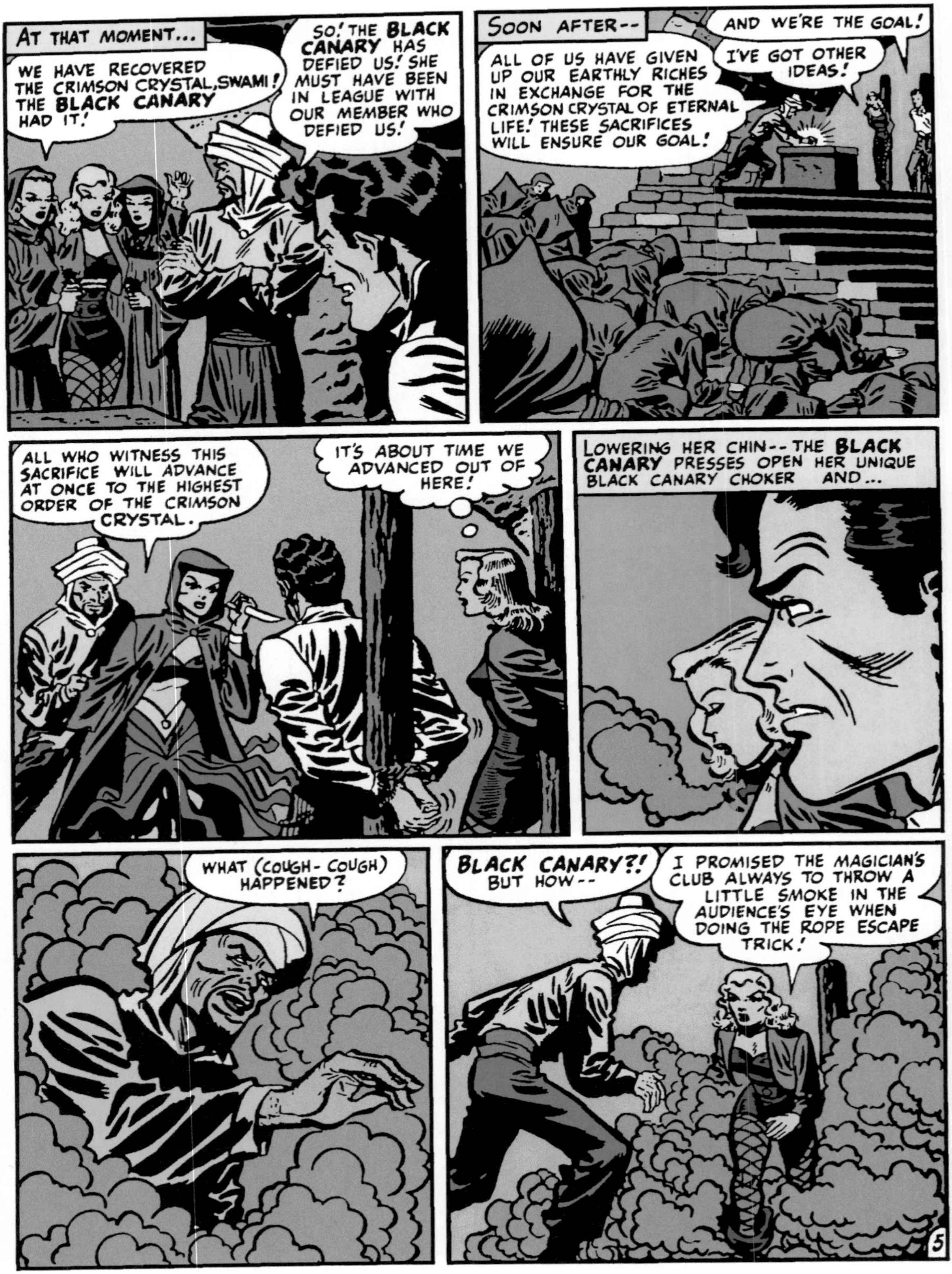

AT THAT MOMENT...
WE HAVE RECOVERED THE CRIMSON CRYSTAL, SWAMI! THE BLACK CANARY HAD IT!
SO! THE BLACK CANARY HAS DEFIED US! SHE MUST HAVE BEEN IN LEAGUE WITH OUR MEMBER WHO DEFIED US!
SOON AFTER--
ALL OF US HAVE GIVEN UP OUR EARTHLY RICHES IN EXCHANGE FOR THE CRIMSON CRYSTAL OF ETERNAL LIFE! THESE SACRIFICES WILL ENSURE OUR GOAL!
AND WE'RE THE GOAL!
I'VE GOT OTHER IDEAS!
ALL WHO WITNESS THIS SACRIFICE WILL ADVANCE AT ONCE TO THE HIGHEST ORDER OF THE CRIMSON CRYSTAL.
IT'S ABOUT TIME WE ADVANCED OUT OF HERE!
LOWERING HER CHIN--THE BLACK CANARY PRESSES OPEN HER UNIQUE BLACK CANARY CHOKER AND...
WHAT (COUGH-COUGH) HAPPENED?
BLACK CANARY?! BUT HOW--
I PROMISED THE MAGICIAN'S CLUB ALWAYS TO THROW A LITTLE SMOKE IN THE AUDIENCE'S EYE WHEN DOING THE ROPE ESCAPE TRICK!
5

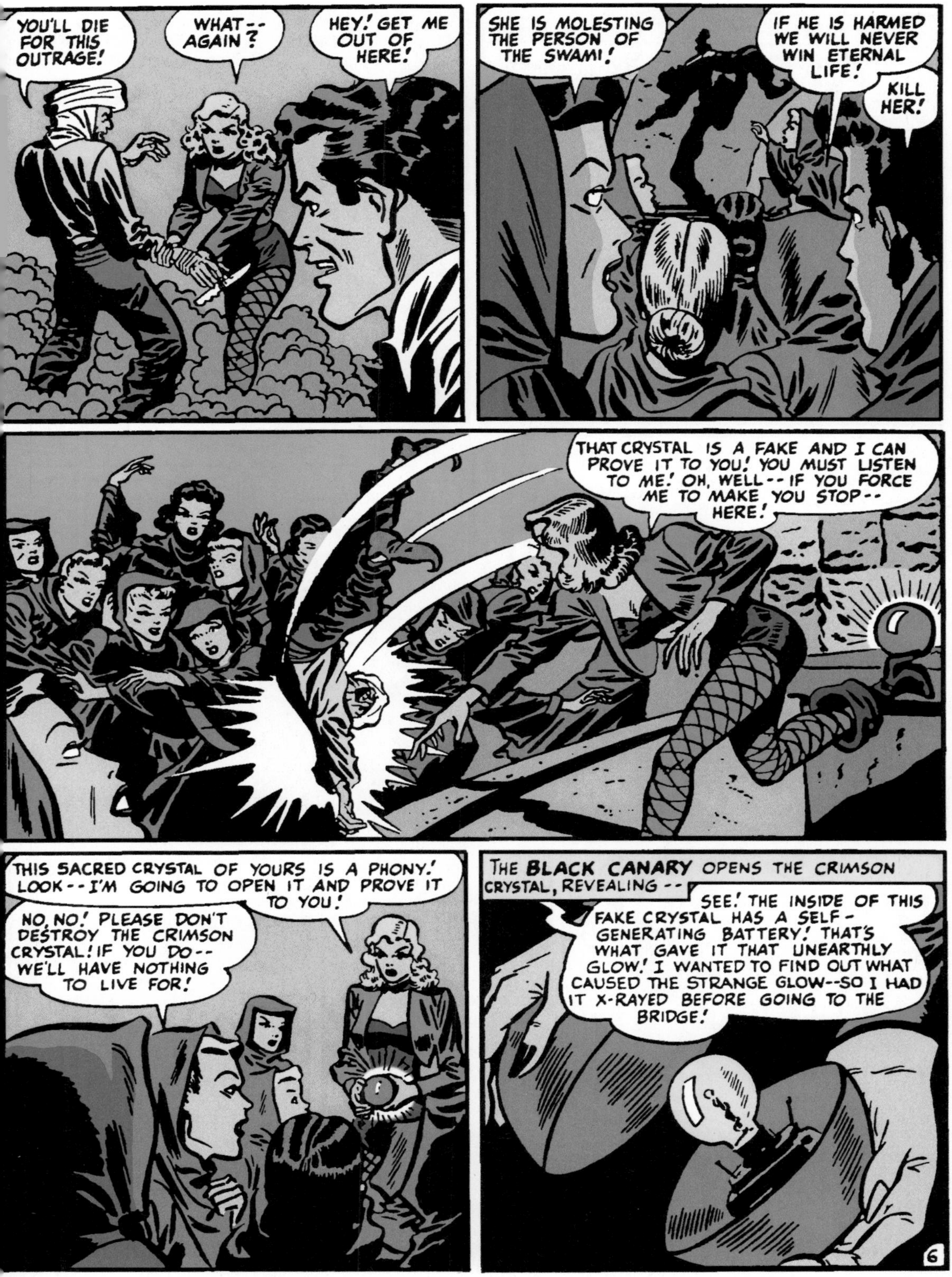
YOU'LL DIE FOR THIS OUTRAGE!
WHAT-- AGAIN?
HEY! GET ME OUT OF HERE!
SHE IS MOLESTING THE PERSON OF THE SWAMI!
IF HE IS HARMED WE WILL NEVER WIN ETERNAL LIFE!
KILL HER!
THAT CRYSTAL IS A FAKE AND I CAN PROVE IT TO YOU! YOU MUST LISTEN TO ME! OH, WELL-- IF YOU FORCE ME TO MAKE YOU STOP-- HERE!
THIS SACRED CRYSTAL OF YOURS IS A PHONY! LOOK--I'M GOING TO OPEN IT AND PROVE IT TO YOU!
NO, NO! PLEASE DON'T DESTROY THE CRIMSON CRYSTAL! IF YOU DO-- WE'LL HAVE NOTHING TO LIVE FOR!
THE BLACK CANARY OPENS THE CRIMSON CRYSTAL, REVEALING--
SEE! THE INSIDE OF THIS FAKE CRYSTAL HAS A SELF-GENERATING BATTERY! THAT'S WHAT GAVE IT THAT UNEARTHLY GLOW! I WANTED TO FIND OUT WHAT CAUSED THE STRANGE GLOW--SO I HAD IT X-RAYED BEFORE GOING TO THE BRIDGE!
6

AS THE **BLACK CANARY** RELEASES LARRY LANCE--

FORGET ABOUT ME, HUH? I'LL GET YOU FOR THIS!

AHHNNN!

LARRY!

BANG! BANG!

YOU'RE NEXT, **BLACK CANARY**-- UGG!

SAVE YOUR BREATH FOR THE CONFESSION, SWAMI!

ON YOUR FEET! WHY--IT'S BULLET BENN-- UNDER A MASK! SO THIS IS HOW YOU EVADED THE POLICE! TALK!

OW! S-S-SURE, **BLACK CANARY!** I'LL TALK!

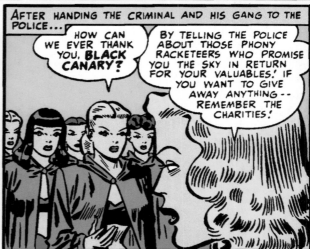

AFTER HANDING THE CRIMINAL AND HIS GANG TO THE POLICE...

HOW CAN WE EVER THANK YOU, **BLACK CANARY?**

BY TELLING THE POLICE ABOUT THOSE PHONY RACKETEERS WHO PROMISE YOU THE SKY IN RETURN FOR YOUR VALUABLES! IF YOU WANT TO GIVE AWAY ANYTHING-- REMEMBER THE CHARITIES!

LATER--

WAIT! WHEN AM I GOING TO SEE YOU AGAIN?

THE NEXT TIME YOU'RE IN TROUBLE!

NEXT MORNING, AT DINAH DRAKE'S FLORIST SHOP--

WHAT A CASE! ONLY THING THAT WORRIES ME IS THAT SOME DAY THE **BLACK CANARY** IS GOING TO GET IN A JAM AND I WON'T BE AROUND TO HELP HER!

I'M SURE YOU'LL BE **ON THE SPOT** AS USUAL!

OF COURSE I'LL BE **ON THE SPOT** -- HUH?

THE END.

7

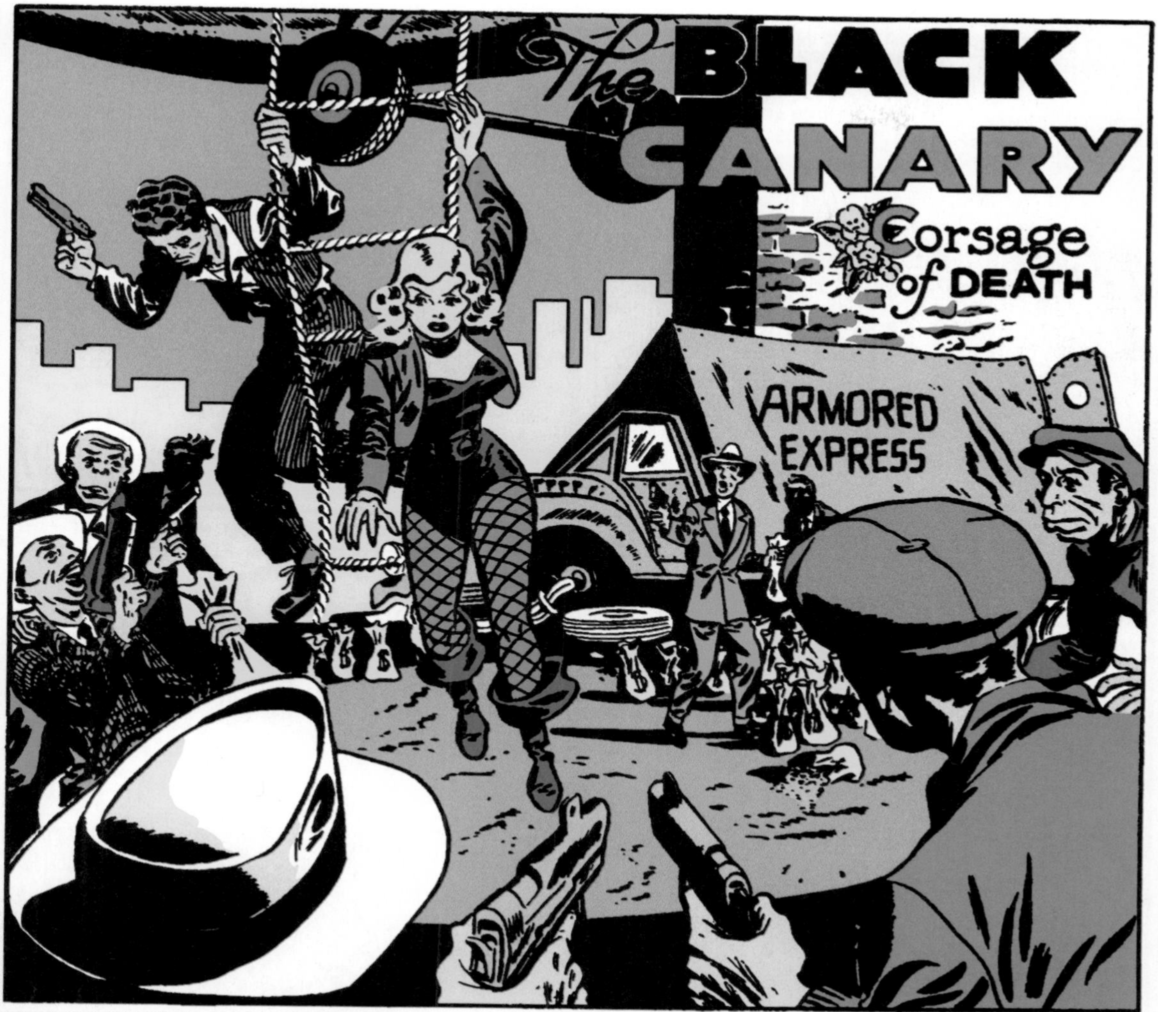
The BLACK CANARY
Corsage of DEATH
ARMORED EXPRESS

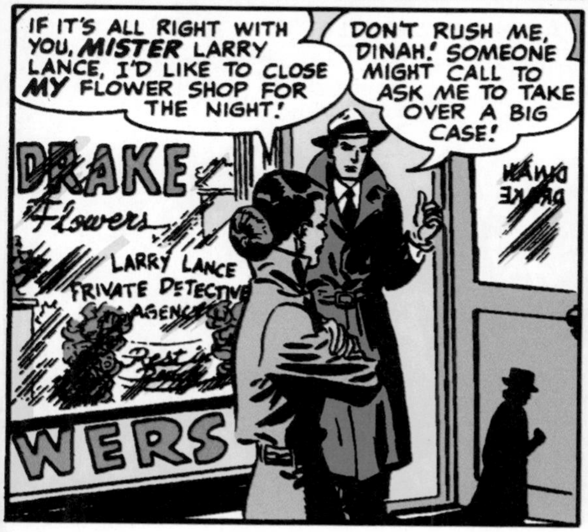
IF IT'S ALL RIGHT WITH YOU, MISTER LARRY LANCE, I'D LIKE TO CLOSE MY FLOWER SHOP FOR THE NIGHT!
DON'T RUSH ME, DINAH! SOMEONE MIGHT CALL TO ASK ME TO TAKE OVER A BIG CASE!
DRAKE Flowers
LARRY LANCE PRIVATE DETECTIVE AGENCY
WERS
DINAH DRAKE

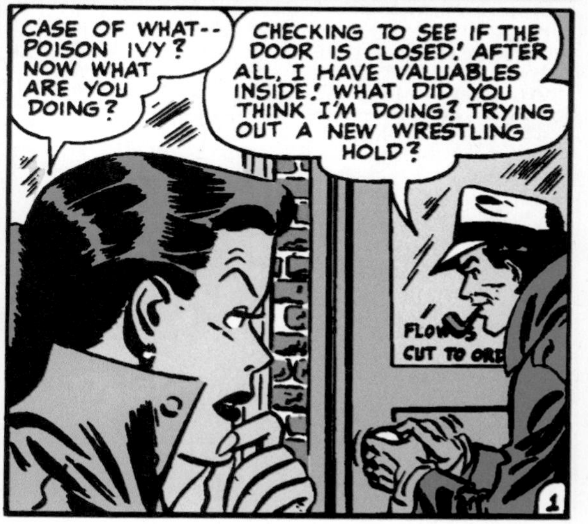
CASE OF WHAT-- POISON IVY? NOW WHAT ARE YOU DOING?
CHECKING TO SEE IF THE DOOR IS CLOSED! AFTER ALL, I HAVE VALUABLES INSIDE! WHAT DID YOU THINK I'M DOING? TRYING OUT A NEW WRESTLING HOLD?
CUT TO ORD
1

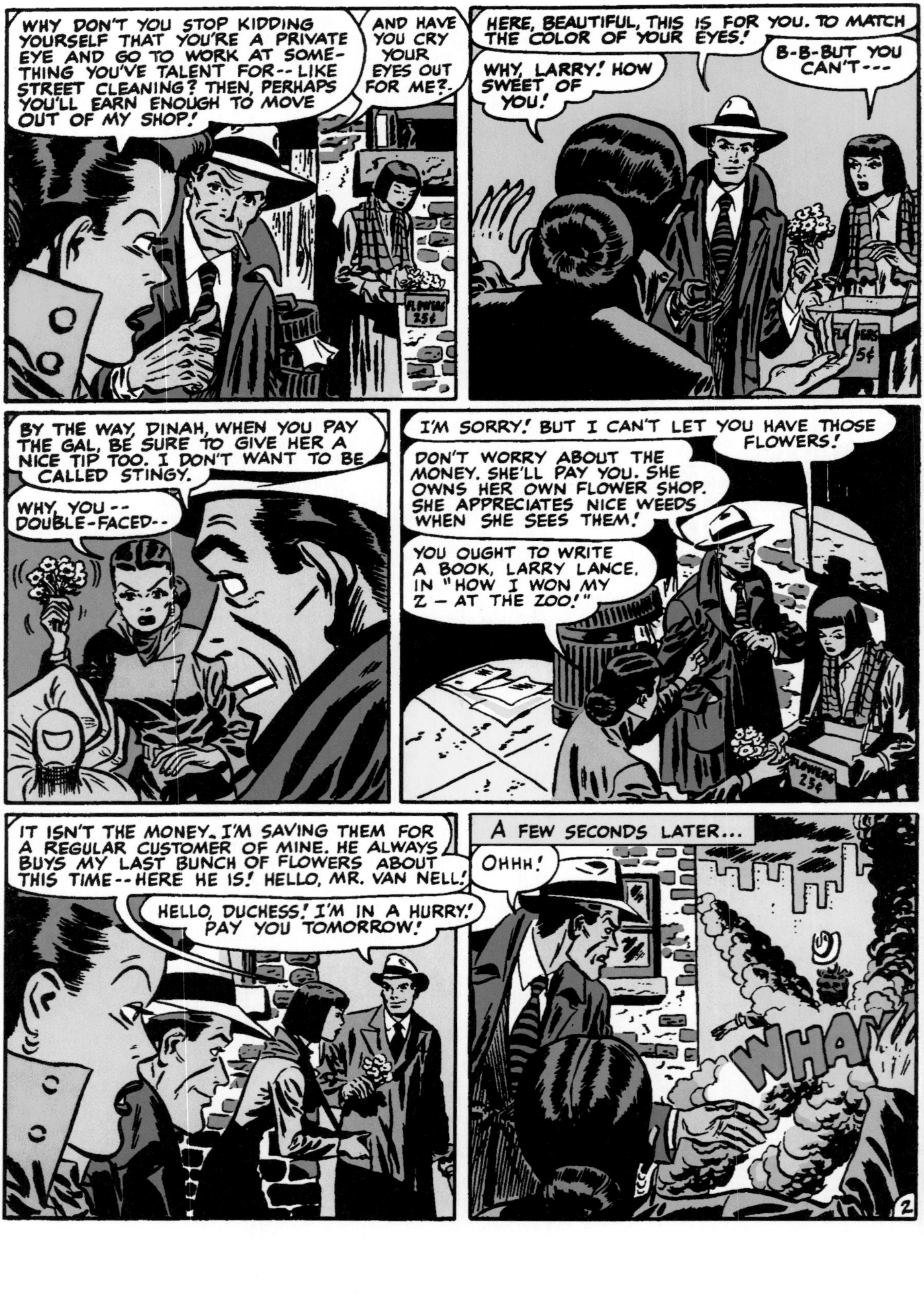
WHY DON'T YOU STOP KIDDING YOURSELF THAT YOU'RE A PRIVATE EYE AND GO TO WORK AT SOMETHING YOU'VE TALENT FOR-- LIKE STREET CLEANING? THEN, PERHAPS YOU'LL EARN ENOUGH TO MOVE OUT OF MY SHOP!
AND HAVE YOU CRY YOUR EYES OUT FOR ME?
FLOWERS 25¢
HERE, BEAUTIFUL, THIS IS FOR YOU. TO MATCH THE COLOR OF YOUR EYES!
WHY, LARRY! HOW SWEET OF YOU!
B-B-BUT YOU CAN'T---
FLOWERS 5¢
BY THE WAY, DINAH, WHEN YOU PAY THE GAL, BE SURE TO GIVE HER A NICE TIP TOO. I DON'T WANT TO BE CALLED STINGY.
WHY, YOU -- DOUBLE-FACED--
I'M SORRY! BUT I CAN'T LET YOU HAVE THOSE FLOWERS!
DON'T WORRY ABOUT THE MONEY. SHE'LL PAY YOU. SHE OWNS HER OWN FLOWER SHOP. SHE APPRECIATES NICE WEEDS WHEN SHE SEES THEM!
YOU OUGHT TO WRITE A BOOK, LARRY LANCE, IN "HOW I WON MY Z - AT THE ZOO!"
FLOWERS 25¢
IT ISN'T THE MONEY. I'M SAVING THEM FOR A REGULAR CUSTOMER OF MINE. HE ALWAYS BUYS MY LAST BUNCH OF FLOWERS ABOUT THIS TIME--HERE HE IS! HELLO, MR. VAN NELL!
HELLO, DUCHESS! I'M IN A HURRY! PAY YOU TOMORROW!
A FEW SECONDS LATER...
OHHH!
WHAM
2

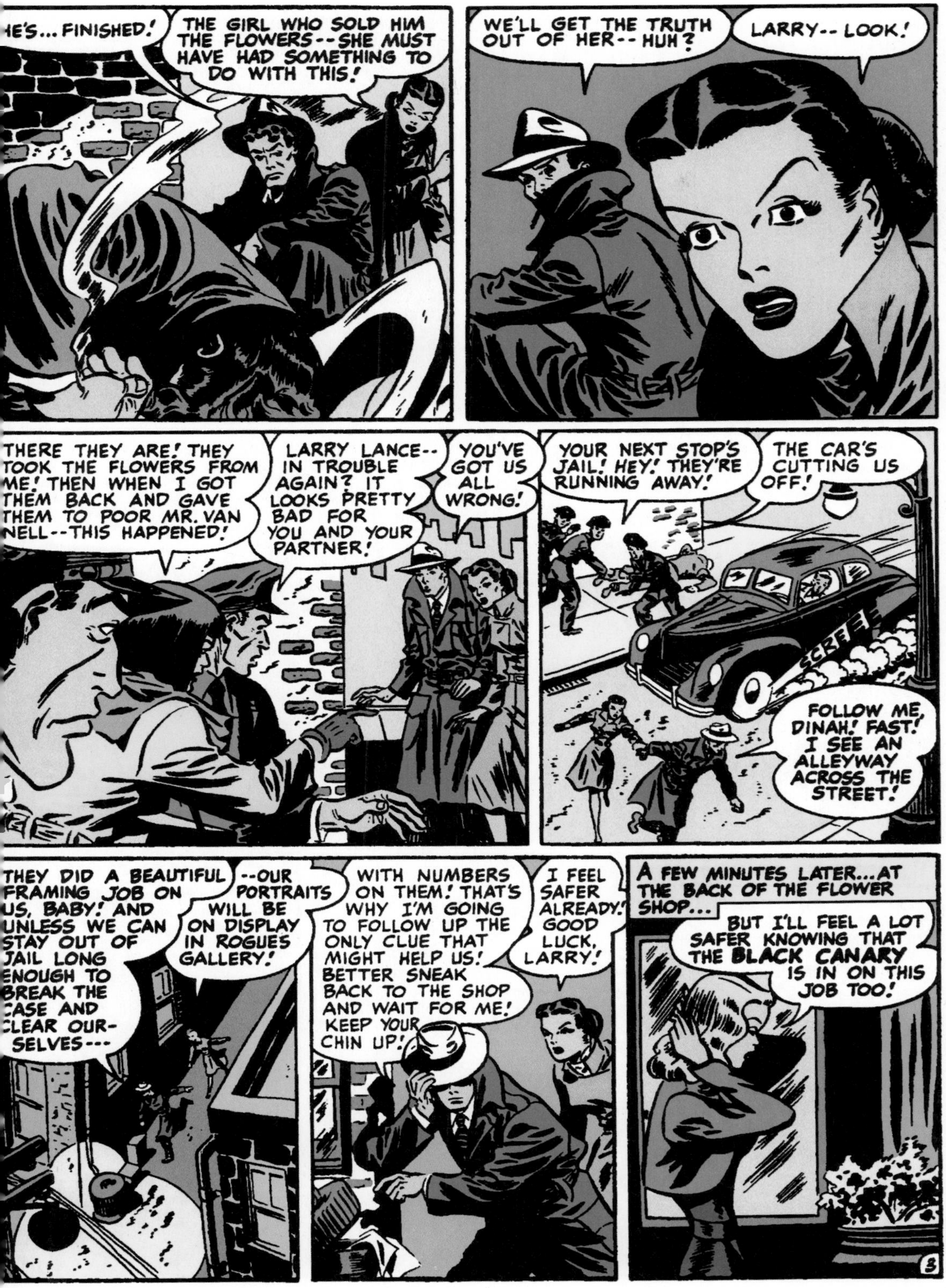
HE'S... FINISHED!
THE GIRL WHO SOLD HIM THE FLOWERS--SHE MUST HAVE HAD SOMETHING TO DO WITH THIS!
WE'LL GET THE TRUTH OUT OF HER--HUH?
LARRY--LOOK!
THERE THEY ARE! THEY TOOK THE FLOWERS FROM ME! THEN WHEN I GOT THEM BACK AND GAVE THEM TO POOR MR. VAN NELL--THIS HAPPENED!
LARRY LANCE--IN TROUBLE AGAIN? IT LOOKS PRETTY BAD FOR YOU AND YOUR PARTNER!
YOU'VE GOT US ALL WRONG!
YOUR NEXT STOP'S JAIL! HEY! THEY'RE RUNNING AWAY!
THE CAR'S CUTTING US OFF!
SCREE
FOLLOW ME, DINAH! FAST! I SEE AN ALLEYWAY ACROSS THE STREET!
THEY DID A BEAUTIFUL FRAMING JOB ON US, BABY! AND UNLESS WE CAN STAY OUT OF JAIL LONG ENOUGH TO BREAK THE CASE AND CLEAR OURSELVES---
--OUR PORTRAITS WILL BE ON DISPLAY IN ROGUES GALLERY!
WITH NUMBERS ON THEM! THAT'S WHY I'M GOING TO FOLLOW UP THE ONLY CLUE THAT MIGHT HELP US! BETTER SNEAK BACK TO THE SHOP AND WAIT FOR ME! KEEP YOUR CHIN UP!
I FEEL SAFER ALREADY! GOOD LUCK, LARRY!
A FEW MINUTES LATER...AT THE BACK OF THE FLOWER SHOP...
BUT I'LL FEEL A LOT SAFER KNOWING THAT THE BLACK CANARY IS IN ON THIS JOB TOO!
3

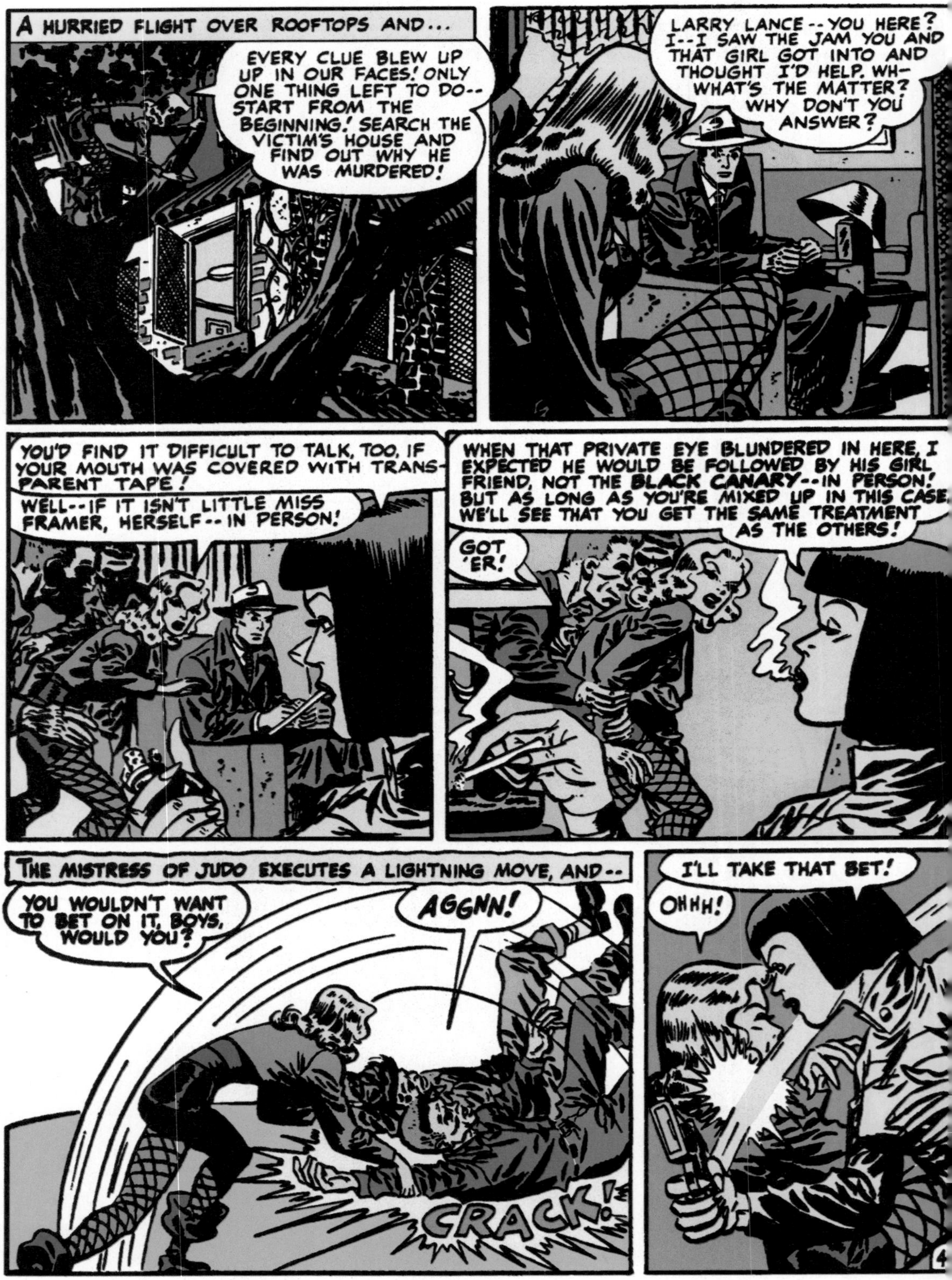

A HURRIED FLIGHT OVER ROOFTOPS AND...
EVERY CLUE BLEW UP UP IN OUR FACES! ONLY ONE THING LEFT TO DO-- START FROM THE BEGINNING! SEARCH THE VICTIM'S HOUSE AND FIND OUT WHY HE WAS MURDERED!
LARRY LANCE--YOU HERE? I--I SAW THE JAM YOU AND THAT GIRL GOT INTO AND THOUGHT I'D HELP. WH-WHAT'S THE MATTER? WHY DON'T YOU ANSWER?
YOU'D FIND IT DIFFICULT TO TALK, TOO, IF YOUR MOUTH WAS COVERED WITH TRANSPARENT TAPE!
WELL--IF IT ISN'T LITTLE MISS FRAMER, HERSELF--IN PERSON!
WHEN THAT PRIVATE EYE BLUNDERED IN HERE, I EXPECTED HE WOULD BE FOLLOWED BY HIS GIRL FRIEND, NOT THE BLACK CANARY--IN PERSON! BUT AS LONG AS YOU'RE MIXED UP IN THIS CASE, WE'LL SEE THAT YOU GET THE SAME TREATMENT AS THE OTHERS!
GOT 'ER!
THE MISTRESS OF JUDO EXECUTES A LIGHTNING MOVE, AND--
YOU WOULDN'T WANT TO BET ON IT, BOYS, WOULD YOU?
AGGNN!
CRACK!
I'LL TAKE THAT BET!
OHHH!
4

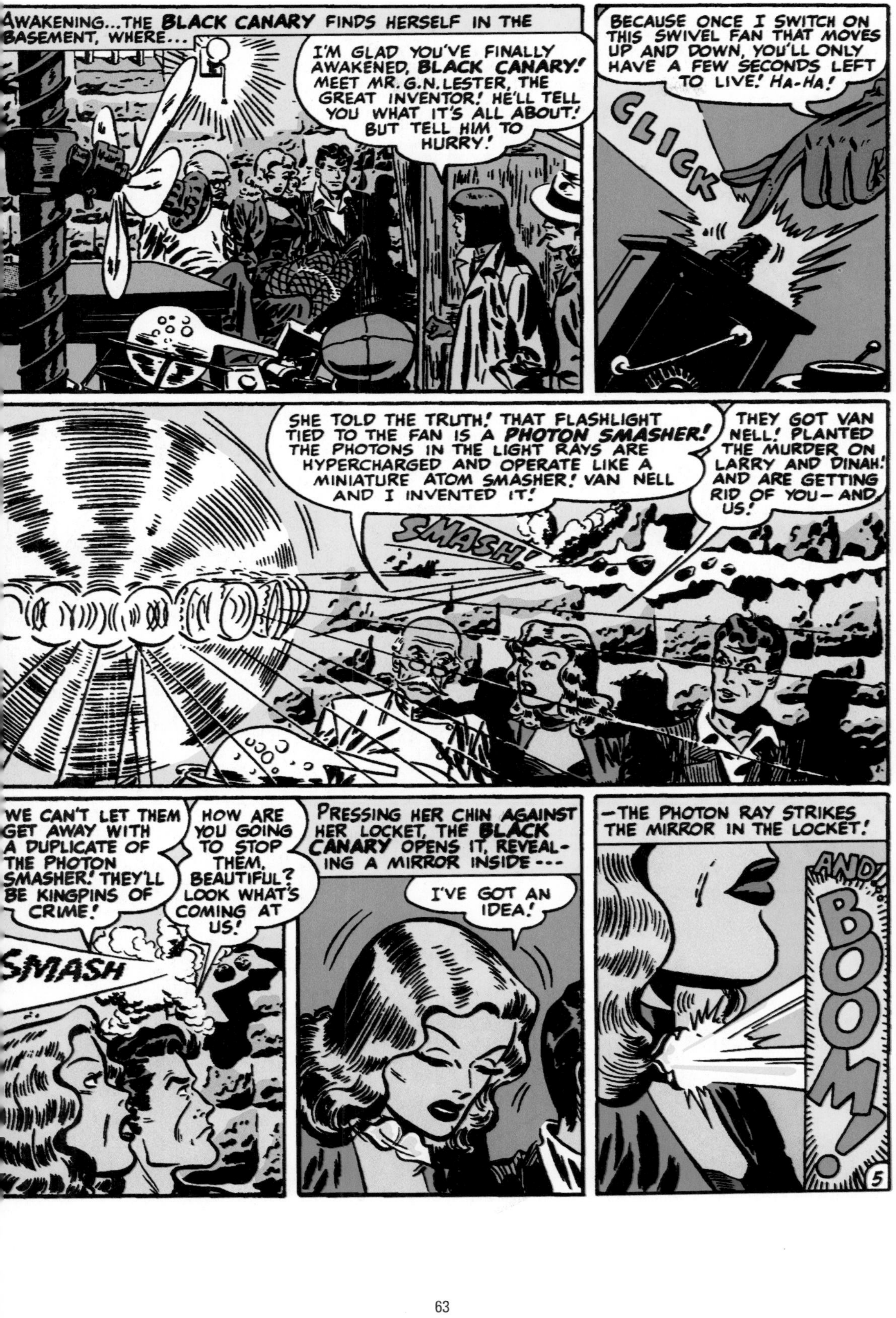
AWAKENING...THE BLACK CANARY FINDS HERSELF IN THE BASEMENT, WHERE...
I'M GLAD YOU'VE FINALLY AWAKENED, BLACK CANARY! MEET MR. G.N. LESTER, THE GREAT INVENTOR! HE'LL TELL YOU WHAT IT'S ALL ABOUT! BUT TELL HIM TO HURRY!
BECAUSE ONCE I SWITCH ON THIS SWIVEL FAN THAT MOVES UP AND DOWN, YOU'LL ONLY HAVE A FEW SECONDS LEFT TO LIVE! HA-HA!
CLICK
SHE TOLD THE TRUTH! THAT FLASHLIGHT TIED TO THE FAN IS A PHOTON SMASHER! THE PHOTONS IN THE LIGHT RAYS ARE HYPERCHARGED AND OPERATE LIKE A MINIATURE ATOM SMASHER! VAN NELL AND I INVENTED IT!
THEY GOT VAN NELL! PLANTED THE MURDER ON LARRY AND DINAH! AND ARE GETTING RID OF YOU—AND US!
SMASH!
WE CAN'T LET THEM GET AWAY WITH A DUPLICATE OF THE PHOTON SMASHER! THEY'LL BE KINGPINS OF CRIME!
HOW ARE YOU GOING TO STOP THEM, BEAUTIFUL? LOOK WHAT'S COMING AT US!
SMASH
PRESSING HER CHIN AGAINST HER LOCKET, THE BLACK CANARY OPENS IT, REVEALING A MIRROR INSIDE---
I'VE GOT AN IDEA!
—THE PHOTON RAY STRIKES THE MIRROR IN THE LOCKET!
AND
BOOM!
5

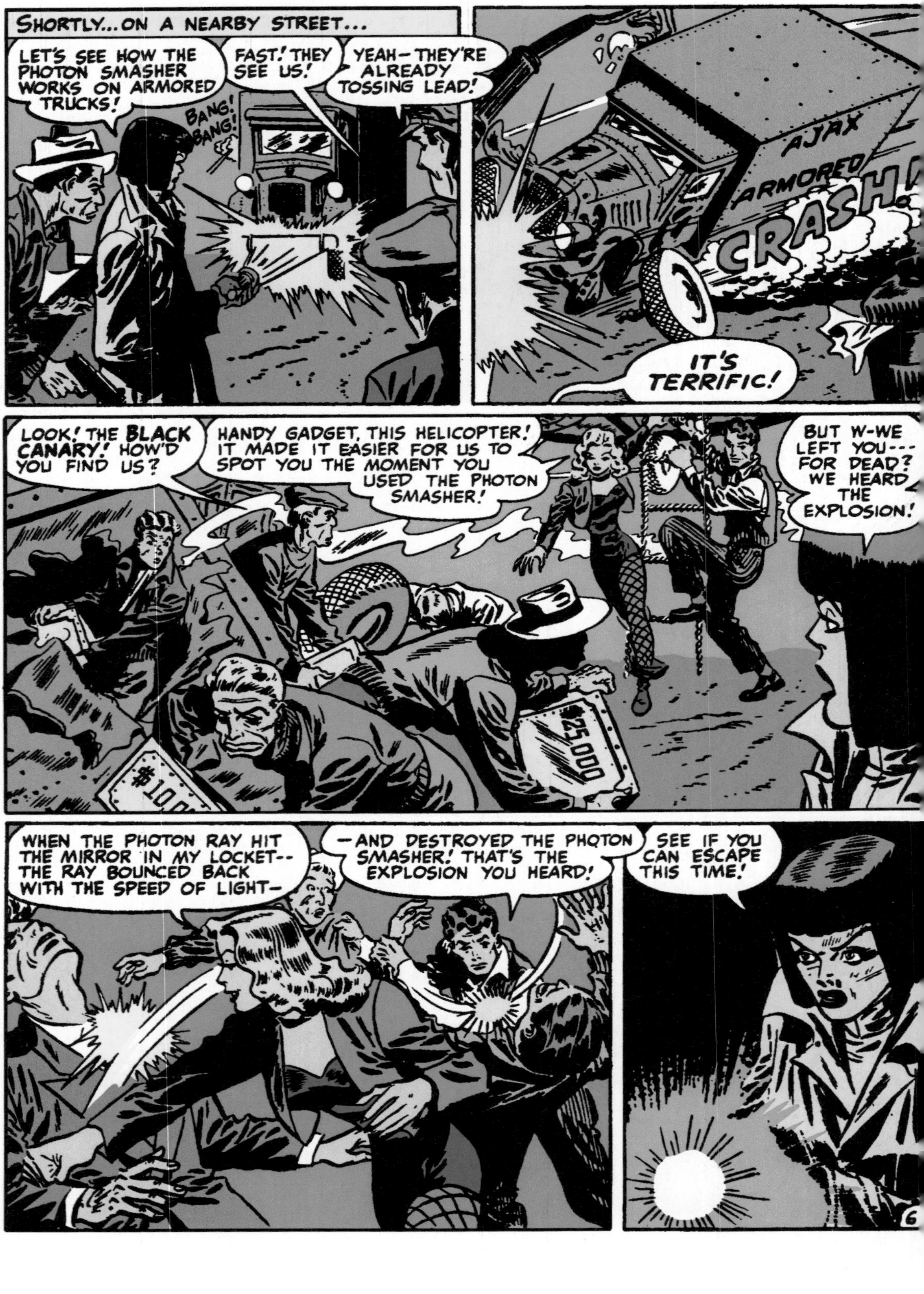
SHORTLY...ON A NEARBY STREET...
LET'S SEE HOW THE PHOTON SMASHER WORKS ON ARMORED TRUCKS!
FAST! THEY SEE US!
YEAH—THEY'RE ALREADY TOSSING LEAD!
BANG! BANG!
AJAX ARMORED
CRASH!
IT'S TERRIFIC!
LOOK! THE BLACK CANARY! HOW'D YOU FIND US?
HANDY GADGET, THIS HELICOPTER! IT MADE IT EASIER FOR US TO SPOT YOU THE MOMENT YOU USED THE PHOTON SMASHER!
BUT W-WE LEFT YOU--- FOR DEAD? WE HEARD THE EXPLOSION!
$25,000
WHEN THE PHOTON RAY HIT THE MIRROR IN MY LOCKET-- THE RAY BOUNCED BACK WITH THE SPEED OF LIGHT—
—AND DESTROYED THE PHOTON SMASHER! THAT'S THE EXPLOSION YOU HEARD!
SEE IF YOU CAN ESCAPE THIS TIME!
6

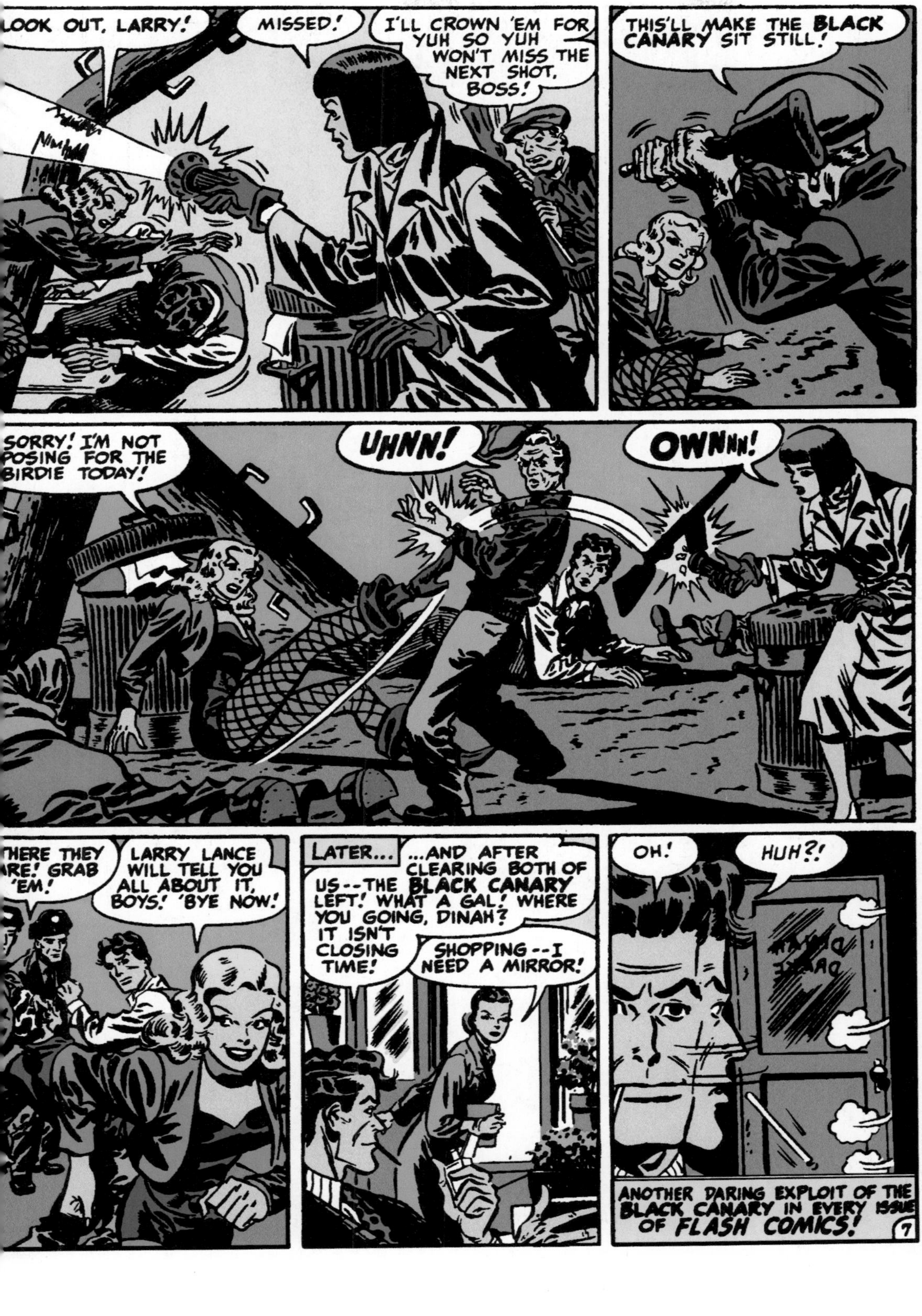
LOOK OUT, LARRY!
MISSED!
I'LL CROWN 'EM FOR YUH SO YUH WON'T MISS THE NEXT SHOT, BOSS!
THIS'LL MAKE THE BLACK CANARY SIT STILL!
SORRY! I'M NOT POSING FOR THE BIRDIE TODAY!
UHNN!
OWNNN!
THERE THEY ARE! GRAB 'EM!
LARRY LANCE WILL TELL YOU ALL ABOUT IT, BOYS! 'BYE NOW!
LATER...
...AND AFTER CLEARING BOTH OF US--THE BLACK CANARY LEFT! WHAT A GAL! WHERE YOU GOING, DINAH? IT ISN'T CLOSING TIME!
SHOPPING--I NEED A MIRROR!
OH!
HUH?!
ANOTHER DARING EXPLOIT OF THE BLACK CANARY IN EVERY ISSUE OF FLASH COMICS!
7

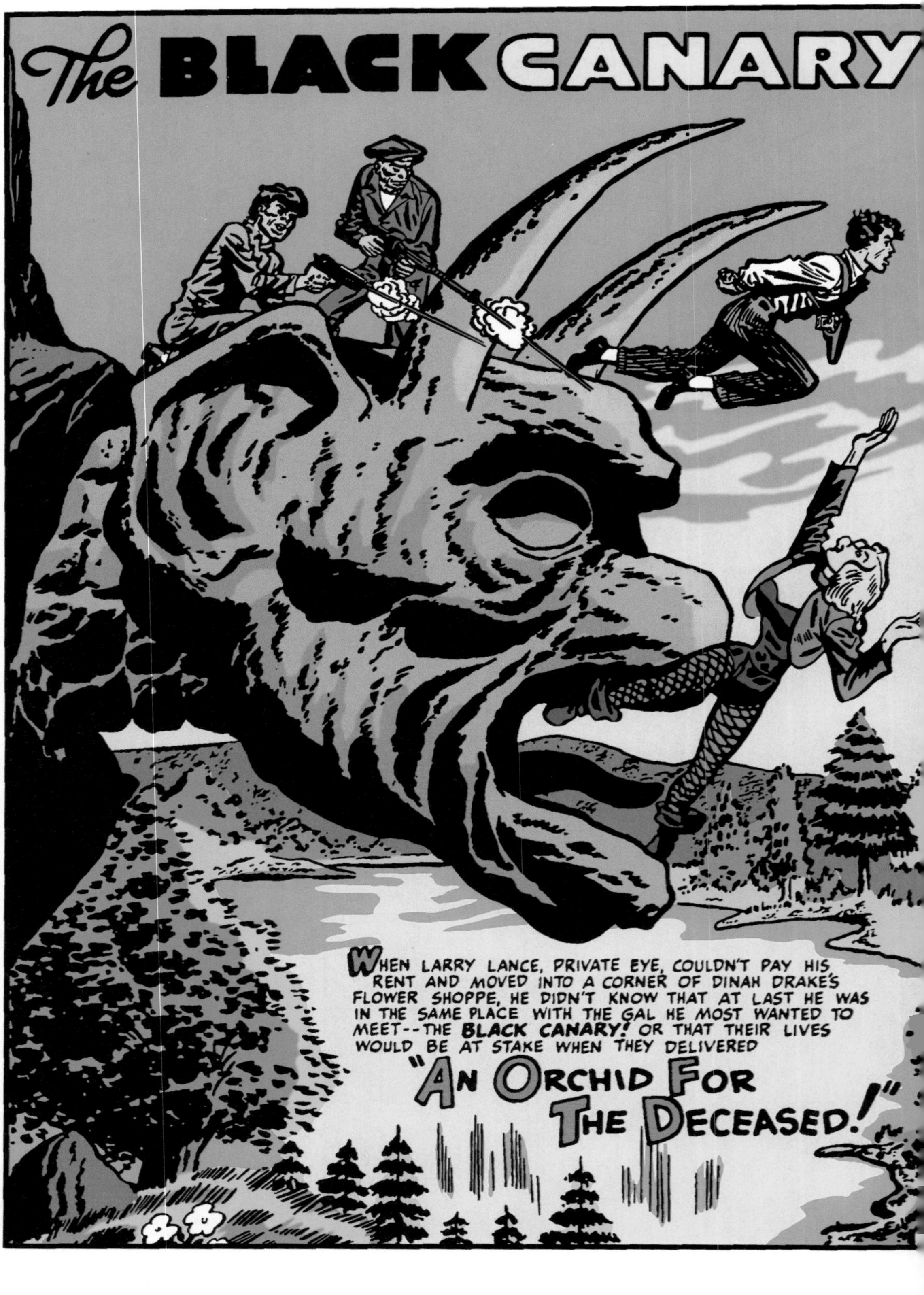
The BLACK CANARY
WHEN LARRY LANCE, PRIVATE EYE, COULDN'T PAY HIS RENT AND MOVED INTO A CORNER OF DINAH DRAKE'S FLOWER SHOPPE, HE DIDN'T KNOW THAT AT LAST HE WAS IN THE SAME PLACE WITH THE GAL HE MOST WANTED TO MEET--THE BLACK CANARY! OR THAT THEIR LIVES WOULD BE AT STAKE WHEN THEY DELIVERED
"AN ORCHID FOR THE DECEASED!"

AS DINAH DRAKE NEARS HER FLOWER SHOP, SHE HASN'T A CARE IN THE WORLD--

GOOD MORNING, MISS DRAKE!

GOOD MORNING, MISS DRAKE!

GOOD MORNING, MISS DRAKE!

GOOD MORNING!

FRUITS VEGETABLES

BUT SUDDENLY--

WHAT IN THE WORLD--?!

LARRY LANCE! WHAT IN THE WORLD DO YOU THINK YOU'RE DOING?

MOVING IN, SUGAR PIE! YOU DIDN'T THINK I WAS GOING TO TAKE THOSE MEASLY LITTLE CASES JUST TO PAY MY LANDLORD, DID YOU?

HA, HA!

DINAH DRAKE
FLOWERS CUT FLOWERS

DINAH DRAKE
FLOWER SHOP
PH. IX-3-2122

SO THOSE CASES WEREN'T GOOD ENOUGH FOR A BIG SHOT LIKE YOU? WELL, YOU BIG APE, IF YOU WANT TO MOVE, WHY DON'T YOU GO TO THE ZOO AND JOIN YOUR RELATIVES?

BECAUSE THEY DON'T HAVE TELEPHONES, HONEY!

DINAH DRAKE
FLOWERS SHOPPE

PICK UP YOUR JUNK AND GO, MR. COMIC! I'LL NEVER LET YOU SET UP YOUR THREE-RING CIRCUS IN MY SHOP! NOT ON YOUR LIFE!

DID ANYONE EVER TELL YOU HOW BEAUTIFUL YOU ARE, BEAUTIFUL? I CAN SIT HERE AND LISTEN TO YOU FOREVER!

1

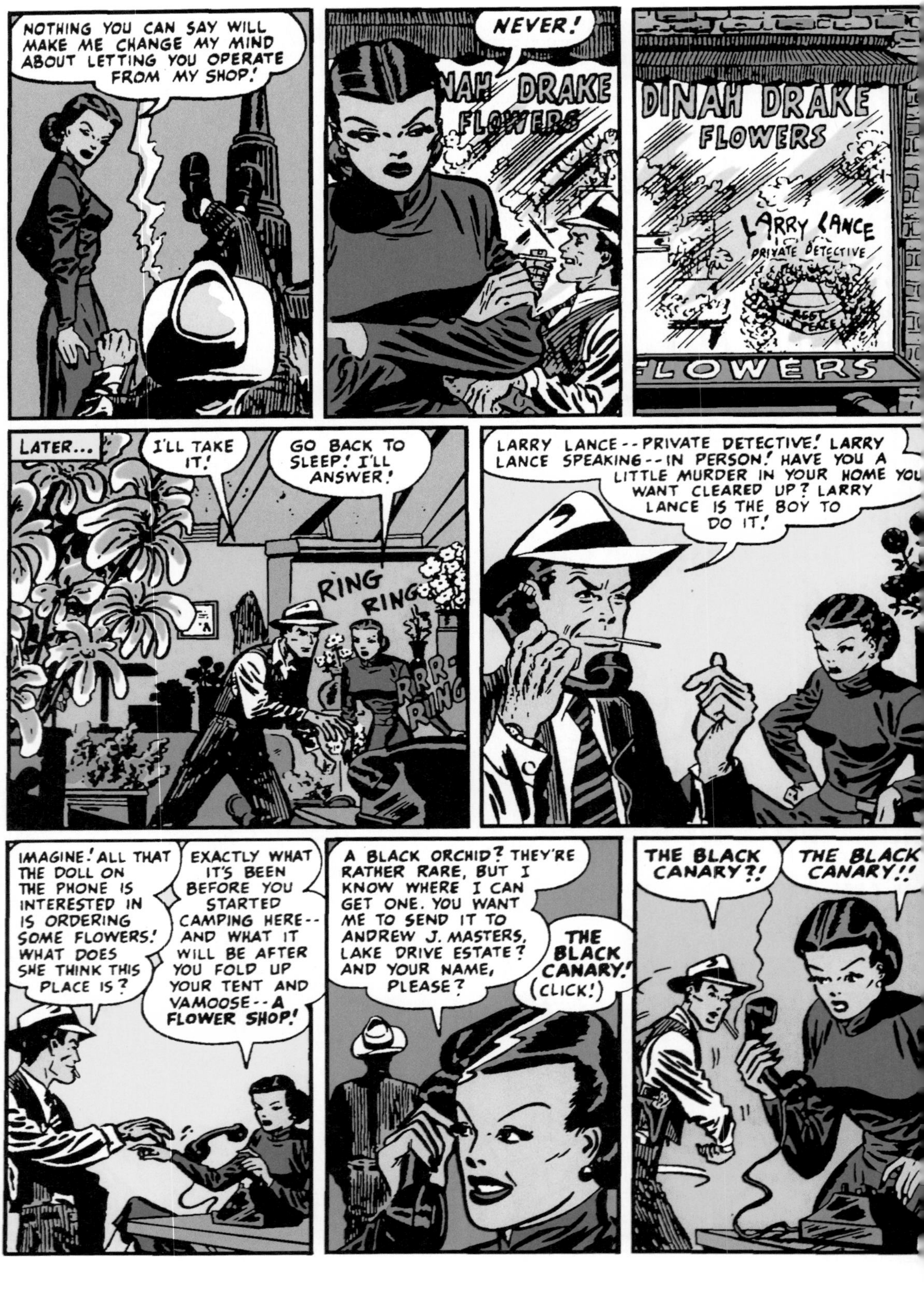
NOTHING YOU CAN SAY WILL MAKE ME CHANGE MY MIND ABOUT LETTING YOU OPERATE FROM MY SHOP!
NEVER!
DINAH DRAKE FLOWERS
DINAH DRAKE FLOWERS
LARRY LANCE PRIVATE DETECTIVE
FLOWERS
LATER...
I'LL TAKE IT!
GO BACK TO SLEEP! I'LL ANSWER!
RING RING
RRR-RING
LARRY LANCE--PRIVATE DETECTIVE! LARRY LANCE SPEAKING--IN PERSON! HAVE YOU A LITTLE MURDER IN YOUR HOME YOU WANT CLEARED UP? LARRY LANCE IS THE BOY TO DO IT!
IMAGINE! ALL THAT THE DOLL ON THE PHONE IS INTERESTED IN IS ORDERING SOME FLOWERS! WHAT DOES SHE THINK THIS PLACE IS?
EXACTLY WHAT IT'S BEEN BEFORE YOU STARTED CAMPING HERE--AND WHAT IT WILL BE AFTER YOU FOLD UP YOUR TENT AND VAMOOSE--A FLOWER SHOP!
A BLACK ORCHID? THEY'RE RATHER RARE, BUT I KNOW WHERE I CAN GET ONE. YOU WANT ME TO SEND IT TO ANDREW J. MASTERS, LAKE DRIVE ESTATE? AND YOUR NAME, PLEASE?
THE BLACK CANARY! (CLICK!)
THE BLACK CANARY?!
THE BLACK CANARY!!

SO THAT WAS THE **BLACK CANARY**?! I'D SURE LIKE TO MEET THAT SWEET POTATO FACE TO FACE --TO SWAP CASES!

THAT MIGHT BE SOONER THAN YOU THINK!

LARRY--I JUST REMEMBERED --THIS RUSH ORDER HAS TO GO OUT IMMEDIATELY! THE ADDRESS IS ATTACHED! YOU'LL DELIVER IT, WON'T YOU, MY SWEET?

UMPF-- FUPH!

I CAN'T SEE! ISN'T THAT KIND OF A TOUGH HANDICAP TO GIVE YOUR DELIVERY BOY?

YOU'LL SOLVE IT, DARLING--LIKE YOU DO EVERYTHING ELSE!

DRAKE FLOWERS

LARRY LAN PRIVATE DETEC

BON VOYAGE

OWERS

RACING TO THE BACK OF THE STORE, DINAH DRAKE OPENS A SECRET WALL PANEL AND --

I LIKE TO HAVE THE BIG MOOSE AROUND!

BUT NOT WHEN I'M CHANGING INTO THE **BLACK CANARY**!

AS SOON AS I WIRE A BLACK ORCHID TO BE SENT TO MR. MASTERS--I'LL FOLLOW AND FIND OUT WHY SOMEONE MASQUERADING AS ME WANTED TO SEND IT!

4

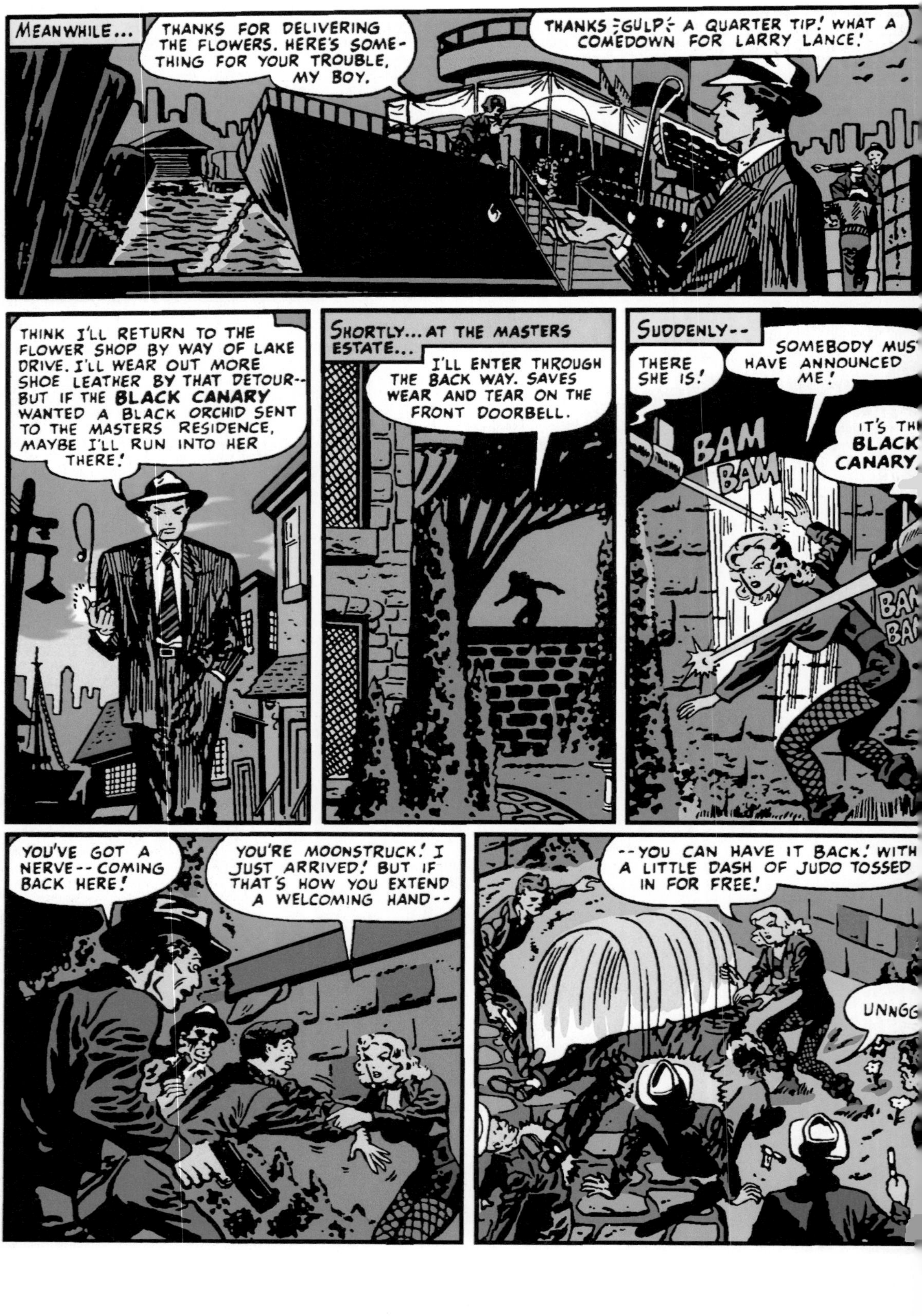

MEANWHILE...
THANKS FOR DELIVERING THE FLOWERS. HERE'S SOMETHING FOR YOUR TROUBLE, MY BOY.
THANKS -GULP!- A QUARTER TIP! WHAT A COMEDOWN FOR LARRY LANCE!
THINK I'LL RETURN TO THE FLOWER SHOP BY WAY OF LAKE DRIVE. I'LL WEAR OUT MORE SHOE LEATHER BY THAT DETOUR--BUT IF THE BLACK CANARY WANTED A BLACK ORCHID SENT TO THE MASTERS RESIDENCE, MAYBE I'LL RUN INTO HER THERE!
SHORTLY...AT THE MASTERS ESTATE...
I'LL ENTER THROUGH THE BACK WAY. SAVES WEAR AND TEAR ON THE FRONT DOORBELL.
SUDDENLY--
THERE SHE IS!
SOMEBODY MUST HAVE ANNOUNCED ME!
IT'S TH BLACK CANARY
BAM BAM
BAM BAM
YOU'VE GOT A NERVE--COMING BACK HERE!
YOU'RE MOONSTRUCK! I JUST ARRIVED! BUT IF THAT'S HOW YOU EXTEND A WELCOMING HAND--
--YOU CAN HAVE IT BACK! WITH A LITTLE DASH OF JUDO TOSSED IN FOR FREE!
UNNGG

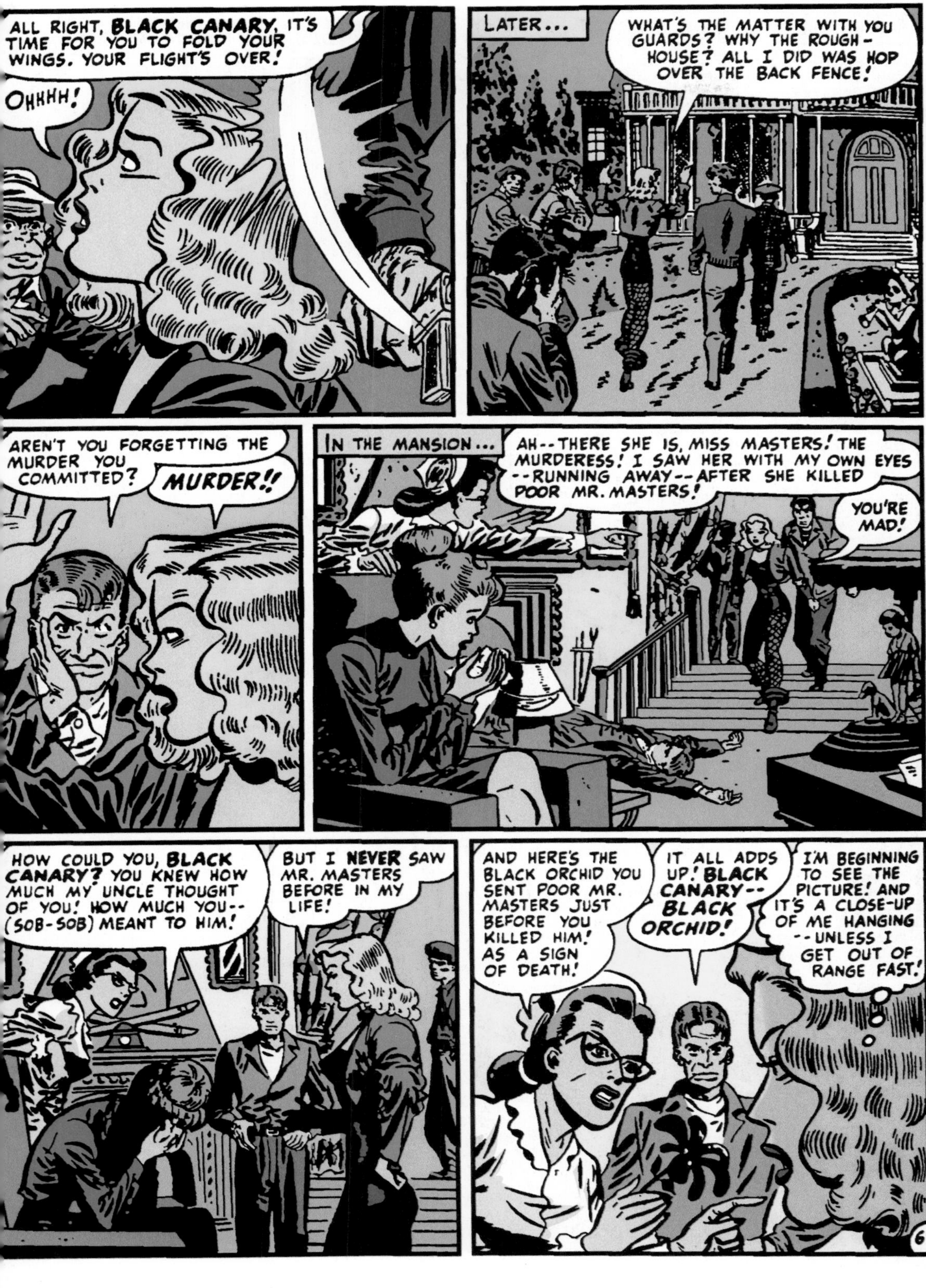

ALL RIGHT, BLACK CANARY, IT'S TIME FOR YOU TO FOLD YOUR WINGS. YOUR FLIGHT'S OVER!
OHHHH!
LATER...
WHAT'S THE MATTER WITH YOU GUARDS? WHY THE ROUGH-HOUSE? ALL I DID WAS HOP OVER THE BACK FENCE!
AREN'T YOU FORGETTING THE MURDER YOU COMMITTED?
MURDER!!
IN THE MANSION...
AH--THERE SHE IS, MISS MASTERS! THE MURDERESS! I SAW HER WITH MY OWN EYES --RUNNING AWAY--AFTER SHE KILLED POOR MR. MASTERS!
YOU'RE MAD!
HOW COULD YOU, BLACK CANARY? YOU KNEW HOW MUCH MY UNCLE THOUGHT OF YOU! HOW MUCH YOU--(SOB-SOB) MEANT TO HIM!
BUT I NEVER SAW MR. MASTERS BEFORE IN MY LIFE!
AND HERE'S THE BLACK ORCHID YOU SENT POOR MR. MASTERS JUST BEFORE YOU KILLED HIM! AS A SIGN OF DEATH!
IT ALL ADDS UP! BLACK CANARY--BLACK ORCHID!
I'M BEGINNING TO SEE THE PICTURE! AND IT'S A CLOSE-UP OF ME HANGING --UNLESS I GET OUT OF RANGE FAST!
6

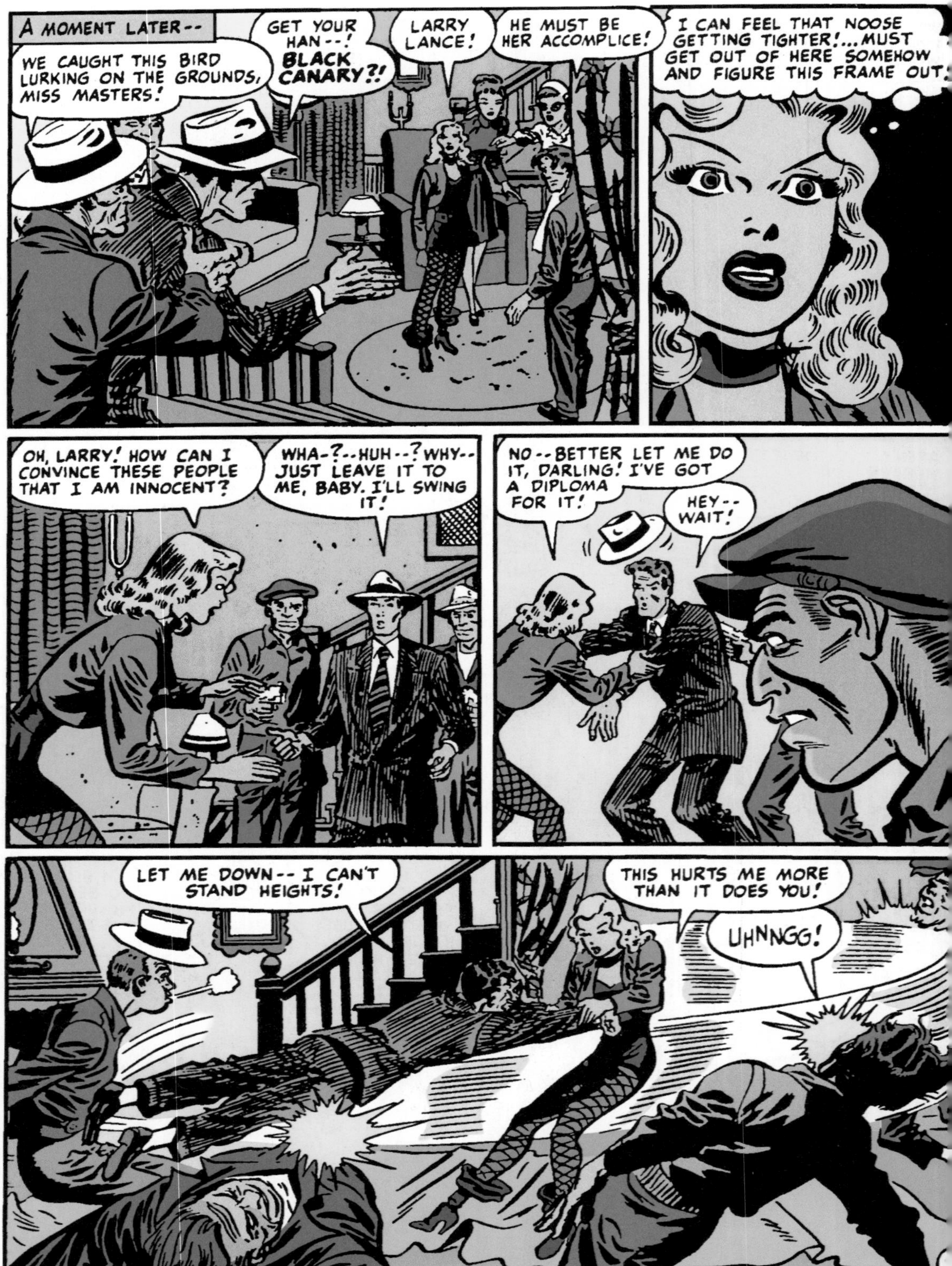
A MOMENT LATER--
WE CAUGHT THIS BIRD LURKING ON THE GROUNDS, MISS MASTERS!
GET YOUR HAN--! BLACK CANARY?!
LARRY LANCE!
HE MUST BE HER ACCOMPLICE!
I CAN FEEL THAT NOOSE GETTING TIGHTER!...MUST GET OUT OF HERE SOMEHOW AND FIGURE THIS FRAME OUT!
OH, LARRY! HOW CAN I CONVINCE THESE PEOPLE THAT I AM INNOCENT?
WHA-?--HUH--? WHY--JUST LEAVE IT TO ME, BABY. I'LL SWING IT!
NO--BETTER LET ME DO IT, DARLING! I'VE GOT A DIPLOMA FOR IT!
HEY--WAIT!
LET ME DOWN--I CAN'T STAND HEIGHTS!
THIS HURTS ME MORE THAN IT DOES YOU!
UHNNGG!

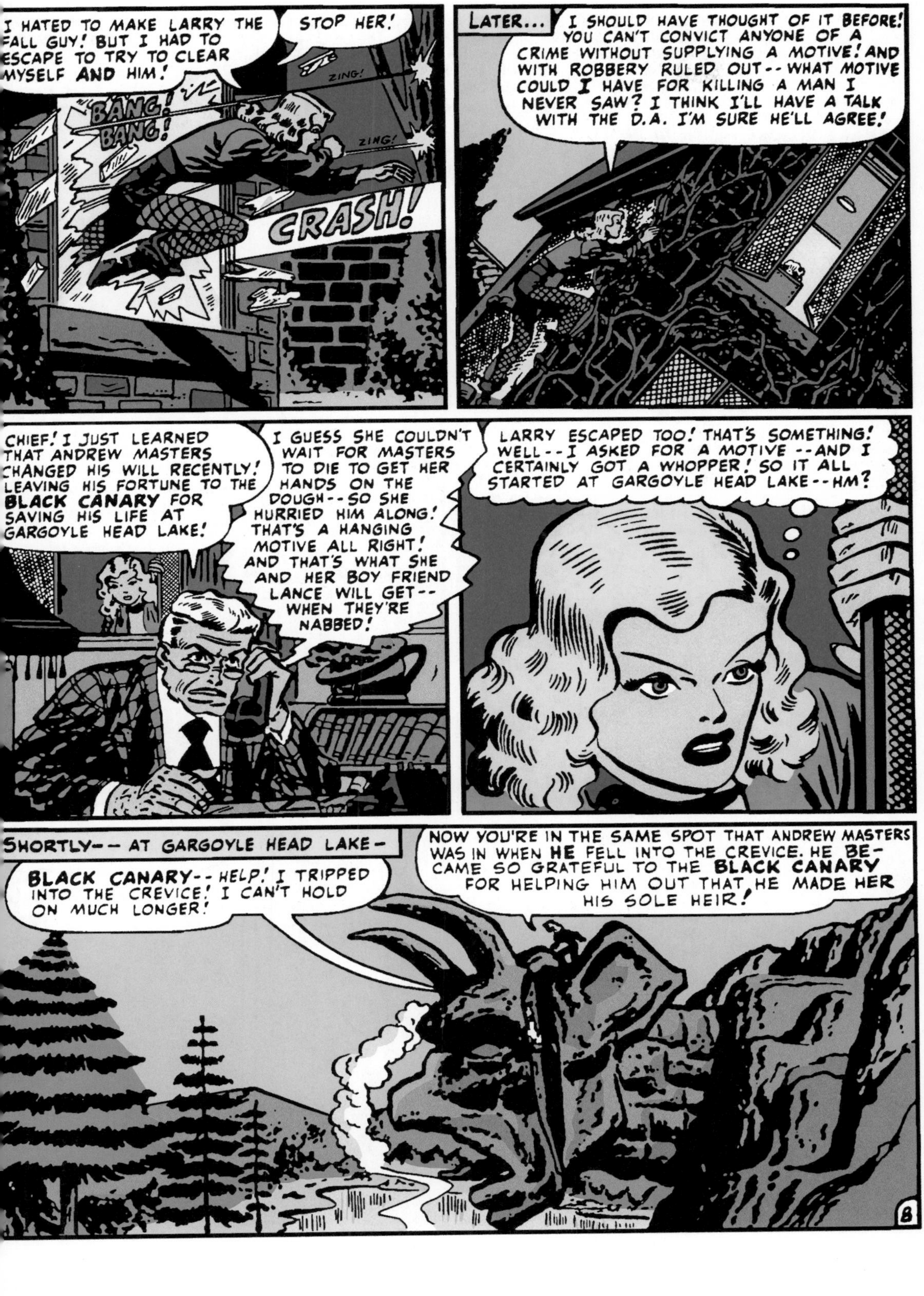
I HATED TO MAKE LARRY THE FALL GUY! BUT I HAD TO ESCAPE TO TRY TO CLEAR MYSELF AND HIM!
STOP HER!
ZING!
BANG! BANG!
ZING!
CRASH!
LATER...
I SHOULD HAVE THOUGHT OF IT BEFORE! YOU CAN'T CONVICT ANYONE OF A CRIME WITHOUT SUPPLYING A MOTIVE! AND WITH ROBBERY RULED OUT -- WHAT MOTIVE COULD I HAVE FOR KILLING A MAN I NEVER SAW? I THINK I'LL HAVE A TALK WITH THE D.A. I'M SURE HE'LL AGREE!
CHIEF! I JUST LEARNED THAT ANDREW MASTERS CHANGED HIS WILL RECENTLY! LEAVING HIS FORTUNE TO THE BLACK CANARY FOR SAVING HIS LIFE AT GARGOYLE HEAD LAKE!
I GUESS SHE COULDN'T WAIT FOR MASTERS TO DIE TO GET HER HANDS ON THE DOUGH -- SO SHE HURRIED HIM ALONG! THAT'S A HANGING MOTIVE ALL RIGHT! AND THAT'S WHAT SHE AND HER BOY FRIEND LANCE WILL GET -- WHEN THEY'RE NABBED!
LARRY ESCAPED TOO! THAT'S SOMETHING! WELL -- I ASKED FOR A MOTIVE -- AND I CERTAINLY GOT A WHOPPER! SO IT ALL STARTED AT GARGOYLE HEAD LAKE -- HM?
SHORTLY -- AT GARGOYLE HEAD LAKE -
BLACK CANARY -- HELP! I TRIPPED INTO THE CREVICE! I CAN'T HOLD ON MUCH LONGER!
NOW YOU'RE IN THE SAME SPOT THAT ANDREW MASTERS WAS IN WHEN HE FELL INTO THE CREVICE. HE BECAME SO GRATEFUL TO THE BLACK CANARY FOR HELPING HIM OUT THAT HE MADE HER HIS SOLE HEIR!
8

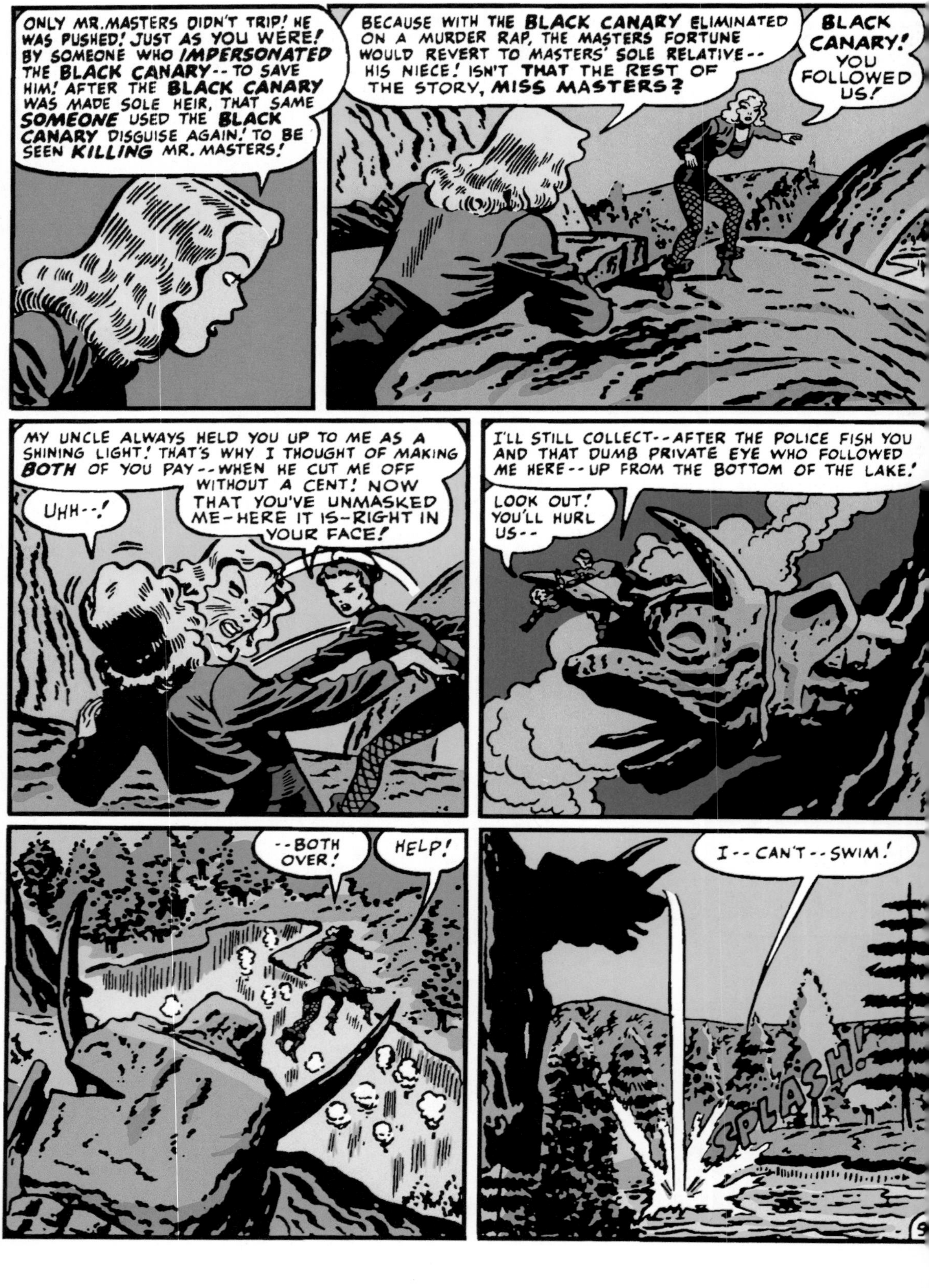
ONLY MR. MASTERS DIDN'T TRIP! HE WAS PUSHED! JUST AS YOU WERE! BY SOMEONE WHO IMPERSONATED THE BLACK CANARY--TO SAVE HIM! AFTER THE BLACK CANARY WAS MADE SOLE HEIR, THAT SAME SOMEONE USED THE BLACK CANARY DISGUISE AGAIN! TO BE SEEN KILLING MR. MASTERS!
BECAUSE WITH THE BLACK CANARY ELIMINATED ON A MURDER RAP, THE MASTERS FORTUNE WOULD REVERT TO MASTERS' SOLE RELATIVE--HIS NIECE! ISN'T THAT THE REST OF THE STORY, MISS MASTERS?
BLACK CANARY! YOU FOLLOWED US!
MY UNCLE ALWAYS HELD YOU UP TO ME AS A SHINING LIGHT! THAT'S WHY I THOUGHT OF MAKING BOTH OF YOU PAY--WHEN HE CUT ME OFF WITHOUT A CENT! NOW THAT YOU'VE UNMASKED ME--HERE IT IS--RIGHT IN YOUR FACE!
UHH--!
I'LL STILL COLLECT--AFTER THE POLICE FISH YOU AND THAT DUMB PRIVATE EYE WHO FOLLOWED ME HERE--UP FROM THE BOTTOM OF THE LAKE!
LOOK OUT! YOU'LL HURL US--
--BOTH OVER!
HELP!
I--CAN'T--SWIM!
SPLASH!

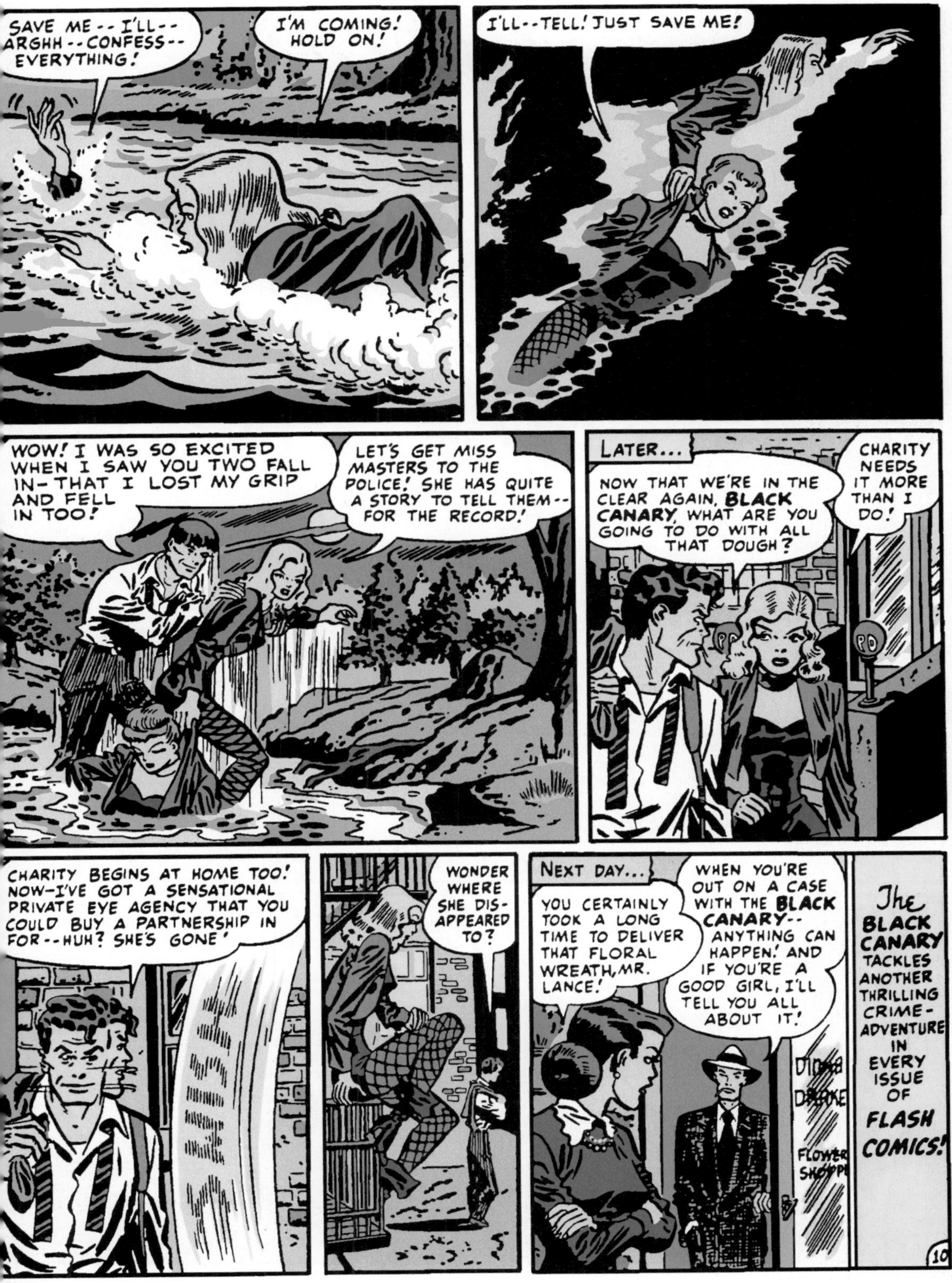
SAVE ME -- I'LL -- ARGHH -- CONFESS -- EVERYTHING!
I'M COMING! HOLD ON!
I'LL -- TELL! JUST SAVE ME!
WOW! I WAS SO EXCITED WHEN I SAW YOU TWO FALL IN -- THAT I LOST MY GRIP AND FELL IN TOO!
LET'S GET MISS MASTERS TO THE POLICE! SHE HAS QUITE A STORY TO TELL THEM -- FOR THE RECORD!
LATER...
NOW THAT WE'RE IN THE CLEAR AGAIN, BLACK CANARY, WHAT ARE YOU GOING TO DO WITH ALL THAT DOUGH?
CHARITY NEEDS IT MORE THAN I DO!
CHARITY BEGINS AT HOME TOO! NOW -- I'VE GOT A SENSATIONAL PRIVATE EYE AGENCY THAT YOU COULD BUY A PARTNERSHIP IN FOR -- HUH? SHE'S GONE!
WONDER WHERE SHE DIS-APPEARED TO?
NEXT DAY...
YOU CERTAINLY TOOK A LONG TIME TO DELIVER THAT FLORAL WREATH, MR. LANCE!
WHEN YOU'RE OUT ON A CASE WITH THE BLACK CANARY -- ANYTHING CAN HAPPEN! AND IF YOU'RE A GOOD GIRL, I'LL TELL YOU ALL ABOUT IT!
FLOWER SHOPPE
The BLACK CANARY TACKLES ANOTHER THRILLING CRIME-ADVENTURE IN EVERY ISSUE OF FLASH COMICS!
10

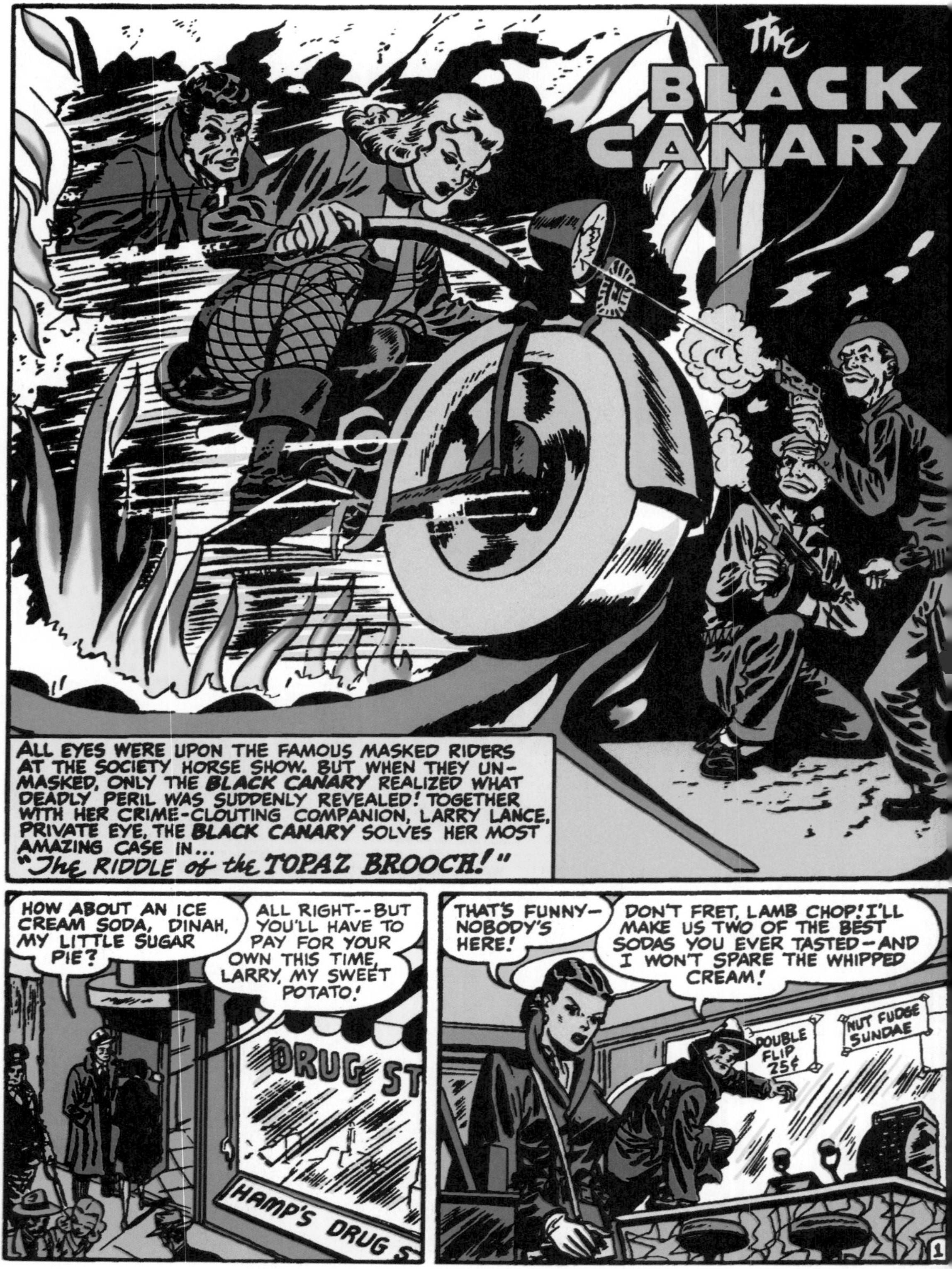
THE BLACK CANARY
ALL EYES WERE UPON THE FAMOUS MASKED RIDERS AT THE SOCIETY HORSE SHOW. BUT WHEN THEY UN-MASKED, ONLY THE BLACK CANARY REALIZED WHAT DEADLY PERIL WAS SUDDENLY REVEALED! TOGETHER WITH HER CRIME-CLOUTING COMPANION, LARRY LANCE, PRIVATE EYE, THE BLACK CANARY SOLVES HER MOST AMAZING CASE IN...
"THE RIDDLE of the TOPAZ BROOCH!"
HOW ABOUT AN ICE CREAM SODA, DINAH, MY LITTLE SUGAR PIE?
ALL RIGHT--BUT YOU'LL HAVE TO PAY FOR YOUR OWN THIS TIME, LARRY, MY SWEET POTATO!
DRUG ST
HAMP'S DRUG S
THAT'S FUNNY-NOBODY'S HERE!
DON'T FRET, LAMB CHOP! I'LL MAKE US TWO OF THE BEST SODAS YOU EVER TASTED--AND I WON'T SPARE THE WHIPPED CREAM!
DOUBLE FLIP 25¢
NUT FUDGE SUNDAE
1

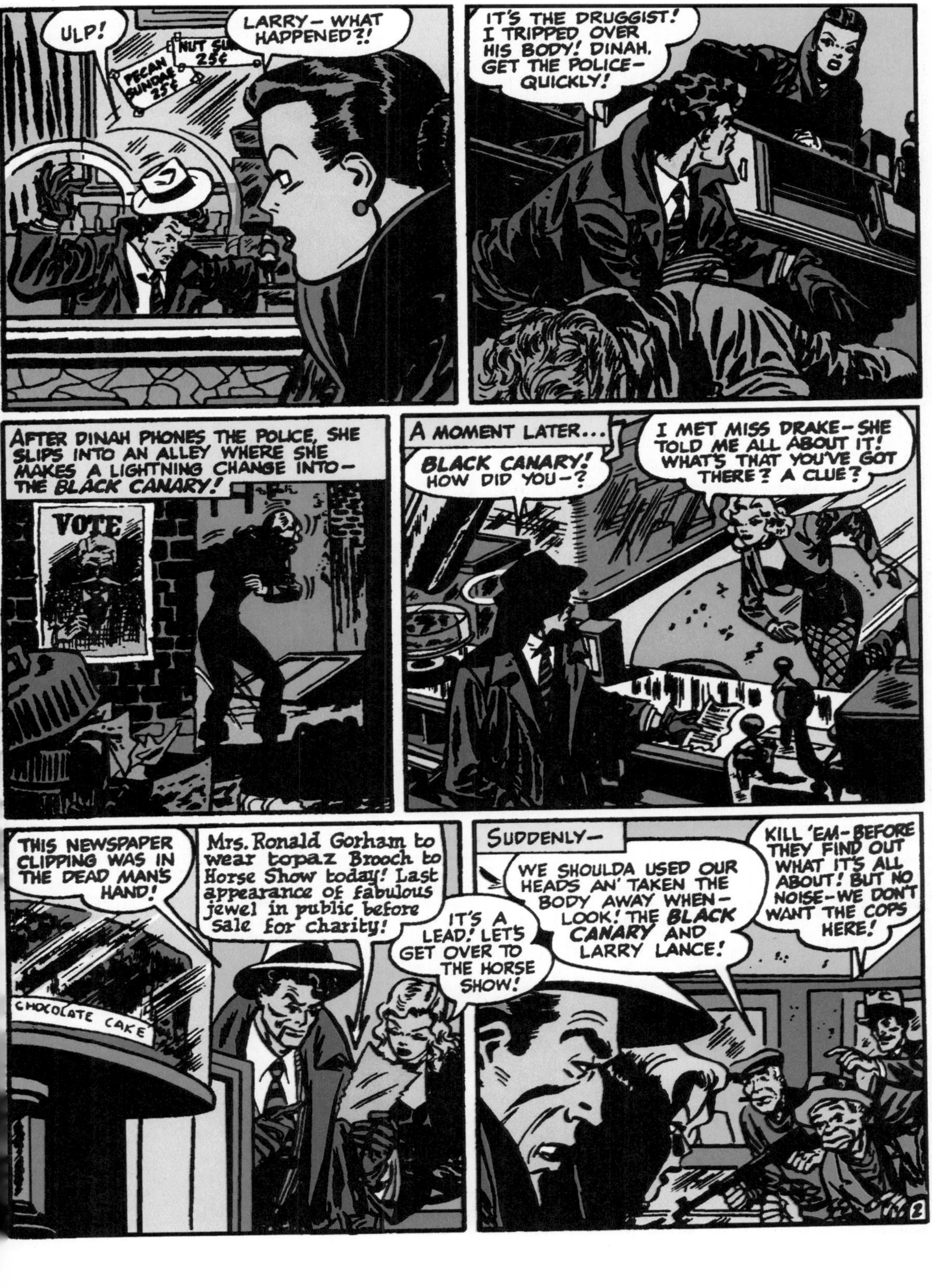

ULP!
LARRY—WHAT HAPPENED?!
PECAN SUNDAE 25¢
NUT SU 25¢
IT'S THE DRUGGIST! I TRIPPED OVER HIS BODY! DINAH, GET THE POLICE—QUICKLY!
AFTER DINAH PHONES THE POLICE, SHE SLIPS INTO AN ALLEY WHERE SHE MAKES A LIGHTNING CHANGE INTO—THE BLACK CANARY!
VOTE
A MOMENT LATER...
BLACK CANARY! HOW DID YOU—?
I MET MISS DRAKE—SHE TOLD ME ALL ABOUT IT! WHAT'S THAT YOU'VE GOT THERE? A CLUE?
THIS NEWSPAPER CLIPPING WAS IN THE DEAD MAN'S HAND!
Mrs. Ronald Gorham to wear topaz Brooch to Horse Show today! Last appearance of fabulous jewel in public before sale for charity!
IT'S A LEAD! LET'S GET OVER TO THE HORSE SHOW!
CHOCOLATE CAKE
SUDDENLY—
WE SHOULDA USED OUR HEADS AN' TAKEN THE BODY AWAY WHEN—LOOK! THE BLACK CANARY AND LARRY LANCE!
KILL 'EM—BEFORE THEY FIND OUT WHAT IT'S ALL ABOUT! BUT NO NOISE—WE DON'T WANT THE COPS HERE!
2

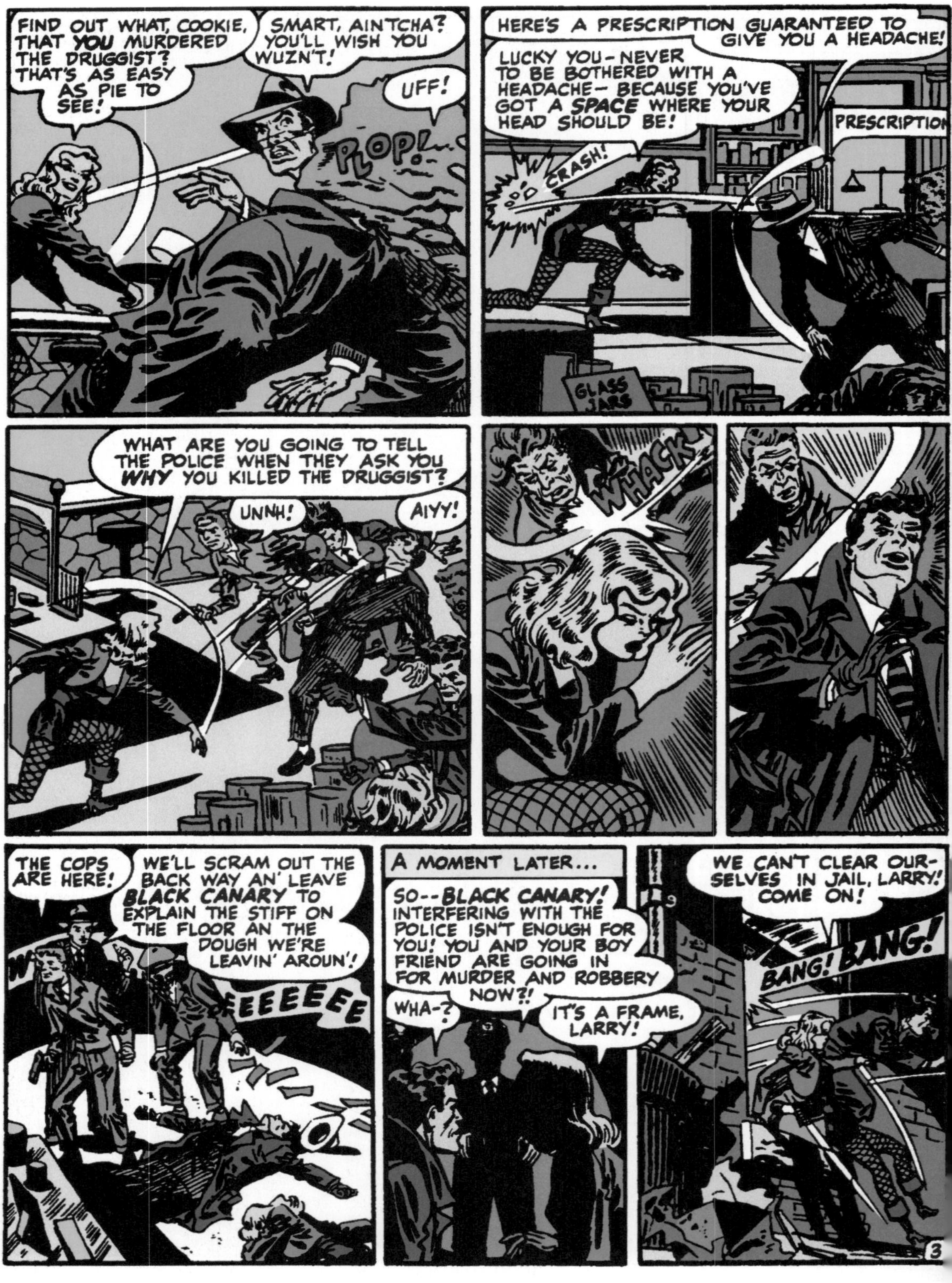
FIND OUT WHAT, COOKIE, THAT YOU MURDERED THE DRUGGIST? THAT'S AS EASY AS PIE TO SEE!
SMART, AIN'TCHA? YOU'LL WISH YOU WUZN'T!
UFF!
PLOP!
HERE'S A PRESCRIPTION GUARANTEED TO GIVE YOU A HEADACHE!
LUCKY YOU-NEVER TO BE BOTHERED WITH A HEADACHE- BECAUSE YOU'VE GOT A SPACE WHERE YOUR HEAD SHOULD BE!
PRESCRIPTION
CRASH!
GLASS JARS
WHAT ARE YOU GOING TO TELL THE POLICE WHEN THEY ASK YOU WHY YOU KILLED THE DRUGGIST?
UNNH!
AIYY!
WHACK
THE COPS ARE HERE!
WE'LL SCRAM OUT THE BACK WAY AN' LEAVE BLACK CANARY TO EXPLAIN THE STIFF ON THE FLOOR AN THE DOUGH WE'RE LEAVIN' AROUN'!
EEEEEEE
A MOMENT LATER...
SO--BLACK CANARY! INTERFERING WITH THE POLICE ISN'T ENOUGH FOR YOU! YOU AND YOUR BOY FRIEND ARE GOING IN FOR MURDER AND ROBBERY NOW?!
WHA-?
IT'S A FRAME, LARRY!
WE CAN'T CLEAR OURSELVES IN JAIL, LARRY! COME ON!
BANG! BANG!
3

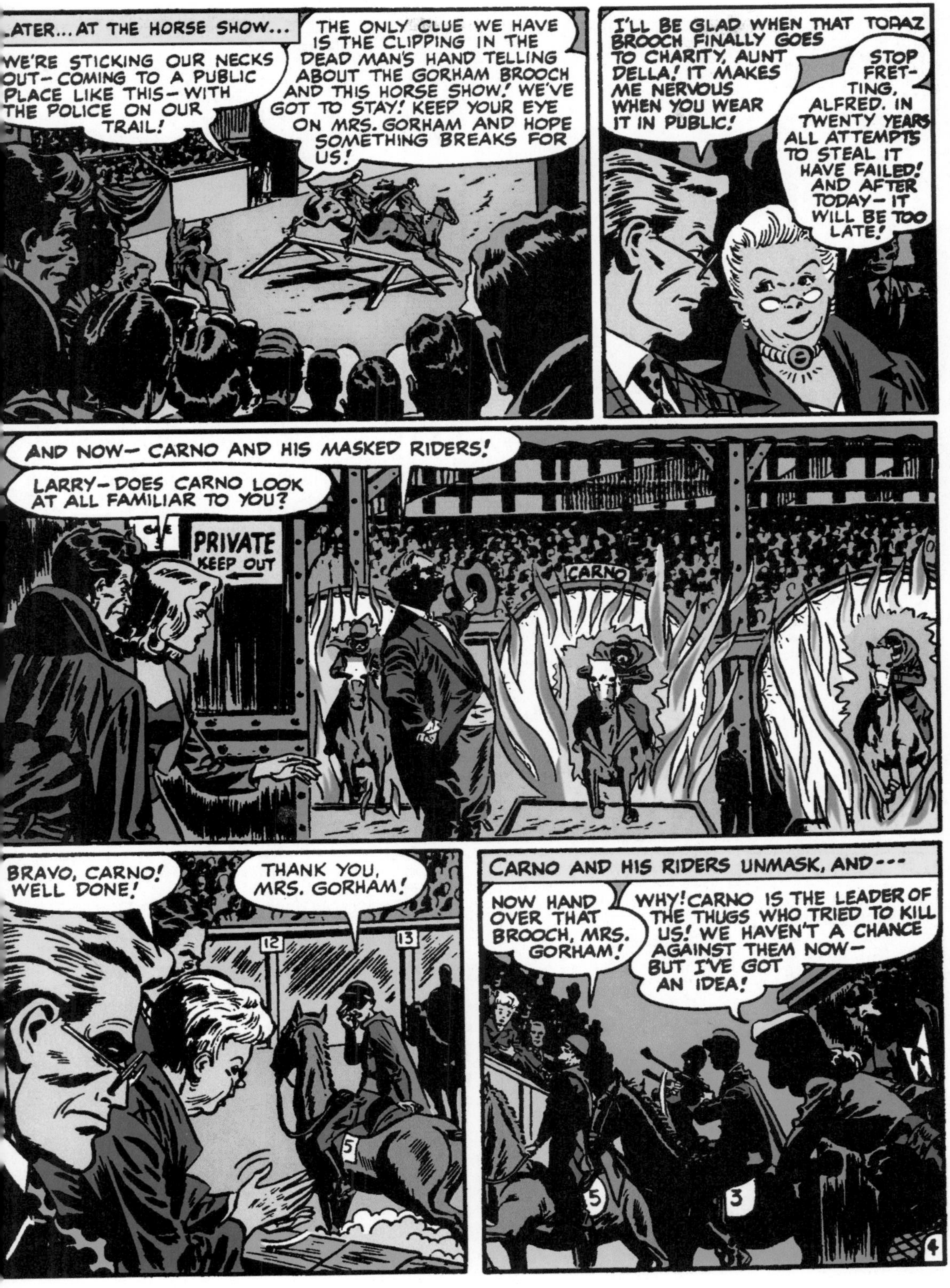
LATER... AT THE HORSE SHOW...
WE'RE STICKING OUR NECKS OUT—COMING TO A PUBLIC PLACE LIKE THIS—WITH THE POLICE ON OUR TRAIL!
THE ONLY CLUE WE HAVE IS THE CLIPPING IN THE DEAD MAN'S HAND TELLING ABOUT THE GORHAM BROOCH AND THIS HORSE SHOW! WE'VE GOT TO STAY! KEEP YOUR EYE ON MRS. GORHAM AND HOPE SOMETHING BREAKS FOR US!
I'LL BE GLAD WHEN THAT TOPAZ BROOCH FINALLY GOES TO CHARITY, AUNT DELLA! IT MAKES ME NERVOUS WHEN YOU WEAR IT IN PUBLIC!
STOP FRETTING, ALFRED. IN TWENTY YEARS ALL ATTEMPTS TO STEAL IT HAVE FAILED! AND AFTER TODAY—IT WILL BE TOO LATE!
AND NOW—CARNO AND HIS MASKED RIDERS!
LARRY—DOES CARNO LOOK AT ALL FAMILIAR TO YOU?
PRIVATE KEEP OUT
CARNO
BRAVO, CARNO! WELL DONE!
THANK YOU, MRS. GORHAM!
12
13
5
CARNO AND HIS RIDERS UNMASK, AND---
NOW HAND OVER THAT BROOCH, MRS. GORHAM!
WHY! CARNO IS THE LEADER OF THE THUGS WHO TRIED TO KILL US! WE HAVEN'T A CHANCE AGAINST THEM NOW—BUT I'VE GOT AN IDEA!
5
3
4

BETTER GIVE THEM THE BROOCH, AUNTIE! THEY MEAN BUSINESS!
D-D-DON'T SHOOT! HERE'S THE BROOCH!
BOSS, LOOK! HERE COMES BLACK CANARY ON A MOTOR-CYCLE!
WE CAN'T WASTE TIME WITH BLACK CANARY— NOW THAT WE'VE GOT THE BROOCH! LET'S GO!
BUT, BOSS—WE'VE GOTTA STOP 'EM!
BANG!
EXIT
THERE! THIS'LL STOP 'EM!
CANARY, LOOK OUT! THAT FLAMING RING IS COMING STRAIGHT TOWARDS US!
5
LT-131
HOLD YOUR BREATH, LARRY, IF YOU DON'T WANT IT SCORCHED!
HURRY—THEY'VE ALREADY GONE THROUGH THE EXIT!
BUT AS THE TWO REACH THE STREET...
THOSE CRAZY HORSEMEN!
THEY CAUSED A TRAFFIC JAM!
HONK!
HONK!
FINALLY EXTRICATING THEMSELVES FROM THE TRAFFIC JAM, BLACK CANARY TRAILS THE HORSEMEN OUTSIDE THE CITY TO--
THERE THEY ARE—MAKING THEIR GETAWAY IN A PLANE!
TAKE IT EASY, CANARY! THIS GROUND WASN'T MEANT FOR A MOTOR-CYCLE TRIP, YOU KNOW!
5

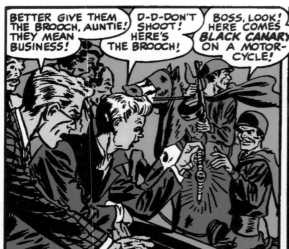

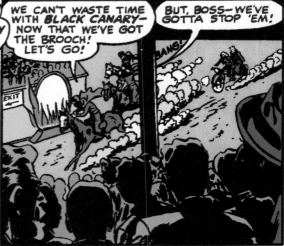

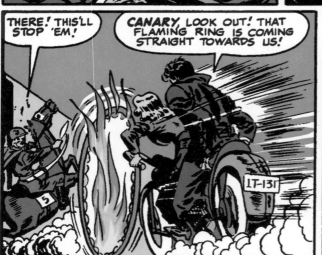

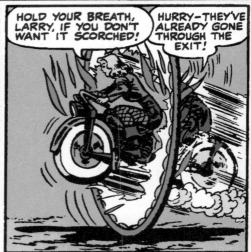

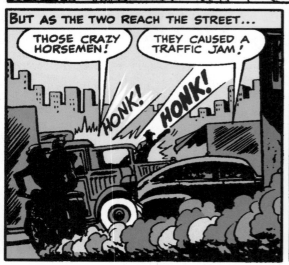

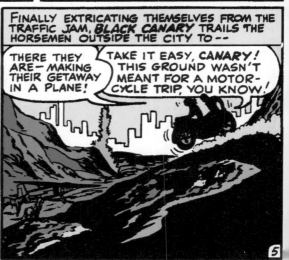

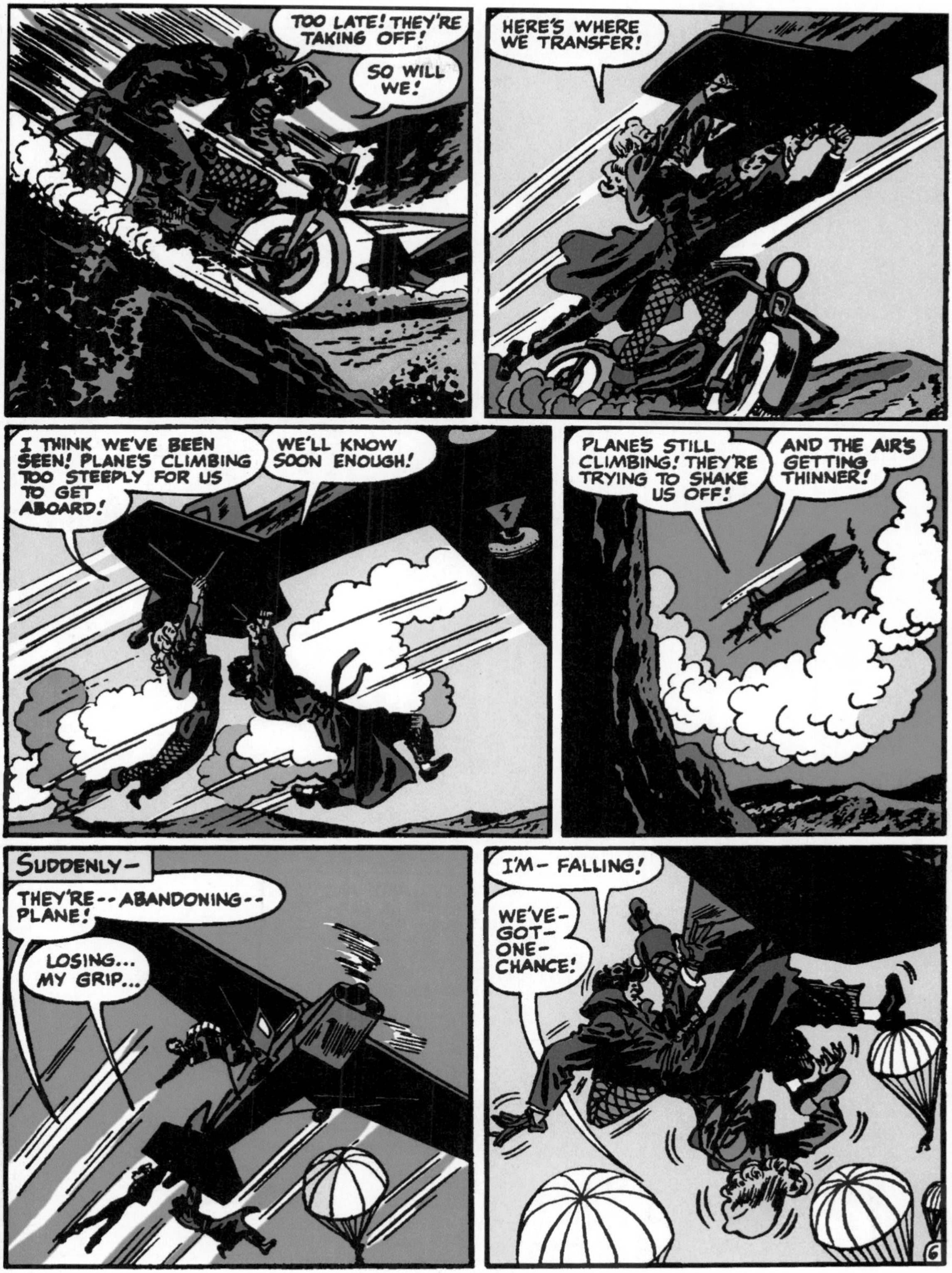
TOO LATE! THEY'RE TAKING OFF!
SO WILL WE!
HERE'S WHERE WE TRANSFER!
I THINK WE'VE BEEN SEEN! PLANE'S CLIMBING TOO STEEPLY FOR US TO GET ABOARD!
WE'LL KNOW SOON ENOUGH!
PLANE'S STILL CLIMBING! THEY'RE TRYING TO SHAKE US OFF!
AND THE AIR'S GETTING THINNER!
SUDDENLY—
THEY'RE--ABANDONING--PLANE!
LOSING... MY GRIP...
I'M—FALLING!
WE'VE—GOT—ONE—CHANCE!
6

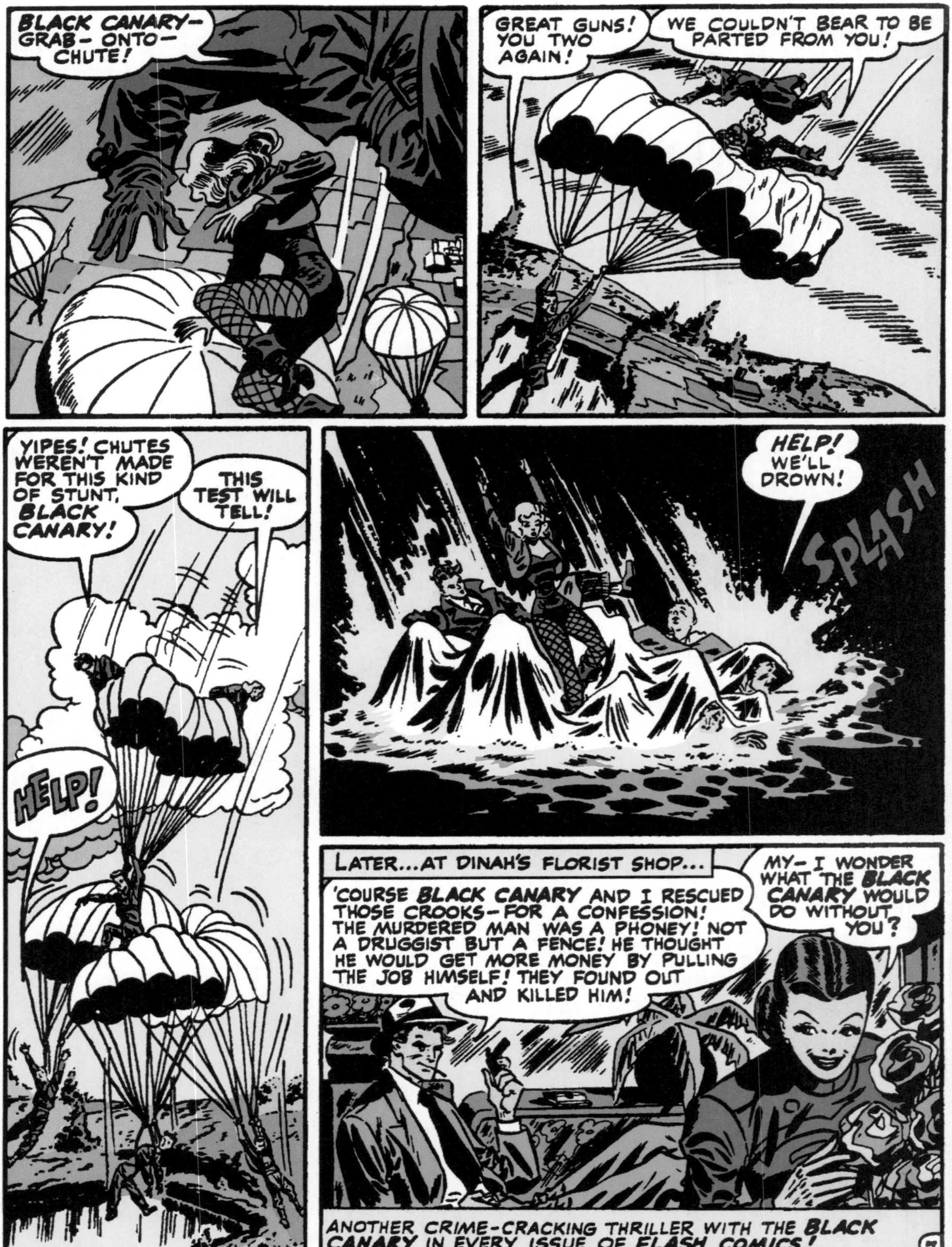
BLACK CANARY— GRAB - ONTO— CHUTE!
GREAT GUNS! YOU TWO AGAIN!
WE COULDN'T BEAR TO BE PARTED FROM YOU!
YIPES! CHUTES WEREN'T MADE FOR THIS KIND OF STUNT, BLACK CANARY!
THIS TEST WILL TELL!
HELP!
HELP! WE'LL DROWN!
SPLASH
LATER...AT DINAH'S FLORIST SHOP...
'COURSE BLACK CANARY AND I RESCUED THOSE CROOKS— FOR A CONFESSION! THE MURDERED MAN WAS A PHONEY! NOT A DRUGGIST BUT A FENCE! HE THOUGHT HE WOULD GET MORE MONEY BY PULLING THE JOB HIMSELF! THEY FOUND OUT AND KILLED HIM!
MY— I WONDER WHAT THE BLACK CANARY WOULD DO WITHOUT YOU?
ANOTHER CRIME-CRACKING THRILLER WITH THE BLACK CANARY IN EVERY ISSUE OF FLASH COMICS!
7

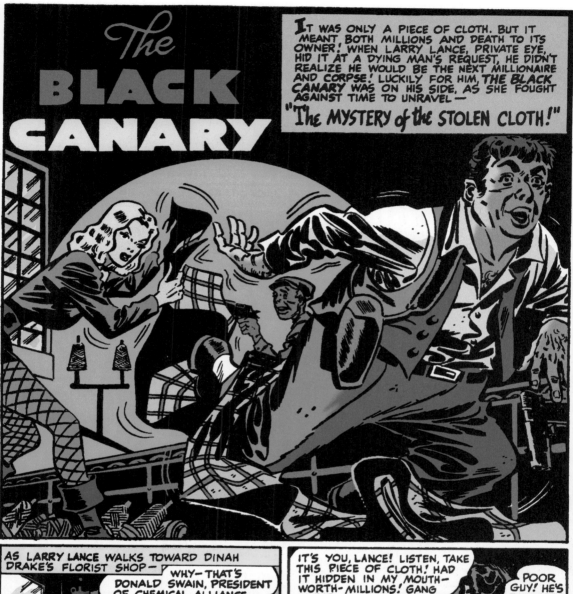

THE BLACK CANARY

IT WAS ONLY A PIECE OF CLOTH. BUT IT MEANT BOTH MILLIONS AND DEATH TO ITS OWNER! WHEN LARRY LANCE, PRIVATE EYE, HID IT AT A DYING MAN'S REQUEST, HE DIDN'T REALIZE HE WOULD BE THE NEXT MILLIONAIRE AND CORPSE! LUCKILY FOR HIM, THE BLACK CANARY WAS ON HIS SIDE, AS SHE FOUGHT AGAINST TIME TO UNRAVEL—

"THE MYSTERY of the STOLEN CLOTH!"

AS LARRY LANCE WALKS TOWARD DINAH DRAKE'S FLORIST SHOP—

WHY—THAT'S DONALD SWAIN, PRESIDENT OF CHEMICAL ALLIANCE, BEING SHOVED OUT OF THAT CAR!

IT'S YOU, LANCE! LISTEN, TAKE THIS PIECE OF CLOTH! HAD IT HIDDEN IN MY MOUTH—WORTH-MILLIONS! GANG AFTER IT—CAREFUL—I-I OHH..

POOR GUY! HE'S FINISHED!

1

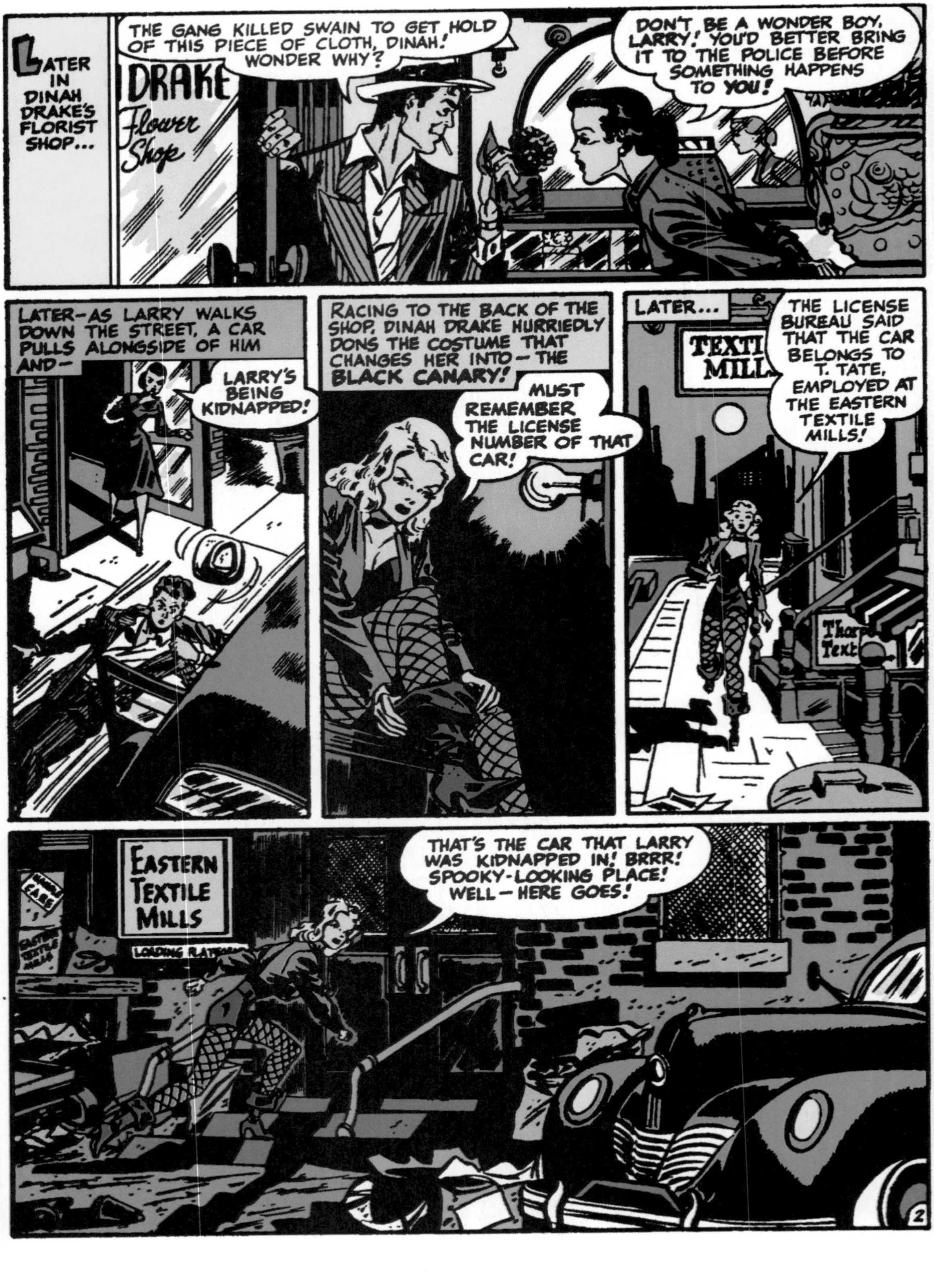
LATER IN DINAH DRAKE'S FLORIST SHOP...
THE GANG KILLED SWAIN TO GET HOLD OF THIS PIECE OF CLOTH, DINAH! WONDER WHY?
DON'T BE A WONDER BOY, LARRY! YOU'D BETTER BRING IT TO THE POLICE BEFORE SOMETHING HAPPENS TO YOU!
DRAKE Flower Shop
LATER—AS LARRY WALKS DOWN THE STREET, A CAR PULLS ALONGSIDE OF HIM AND—
LARRY'S BEING KIDNAPPED!
RACING TO THE BACK OF THE SHOP, DINAH DRAKE HURRIEDLY DONS THE COSTUME THAT CHANGES HER INTO—THE BLACK CANARY!
MUST REMEMBER THE LICENSE NUMBER OF THAT CAR!
LATER...
THE LICENSE BUREAU SAID THAT THE CAR BELONGS TO T. TATE, EMPLOYED AT THE EASTERN TEXTILE MILLS!
EASTERN TEXTILE MILLS
THAT'S THE CAR THAT LARRY WAS KIDNAPPED IN! BRRR! SPOOKY-LOOKING PLACE! WELL—HERE GOES!
2

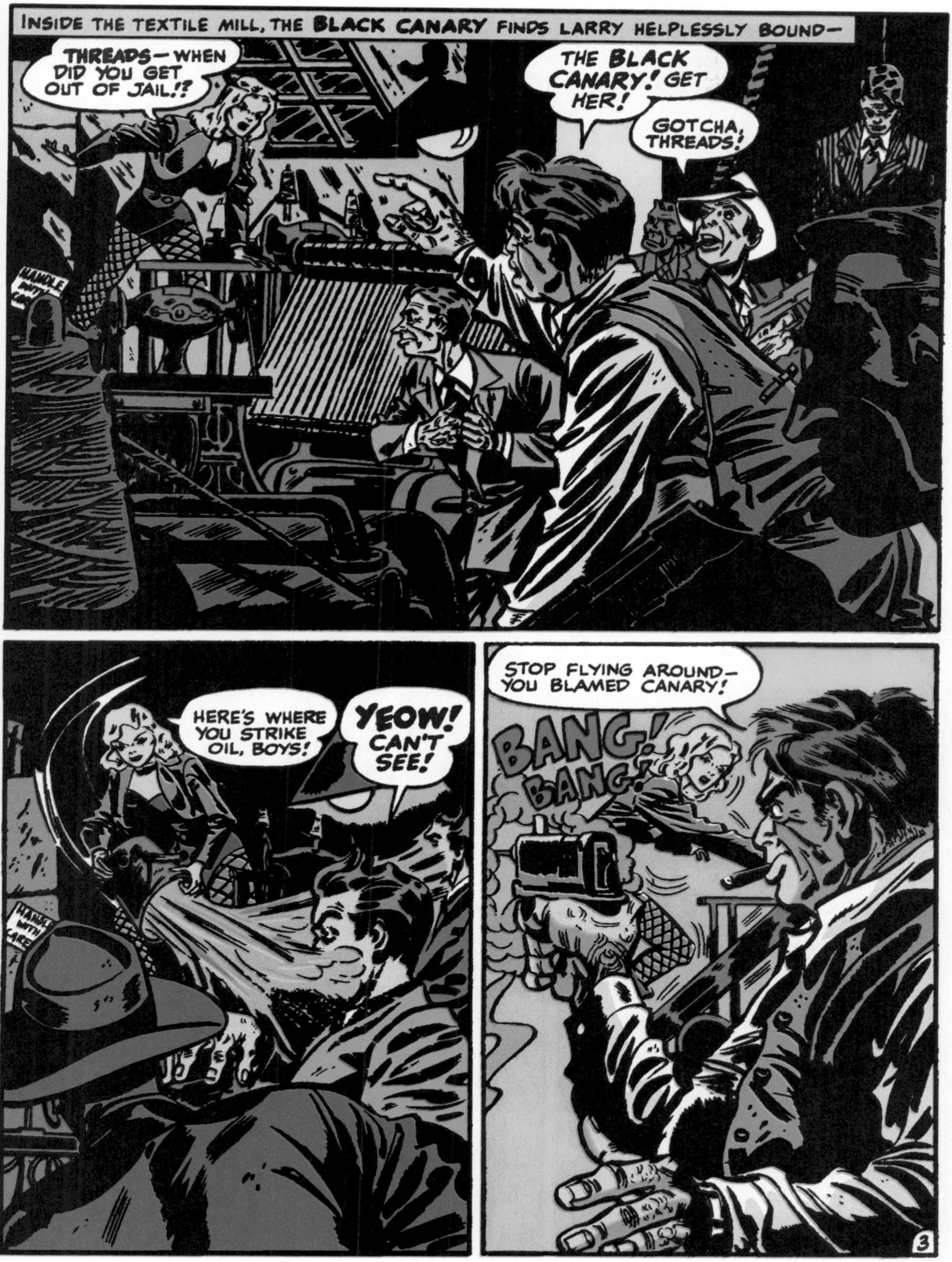
INSIDE THE TEXTILE MILL, THE BLACK CANARY FINDS LARRY HELPLESSLY BOUND—
THREADS—WHEN DID YOU GET OUT OF JAIL!?
THE BLACK CANARY! GET HER!
GOTCHA, THREADS!
HERE'S WHERE YOU STRIKE OIL, BOYS!
YEOW! CAN'T SEE!
STOP FLYING AROUND—YOU BLAMED CANARY!
BANG! BANG!

OUT OF BULLETS, **THREADS?** TSK-TSK-TSK! HOW ARE YOU GOING TO STOP ME NOW?

WITH A LITTLE SWITCHEROO! WATCH!

THE SWITCH STARTS THE BELT MOVING, ON WHICH THE **BLACK CANARY** IS STANDING--

OHHH! LOSING MY BALANCE!

WHACK!

THE **BLACK CANARY** IS TIED TO A BOBBIN BESIDE LARRY, AND—

OKAY, PRIVATE EYE! WHERE'S THAT PIECE OF CLOTH YOU TOOK FROM OLD MAN SWAIN?

DON'T TELL HIM A THING, LARRY!

DON'T WORRY ABOUT ME, DREAM-BOAT!

AS THE BOBBINS START SPINNING, THE THREADS ENVELOP THE HELP-LESS DUO!

WHEN YOU FEEL LIKE TALKING!

YEO-OW!

CALL OUT WHEN YOU FEEL LIKE TALKING!

THEY'RE READY!

WHEN THE CURRENT IS SHUT OFF—

WHO FEELS LIKE TALKING? WE WERE JUST SINGING!

A LITTLE BARBER SHOP HARMONY! ONLY WE'RE HALF A QUARTET! WANT TO JOIN US?

I'LL BE BACK IN TEN MINUTES! EITHER YOU'LL SING AND TELL ME WHERE YOU HID THAT CLOTH – OR I'LL LEAVE YOU IN DEAD STORAGE!

4

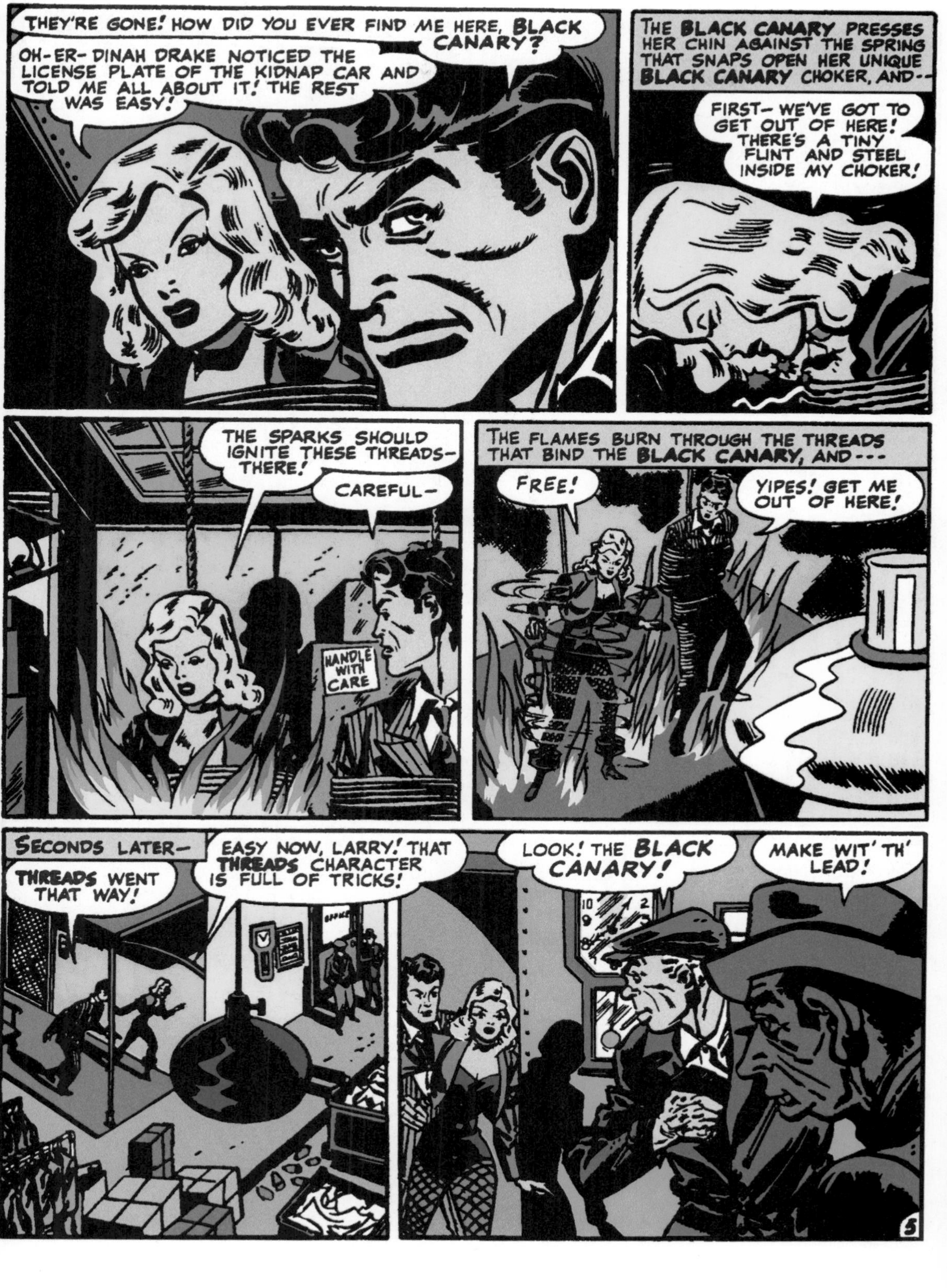
THEY'RE GONE! HOW DID YOU EVER FIND ME HERE, BLACK CANARY?
OH-ER- DINAH DRAKE NOTICED THE LICENSE PLATE OF THE KIDNAP CAR AND TOLD ME ALL ABOUT IT! THE REST WAS EASY!
THE BLACK CANARY PRESSES HER CHIN AGAINST THE SPRING THAT SNAPS OPEN HER UNIQUE BLACK CANARY CHOKER, AND--
FIRST- WE'VE GOT TO GET OUT OF HERE! THERE'S A TINY FLINT AND STEEL INSIDE MY CHOKER!
THE SPARKS SHOULD IGNITE THESE THREADS- THERE!
CAREFUL-
HANDLE WITH CARE
THE FLAMES BURN THROUGH THE THREADS THAT BIND THE BLACK CANARY, AND---
FREE!
YIPES! GET ME OUT OF HERE!
SECONDS LATER-
THREADS WENT THAT WAY!
EASY NOW, LARRY! THAT THREADS CHARACTER IS FULL OF TRICKS!
LOOK! THE BLACK CANARY!
MAKE WIT' TH' LEAD!
5

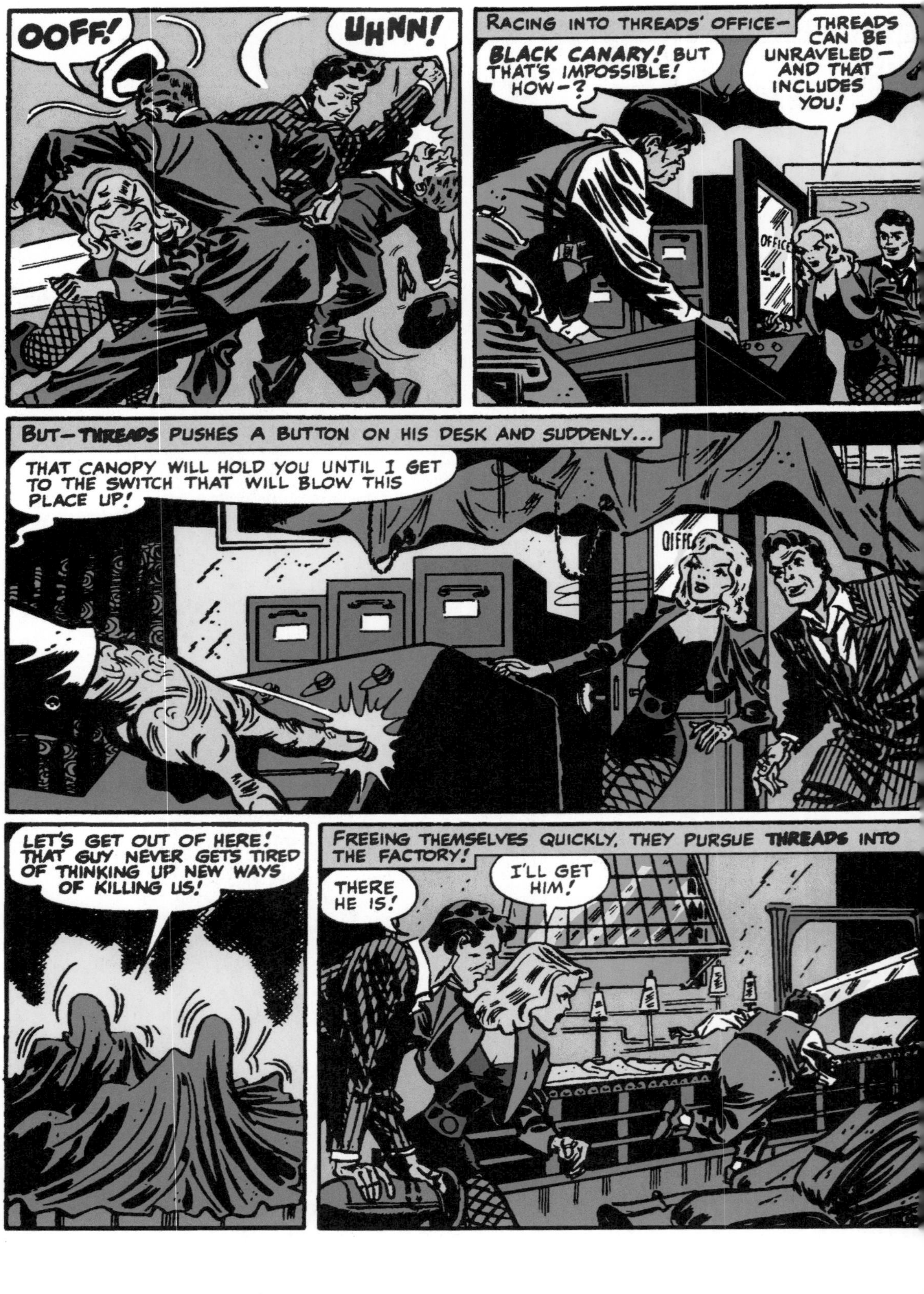

OOFF!
UHNN!
RACING INTO THREADS' OFFICE—
BLACK CANARY! BUT THAT'S IMPOSSIBLE! HOW—?
THREADS CAN BE UNRAVELED—AND THAT INCLUDES YOU!
OFFICE
BUT—THREADS PUSHES A BUTTON ON HIS DESK AND SUDDENLY...
THAT CANOPY WILL HOLD YOU UNTIL I GET TO THE SWITCH THAT WILL BLOW THIS PLACE UP!
LET'S GET OUT OF HERE! THAT GUY NEVER GETS TIRED OF THINKING UP NEW WAYS OF KILLING US!
FREEING THEMSELVES QUICKLY, THEY PURSUE THREADS INTO THE FACTORY!
THERE HE IS!
I'LL GET HIM!

BLACK CANARY HURLS A BOLT OF CLOTH AT THE FLEEING THUG!

HERE'S WHERE I ROLL UP THE CASE!

UFFF! WHAT TRIPPED ME?

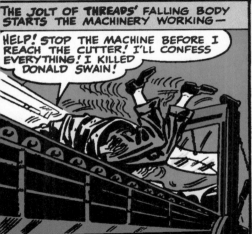

THE JOLT OF THREADS' FALLING BODY STARTS THE MACHINERY WORKING—

HELP! STOP THE MACHINE BEFORE I REACH THE CUTTER! I'LL CONFESS EVERYTHING! I KILLED DONALD SWAIN!

TALK FAST!

HE KEPT A PRICELESS FORMULA FOR A NEW DYE HIDDEN IN A PIECE OF CLOTH! I FOUND OUT— AND KILLED HIM— TRYING TO GET IT!

CLICK!

JUST THINK! I HAD THE FORMULA AROUND MY NECK ALL ALONG! I MADE IT INTO A TIE— SO NO ONE WOULD SUSPECT!

LARRY, YOU'RE SO CLEVER!

NEXT DAY...

—AFTER I HANDED THREADS AND HIS THUSS OVER TO THE POLICE, I RETURNED THE FORMULA TO CHEMICAL ALLIANCE. THE JOB WAS A SNAP FOR ME... AND THE BLACK CANARY!

I WONDER WHAT THE BLACK CANARY WOULD DO WITHOUT YOU?

THE END

ANOTHER CRIME-TINGLING ADVENTURE WITH THE BLACK CANARY IN EVERY ISSUE OF FLASH COMICS

7

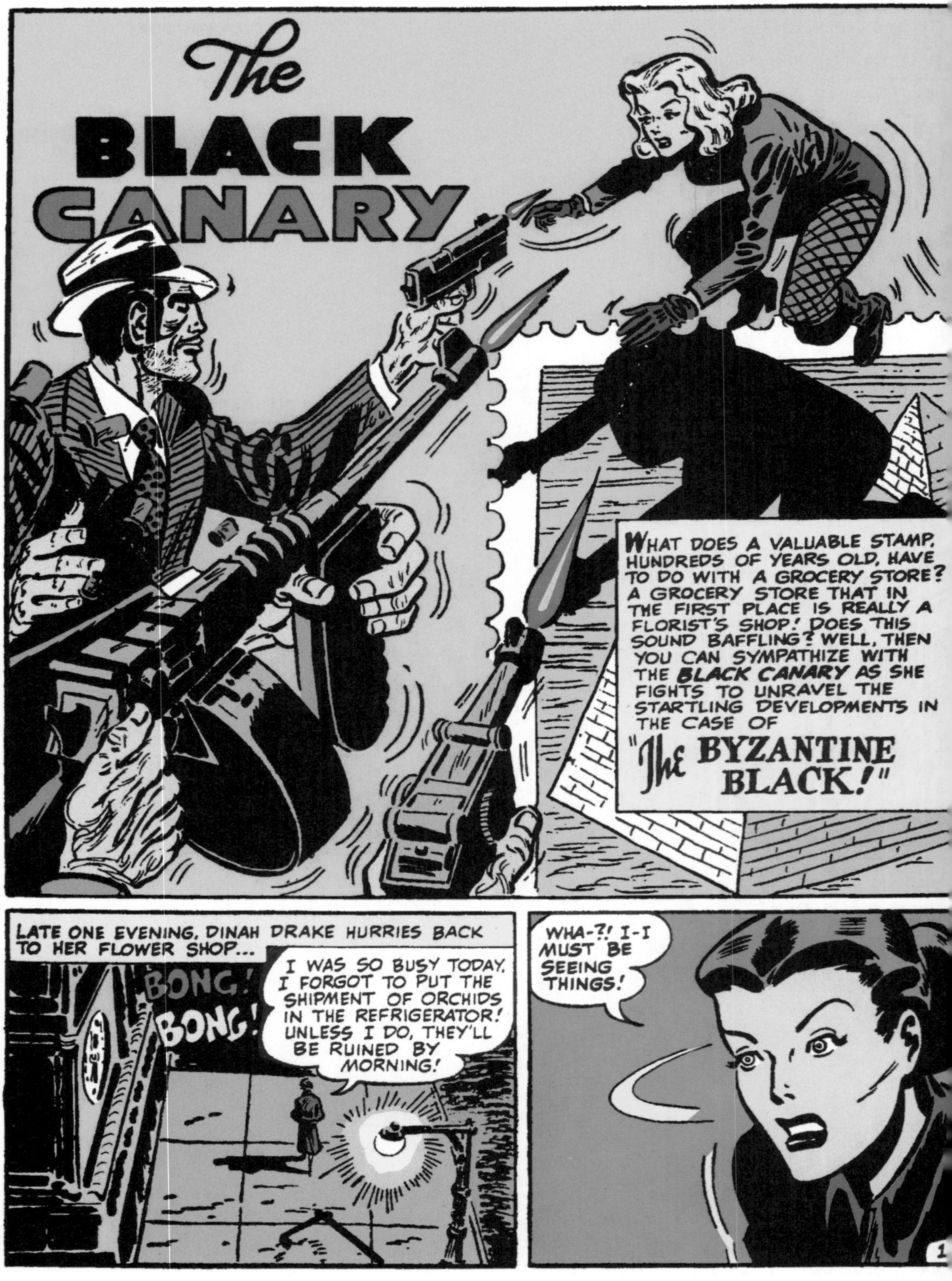
The BLACK CANARY
WHAT DOES A VALUABLE STAMP, HUNDREDS OF YEARS OLD, HAVE TO DO WITH A GROCERY STORE? A GROCERY STORE THAT IN THE FIRST PLACE IS REALLY A FLORIST'S SHOP! DOES THIS SOUND BAFFLING? WELL, THEN YOU CAN SYMPATHIZE WITH THE BLACK CANARY AS SHE FIGHTS TO UNRAVEL THE STARTLING DEVELOPMENTS IN THE CASE OF
"The BYZANTINE BLACK!"
LATE ONE EVENING, DINAH DRAKE HURRIES BACK TO HER FLOWER SHOP...
BONG! BONG!
I WAS SO BUSY TODAY, I FORGOT TO PUT THE SHIPMENT OF ORCHIDS IN THE REFRIGERATOR! UNLESS I DO, THEY'LL BE RUINED BY MORNING!
WHA-?! I-I MUST BE SEEING THINGS!
1

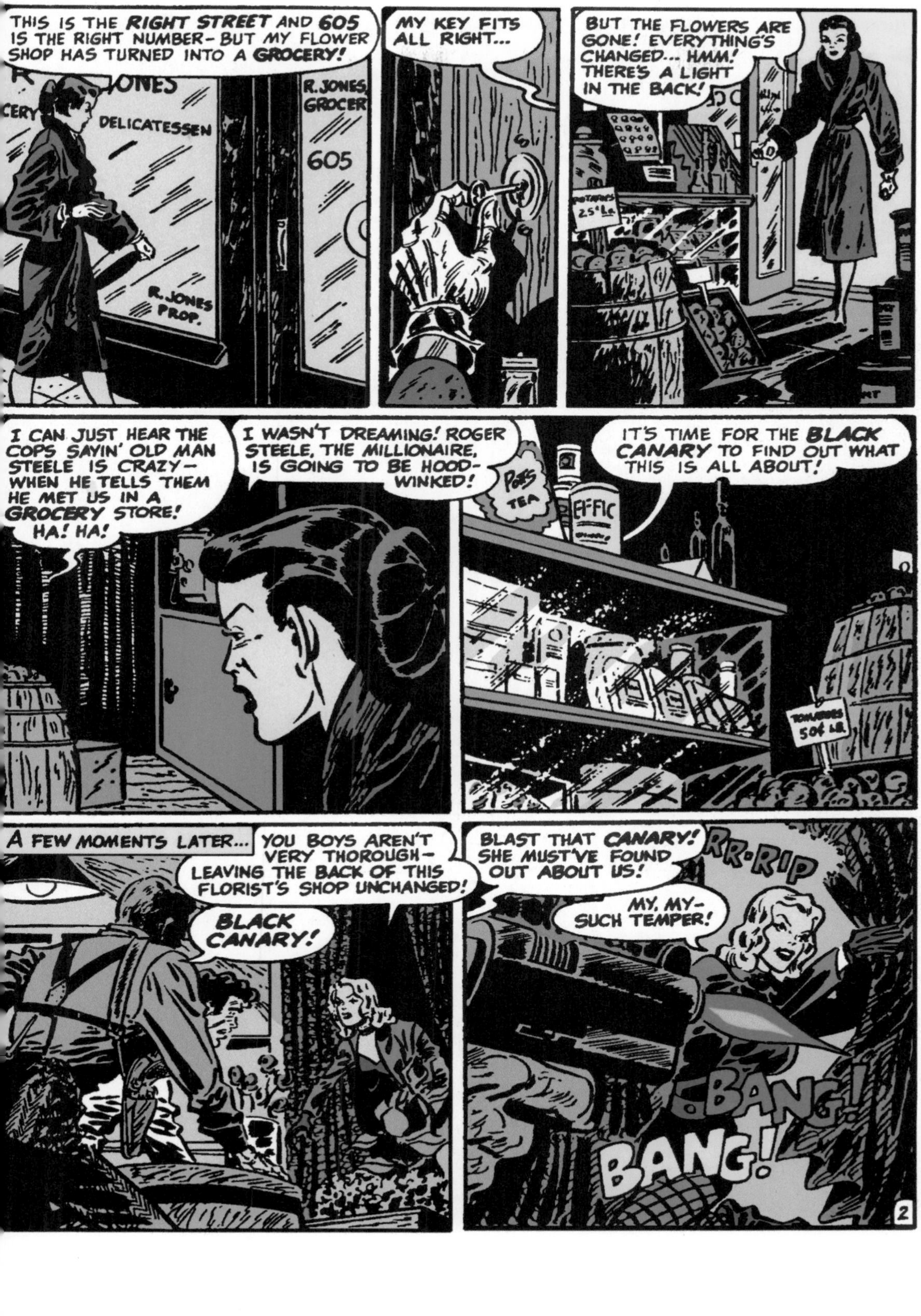

THIS IS THE RIGHT STREET AND 605 IS THE RIGHT NUMBER– BUT MY FLOWER SHOP HAS TURNED INTO A GROCERY!
DELICATESSEN
R. JONES, GROCER
605
R. JONES PROP.
MY KEY FITS ALL RIGHT...
BUT THE FLOWERS ARE GONE! EVERYTHING'S CHANGED... HMM! THERE'S A LIGHT IN THE BACK!
I CAN JUST HEAR THE COPS SAYIN' OLD MAN STEELE IS CRAZY– WHEN HE TELLS THEM HE MET US IN A GROCERY STORE! HA! HA!
I WASN'T DREAMING! ROGER STEELE, THE MILLIONAIRE, IS GOING TO BE HOOD-WINKED!
IT'S TIME FOR THE BLACK CANARY TO FIND OUT WHAT THIS IS ALL ABOUT!
TEA
A FEW MOMENTS LATER...
YOU BOYS AREN'T VERY THOROUGH– LEAVING THE BACK OF THIS FLORIST'S SHOP UNCHANGED!
BLACK CANARY!
BLAST THAT CANARY! SHE MUST'VE FOUND OUT ABOUT US!
RR-RIP
MY, MY– SUCH TEMPER!
BANG!
BANG!
2

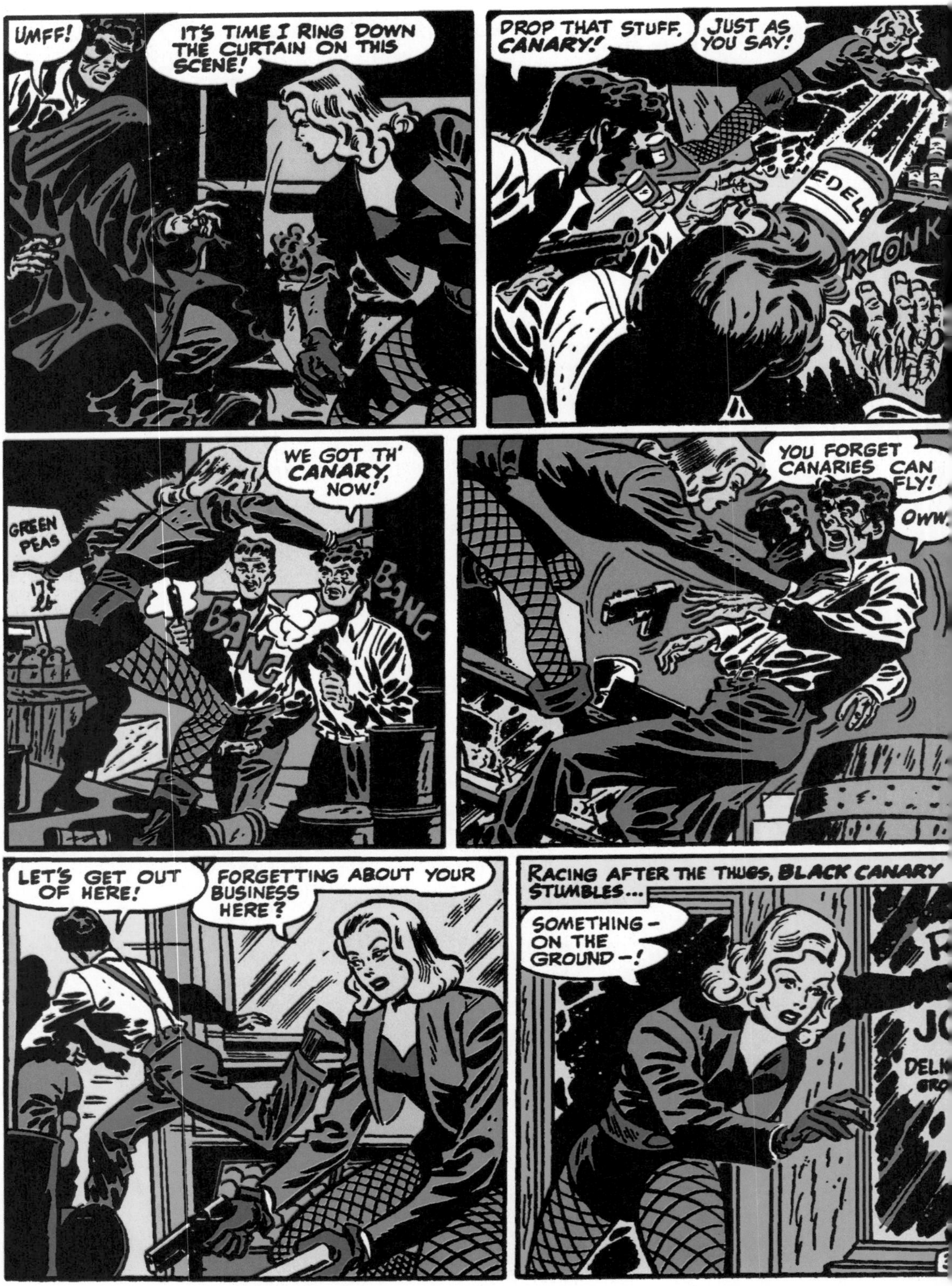
UMFF!
IT'S TIME I RING DOWN THE CURTAIN ON THIS SCENE!
DROP THAT STUFF, CANARY!
JUST AS YOU SAY!
KLONK
WE GOT TH' CANARY, NOW!
GREEN PEAS
BANG
BANG
BANG
YOU FORGET CANARIES CAN FLY!
OWW
LET'S GET OUT OF HERE!
FORGETTING ABOUT YOUR BUSINESS HERE?
RACING AFTER THE THUGS, BLACK CANARY STUMBLES...
SOMETHING -- ON THE GROUND --!

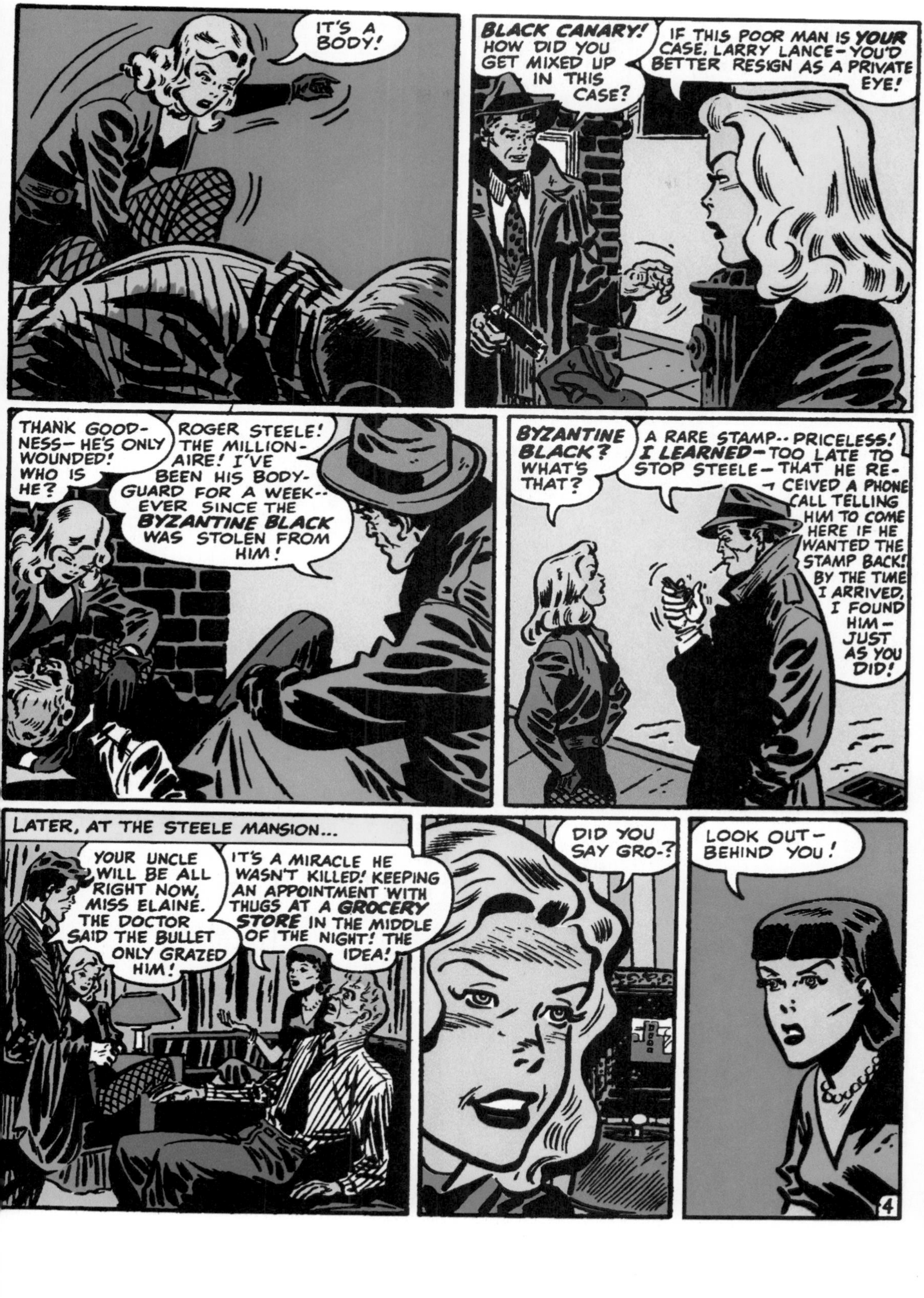
IT'S A BODY!
BLACK CANARY! HOW DID YOU GET MIXED UP IN THIS CASE?
IF THIS POOR MAN IS YOUR CASE, LARRY LANCE–YOU'D BETTER RESIGN AS A PRIVATE EYE!
THANK GOODNESS–HE'S ONLY WOUNDED! WHO IS HE?
ROGER STEELE! THE MILLIONAIRE! I'VE BEEN HIS BODYGUARD FOR A WEEK-- EVER SINCE THE BYZANTINE BLACK WAS STOLEN FROM HIM!
BYZANTINE BLACK? WHAT'S THAT?
A RARE STAMP-- PRICELESS! I LEARNED–TOO LATE TO STOP STEELE–THAT HE RECEIVED A PHONE CALL TELLING HIM TO COME HERE IF HE WANTED THE STAMP BACK! BY THE TIME I ARRIVED, I FOUND HIM–JUST AS YOU DID!
LATER, AT THE STEELE MANSION...
YOUR UNCLE WILL BE ALL RIGHT NOW, MISS ELAINE. THE DOCTOR SAID THE BULLET ONLY GRAZED HIM!
IT'S A MIRACLE HE WASN'T KILLED! KEEPING AN APPOINTMENT WITH THUGS AT A GROCERY STORE IN THE MIDDLE OF THE NIGHT! THE IDEA!
DID YOU SAY GRO-?
LOOK OUT–BEHIND YOU!
4

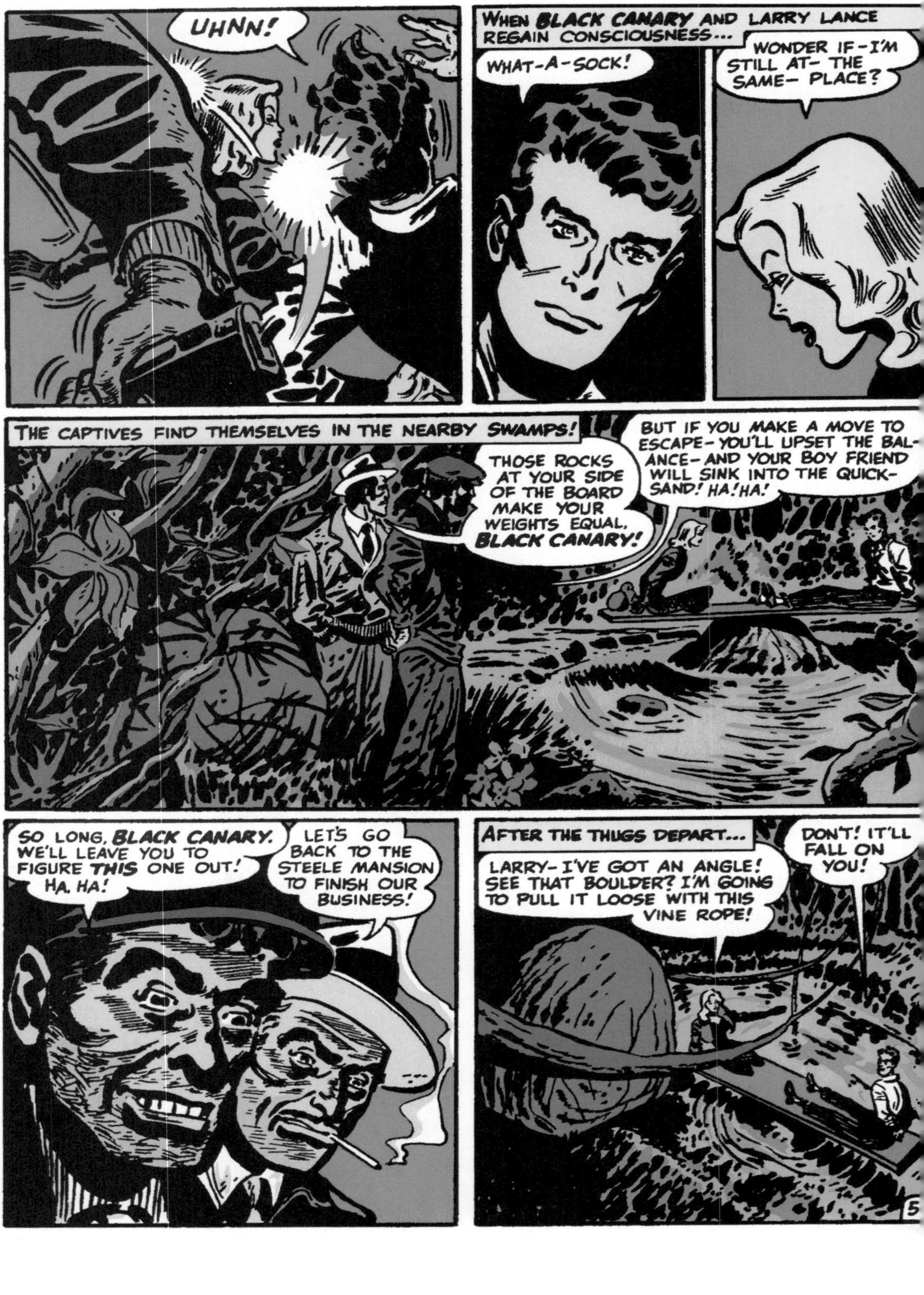
UHNN!
WHEN BLACK CANARY AND LARRY LANCE REGAIN CONSCIOUSNESS...
WHAT-A-SOCK!
WONDER IF-I'M STILL AT- THE SAME- PLACE?
THE CAPTIVES FIND THEMSELVES IN THE NEARBY SWAMPS!
THOSE ROCKS AT YOUR SIDE OF THE BOARD MAKE YOUR WEIGHTS EQUAL, BLACK CANARY!
BUT IF YOU MAKE A MOVE TO ESCAPE- YOU'LL UPSET THE BAL-ANCE- AND YOUR BOY FRIEND WILL SINK INTO THE QUICK-SAND! HA! HA!
SO LONG, BLACK CANARY. WE'LL LEAVE YOU TO FIGURE THIS ONE OUT! HA, HA!
LET'S GO BACK TO THE STEELE MANSION TO FINISH OUR BUSINESS!
AFTER THE THUGS DEPART...
LARRY- I'VE GOT AN ANGLE! SEE THAT BOULDER? I'M GOING TO PULL IT LOOSE WITH THIS VINE ROPE!
DON'T! IT'LL FALL ON YOU!
5

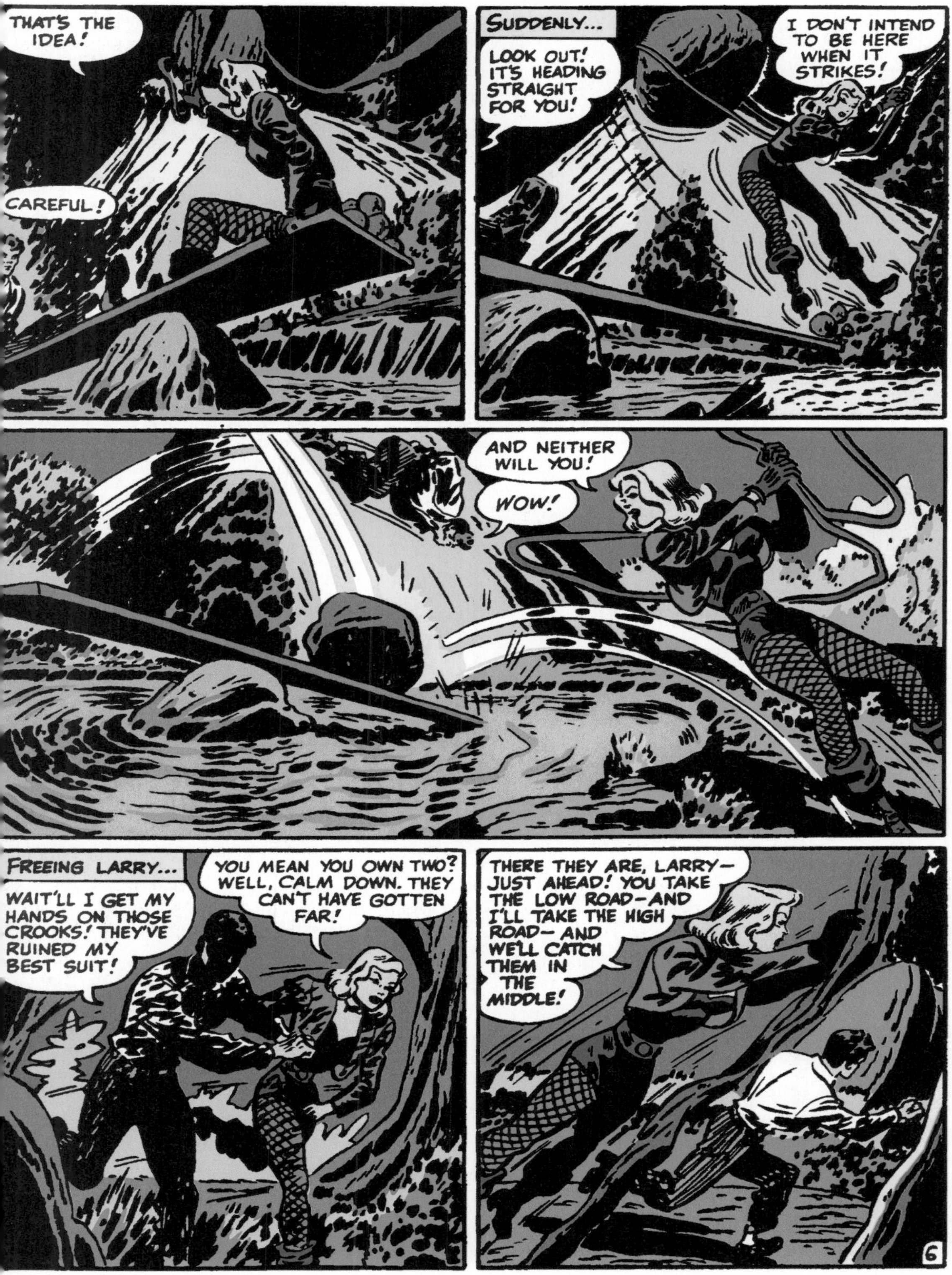

THAT'S THE IDEA!
CAREFUL!
SUDDENLY...
LOOK OUT! IT'S HEADING STRAIGHT FOR YOU!
I DON'T INTEND TO BE HERE WHEN IT STRIKES!
AND NEITHER WILL YOU!
WOW!
FREEING LARRY...
WAIT'LL I GET MY HANDS ON THOSE CROOKS! THEY'VE RUINED MY BEST SUIT!
YOU MEAN YOU OWN TWO? WELL, CALM DOWN. THEY CAN'T HAVE GOTTEN FAR!
THERE THEY ARE, LARRY— JUST AHEAD! YOU TAKE THE LOW ROAD—AND I'LL TAKE THE HIGH ROAD—AND WE'LL CATCH THEM IN THE MIDDLE!
6

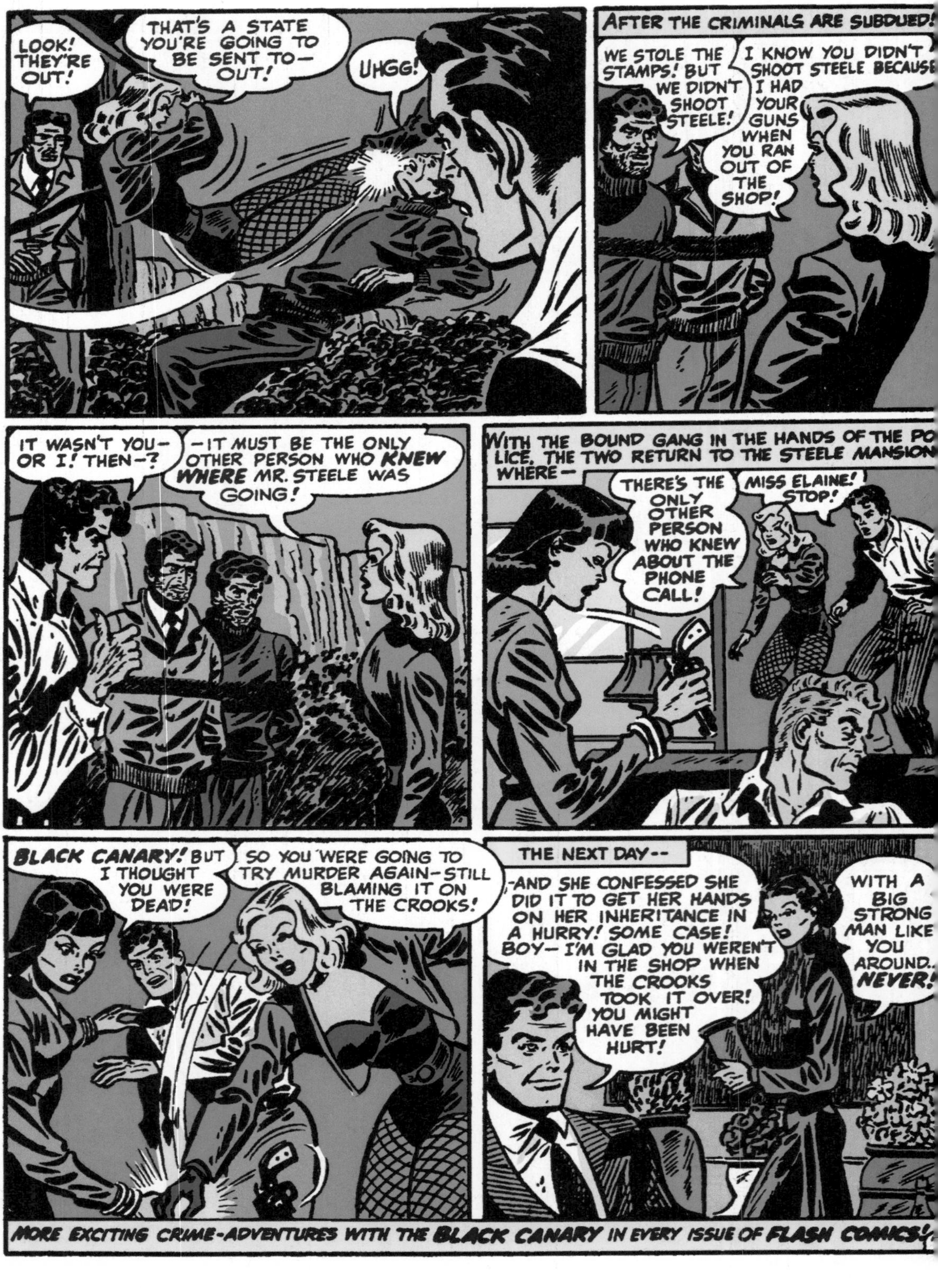
LOOK! THEY'RE OUT!
THAT'S A STATE YOU'RE GOING TO BE SENT TO—OUT!
UHGG!
AFTER THE CRIMINALS ARE SUBDUED!
WE STOLE THE STAMPS! BUT WE DIDN'T SHOOT STEELE!
I KNOW YOU DIDN'T SHOOT STEELE BECAUSE I HAD YOUR GUNS WHEN YOU RAN OUT OF THE SHOP!
IT WASN'T YOU—OR I! THEN—?
—IT MUST BE THE ONLY OTHER PERSON WHO KNEW WHERE MR. STEELE WAS GOING!
WITH THE BOUND GANG IN THE HANDS OF THE PO LICE, THE TWO RETURN TO THE STEELE MANSION WHERE—
THERE'S THE ONLY OTHER PERSON WHO KNEW ABOUT THE PHONE CALL!
MISS ELAINE! STOP!
BLACK CANARY! BUT I THOUGHT YOU WERE DEAD!
SO YOU WERE GOING TO TRY MURDER AGAIN—STILL BLAMING IT ON THE CROOKS!
THE NEXT DAY--
-AND SHE CONFESSED SHE DID IT TO GET HER HANDS ON HER INHERITANCE IN A HURRY! SOME CASE! BOY—I'M GLAD YOU WEREN'T IN THE SHOP WHEN THE CROOKS TOOK IT OVER! YOU MIGHT HAVE BEEN HURT!
WITH A BIG STRONG MAN LIKE YOU AROUND.. NEVER!
MORE EXCITING CRIME-ADVENTURES WITH THE BLACK CANARY IN EVERY ISSUE OF FLASH COMICS!

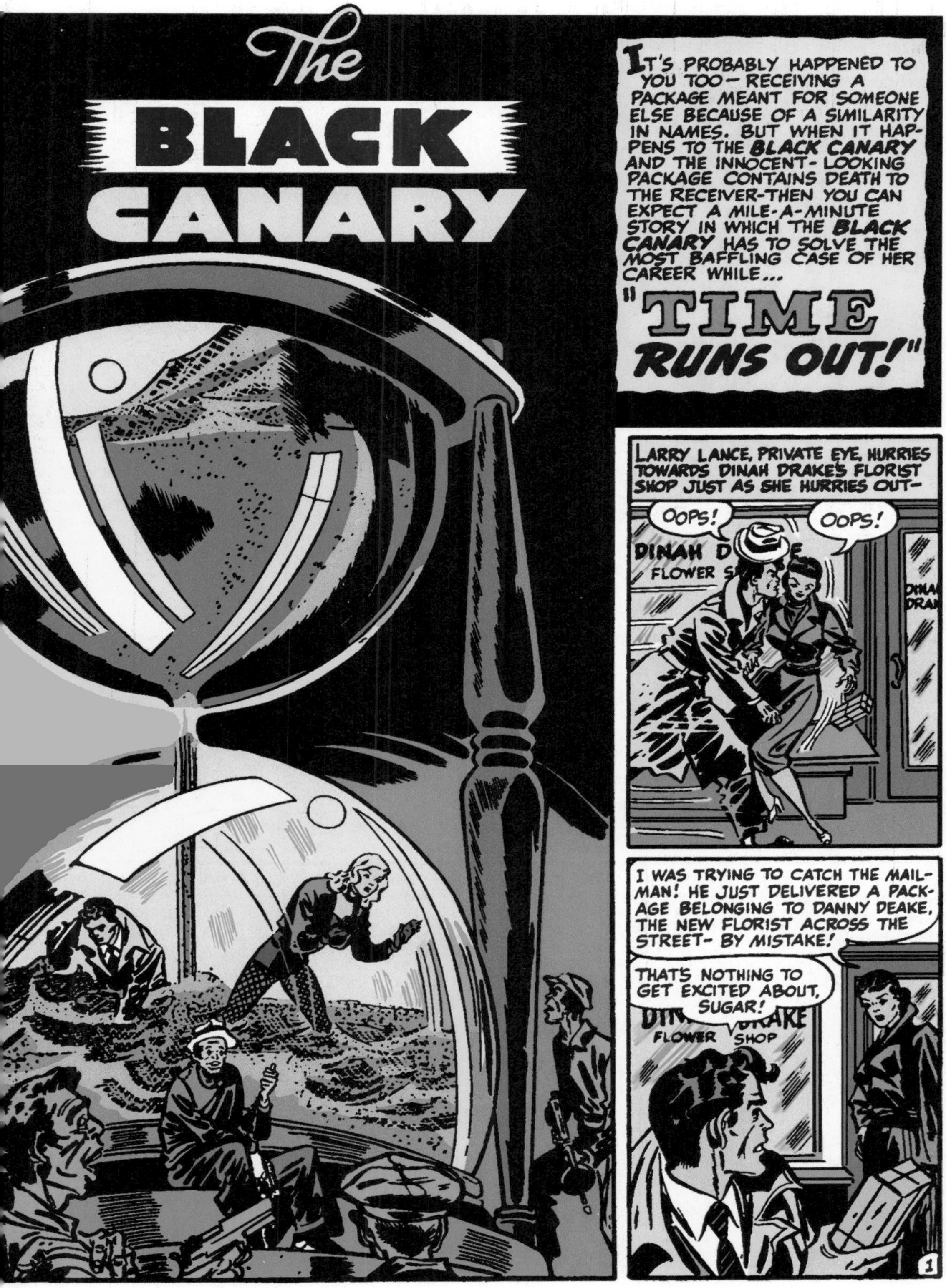

The BLACK CANARY
IT'S PROBABLY HAPPENED TO YOU TOO—RECEIVING A PACKAGE MEANT FOR SOMEONE ELSE BECAUSE OF A SIMILARITY IN NAMES. BUT WHEN IT HAPPENS TO THE BLACK CANARY AND THE INNOCENT-LOOKING PACKAGE CONTAINS DEATH TO THE RECEIVER—THEN YOU CAN EXPECT A MILE-A-MINUTE STORY IN WHICH THE BLACK CANARY HAS TO SOLVE THE MOST BAFFLING CASE OF HER CAREER WHILE...
"TIME RUNS OUT!"
LARRY LANCE, PRIVATE EYE, HURRIES TOWARDS DINAH DRAKE'S FLORIST SHOP JUST AS SHE HURRIES OUT—
OOPS!
OOPS!
I WAS TRYING TO CATCH THE MAILMAN! HE JUST DELIVERED A PACKAGE BELONGING TO DANNY DEAKE, THE NEW FLORIST ACROSS THE STREET—BY MISTAKE!
THAT'S NOTHING TO GET EXCITED ABOUT, SUGAR!
FLOWER SHOP
1

THINK HOW EXCITED I AM TRYING TO TRACE A MILLION DOLLARS' WORTH OF STOLEN RADIOACTIVE VINIUM... UH-OH! YOU'RE BEING PAGED!

MISS DRAKE!

IT'S DEAKE- THE NEW FLORIST!

THAT PACKAGE (PANT- PANT) IS MINE!

WHO SAID IT WASN'T? WHAT'S YOUR FRENZY, FRIEND?

YES, NO ONE'S TAKING YOUR OLD PACKAGE.

SUDDENLY...

THAT'S LARRY LANCE, TH' PRIVATE EYE! TH' BOSS FIGURED DEAKE MIGHT SPILL TH' BEANS! GET TH' PACKAGE!

UHNN-!

HIT THE DECK, DINAH! THOSE AREN'T FIRE CRACKERS!

DINAH DRAKE FLOWER SHOP

THOSE GORILLAS DON'T SEE ME! NOW'S MY CHANCE TO SNEAK INTO THE BACK OF THE SHOP!

DINAH DRAKE SWIFTLY CHANGES INTO THE BLACK CANARY!

LARRY MAY THINK THAT DINAH ISN'T DOING A THING TO HELP HIM- AND HE'S RIGHT! DINAH ISN'T- BUT THE BLACK CANARY WILL!

RETURNING TO THE FRONT OF THE SHOP—

THEY'VE GOT LARRY!

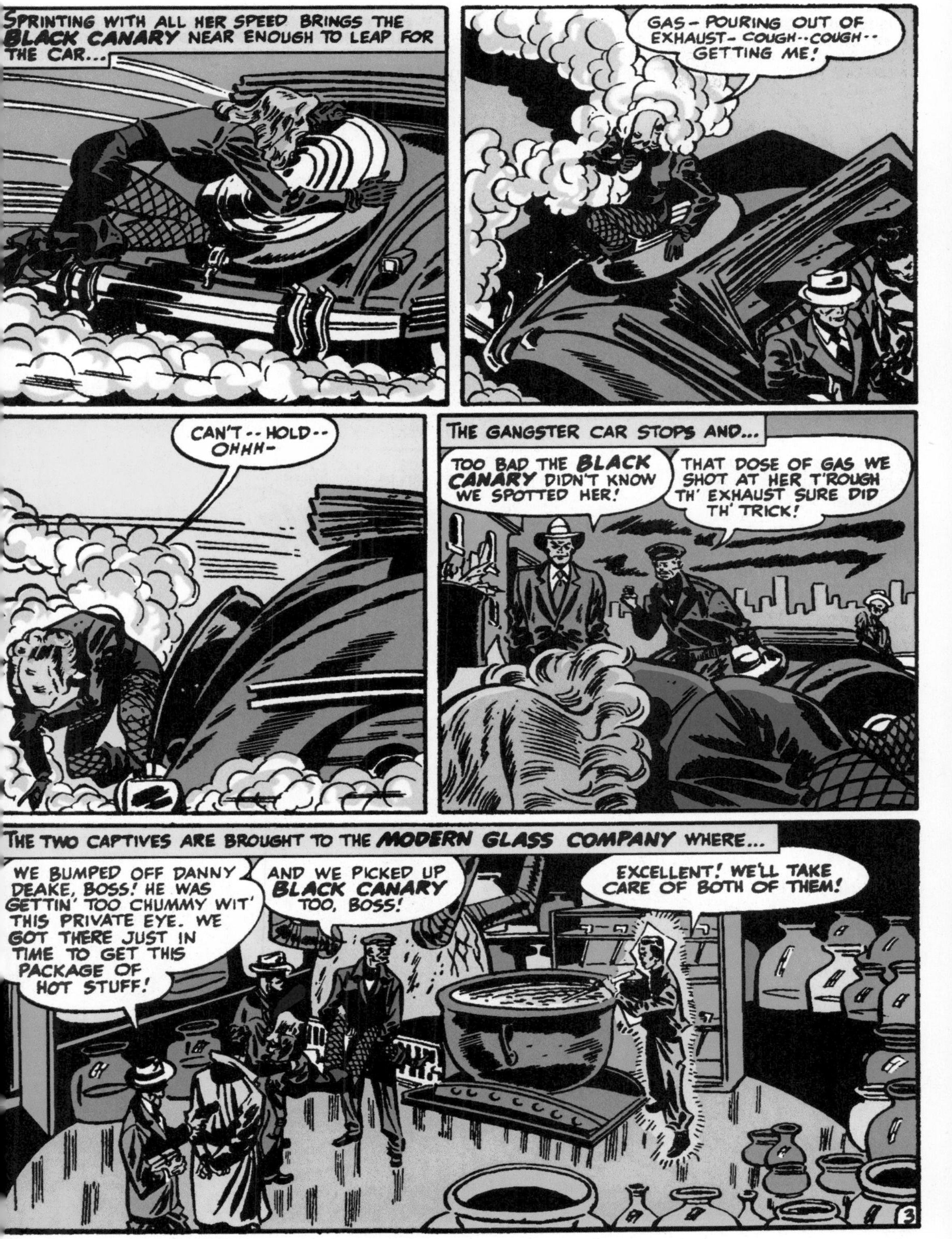
SPRINTING WITH ALL HER SPEED BRINGS THE BLACK CANARY NEAR ENOUGH TO LEAP FOR THE CAR...
GAS-POURING OUT OF EXHAUST-COUGH--COUGH--GETTING ME!
CAN'T--HOLD--OHHH-
THE GANGSTER CAR STOPS AND...
TOO BAD THE BLACK CANARY DIDN'T KNOW WE SPOTTED HER!
THAT DOSE OF GAS WE SHOT AT HER T'ROUGH TH' EXHAUST SURE DID TH' TRICK!
THE TWO CAPTIVES ARE BROUGHT TO THE MODERN GLASS COMPANY WHERE...
WE BUMPED OFF DANNY DEAKE, BOSS! HE WAS GETTIN' TOO CHUMMY WIT' THIS PRIVATE EYE. WE GOT THERE JUST IN TIME TO GET THIS PACKAGE OF HOT STUFF!
AND WE PICKED UP BLACK CANARY TOO, BOSS!
EXCELLENT! WE'LL TAKE CARE OF BOTH OF THEM!
3

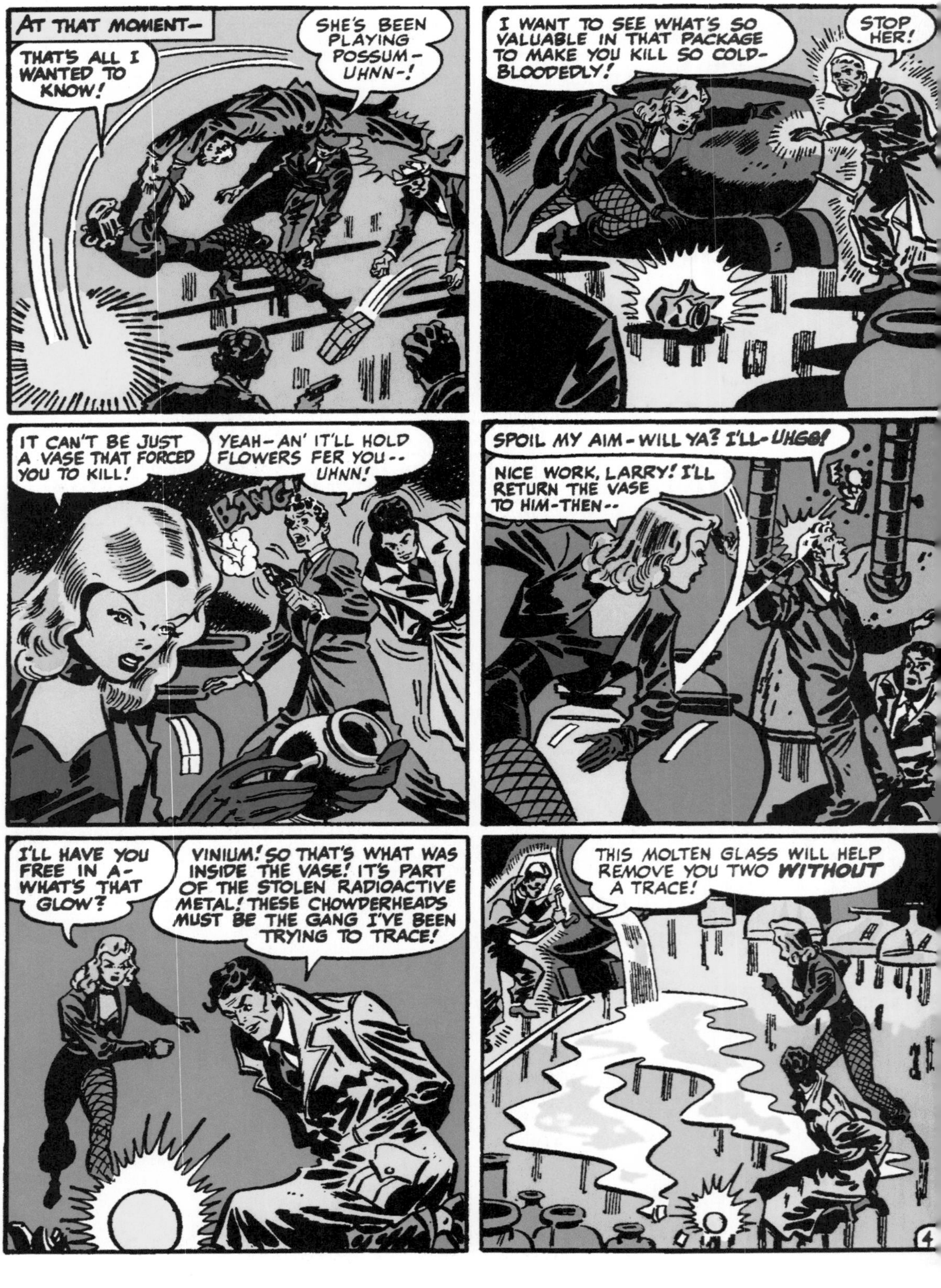
AT THAT MOMENT—
THAT'S ALL I WANTED TO KNOW!
SHE'S BEEN PLAYING POSSUM— UHNN-!
I WANT TO SEE WHAT'S SO VALUABLE IN THAT PACKAGE TO MAKE YOU KILL SO COLD-BLOODEDLY!
STOP HER!
IT CAN'T BE JUST A VASE THAT FORCED YOU TO KILL!
YEAH—AN' IT'LL HOLD FLOWERS FER YOU-- UHNN!
BANG!
SPOIL MY AIM—WILL YA? I'LL—UHGG!
NICE WORK, LARRY! I'LL RETURN THE VASE TO HIM—THEN--
I'LL HAVE YOU FREE IN A— WHAT'S THAT GLOW?
VINIUM! SO THAT'S WHAT WAS INSIDE THE VASE! IT'S PART OF THE STOLEN RADIOACTIVE METAL! THESE CHOWDERHEADS MUST BE THE GANG I'VE BEEN TRYING TO TRACE!
THIS MOLTEN GLASS WILL HELP REMOVE YOU TWO WITHOUT A TRACE!
4

CAN'T MOVE!
NEITHER CAN I!
HOW UNFORTUNATE!
SEE WHAT I MEAN?!
UHNNG!
HE BLACK CANARY AND LARRY AWAKE IN A GIANT HOURGLASS...
NO USE STRUGGLING! EVEN IF YOUR HANDS WERE FREE - YOU OULDN'T BREAK THAT LASS! IT'S AN INCH HICK! IT TAKES EXACTLY NE HOUR FOR THE SAND TO FILL YOUR PART OF THE HOUR GLASS-THAT'S HOW ONG YOU'VE GOT TO LIVE!
A, HA!
5

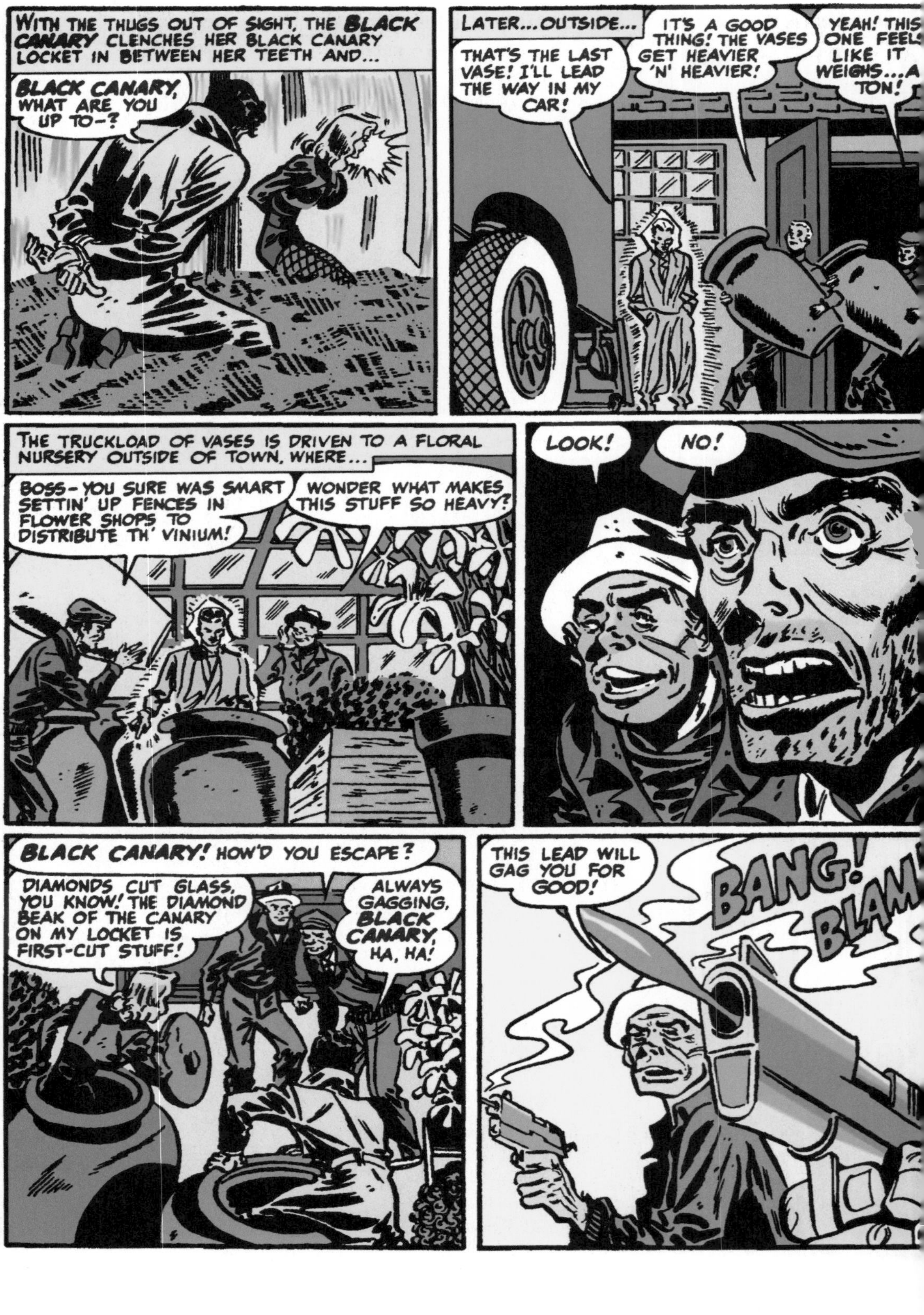

WITH THE THUGS OUT OF SIGHT, THE BLACK CANARY CLENCHES HER BLACK CANARY LOCKET IN BETWEEN HER TEETH AND...
BLACK CANARY, WHAT ARE YOU UP TO-?
LATER...OUTSIDE...
THAT'S THE LAST VASE! I'LL LEAD THE WAY IN MY CAR!
IT'S A GOOD THING! THE VASES GET HEAVIER 'N' HEAVIER!
YEAH! THIS ONE FEELS LIKE IT WEIGHS...A TON!
THE TRUCKLOAD OF VASES IS DRIVEN TO A FLORAL NURSERY OUTSIDE OF TOWN, WHERE...
BOSS- YOU SURE WAS SMART SETTIN' UP FENCES IN FLOWER SHOPS TO DISTRIBUTE TH' VINIUM!
WONDER WHAT MAKES THIS STUFF SO HEAVY?
LOOK!
NO!
BLACK CANARY! HOW'D YOU ESCAPE?
DIAMONDS CUT GLASS, YOU KNOW! THE DIAMOND BEAK OF THE CANARY ON MY LOCKET IS FIRST-CUT STUFF!
ALWAYS GAGGING, BLACK CANARY, HA, HA!
THIS LEAD WILL GAG YOU FOR GOOD!
BANG!
BLAM

NOW IT'S *OUR* TURN TO TAKE A POTSHOT AT YOU!

BANG! BANG!

UPFFF!

YOU WON'T ESCAPE THIS TIME, LANCE--! HEY, LEGGO MY ARM--!

NOW, NOW! TEMPER-- TEMPER!

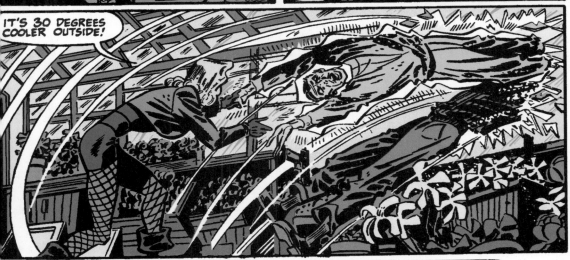

IT'S 30 DEGREES COOLER OUTSIDE!

LATER, WITH THE THUGS IN THE HANDS OF THE POLICE...

NOW, *BLACK CANARY!* IT ISN'T FAIR! EVERY TIME I WANT TO GET ACQUAINTED-- YOU DISAPPEAR!

DON'T WORRY, LARRY. YOU'LL SEE ME SOON ENOUGH!

AT THE FLORIST SHOP AGAIN...

BLACK CANARY SAID I'D SEE HER SOON BUT SHE DIDN'T SAY WHERE THAT WOULD BE! (SIGH!)

ANOTHER EXCITING CRIME-CRACKING ADVENTURE WITH

The BLACK CANARY in EVERY ISSUE OF

FLASH COMICS!

7

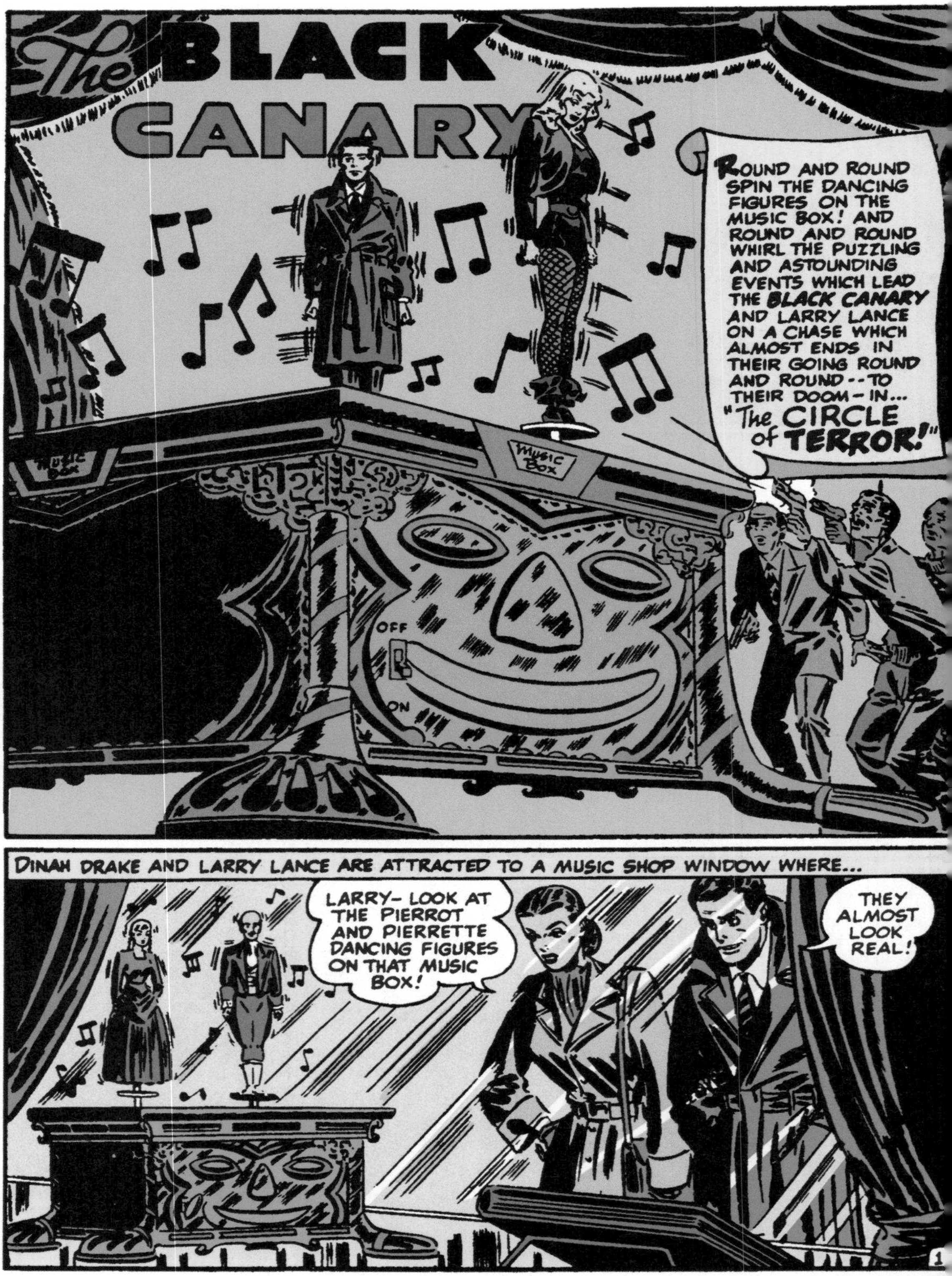
The BLACK CANARY
ROUND AND ROUND SPIN THE DANCING FIGURES ON THE MUSIC BOX! AND ROUND AND ROUND WHIRL THE PUZZLING AND ASTOUNDING EVENTS WHICH LEAD THE BLACK CANARY AND LARRY LANCE ON A CHASE WHICH ALMOST ENDS IN THEIR GOING ROUND AND ROUND--TO THEIR DOOM-IN... "The CIRCLE of TERROR!"
MUSIC BOX
OFF
ON
DINAH DRAKE AND LARRY LANCE ARE ATTRACTED TO A MUSIC SHOP WINDOW WHERE...
LARRY- LOOK AT THE PIERROT AND PIERRETTE DANCING FIGURES ON THAT MUSIC BOX!
THEY ALMOST LOOK REAL!
1

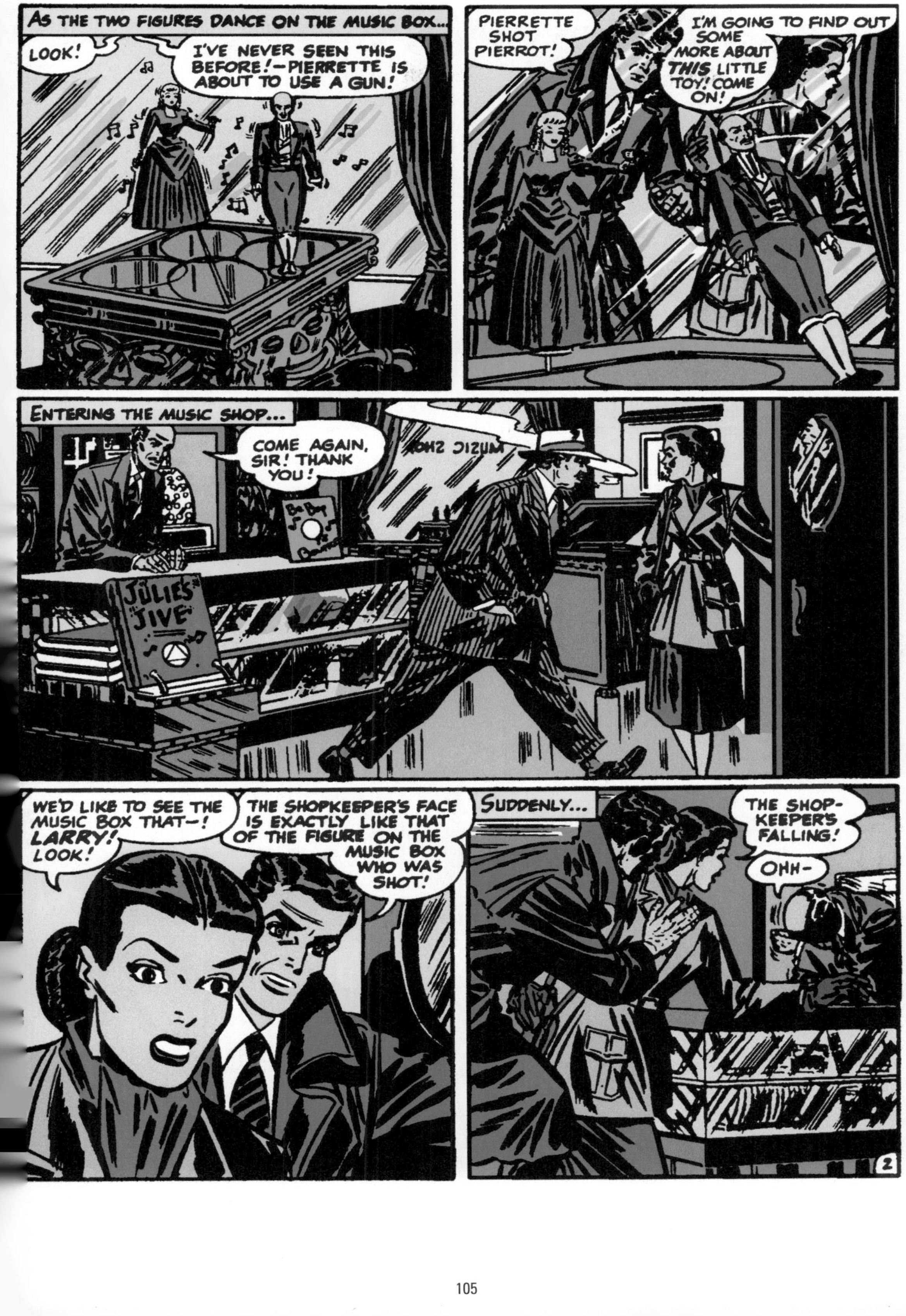
AS THE TWO FIGURES DANCE ON THE MUSIC BOX...
LOOK!
I'VE NEVER SEEN THIS BEFORE!—PIERRETTE IS ABOUT TO USE A GUN!
PIERRETTE SHOT PIERROT!
I'M GOING TO FIND OUT SOME MORE ABOUT THIS LITTLE TOY! COME ON!
ENTERING THE MUSIC SHOP...
COME AGAIN, SIR! THANK YOU!
MUSIC SHOP
JULIE'S JIVE
WE'D LIKE TO SEE THE MUSIC BOX THAT—! LARRY! LOOK!
THE SHOPKEEPER'S FACE IS EXACTLY LIKE THAT OF THE FIGURE ON THE MUSIC BOX WHO WAS SHOT!
SUDDENLY...
THE SHOP-KEEPER'S FALLING!
OHH-
2

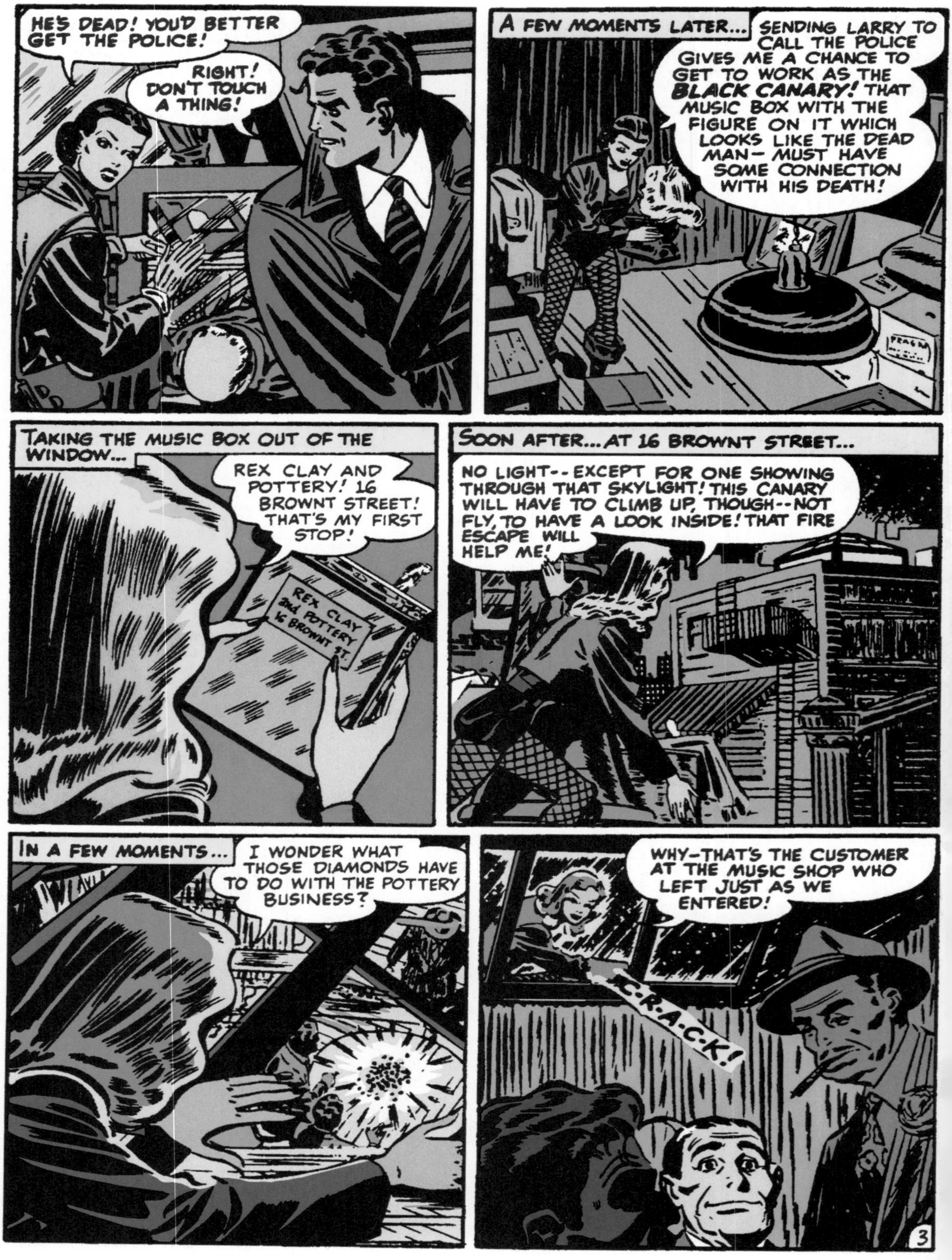
HE'S DEAD! YOU'D BETTER GET THE POLICE!
RIGHT! DON'T TOUCH A THING!
A FEW MOMENTS LATER...
SENDING LARRY TO CALL THE POLICE GIVES ME A CHANCE TO GET TO WORK AS THE BLACK CANARY! THAT MUSIC BOX WITH THE FIGURE ON IT WHICH LOOKS LIKE THE DEAD MAN— MUST HAVE SOME CONNECTION WITH HIS DEATH!
TAKING THE MUSIC BOX OUT OF THE WINDOW...
REX CLAY AND POTTERY! 16 BROWNT STREET! THAT'S MY FIRST STOP!
REX CLAY and POTTERY 16 BROWNT ST.
SOON AFTER... AT 16 BROWNT STREET...
NO LIGHT-- EXCEPT FOR ONE SHOWING THROUGH THAT SKYLIGHT! THIS CANARY WILL HAVE TO CLIMB UP, THOUGH--NOT FLY, TO HAVE A LOOK INSIDE! THAT FIRE ESCAPE WILL HELP ME!
IN A FEW MOMENTS...
I WONDER WHAT THOSE DIAMONDS HAVE TO DO WITH THE POTTERY BUSINESS?
WHY—THAT'S THE CUSTOMER AT THE MUSIC SHOP WHO LEFT JUST AS WE ENTERED!
C-R-A-C-K!
3

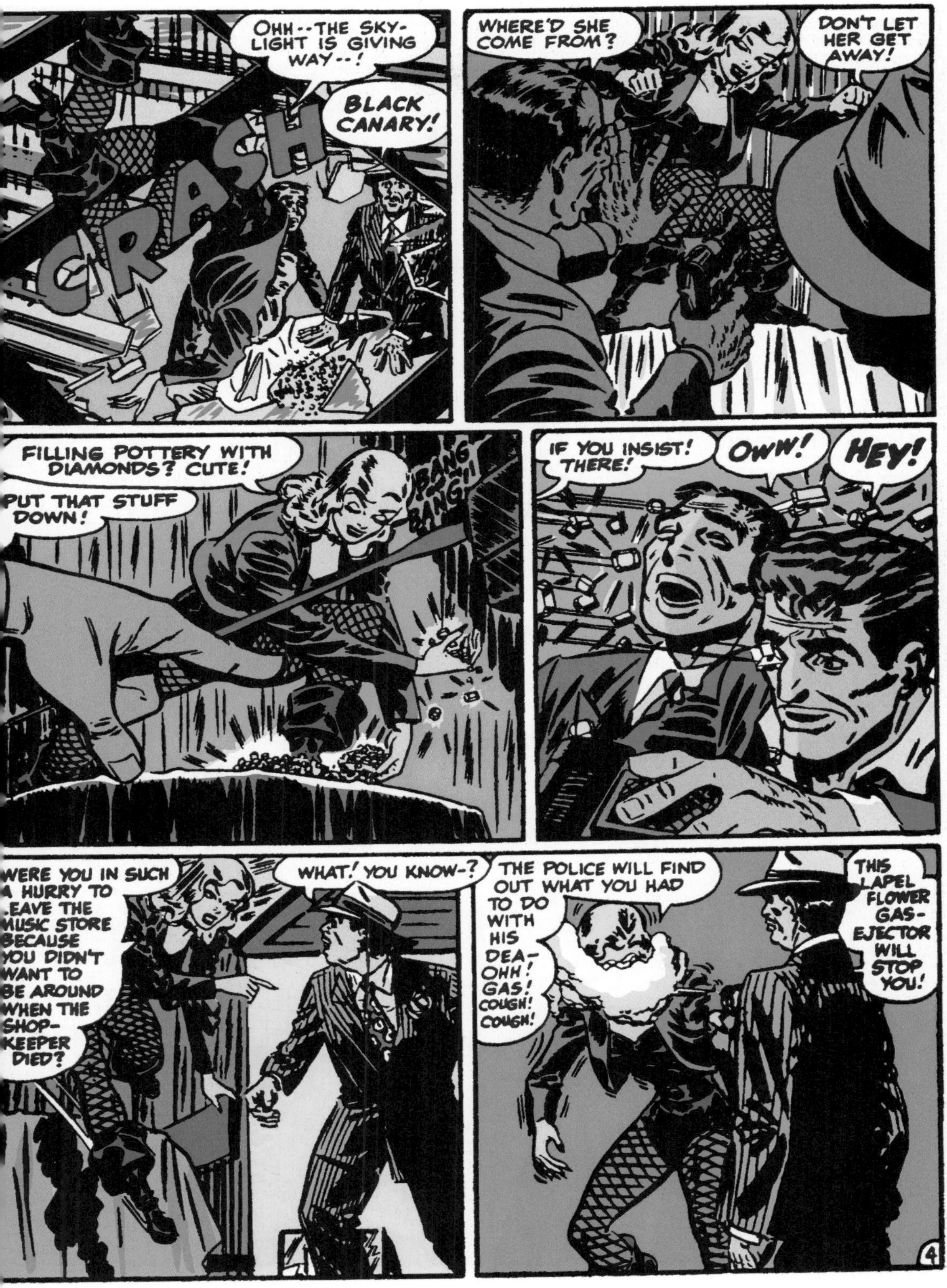

OHH--THE SKY-LIGHT IS GIVING WAY--!
BLACK CANARY!
CRASH
WHERE'D SHE COME FROM?
DON'T LET HER GET AWAY!
FILLING POTTERY WITH DIAMONDS? CUTE!
PUT THAT STUFF DOWN!
BANG BANG
IF YOU INSIST! THERE!
OWW!
HEY!
WERE YOU IN SUCH A HURRY TO LEAVE THE MUSIC STORE BECAUSE YOU DIDN'T WANT TO BE AROUND WHEN THE SHOP-KEEPER DIED?
WHAT! YOU KNOW-?
THE POLICE WILL FIND OUT WHAT YOU HAD TO DO WITH HIS DEA- OHH! GAS! COUGH! COUGH!
THIS LAPEL FLOWER GAS-EJECTOR WILL STOP YOU!
4

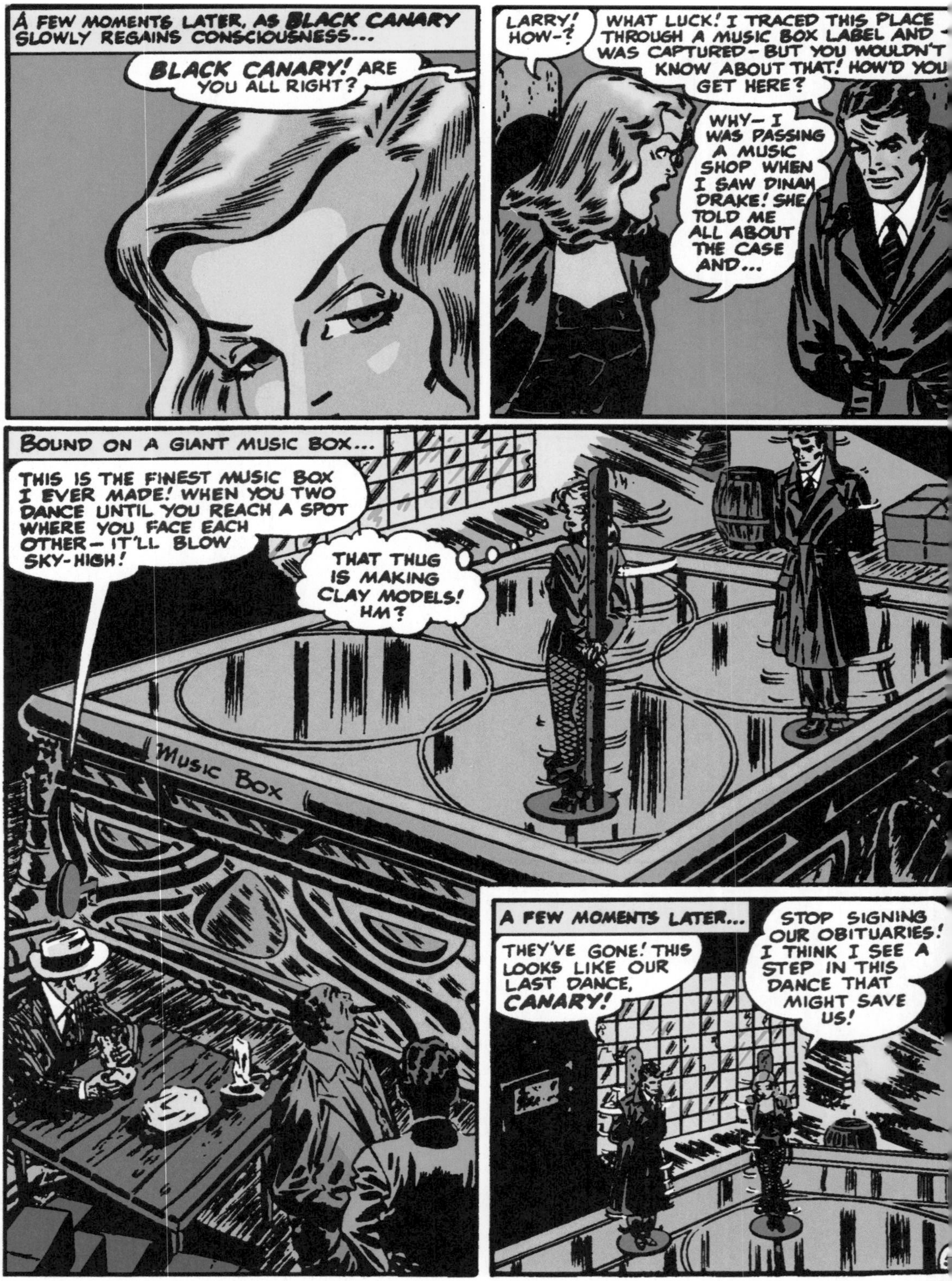
A FEW MOMENTS LATER, AS BLACK CANARY SLOWLY REGAINS CONSCIOUSNESS...
BLACK CANARY! ARE YOU ALL RIGHT?
LARRY! HOW-?
WHAT LUCK! I TRACED THIS PLACE THROUGH A MUSIC BOX LABEL AND WAS CAPTURED-BUT YOU WOULDN'T KNOW ABOUT THAT! HOW'D YOU GET HERE?
WHY-I WAS PASSING A MUSIC SHOP WHEN I SAW DINAH DRAKE! SHE TOLD ME ALL ABOUT THE CASE AND...
BOUND ON A GIANT MUSIC BOX...
THIS IS THE FINEST MUSIC BOX I EVER MADE! WHEN YOU TWO DANCE UNTIL YOU REACH A SPOT WHERE YOU FACE EACH OTHER-IT'LL BLOW SKY-HIGH!
THAT THUG IS MAKING CLAY MODELS! HM?
MUSIC BOX
A FEW MOMENTS LATER...
THEY'VE GONE! THIS LOOKS LIKE OUR LAST DANCE, CANARY!
STOP SIGNING OUR OBITUARIES! I THINK I SEE A STEP IN THIS DANCE THAT MIGHT SAVE US!

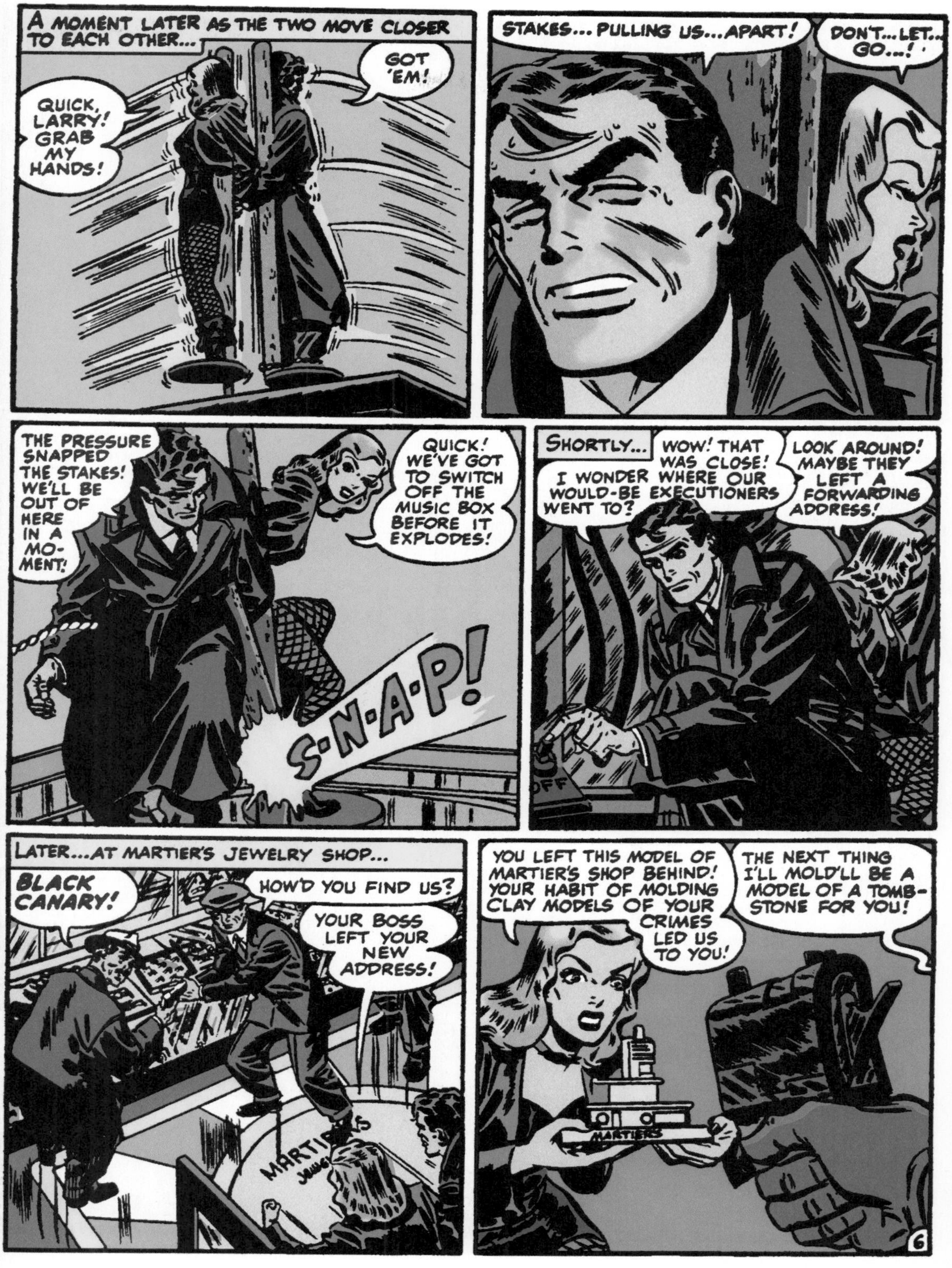
A MOMENT LATER AS THE TWO MOVE CLOSER TO EACH OTHER...
GOT 'EM!
QUICK, LARRY! GRAB MY HANDS!
STAKES... PULLING US... APART!
DON'T... LET... GO...!
THE PRESSURE SNAPPED THE STAKES! WE'LL BE OUT OF HERE IN A MO-MENT!
QUICK! WE'VE GOT TO SWITCH OFF THE MUSIC BOX BEFORE IT EXPLODES!
S-N-A-P!
SHORTLY...
WOW! THAT WAS CLOSE! I WONDER WHERE OUR WOULD-BE EXECUTIONERS WENT TO?
LOOK AROUND! MAYBE THEY LEFT A FORWARDING ADDRESS!
OFF
LATER...AT MARTIER'S JEWELRY SHOP...
BLACK CANARY!
HOW'D YOU FIND US?
YOUR BOSS LEFT YOUR NEW ADDRESS!
MARTIER'S
YOU LEFT THIS MODEL OF MARTIER'S SHOP BEHIND! YOUR HABIT OF MOLDING CLAY MODELS OF YOUR CRIMES LED US TO YOU!
THE NEXT THING I'LL MOLD'LL BE A MODEL OF A TOMB-STONE FOR YOU!
MARTIERS
6

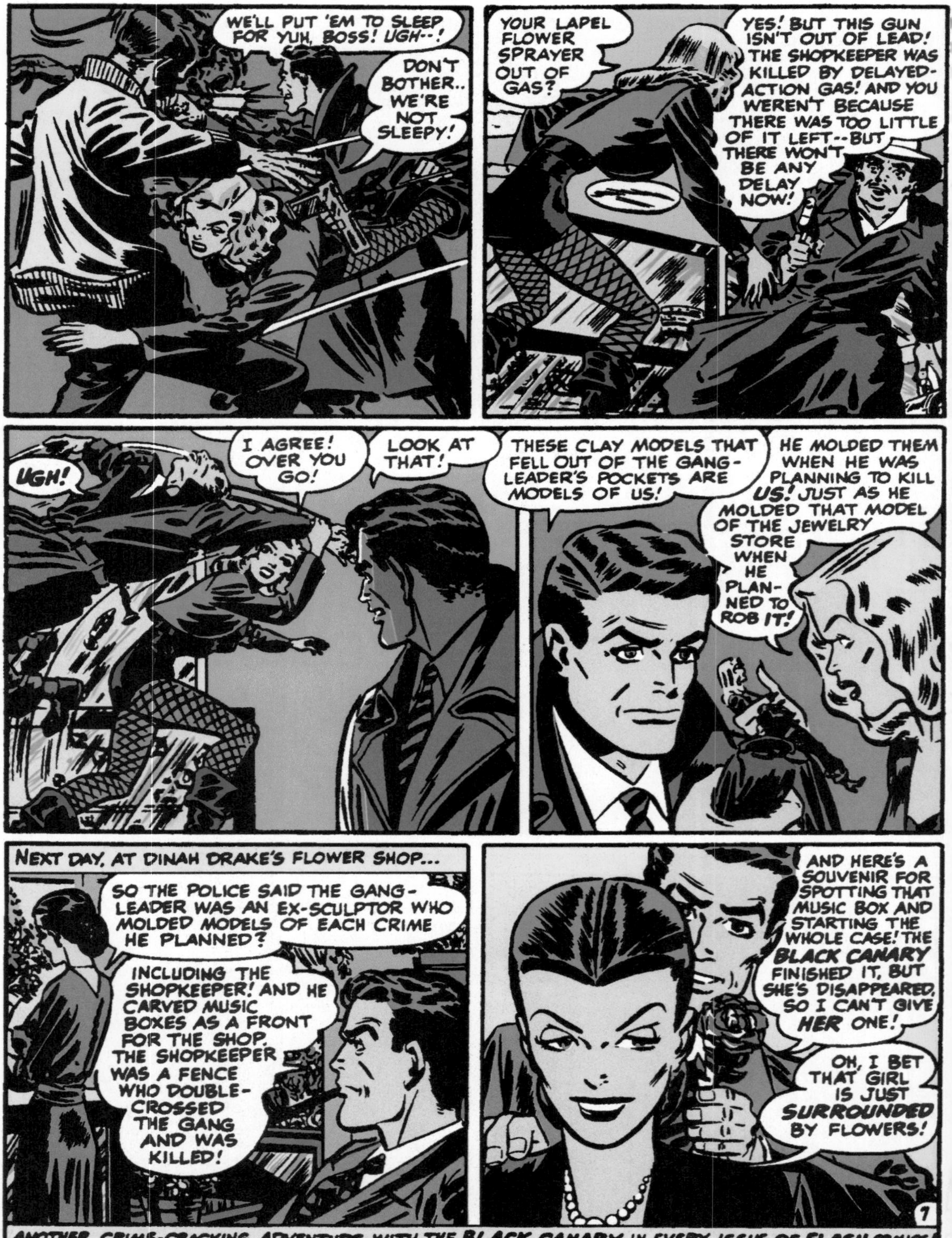

WE'LL PUT 'EM TO SLEEP FOR YUH, BOSS! UGH--!
DON'T BOTHER.. WE'RE NOT SLEEPY!
YOUR LAPEL FLOWER SPRAYER OUT OF GAS?
YES! BUT THIS GUN ISN'T OUT OF LEAD! THE SHOPKEEPER WAS KILLED BY DELAYED-ACTION GAS! AND YOU WEREN'T BECAUSE THERE WAS TOO LITTLE OF IT LEFT--BUT THERE WON'T BE ANY DELAY NOW!
UGH!
I AGREE! OVER YOU GO!
LOOK AT THAT!
THESE CLAY MODELS THAT FELL OUT OF THE GANG-LEADER'S POCKETS ARE MODELS OF US!
HE MOLDED THEM WHEN HE WAS PLANNING TO KILL US! JUST AS HE MOLDED THAT MODEL OF THE JEWELRY STORE WHEN HE PLANNED TO ROB IT!
NEXT DAY, AT DINAH DRAKE'S FLOWER SHOP...
SO THE POLICE SAID THE GANG-LEADER WAS AN EX-SCULPTOR WHO MOLDED MODELS OF EACH CRIME HE PLANNED?
INCLUDING THE SHOPKEEPER! AND HE CARVED MUSIC BOXES AS A FRONT FOR THE SHOP. THE SHOPKEEPER WAS A FENCE WHO DOUBLE-CROSSED THE GANG AND WAS KILLED!
AND HERE'S A SOUVENIR FOR SPOTTING THAT MUSIC BOX AND STARTING THE WHOLE CASE! THE BLACK CANARY FINISHED IT, BUT SHE'S DISAPPEARED, SO I CAN'T GIVE HER ONE!
OH, I BET THAT GIRL IS JUST SURROUNDED BY FLOWERS!
7
ANOTHER CRIME-CRACKING ADVENTURE WITH THE BLACK CANARY IN EVERY ISSUE OF FLASH COMICS!

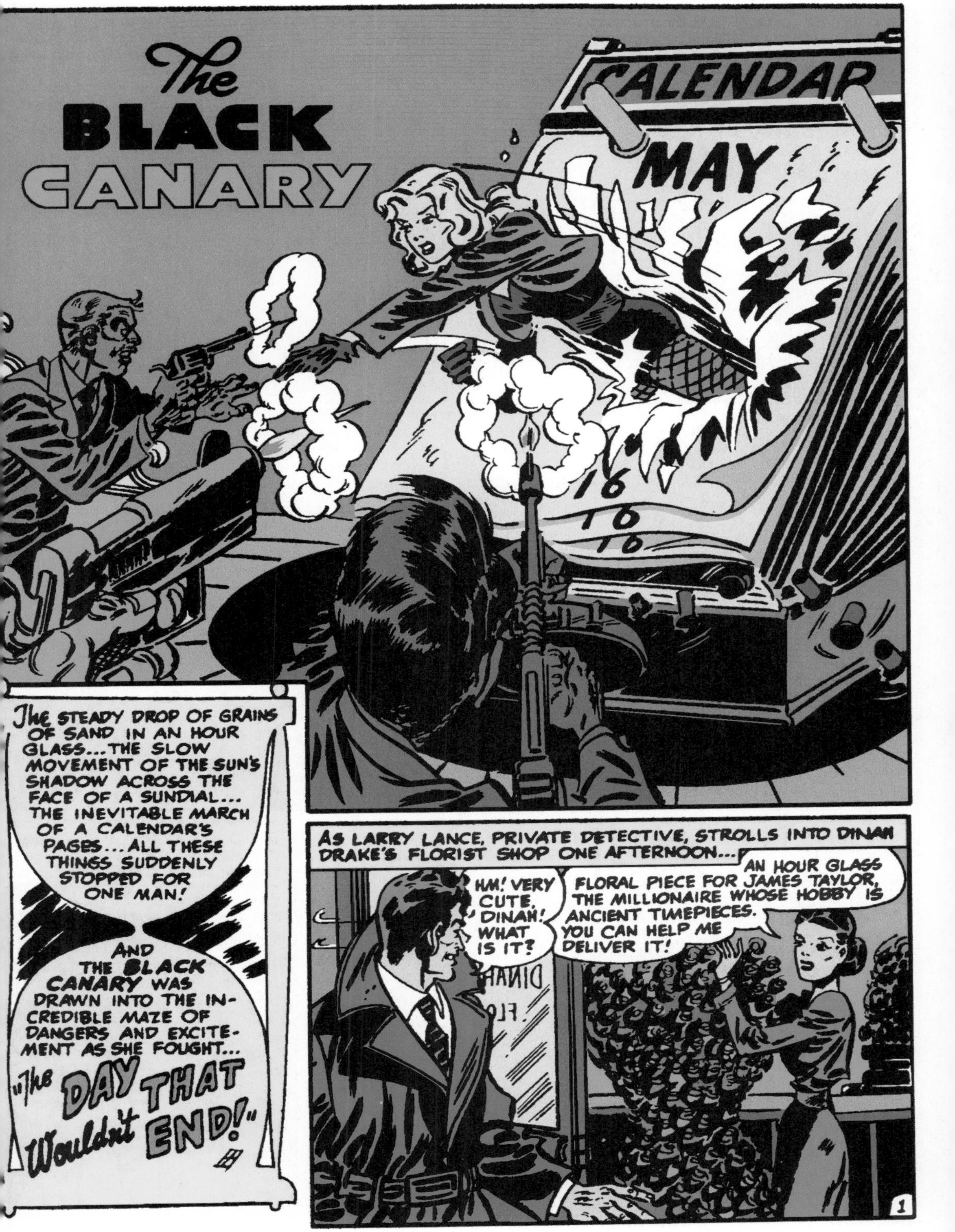
The BLACK CANARY
CALENDAR
MAY
16
16
16
THE STEADY DROP OF GRAINS OF SAND IN AN HOUR GLASS... THE SLOW MOVEMENT OF THE SUN'S SHADOW ACROSS THE FACE OF A SUNDIAL... THE INEVITABLE MARCH OF A CALENDAR'S PAGES... ALL THESE THINGS SUDDENLY STOPPED FOR ONE MAN!
AND THE BLACK CANARY WAS DRAWN INTO THE INCREDIBLE MAZE OF DANGERS AND EXCITEMENT AS SHE FOUGHT... "The DAY THAT Wouldn't END!"
AS LARRY LANCE, PRIVATE DETECTIVE, STROLLS INTO DINAH DRAKE'S FLORIST SHOP ONE AFTERNOON...
HM! VERY CUTE, DINAH! WHAT IS IT?
AN HOUR GLASS FLORAL PIECE FOR JAMES TAYLOR, THE MILLIONAIRE WHOSE HOBBY IS ANCIENT TIMEPIECES. YOU CAN HELP ME DELIVER IT!
1

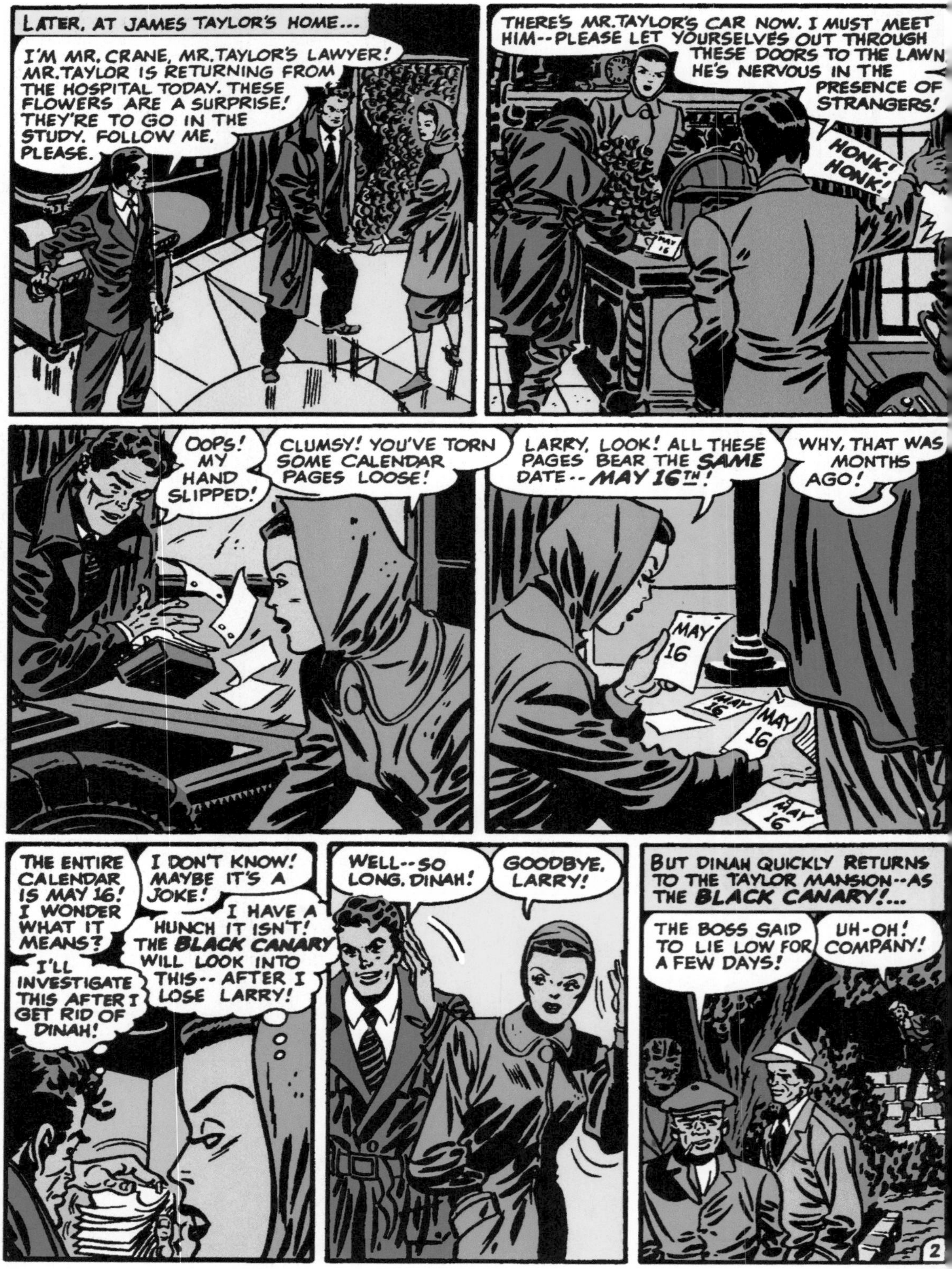
LATER, AT JAMES TAYLOR'S HOME...
I'M MR. CRANE, MR. TAYLOR'S LAWYER! MR. TAYLOR IS RETURNING FROM THE HOSPITAL TODAY. THESE FLOWERS ARE A SURPRISE! THEY'RE TO GO IN THE STUDY. FOLLOW ME, PLEASE.
THERE'S MR. TAYLOR'S CAR NOW. I MUST MEET HIM--PLEASE LET YOURSELVES OUT THROUGH THESE DOORS TO THE LAWN. HE'S NERVOUS IN THE PRESENCE OF STRANGERS!
HONK! HONK!
MAY 16
OOPS! MY HAND SLIPPED!
CLUMSY! YOU'VE TORN SOME CALENDAR PAGES LOOSE!
LARRY, LOOK! ALL THESE PAGES BEAR THE SAME DATE--MAY 16TH!
WHY, THAT WAS MONTHS AGO!
MAY 16
MAY 16
MAY 16
MAY 16
THE ENTIRE CALENDAR IS MAY 16! I WONDER WHAT IT MEANS?
I DON'T KNOW! MAYBE IT'S A JOKE!
I'LL INVESTIGATE THIS AFTER I GET RID OF DINAH!
I HAVE A HUNCH IT ISN'T! THE BLACK CANARY WILL LOOK INTO THIS--AFTER I LOSE LARRY!
WELL--SO LONG, DINAH!
GOODBYE, LARRY!
BUT DINAH QUICKLY RETURNS TO THE TAYLOR MANSION--AS THE BLACK CANARY!...
THE BOSS SAID TO LIE LOW FOR A FEW DAYS!
UH-OH! COMPANY!
2

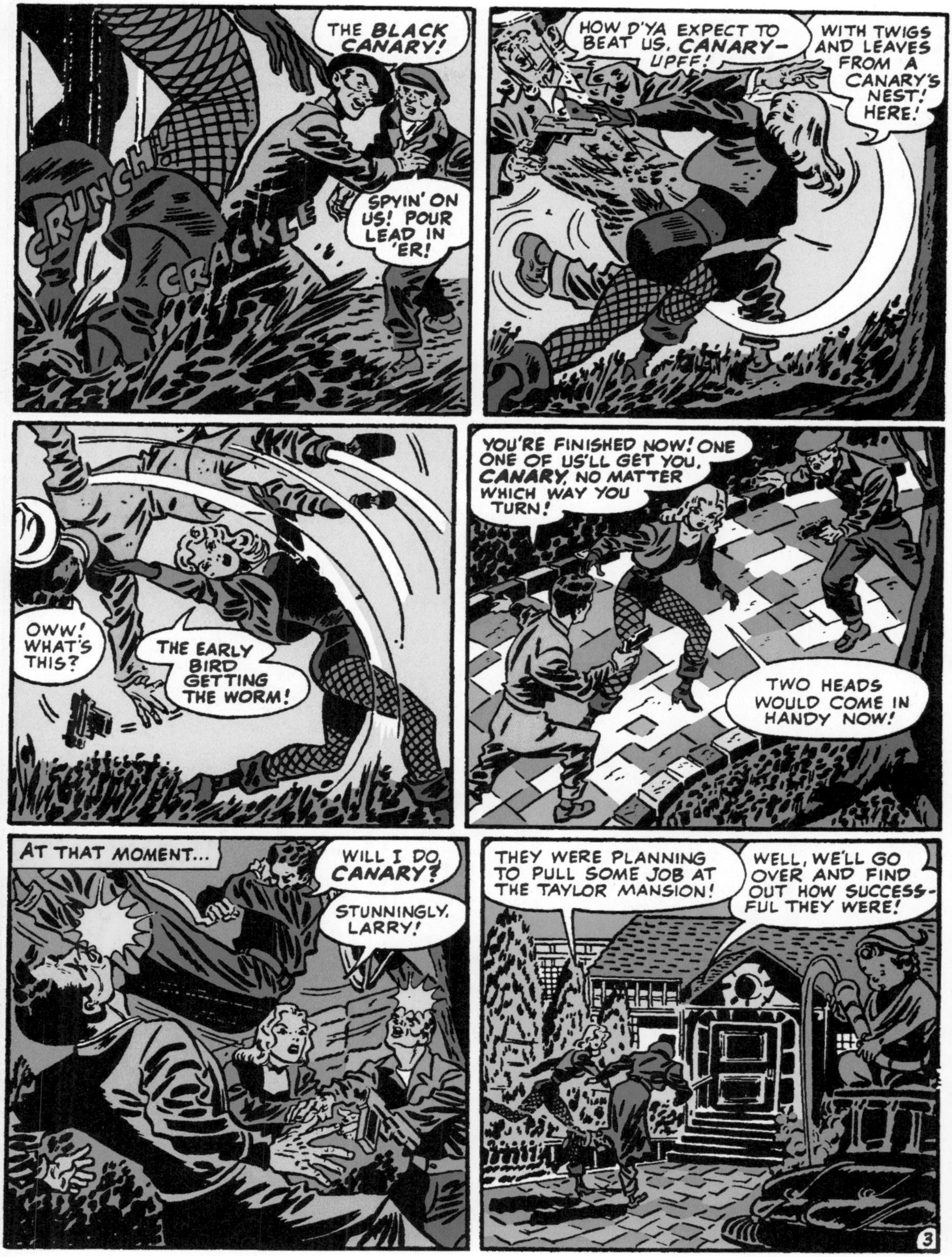
THE BLACK CANARY!
CRUNCH!
CRACKLE
SPYIN' ON US! POUR LEAD IN 'ER!
HOW D'YA EXPECT TO BEAT US, CANARY- UPFF!
WITH TWIGS AND LEAVES FROM A CANARY'S NEST! HERE!
OWW! WHAT'S THIS?
THE EARLY BIRD GETTING THE WORM!
YOU'RE FINISHED NOW! ONE ONE OF US'LL GET YOU, CANARY, NO MATTER WHICH WAY YOU TURN!
TWO HEADS WOULD COME IN HANDY NOW!
AT THAT MOMENT...
WILL I DO, CANARY?
STUNNINGLY, LARRY!
THEY WERE PLANNING TO PULL SOME JOB AT THE TAYLOR MANSION!
WELL, WE'LL GO OVER AND FIND OUT HOW SUCCESSFUL THEY WERE!
3

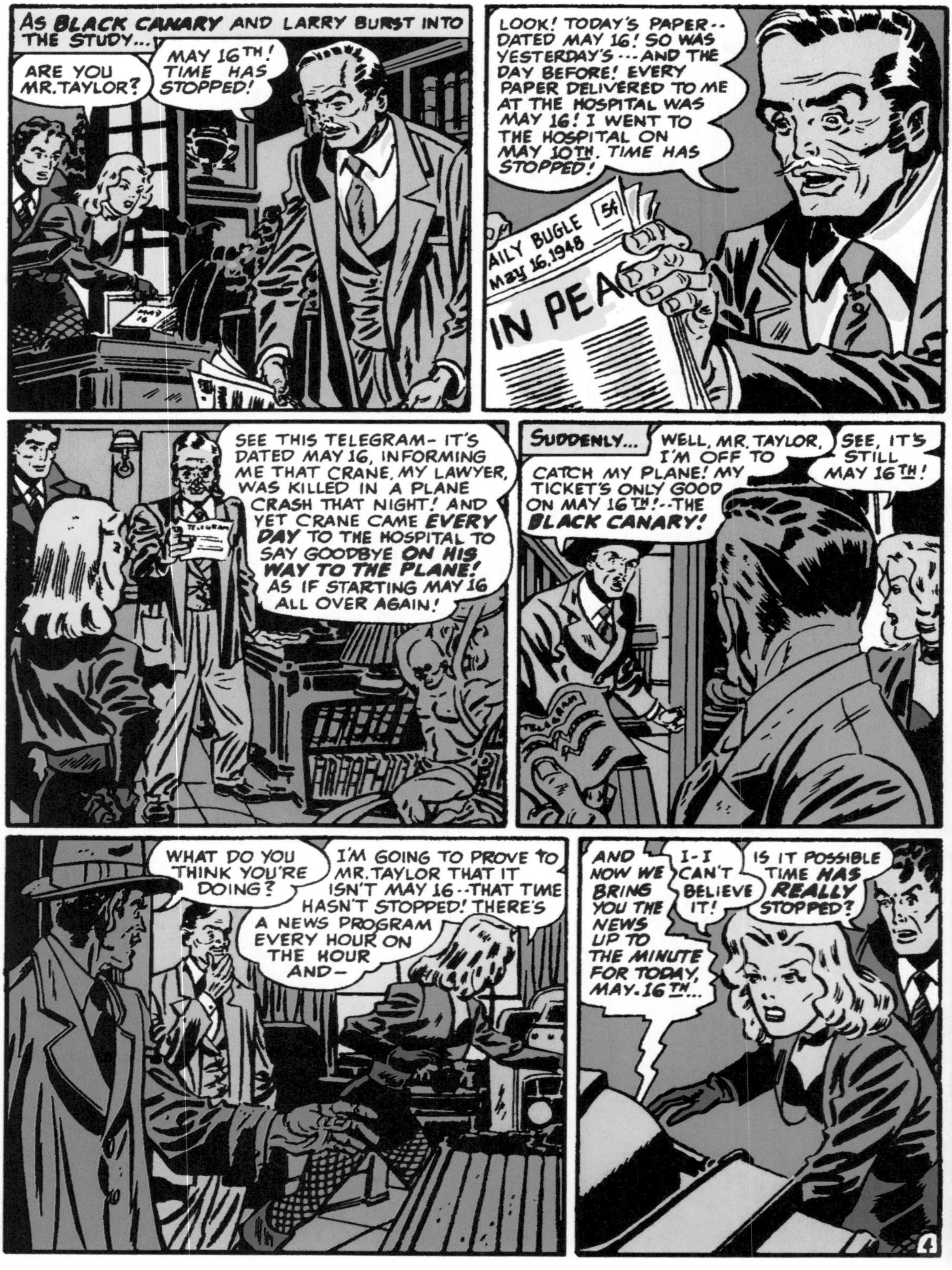
AS BLACK CANARY AND LARRY BURST INTO THE STUDY...
ARE YOU MR. TAYLOR?
MAY 16TH! TIME HAS STOPPED!
MAY 16
LOOK! TODAY'S PAPER-- DATED MAY 16! SO WAS YESTERDAY'S --- AND THE DAY BEFORE! EVERY PAPER DELIVERED TO ME AT THE HOSPITAL WAS MAY 16! I WENT TO THE HOSPITAL ON MAY 10TH. TIME HAS STOPPED!
AILY BUGLE 5¢
MAY 16, 1948
IN PEA
SEE THIS TELEGRAM- IT'S DATED MAY 16, INFORMING ME THAT CRANE, MY LAWYER, WAS KILLED IN A PLANE CRASH THAT NIGHT! AND YET CRANE CAME EVERY DAY TO THE HOSPITAL TO SAY GOODBYE ON HIS WAY TO THE PLANE! AS IF STARTING MAY 16 ALL OVER AGAIN!
SUDDENLY...
WELL, MR. TAYLOR, I'M OFF TO CATCH MY PLANE! MY TICKET'S ONLY GOOD ON MAY 16TH!--THE BLACK CANARY!
SEE, IT'S STILL MAY 16TH!
TELEGRAM
WHAT DO YOU THINK YOU'RE DOING?
I'M GOING TO PROVE TO MR. TAYLOR THAT IT ISN'T MAY 16--THAT TIME HASN'T STOPPED! THERE'S A NEWS PROGRAM EVERY HOUR ON THE HOUR AND-
AND NOW WE BRING YOU THE NEWS UP TO THE MINUTE FOR TODAY, MAY. 16TH...
I-I CAN'T BELIEVE IT!
IS IT POSSIBLE TIME HAS REALLY STOPPED?
4

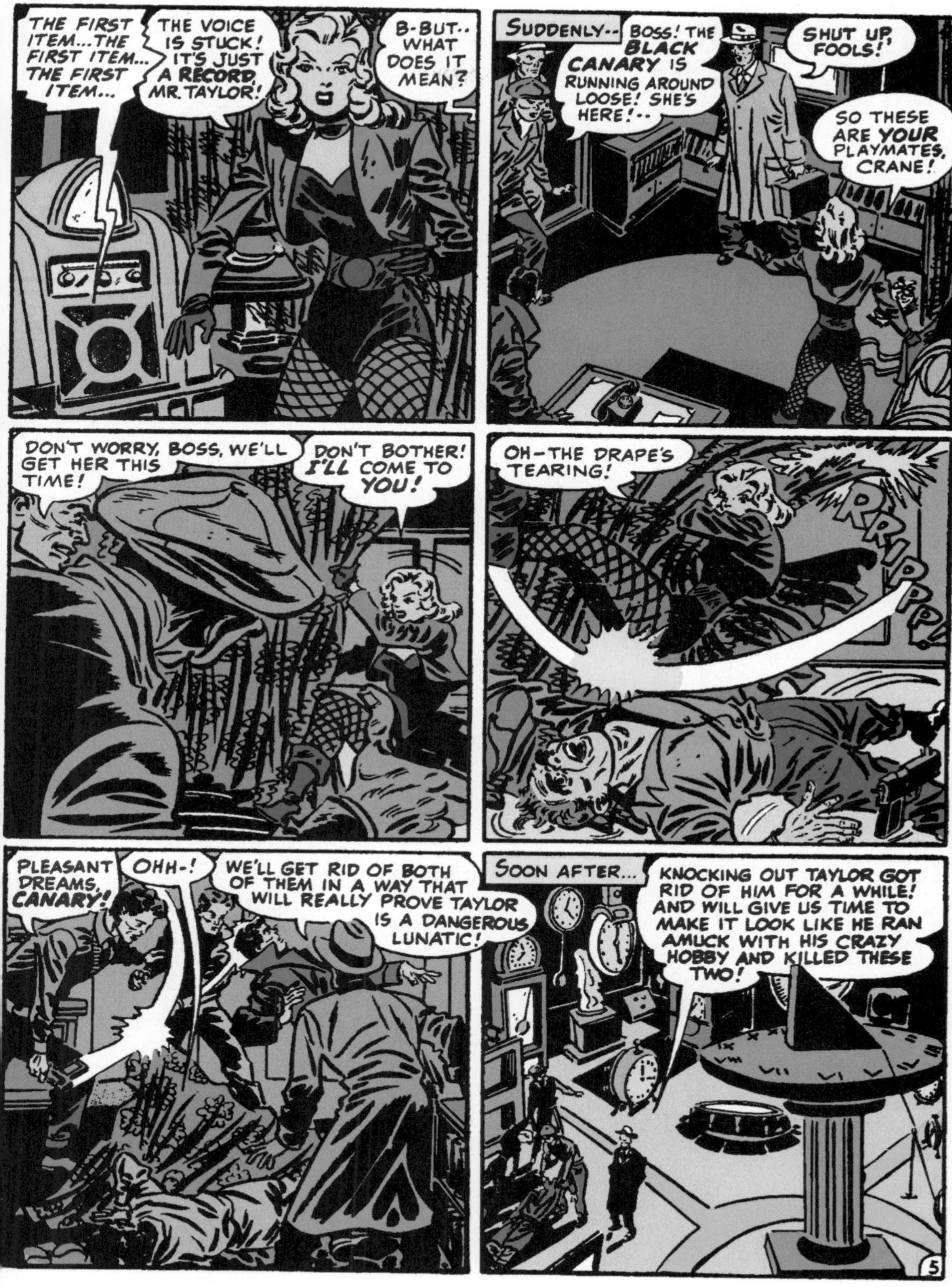
THE FIRST ITEM...THE FIRST ITEM... THE FIRST ITEM...
THE VOICE IS STUCK! IT'S JUST A RECORD, MR. TAYLOR!
B-BUT.. WHAT DOES IT MEAN?
SUDDENLY--
BOSS! THE BLACK CANARY IS RUNNING AROUND LOOSE! SHE'S HERE!--
SHUT UP, FOOLS!
SO THESE ARE YOUR PLAYMATES, CRANE!
DON'T WORRY, BOSS, WE'LL GET HER THIS TIME!
DON'T BOTHER! I'LL COME TO YOU!
OH-THE DRAPE'S TEARING!
RRIPP!
PLEASANT DREAMS, CANARY!
OHH-!
WE'LL GET RID OF BOTH OF THEM IN A WAY THAT WILL REALLY PROVE TAYLOR IS A DANGEROUS LUNATIC!
SOON AFTER...
KNOCKING OUT TAYLOR GOT RID OF HIM FOR A WHILE! AND WILL GIVE US TIME TO MAKE IT LOOK LIKE HE RAN AMUCK WITH HIS CRAZY HOBBY AND KILLED THESE TWO!
5

THE *BLACK CANARY* AND LARRY ARE TURNED INTO HUMAN SUNDIAL POINTERS!...

WHEN THE SHADOW POINTS TO THREE O'CLOCK, A TIME DEVICE WILL SET OFF THAT DYNAMITE!

I HOPE THE EXPLOSION DOESN'T BOTHER THE ORCHIDS, HA, HA! LET'S GO!

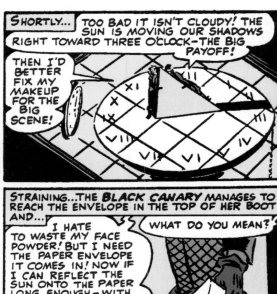

SHORTLY... TOO BAD IT ISN'T CLOUDY! THE SUN IS MOVING OUR SHADOWS RIGHT TOWARD THREE O'CLOCK—THE BIG PAYOFF!

THEN I'D BETTER FIX MY MAKEUP FOR THE BIG SCENE!

STRAINING...THE *BLACK CANARY* MANAGES TO REACH THE ENVELOPE IN THE TOP OF HER BOOT AND...

I HATE TO WASTE MY FACE POWDER! BUT I NEED THE PAPER ENVELOPE IT COMES IN! NOW IF I CAN REFLECT THE SUN ONTO THE PAPER LONG ENOUGH—WITH THE MAGNIFYING GLASS IN MY LOCKET!

WHAT DO YOU MEAN?

WHAT MAGNIFYING GLASS?

THE ONE I CARRY FOR EXAMINING FINGER-PRINTS!

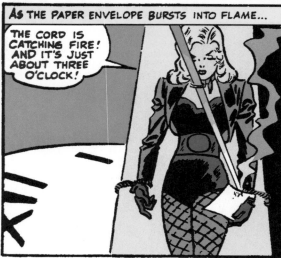

AS THE PAPER ENVELOPE BURSTS INTO FLAME...

THE CORD IS CATCHING FIRE! AND IT'S JUST ABOUT THREE O'CLOCK!

UNTYING HER BONDS, *BLACK CANARY* RACES TO THE CONTROL BOX AND...

WOW! YOU BROKE THE CONNECTION JUST IN TIME!

YOU CAN SAY THAT AGAIN!

6

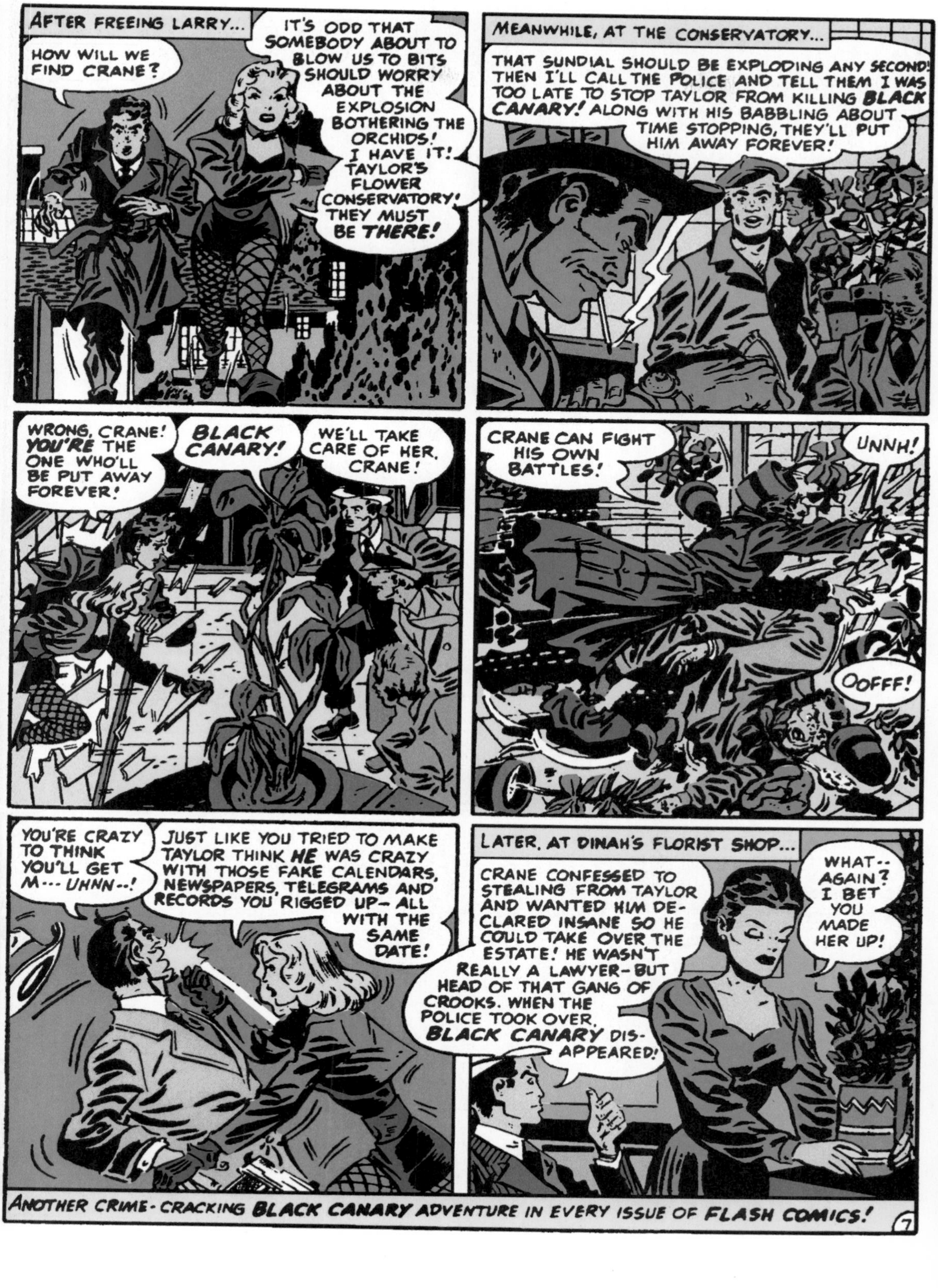
AFTER FREEING LARRY...
HOW WILL WE FIND CRANE?
IT'S ODD THAT SOMEBODY ABOUT TO BLOW US TO BITS SHOULD WORRY ABOUT THE EXPLOSION BOTHERING THE ORCHIDS! I HAVE IT! TAYLOR'S FLOWER CONSERVATORY! THEY MUST BE THERE!
MEANWHILE, AT THE CONSERVATORY...
THAT SUNDIAL SHOULD BE EXPLODING ANY SECOND! THEN I'LL CALL THE POLICE AND TELL THEM I WAS TOO LATE TO STOP TAYLOR FROM KILLING BLACK CANARY! ALONG WITH HIS BABBLING ABOUT TIME STOPPING, THEY'LL PUT HIM AWAY FOREVER!
WRONG, CRANE! YOU'RE THE ONE WHO'LL BE PUT AWAY FOREVER!
BLACK CANARY!
WE'LL TAKE CARE OF HER, CRANE!
CRANE CAN FIGHT HIS OWN BATTLES!
UNNH!
OOFFF!
YOU'RE CRAZY TO THINK YOU'LL GET M--- UHNN--!
JUST LIKE YOU TRIED TO MAKE TAYLOR THINK HE WAS CRAZY WITH THOSE FAKE CALENDARS, NEWSPAPERS, TELEGRAMS AND RECORDS YOU RIGGED UP-- ALL WITH THE SAME DATE!
LATER, AT DINAH'S FLORIST SHOP...
CRANE CONFESSED TO STEALING FROM TAYLOR AND WANTED HIM DE-CLARED INSANE SO HE COULD TAKE OVER THE ESTATE! HE WASN'T REALLY A LAWYER-- BUT HEAD OF THAT GANG OF CROOKS. WHEN THE POLICE TOOK OVER, BLACK CANARY DIS-APPEARED!
WHAT-- AGAIN? I BET YOU MADE HER UP!
ANOTHER CRIME-CRACKING BLACK CANARY ADVENTURE IN EVERY ISSUE OF FLASH COMICS!
7

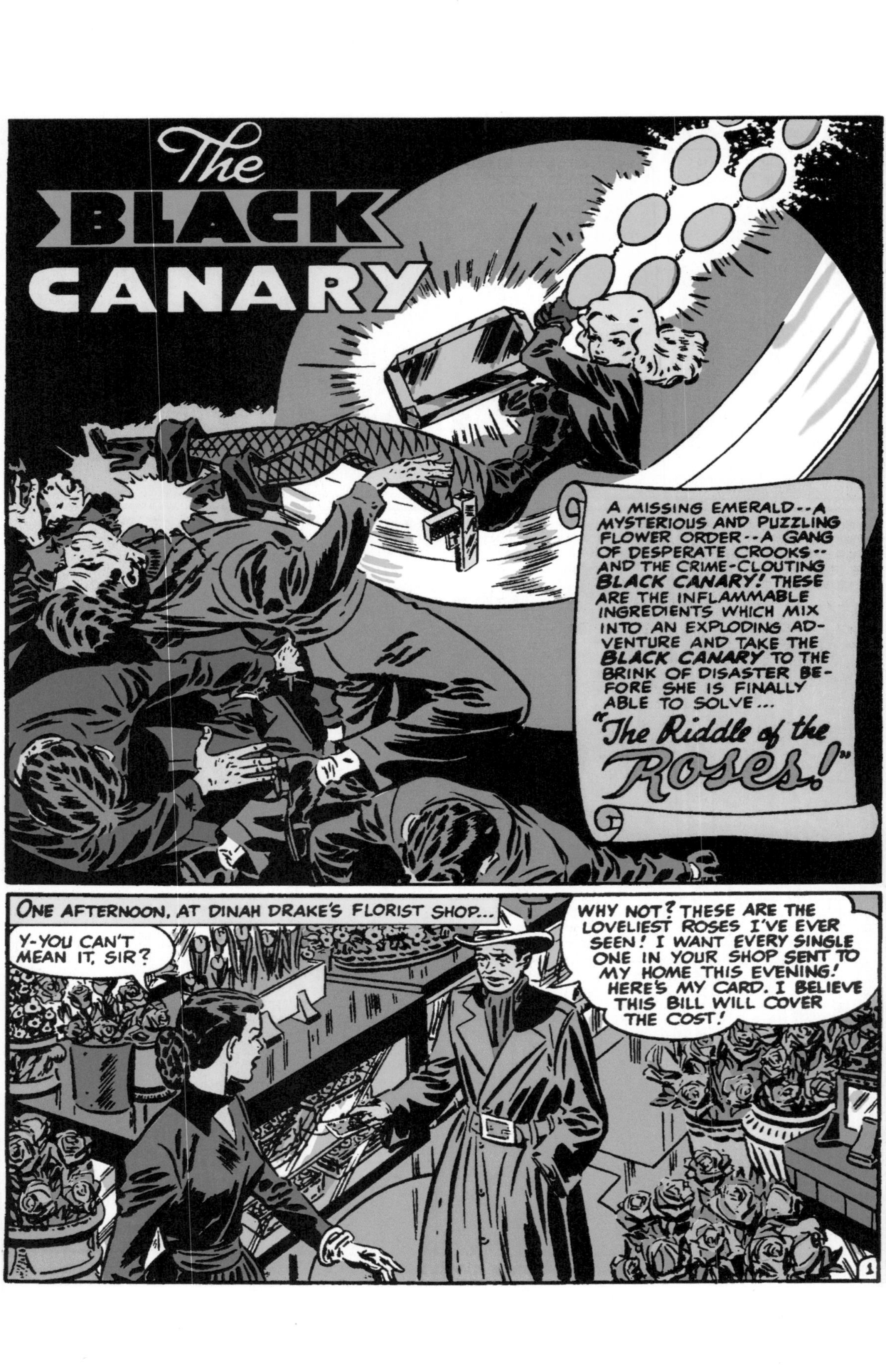
The BLACK CANARY
A MISSING EMERALD--A MYSTERIOUS AND PUZZLING FLOWER ORDER--A GANG OF DESPERATE CROOKS--AND THE CRIME-CLOUTING BLACK CANARY! THESE ARE THE INFLAMMABLE INGREDIENTS WHICH MIX INTO AN EXPLODING ADVENTURE AND TAKE THE BLACK CANARY TO THE BRINK OF DISASTER BEFORE SHE IS FINALLY ABLE TO SOLVE...
"The Riddle of the Roses!"
ONE AFTERNOON, AT DINAH DRAKE'S FLORIST SHOP...
Y-YOU CAN'T MEAN IT, SIR?
WHY NOT? THESE ARE THE LOVELIEST ROSES I'VE EVER SEEN! I WANT EVERY SINGLE ONE IN YOUR SHOP SENT TO MY HOME THIS EVENING! HERE'S MY CARD. I BELIEVE THIS BILL WILL COVER THE COST!
1

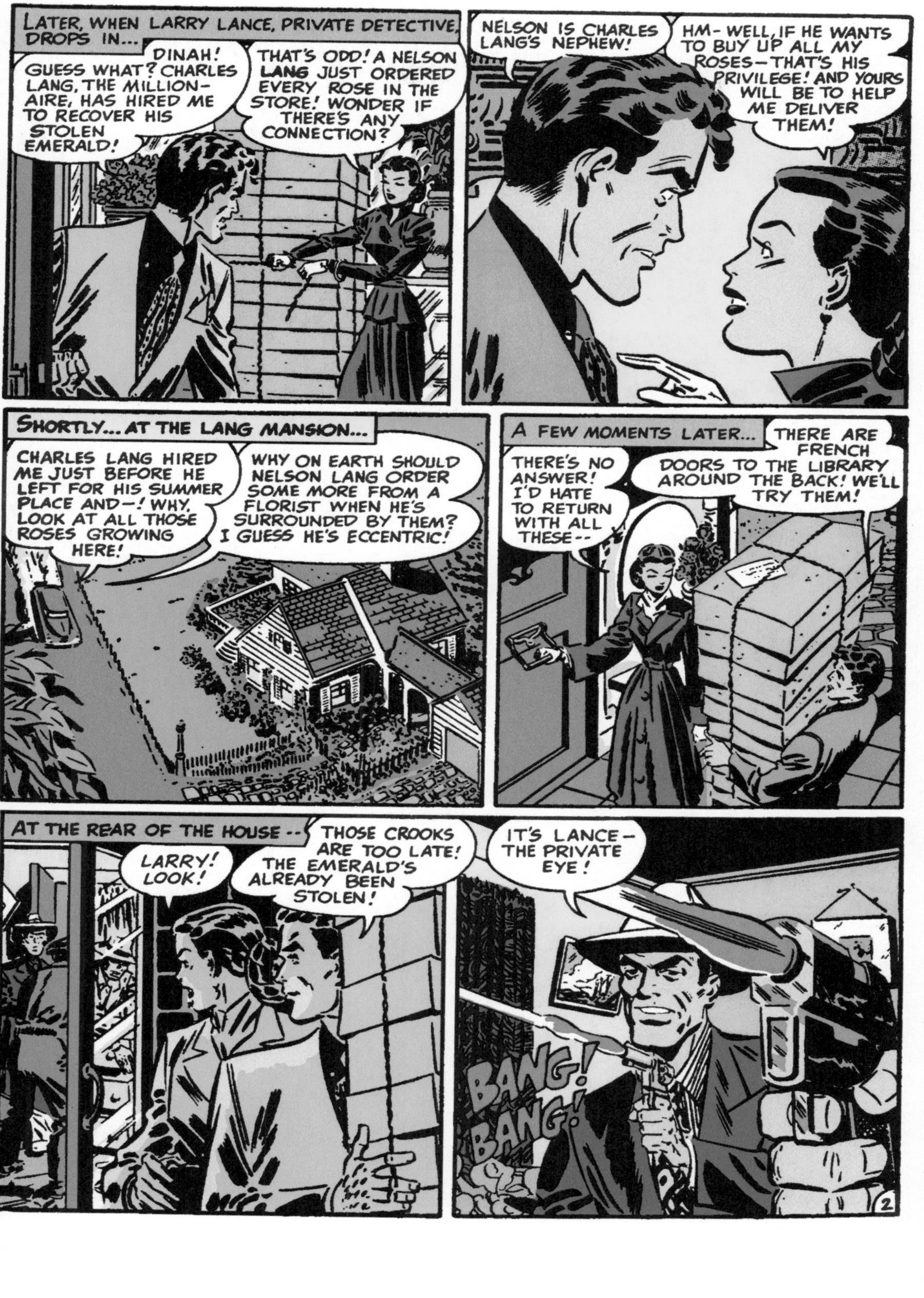
LATER, WHEN LARRY LANCE, PRIVATE DETECTIVE, DROPS IN...
DINAH! GUESS WHAT? CHARLES LANG, THE MILLIONAIRE, HAS HIRED ME TO RECOVER HIS STOLEN EMERALD!
THAT'S ODD! A NELSON LANG JUST ORDERED EVERY ROSE IN THE STORE! WONDER IF THERE'S ANY CONNECTION?
NELSON IS CHARLES LANG'S NEPHEW!
HM- WELL, IF HE WANTS TO BUY UP ALL MY ROSES—THAT'S HIS PRIVILEGE! AND YOURS WILL BE TO HELP ME DELIVER THEM!
SHORTLY... AT THE LANG MANSION...
CHARLES LANG HIRED ME JUST BEFORE HE LEFT FOR HIS SUMMER PLACE AND—! WHY, LOOK AT ALL THOSE ROSES GROWING HERE!
WHY ON EARTH SHOULD NELSON LANG ORDER SOME MORE FROM A FLORIST WHEN HE'S SURROUNDED BY THEM? I GUESS HE'S ECCENTRIC!
A FEW MOMENTS LATER...
THERE'S NO ANSWER! I'D HATE TO RETURN WITH ALL THESE--
THERE ARE FRENCH DOORS TO THE LIBRARY AROUND THE BACK! WE'LL TRY THEM!
AT THE REAR OF THE HOUSE --
LARRY! LOOK!
THOSE CROOKS ARE TOO LATE! THE EMERALD'S ALREADY BEEN STOLEN!
IT'S LANCE— THE PRIVATE EYE!
BANG! BANG!
2

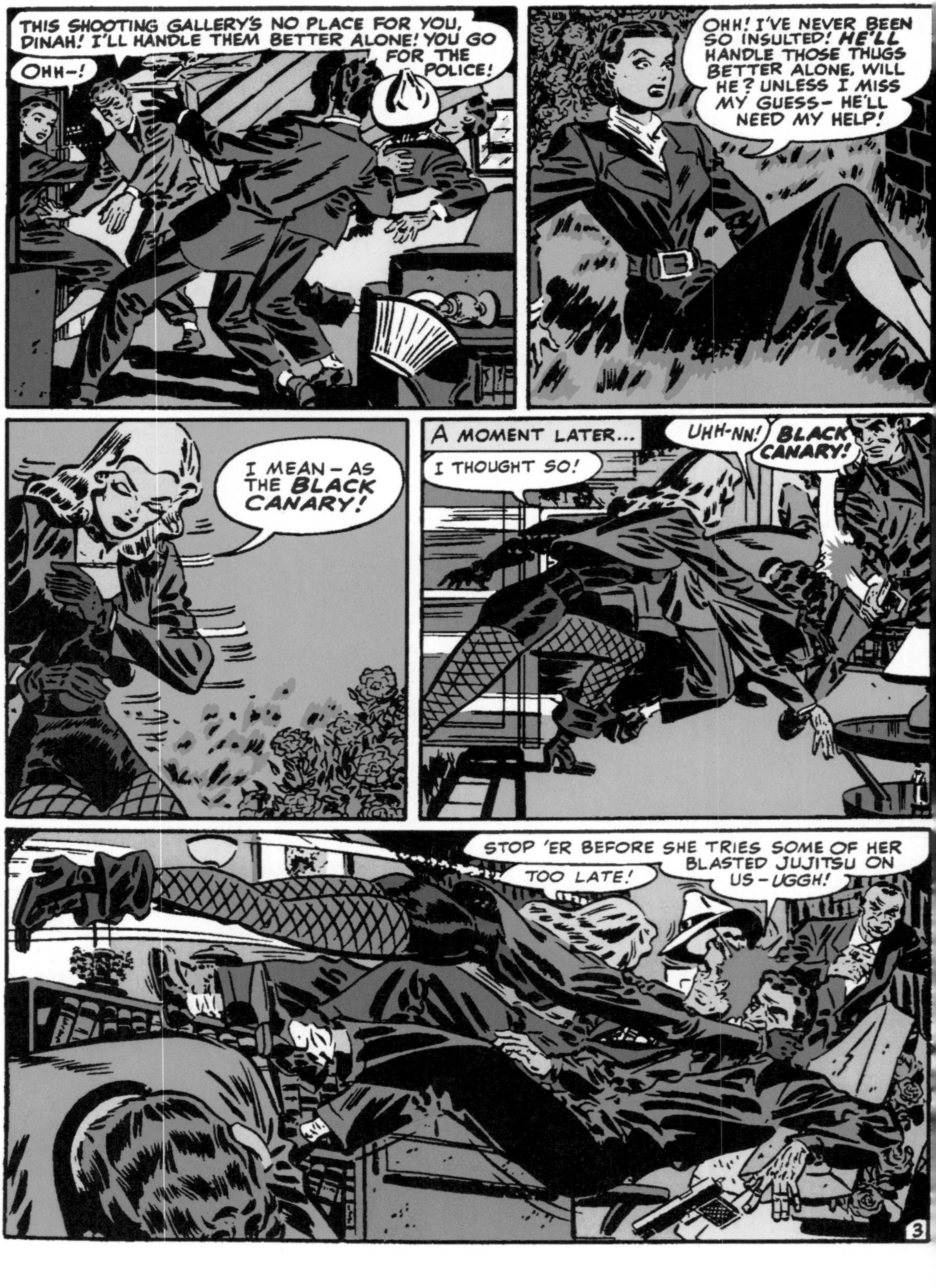
THIS SHOOTING GALLERY'S NO PLACE FOR YOU, DINAH! I'LL HANDLE THEM BETTER ALONE! YOU GO FOR THE POLICE!
OHH-!
OHH! I'VE NEVER BEEN SO INSULTED! HE'LL HANDLE THOSE THUGS BETTER ALONE, WILL HE? UNLESS I MISS MY GUESS- HE'LL NEED MY HELP!
I MEAN-AS THE BLACK CANARY!
A MOMENT LATER...
I THOUGHT SO!
UHH-NN! BLACK CANARY!
STOP 'ER BEFORE SHE TRIES SOME OF HER BLASTED JUJITSU ON US-UGGH!
TOO LATE!
3

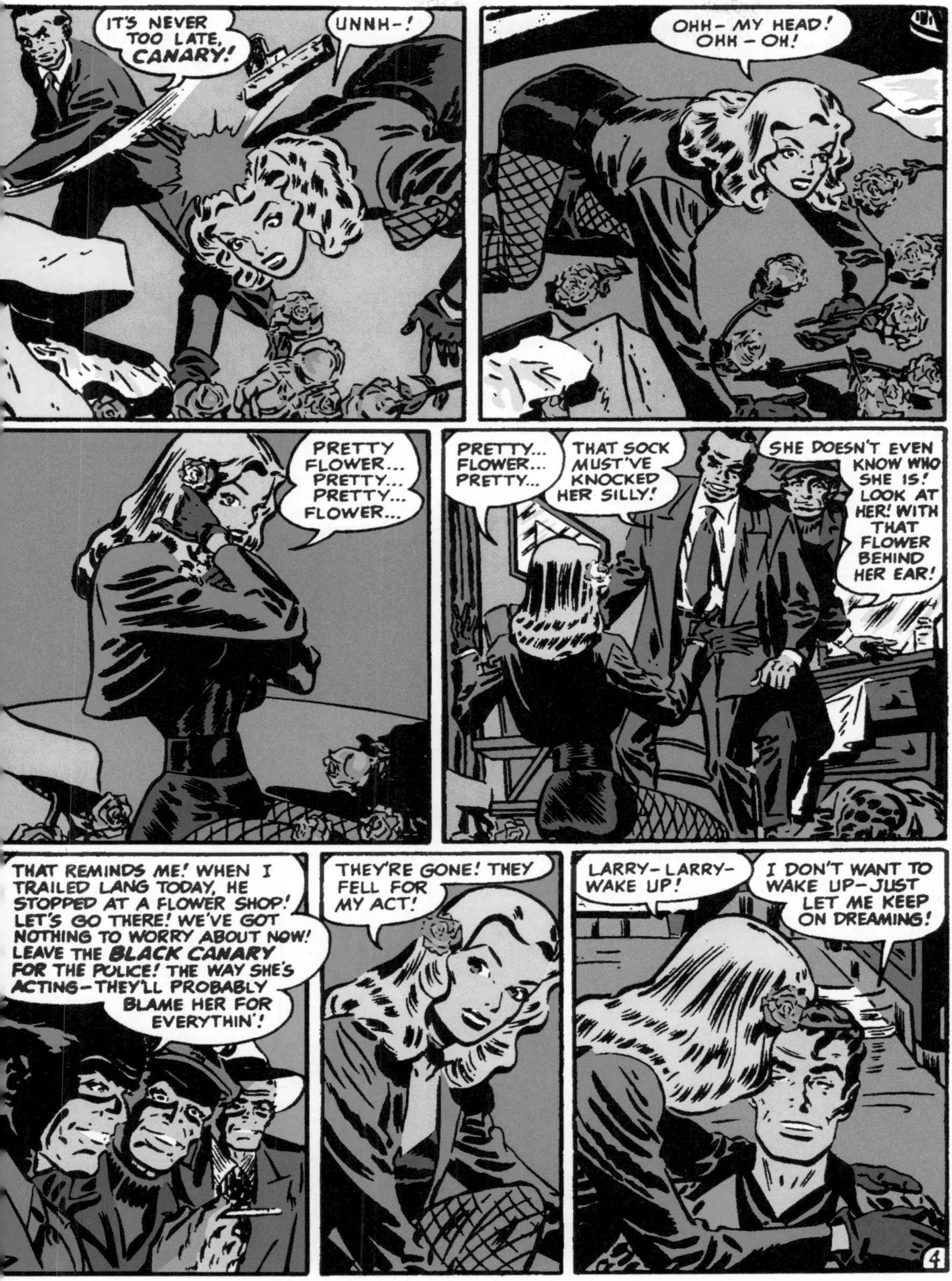
IT'S NEVER TOO LATE, CANARY!
UNNH-!
OHH- MY HEAD! OHH - OH!
PRETTY FLOWER... PRETTY... PRETTY... FLOWER...
PRETTY... FLOWER... PRETTY...
THAT SOCK MUST'VE KNOCKED HER SILLY!
SHE DOESN'T EVEN KNOW WHO SHE IS! LOOK AT HER! WITH THAT FLOWER BEHIND HER EAR!
THAT REMINDS ME! WHEN I TRAILED LANG TODAY, HE STOPPED AT A FLOWER SHOP! LET'S GO THERE! WE'VE GOT NOTHING TO WORRY ABOUT NOW! LEAVE THE BLACK CANARY FOR THE POLICE! THE WAY SHE'S ACTING- THEY'LL PROBABLY BLAME HER FOR EVERYTHIN'!
THEY'RE GONE! THEY FELL FOR MY ACT!
LARRY- LARRY- WAKE UP!
I DON'T WANT TO WAKE UP- JUST LET ME KEEP ON DREAMING!
4

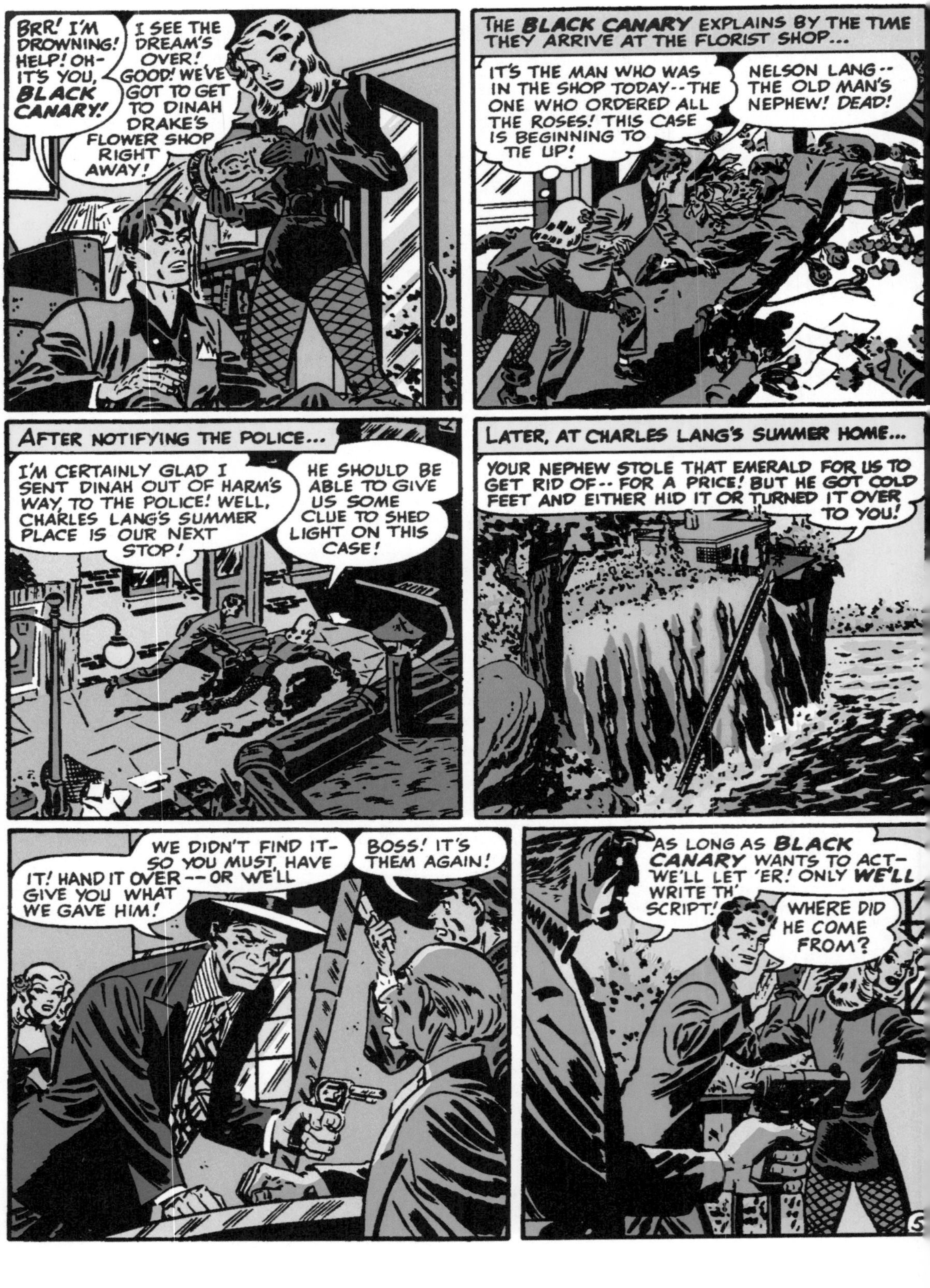
BRR! I'M DROWNING! HELP! OH-- IT'S YOU, BLACK CANARY!
I SEE THE DREAM'S OVER! GOOD! WE'VE GOT TO GET TO DINAH DRAKE'S FLOWER SHOP RIGHT AWAY!
THE BLACK CANARY EXPLAINS BY THE TIME THEY ARRIVE AT THE FLORIST SHOP...
IT'S THE MAN WHO WAS IN THE SHOP TODAY--THE ONE WHO ORDERED ALL THE ROSES! THIS CASE IS BEGINNING TO TIE UP!
NELSON LANG--THE OLD MAN'S NEPHEW! DEAD!
AFTER NOTIFYING THE POLICE...
I'M CERTAINLY GLAD I SENT DINAH OUT OF HARM'S WAY, TO THE POLICE! WELL, CHARLES LANG'S SUMMER PLACE IS OUR NEXT STOP!
HE SHOULD BE ABLE TO GIVE US SOME CLUE TO SHED LIGHT ON THIS CASE!
LATER, AT CHARLES LANG'S SUMMER HOME...
YOUR NEPHEW STOLE THAT EMERALD FOR US TO GET RID OF-- FOR A PRICE! BUT HE GOT COLD FEET AND EITHER HID IT OR TURNED IT OVER TO YOU!
WE DIDN'T FIND IT-SO YOU MUST HAVE IT! HAND IT OVER--OR WE'LL GIVE YOU WHAT WE GAVE HIM!
BOSS! IT'S THEM AGAIN!
AS LONG AS BLACK CANARY WANTS TO ACT-WE'LL LET 'ER! ONLY WE'LL WRITE TH' SCRIPT!
WHERE DID HE COME FROM?
5

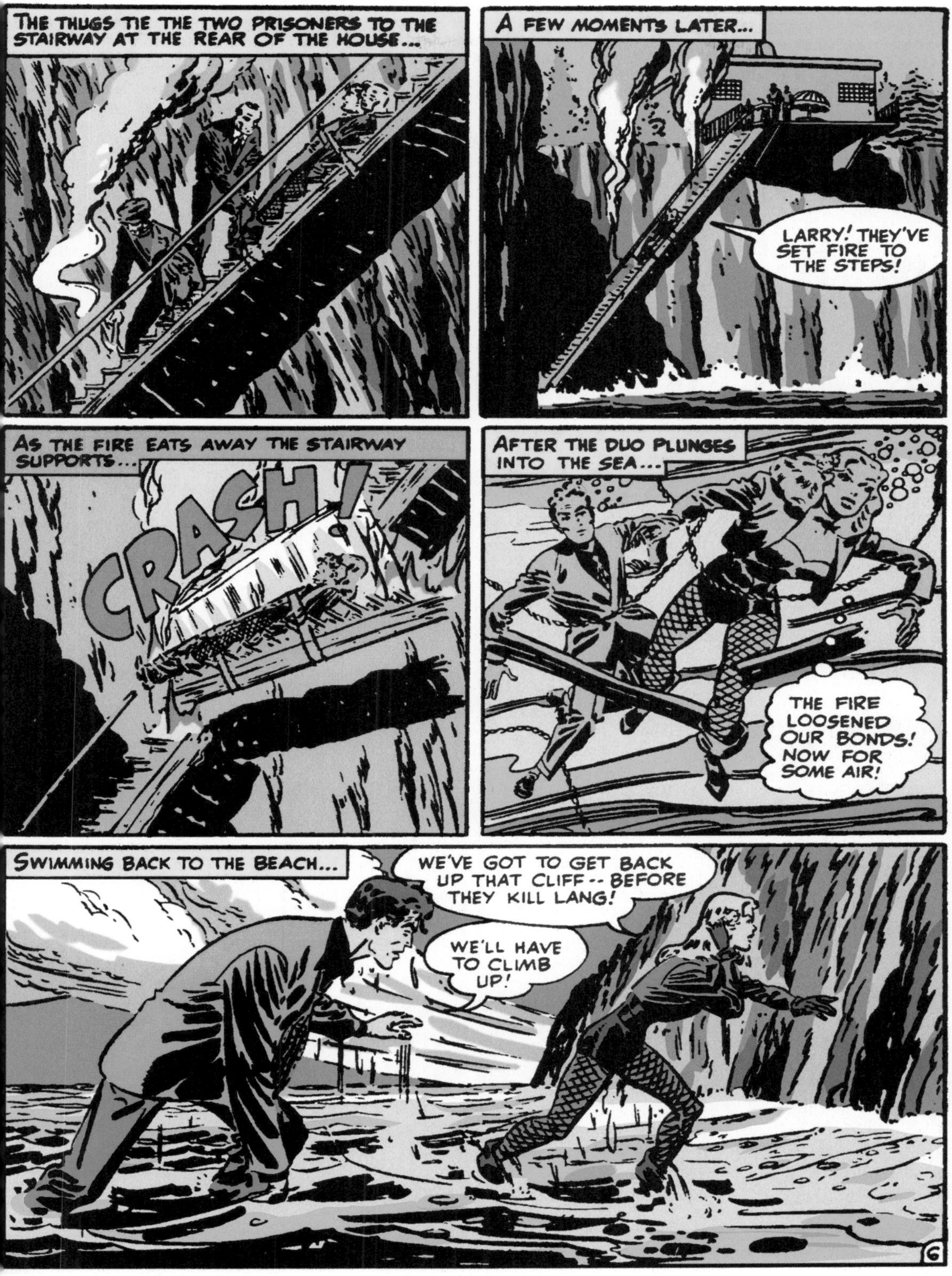
THE THUGS TIE THE TWO PRISONERS TO THE STAIRWAY AT THE REAR OF THE HOUSE...
A FEW MOMENTS LATER...
LARRY! THEY'VE SET FIRE TO THE STEPS!
AS THE FIRE EATS AWAY THE STAIRWAY SUPPORTS...
CRASH!
AFTER THE DUO PLUNGES INTO THE SEA...
THE FIRE LOOSENED OUR BONDS! NOW FOR SOME AIR!
SWIMMING BACK TO THE BEACH...
WE'VE GOT TO GET BACK UP THAT CLIFF -- BEFORE THEY KILL LANG!
WE'LL HAVE TO CLIMB UP!
6

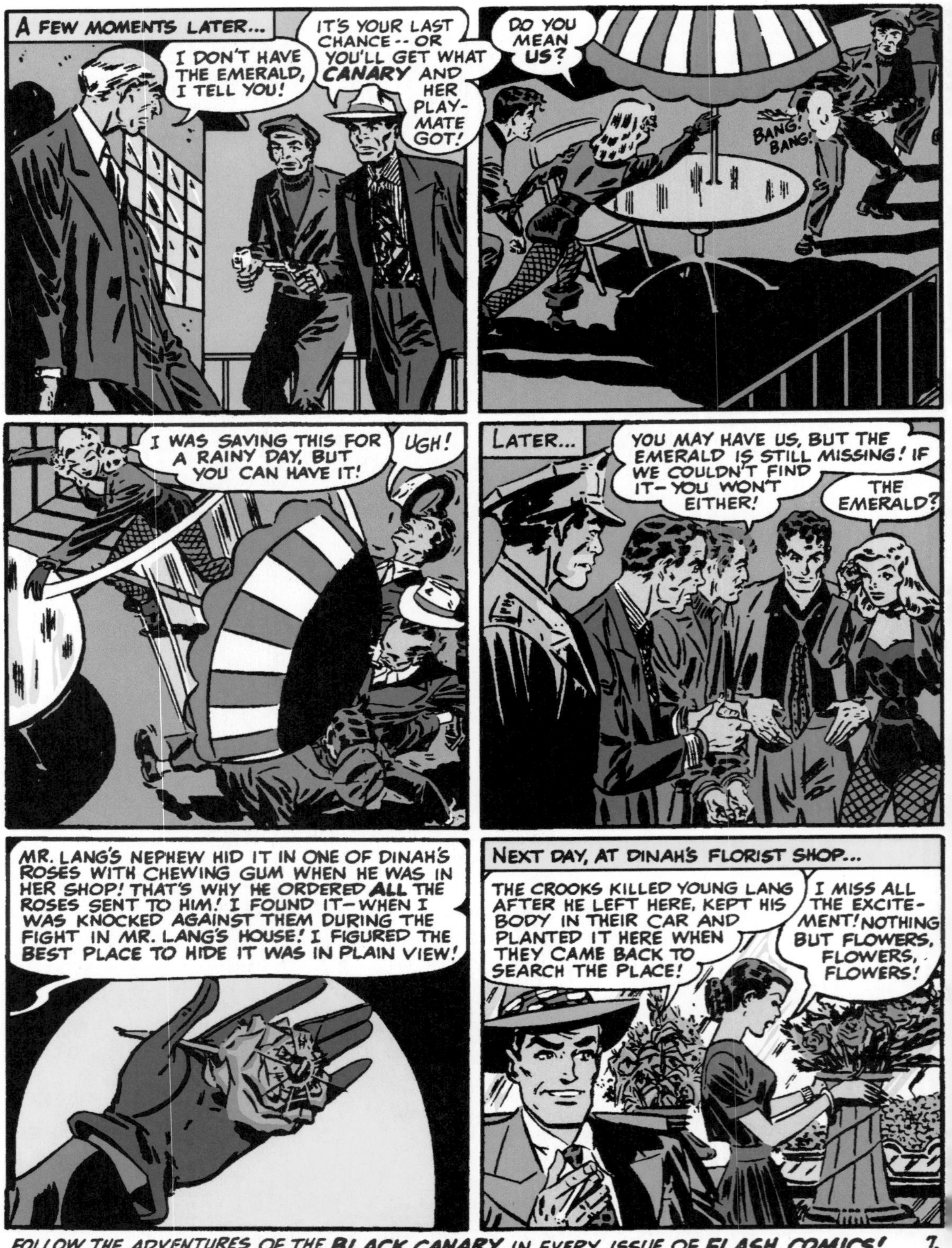
A FEW MOMENTS LATER...
IT'S YOUR LAST CHANCE -- OR YOU'LL GET WHAT CANARY AND HER PLAYMATE GOT!
I DON'T HAVE THE EMERALD, I TELL YOU!
DO YOU MEAN US?
BANG! BANG!
I WAS SAVING THIS FOR A RAINY DAY, BUT YOU CAN HAVE IT!
UGH!
LATER...
YOU MAY HAVE US, BUT THE EMERALD IS STILL MISSING! IF WE COULDN'T FIND IT– YOU WON'T EITHER!
THE EMERALD?
MR. LANG'S NEPHEW HID IT IN ONE OF DINAH'S ROSES WITH CHEWING GUM WHEN HE WAS IN HER SHOP! THAT'S WHY HE ORDERED ALL THE ROSES SENT TO HIM! I FOUND IT–WHEN I WAS KNOCKED AGAINST THEM DURING THE FIGHT IN MR. LANG'S HOUSE! I FIGURED THE BEST PLACE TO HIDE IT WAS IN PLAIN VIEW!
NEXT DAY, AT DINAH'S FLORIST SHOP...
THE CROOKS KILLED YOUNG LANG AFTER HE LEFT HERE, KEPT HIS BODY IN THEIR CAR AND PLANTED IT HERE WHEN THEY CAME BACK TO SEARCH THE PLACE!
I MISS ALL THE EXCITEMENT! NOTHING BUT FLOWERS, FLOWERS, FLOWERS!

FOLLOW THE ADVENTURES OF THE **BLACK CANARY** IN EVERY ISSUE OF **FLASH COMICS!** 7.

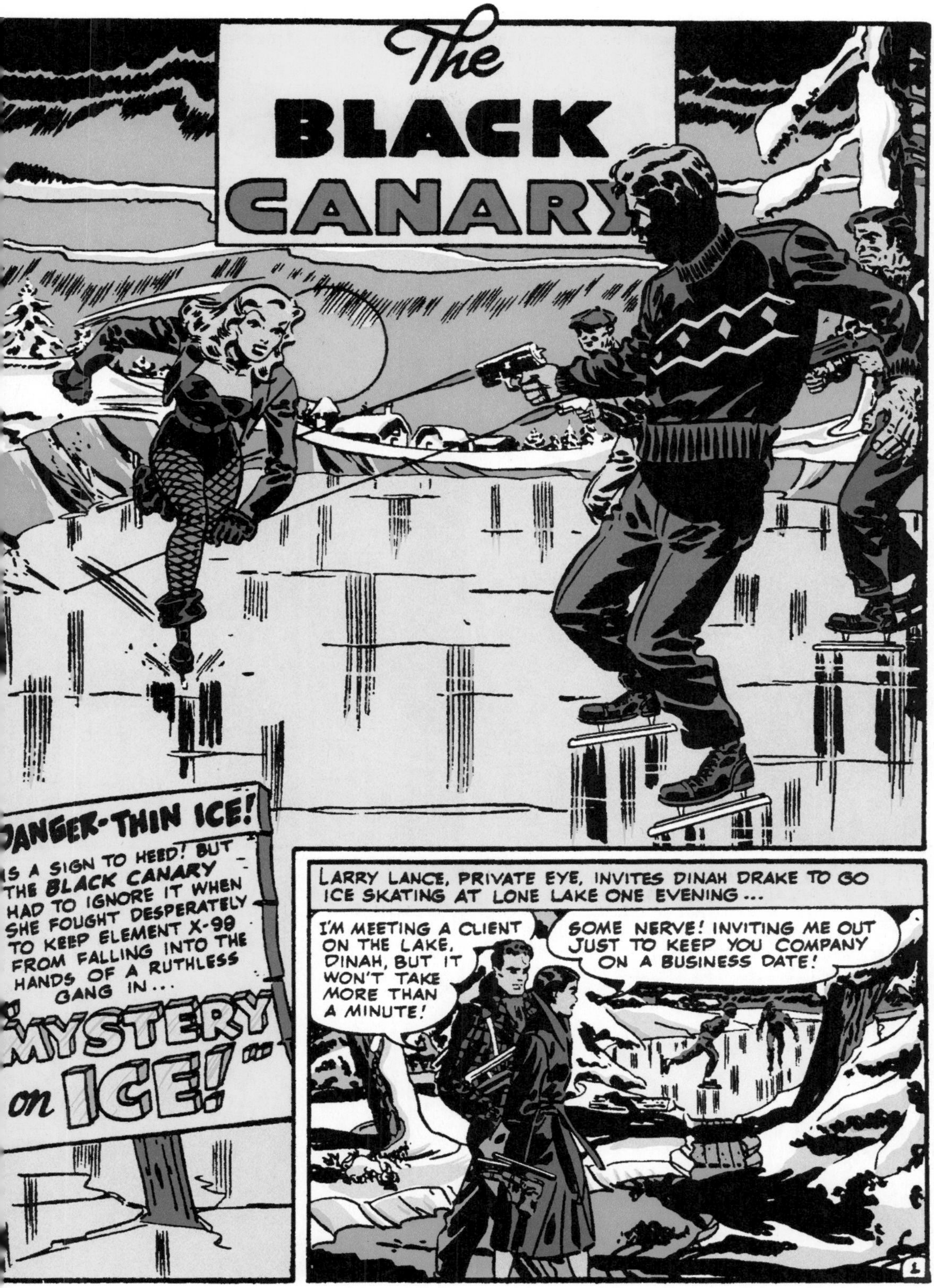

The BLACK CANARY
DANGER-THIN ICE!
IS A SIGN TO HEED! BUT THE BLACK CANARY HAD TO IGNORE IT WHEN SHE FOUGHT DESPERATELY TO KEEP ELEMENT X-99 FROM FALLING INTO THE HANDS OF A RUTHLESS GANG IN...
"MYSTERY on ICE!"
LARRY LANCE, PRIVATE EYE, INVITES DINAH DRAKE TO GO ICE SKATING AT LONE LAKE ONE EVENING...
I'M MEETING A CLIENT ON THE LAKE, DINAH, BUT IT WON'T TAKE MORE THAN A MINUTE!
SOME NERVE! INVITING ME OUT JUST TO KEEP YOU COMPANY ON A BUSINESS DATE!
1

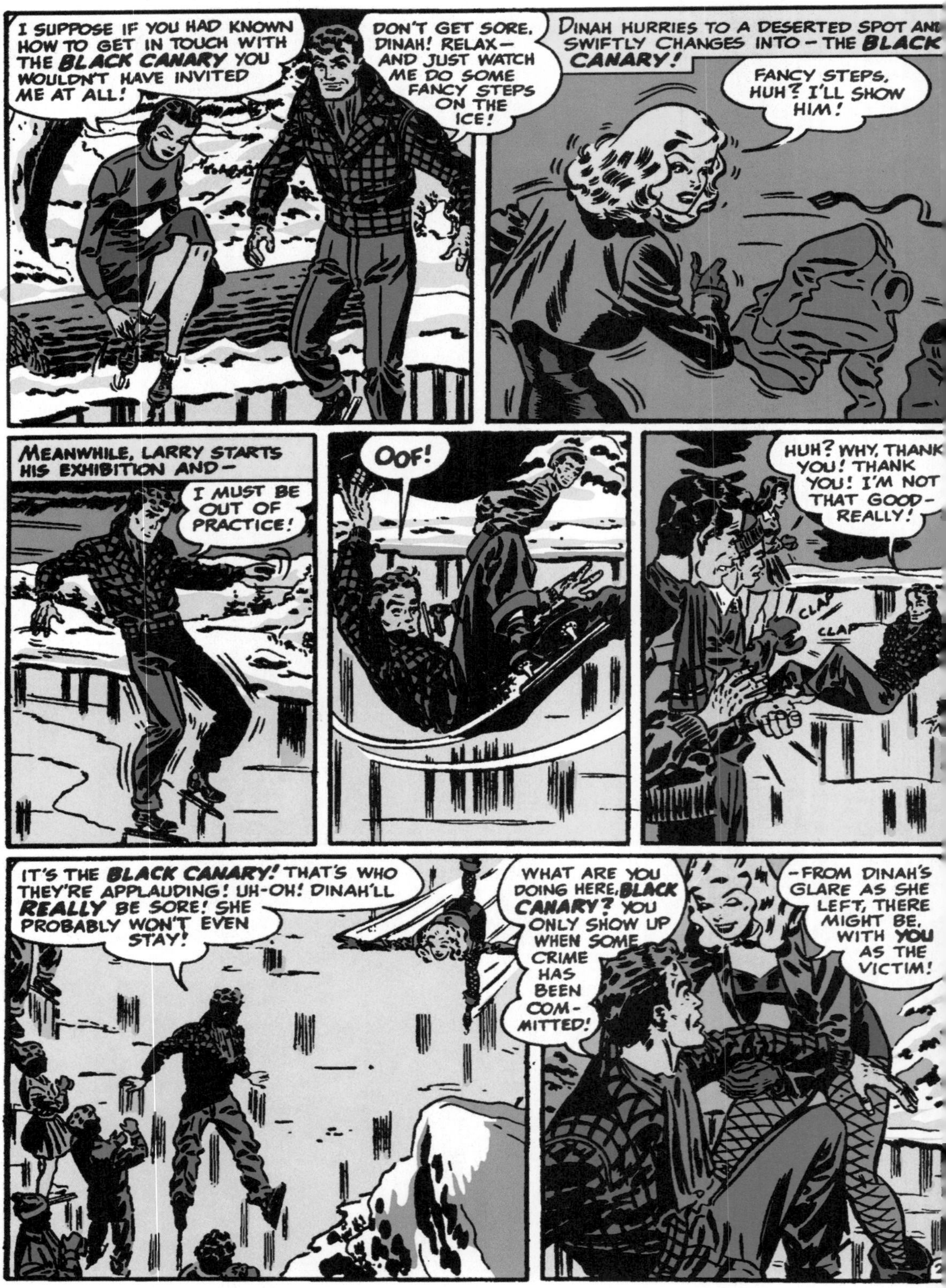
I SUPPOSE IF YOU HAD KNOWN HOW TO GET IN TOUCH WITH THE BLACK CANARY YOU WOULDN'T HAVE INVITED ME AT ALL!
DON'T GET SORE, DINAH! RELAX— AND JUST WATCH ME DO SOME FANCY STEPS ON THE ICE!
DINAH HURRIES TO A DESERTED SPOT AND SWIFTLY CHANGES INTO—THE BLACK CANARY!
FANCY STEPS, HUH? I'LL SHOW HIM!
MEANWHILE, LARRY STARTS HIS EXHIBITION AND—
I MUST BE OUT OF PRACTICE!
OOF!
HUH? WHY, THANK YOU! THANK YOU! I'M NOT THAT GOOD—REALLY!
CLAP
CLAP
IT'S THE BLACK CANARY! THAT'S WHO THEY'RE APPLAUDING! UH-OH! DINAH'LL REALLY BE SORE! SHE PROBABLY WON'T EVEN STAY!
WHAT ARE YOU DOING HERE, BLACK CANARY? YOU ONLY SHOW UP WHEN SOME CRIME HAS BEEN COMMITTED!
—FROM DINAH'S GLARE AS SHE LEFT, THERE MIGHT BE, WITH YOU AS THE VICTIM!

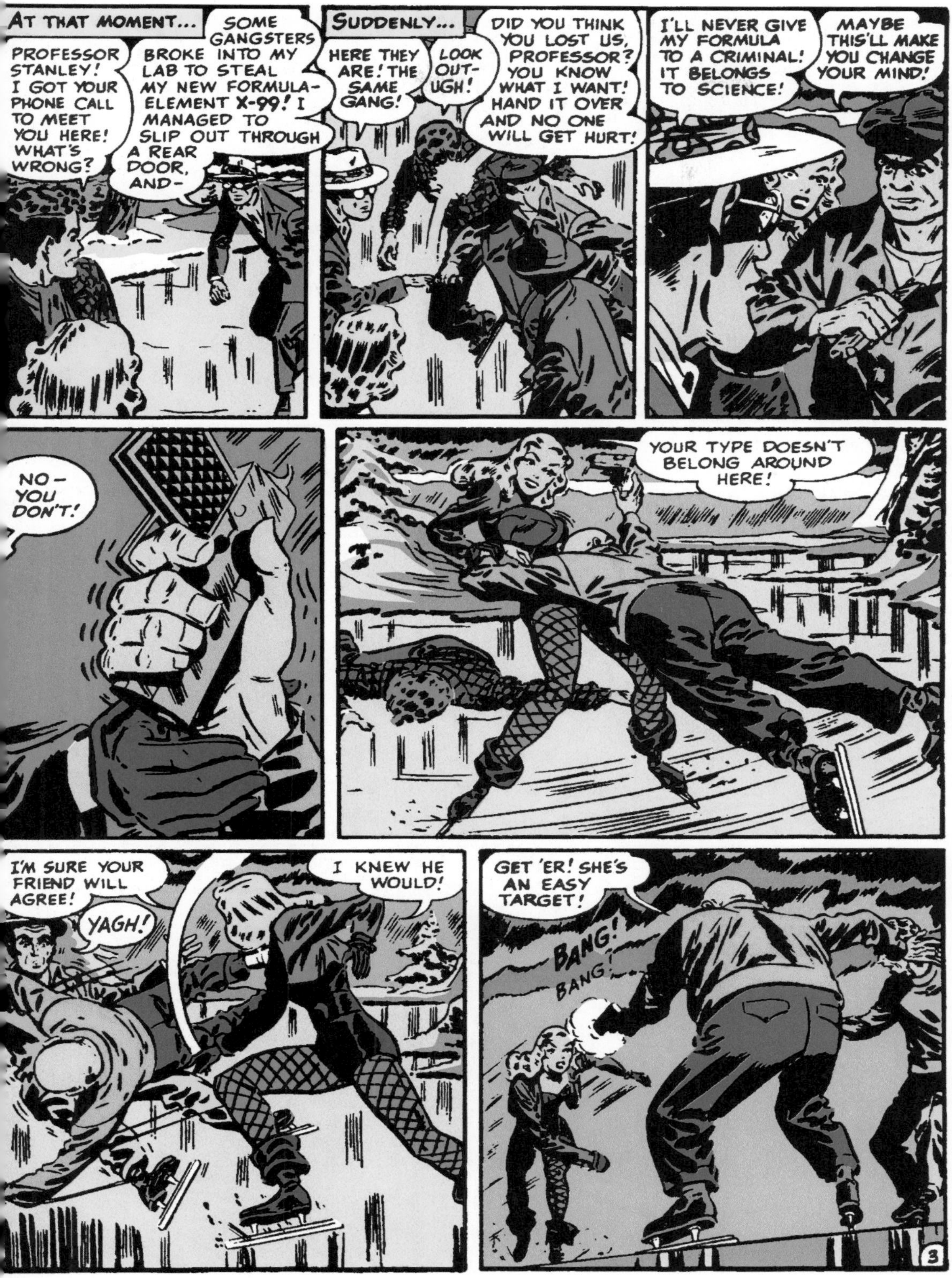
AT THAT MOMENT...
PROFESSOR STANLEY! I GOT YOUR PHONE CALL TO MEET YOU HERE! WHAT'S WRONG?
SOME GANGSTERS BROKE INTO MY LAB TO STEAL MY NEW FORMULA-ELEMENT X-99! I MANAGED TO SLIP OUT THROUGH A REAR DOOR, AND-
SUDDENLY...
HERE THEY ARE! THE SAME GANG!
LOOK OUT- UGH!
DID YOU THINK YOU LOST US, PROFESSOR? YOU KNOW WHAT I WANT! HAND IT OVER AND NO ONE WILL GET HURT!
I'LL NEVER GIVE MY FORMULA TO A CRIMINAL! IT BELONGS TO SCIENCE!
MAYBE THIS'LL MAKE YOU CHANGE YOUR MIND!
NO - YOU DON'T!
YOUR TYPE DOESN'T BELONG AROUND HERE!
I'M SURE YOUR FRIEND WILL AGREE!
YAGH!
I KNEW HE WOULD!
GET 'ER! SHE'S AN EASY TARGET!
BANG!
BANG!
3

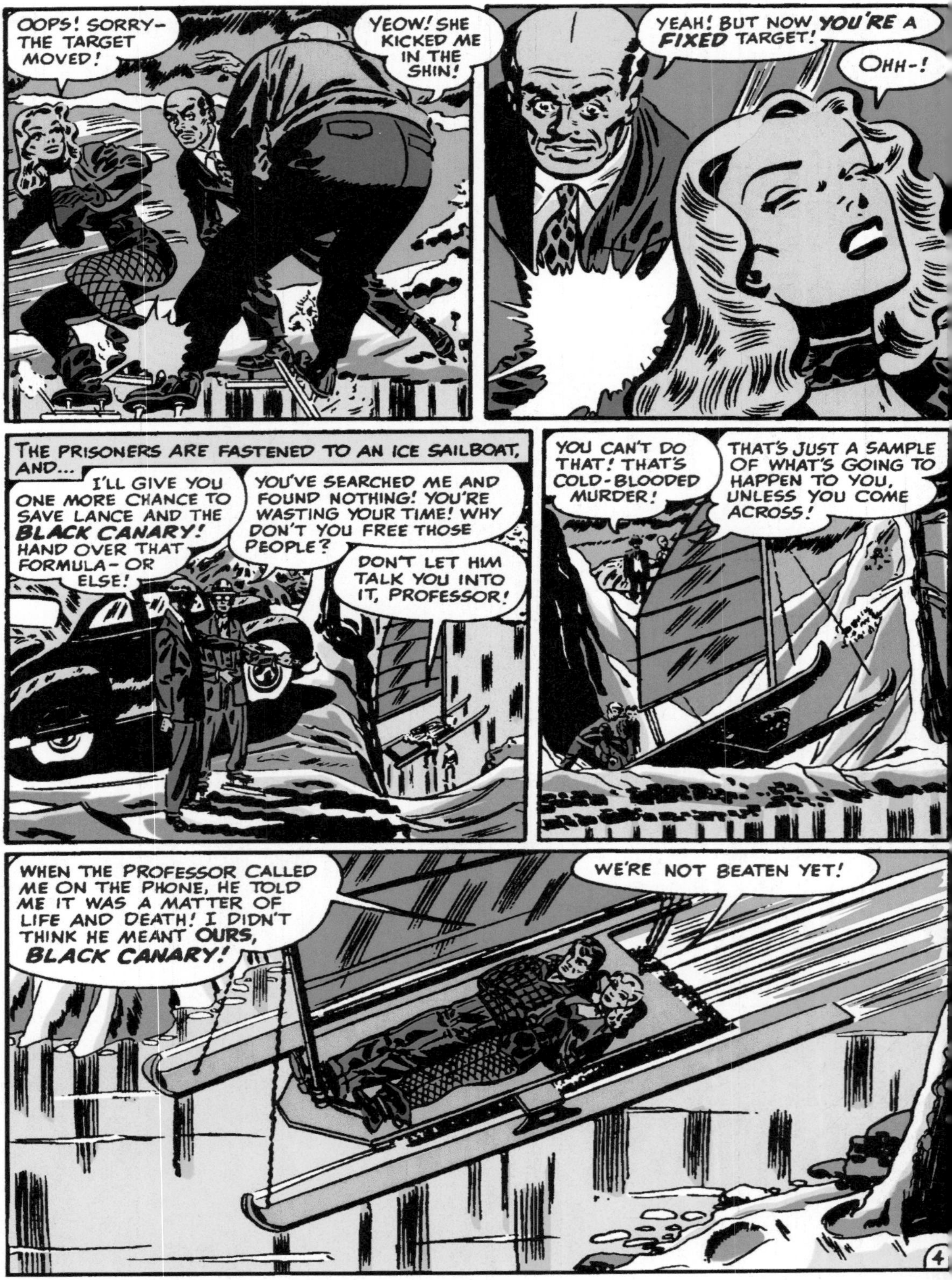
OOPS! SORRY- THE TARGET MOVED!
YEOW! SHE KICKED ME IN THE SHIN!
YEAH! BUT NOW YOU'RE A FIXED TARGET!
OHH-!
THE PRISONERS ARE FASTENED TO AN ICE SAILBOAT, AND...
I'LL GIVE YOU ONE MORE CHANCE TO SAVE LANCE AND THE BLACK CANARY! HAND OVER THAT FORMULA- OR ELSE!
YOU'VE SEARCHED ME AND FOUND NOTHING! YOU'RE WASTING YOUR TIME! WHY DON'T YOU FREE THOSE PEOPLE?
DON'T LET HIM TALK YOU INTO IT, PROFESSOR!
YOU CAN'T DO THAT! THAT'S COLD-BLOODED MURDER!
THAT'S JUST A SAMPLE OF WHAT'S GOING TO HAPPEN TO YOU, UNLESS YOU COME ACROSS!
WHEN THE PROFESSOR CALLED ME ON THE PHONE, HE TOLD ME IT WAS A MATTER OF LIFE AND DEATH! I DIDN'T THINK HE MEANT OURS, BLACK CANARY!
WE'RE NOT BEATEN YET!
4

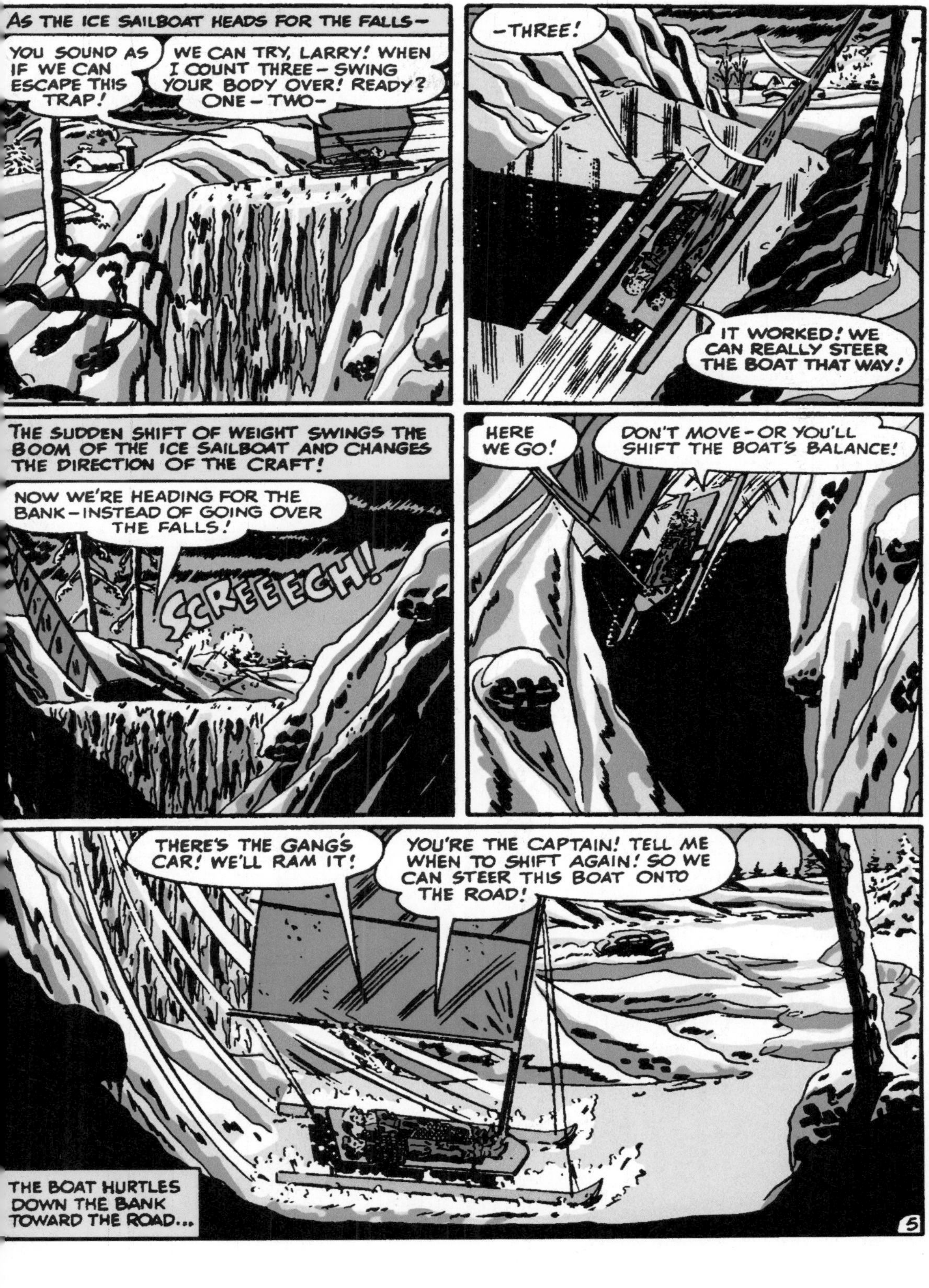
AS THE ICE SAILBOAT HEADS FOR THE FALLS—
YOU SOUND AS IF WE CAN ESCAPE THIS TRAP!
WE CAN TRY, LARRY! WHEN I COUNT THREE—SWING YOUR BODY OVER! READY? ONE—TWO—
—THREE!
IT WORKED! WE CAN REALLY STEER THE BOAT THAT WAY!
THE SUDDEN SHIFT OF WEIGHT SWINGS THE BOOM OF THE ICE SAILBOAT AND CHANGES THE DIRECTION OF THE CRAFT!
NOW WE'RE HEADING FOR THE BANK—INSTEAD OF GOING OVER THE FALLS!
SCREEECH!!
HERE WE GO!
DON'T MOVE—OR YOU'LL SHIFT THE BOAT'S BALANCE!
THERE'S THE GANG'S CAR! WE'LL RAM IT!
YOU'RE THE CAPTAIN! TELL ME WHEN TO SHIFT AGAIN! SO WE CAN STEER THIS BOAT ONTO THE ROAD!
THE BOAT HURTLES DOWN THE BANK TOWARD THE ROAD...
5

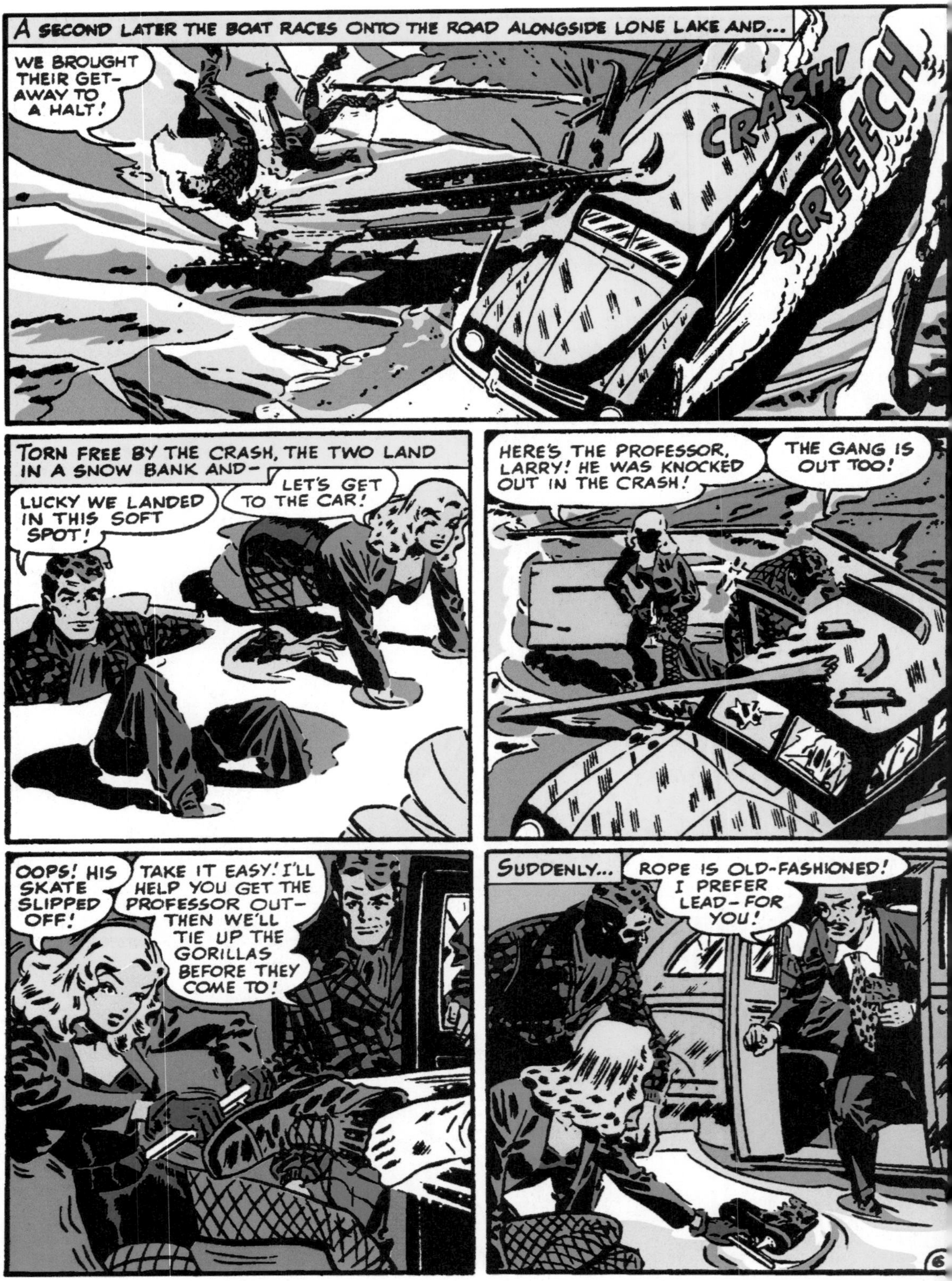
A SECOND LATER THE BOAT RACES ONTO THE ROAD ALONGSIDE LONE LAKE AND...
WE BROUGHT THEIR GET-AWAY TO A HALT!
CRASH!
SCREEECH
TORN FREE BY THE CRASH, THE TWO LAND IN A SNOW BANK AND—
LUCKY WE LANDED IN THIS SOFT SPOT!
LET'S GET TO THE CAR!
HERE'S THE PROFESSOR, LARRY! HE WAS KNOCKED OUT IN THE CRASH!
THE GANG IS OUT TOO!
OOPS! HIS SKATE SLIPPED OFF!
TAKE IT EASY! I'LL HELP YOU GET THE PROFESSOR OUT—THEN WE'LL TIE UP THE GORILLAS BEFORE THEY COME TO!
SUDDENLY...
ROPE IS OLD-FASHIONED! I PREFER LEAD—FOR YOU!
6

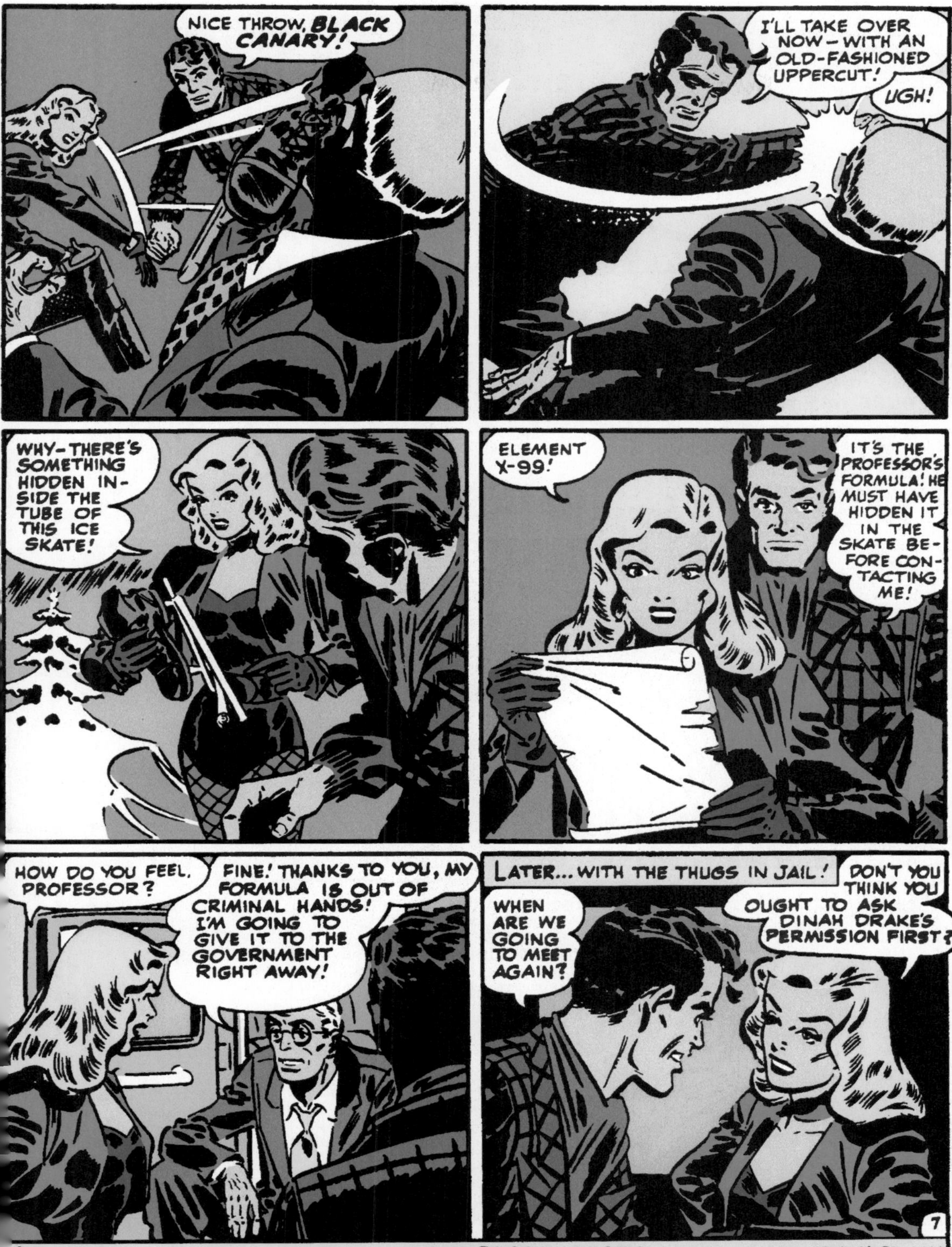

NICE THROW, BLACK CANARY!
I'LL TAKE OVER NOW—WITH AN OLD-FASHIONED UPPERCUT!
UGH!
WHY—THERE'S SOMETHING HIDDEN INSIDE THE TUBE OF THIS ICE SKATE!
ELEMENT X-99!
IT'S THE PROFESSOR'S FORMULA! HE MUST HAVE HIDDEN IT IN THE SKATE BEFORE CONTACTING ME!
HOW DO YOU FEEL, PROFESSOR?
FINE! THANKS TO YOU, MY FORMULA IS OUT OF CRIMINAL HANDS! I'M GOING TO GIVE IT TO THE GOVERNMENT RIGHT AWAY!
LATER... WITH THE THUGS IN JAIL!
WHEN ARE WE GOING TO MEET AGAIN?
DON'T YOU THINK YOU OUGHT TO ASK DINAH DRAKE'S PERMISSION FIRST?
7
ANOTHER EXCITING CRIME-ADVENTURE WITH THE BLACK CANARY IN EVERY ISSUE OF FLASH COMICS.

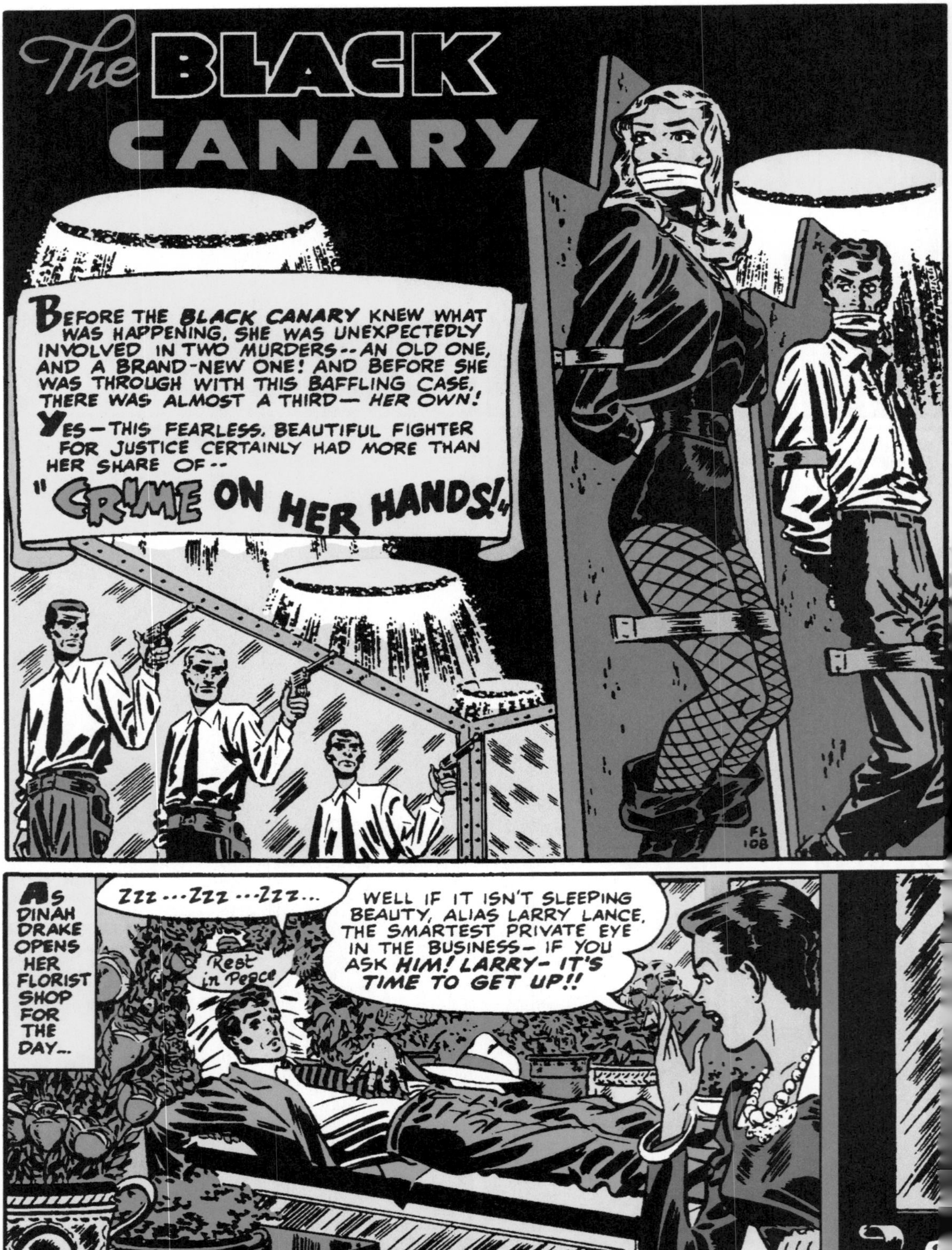

The BLACK CANARY
BEFORE THE BLACK CANARY KNEW WHAT WAS HAPPENING, SHE WAS UNEXPECTEDLY INVOLVED IN TWO MURDERS--AN OLD ONE, AND A BRAND-NEW ONE! AND BEFORE SHE WAS THROUGH WITH THIS BAFFLING CASE, THERE WAS ALMOST A THIRD— HER OWN! YES—THIS FEARLESS, BEAUTIFUL FIGHTER FOR JUSTICE CERTAINLY HAD MORE THAN HER SHARE OF--
"CRIME ON HER HANDS!"
AS DINAH DRAKE OPENS HER FLORIST SHOP FOR THE DAY...
ZZZ...ZZZ...ZZZ...
Rest in Peace
WELL IF IT ISN'T SLEEPING BEAUTY, ALIAS LARRY LANCE, THE SMARTEST PRIVATE EYE IN THE BUSINESS— IF YOU ASK HIM! LARRY— IT'S TIME TO GET UP!!

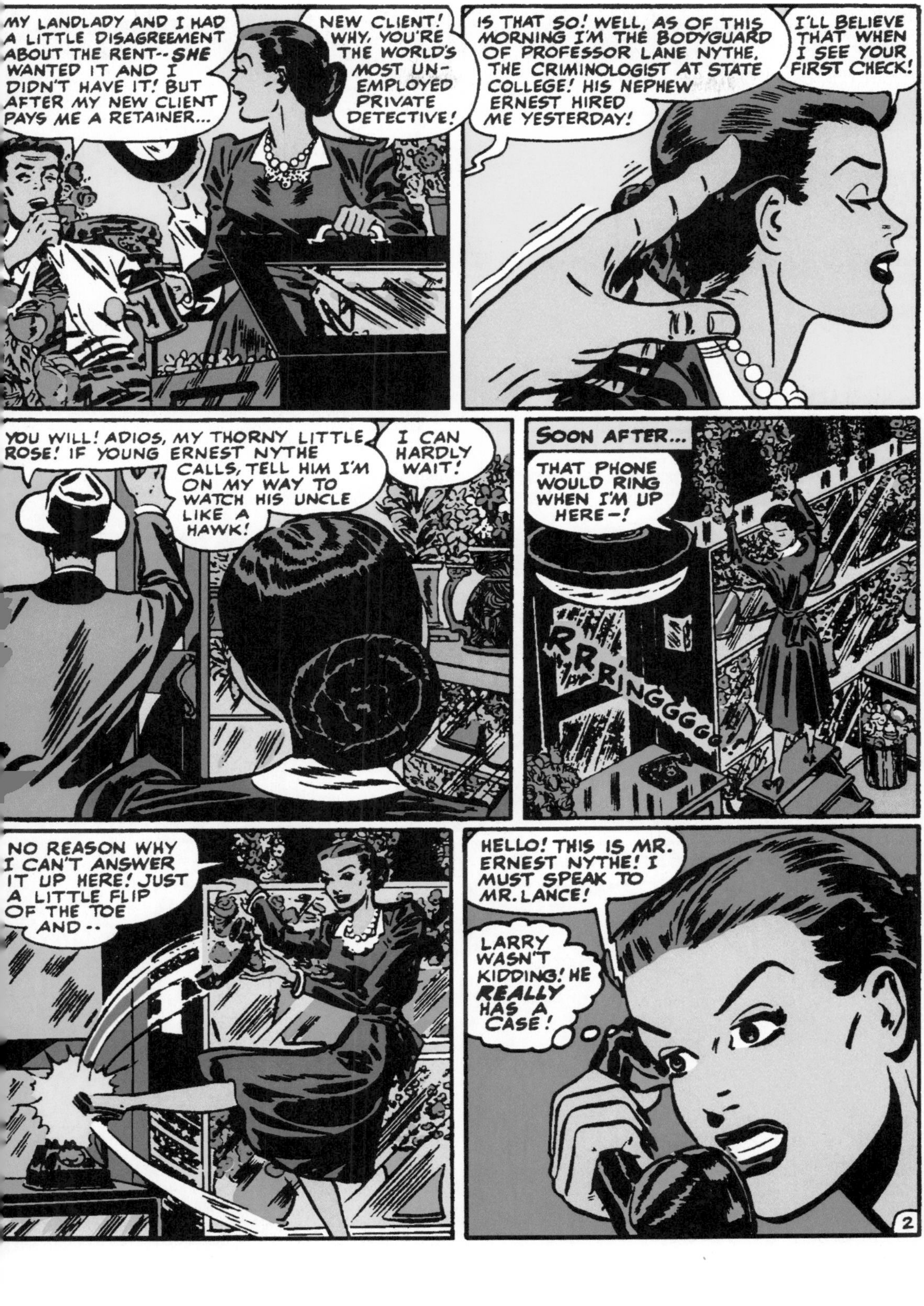
MY LANDLADY AND I HAD A LITTLE DISAGREEMENT ABOUT THE RENT--SHE WANTED IT AND I DIDN'T HAVE IT! BUT AFTER MY NEW CLIENT PAYS ME A RETAINER...
NEW CLIENT! WHY, YOU'RE THE WORLD'S MOST UN-EMPLOYED PRIVATE DETECTIVE!
IS THAT SO! WELL, AS OF THIS MORNING I'M THE BODYGUARD OF PROFESSOR LANE NYTHE, THE CRIMINOLOGIST AT STATE COLLEGE! HIS NEPHEW ERNEST HIRED ME YESTERDAY!
I'LL BELIEVE THAT WHEN I SEE YOUR FIRST CHECK!
YOU WILL! ADIOS, MY THORNY LITTLE ROSE! IF YOUNG ERNEST NYTHE CALLS, TELL HIM I'M ON MY WAY TO WATCH HIS UNCLE LIKE A HAWK!
I CAN HARDLY WAIT!
SOON AFTER...
THAT PHONE WOULD RING WHEN I'M UP HERE-!
RRRINGGGGG
NO REASON WHY I CAN'T ANSWER IT UP HERE! JUST A LITTLE FLIP OF THE TOE AND--
HELLO! THIS IS MR. ERNEST NYTHE! I MUST SPEAK TO MR. LANCE!
LARRY WASN'T KIDDING! HE REALLY HAS A CASE!
2

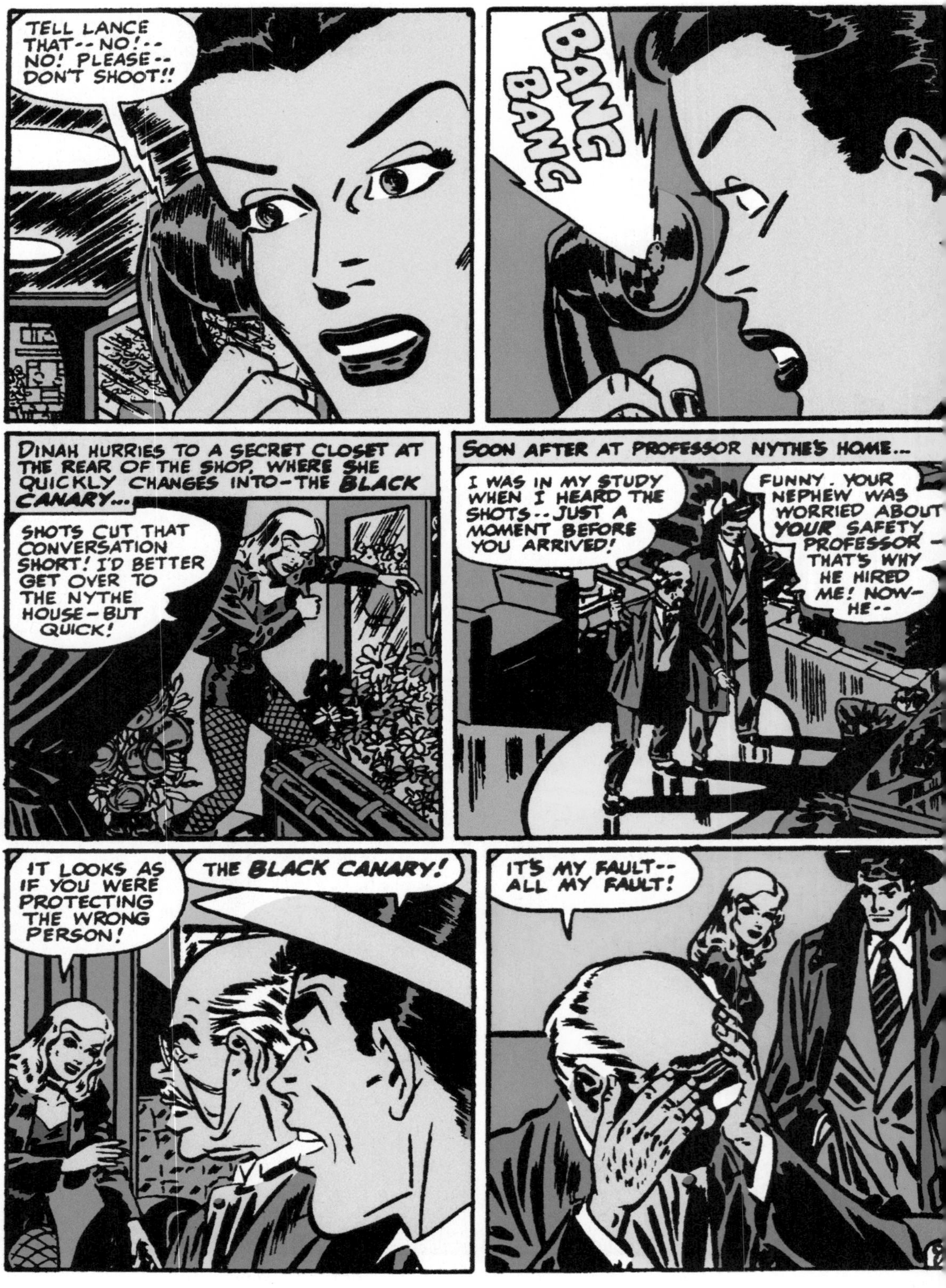
TELL LANCE THAT--NO!-- NO! PLEASE-- DON'T SHOOT!!
BANG BANG
DINAH HURRIES TO A SECRET CLOSET AT THE REAR OF THE SHOP, WHERE SHE QUICKLY CHANGES INTO-THE BLACK CANARY...
SHOTS CUT THAT CONVERSATION SHORT! I'D BETTER GET OVER TO THE NYTHE HOUSE-BUT QUICK!
SOON AFTER AT PROFESSOR NYTHE'S HOME...
I WAS IN MY STUDY WHEN I HEARD THE SHOTS--JUST A MOMENT BEFORE YOU ARRIVED!
FUNNY. YOUR NEPHEW WAS WORRIED ABOUT YOUR SAFETY PROFESSOR-THAT'S WHY HE HIRED ME! NOW-HE--
IT LOOKS AS IF YOU WERE PROTECTING THE WRONG PERSON!
THE BLACK CANARY!
IT'S MY FAULT-- ALL MY FAULT!

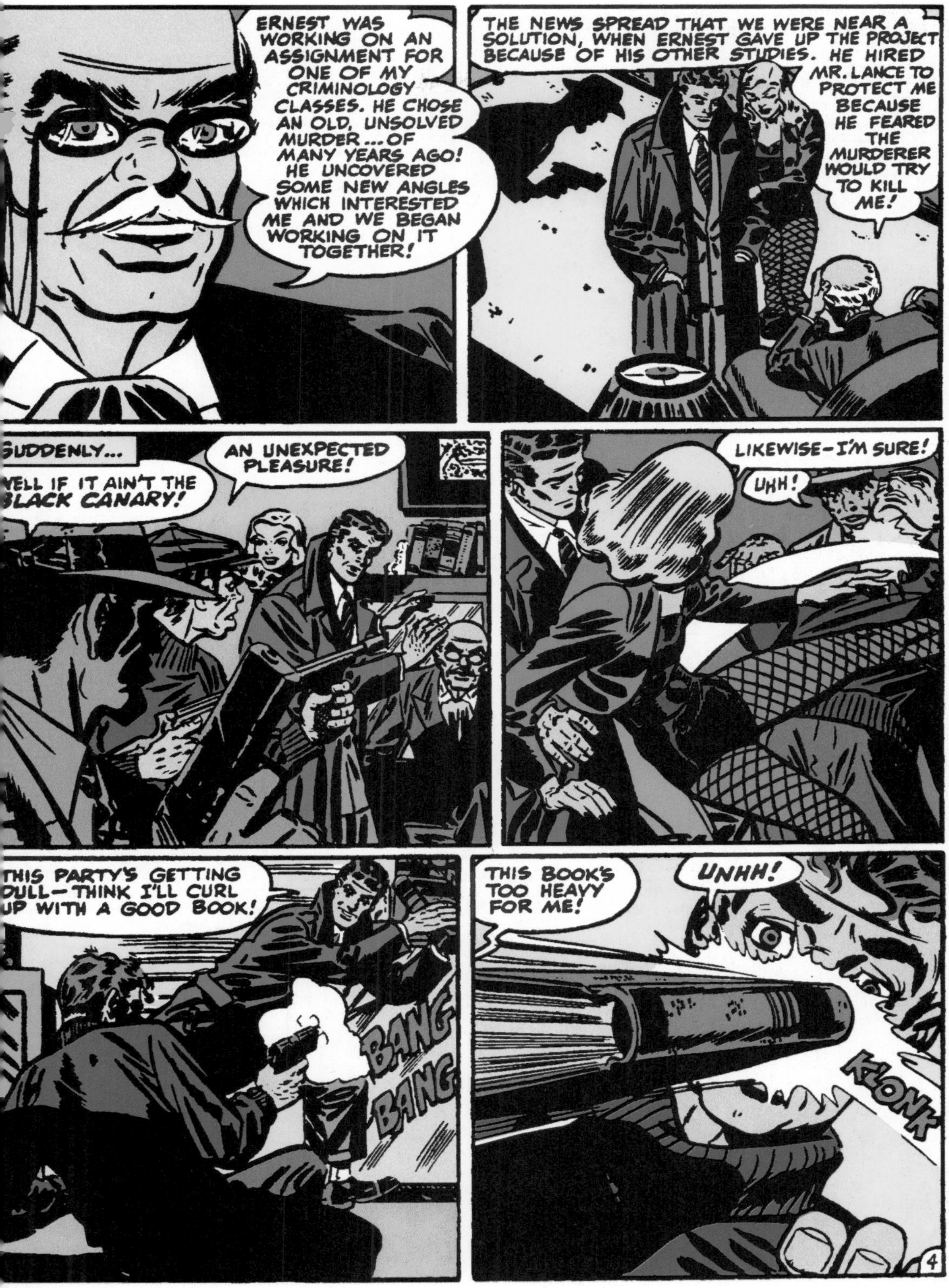
ERNEST WAS WORKING ON AN ASSIGNMENT FOR ONE OF MY CRIMINOLOGY CLASSES. HE CHOSE AN OLD, UNSOLVED MURDER ... OF MANY YEARS AGO! HE UNCOVERED SOME NEW ANGLES WHICH INTERESTED ME AND WE BEGAN WORKING ON IT TOGETHER!
THE NEWS SPREAD THAT WE WERE NEAR A SOLUTION, WHEN ERNEST GAVE UP THE PROJECT BECAUSE OF HIS OTHER STUDIES. HE HIRED MR. LANCE TO PROTECT ME BECAUSE HE FEARED THE MURDERER WOULD TRY TO KILL ME!
SUDDENLY...
WELL IF IT AIN'T THE BLACK CANARY!
AN UNEXPECTED PLEASURE!
LIKEWISE—I'M SURE!
UHH!
THIS PARTY'S GETTING DULL—THINK I'LL CURL UP WITH A GOOD BOOK!
BANG
BANG
THIS BOOK'S TOO HEAVY FOR ME!
UNHH!
K'LONK
4

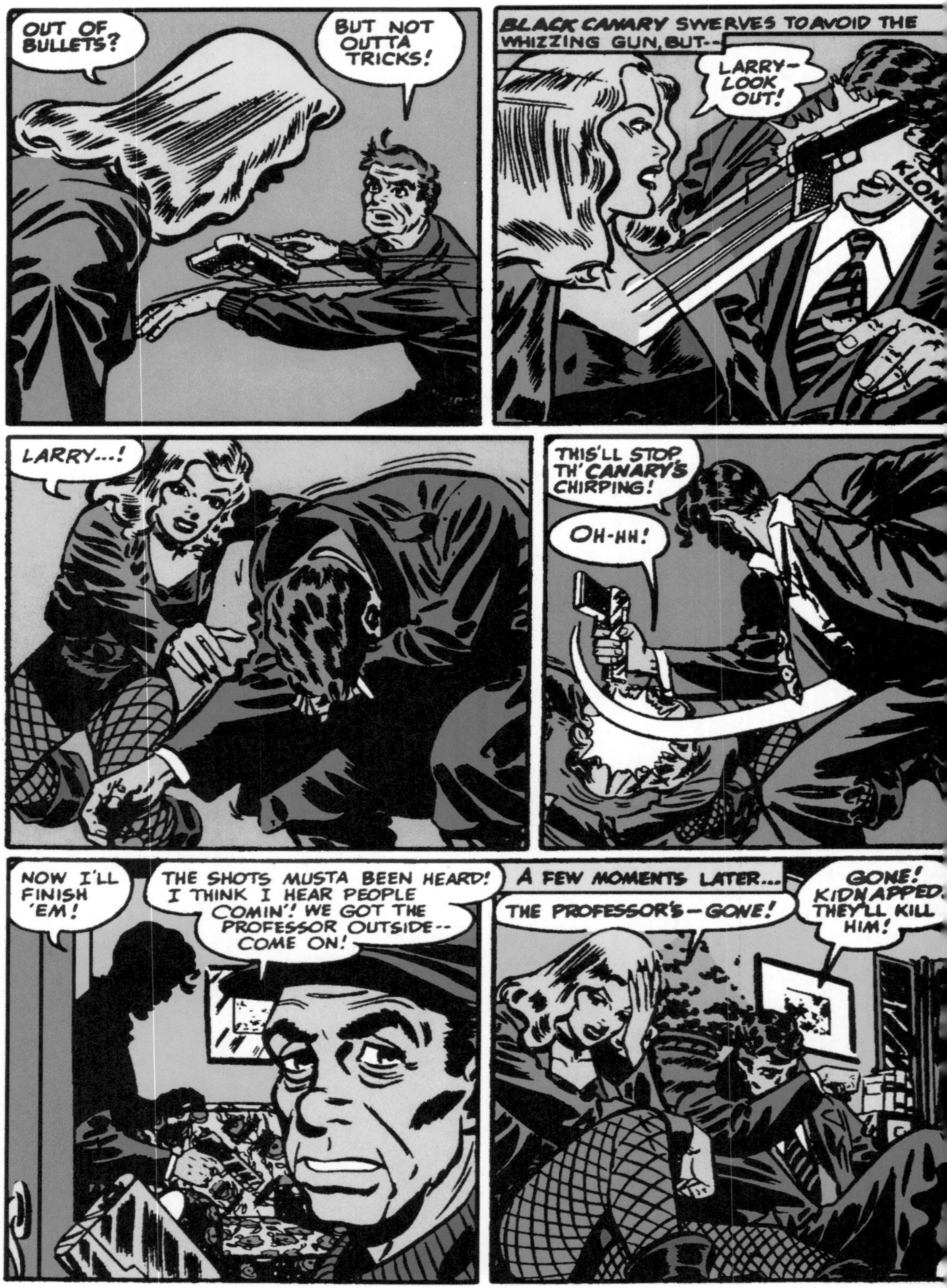
OUT OF BULLETS?
BUT NOT OUTTA TRICKS!
BLACK CANARY SWERVES TO AVOID THE WHIZZING GUN, BUT--
LARRY-LOOK OUT!
KLONK
LARRY...!
THIS'LL STOP TH' CANARY'S CHIRPING!
OH-HH!
NOW I'LL FINISH 'EM!
THE SHOTS MUSTA BEEN HEARD! I THINK I HEAR PEOPLE COMIN'! WE GOT THE PROFESSOR OUTSIDE--COME ON!
A FEW MOMENTS LATER...
THE PROFESSOR'S--GONE!
GONE! KIDNAPPED. THEY'LL KILL HIM!

WE HAVEN'T A SINGLE LEAD...

LARRY! COME HERE-- LOOK AT THIS!

FOOTPRINTS MADE BY THE THUGS!

IT HAS A CHALKY, ROUGH TEXTURE!

...AND IT BURNS! IT MUST BE LIME! THERE'S ONLY ONE LIME-KILN IN THIS TOWN! IT'S CLOSED DOWN! THE THUGS MUST BE USING IT AS A HIDEOUT!

THAT'S OUR NEXT STOP!

SOON AFTER...

LOOK! SMOKE COMING FROM THE LIME-KILN! THERE'S SOMEONE THERE ALL RIGHT!

I HOPE WE'RE NOT TOO LATE!

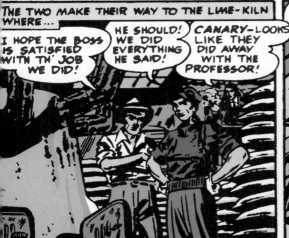

THE TWO MAKE THEIR WAY TO THE LIME-KILN WHERE...

I HOPE THE BOSS IS SATISFIED WITH TH' JOB WE DID!

HE SHOULD! WE DID EVERYTHING HE SAID!

CANARY-LOOKS LIKE THEY DID AWAY WITH THE PROFESSOR!

LOOK-BLACK CANARY AND LANCE! THEY MUST'VE TRAILED US!

MAKE THIS A DEAD END FOR 'EM!

BANG BANG

6

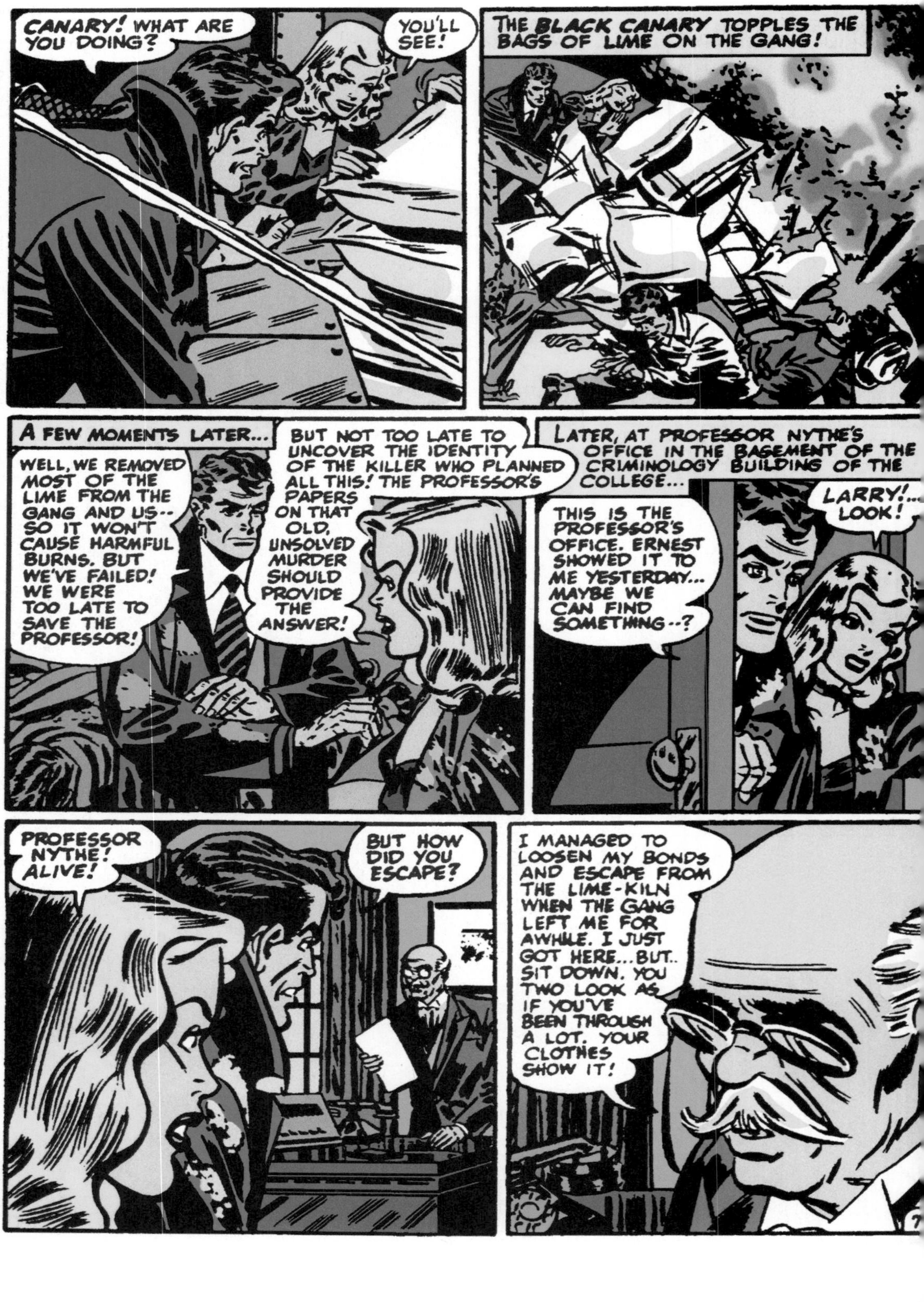
CANARY! WHAT ARE YOU DOING?
YOU'LL SEE!
THE BLACK CANARY TOPPLES THE BAGS OF LIME ON THE GANG!
A FEW MOMENTS LATER...
WELL, WE REMOVED MOST OF THE LIME FROM THE GANG AND US-- SO IT WON'T CAUSE HARMFUL BURNS. BUT WE'VE FAILED! WE WERE TOO LATE TO SAVE THE PROFESSOR!
BUT NOT TOO LATE TO UNCOVER THE IDENTITY OF THE KILLER WHO PLANNED ALL THIS! THE PROFESSOR'S PAPERS ON THAT OLD, UNSOLVED MURDER SHOULD PROVIDE THE ANSWER!
LATER, AT PROFESSOR NYTHE'S OFFICE IN THE BASEMENT OF THE CRIMINOLOGY BUILDING OF THE COLLEGE...
THIS IS THE PROFESSOR'S OFFICE. ERNEST SHOWED IT TO ME YESTERDAY... MAYBE WE CAN FIND SOMETHING--?
LARRY!... LOOK!
PROFESSOR NYTHE! ALIVE!
BUT HOW DID YOU ESCAPE?
I MANAGED TO LOOSEN MY BONDS AND ESCAPE FROM THE LIME-KILN WHEN THE GANG LEFT ME FOR AWHILE. I JUST GOT HERE...BUT.. SIT DOWN. YOU TWO LOOK AS IF YOU'VE BEEN THROUGH A LOT. YOUR CLOTHES SHOW IT!

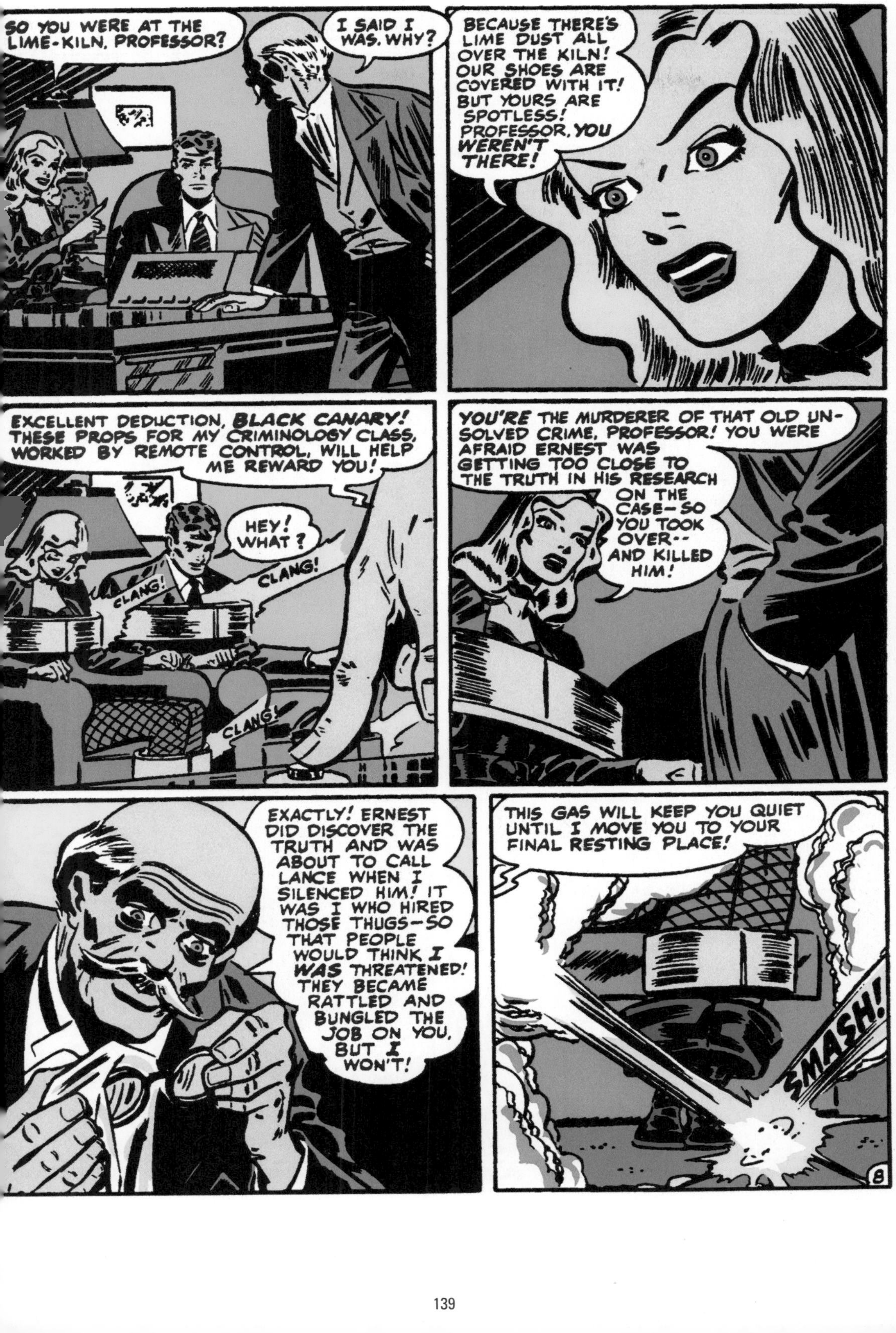

SO YOU WERE AT THE LIME-KILN, PROFESSOR?
I SAID I WAS. WHY?
BECAUSE THERE'S LIME DUST ALL OVER THE KILN! OUR SHOES ARE COVERED WITH IT! BUT YOURS ARE SPOTLESS! PROFESSOR, YOU WEREN'T THERE!
EXCELLENT DEDUCTION, BLACK CANARY! THESE PROPS FOR MY CRIMINOLOGY CLASS, WORKED BY REMOTE CONTROL, WILL HELP ME REWARD YOU!
HEY! WHAT?
CLANG!
CLANG!
CLANG!
YOU'RE THE MURDERER OF THAT OLD UNSOLVED CRIME, PROFESSOR! YOU WERE AFRAID ERNEST WAS GETTING TOO CLOSE TO THE TRUTH IN HIS RESEARCH ON THE CASE--SO YOU TOOK OVER-- AND KILLED HIM!
EXACTLY! ERNEST DID DISCOVER THE TRUTH AND WAS ABOUT TO CALL LANCE WHEN I SILENCED HIM! IT WAS I WHO HIRED THOSE THUGS--SO THAT PEOPLE WOULD THINK I WAS THREATENED! THEY BECAME RATTLED AND BUNGLED THE JOB ON YOU, BUT I WON'T!
THIS GAS WILL KEEP YOU QUIET UNTIL I MOVE YOU TO YOUR FINAL RESTING PLACE!
SMASH!
8

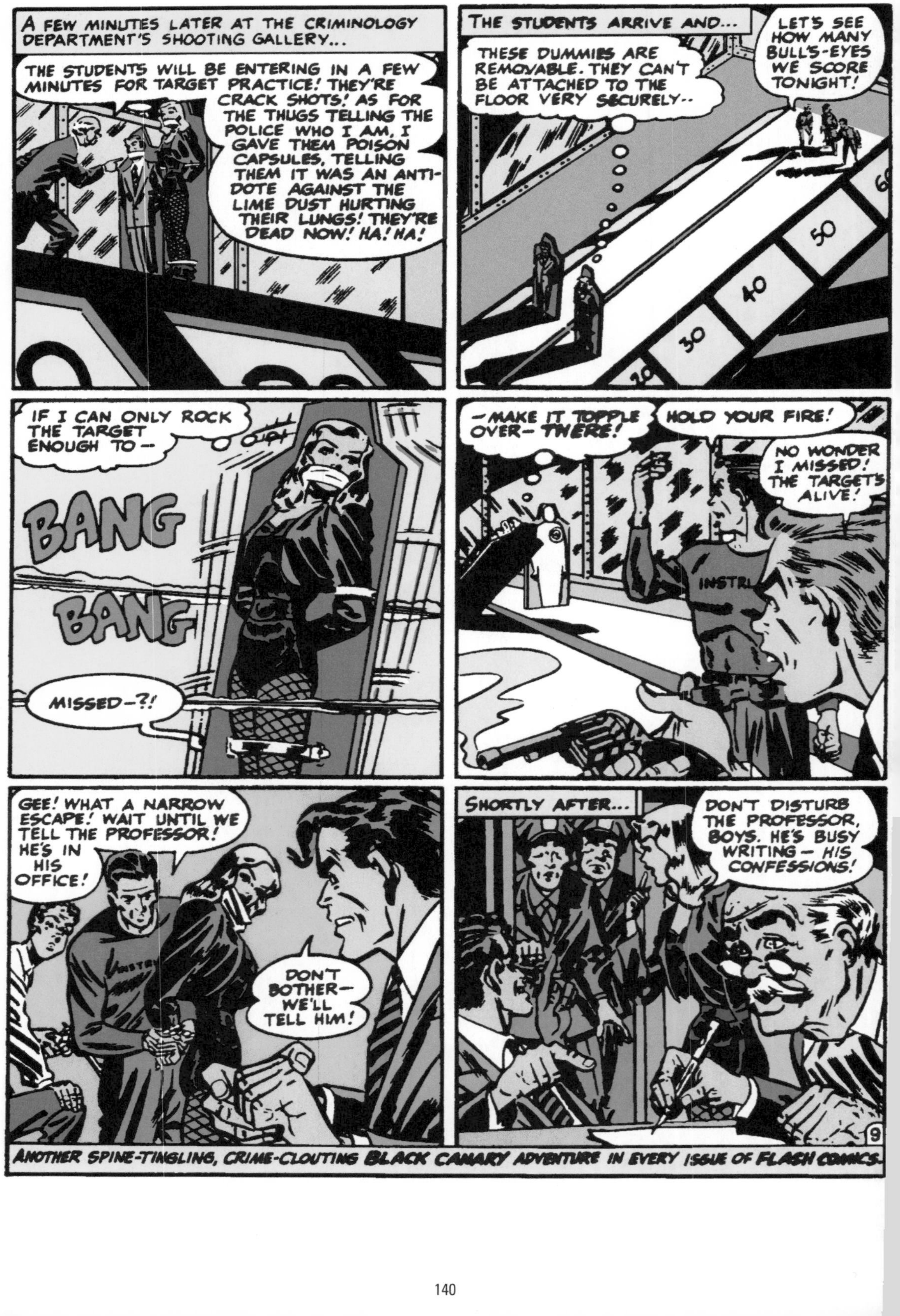
A FEW MINUTES LATER AT THE CRIMINOLOGY DEPARTMENT'S SHOOTING GALLERY...
THE STUDENTS WILL BE ENTERING IN A FEW MINUTES FOR TARGET PRACTICE! THEY'RE CRACK SHOTS! AS FOR THE THUGS TELLING THE POLICE WHO I AM, I GAVE THEM POISON CAPSULES, TELLING THEM IT WAS AN ANTIDOTE AGAINST THE LIME DUST HURTING THEIR LUNGS! THEY'RE DEAD NOW! HA! HA!
THE STUDENTS ARRIVE AND...
THESE DUMMIES ARE REMOVABLE. THEY CAN'T BE ATTACHED TO THE FLOOR VERY SECURELY..
LET'S SEE HOW MANY BULL'S-EYES WE SCORE TONIGHT!
30
40
50
IF I CAN ONLY ROCK THE TARGET ENOUGH TO --
BANG
BANG
MISSED--?!
--MAKE IT TOPPLE OVER-- THERE!
HOLD YOUR FIRE!
NO WONDER I MISSED! THE TARGET'S ALIVE!
GEE! WHAT A NARROW ESCAPE! WAIT UNTIL WE TELL THE PROFESSOR! HE'S IN HIS OFFICE!
DON'T BOTHER-- WE'LL TELL HIM!
SHORTLY AFTER...
DON'T DISTURB THE PROFESSOR, BOYS. HE'S BUSY WRITING -- HIS CONFESSIONS!
9
ANOTHER SPINE-TINGLING, CRIME-CLOUTING BLACK CANARY ADVENTURE IN EVERY ISSUE OF FLASH COMICS.

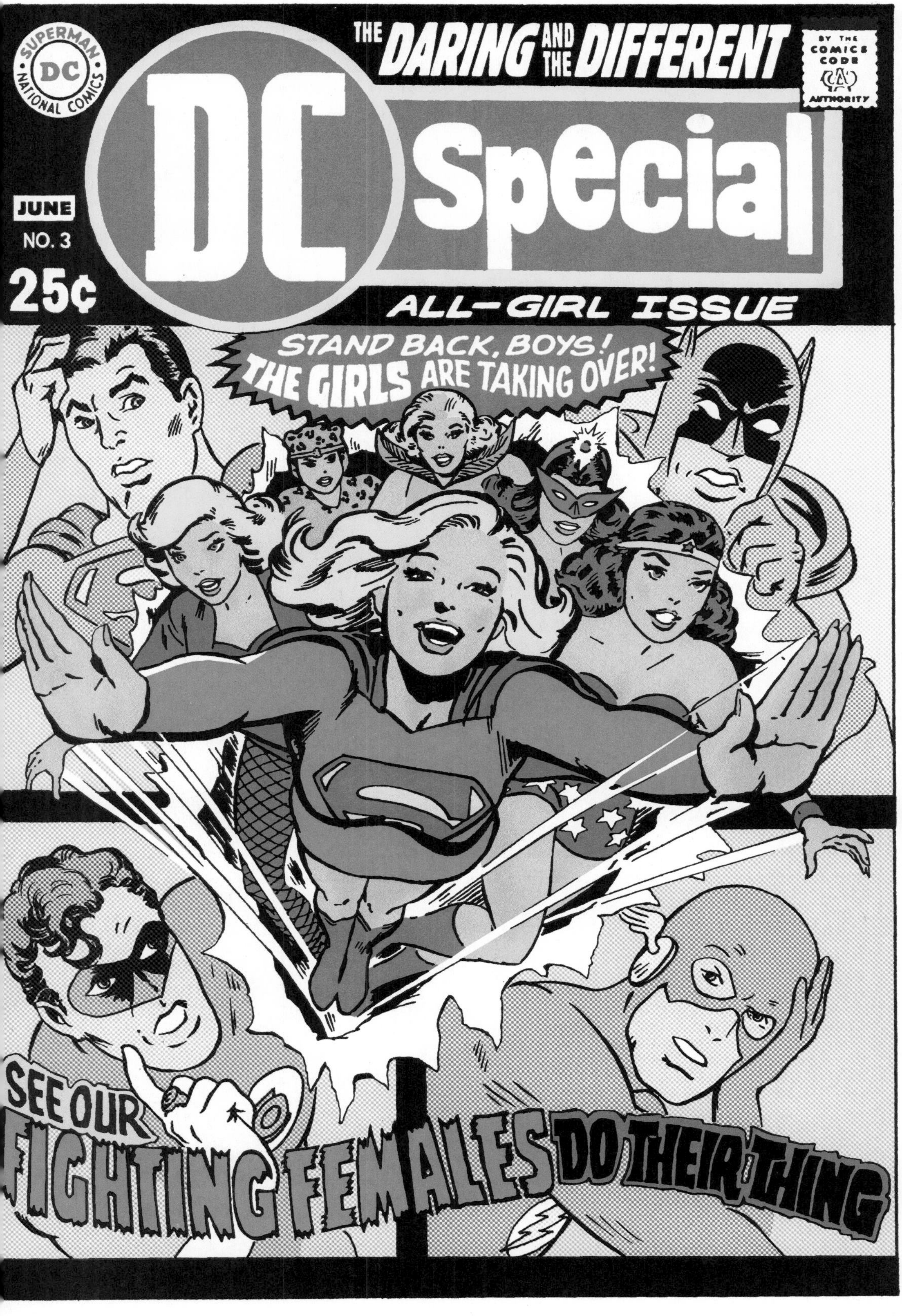
SUPERMAN DC NATIONAL COMICS
THE DARING AND THE DIFFERENT
BY THE COMICS CODE AUTHORITY
DC Special
JUNE
NO. 3
25¢
ALL-GIRL ISSUE
STAND BACK, BOYS! THE GIRLS ARE TAKING OVER!
SEE OUR FIGHTING FEMALES DO THEIR THING

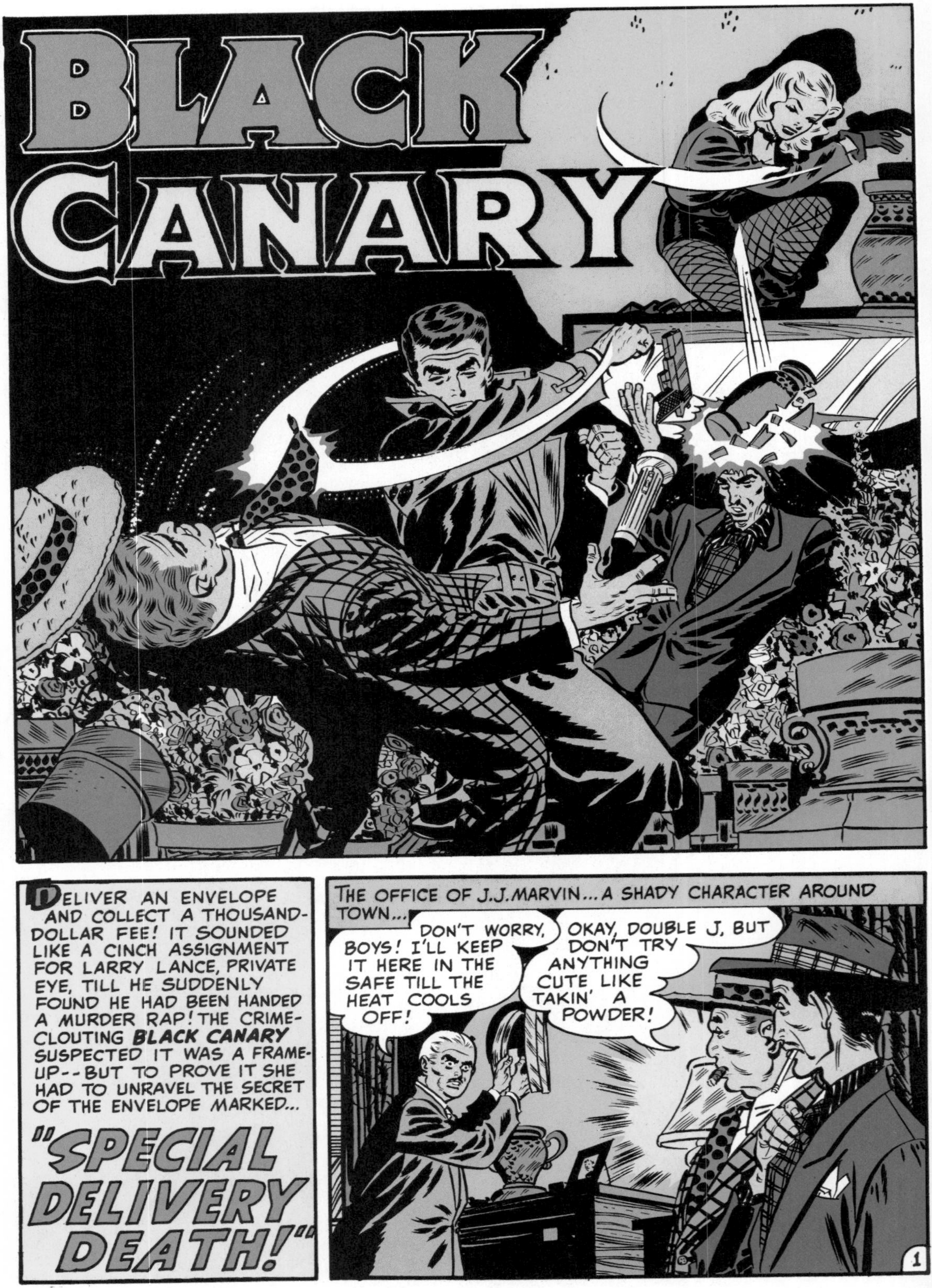
BLACK CANARY
DELIVER AN ENVELOPE AND COLLECT A THOUSAND-DOLLAR FEE! IT SOUNDED LIKE A CINCH ASSIGNMENT FOR LARRY LANCE, PRIVATE EYE, TILL HE SUDDENLY FOUND HE HAD BEEN HANDED A MURDER RAP! THE CRIME-CLOUTING BLACK CANARY SUSPECTED IT WAS A FRAME-UP--BUT TO PROVE IT SHE HAD TO UNRAVEL THE SECRET OF THE ENVELOPE MARKED...
"SPECIAL DELIVERY DEATH!"
THE OFFICE OF J.J. MARVIN... A SHADY CHARACTER AROUND TOWN...
DON'T WORRY, BOYS! I'LL KEEP IT HERE IN THE SAFE TILL THE HEAT COOLS OFF!
OKAY, DOUBLE J, BUT DON'T TRY ANYTHING CUTE LIKE TAKIN' A POWDER!
1

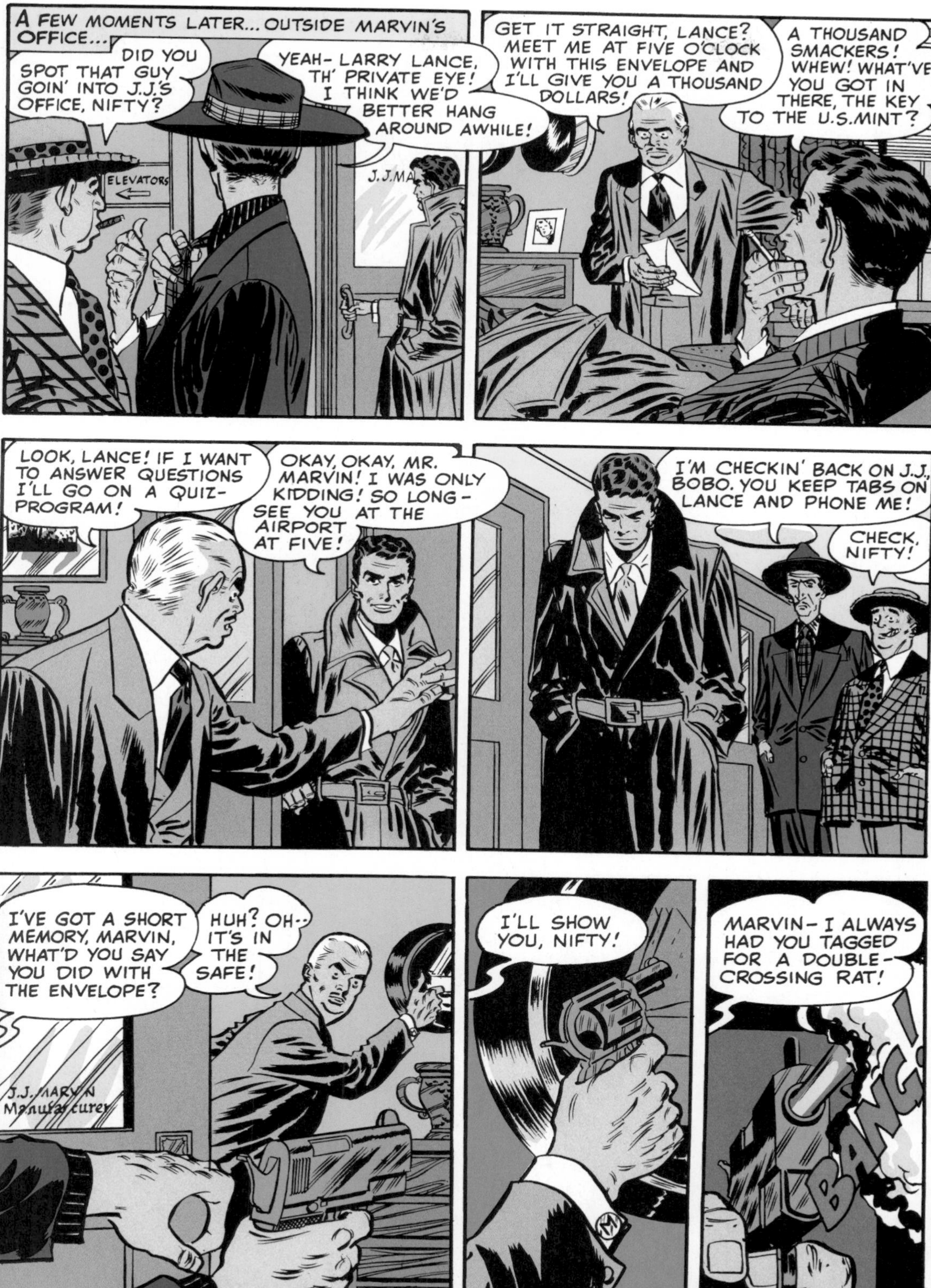
A FEW MOMENTS LATER... OUTSIDE MARVIN'S OFFICE...
DID YOU SPOT THAT GUY GOIN' INTO J.J.'S OFFICE, NIFTY?
YEAH- LARRY LANCE, TH' PRIVATE EYE! I THINK WE'D BETTER HANG AROUND AWHILE!
ELEVATORS
J.J.MA
GET IT STRAIGHT, LANCE? MEET ME AT FIVE O'CLOCK WITH THIS ENVELOPE AND I'LL GIVE YOU A THOUSAND DOLLARS!
A THOUSAND SMACKERS! WHEW! WHAT'VE YOU GOT IN THERE, THE KEY TO THE U.S.MINT?
LOOK, LANCE! IF I WANT TO ANSWER QUESTIONS I'LL GO ON A QUIZ-PROGRAM!
OKAY, OKAY, MR. MARVIN! I WAS ONLY KIDDING! SO LONG- SEE YOU AT THE AIRPORT AT FIVE!
I'M CHECKIN' BACK ON J.J., BOBO. YOU KEEP TABS ON LANCE AND PHONE ME!
CHECK, NIFTY!
I'VE GOT A SHORT MEMORY, MARVIN, WHAT'D YOU SAY YOU DID WITH THE ENVELOPE?
HUH? OH-- IT'S IN THE SAFE!
J.J. MARVIN Manufacturer
I'LL SHOW YOU, NIFTY!
MARVIN- I ALWAYS HAD YOU TAGGED FOR A DOUBLE-CROSSING RAT!
BANG!
2

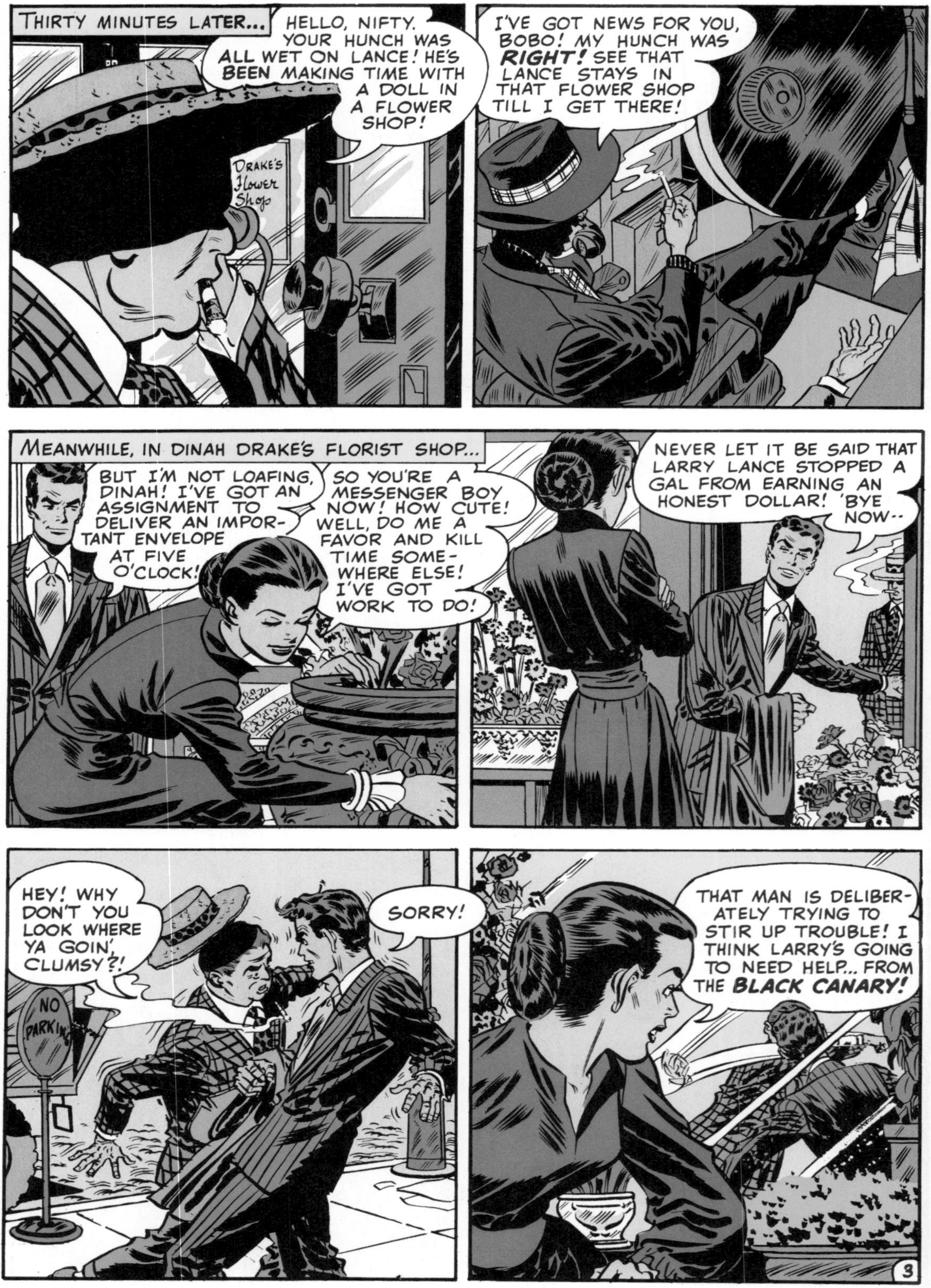

THIRTY MINUTES LATER...
HELLO, NIFTY. YOUR HUNCH WAS ALL WET ON LANCE! HE'S BEEN MAKING TIME WITH A DOLL IN A FLOWER SHOP!
DRAKE'S Flower Shop
I'VE GOT NEWS FOR YOU, BOBO! MY HUNCH WAS RIGHT! SEE THAT LANCE STAYS IN THAT FLOWER SHOP TILL I GET THERE!
MEANWHILE, IN DINAH DRAKE'S FLORIST SHOP...
BUT I'M NOT LOAFING, DINAH! I'VE GOT AN ASSIGNMENT TO DELIVER AN IMPORTANT ENVELOPE AT FIVE O'CLOCK!
SO YOU'RE A MESSENGER BOY NOW! HOW CUTE! WELL, DO ME A FAVOR AND KILL TIME SOMEWHERE ELSE! I'VE GOT WORK TO DO!
NEVER LET IT BE SAID THAT LARRY LANCE STOPPED A GAL FROM EARNING AN HONEST DOLLAR! 'BYE NOW--
HEY! WHY DON'T YOU LOOK WHERE YA GOIN', CLUMSY?!
SORRY!
NO PARKING
THAT MAN IS DELIBERATELY TRYING TO STIR UP TROUBLE! I THINK LARRY'S GOING TO NEED HELP... FROM THE BLACK CANARY!
3

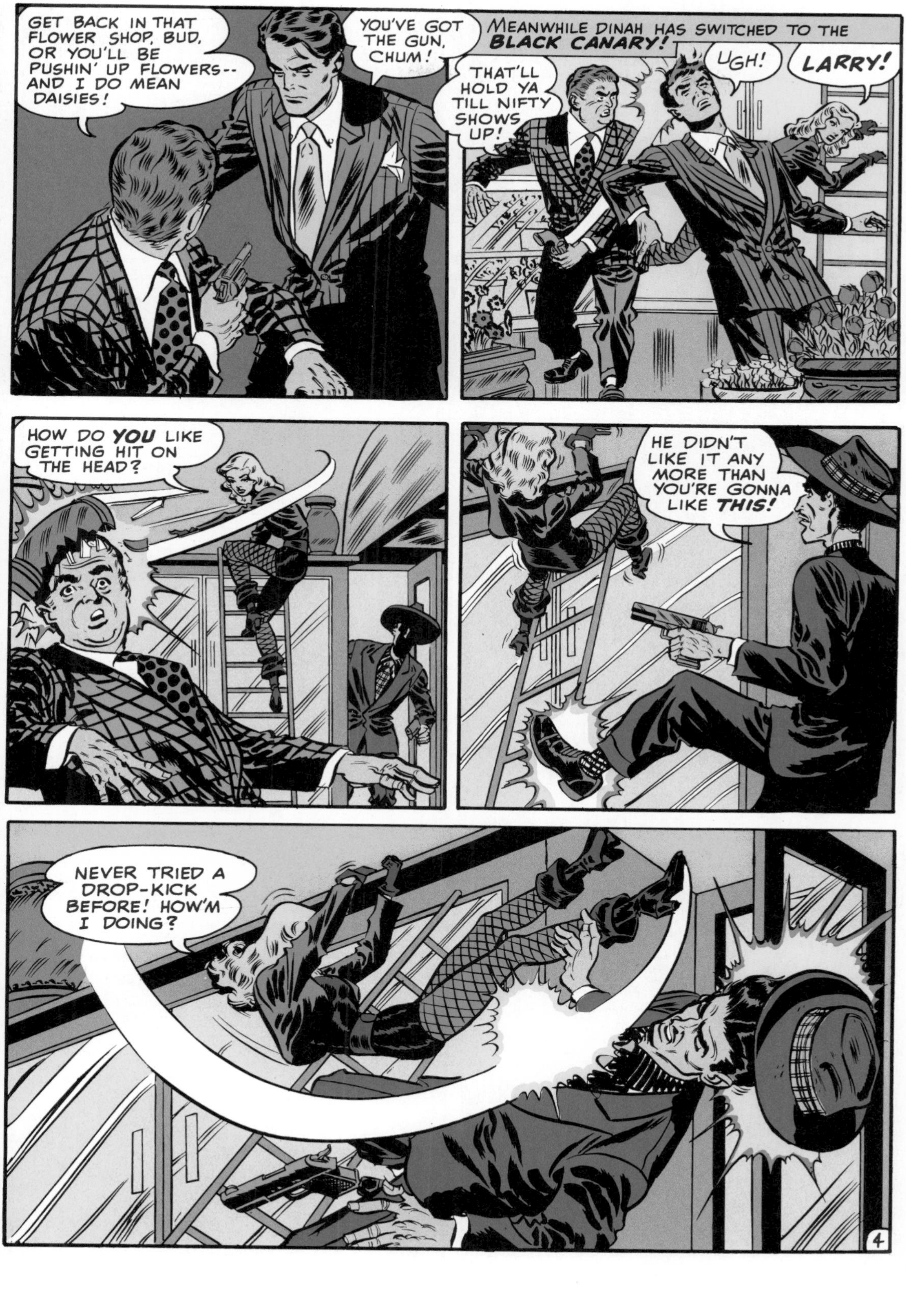
GET BACK IN THAT FLOWER SHOP, BUD, OR YOU'LL BE PUSHIN' UP FLOWERS-- AND I DO MEAN DAISIES!
YOU'VE GOT THE GUN, CHUM!
MEANWHILE DINAH HAS SWITCHED TO THE BLACK CANARY!
THAT'LL HOLD YA TILL NIFTY SHOWS UP!
UGH!
LARRY!
HOW DO YOU LIKE GETTING HIT ON THE HEAD?
HE DIDN'T LIKE IT ANY MORE THAN YOU'RE GONNA LIKE THIS!
NEVER TRIED A DROP-KICK BEFORE! HOW'M I DOING?
4

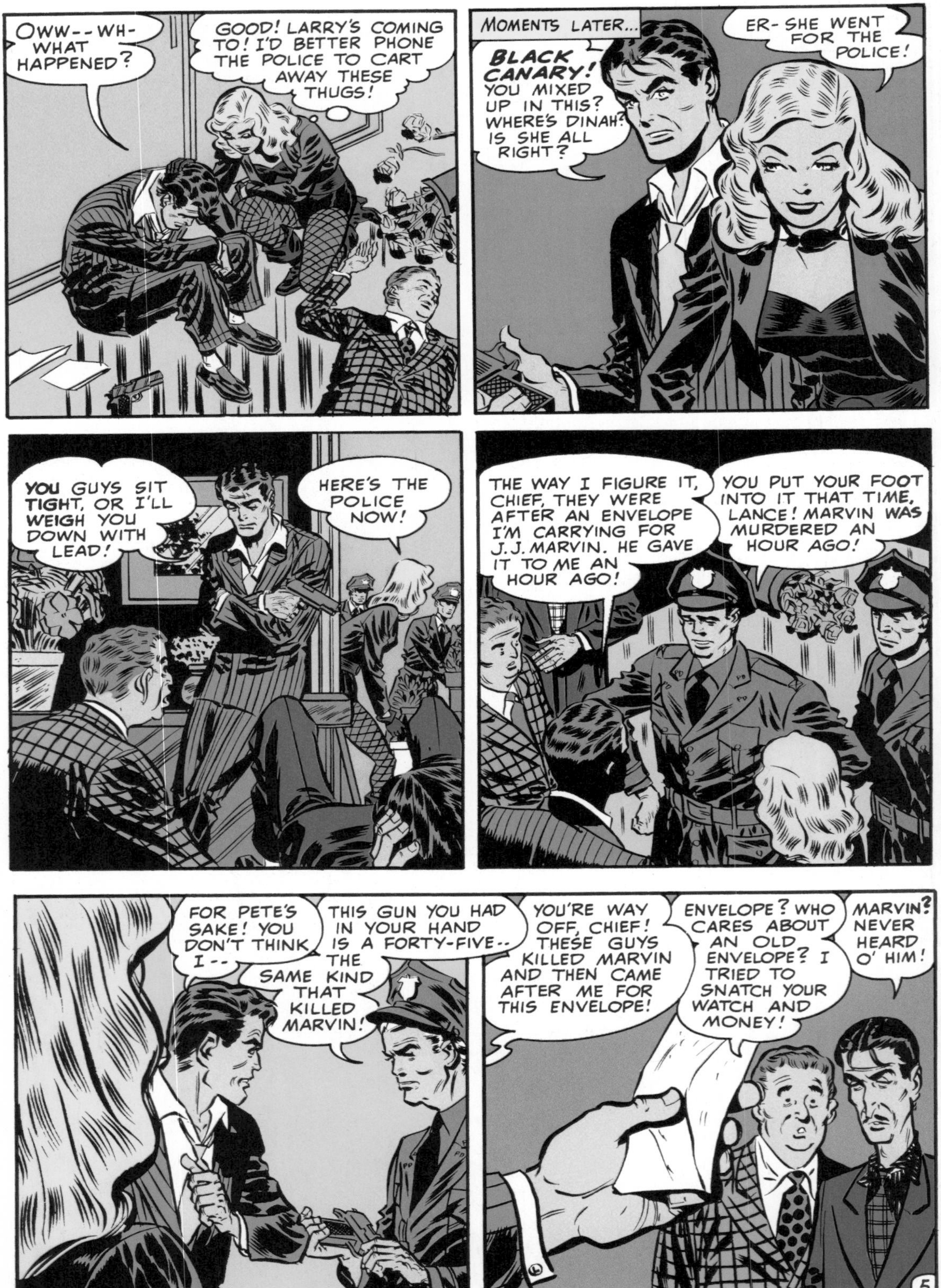

OWW--WH- WHAT HAPPENED?
GOOD! LARRY'S COMING TO! I'D BETTER PHONE THE POLICE TO CART AWAY THESE THUGS!
MOMENTS LATER...
BLACK CANARY! YOU MIXED UP IN THIS? WHERE'S DINAH? IS SHE ALL RIGHT?
ER- SHE WENT FOR THE POLICE!
YOU GUYS SIT TIGHT, OR I'LL WEIGH YOU DOWN WITH LEAD!
HERE'S THE POLICE NOW!
THE WAY I FIGURE IT, CHIEF, THEY WERE AFTER AN ENVELOPE I'M CARRYING FOR J.J. MARVIN. HE GAVE IT TO ME AN HOUR AGO!
YOU PUT YOUR FOOT INTO IT THAT TIME, LANCE! MARVIN WAS MURDERED AN HOUR AGO!
FOR PETE'S SAKE! YOU DON'T THINK I--
THIS GUN YOU HAD IN YOUR HAND IS A FORTY-FIVE-- THE SAME KIND THAT KILLED MARVIN!
YOU'RE WAY OFF, CHIEF! THESE GUYS KILLED MARVIN AND THEN CAME AFTER ME FOR THIS ENVELOPE!
ENVELOPE? WHO CARES ABOUT AN OLD ENVELOPE? I TRIED TO SNATCH YOUR WATCH AND MONEY!
MARVIN? NEVER HEARD O' HIM!
5

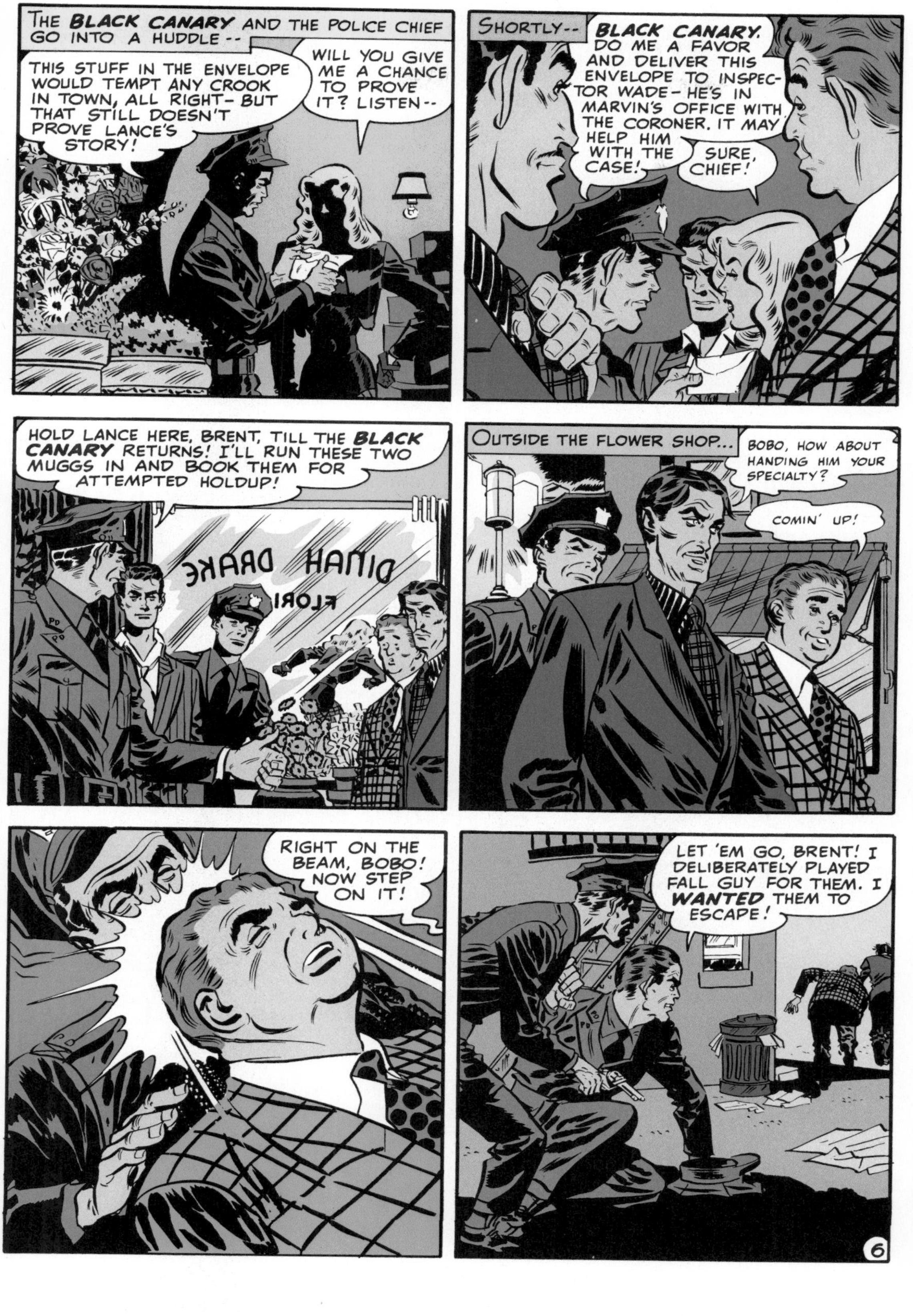

THE BLACK CANARY AND THE POLICE CHIEF GO INTO A HUDDLE --
THIS STUFF IN THE ENVELOPE WOULD TEMPT ANY CROOK IN TOWN, ALL RIGHT- BUT THAT STILL DOESN'T PROVE LANCE'S STORY!
WILL YOU GIVE ME A CHANCE TO PROVE IT? LISTEN --
SHORTLY--
BLACK CANARY. DO ME A FAVOR AND DELIVER THIS ENVELOPE TO INSPECTOR WADE- HE'S IN MARVIN'S OFFICE WITH THE CORONER. IT MAY HELP HIM WITH THE CASE!
SURE, CHIEF!
HOLD LANCE HERE, BRENT, TILL THE BLACK CANARY RETURNS! I'LL RUN THESE TWO MUGGS IN AND BOOK THEM FOR ATTEMPTED HOLDUP!
OUTSIDE THE FLOWER SHOP...
BOBO, HOW ABOUT HANDING HIM YOUR SPECIALTY?
COMIN' UP!
RIGHT ON THE BEAM, BOBO! NOW STEP ON IT!
LET 'EM GO, BRENT! I DELIBERATELY PLAYED FALL GUY FOR THEM. I WANTED THEM TO ESCAPE!
6

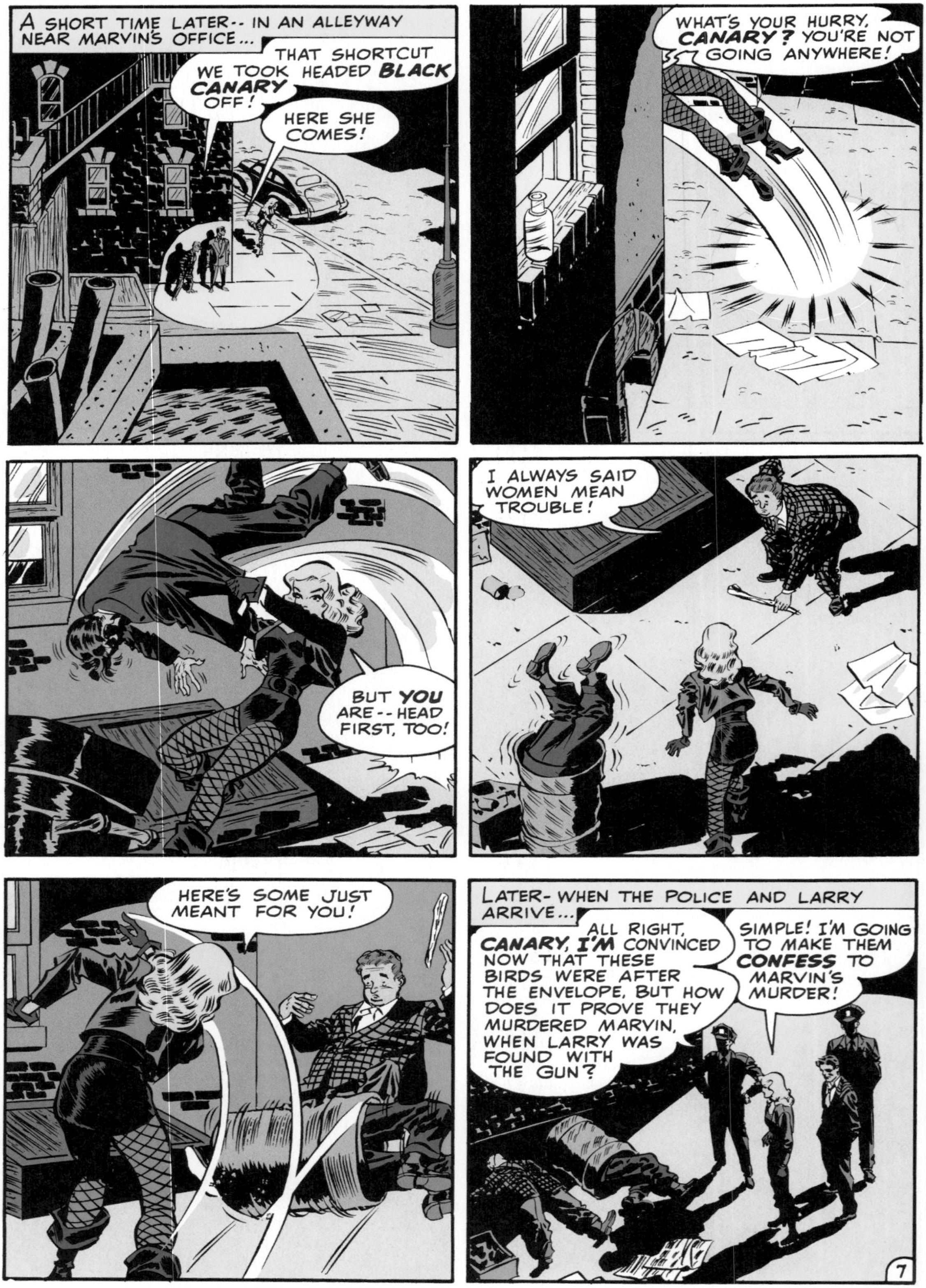
A SHORT TIME LATER-- IN AN ALLEYWAY NEAR MARVIN'S OFFICE...
THAT SHORTCUT WE TOOK HEADED BLACK CANARY OFF!
HERE SHE COMES!
WHAT'S YOUR HURRY, CANARY? YOU'RE NOT GOING ANYWHERE!
BUT YOU ARE--HEAD FIRST, TOO!
I ALWAYS SAID WOMEN MEAN TROUBLE!
HERE'S SOME JUST MEANT FOR YOU!
LATER- WHEN THE POLICE AND LARRY ARRIVE...
ALL RIGHT, CANARY, I'M CONVINCED NOW THAT THESE BIRDS WERE AFTER THE ENVELOPE, BUT HOW DOES IT PROVE THEY MURDERED MARVIN, WHEN LARRY WAS FOUND WITH THE GUN?
SIMPLE! I'M GOING TO MAKE THEM CONFESS TO MARVIN'S MURDER!
7

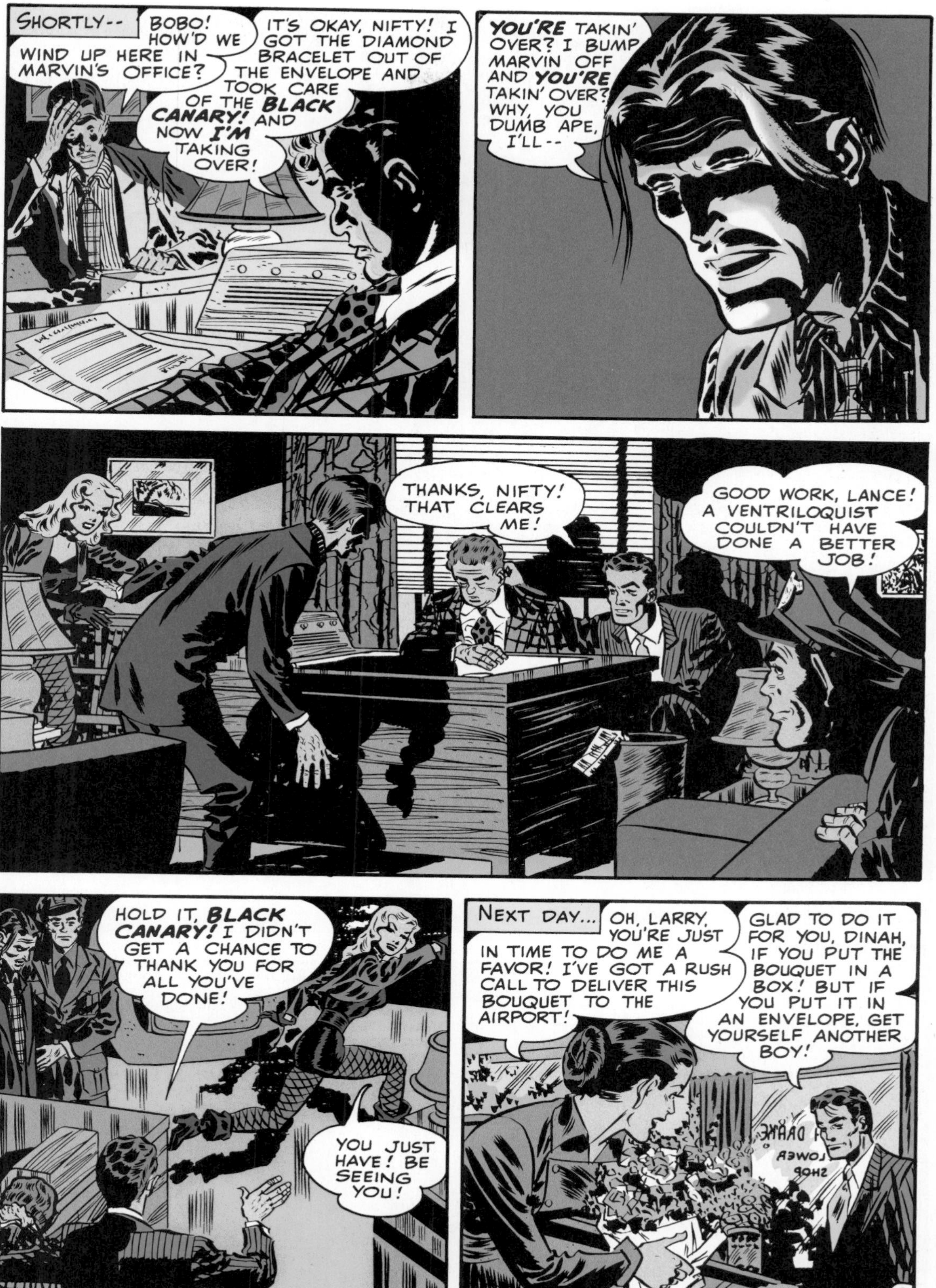
SHORTLY--
BOBO! HOW'D WE WIND UP HERE IN MARVIN'S OFFICE?
IT'S OKAY, NIFTY! I GOT THE DIAMOND BRACELET OUT OF THE ENVELOPE AND TOOK CARE OF THE BLACK CANARY! AND NOW I'M TAKING OVER!
YOU'RE TAKIN' OVER? I BUMP MARVIN OFF AND YOU'RE TAKIN' OVER? WHY, YOU DUMB APE, I'LL--
THANKS, NIFTY! THAT CLEARS ME!
GOOD WORK, LANCE! A VENTRILOQUIST COULDN'T HAVE DONE A BETTER JOB!
HOLD IT, BLACK CANARY! I DIDN'T GET A CHANCE TO THANK YOU FOR ALL YOU'VE DONE!
YOU JUST HAVE! BE SEEING YOU!
NEXT DAY...
OH, LARRY, YOU'RE JUST IN TIME TO DO ME A FAVOR! I'VE GOT A RUSH CALL TO DELIVER THIS BOUQUET TO THE AIRPORT!
GLAD TO DO IT FOR YOU, DINAH, IF YOU PUT THE BOUQUET IN A BOX! BUT IF YOU PUT IT IN AN ENVELOPE, GET YOURSELF ANOTHER BOY!
THE END.
8

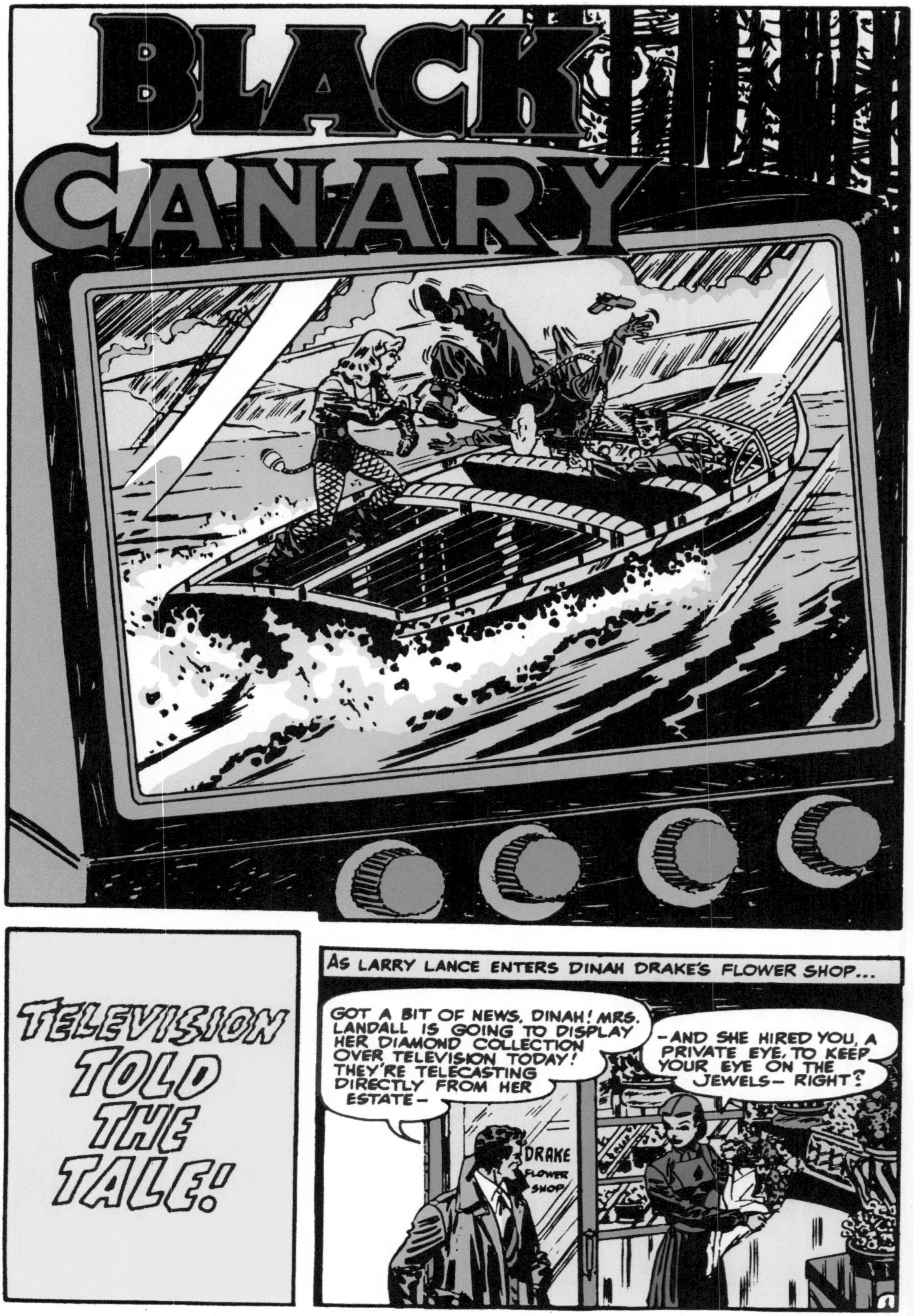
BLACK CANARY
TELEVISION TOLD THE TALE!
AS LARRY LANCE ENTERS DINAH DRAKE'S FLOWER SHOP...
GOT A BIT OF NEWS, DINAH! MRS. LANDALL IS GOING TO DISPLAY HER DIAMOND COLLECTION OVER TELEVISION TODAY! THEY'RE TELECASTING DIRECTLY FROM HER ESTATE—
—AND SHE HIRED YOU, A PRIVATE EYE, TO KEEP YOUR EYE ON THE JEWELS— RIGHT?
DRAKE FLOWER SHOP

HOW'D **YOU** KNOW, MISS FORTUNE-TELLER?

MRS. LANDALL TOLD ME ALL ABOUT IT, LARRY. I'M MAKING THE FLORAL ARRANGEMENTS FOR HER! AND SINCE YOU'RE HERE, YOU CAN HELP ME INTO A CAB!

SOON AFTER... AT THE LANDALL ESTATE...

QUITE A PLACE! PARTLY ON LAND — PARTLY ON WATER!

IT'S A WONDERFUL SPOT FROM WHICH TO WATCH THE MOTOR-BOAT RACES THIS AFTERNOON! WISH I COULD STAY — BUT I HAVE TO GET BACK TO THE SHOP!

A FEW MINUTES LATER...

AREN'T YOU GOING TO WAIT FOR THE TELEVISION SHOW, DINAH?

IT GOES ON JUST BEFORE THE MOTOR-BOAT RACES. I'LL SEE IT OVER MY SET!

'BYE, LARRY! SEE YOU ON TELEVISION!

THE LIGHTING'S PERFECT, MAC! READY?

ALL SET HERE!

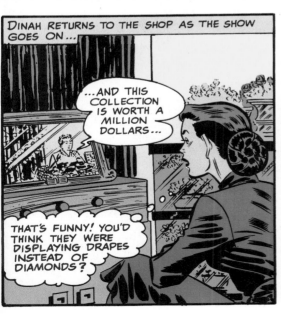

DINAH RETURNS TO THE SHOP AS THE SHOW GOES ON...

...AND THIS COLLECTION IS WORTH A MILLION DOLLARS...

THAT'S FUNNY! YOU'D THINK THEY WERE DISPLAYING DRAPES INSTEAD OF DIAMONDS?

THE LARGE DIAMOND ON THE RIGHT WAS ORIGINALLY WORN BY PRINCESS CASSANDRA AND...

THAT CAMERA ISN'T FOCUSING ON MRS. LANDALL...

AND THIS DIAMOND IS A PERFECT BLUE-WHITE STONE WHICH WAS PURCHASED...

AND I THINK I KNOW WHAT IT IS!

②

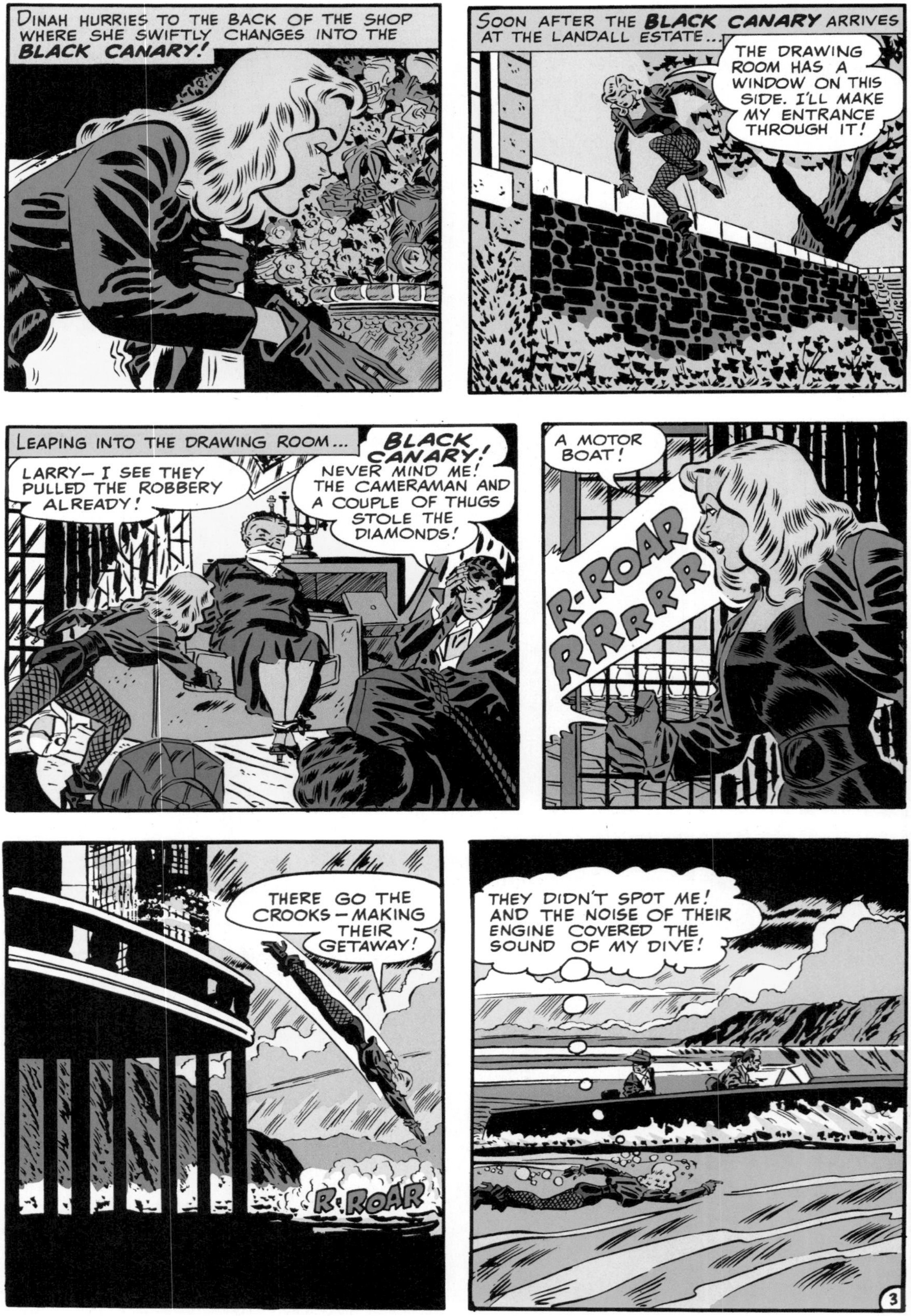
DINAH HURRIES TO THE BACK OF THE SHOP WHERE SHE SWIFTLY CHANGES INTO THE BLACK CANARY!
SOON AFTER THE BLACK CANARY ARRIVES AT THE LANDALL ESTATE...
THE DRAWING ROOM HAS A WINDOW ON THIS SIDE. I'LL MAKE MY ENTRANCE THROUGH IT!
LEAPING INTO THE DRAWING ROOM...
LARRY— I SEE THEY PULLED THE ROBBERY ALREADY!
BLACK CANARY! NEVER MIND ME! THE CAMERAMAN AND A COUPLE OF THUGS STOLE THE DIAMONDS!
A MOTOR BOAT!
R-ROAR RRRRR
THERE GO THE CROOKS — MAKING THEIR GETAWAY!
R-ROAR
THEY DIDN'T SPOT ME! AND THE NOISE OF THEIR ENGINE COVERED THE SOUND OF MY DIVE!
3

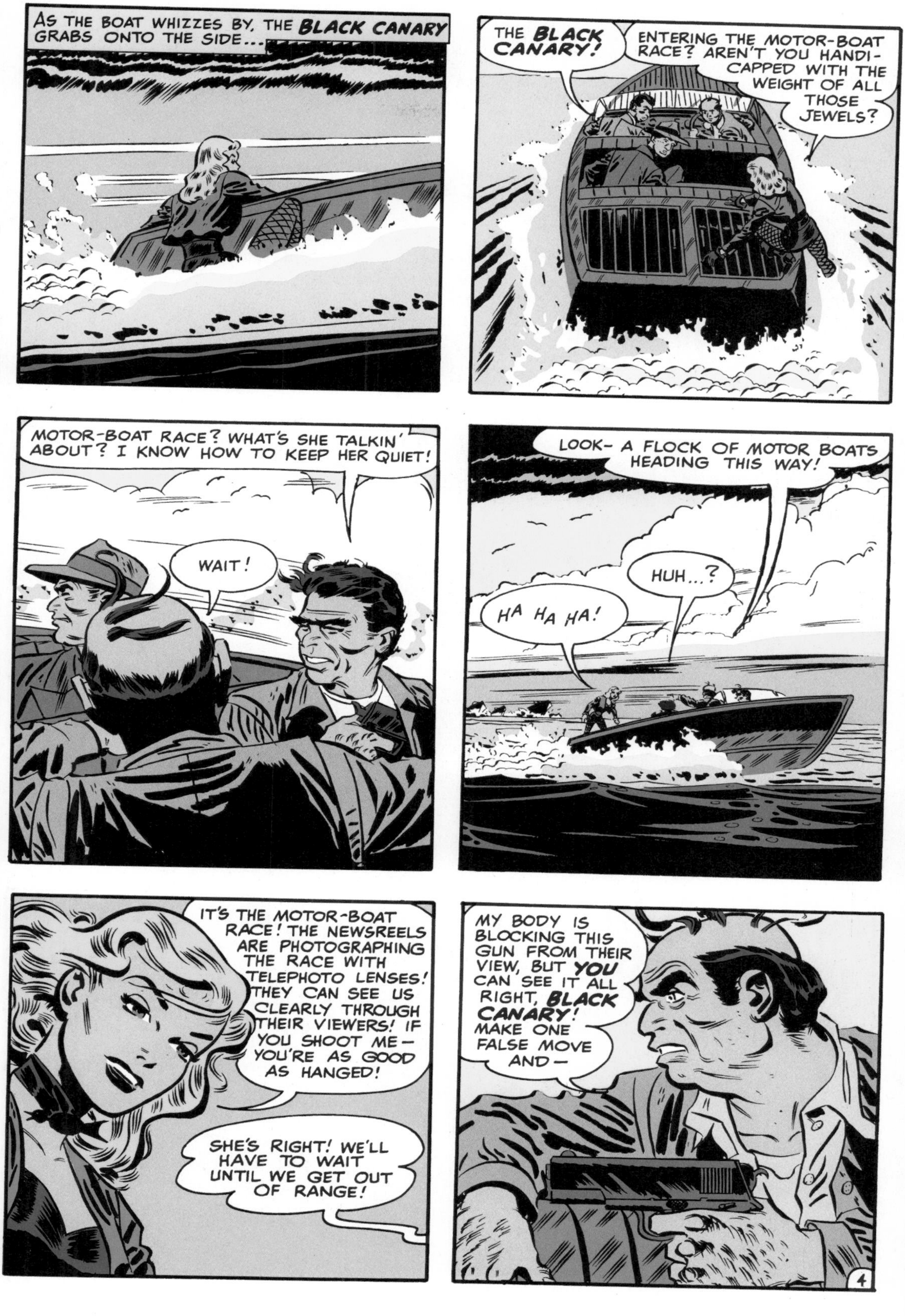
AS THE BOAT WHIZZES BY, THE BLACK CANARY GRABS ONTO THE SIDE...
THE BLACK CANARY!
ENTERING THE MOTOR-BOAT RACE? AREN'T YOU HANDI-CAPPED WITH THE WEIGHT OF ALL THOSE JEWELS?
MOTOR-BOAT RACE? WHAT'S SHE TALKIN' ABOUT? I KNOW HOW TO KEEP HER QUIET!
WAIT!
LOOK- A FLOCK OF MOTOR BOATS HEADING THIS WAY!
HUH...?
HA HA HA!
IT'S THE MOTOR-BOAT RACE! THE NEWSREELS ARE PHOTOGRAPHING THE RACE WITH TELEPHOTO LENSES! THEY CAN SEE US CLEARLY THROUGH THEIR VIEWERS! IF YOU SHOOT ME — YOU'RE AS GOOD AS HANGED!
SHE'S RIGHT! WE'LL HAVE TO WAIT UNTIL WE GET OUT OF RANGE!
MY BODY IS BLOCKING THIS GUN FROM THEIR VIEW, BUT YOU CAN SEE IT ALL RIGHT, BLACK CANARY! MAKE ONE FALSE MOVE AND—
4

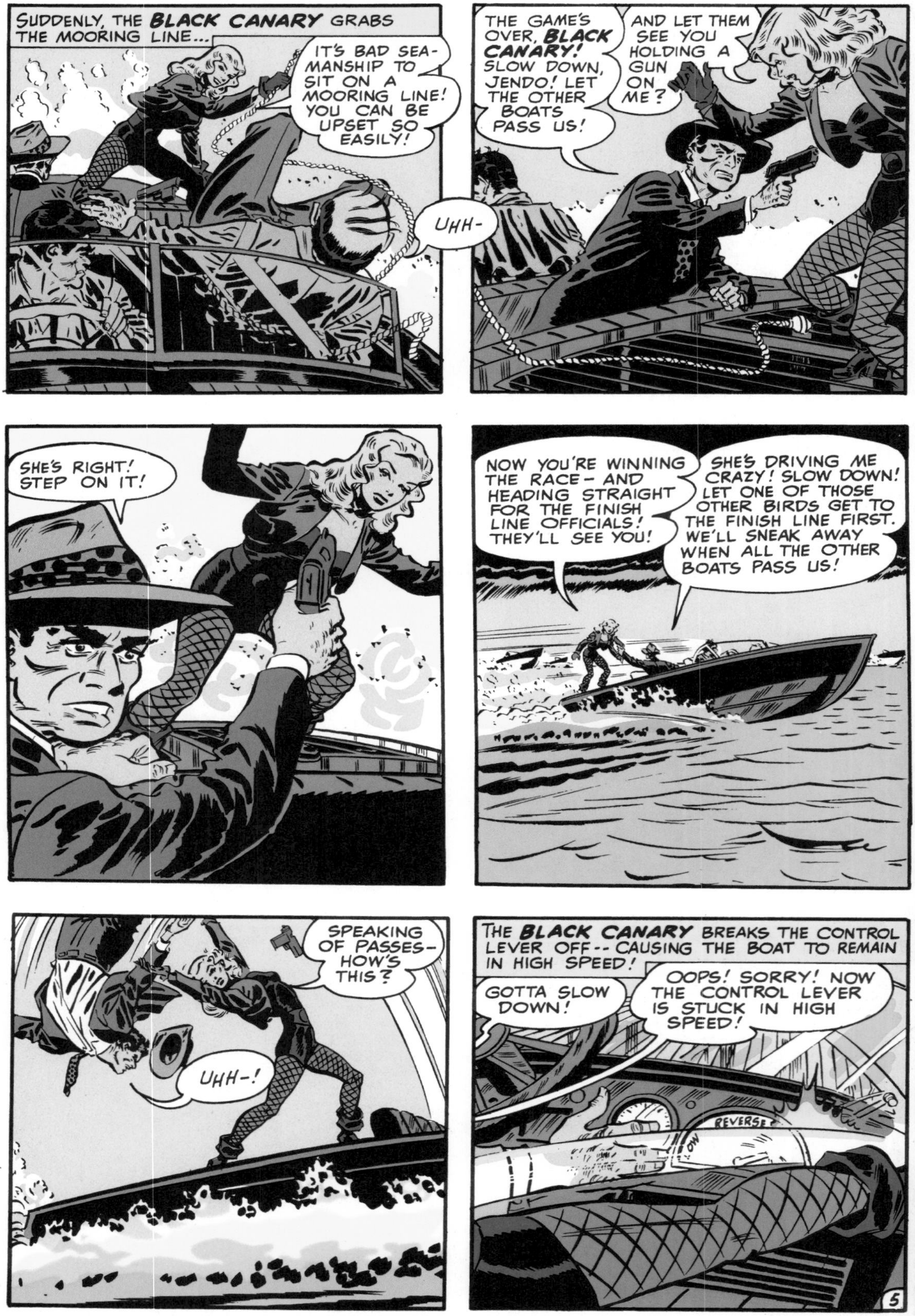
SUDDENLY, THE BLACK CANARY GRABS THE MOORING LINE...
IT'S BAD SEAMANSHIP TO SIT ON A MOORING LINE! YOU CAN BE UPSET SO EASILY!
UHH-
THE GAME'S OVER, BLACK CANARY! SLOW DOWN, JENDO! LET THE OTHER BOATS PASS US!
AND LET THEM SEE YOU HOLDING A GUN ON ME?
SHE'S RIGHT! STEP ON IT!
NOW YOU'RE WINNING THE RACE-AND HEADING STRAIGHT FOR THE FINISH LINE OFFICIALS! THEY'LL SEE YOU!
SHE'S DRIVING ME CRAZY! SLOW DOWN! LET ONE OF THOSE OTHER BIRDS GET TO THE FINISH LINE FIRST. WE'LL SNEAK AWAY WHEN ALL THE OTHER BOATS PASS US!
SPEAKING OF PASSES-HOW'S THIS?
UHH-!
THE BLACK CANARY BREAKS THE CONTROL LEVER OFF--CAUSING THE BOAT TO REMAIN IN HIGH SPEED!
GOTTA SLOW DOWN!
OOPS! SORRY! NOW THE CONTROL LEVER IS STUCK IN HIGH SPEED!
REVERSE
5

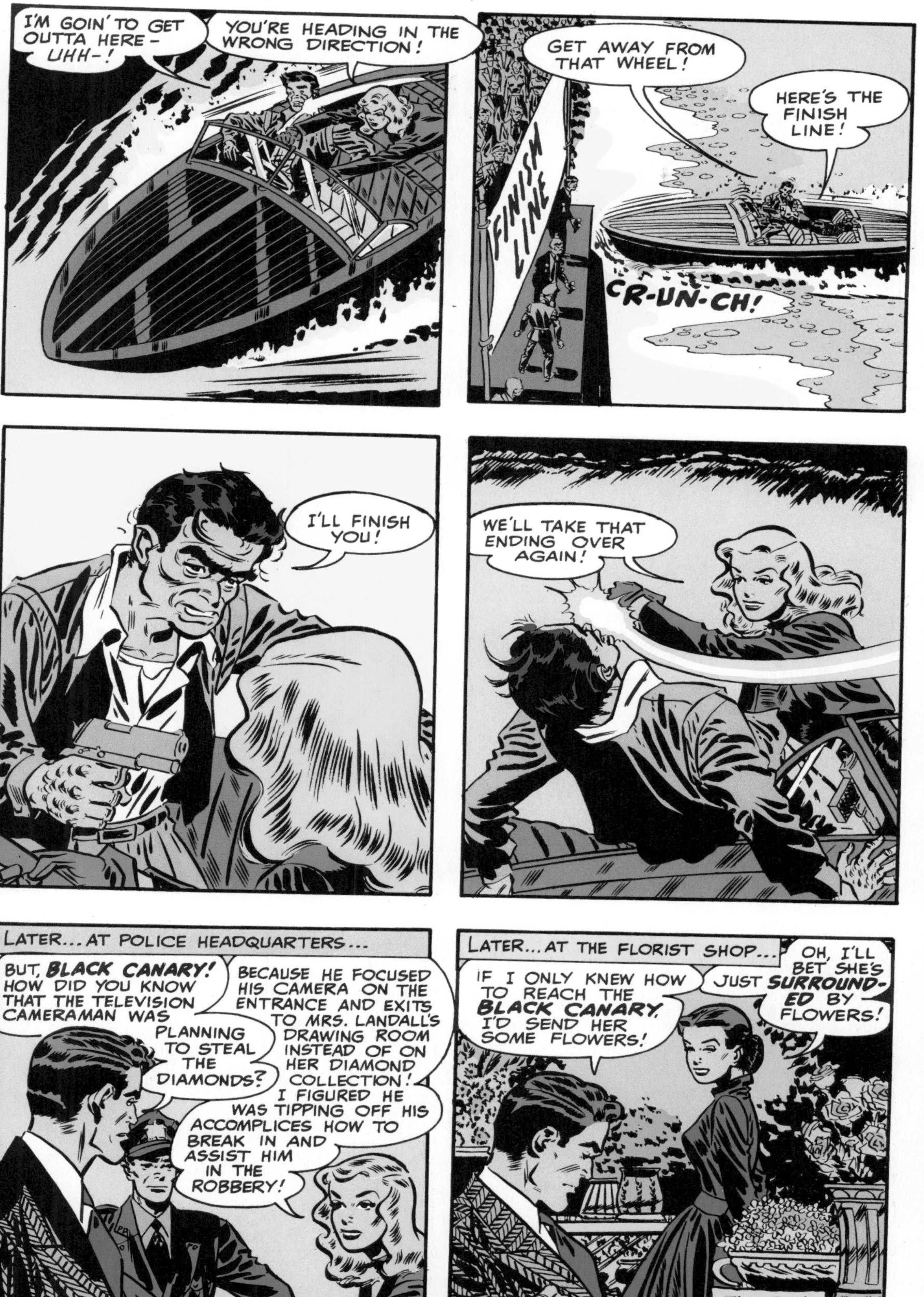

I'M GOIN' TO GET OUTTA HERE– UHH–!
YOU'RE HEADING IN THE WRONG DIRECTION!
GET AWAY FROM THAT WHEEL!
HERE'S THE FINISH LINE!
FINISH LINE
CR-UN-CH!
I'LL FINISH YOU!
WE'LL TAKE THAT ENDING OVER AGAIN!
LATER... AT POLICE HEADQUARTERS...
BUT, BLACK CANARY! HOW DID YOU KNOW THAT THE TELEVISION CAMERAMAN WAS PLANNING TO STEAL THE DIAMONDS?
BECAUSE HE FOCUSED HIS CAMERA ON THE ENTRANCE AND EXITS TO MRS. LANDALL'S DRAWING ROOM INSTEAD OF ON HER DIAMOND COLLECTION! I FIGURED HE WAS TIPPING OFF HIS ACCOMPLICES HOW TO BREAK IN AND ASSIST HIM IN THE ROBBERY!
LATER... AT THE FLORIST SHOP...
IF I ONLY KNEW HOW TO REACH THE BLACK CANARY, I'D SEND HER SOME FLOWERS!
OH, I'LL BET SHE'S JUST SURROUNDED BY FLOWERS!
The End.
6

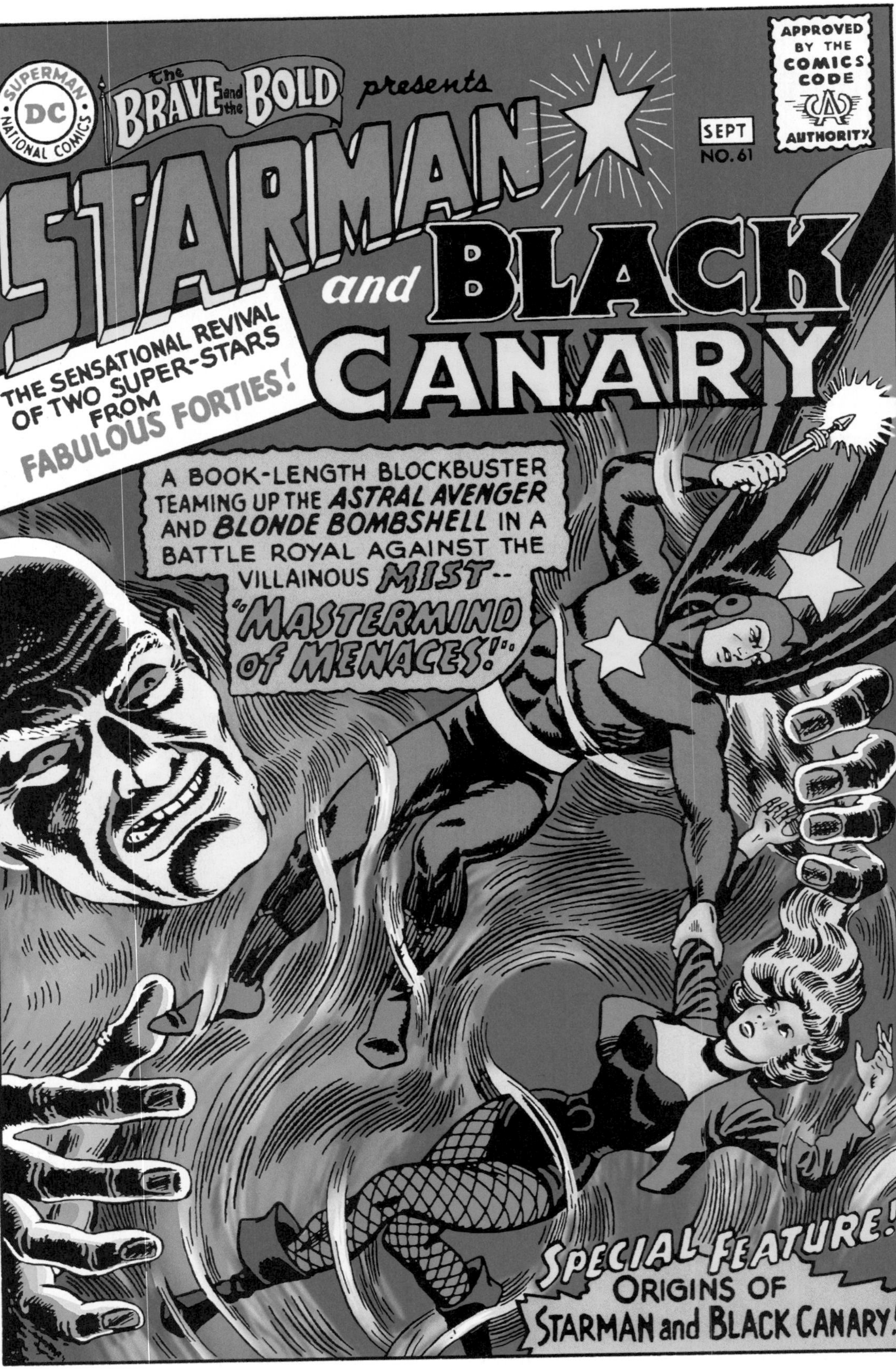
SUPERMAN DC NATIONAL COMICS
The BRAVE and the BOLD presents
APPROVED BY THE COMICS CODE AUTHORITY
SEPT NO. 61
STARMAN and BLACK CANARY
THE SENSATIONAL REVIVAL OF TWO SUPER-STARS FROM FABULOUS FORTIES!
A BOOK-LENGTH BLOCKBUSTER TEAMING UP THE ASTRAL AVENGER AND BLONDE BOMBSHELL IN A BATTLE ROYAL AGAINST THE VILLAINOUS MIST-- "MASTERMIND of MENACES!"
SPECIAL FEATURE! ORIGINS OF STARMAN and BLACK CANARY!

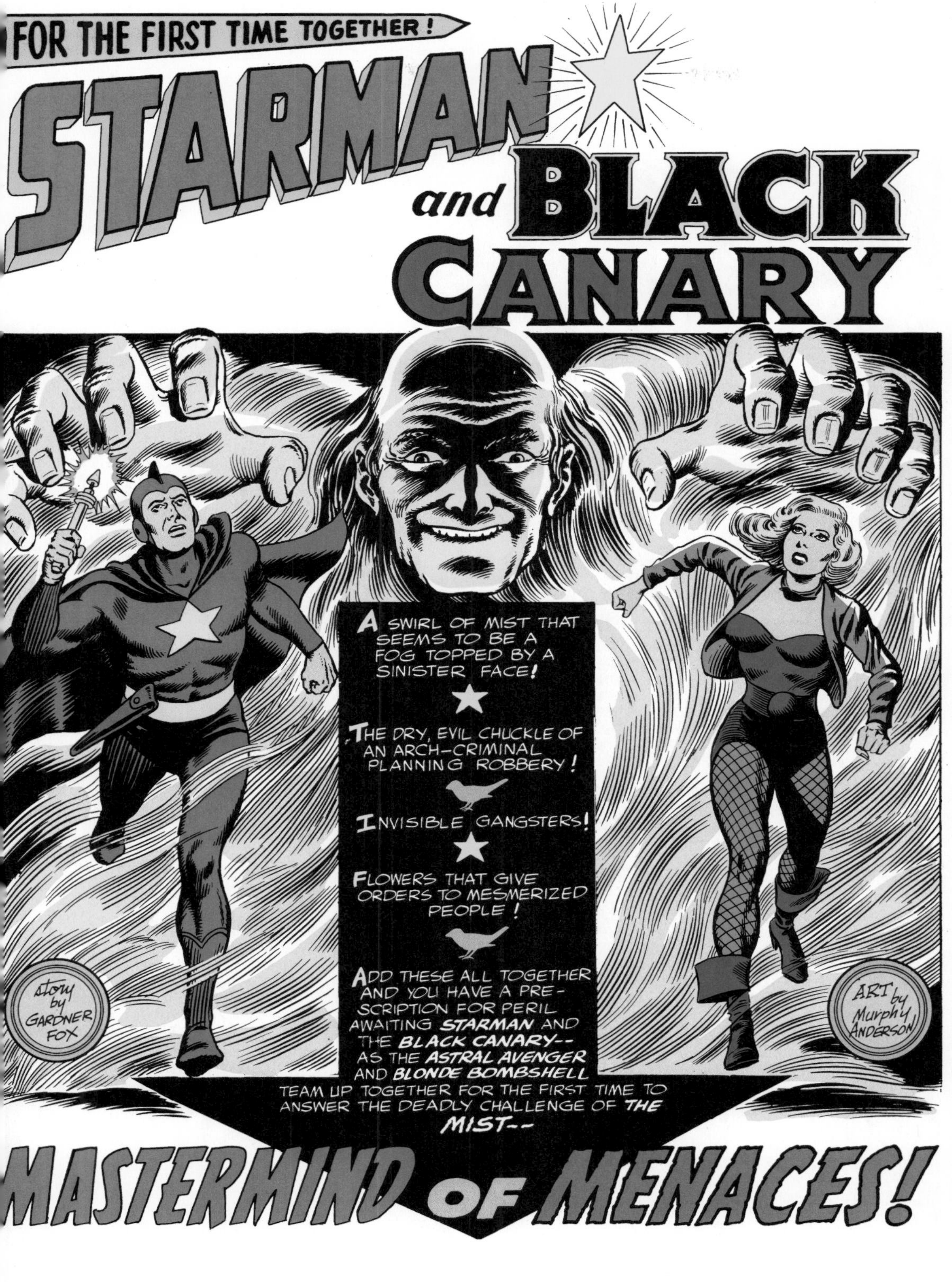
FOR THE FIRST TIME TOGETHER!
STARMAN
and BLACK CANARY
A SWIRL OF MIST THAT SEEMS TO BE A FOG TOPPED BY A SINISTER FACE!
THE DRY, EVIL CHUCKLE OF AN ARCH-CRIMINAL PLANNING ROBBERY!
INVISIBLE GANGSTERS!
FLOWERS THAT GIVE ORDERS TO MESMERIZED PEOPLE!
ADD THESE ALL TOGETHER AND YOU HAVE A PRE-SCRIPTION FOR PERIL AWAITING STARMAN AND THE BLACK CANARY-- AS THE ASTRAL AVENGER AND BLONDE BOMBSHELL TEAM UP TOGETHER FOR THE FIRST TIME TO ANSWER THE DEADLY CHALLENGE OF THE MIST--
story by GARDNER FOX
ART by Murphy ANDERSON
MASTERMIND OF MENACES!

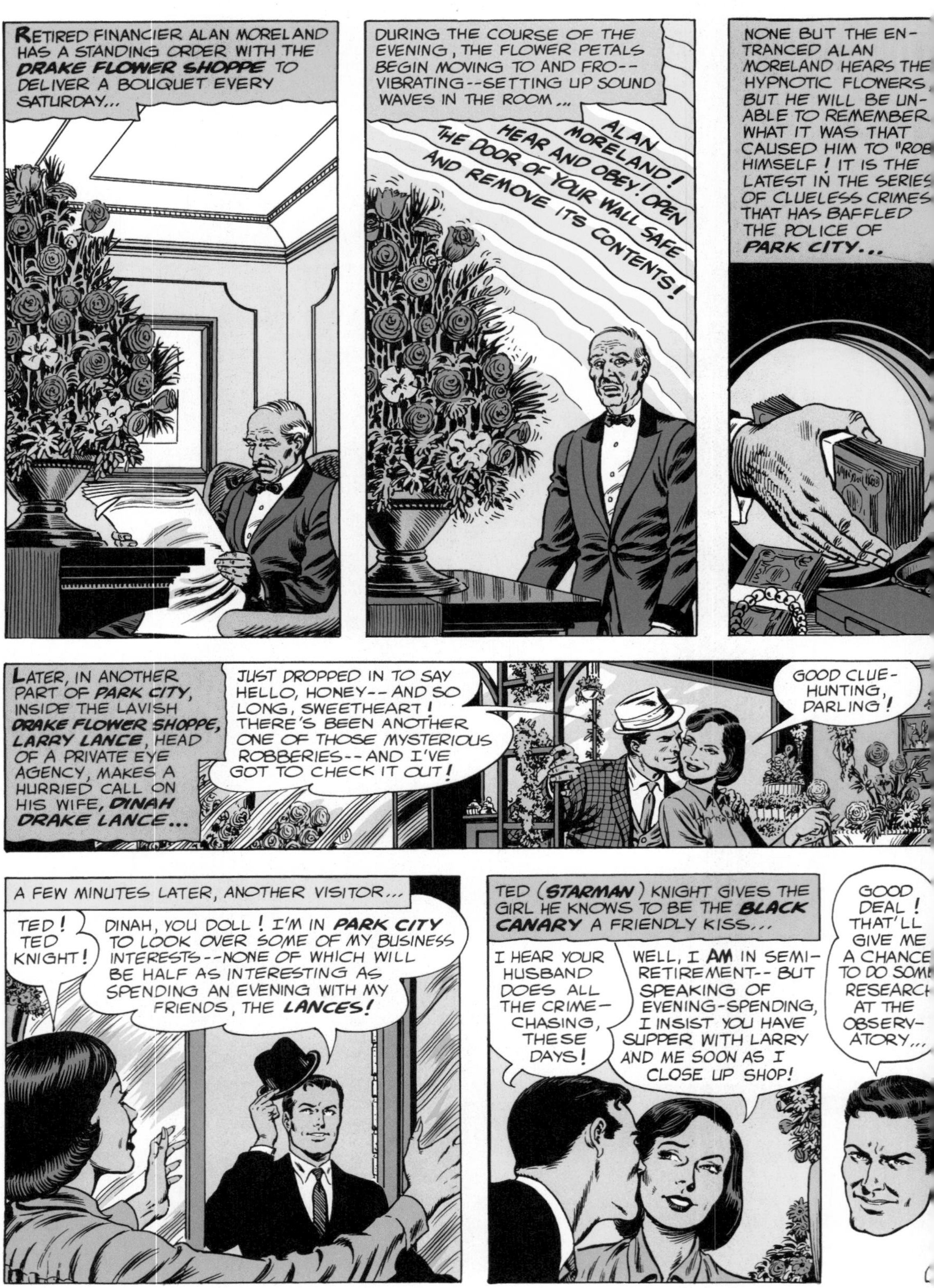
RETIRED FINANCIER ALAN MORELAND HAS A STANDING ORDER WITH THE DRAKE FLOWER SHOPPE TO DELIVER A BOUQUET EVERY SATURDAY...
DURING THE COURSE OF THE EVENING, THE FLOWER PETALS BEGIN MOVING TO AND FRO--VIBRATING--SETTING UP SOUND WAVES IN THE ROOM...
ALAN MORELAND! HEAR AND OBEY! OPEN THE DOOR OF YOUR WALL SAFE AND REMOVE ITS CONTENTS!
NONE BUT THE ENTRANCED ALAN MORELAND HEARS THE HYPNOTIC FLOWERS, BUT HE WILL BE UNABLE TO REMEMBER WHAT IT WAS THAT CAUSED HIM TO "ROB HIMSELF! IT IS THE LATEST IN THE SERIES OF CLUELESS CRIMES THAT HAS BAFFLED THE POLICE OF PARK CITY...
LATER, IN ANOTHER PART OF PARK CITY, INSIDE THE LAVISH DRAKE FLOWER SHOPPE, LARRY LANCE, HEAD OF A PRIVATE EYE AGENCY, MAKES A HURRIED CALL ON HIS WIFE, DINAH DRAKE LANCE...
JUST DROPPED IN TO SAY HELLO, HONEY-- AND SO LONG, SWEETHEART! THERE'S BEEN ANOTHER ONE OF THOSE MYSTERIOUS ROBBERIES-- AND I'VE GOT TO CHECK IT OUT!
GOOD CLUE-HUNTING, DARLING!
A FEW MINUTES LATER, ANOTHER VISITOR...
TED! TED KNIGHT!
DINAH, YOU DOLL! I'M IN PARK CITY TO LOOK OVER SOME OF MY BUSINESS INTERESTS--NONE OF WHICH WILL BE HALF AS INTERESTING AS SPENDING AN EVENING WITH MY FRIENDS, THE LANCES!
TED (STARMAN) KNIGHT GIVES THE GIRL HE KNOWS TO BE THE BLACK CANARY A FRIENDLY KISS...
I HEAR YOUR HUSBAND DOES ALL THE CRIME-CHASING, THESE DAYS!
WELL, I AM IN SEMI-RETIREMENT-- BUT SPEAKING OF EVENING-SPENDING, I INSIST YOU HAVE SUPPER WITH LARRY AND ME SOON AS I CLOSE UP SHOP!
GOOD DEAL! THAT'LL GIVE ME A CHANCE TO DO SOM RESEARC AT THE OBSERV-ATORY...

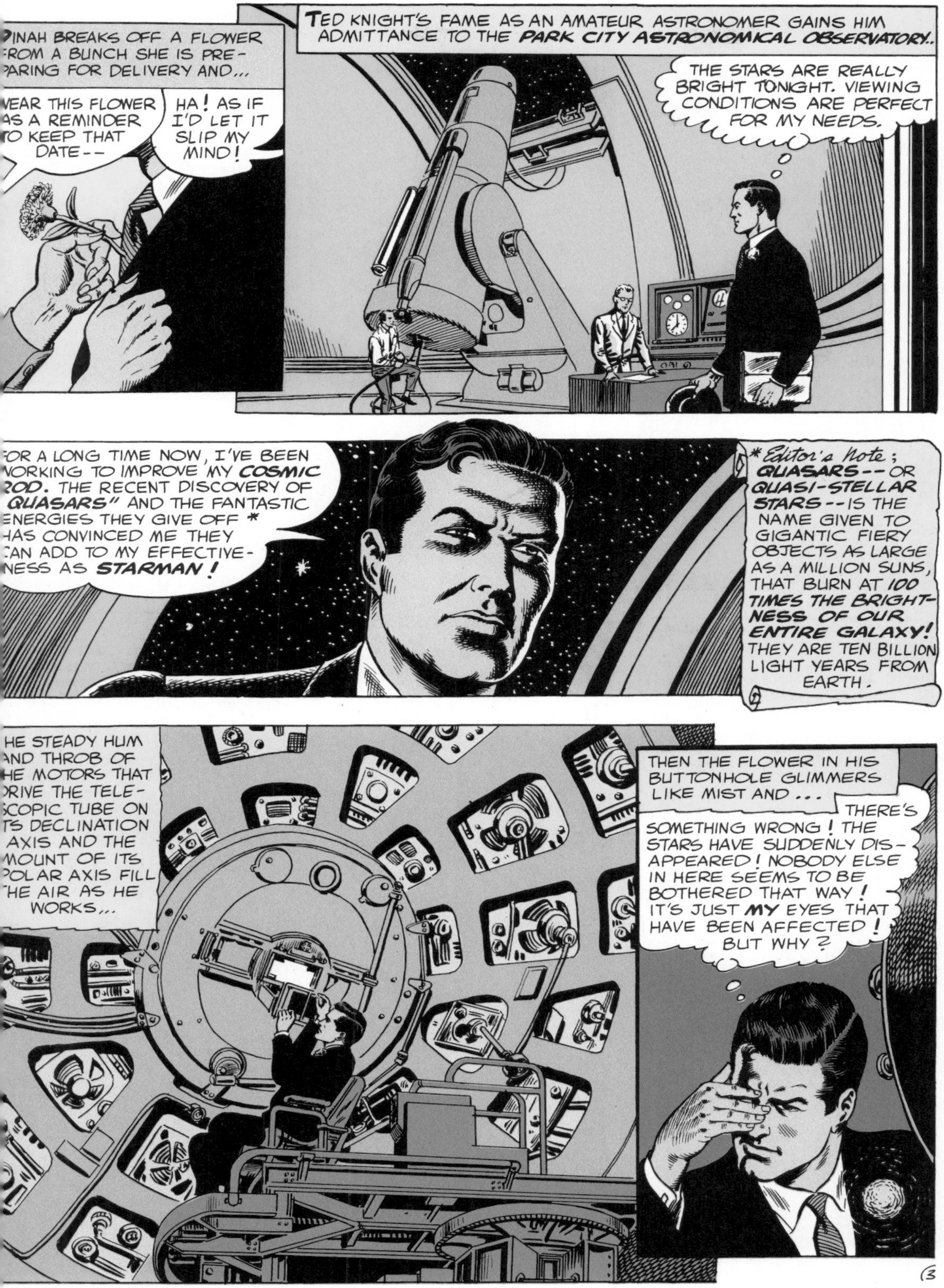
DINAH BREAKS OFF A FLOWER FROM A BUNCH SHE IS PRE-PARING FOR DELIVERY AND...
WEAR THIS FLOWER AS A REMINDER TO KEEP THAT DATE--
HA! AS IF I'D LET IT SLIP MY MIND!
TED KNIGHT'S FAME AS AN AMATEUR ASTRONOMER GAINS HIM ADMITTANCE TO THE PARK CITY ASTRONOMICAL OBSERVATORY..
THE STARS ARE REALLY BRIGHT TONIGHT. VIEWING CONDITIONS ARE PERFECT FOR MY NEEDS.
FOR A LONG TIME NOW, I'VE BEEN WORKING TO IMPROVE MY COSMIC ROD. THE RECENT DISCOVERY OF "QUASARS" AND THE FANTASTIC ENERGIES THEY GIVE OFF * HAS CONVINCED ME THEY CAN ADD TO MY EFFECTIVE-NESS AS STARMAN!
* Editor's Note; QUASARS--OR QUASI-STELLAR STARS--IS THE NAME GIVEN TO GIGANTIC FIERY OBJECTS AS LARGE AS A MILLION SUNS, THAT BURN AT 100 TIMES THE BRIGHT-NESS OF OUR ENTIRE GALAXY! THEY ARE TEN BILLION LIGHT YEARS FROM EARTH.
THE STEADY HUM AND THROB OF THE MOTORS THAT DRIVE THE TELE-SCOPIC TUBE ON ITS DECLINATION AXIS AND THE MOUNT OF ITS POLAR AXIS FILL THE AIR AS HE WORKS...
THEN THE FLOWER IN HIS BUTTONHOLE GLIMMERS LIKE MIST AND ...
THERE'S SOMETHING WRONG! THE STARS HAVE SUDDENLY DIS-APPEARED! NOBODY ELSE IN HERE SEEMS TO BE BOTHERED THAT WAY! IT'S JUST MY EYES THAT HAVE BEEN AFFECTED! BUT WHY?
3

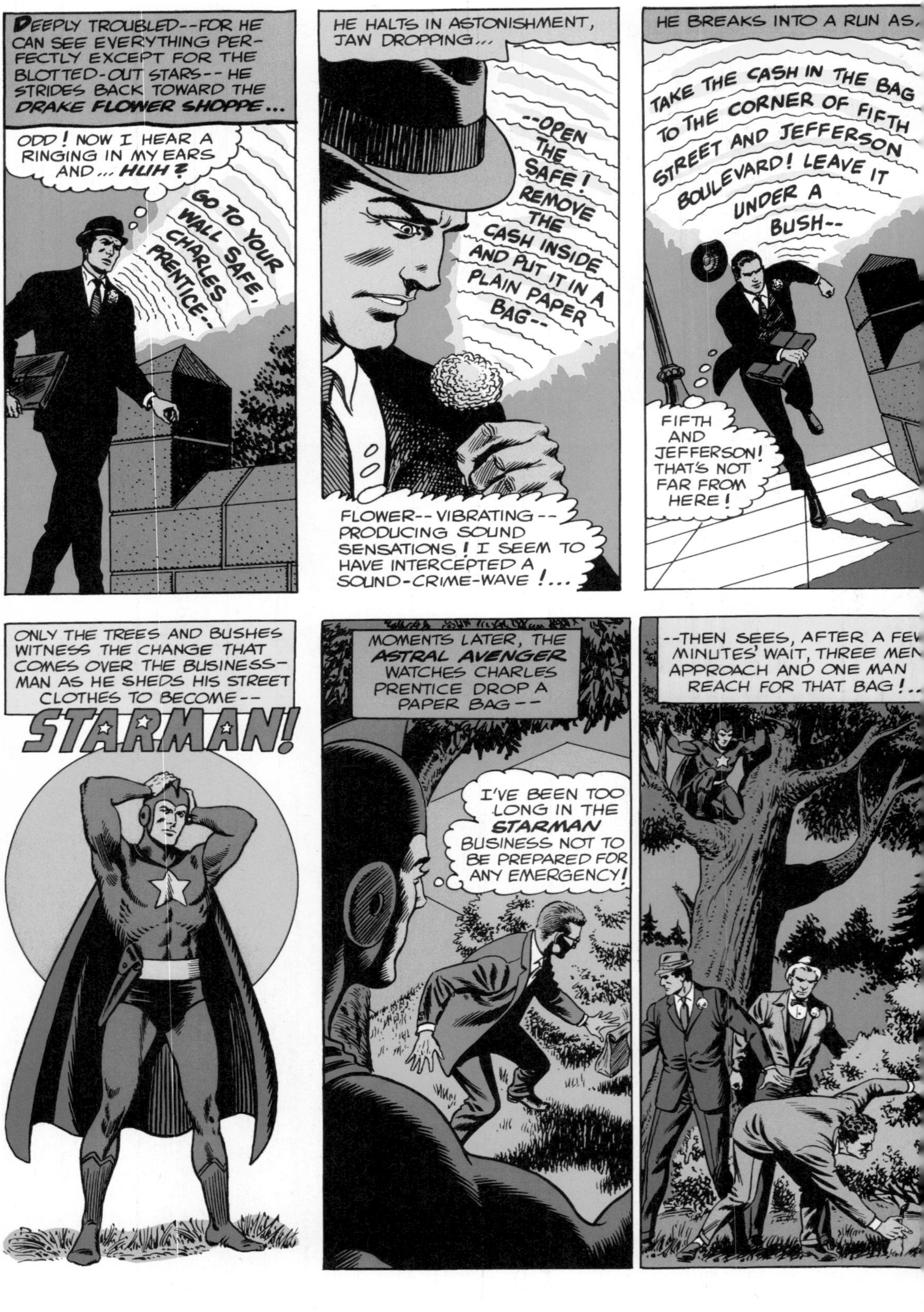
DEEPLY TROUBLED--FOR HE CAN SEE EVERYTHING PERFECTLY EXCEPT FOR THE BLOTTED-OUT STARS--HE STRIDES BACK TOWARD THE DRAKE FLOWER SHOPPE...
ODD! NOW I HEAR A RINGING IN MY EARS AND... HUH?
GO TO YOUR WALL SAFE, CHARLES PRENTICE--
HE HALTS IN ASTONISHMENT, JAW DROPPING...
--OPEN THE SAFE! REMOVE THE CASH INSIDE AND PUT IT IN A PLAIN PAPER BAG--
FLOWER--VIBRATING--PRODUCING SOUND SENSATIONS! I SEEM TO HAVE INTERCEPTED A SOUND-CRIME-WAVE!...
HE BREAKS INTO A RUN AS,
TAKE THE CASH IN THE BAG TO THE CORNER OF FIFTH STREET AND JEFFERSON BOULEVARD! LEAVE IT UNDER A BUSH--
FIFTH AND JEFFERSON! THAT'S NOT FAR FROM HERE!
ONLY THE TREES AND BUSHES WITNESS THE CHANGE THAT COMES OVER THE BUSINESSMAN AS HE SHEDS HIS STREET CLOTHES TO BECOME--
STARMAN!
MOMENTS LATER, THE ASTRAL AVENGER WATCHES CHARLES PRENTICE DROP A PAPER BAG--
I'VE BEEN TOO LONG IN THE STARMAN BUSINESS NOT TO BE PREPARED FOR ANY EMERGENCY!
--THEN SEES, AFTER A FEW MINUTES' WAIT, THREE MEN APPROACH AND ONE MAN REACH FOR THAT BAG!...

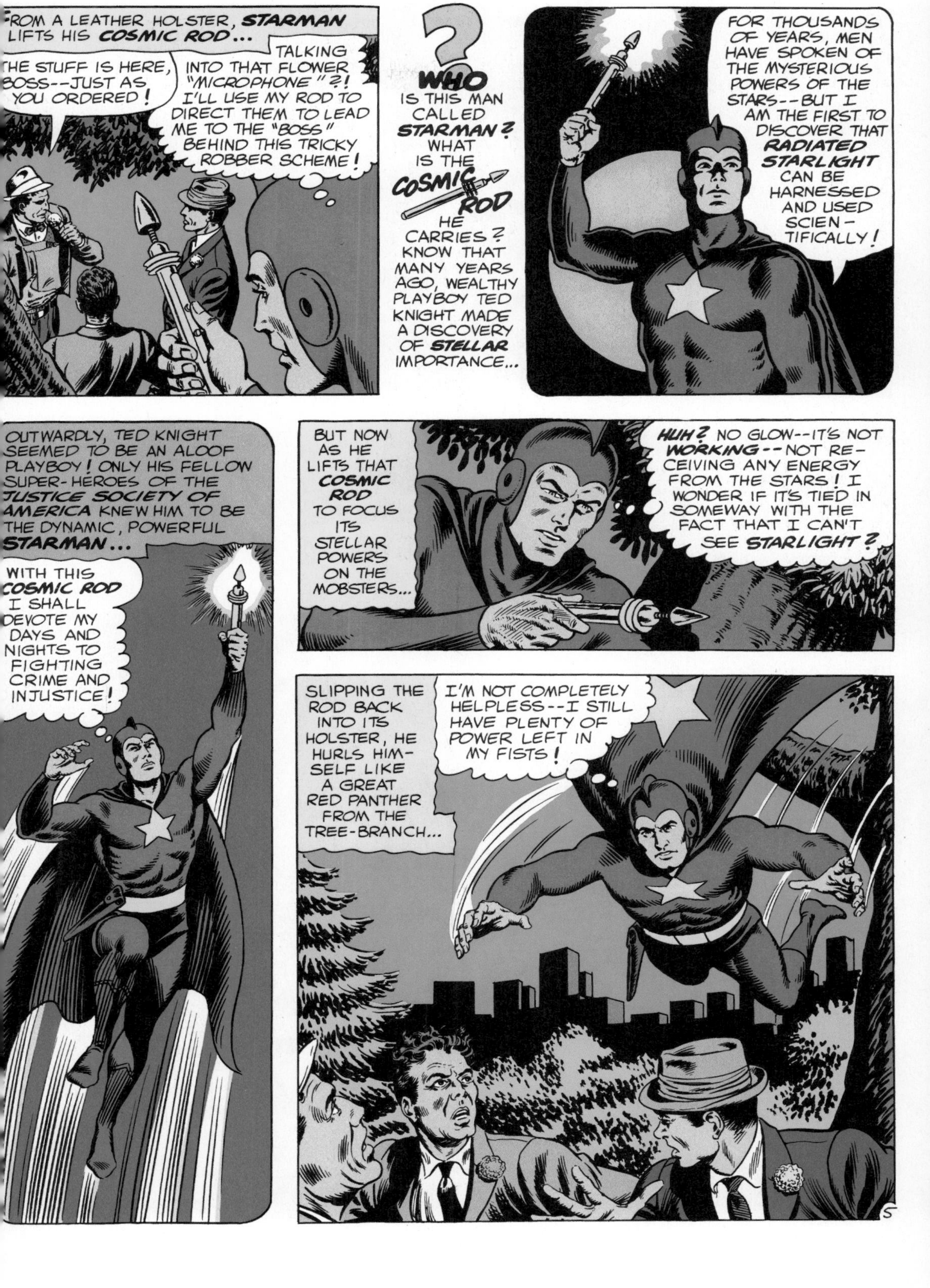
FROM A LEATHER HOLSTER, STARMAN LIFTS HIS COSMIC ROD...
THE STUFF IS HERE, BOSS--JUST AS YOU ORDERED!
TALKING INTO THAT FLOWER "MICROPHONE"?! I'LL USE MY ROD TO DIRECT THEM TO LEAD ME TO THE "BOSS" BEHIND THIS TRICKY ROBBER SCHEME!
? WHO IS THIS MAN CALLED STARMAN? WHAT IS THE COSMIC ROD HE CARRIES? KNOW THAT MANY YEARS AGO, WEALTHY PLAYBOY TED KNIGHT MADE A DISCOVERY OF STELLAR IMPORTANCE...
FOR THOUSANDS OF YEARS, MEN HAVE SPOKEN OF THE MYSTERIOUS POWERS OF THE STARS--BUT I AM THE FIRST TO DISCOVER THAT RADIATED STARLIGHT CAN BE HARNESSED AND USED SCIEN-TIFICALLY!
OUTWARDLY, TED KNIGHT SEEMED TO BE AN ALOOF PLAYBOY! ONLY HIS FELLOW SUPER-HEROES OF THE JUSTICE SOCIETY OF AMERICA KNEW HIM TO BE THE DYNAMIC, POWERFUL STARMAN...
WITH THIS COSMIC ROD I SHALL DEVOTE MY DAYS AND NIGHTS TO FIGHTING CRIME AND INJUSTICE!
BUT NOW AS HE LIFTS THAT COSMIC ROD TO FOCUS ITS STELLAR POWERS ON THE MOBSTERS...
HUH? NO GLOW--IT'S NOT WORKING--NOT RE-CEIVING ANY ENERGY FROM THE STARS! I WONDER IF IT'S TIED IN SOMEWAY WITH THE FACT THAT I CAN'T SEE STARLIGHT?
SLIPPING THE ROD BACK INTO ITS HOLSTER, HE HURLS HIM-SELF LIKE A GREAT RED PANTHER FROM THE TREE-BRANCH...
I'M NOT COMPLETELY HELPLESS--I STILL HAVE PLENTY OF POWER LEFT IN MY FISTS!
5

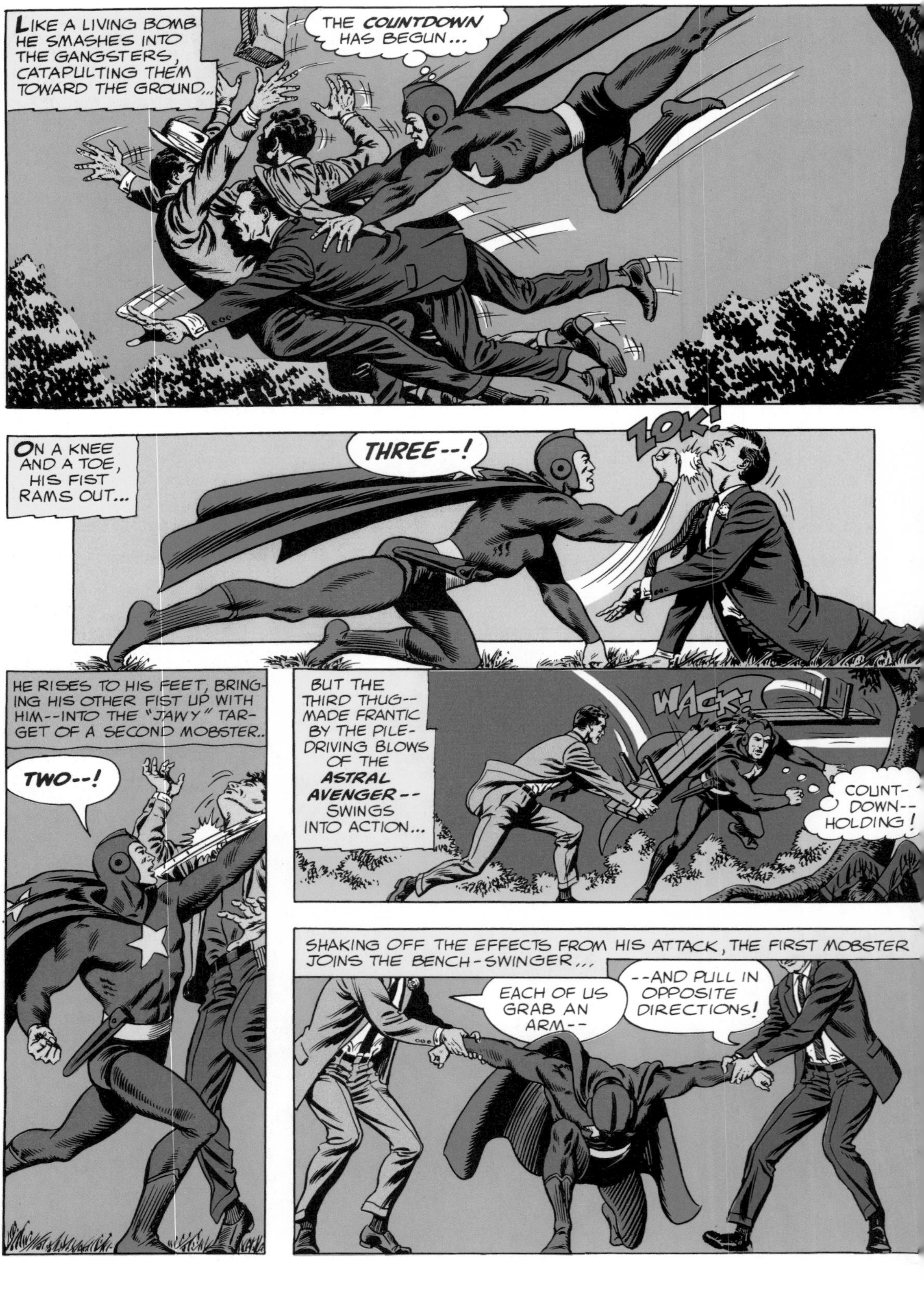

LIKE A LIVING BOMB HE SMASHES INTO THE GANGSTERS, CATAPULTING THEM TOWARD THE GROUND...
THE COUNTDOWN HAS BEGUN...
ON A KNEE AND A TOE, HIS FIST RAMS OUT...
THREE--!
ZOK!
HE RISES TO HIS FEET, BRINGING HIS OTHER FIST UP WITH HIM--INTO THE "JAWY" TARGET OF A SECOND MOBSTER..
TWO--!
BUT THE THIRD THUG--MADE FRANTIC BY THE PILE-DRIVING BLOWS OF THE ASTRAL AVENGER--SWINGS INTO ACTION...
WACK!
COUNT-DOWN--HOLDING!
SHAKING OFF THE EFFECTS FROM HIS ATTACK, THE FIRST MOBSTER JOINS THE BENCH-SWINGER...
EACH OF US GRAB AN ARM--
--AND PULL IN OPPOSITE DIRECTIONS!

DRAWING ON HIS RESERVE STRENGTH, STARMAN PLUNGES FORWARD, CARRYING THE GANGSTERS WITH HIM...

GOT ONE CHANCE TO DISLODGE THEM--BY JARRING THEM LOOSE!

LIKE A FULLBACK HITTING THE LINE, HE DRIVES A SHOULDER INTO TREE BOLE --SIMULTANEOUSLY WHIPPING HIS ARMS AROUND ON EITHER SIDE OF THAT THICK TRUNK...

THUMMMP!

I CAN'T HANG ON!

HIS PERFECTLY CONDITIONED BODY QUICKLY RECOVERING FROM THAT BLASTING BLOW, STARMAN WHIRLS AND HURLS HIMSELF THROUGH THE AIR, TO GRIP AND LIFT A GANGSTER...

UP YOU GO!

SLAMMING HIM FLAT UPON THE GROUND, HE DIVES OVER HIM TOWARD THE REMAINING MOBSTER STRUGGLING TO HIS FEET...

NOW TO ZERO OFF MY DELAYED COUNTDOWN --

SUDDENLY, FROM THE FLOWER IN THE MOBSTER'S JACKET COMES A HIGH-PITCHED SERIES OF EAR-SPLITTING FREQUENCIES...

KKKIVEEEEE

THOSE SOUNDS -- STRIKING INTO MY VERY BRAIN -- BLACKING ME OUT!

HA! I KNEW THE BOSS WOULDN'T FAIL US!

7

BY THE TIME THE SOUNDS DIE AWAY, AND A SHAKEN *STARMAN* STAGGERS FROM THE SCENE...

THEY'RE GONE! WHILE I WAS BEING BATTERED BY THOSE SOUND-WAVES, THEY MADE THEIR GETAWAY-- AND I LOST MY CHANCE TO TRACK DOWN THEIR "BOSS"!

ELSEWHERE IN THE CITY, AN OLD FOE--*THE MIST*-- IS GLOATING OVER *STARMAN'S* DEFEAT...

MY LONG-TIME EMEMY-- BACK AGAIN! *Ah*, IT SEEMS LIKE OLD TIMES PITTING MY INGENIOUS CRIMINAL MIND AND POWERS AGAINST *STARMAN'S* STAR-POWERED STUNTS!

YES, THIS IS *THE MIST!* THE MASTER OF THAT *INVISO-SOLUTION* WHICH ENABLES HIM TO MAKE ANY OBJECT WITH WHICH IT IS COATED-- DISAPPEAR FROM VIEW!

EVEN THE VERY CLOAK HE WEARS SEEMS TO BE A *MIST* OUT OF WHICH HIS HEAD PROTRUDES...

WITH THIS SAME SOLUTION HE HAS LEARNED TO TRANSMIT HYPNOTIC INFLUENCES TO VICTIMS HE CHOOSES TO ROB...

JUST AS I SENT SOUND-SHOCK WAVES TO THE FLOWER WORN BY MY HIRELING -- WHO WAS PRO-TECTED AGAINST IT--TO KNOCK OUT *STARMAN!* WHAT PUZZLES ME IS, HOW DID *STARMAN* GET WISE TO MY LATEST RACKET? I MUST ASK MY MEN WHEN THEY ARRIVE!

BLACK CANARY

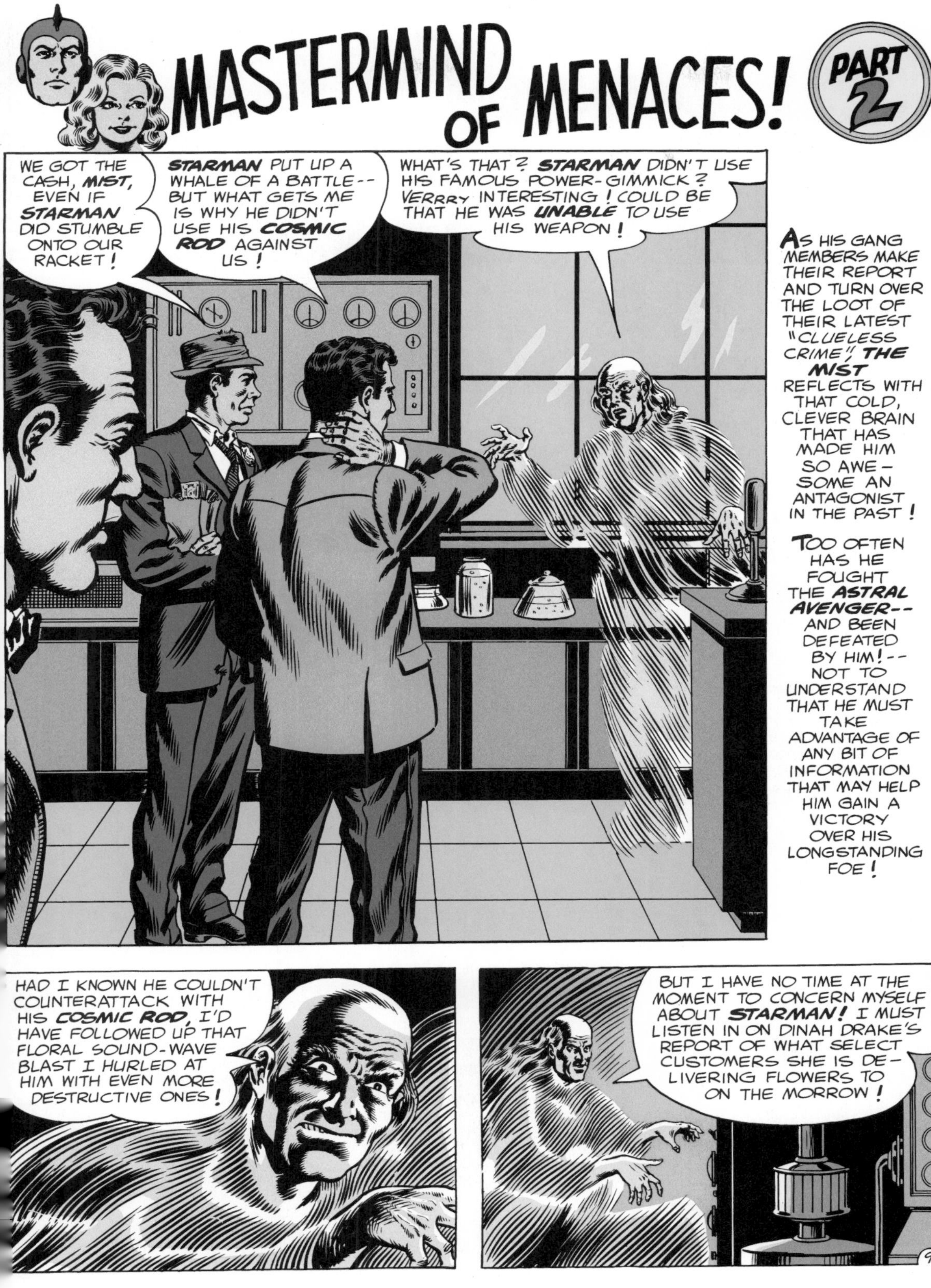
MASTERMIND MENACES! OF
PART 2
WE GOT THE CASH, MIST, EVEN IF STARMAN DID STUMBLE ONTO OUR RACKET!
STARMAN PUT UP A WHALE OF A BATTLE-- BUT WHAT GETS ME IS WHY HE DIDN'T USE HIS COSMIC ROD AGAINST US!
WHAT'S THAT? STARMAN DIDN'T USE HIS FAMOUS POWER-GIMMICK? VERRRY INTERESTING! COULD BE THAT HE WAS UNABLE TO USE HIS WEAPON!
AS HIS GANG MEMBERS MAKE THEIR REPORT AND TURN OVER THE LOOT OF THEIR LATEST "CLUELESS CRIME", THE MIST REFLECTS WITH THAT COLD, CLEVER BRAIN THAT HAS MADE HIM SO AWE-SOME AN ANTAGONIST IN THE PAST!
TOO OFTEN HAS HE FOUGHT THE ASTRAL AVENGER-- AND BEEN DEFEATED BY HIM!-- NOT TO UNDERSTAND THAT HE MUST TAKE ADVANTAGE OF ANY BIT OF INFORMATION THAT MAY HELP HIM GAIN A VICTORY OVER HIS LONGSTANDING FOE!
HAD I KNOWN HE COULDN'T COUNTERATTACK WITH HIS COSMIC ROD, I'D HAVE FOLLOWED UP THAT FLORAL SOUND-WAVE BLAST I HURLED AT HIM WITH EVEN MORE DESTRUCTIVE ONES!
BUT I HAVE NO TIME AT THE MOMENT TO CONCERN MYSELF ABOUT STARMAN! I MUST LISTEN IN ON DINAH DRAKE'S REPORT OF WHAT SELECT CUSTOMERS SHE IS DE-LIVERING FLOWERS TO ON THE MORROW!
9

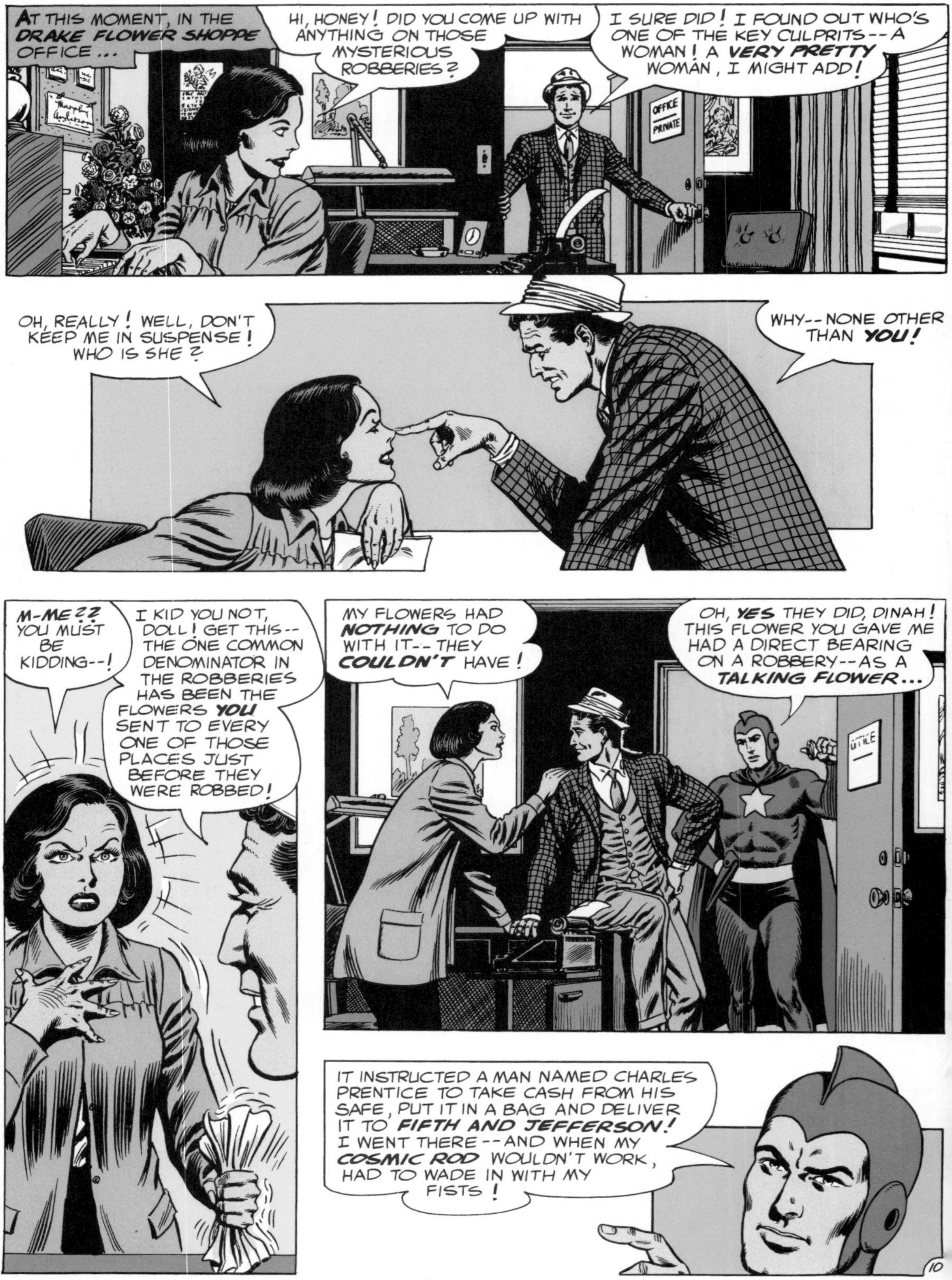
AT THIS MOMENT, IN THE DRAKE FLOWER SHOPPE OFFICE...
HI, HONEY! DID YOU COME UP WITH ANYTHING ON THOSE MYSTERIOUS ROBBERIES?
I SURE DID! I FOUND OUT WHO'S ONE OF THE KEY CULPRITS--A WOMAN! A VERY PRETTY WOMAN, I MIGHT ADD!
OFFICE PRIVATE
OH, REALLY! WELL, DON'T KEEP ME IN SUSPENSE! WHO IS SHE?
WHY--NONE OTHER THAN YOU!
M-ME?? YOU MUST BE KIDDING--!
I KID YOU NOT, DOLL! GET THIS--THE ONE COMMON DENOMINATOR IN THE ROBBERIES HAS BEEN THE FLOWERS YOU SENT TO EVERY ONE OF THOSE PLACES JUST BEFORE THEY WERE ROBBED!
MY FLOWERS HAD NOTHING TO DO WITH IT--THEY COULDN'T HAVE!
OH, YES THEY DID, DINAH! THIS FLOWER YOU GAVE ME HAD A DIRECT BEARING ON A ROBBERY--AS A TALKING FLOWER...
IT INSTRUCTED A MAN NAMED CHARLES PRENTICE TO TAKE CASH FROM HIS SAFE, PUT IT IN A BAG AND DELIVER IT TO FIFTH AND JEFFERSON! I WENT THERE--AND WHEN MY COSMIC ROD WOULDN'T WORK, HAD TO WADE IN WITH MY FISTS!
10

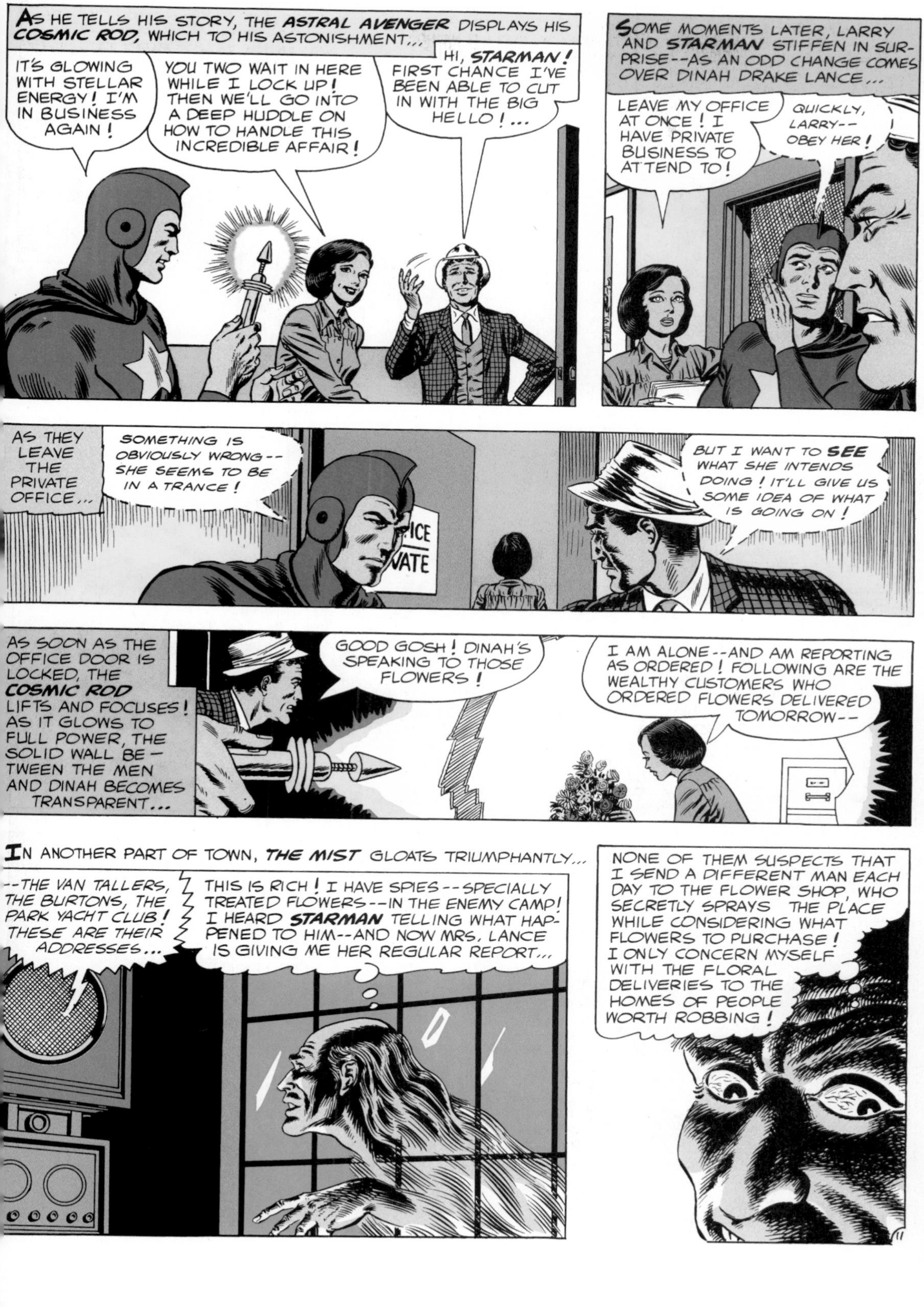
AS HE TELLS HIS STORY, THE ASTRAL AVENGER DISPLAYS HIS COSMIC ROD, WHICH TO HIS ASTONISHMENT...
IT'S GLOWING WITH STELLAR ENERGY! I'M IN BUSINESS AGAIN!
YOU TWO WAIT IN HERE WHILE I LOCK UP! THEN WE'LL GO INTO A DEEP HUDDLE ON HOW TO HANDLE THIS INCREDIBLE AFFAIR!
HI, STARMAN! FIRST CHANCE I'VE BEEN ABLE TO CUT IN WITH THE BIG HELLO!...
SOME MOMENTS LATER, LARRY AND STARMAN STIFFEN IN SURPRISE--AS AN ODD CHANGE COMES OVER DINAH DRAKE LANCE...
LEAVE MY OFFICE AT ONCE! I HAVE PRIVATE BUSINESS TO ATTEND TO!
QUICKLY, LARRY-- OBEY HER!
AS THEY LEAVE THE PRIVATE OFFICE...
SOMETHING IS OBVIOUSLY WRONG-- SHE SEEMS TO BE IN A TRANCE!
BUT I WANT TO SEE WHAT SHE INTENDS DOING! IT'LL GIVE US SOME IDEA OF WHAT IS GOING ON!
AS SOON AS THE OFFICE DOOR IS LOCKED, THE COSMIC ROD LIFTS AND FOCUSES! AS IT GLOWS TO FULL POWER, THE SOLID WALL BETWEEN THE MEN AND DINAH BECOMES TRANSPARENT...
GOOD GOSH! DINAH'S SPEAKING TO THOSE FLOWERS!
I AM ALONE--AND AM REPORTING AS ORDERED! FOLLOWING ARE THE WEALTHY CUSTOMERS WHO ORDERED FLOWERS DELIVERED TOMORROW--
IN ANOTHER PART OF TOWN, THE MIST GLOATS TRIUMPHANTLY...
--THE VAN TALLERS, THE BURTONS, THE PARK YACHT CLUB! THESE ARE THEIR ADDRESSES...
THIS IS RICH! I HAVE SPIES--SPECIALLY TREATED FLOWERS--IN THE ENEMY CAMP! I HEARD STARMAN TELLING WHAT HAPPENED TO HIM--AND NOW MRS. LANCE IS GIVING ME HER REGULAR REPORT...
NONE OF THEM SUSPECTS THAT I SEND A DIFFERENT MAN EACH DAY TO THE FLOWER SHOP, WHO SECRETLY SPRAYS THE PLACE WHILE CONSIDERING WHAT FLOWERS TO PURCHASE! I ONLY CONCERN MYSELF WITH THE FLORAL DELIVERIES TO THE HOMES OF PEOPLE WORTH ROBBING!
11

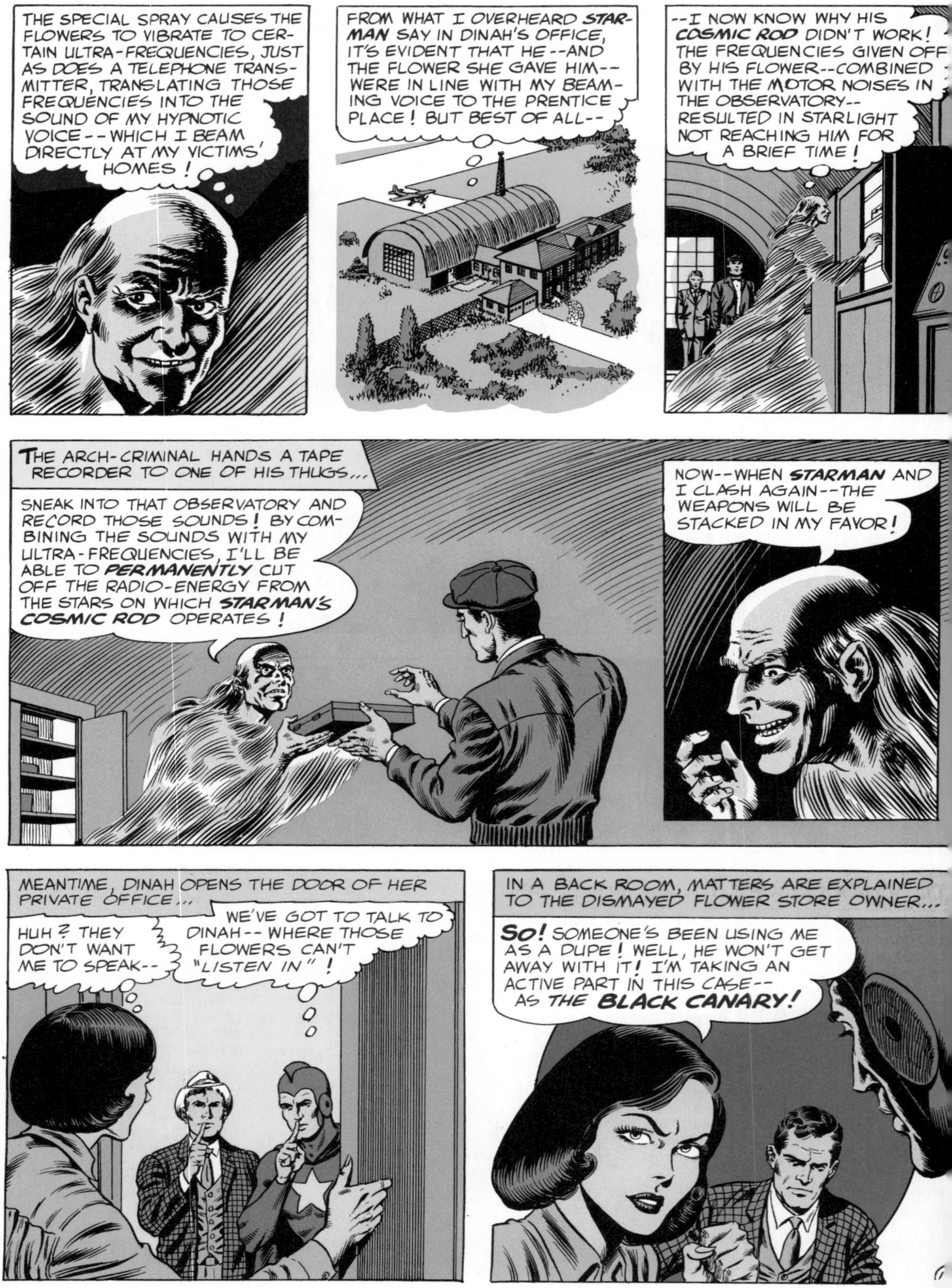
THE SPECIAL SPRAY CAUSES THE FLOWERS TO VIBRATE TO CERTAIN ULTRA-FREQUENCIES, JUST AS DOES A TELEPHONE TRANSMITTER, TRANSLATING THOSE FREQUENCIES INTO THE SOUND OF MY HYPNOTIC VOICE--WHICH I BEAM DIRECTLY AT MY VICTIMS' HOMES!
FROM WHAT I OVERHEARD STARMAN SAY IN DINAH'S OFFICE, IT'S EVIDENT THAT HE--AND THE FLOWER SHE GAVE HIM--WERE IN LINE WITH MY BEAMING VOICE TO THE PRENTICE PLACE! BUT BEST OF ALL--
--I NOW KNOW WHY HIS COSMIC ROD DIDN'T WORK! THE FREQUENCIES GIVEN OFF BY HIS FLOWER--COMBINED WITH THE MOTOR NOISES IN THE OBSERVATORY--RESULTED IN STARLIGHT NOT REACHING HIM FOR A BRIEF TIME!
THE ARCH-CRIMINAL HANDS A TAPE RECORDER TO ONE OF HIS THUGS...
SNEAK INTO THAT OBSERVATORY AND RECORD THOSE SOUNDS! BY COMBINING THE SOUNDS WITH MY ULTRA-FREQUENCIES, I'LL BE ABLE TO PERMANENTLY CUT OFF THE RADIO-ENERGY FROM THE STARS ON WHICH STARMAN'S COSMIC ROD OPERATES!
NOW--WHEN STARMAN AND I CLASH AGAIN--THE WEAPONS WILL BE STACKED IN MY FAVOR!
MEANTIME, DINAH OPENS THE DOOR OF HER PRIVATE OFFICE...
HUH? THEY DON'T WANT ME TO SPEAK--
WE'VE GOT TO TALK TO DINAH--WHERE THOSE FLOWERS CAN'T "LISTEN IN"!
IN A BACK ROOM, MATTERS ARE EXPLAINED TO THE DISMAYED FLOWER STORE OWNER...
SO! SOMEONE'S BEEN USING ME AS A DUPE! WELL, HE WON'T GET AWAY WITH IT! I'M TAKING AN ACTIVE PART IN THIS CASE--AS THE BLACK CANARY!

IN HER SPECIAL DRESS-ING ROOM, ANGRY FINGERS LIFT AND FIT THE DARK FABRIC OF HER COSTUME OVER THE FLUSHED GIRL...

THE NERVE OF THAT GUY--WHOEVER HE IS! USING ME AND MY FLOWERS TO HELP HIM ROB!

A BLONDE WIG IS FITTED OVER HER BLACK HAIR AND NOW SHE IS READY TO FACE THE WORLD AS THE CRIME-BUSTING

BLACK CANARY...

YOU GAVE THE CROOK THREE ADDRESSES, HONEY! I SUGGEST WE EACH GO TO ONE AND NAB THEM!

GOOD IDEA, LARRY--WITH ONE ADDITION! *YOU* WILL GO THERE ONLY TO WATCH AND OBSERVE-- AND THEN *FOLLOW* THE ROBBERS TO THEIR HIDE-OUT!

BLACK CANARY'S RIGHT! WE MUST FIND THE MASTER-MIND BEHIND ALL THIS--BY HAVING ONE OF US FOLLOW THE MOBSTERS!

BUT WHY ELECT *ME*? I'M A PRETTY GOOD CROOK-CATCHER, YOU KNOW!

DEAR, YOU'RE AN EXPERIENCED DETECTIVE--A CRACKERJACK AT SHADOWING PEOPLE WITHOUT THEIR KNOWING IT!

SURE--THE RIGHT MAN FOR THE RIGHT JOB! WITH YOUR DETECTIVE GIMMICKS, YOU CAN CONTACT US AND PINPOINT THE HIDE-OUT'S LOCATION!

FLATTERY SURE GOT YOU SOMEWHERE! WHAT CAN I SAY BUT--*OKAY!*

HERE'S AN ADDRESS FOR EACH OF YOU! I'LL TAKE THE *VAN TALLER* HOUSE! LARRY, YOU GO TO THE BURTONS'! *STARMAN*, I'M PUTTING THE YACHT CLUB INTO YOUR KEEPING!

JUST AS I'M PUTTING THIS *MINIATURE COSMIC ROD* INTO YOURS, *BLACK CANARY!*

I WANT YOU TO USE IT AS A SECRET WEAPON AGAINST OUR FOE--IF MY REGULAR ONE FAILS TO WORK AGAIN, AS I SUSPECT! IT DRAWS ITS POWER FROM *QUASARS*, THE GREATEST KNOWN SOURCE OF ENERGY IN THE UNIVERSE! I'VE BEEN WORKING ON IT FOR SOME MONTHS--FINALLY FINISHING IT TODAY AT THE OBSERVATORY ...

NEXT DAY, AFTER THE SPRAYED FLOWERS HAVE BEEN DELIVERED...

FREDA VAN TALLER, GATHER ALL YOUR EMERALDS AND LEAVE THEM ON YOUR VANITY TABLE! OPEN A DOWNSTAIRS WINDOW-- THEN LEAVE THE HOUSE FOR AN HOUR

A FEW MINUTES AFTER THE WEALTHY WOMAN HAS LEFT HER HOME...

LET'S GO! SHE DID JUST WHAT *THE MIST* TOLD HER TO...

DON'T THEY ALWAYS? HE'S COME UP WITH THE NEATEST ROBBERY SCHEME OF ALL TIME!

IN THE BEDROOM ABOVE, INVISIBLE FINGERS LIFT AND DISPLAY GREEN FIRE IN THE SHAPE OF COSTLY EMERALDS...

MAN, WHEN IT COMES TO GREEN STUFF, I'LL TAKE EMERALDS OVER BUCKS ANY TIME!

BELOW, A *BLONDE BOMB-SHELL* LEAPS THROUGH THE OPEN WINDOW...

I DIDN'T SEE ANYONE COME IN BUT I KNOW SOMEONE'S HERE --

FROM THE AMULET ABOUT HER THROAT, *BLACK CANARY* REMOVES A PELLET OF REDDISH POWDER AND BREAKS IT IN HER PALM...

I HEAR FOOTSTEPS AND VOICES UPSTAIRS! IT WAS GOOD OF *STARMAN* TO LET ME HAVE THAT *TINY COSMIC ROD*--BUT I HAVE WAYS OF MY OWN FOR DEALING WITH INVISIBLE CROOKS!

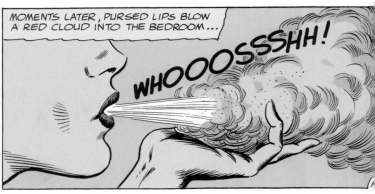

MOMENTS LATER, PURSED LIPS BLOW A RED CLOUD INTO THE BEDROOM...

WHOOOSSSHH!

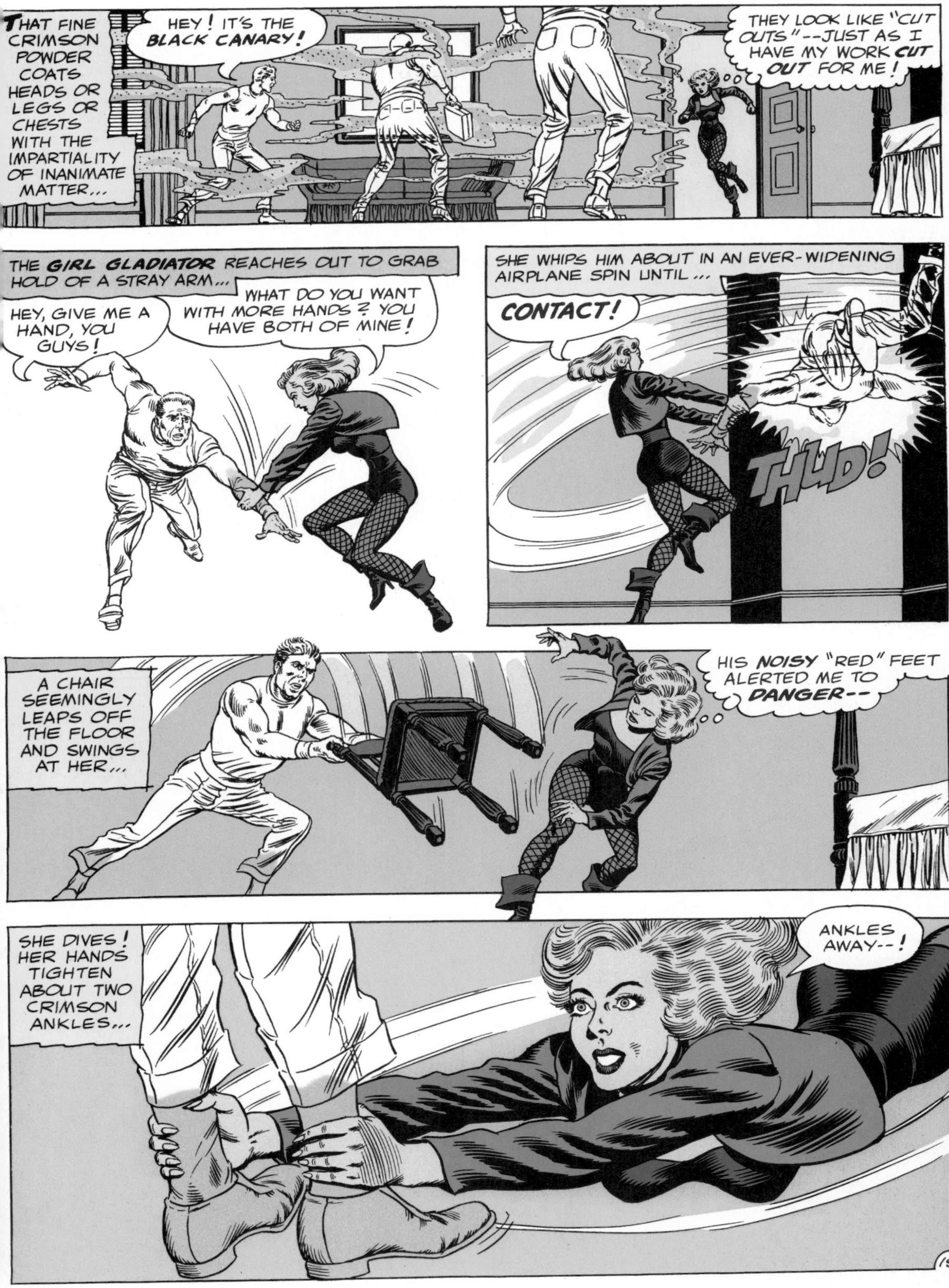
THAT FINE CRIMSON POWDER COATS HEADS OR LEGS OR CHESTS WITH THE IMPARTIALITY OF INANIMATE MATTER...
HEY! IT'S THE BLACK CANARY!
THEY LOOK LIKE "CUT OUTS" --JUST AS I HAVE MY WORK CUT OUT FOR ME!
THE GIRL GLADIATOR REACHES OUT TO GRAB HOLD OF A STRAY ARM...
HEY, GIVE ME A HAND, YOU GUYS!
WHAT DO YOU WANT WITH MORE HANDS? YOU HAVE BOTH OF MINE!
SHE WHIPS HIM ABOUT IN AN EVER-WIDENING AIRPLANE SPIN UNTIL...
CONTACT!
THUD!
A CHAIR SEEMINGLY LEAPS OFF THE FLOOR AND SWINGS AT HER...
HIS NOISY "RED" FEET ALERTED ME TO DANGER--
SHE DIVES! HER HANDS TIGHTEN ABOUT TWO CRIMSON ANKLES...
ANKLES AWAY--!
15

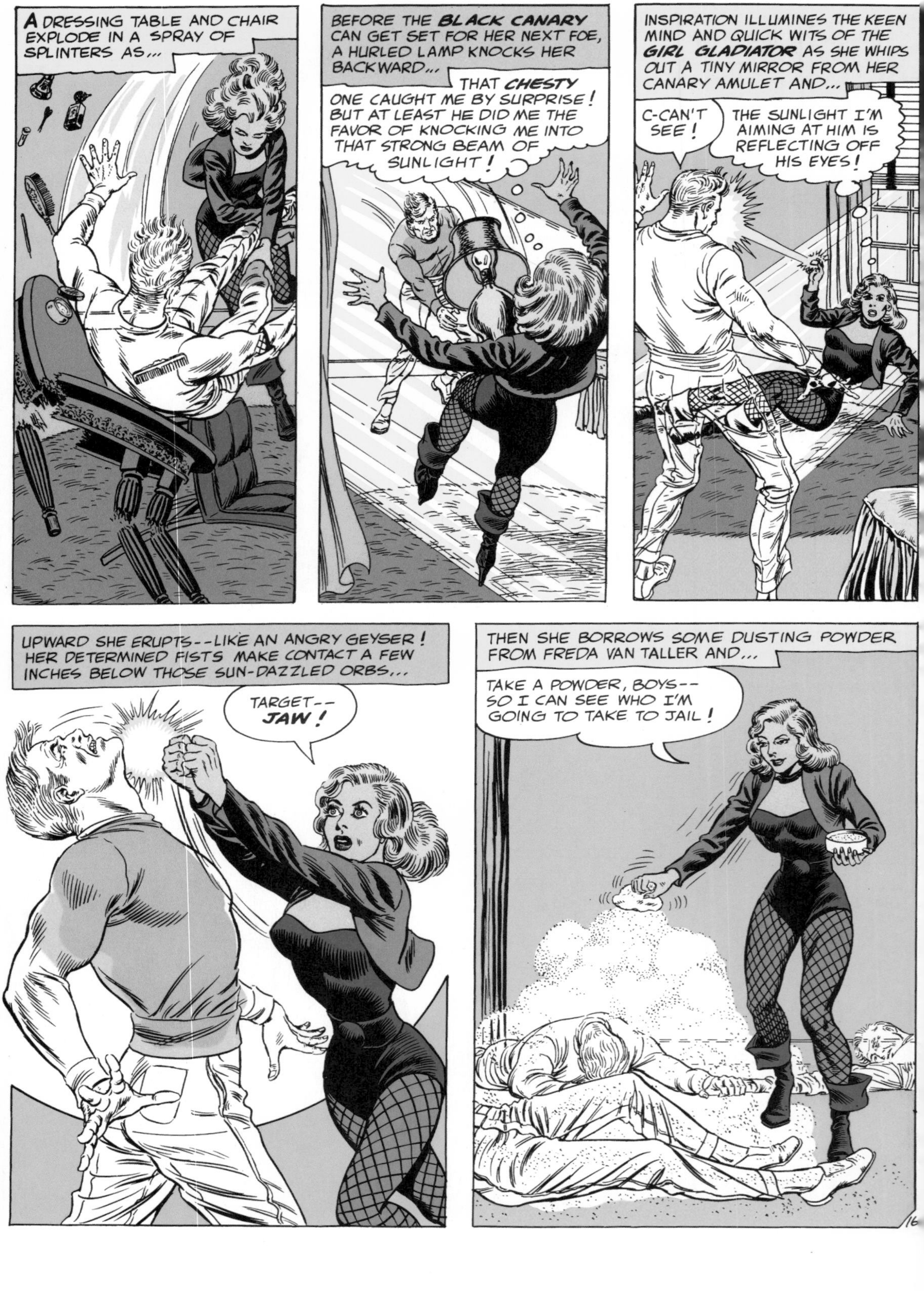
A DRESSING TABLE AND CHAIR EXPLODE IN A SPRAY OF SPLINTERS AS...
BEFORE THE BLACK CANARY CAN GET SET FOR HER NEXT FOE, A HURLED LAMP KNOCKS HER BACKWARD...
THAT CHESTY ONE CAUGHT ME BY SURPRISE! BUT AT LEAST HE DID ME THE FAVOR OF KNOCKING ME INTO THAT STRONG BEAM OF SUNLIGHT!
INSPIRATION ILLUMINES THE KEEN MIND AND QUICK WITS OF THE GIRL GLADIATOR AS SHE WHIPS OUT A TINY MIRROR FROM HER CANARY AMULET AND...
C-CAN'T SEE!
THE SUNLIGHT I'M AIMING AT HIM IS REFLECTING OFF HIS EYES!
UPWARD SHE ERUPTS--LIKE AN ANGRY GEYSER! HER DETERMINED FISTS MAKE CONTACT A FEW INCHES BELOW THOSE SUN-DAZZLED ORBS...
TARGET--JAW!
THEN SHE BORROWS SOME DUSTING POWDER FROM FREDA VAN TALLER AND...
TAKE A POWDER, BOYS--SO I CAN SEE WHO I'M GOING TO TAKE TO JAIL!
16

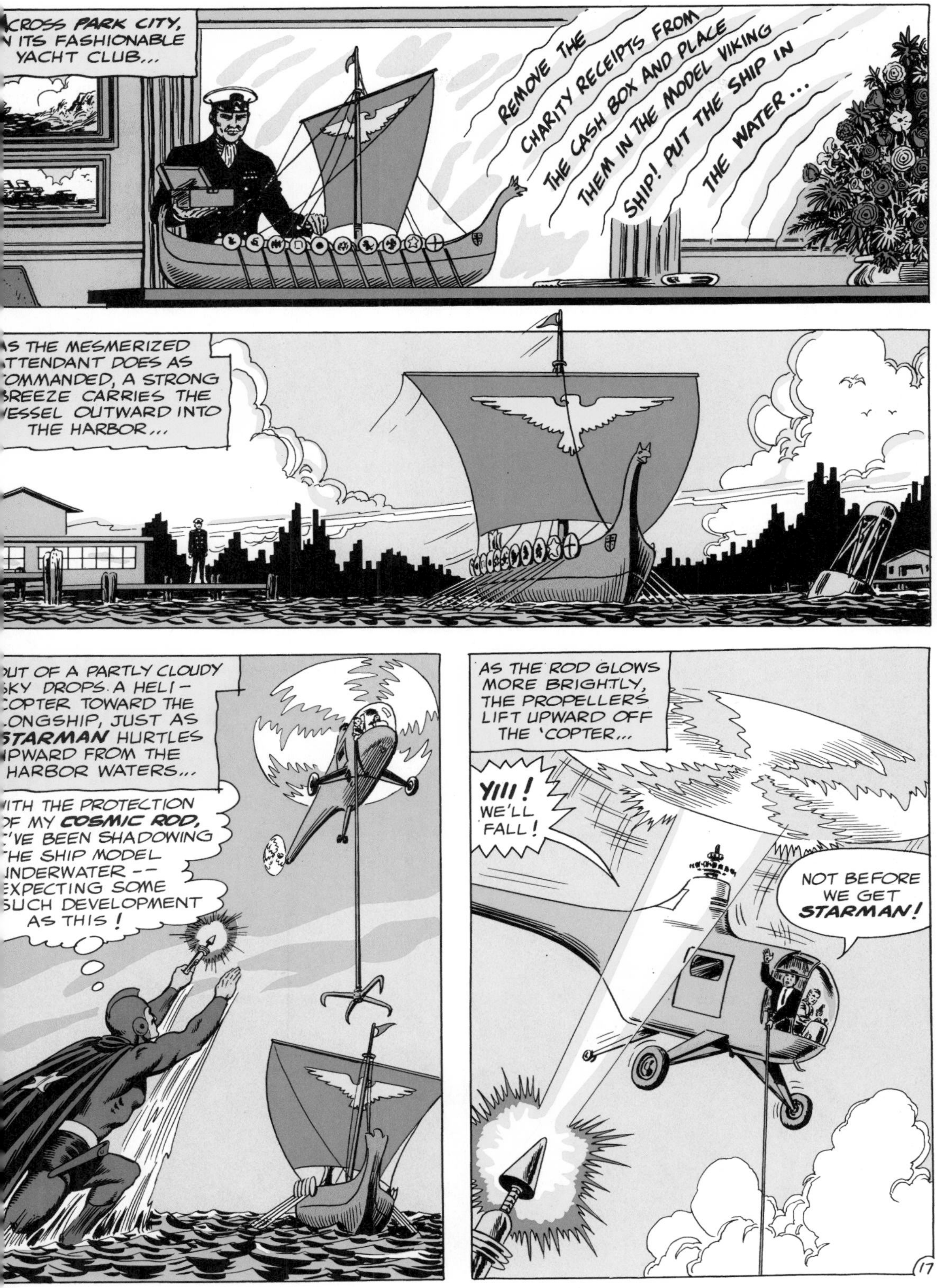
ACROSS PARK CITY, IN ITS FASHIONABLE YACHT CLUB...
REMOVE THE CHARITY RECEIPTS FROM THE CASH BOX AND PLACE THEM IN THE MODEL VIKING SHIP! PUT THE SHIP IN THE WATER...
AS THE MESMERIZED ATTENDANT DOES AS COMMANDED, A STRONG BREEZE CARRIES THE VESSEL OUTWARD INTO THE HARBOR...
OUT OF A PARTLY CLOUDY SKY DROPS A HELI-COPTER TOWARD THE LONGSHIP, JUST AS STARMAN HURTLES UPWARD FROM THE HARBOR WATERS...
WITH THE PROTECTION OF MY COSMIC ROD, I'VE BEEN SHADOWING THE SHIP MODEL UNDERWATER -- EXPECTING SOME SUCH DEVELOPMENT AS THIS!
AS THE ROD GLOWS MORE BRIGHTLY, THE PROPELLERS LIFT UPWARD OFF THE 'COPTER...
YIII! WE'LL FALL!
NOT BEFORE WE GET STARMAN!
17

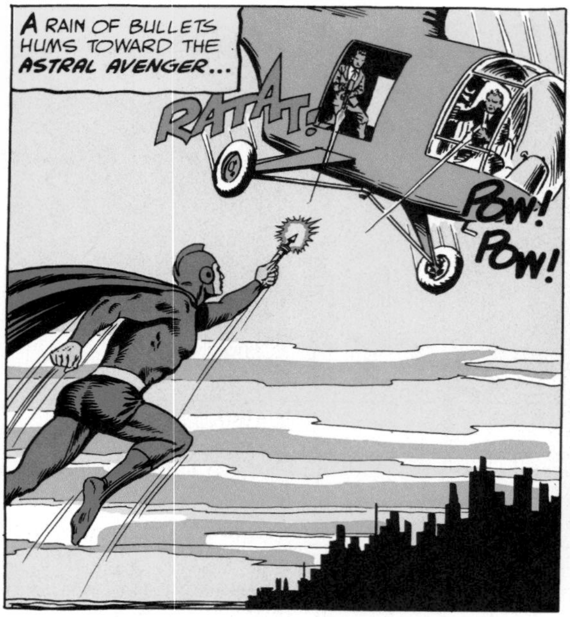
A RAIN OF BULLETS HUMS TOWARD THE ASTRAL AVENGER...
RATAT!
POW! POW!

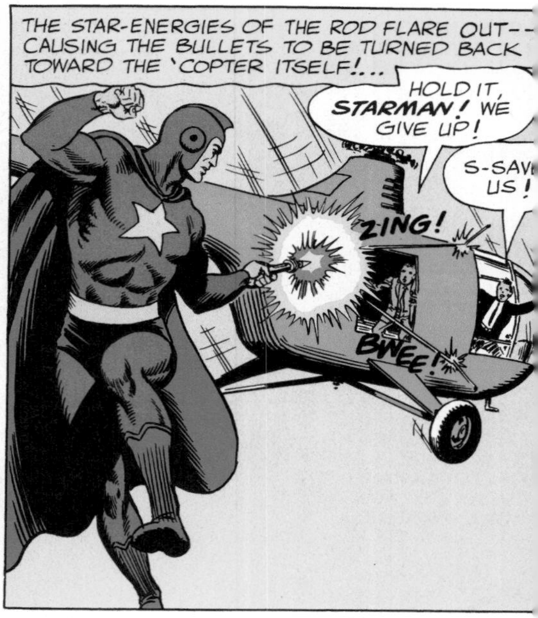
THE STAR-ENERGIES OF THE ROD FLARE OUT-- CAUSING THE BULLETS TO BE TURNED BACK TOWARD THE 'COPTER ITSELF!...
HOLD IT, STARMAN! WE GIVE UP!
S-SAV US!
ZING!
BWEE!

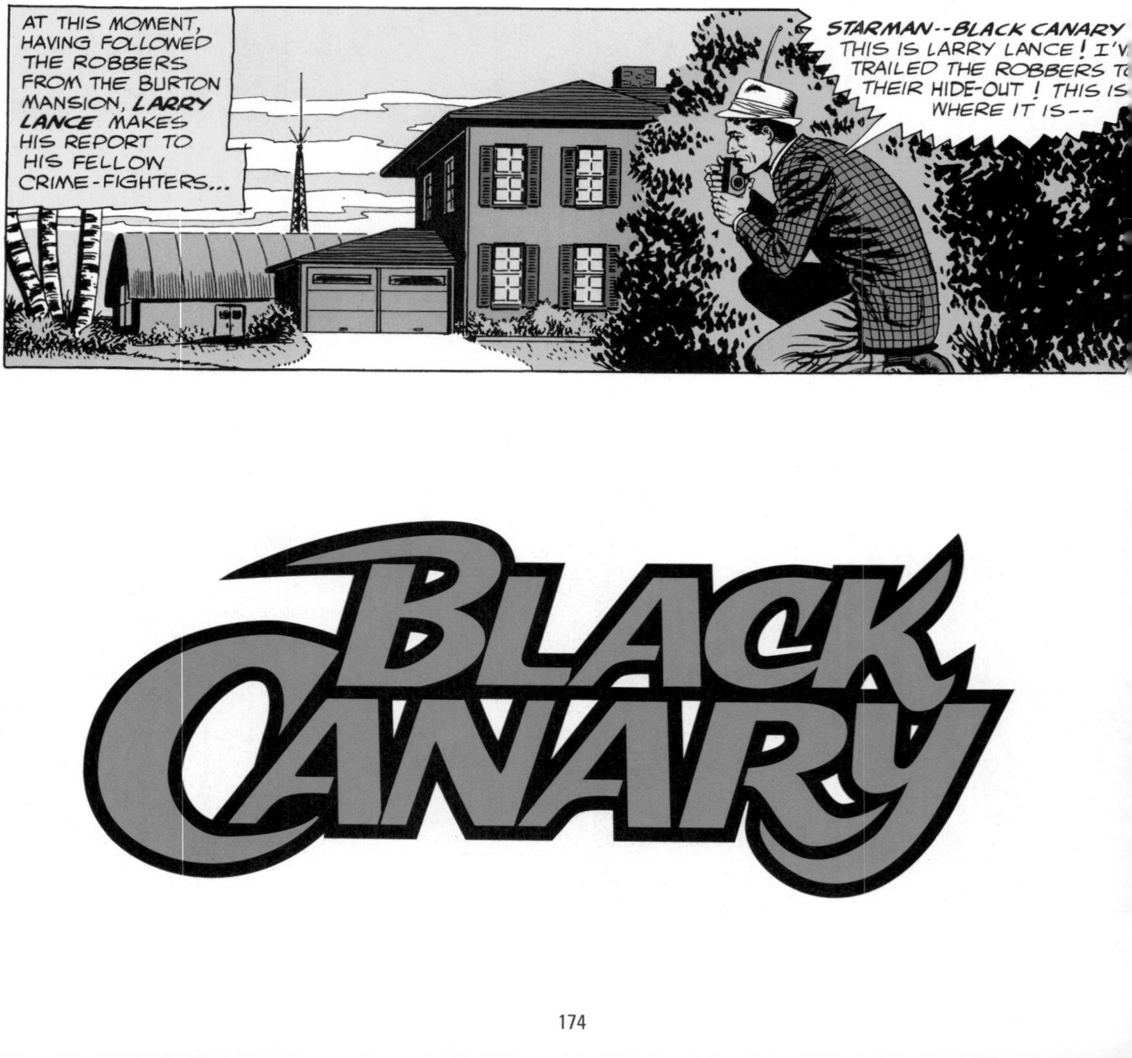
AT THIS MOMENT, HAVING FOLLOWED THE ROBBERS FROM THE BURTON MANSION, LARRY LANCE MAKES HIS REPORT TO HIS FELLOW CRIME-FIGHTERS...
STARMAN--BLACK CANARY THIS IS LARRY LANCE! I'V TRAILED THE ROBBERS T THEIR HIDE-OUT! THIS IS WHERE IT IS--

BLACK CANARY

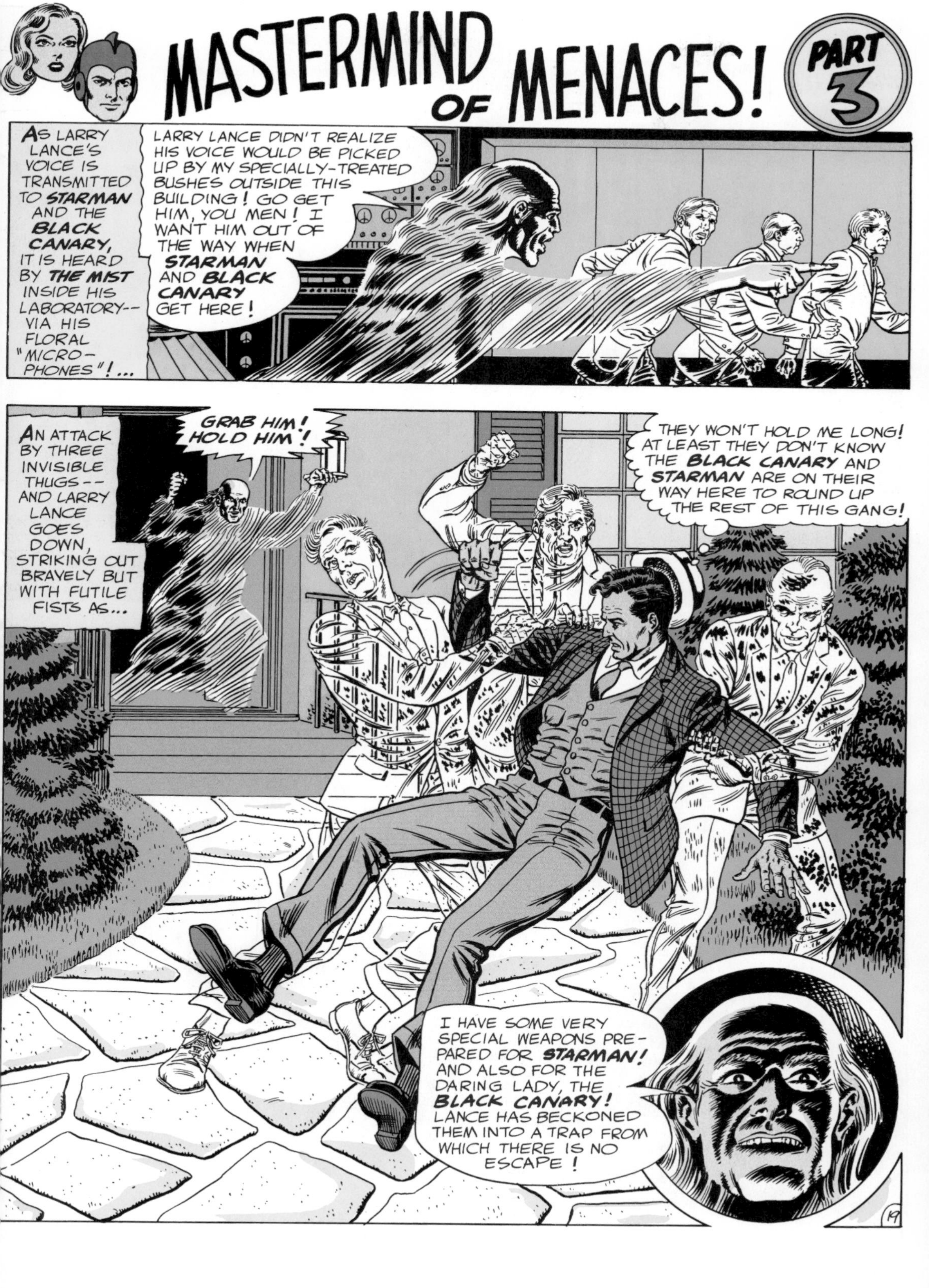
MASTERMIND OF MENACES!
PART 3
AS LARRY LANCE'S VOICE IS TRANSMITTED TO STARMAN AND THE BLACK CANARY, IT IS HEARD BY THE MIST INSIDE HIS LABORATORY-- VIA HIS FLORAL "MICRO-PHONES"!...
LARRY LANCE DIDN'T REALIZE HIS VOICE WOULD BE PICKED UP BY MY SPECIALLY-TREATED BUSHES OUTSIDE THIS BUILDING! GO GET HIM, YOU MEN! I WANT HIM OUT OF THE WAY WHEN STARMAN AND BLACK CANARY GET HERE!
AN ATTACK BY THREE INVISIBLE THUGS -- AND LARRY LANCE GOES DOWN, STRIKING OUT BRAVELY BUT WITH FUTILE FISTS AS...
GRAB HIM! HOLD HIM!
THEY WON'T HOLD ME LONG! AT LEAST THEY DON'T KNOW THE BLACK CANARY AND STARMAN ARE ON THEIR WAY HERE TO ROUND UP THE REST OF THIS GANG!
I HAVE SOME VERY SPECIAL WEAPONS PRE-PARED FOR STARMAN! AND ALSO FOR THE DARING LADY, THE BLACK CANARY! LANCE HAS BECKONED THEM INTO A TRAP FROM WHICH THERE IS NO ESCAPE!
19

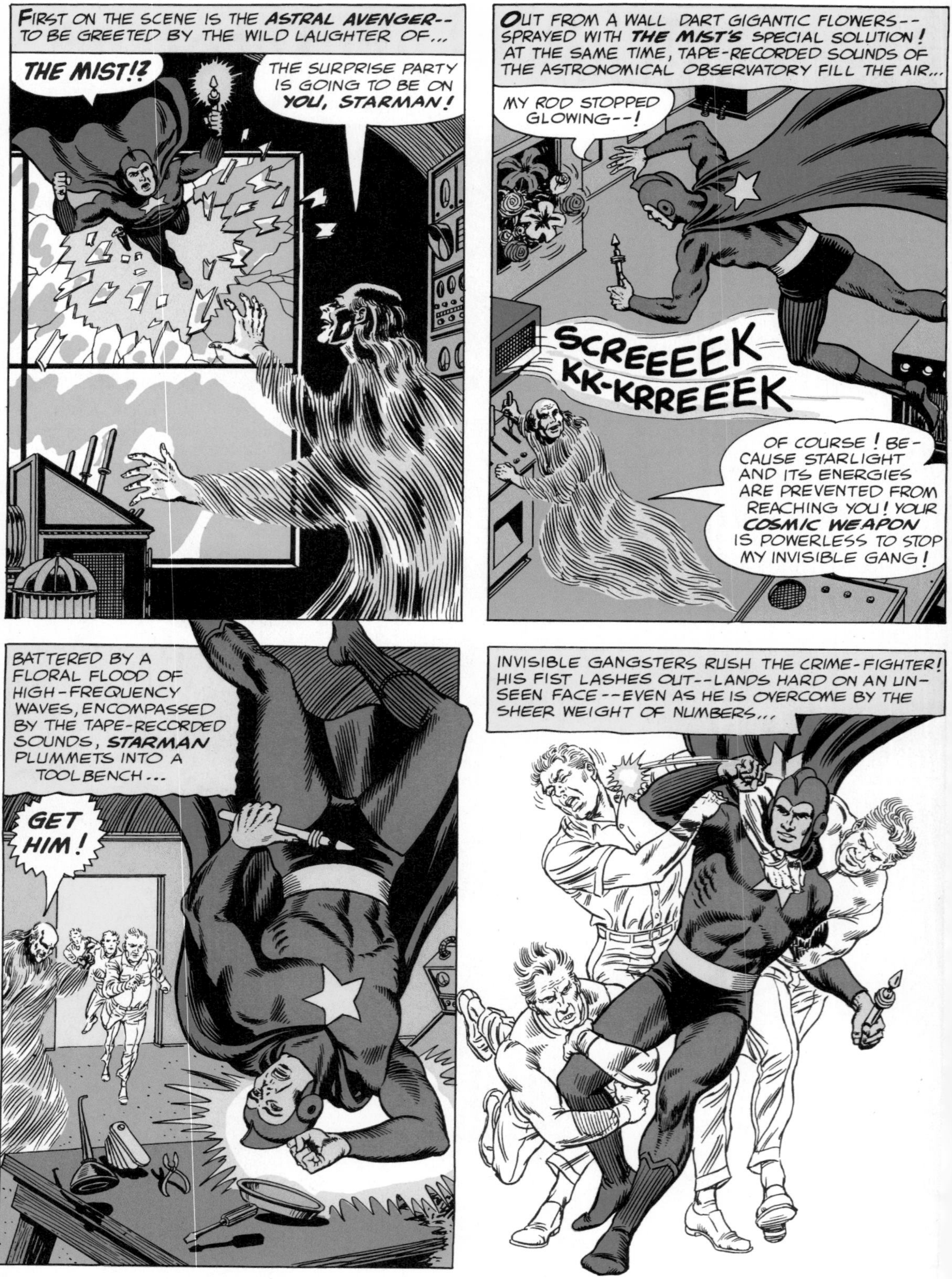
FIRST ON THE SCENE IS THE ASTRAL AVENGER-- TO BE GREETED BY THE WILD LAUGHTER OF...
THE MIST!?
THE SURPRISE PARTY IS GOING TO BE ON YOU, STARMAN!
OUT FROM A WALL DART GIGANTIC FLOWERS-- SPRAYED WITH THE MIST'S SPECIAL SOLUTION! AT THE SAME TIME, TAPE-RECORDED SOUNDS OF THE ASTRONOMICAL OBSERVATORY FILL THE AIR...
MY ROD STOPPED GLOWING--!
SCREEEEEK KK-KRREEEK
OF COURSE! BE-CAUSE STARLIGHT AND ITS ENERGIES ARE PREVENTED FROM REACHING YOU! YOUR COSMIC WEAPON IS POWERLESS TO STOP MY INVISIBLE GANG!
BATTERED BY A FLORAL FLOOD OF HIGH-FREQUENCY WAVES, ENCOMPASSED BY THE TAPE-RECORDED SOUNDS, STARMAN PLUMMETS INTO A TOOLBENCH...
GET HIM!
INVISIBLE GANGSTERS RUSH THE CRIME-FIGHTER! HIS FIST LASHES OUT--LANDS HARD ON AN UN-SEEN FACE--EVEN AS HE IS OVERCOME BY THE SHEER WEIGHT OF NUMBERS...

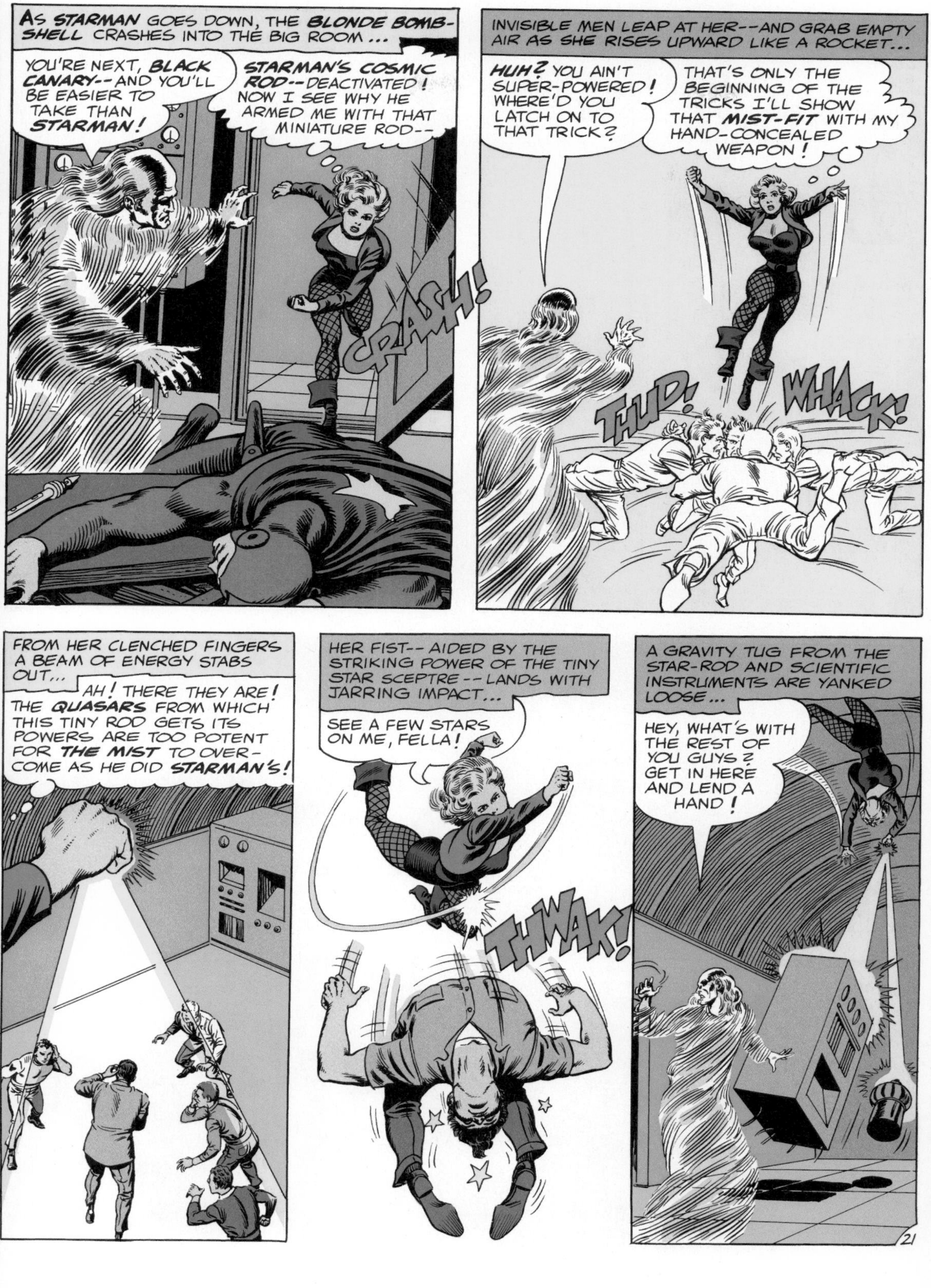

AS STARMAN GOES DOWN, THE BLONDE BOMBSHELL CRASHES INTO THE BIG ROOM...
YOU'RE NEXT, BLACK CANARY-- AND YOU'LL BE EASIER TO TAKE THAN STARMAN!
STARMAN'S COSMIC ROD--DEACTIVATED! NOW I SEE WHY HE ARMED ME WITH THAT MINIATURE ROD--
CRASH!
INVISIBLE MEN LEAP AT HER--AND GRAB EMPTY AIR AS SHE RISES UPWARD LIKE A ROCKET...
HUH? YOU AIN'T SUPER-POWERED! WHERE'D YOU LATCH ON TO THAT TRICK?
THAT'S ONLY THE BEGINNING OF THE TRICKS I'LL SHOW THAT MIST-FIT WITH MY HAND-CONCEALED WEAPON!
THUD!
WHACK!
FROM HER CLENCHED FINGERS A BEAM OF ENERGY STABS OUT...
AH! THERE THEY ARE! THE QUASARS FROM WHICH THIS TINY ROD GETS ITS POWERS ARE TOO POTENT FOR THE MIST TO OVERCOME AS HE DID STARMAN'S!
HER FIST-- AIDED BY THE STRIKING POWER OF THE TINY STAR SCEPTRE -- LANDS WITH JARRING IMPACT...
SEE A FEW STARS ON ME, FELLA!
THWAK!
A GRAVITY TUG FROM THE STAR-ROD AND SCIENTIFIC INSTRUMENTS ARE YANKED LOOSE...
HEY, WHAT'S WITH THE REST OF YOU GUYS? GET IN HERE AND LEND A HAND!
21

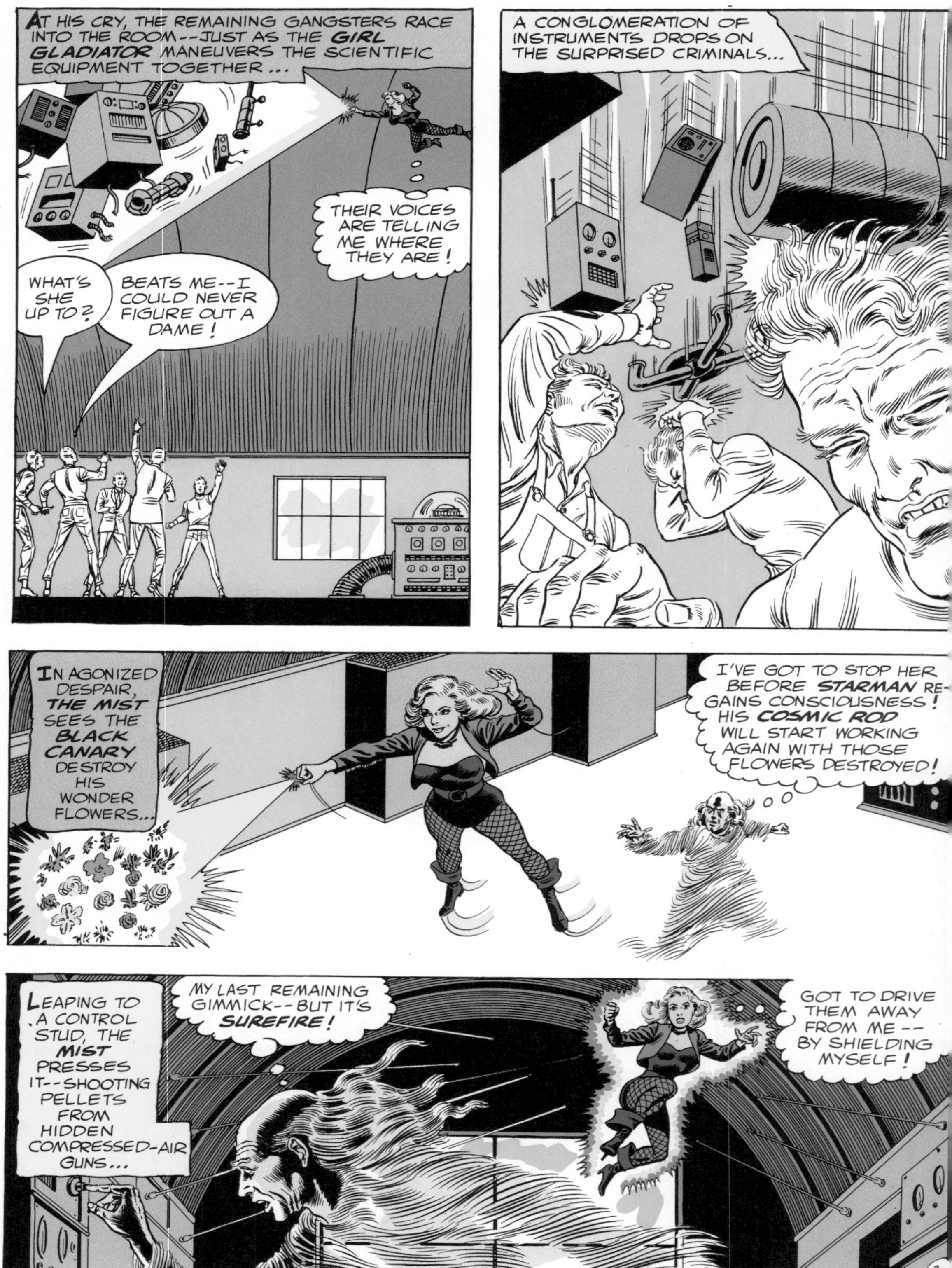
AT HIS CRY, THE REMAINING GANGSTERS RACE INTO THE ROOM--JUST AS THE GIRL GLADIATOR MANEUVERS THE SCIENTIFIC EQUIPMENT TOGETHER...
THEIR VOICES ARE TELLING ME WHERE THEY ARE!
WHAT'S SHE UP TO?
BEATS ME--I COULD NEVER FIGURE OUT A DAME!
A CONGLOMERATION OF INSTRUMENTS DROPS ON THE SURPRISED CRIMINALS...
IN AGONIZED DESPAIR, THE MIST SEES THE BLACK CANARY DESTROY HIS WONDER FLOWERS...
I'VE GOT TO STOP HER BEFORE STARMAN RE-GAINS CONSCIOUSNESS! HIS COSMIC ROD WILL START WORKING AGAIN WITH THOSE FLOWERS DESTROYED!
LEAPING TO A CONTROL STUD, THE MIST PRESSES IT--SHOOTING PELLETS FROM HIDDEN COMPRESSED-AIR GUNS...
MY LAST REMAINING GIMMICK--BUT IT'S SUREFIRE!
GOT TO DRIVE THEM AWAY FROM ME--BY SHIELDING MYSELF!
22

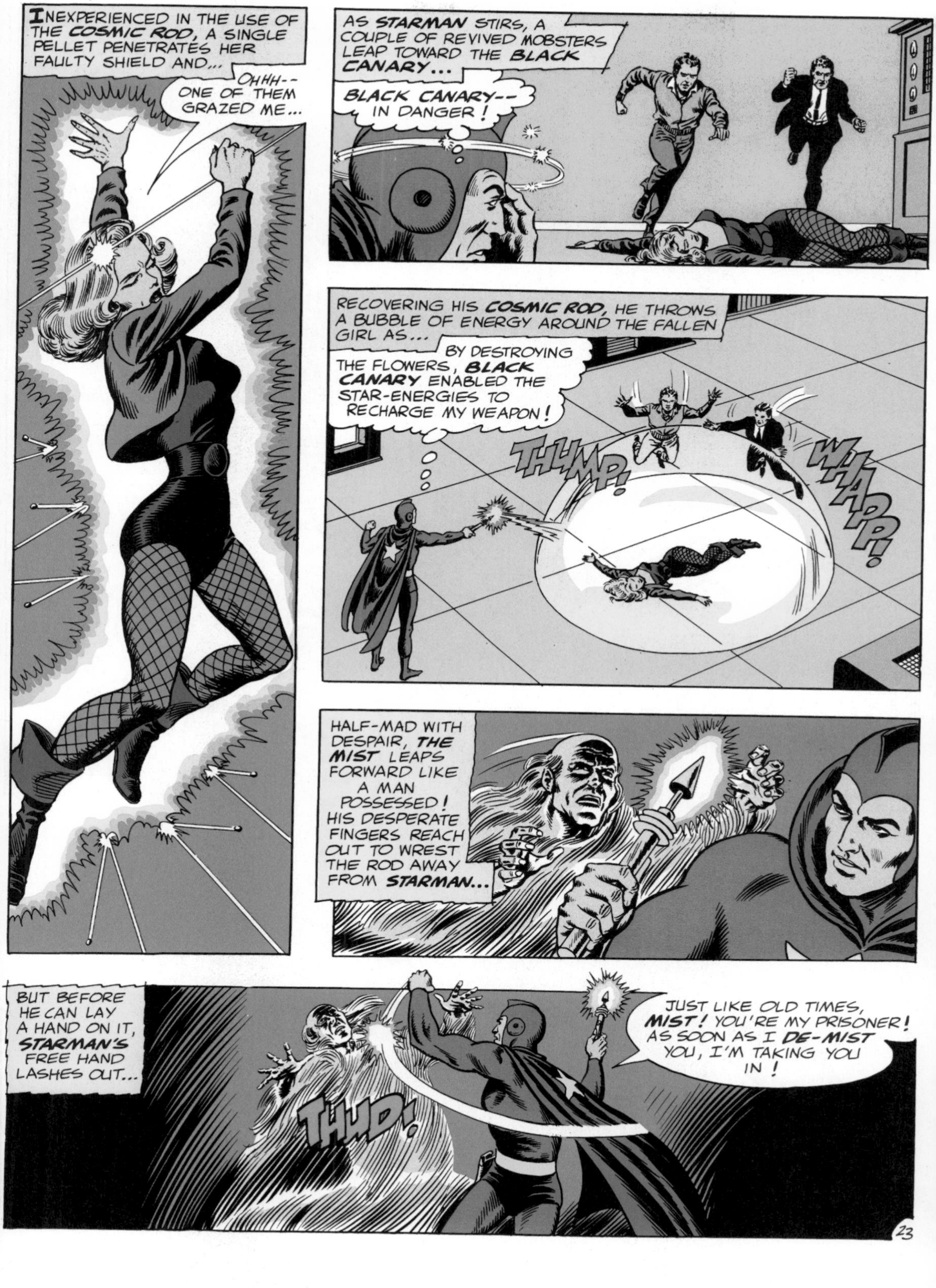
INEXPERIENCED IN THE USE OF THE COSMIC ROD, A SINGLE PELLET PENETRATES HER FAULTY SHIELD AND...
OHHH-- ONE OF THEM GRAZED ME...
AS STARMAN STIRS, A COUPLE OF REVIVED MOBSTERS LEAP TOWARD THE BLACK CANARY...
BLACK CANARY-- IN DANGER!
RECOVERING HIS COSMIC ROD, HE THROWS A BUBBLE OF ENERGY AROUND THE FALLEN GIRL AS...
BY DESTROYING THE FLOWERS, BLACK CANARY ENABLED THE STAR-ENERGIES TO RECHARGE MY WEAPON!
THUMP!
WHAPP!
HALF-MAD WITH DESPAIR, THE MIST LEAPS FORWARD LIKE A MAN POSSESSED! HIS DESPERATE FINGERS REACH OUT TO WREST THE ROD AWAY FROM STARMAN...
BUT BEFORE HE CAN LAY A HAND ON IT, STARMAN'S FREE HAND LASHES OUT...
JUST LIKE OLD TIMES, MIST! YOU'RE MY PRISONER! AS SOON AS I DE-MIST YOU, I'M TAKING YOU IN!
THUD!
23

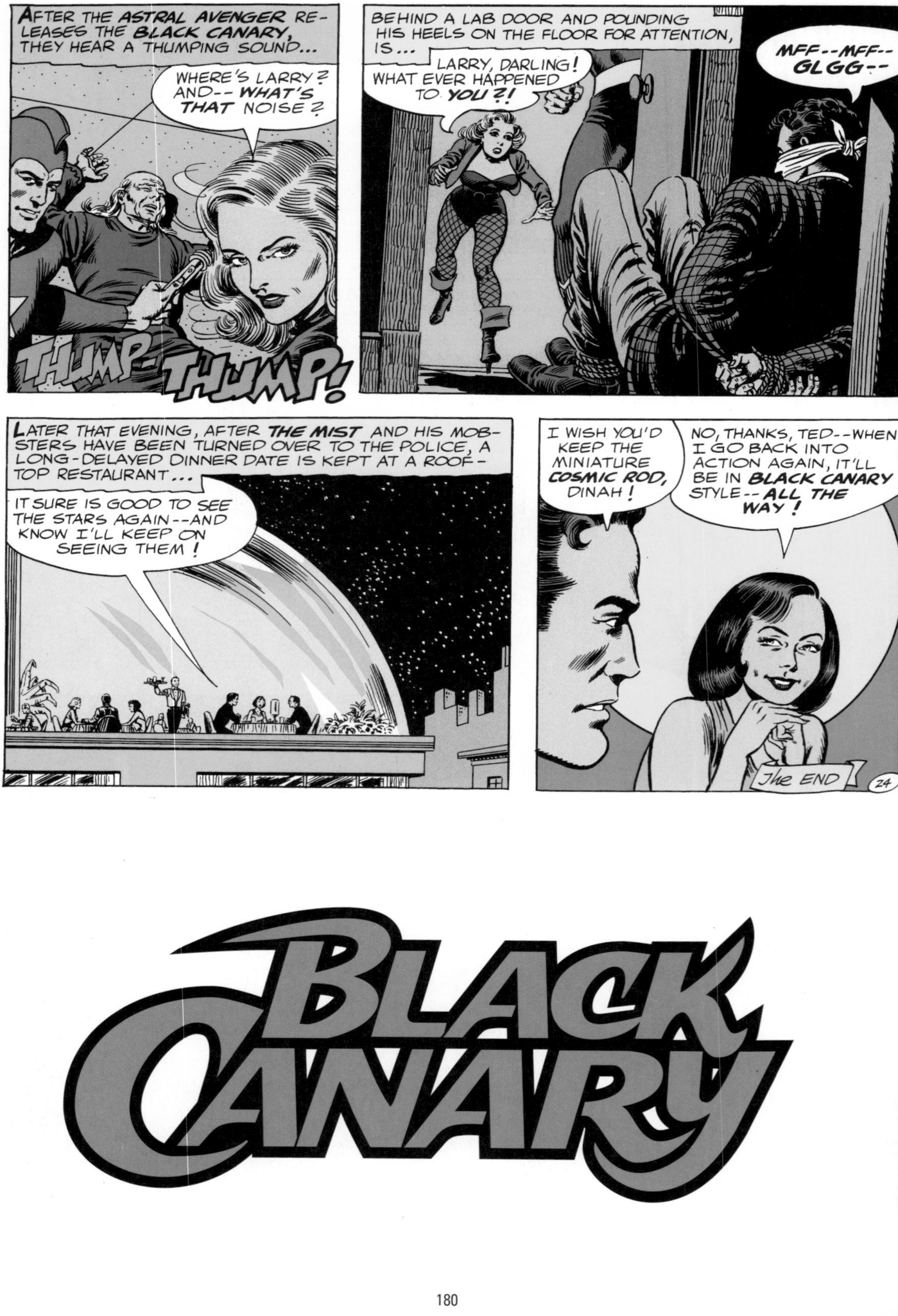
AFTER THE ASTRAL AVENGER RELEASES THE BLACK CANARY, THEY HEAR A THUMPING SOUND...
WHERE'S LARRY? AND-- WHAT'S THAT NOISE?
THUMP-THUMP!
BEHIND A LAB DOOR AND POUNDING HIS HEELS ON THE FLOOR FOR ATTENTION, IS...
LARRY, DARLING! WHAT EVER HAPPENED TO YOU?!
MFF--MFF--GLGG--
LATER THAT EVENING, AFTER THE MIST AND HIS MOBSTERS HAVE BEEN TURNED OVER TO THE POLICE, A LONG-DELAYED DINNER DATE IS KEPT AT A ROOF-TOP RESTAURANT...
IT SURE IS GOOD TO SEE THE STARS AGAIN--AND KNOW I'LL KEEP ON SEEING THEM!
I WISH YOU'D KEEP THE MINIATURE COSMIC ROD, DINAH!
NO, THANKS, TED--WHEN I GO BACK INTO ACTION AGAIN, IT'LL BE IN BLACK CANARY STYLE--ALL THE WAY!
The END
24

BLACK CANARY

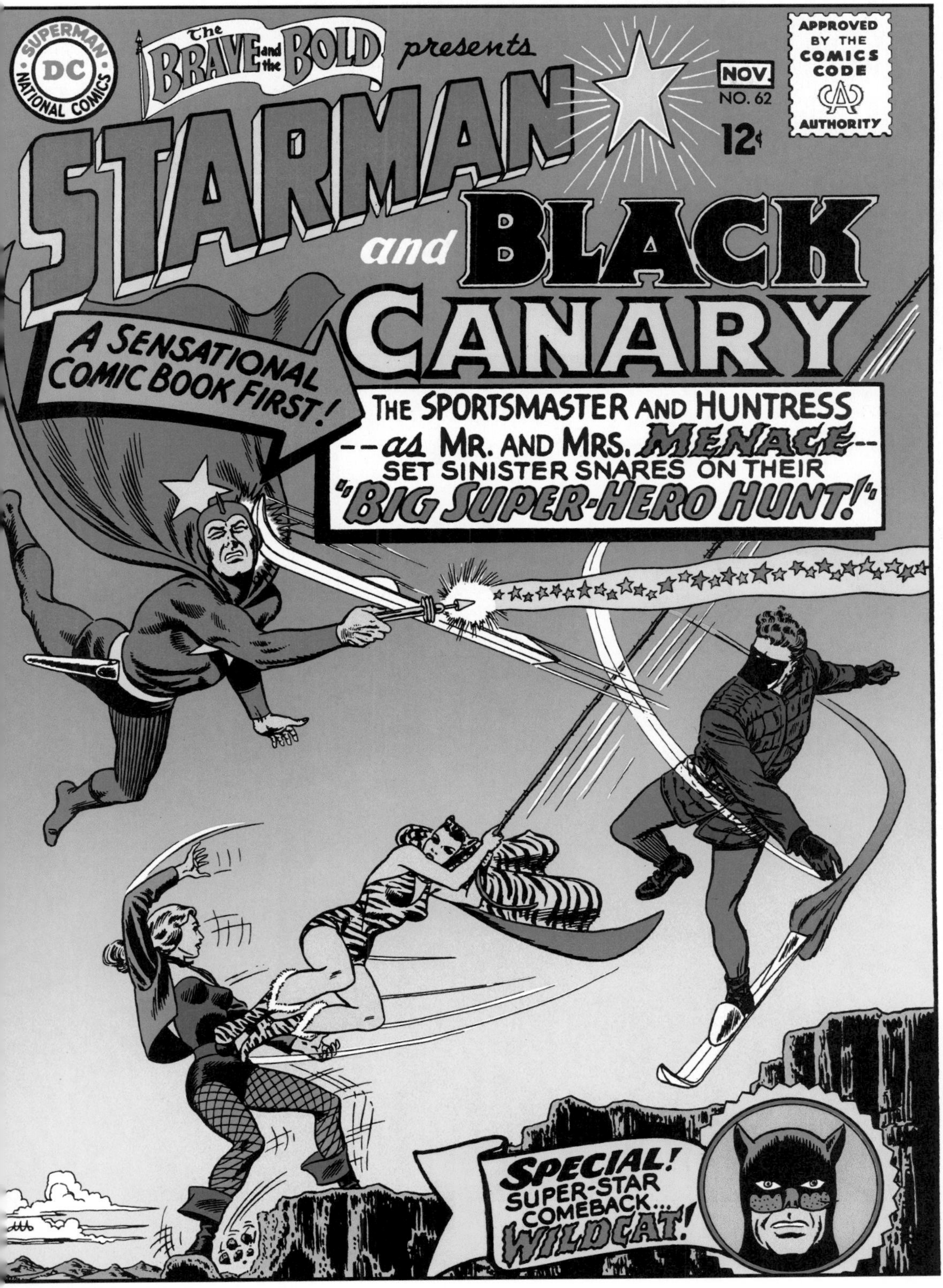
SUPERMAN DC NATIONAL COMICS
The BRAVE and the BOLD presents
NOV. NO. 62
12¢
APPROVED BY THE COMICS CODE AUTHORITY
STARMAN
and BLACK CANARY
A SENSATIONAL COMIC BOOK FIRST!
THE SPORTSMASTER AND HUNTRESS --as MR. AND MRS. MENACE-- SET SINISTER SNARES ON THEIR "BIG SUPER-HERO HUNT!"
SPECIAL! SUPER-STAR COMEBACK... WILDCAT!

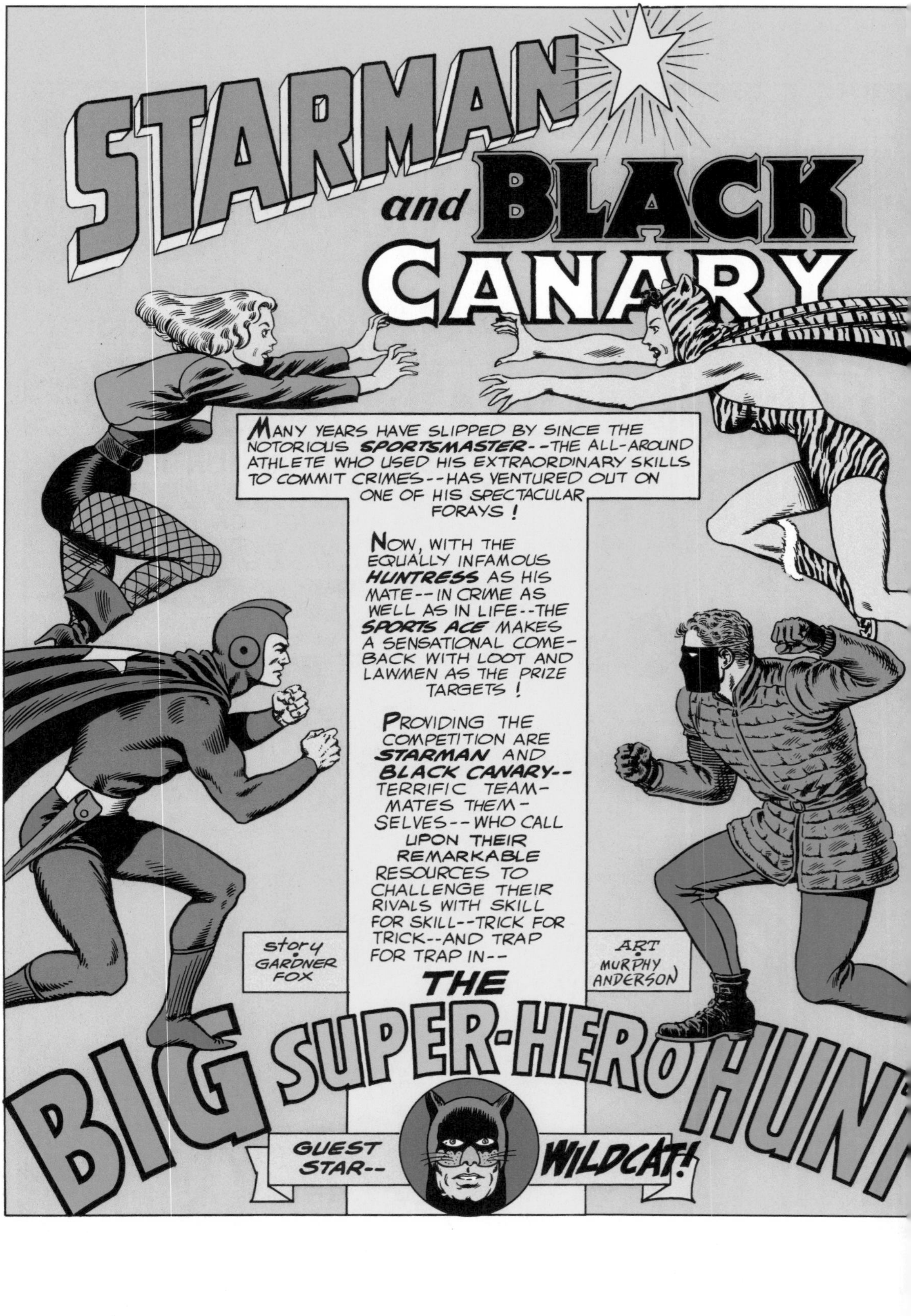

STARMAN and BLACK CANARY
MANY YEARS HAVE SLIPPED BY SINCE THE NOTORIOUS SPORTSMASTER--THE ALL-AROUND ATHLETE WHO USED HIS EXTRAORDINARY SKILLS TO COMMIT CRIMES--HAS VENTURED OUT ON ONE OF HIS SPECTACULAR FORAYS!
NOW, WITH THE EQUALLY INFAMOUS HUNTRESS AS HIS MATE--IN CRIME AS WELL AS IN LIFE--THE SPORTS ACE MAKES A SENSATIONAL COME-BACK WITH LOOT AND LAWMEN AS THE PRIZE TARGETS!
PROVIDING THE COMPETITION ARE STARMAN AND BLACK CANARY--TERRIFIC TEAM-MATES THEM-SELVES--WHO CALL UPON THEIR REMARKABLE RESOURCES TO CHALLENGE THEIR RIVALS WITH SKILL FOR SKILL--TRICK FOR TRICK--AND TRAP FOR TRAP IN--
story GARDNER FOX
ART MURPHY ANDERSON
THE BIG SUPER-HERO HUNT
GUEST STAR--WILDCAT!

AN ARTISTRY OF GENIUS HAS SHAPED THE WAX MANNIKINS AT THE ANNUAL *SPORTSMAN'S SHOW* IN *FEDERAL CITY!* THE GREAT GREEK BOXER *MILO* STANDS BESIDE *DISCOBOLUS,* AND BEYOND THEM IS THE MARATHON RUNNER, *PHEIPPIDES...*

I NEVER SAW ANYTHING SO REAL!

THEY'RE ABSOLUTELY LIFE-LIKE!

LIFE-LIKE? HOW TRUE! FOR EVEN AS ADMIRING EYES STARE UPWARD AT THE DISCUS THROWER CARVED BY *MYRON,* THE WAXEN IMAGE STIRS..

OHHHH! IT'S --STARTING TO MOVE--!

LET'S GET OUT OF HERE!

DISCOBOLUS STANDS ERECT! THE WAX OF HIS ARMS AND LEGS, CHEST AND TORSO, CRACKS WIDE OPEN TO REVEAL --A FISHERMAN -- GARBED FIGURE ...

HA! HA! NO NEED TO SHRIEK, MY GOOD LADIES -- I SHALL NOT HARM YOU -- NOR ANYONE ELSE WHO DOES NOT STAND IN MY WAY OF FISHING FOR A PRIZE CATCH!

EEEK!

OUTWARD FLIES A TROUT LURE TOWARD THE FAMOUS *PARKER TROPHY,* AWARDED TO THE OUTSTANDING ATHLETE OF THE YEAR! THE TROUT-ROD BENDS AND THE REEL WHIZZES...

OBSERVE MY PERFECT CAST, FOLKS! IF YOU WEREN'T SO FRIGHTENED, I'M SURE YOU'D BE APPLAUDING IT!

A HOOK SNATCHES UP THE *PARKER TROPHY!* IN RESPONSE TO THE STRONG TUG OF THE ANGLER, THE CUP FLIES UP-WARD AND ACROSS THE ROOM...

WHY DOESN'T SOMEBODY STOP HIM?

WHAT'S HAPPENED TO THE GUARDS?

2

A POWERFUL HAND TIGHTENS ON THE PRIZE CUP! ANOTHER HAND SENDS THE FLY DARTING OUTWARD LIKE THE TONGUE OF AN ASP,...

STOP ME IF YOU CAN--I WELCOME IT! IT'LL GIVE ZEST TO MY THEFT!

SINCE I MADE ALL THESE WAX FIGURES HERE--I WAS ABLE TO GIMMICK THEM TO SERVE MY PURPOSES!

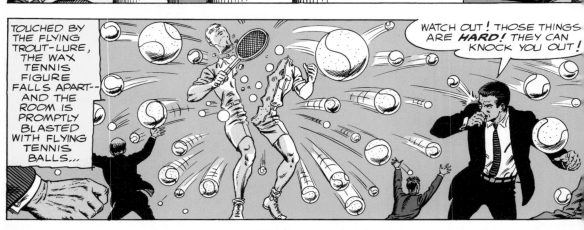

TOUCHED BY THE FLYING TROUT-LURE, THE WAX TENNIS FIGURE FALLS APART-- AND THE ROOM IS PROMPTLY BLASTED WITH FLYING TENNIS BALLS...

WATCH OUT! THOSE THINGS ARE HARD! THEY CAN KNOCK YOU OUT!

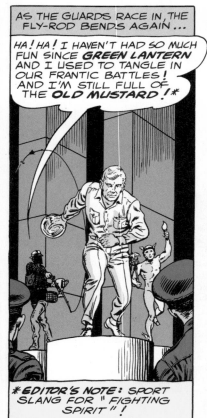

AS THE GUARDS RACE IN, THE FLY-ROD BENDS AGAIN...

HA! HA! I HAVEN'T HAD SO MUCH FUN SINCE GREEN LANTERN AND I USED TO TANGLE IN OUR FRANTIC BATTLES! AND I'M STILL FULL OF THE OLD MUSTARD!*

*EDITOR'S NOTE: SPORT SLANG FOR "FIGHTING SPIRIT"!

ANOTHER STATUE CRACKS WIDE OPEN AND NOW THE ROOM BECOMES A DEADLY BOWLING ALLEY AS...

NOT EVEN THE SPECIAL OPERATIVES FROM THE LARRY LANCE DETECTIVE AGENCY CAN STOP THAT GUY!

MEANWHILE, UNAWARE OF TH GOINGS-ON IN THE ROOM ABOVE THEM, THE DIRECTO OF THE SPORTSMAN'S SHOW IS DINING WITH MRS. LARRY LANCE ...

LARRY WAS WRAPPED UP IN AN URGENT CASE, MR. BENSON-- SO HE ASKED ME TO FILL IN FOR HIM!

I ASSURE YOU, MRS. LANCE I'M MORE THAN SATISFIED WITH THE SUBSTITUTION

WHEN THEY LEISURELY MAKE THEIR WAY TO THE SHOW FLOOR...

I NEVER ENJOYED DINNER SO MUCH AND--LOOK! THAT FISHERMAN HAS THE PARKER TROPHY!

HE WAS A FISHERMAN--

OUT OF ONE SPORTS COSTUME--INTO ANOTHER! INSTEAD OF TROUT BOOTS, THE SPORTS-MASTER SWITCHES TO JET-SKIS...

NOW HE'S A SKIER!

MRS. LANCE--YOUR MEN WERE HIRED TO PROTECT THE PARKER TROPHY! YOU'RE IN CHARGE HERE--WHAT ARE YOU GOING TO DO ABOUT IT?

THOSE JET-SKIS ERUPT WITH POWER THAT CARRIES THE ATHLETIC ARCH-CRIMINAL UPWARD TOWARD A HIGH WINDOW...

I'M THE ONLY COSTUMED VILLAIN WHO MASQUERADES IN A UNIFORM TO SUIT THE OCCASION! HERE'S WHERE I TAKE OFF ON AN "UPHILL SLALOM"!

I'LL DO SOMETHING, ALL RIGHT--BUT NOT AS DINAH DRAKE LANCE!

IN A DESERTED LOUNGE ROOM OF THE GREAT SHOW PALACE, SHE SWIFTLY CHANGES HER GARMENTS WITH THE EASE OF LONG PRACTICE...

NOW I'M ALL SET TO GO--AS THE BLACK CANARY!

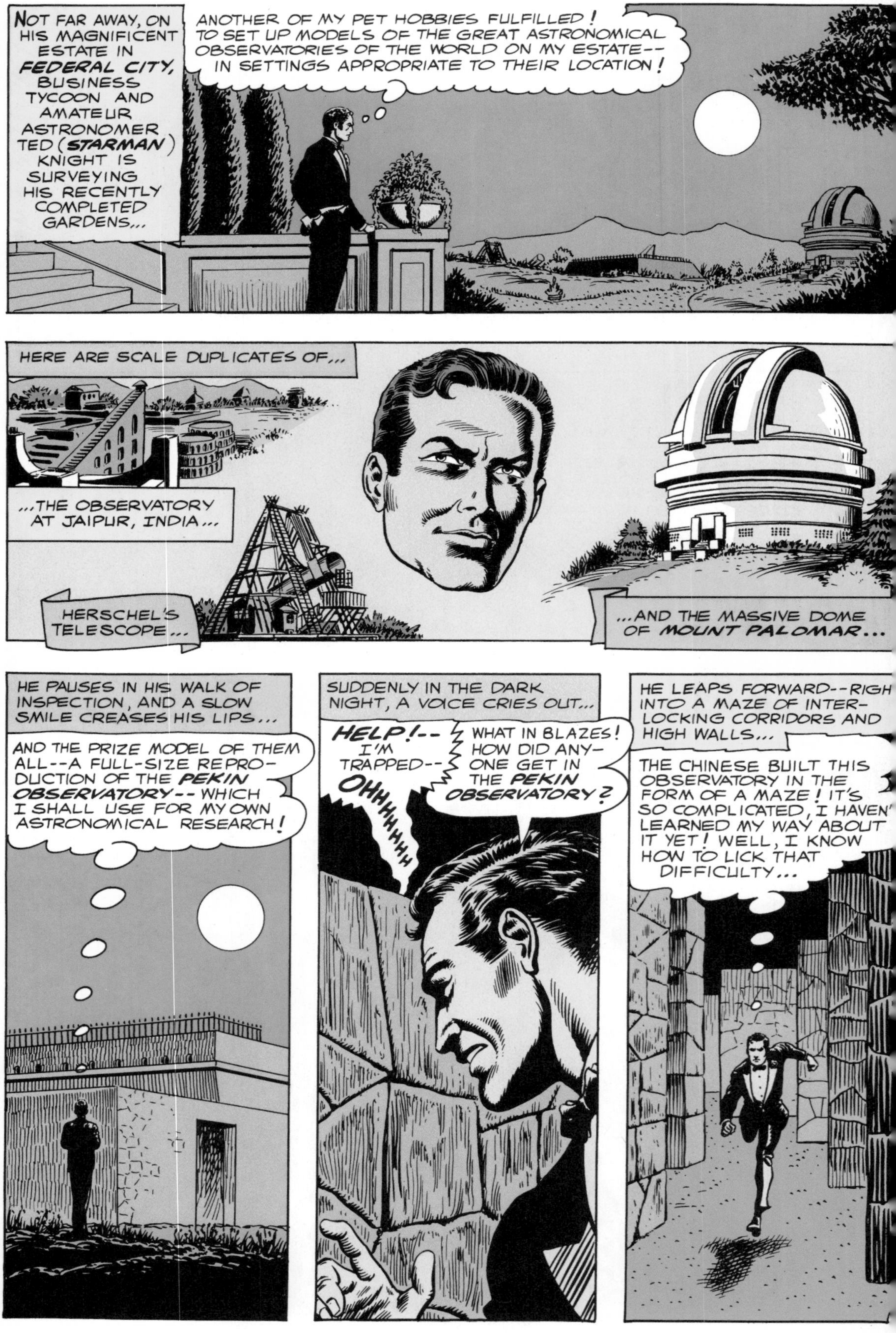
NOT FAR AWAY, ON HIS MAGNIFICENT ESTATE IN FEDERAL CITY, BUSINESS TYCOON AND AMATEUR ASTRONOMER TED (STARMAN) KNIGHT IS SURVEYING HIS RECENTLY COMPLETED GARDENS...
ANOTHER OF MY PET HOBBIES FULFILLED! TO SET UP MODELS OF THE GREAT ASTRONOMICAL OBSERVATORIES OF THE WORLD ON MY ESTATE-- IN SETTINGS APPROPRIATE TO THEIR LOCATION!
HERE ARE SCALE DUPLICATES OF...
...THE OBSERVATORY AT JAIPUR, INDIA...
HERSCHEL'S TELESCOPE...
...AND THE MASSIVE DOME OF MOUNT PALOMAR...
HE PAUSES IN HIS WALK OF INSPECTION, AND A SLOW SMILE CREASES HIS LIPS...
AND THE PRIZE MODEL OF THEM ALL--A FULL-SIZE REPRODUCTION OF THE PEKIN OBSERVATORY-- WHICH I SHALL USE FOR MY OWN ASTRONOMICAL RESEARCH!
SUDDENLY IN THE DARK NIGHT, A VOICE CRIES OUT...
HELP!-- I'M TRAPPED-- OHHHHHHH
WHAT IN BLAZES! HOW DID ANYONE GET IN THE PEKIN OBSERVATORY?
HE LEAPS FORWARD--RIGH INTO A MAZE OF INTERLOCKING CORRIDORS AND HIGH WALLS...
THE CHINESE BUILT THIS OBSERVATORY IN THE FORM OF A MAZE! IT'S SO COMPLICATED, I HAVEN' LEARNED MY WAY ABOUT IT YET! WELL, I KNOW HOW TO LICK THAT DIFFICULTY...

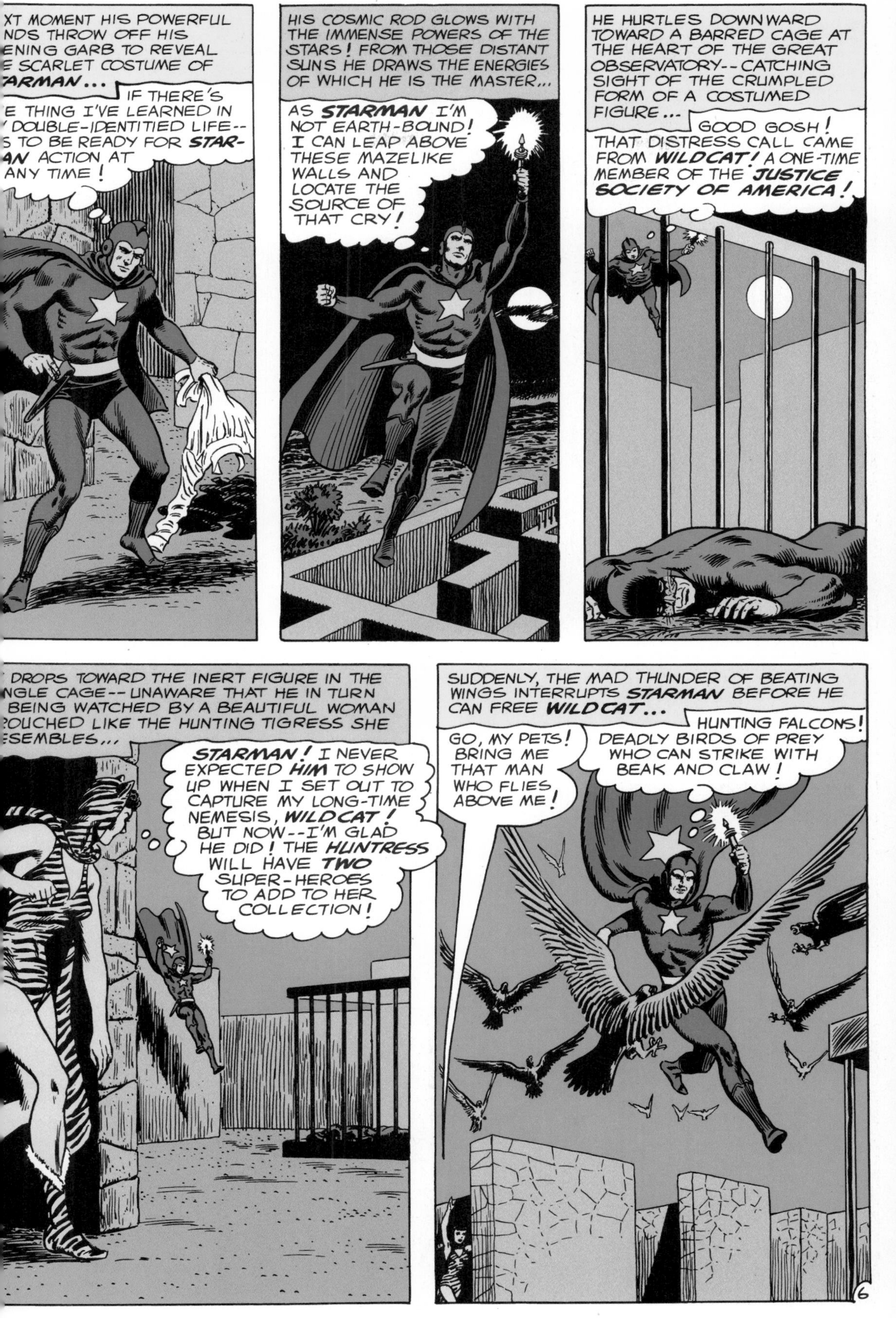
XT MOMENT HIS POWERFUL NDS THROW OFF HIS ENING GARB TO REVEAL E SCARLET COSTUME OF STARMAN...
IF THERE'S E THING I'VE LEARNED IN DOUBLE-IDENTITIED LIFE-- S TO BE READY FOR STAR-AN ACTION AT ANY TIME!
HIS COSMIC ROD GLOWS WITH THE IMMENSE POWERS OF THE STARS! FROM THOSE DISTANT SUNS HE DRAWS THE ENERGIES OF WHICH HE IS THE MASTER...
AS STARMAN I'M NOT EARTH-BOUND! I CAN LEAP ABOVE THESE MAZELIKE WALLS AND LOCATE THE SOURCE OF THAT CRY!
HE HURTLES DOWNWARD TOWARD A BARRED CAGE AT THE HEART OF THE GREAT OBSERVATORY--CATCHING SIGHT OF THE CRUMPLED FORM OF A COSTUMED FIGURE...
GOOD GOSH! THAT DISTRESS CALL CAME FROM WILDCAT! A ONE-TIME MEMBER OF THE JUSTICE SOCIETY OF AMERICA!
DROPS TOWARD THE INERT FIGURE IN THE NGLE CAGE--UNAWARE THAT HE IN TURN BEING WATCHED BY A BEAUTIFUL WOMAN ROUCHED LIKE THE HUNTING TIGRESS SHE ESEMBLES...
STARMAN! I NEVER EXPECTED HIM TO SHOW UP WHEN I SET OUT TO CAPTURE MY LONG-TIME NEMESIS, WILDCAT! BUT NOW--I'M GLAD HE DID! THE HUNTRESS WILL HAVE TWO SUPER-HEROES TO ADD TO HER COLLECTION!
SUDDENLY, THE MAD THUNDER OF BEATING WINGS INTERRUPTS STARMAN BEFORE HE CAN FREE WILDCAT...
GO, MY PETS! BRING ME THAT MAN WHO FLIES ABOVE ME!
HUNTING FALCONS! DEADLY BIRDS OF PREY WHO CAN STRIKE WITH BEAK AND CLAW!
6

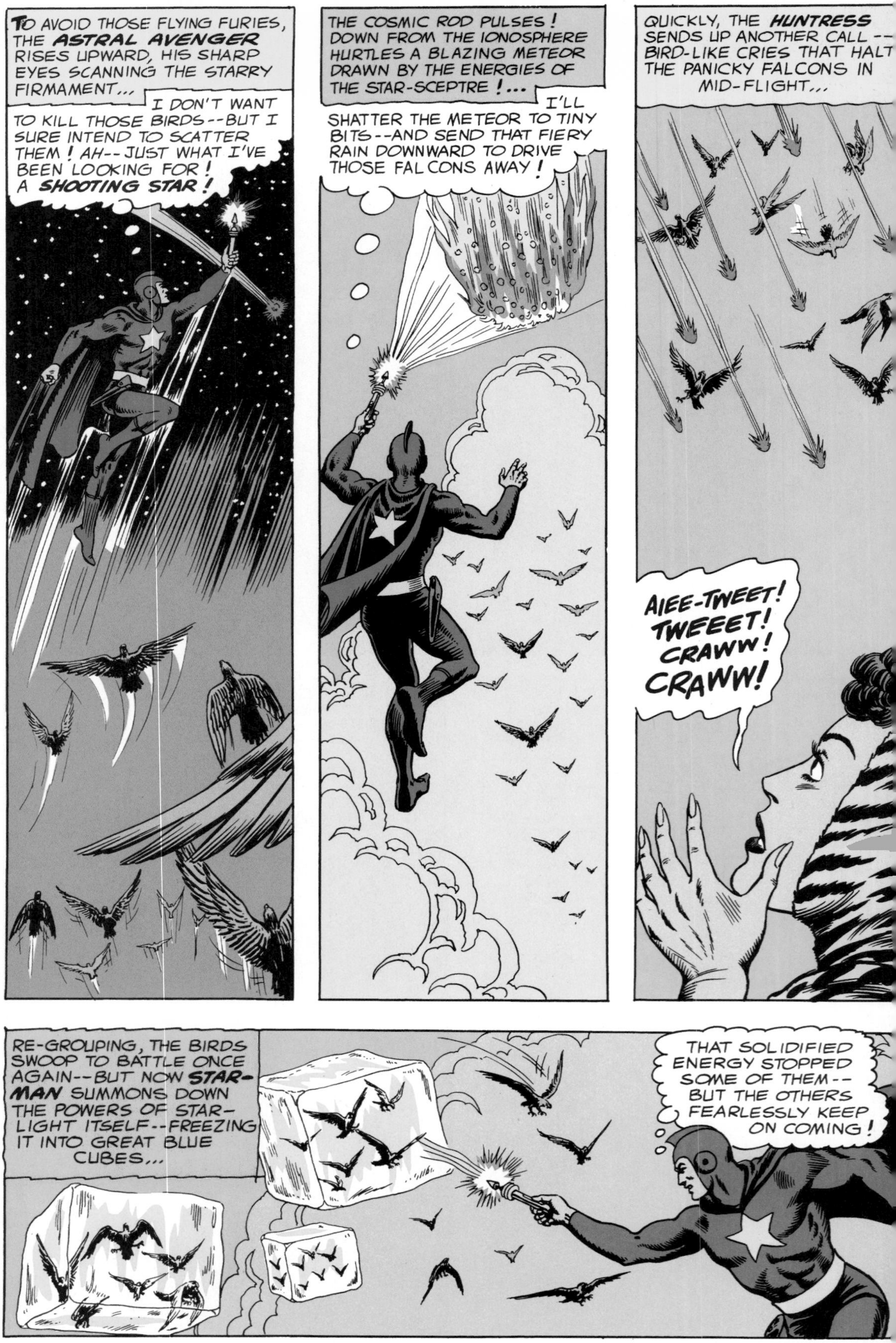
TO AVOID THOSE FLYING FURIES, THE ASTRAL AVENGER RISES UPWARD, HIS SHARP EYES SCANNING THE STARRY FIRMAMENT...
I DON'T WANT TO KILL THOSE BIRDS--BUT I SURE INTEND TO SCATTER THEM! AH--JUST WHAT I'VE BEEN LOOKING FOR! A SHOOTING STAR!
THE COSMIC ROD PULSES! DOWN FROM THE IONOSPHERE HURTLES A BLAZING METEOR DRAWN BY THE ENERGIES OF THE STAR-SCEPTRE!...
I'LL SHATTER THE METEOR TO TINY BITS--AND SEND THAT FIERY RAIN DOWNWARD TO DRIVE THOSE FALCONS AWAY!
QUICKLY, THE HUNTRESS SENDS UP ANOTHER CALL--BIRD-LIKE CRIES THAT HALT THE PANICKY FALCONS IN MID-FLIGHT...
AIEE-TWEET! TWEEET! CRAWW! CRAWW!
RE-GROUPING, THE BIRDS SWOOP TO BATTLE ONCE AGAIN--BUT NOW STAR-MAN SUMMONS DOWN THE POWERS OF STAR-LIGHT ITSELF--FREEZING IT INTO GREAT BLUE CUBES...
THAT SOLIDIFIED ENERGY STOPPED SOME OF THEM--BUT THE OTHERS FEARLESSLY KEEP ON COMING!

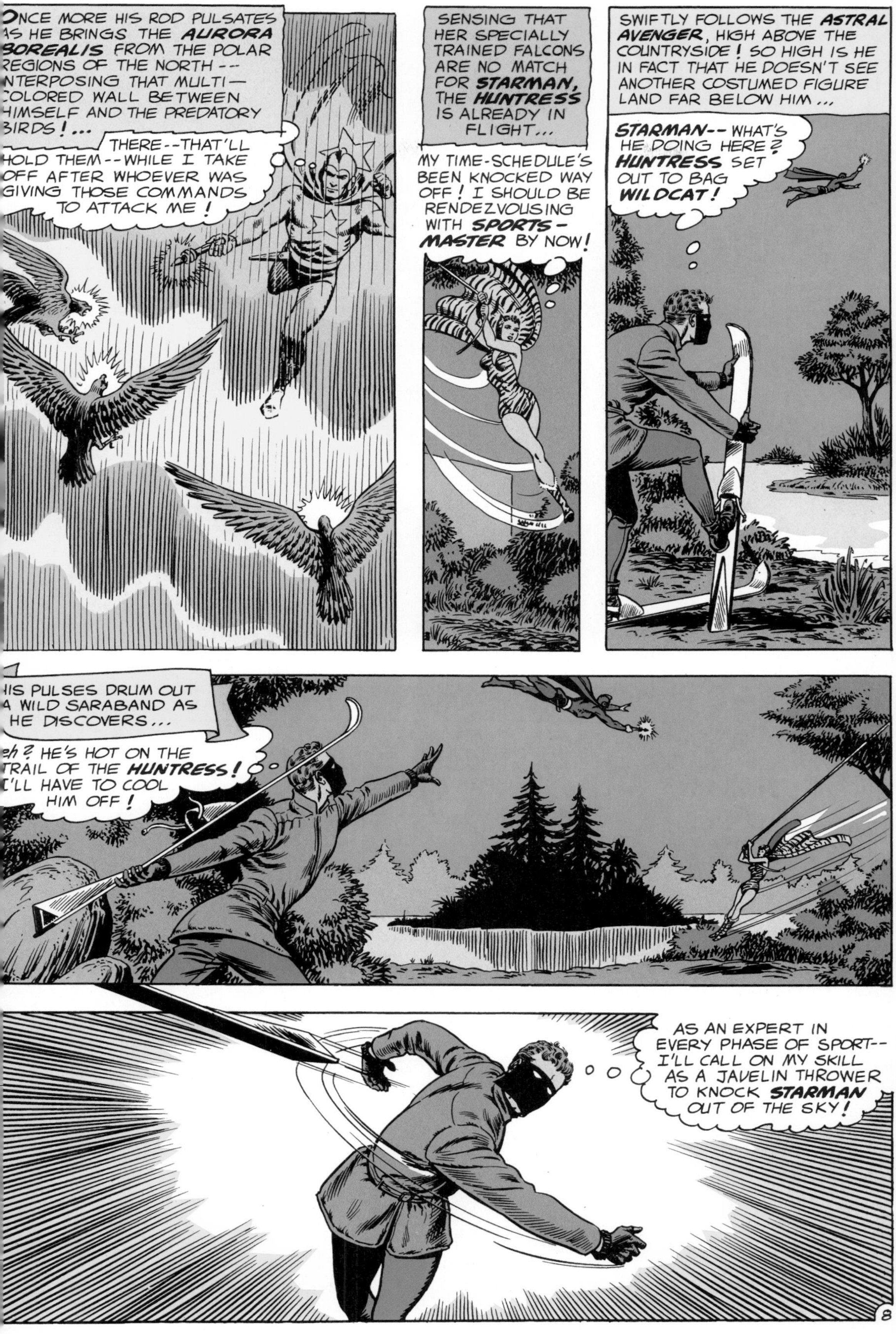
ONCE MORE HIS ROD PULSATES AS HE BRINGS THE AURORA BOREALIS FROM THE POLAR REGIONS OF THE NORTH -- INTERPOSING THAT MULTI-COLORED WALL BETWEEN HIMSELF AND THE PREDATORY BIRDS! ...
THERE--THAT'LL HOLD THEM--WHILE I TAKE OFF AFTER WHOEVER WAS GIVING THOSE COMMANDS TO ATTACK ME!
SENSING THAT HER SPECIALLY TRAINED FALCONS ARE NO MATCH FOR STARMAN, THE HUNTRESS IS ALREADY IN FLIGHT...
MY TIME-SCHEDULE'S BEEN KNOCKED WAY OFF! I SHOULD BE RENDEZVOUSING WITH SPORTS-MASTER BY NOW!
SWIFTLY FOLLOWS THE ASTRAL AVENGER, HIGH ABOVE THE COUNTRYSIDE! SO HIGH IS HE IN FACT THAT HE DOESN'T SEE ANOTHER COSTUMED FIGURE LAND FAR BELOW HIM...
STARMAN-- WHAT'S HE DOING HERE? HUNTRESS SET OUT TO BAG WILDCAT!
HIS PULSES DRUM OUT A WILD SARABAND AS HE DISCOVERS...
EH? HE'S HOT ON THE TRAIL OF THE HUNTRESS! I'LL HAVE TO COOL HIM OFF!
AS AN EXPERT IN EVERY PHASE OF SPORT-- I'LL CALL ON MY SKILL AS A JAVELIN THROWER TO KNOCK STARMAN OUT OF THE SKY!
8

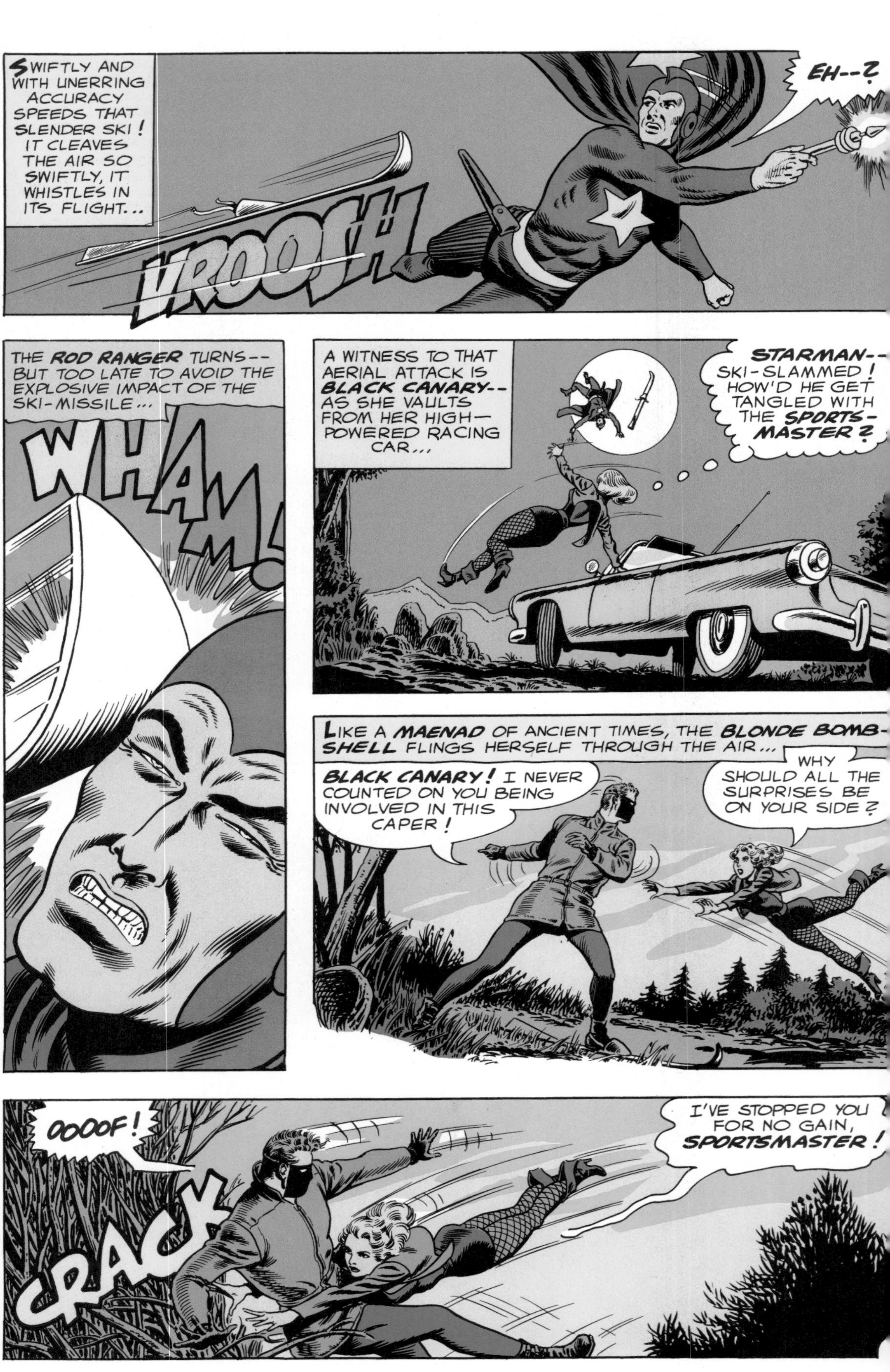
SWIFTLY AND WITH UNERRING ACCURACY SPEEDS THAT SLENDER SKI! IT CLEAVES THE AIR SO SWIFTLY, IT WHISTLES IN ITS FLIGHT...
EH--?
VROOSH
THE ROD RANGER TURNS-- BUT TOO LATE TO AVOID THE EXPLOSIVE IMPACT OF THE SKI-MISSILE...
WHAM!
A WITNESS TO THAT AERIAL ATTACK IS BLACK CANARY-- AS SHE VAULTS FROM HER HIGH-POWERED RACING CAR...
STARMAN-- SKI-SLAMMED! HOW'D HE GET TANGLED WITH THE SPORTSMASTER?
LIKE A MAENAD OF ANCIENT TIMES, THE BLONDE BOMBSHELL FLINGS HERSELF THROUGH THE AIR...
BLACK CANARY! I NEVER COUNTED ON YOU BEING INVOLVED IN THIS CAPER!
WHY SHOULD ALL THE SURPRISES BE ON YOUR SIDE?
OOOOF!
CRACK
I'VE STOPPED YOU FOR NO GAIN, SPORTSMASTER!

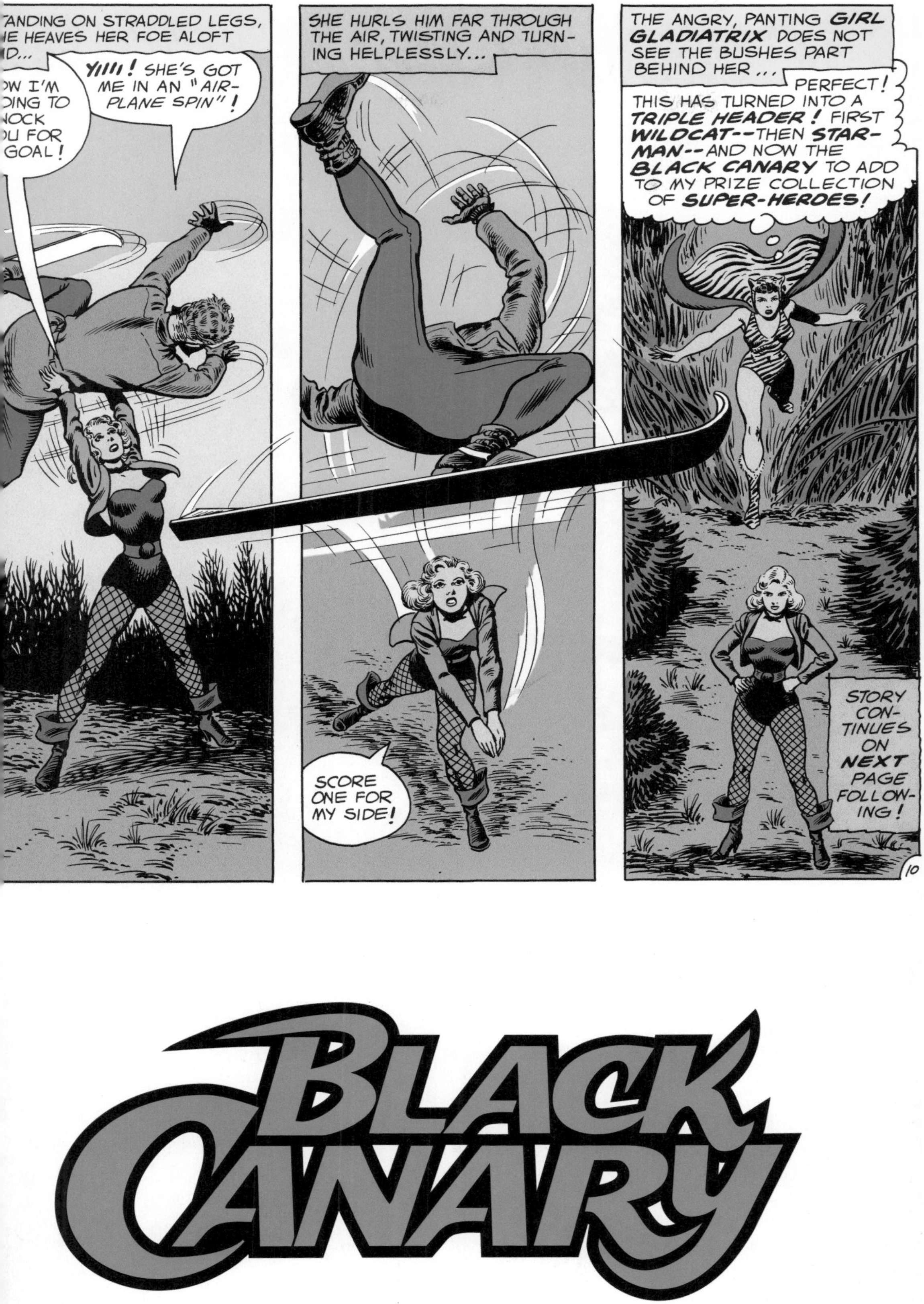

TANDING ON STRADDLED LEGS, HE HEAVES HER FOE ALOFT D...
OW I'M OING TO NOCK U FOR GOAL!
YIIII! SHE'S GOT ME IN AN "AIR-PLANE SPIN"!
SHE HURLS HIM FAR THROUGH THE AIR, TWISTING AND TURN-ING HELPLESSLY...
SCORE ONE FOR MY SIDE!
THE ANGRY, PANTING GIRL GLADIATRIX DOES NOT SEE THE BUSHES PART BEHIND HER...
PERFECT! THIS HAS TURNED INTO A TRIPLE HEADER! FIRST WILDCAT--THEN STAR-MAN--AND NOW THE BLACK CANARY TO ADD TO MY PRIZE COLLECTION OF SUPER-HEROES!
STORY CON-TINUES ON NEXT PAGE FOLLOW-ING!
10

BLACK CANARY

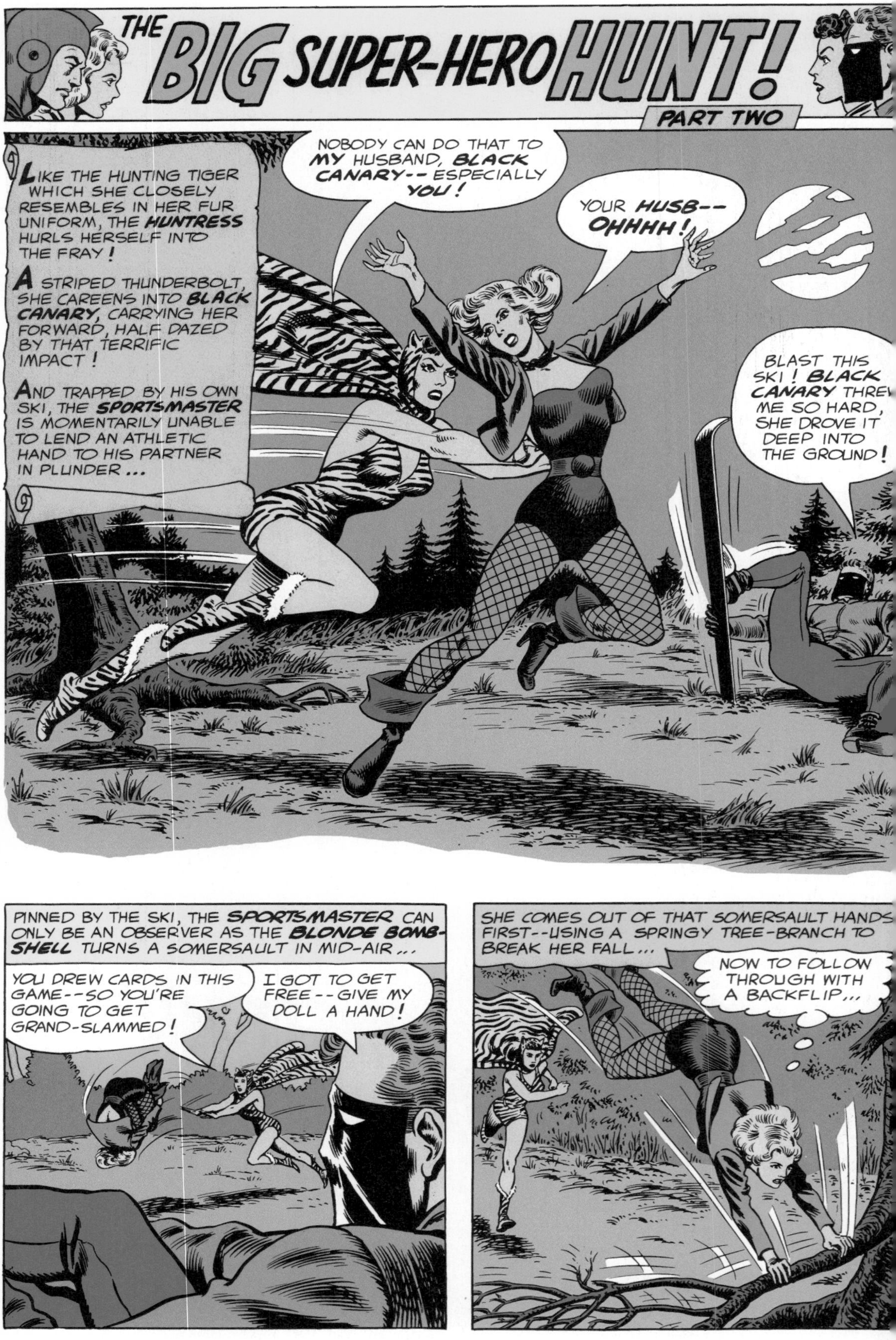
THE BIG SUPER-HERO HUNT!
PART TWO
LIKE THE HUNTING TIGER WHICH SHE CLOSELY RESEMBLES IN HER FUR UNIFORM, THE HUNTRESS HURLS HERSELF INTO THE FRAY!
A STRIPED THUNDERBOLT, SHE CAREENS INTO BLACK CANARY, CARRYING HER FORWARD, HALF DAZED BY THAT TERRIFIC IMPACT!
AND TRAPPED BY HIS OWN SKI, THE SPORTSMASTER IS MOMENTARILY UNABLE TO LEND AN ATHLETIC HAND TO HIS PARTNER IN PLUNDER...
NOBODY CAN DO THAT TO MY HUSBAND, BLACK CANARY-- ESPECIALLY YOU!
YOUR HUSB-- OHHHH!
BLAST THIS SKI! BLACK CANARY THREW ME SO HARD, SHE DROVE IT DEEP INTO THE GROUND!
PINNED BY THE SKI, THE SPORTSMASTER CAN ONLY BE AN OBSERVER AS THE BLONDE BOMBSHELL TURNS A SOMERSAULT IN MID-AIR...
YOU DREW CARDS IN THIS GAME--SO YOU'RE GOING TO GET GRAND-SLAMMED!
I GOT TO GET FREE--GIVE MY DOLL A HAND!
SHE COMES OUT OF THAT SOMERSAULT HANDS FIRST--USING A SPRINGY TREE-BRANCH TO BREAK HER FALL...
NOW TO FOLLOW THROUGH WITH A BACKFLIP...

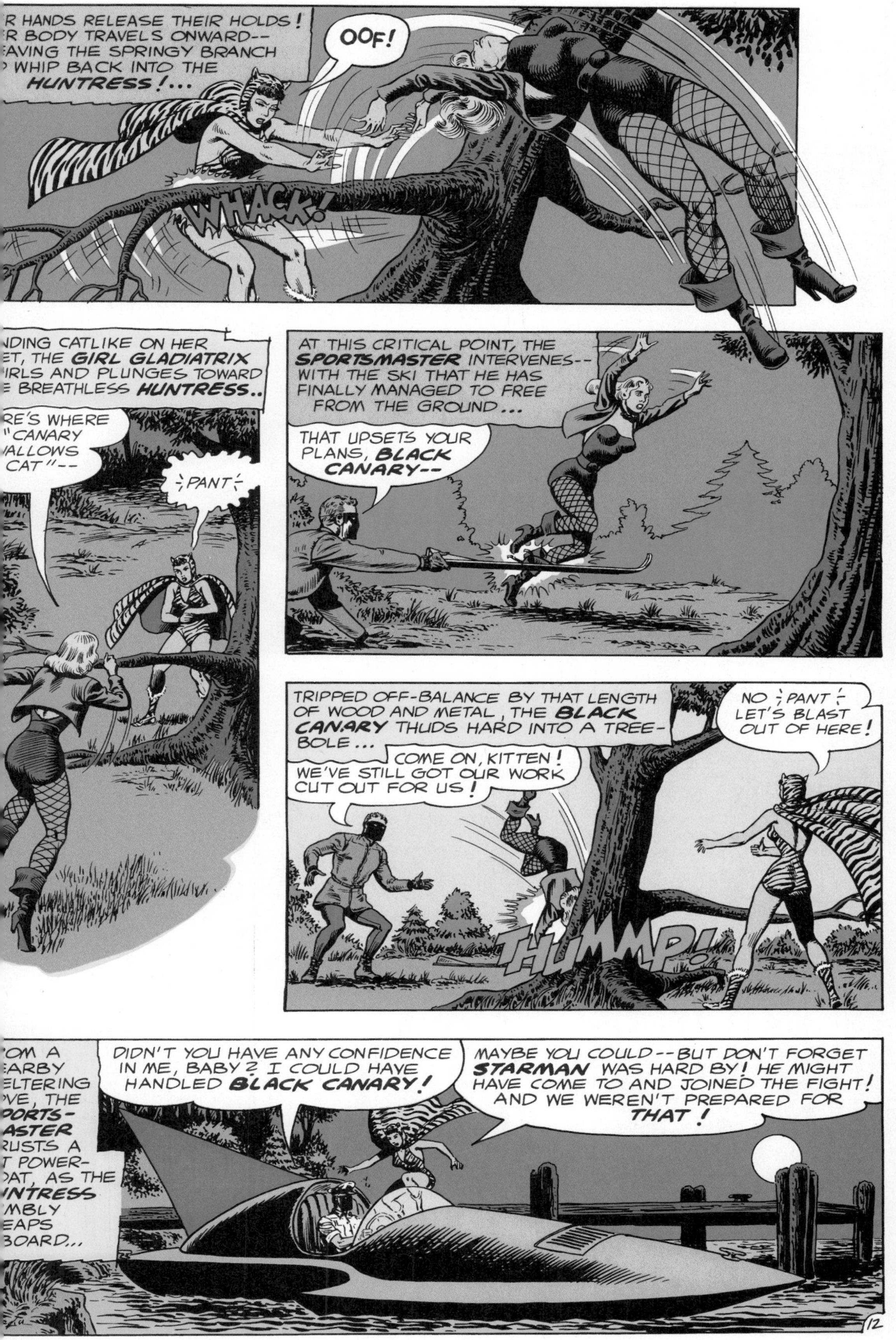

R HANDS RELEASE THEIR HOLDS! R BODY TRAVELS ONWARD-- EAVING THE SPRINGY BRANCH WHIP BACK INTO THE HUNTRESS!...
OOF!
WHACK!
NDING CATLIKE ON HER ET, THE GIRL GLADIATRIX IRLS AND PLUNGES TOWARD E BREATHLESS HUNTRESS..
RE'S WHERE "CANARY ALLOWS CAT"--
PANT
AT THIS CRITICAL POINT, THE SPORTSMASTER INTERVENES-- WITH THE SKI THAT HE HAS FINALLY MANAGED TO FREE FROM THE GROUND...
THAT UPSETS YOUR PLANS, BLACK CANARY--
TRIPPED OFF-BALANCE BY THAT LENGTH OF WOOD AND METAL, THE BLACK CANARY THUDS HARD INTO A TREE-BOLE...
COME ON, KITTEN! WE'VE STILL GOT OUR WORK CUT OUT FOR US!
NO PANT LET'S BLAST OUT OF HERE!
THUMMP!
OM A EARBY ELTERING VE, THE PORTS-ASTER RUSTS A T POWER-OAT, AS THE NTRESS MBLY EAPS BOARD...
DIDN'T YOU HAVE ANY CONFIDENCE IN ME, BABY? I COULD HAVE HANDLED BLACK CANARY!
MAYBE YOU COULD--BUT DON'T FORGET STARMAN WAS HARD BY! HE MIGHT HAVE COME TO AND JOINED THE FIGHT! AND WE WEREN'T PREPARED FOR THAT!
12

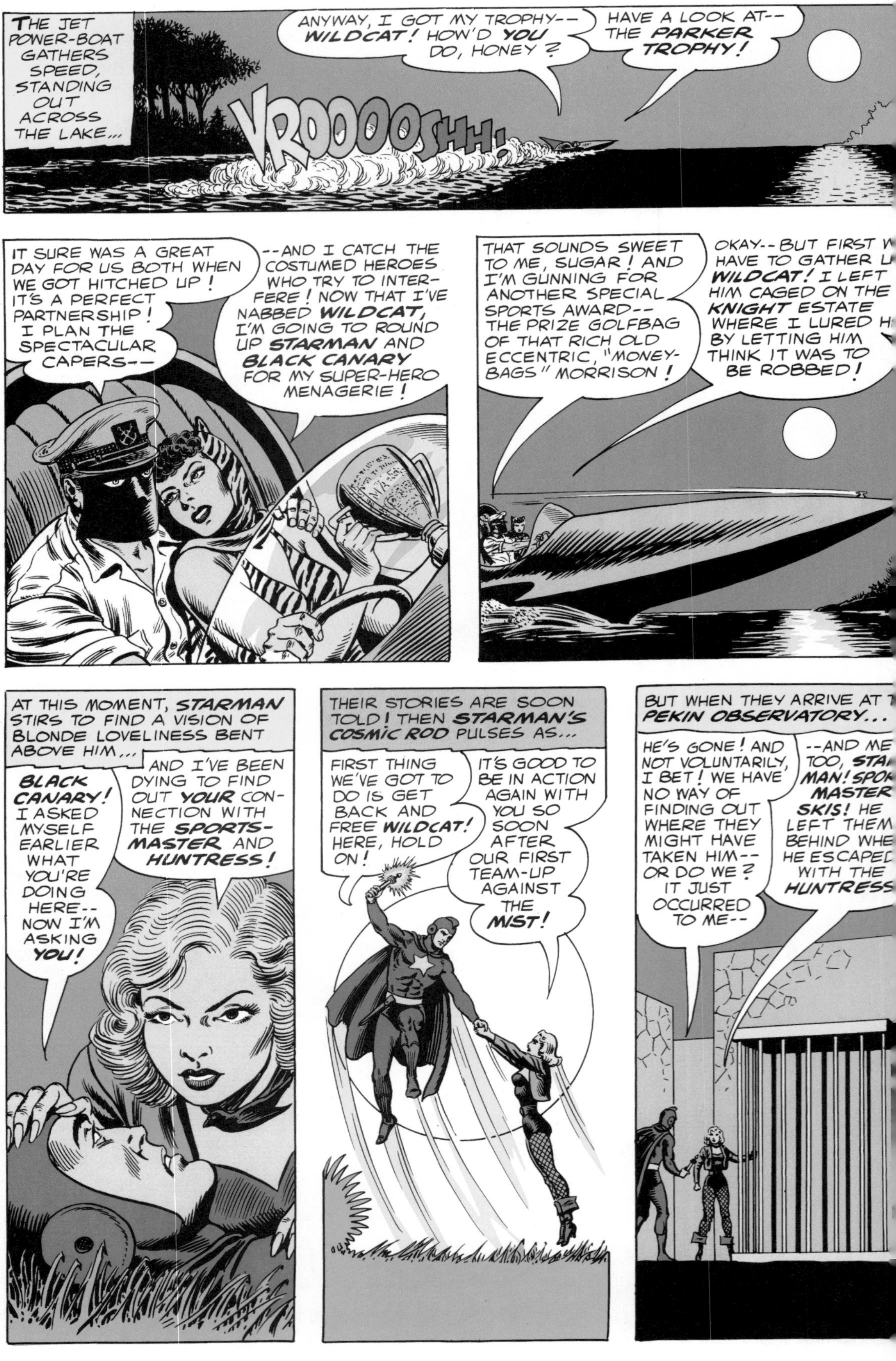

THE JET POWER-BOAT GATHERS SPEED, STANDING OUT ACROSS THE LAKE...
ANYWAY, I GOT MY TROPHY-- WILDCAT! HOW'D YOU DO, HONEY?
HAVE A LOOK AT-- THE PARKER TROPHY!
VROOOOOSHH!
IT SURE WAS A GREAT DAY FOR US BOTH WHEN WE GOT HITCHED UP! IT'S A PERFECT PARTNERSHIP! I PLAN THE SPECTACULAR CAPERS--
--AND I CATCH THE COSTUMED HEROES WHO TRY TO INTER-FERE! NOW THAT I'VE NABBED WILDCAT, I'M GOING TO ROUND UP STARMAN AND BLACK CANARY FOR MY SUPER-HERO MENAGERIE!
THAT SOUNDS SWEET TO ME, SUGAR! AND I'M GUNNING FOR ANOTHER SPECIAL SPORTS AWARD-- THE PRIZE GOLFBAG OF THAT RICH OLD ECCENTRIC, "MONEY-BAGS" MORRISON!
OKAY--BUT FIRST W HAVE TO GATHER U WILDCAT! I LEFT HIM CAGED ON THE KNIGHT ESTATE WHERE I LURED H BY LETTING HIM THINK IT WAS TO BE ROBBED!
AT THIS MOMENT, STARMAN STIRS TO FIND A VISION OF BLONDE LOVELINESS BENT ABOVE HIM...
BLACK CANARY! I ASKED MYSELF EARLIER WHAT YOU'RE DOING HERE-- NOW I'M ASKING YOU!
AND I'VE BEEN DYING TO FIND OUT YOUR CON-NECTION WITH THE SPORTS-MASTER AND HUNTRESS!
THEIR STORIES ARE SOON TOLD! THEN STARMAN'S COSMIC ROD PULSES AS...
FIRST THING WE'VE GOT TO DO IS GET BACK AND FREE WILDCAT! HERE, HOLD ON!
IT'S GOOD TO BE IN ACTION AGAIN WITH YOU SO SOON AFTER OUR FIRST TEAM-UP AGAINST THE MIST!
BUT WHEN THEY ARRIVE AT T PEKIN OBSERVATORY...
HE'S GONE! AND NOT VOLUNTARILY, I BET! WE HAVE NO WAY OF FINDING OUT WHERE THEY MIGHT HAVE TAKEN HIM-- OR DO WE? IT JUST OCCURRED TO ME--
--AND ME TOO, STA MAN! SPOR MASTER SKIS! HE LEFT THEM BEHIND WHE HE ESCAPED WITH THE HUNTRESS

ALL NIGHT LONG BESIDE THE LAKE, TWO GRIM FIGURES CROUCH, IGNORING THE WIND WHISTLING THROUGH THE UNDERBRUSH, INTENT ONLY ON THE SKIS OF THEIR SPORTS FOE...

SPORTSMASTER WAS TOO INTENT ON ESCAPE TO GRAB UP HIS SKIS!

HE VALUES THEM TOO MUCH TO ABANDON THEM! HE'LL BE COMING BACK FOR THEM!

THEN--AT DAWN--THE SKIS STIR--AND SUDDENLY TAKE OFF INTO THE AIR...

SPORTSMASTER'S BRINGING THE SKIS TO HIM--BY REMOTE-CONTROL!

WHERE THEY GO, WE GO, BLACK CANARY! IT'S HAND-OUT TIME AGAIN! HOLD ON--!

LIKE HOMING PIGEONS THE JET-SKIS STREAK TOWARD A HEAVILY WOODED AREA...

THEY'RE DROPPING DOWN--BUT NO SIGN OF ANY HIDE-OUT!

IT MAY BE A CLEVER CAMOUFLAGE JOB--

SURE ENOUGH, WHEN THEY DROP LOWER THEY SEE A GREAT CHALET NESTLED IN AMONG A STAND OF TOWERING TREES, HIDDEN FROM OVERHEAD DISCOVERY...

NO SIGN OF OUR QUARRY, EITHER!

IF I KNOW THEM--THEY'RE PROBABLY ON THEIR WAY TO ANOTHER CRIME! BUT FIRST--LET'S SEE IF WE CAN FIND WILDCAT!

A QUICK SEARCH LEADS TO A VAST CELLAR WHERE...

BLACK CANARY! STARMAN! WOULDN'T YOU KNOW? MY FIRST CASE AFTER COMING OUT OF RETIREMENT--AND I NOT ONLY BOTCH THE JOB, BUT I WIND UP A PRISONER OF THE HUNTRESS!

14

GRIPPING THE BARS OF THE CAGE, THE TWO CRIME-FIGHTERS RELEASE THE LOCK AND LIFT THE DOOR OF WILDCAT'S CELL...

SO THE *HUNTRESS* KEEPS ALL SORTS OF WILD ANIMALS DOWN HERE! LUCKILY, THEY'RE BEHIND BARS!

I OVERHEARD HER SAY SHE'S PLANNING ON ADDING YOU AND *STARMAN* TO HER COLLECTION, TOO!

BUT AS THE CELL-DOOR IS RAISED-- THE BARS OF THE OTHER CAGES ARE AUTOMATICALLY RAISED AS WELL..

THAT *HUNTRESS* IS A CUTIE! SHE GIMMICKED HER CAGES SO THAT IF *WILDCAT* FREED HIMSELF --THE WILD ANIMALS WOULD BE RELEASED TOO--

--DOOMING *WILDCAT!* OK FELLOW LAWMEN-- LET'S START FIGHTIN'!

A KANGAROO LEAPS THROUGH THE AIR! ITS PAWS RAM WITH THE KICK OF A MISSOURI MULE INTO *WILDCAT'S* CHEST...

OOOOF! MUST BE RUSTIER THAN I THOUGHT--TO LET HIM GET IN THE FIRST BLOW!

THUD!

GREAT MUSCLES FLEX AND BULGE! A BODY THAT IS LIKE A STEEL SPRING ERUPTS IN FURIOUS ACTION AS...

I'M STILL THE SAME *TED GRANT* WHO WAS THE UNDEFEATED HEAVYWEIGHT CHAMPION OF THE WORLD BEFORE I RETIRED!

WHAK!

AS A POWERHOUSE LEFT FLASHES IN AN OVERHAND BLOW TO KAYO THE MARSUPIAL -- A GIANT POLAR BEAR RISES UPWARD BEHIND HIM...

I STILL HAVEN' LOST KNOCKC PUNCH

SOK!

FROM BEHIND, A GREAT WHITE-FURRED PAW SLAMS INTO **WILDCAT**...

GRRRKRRRROWW!

MMMppFFF!

I'LL SHOW THAT ARCTIC BEAST I'M STILL ABLE TO "TAKE" A PUNCH!

WITHOUT TAKING COUNT, THE K-CHAMP ZOOMS BACK AT HIS OPPONENT...

BROTHER BEAR-- YOU'RE A SUCKER FOR A LEFT!

MEANWHILE, **STARMAN** HAS BEEN RAMMED INTO THE BARS OF A CELL BY THE LEAP OF A GREAT BLACK PANTHER...

GOT TO COSMIC-ROD HIM AWAY FROM ME!

FROM THE COSMIC RAYS THAT TRAVEL EVERYWHERE, HE SUMMONS ANTI-GRAVITIC POWER TO LIFT THE SCREECHING FELINE HIGH INTO THE AIR...

UP YOU GO, FELLA!

AS THE PANTHER CRASHES HARD INTO THE STONE CEILING--A WILD-EYED TUSKER THUNDERS FROM THE SHADOWS...

THAT BOAR THINKS HE HAS A CLEAR SHOT AT ME--!

THUMP!

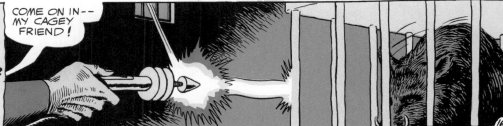

DRAWING AN ERRANT MOONBEAM THROUGH A BARRED WINDOW, THE **ROD RANGER** CONVERTS IT TO A CAGE BEFORE THE ONRUSHING ANIMAL...

COME ON IN-- MY CAGEY FRIEND!

16

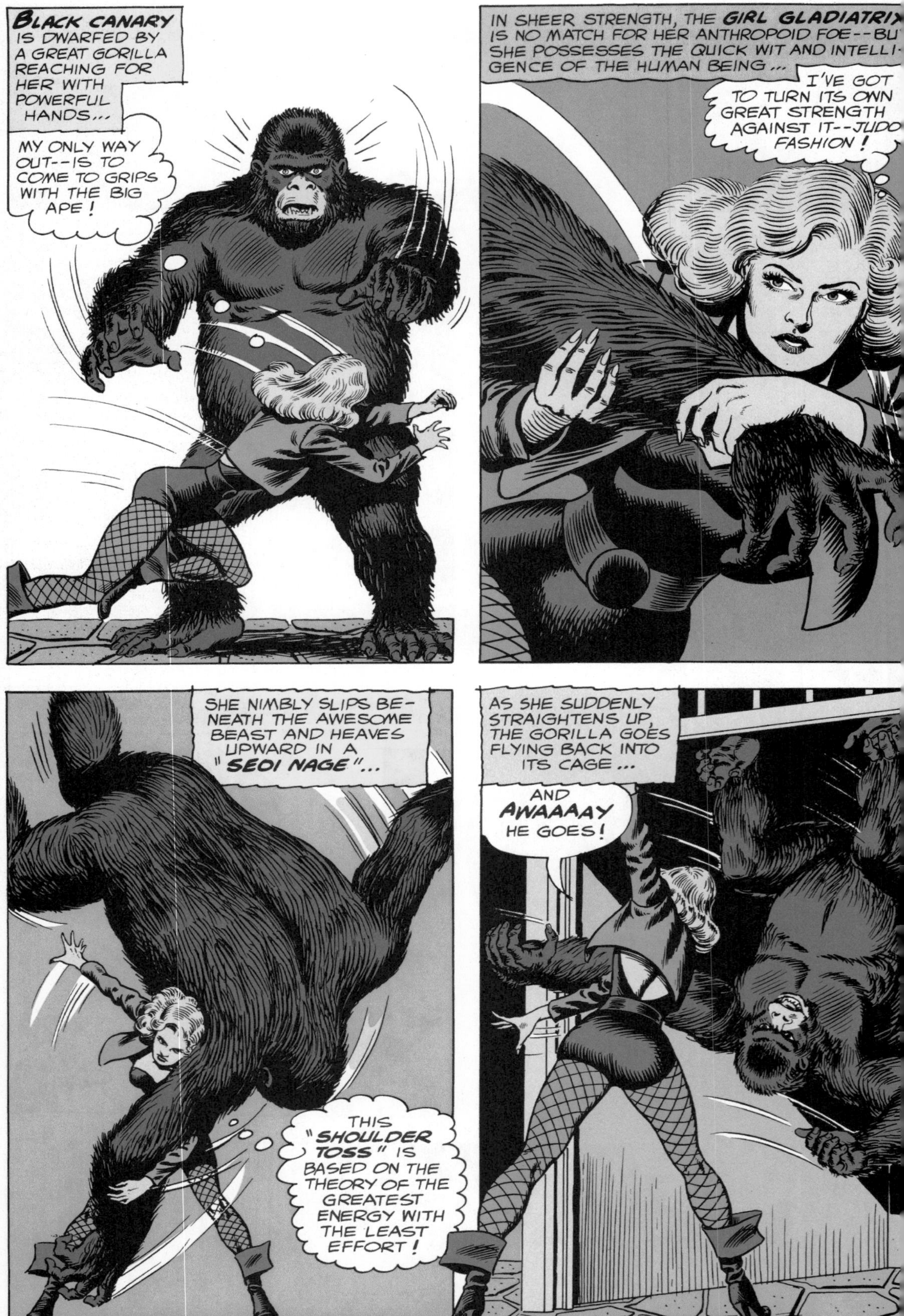
BLACK CANARY IS DWARFED BY A GREAT GORILLA REACHING FOR HER WITH POWERFUL HANDS...
MY ONLY WAY OUT--IS TO COME TO GRIPS WITH THE BIG APE!
IN SHEER STRENGTH, THE GIRL GLADIATRIX IS NO MATCH FOR HER ANTHROPOID FOE--BUT SHE POSSESSES THE QUICK WIT AND INTELLI- GENCE OF THE HUMAN BEING...
I'VE GOT TO TURN ITS OWN GREAT STRENGTH AGAINST IT--JUDO FASHION!
SHE NIMBLY SLIPS BE- NEATH THE AWESOME BEAST AND HEAVES UPWARD IN A "SEOI NAGE"...
THIS "SHOULDER TOSS" IS BASED ON THE THEORY OF THE GREATEST ENERGY WITH THE LEAST EFFORT!
AS SHE SUDDENLY STRAIGHTENS UP, THE GORILLA GOES FLYING BACK INTO ITS CAGE...
AND AWAAAAY HE GOES!

EXT MOMENT, STARMAN ACTIVATES THE MOON-LIGHT INTO TONGUES OF FLAME, EFORE WHICH THE OTHER EASTS SLINK BACK INTO HEIR CAGES...
AS SOON AS THEY'RE ALL BEHIND BARS --SLAM THOSE CELL DOORS SHUT!
EANWHILE, MILES WAY, SPORTS-ASTER AND UNTRESS ARE TEPPING ONTO A UTTING GREEN OMPLETELY SUR-OUNDED BY TREES ORDERING A GOLF FAIRWAY...
NO NEWFANGLED GOLFING ATTIRE FOR ME! I LIKE THESE OLD-FASHIONED PLUS-FOURS WHEN I GO GOLFING!
GOOD HUNTING FOR BOTH OF US! THE MONEY-FILLED GOLF-BAG FOR YOU--STAR-MAN AND BLACK CANARY FOR ME!
S THE ATHLETIC ARCHCRIMINAL TRIPS A ECRET SWITCH IN THE PUTTING GREEN, IT RISES TO THE AIR...
DO YOU HINK THOSE TWO CRIME-USTERS WILL SHOW UP ERE --TO TRY AND CAPTURE US?
OF COURSE, HUSBAND DEAR! WE PLANNED IT THAT WAY!
BY NOW THEY WILL HAVE FOLLOWED YOUR SKIS TO THE CHALET! IN ATTEMPTING TO FREE WILDCAT, THEY'LL HAVE BEEN DELAYED BY MY TRAINED ANIMALS! AFTER THAT, WILDCAT WILL TIP THEM WHERE WE'VE GONE--WHICH I CON-VENIENTLY LET HIM OVERHEAR! ONCE I CAPTURE THEM--IT'LL BE A SNAP TO RE-CAPTURE WILDCAT!

BLACK CANARY

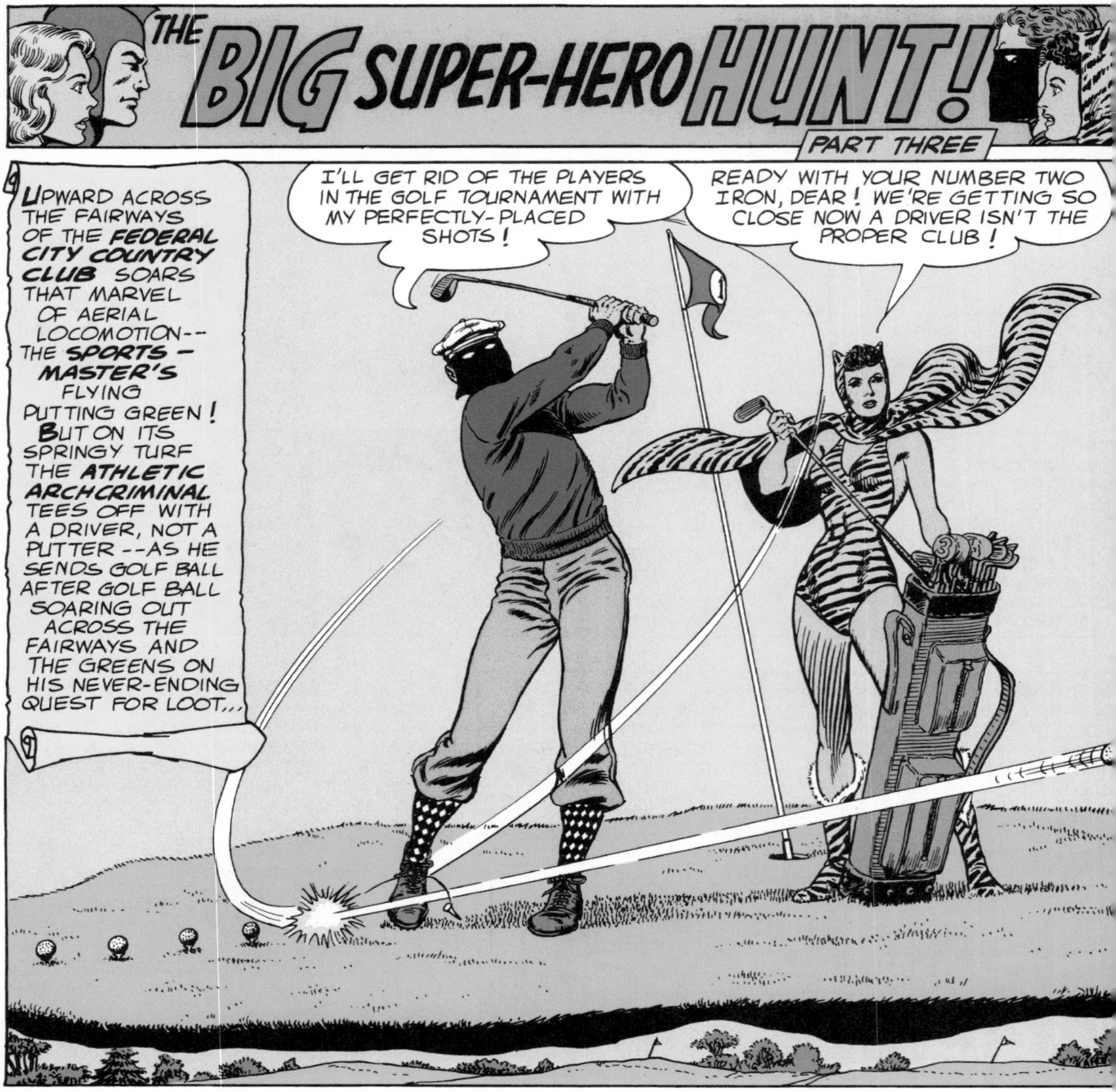
THE BIG SUPER-HERO HUNT!
PART THREE
UPWARD ACROSS THE FAIRWAYS OF THE FEDERAL CITY COUNTRY CLUB SOARS THAT MARVEL OF AERIAL LOCOMOTION-- THE SPORTS-MASTER'S FLYING PUTTING GREEN! BUT ON ITS SPRINGY TURF THE ATHLETIC ARCHCRIMINAL TEES OFF WITH A DRIVER, NOT A PUTTER --AS HE SENDS GOLF BALL AFTER GOLF BALL SOARING OUT ACROSS THE FAIRWAYS AND THE GREENS ON HIS NEVER-ENDING QUEST FOR LOOT...
I'LL GET RID OF THE PLAYERS IN THE GOLF TOURNAMENT WITH MY PERFECTLY-PLACED SHOTS!
READY WITH YOUR NUMBER TWO IRON, DEAR! WE'RE GETTING SO CLOSE NOW A DRIVER ISN'T THE PROPER CLUB!

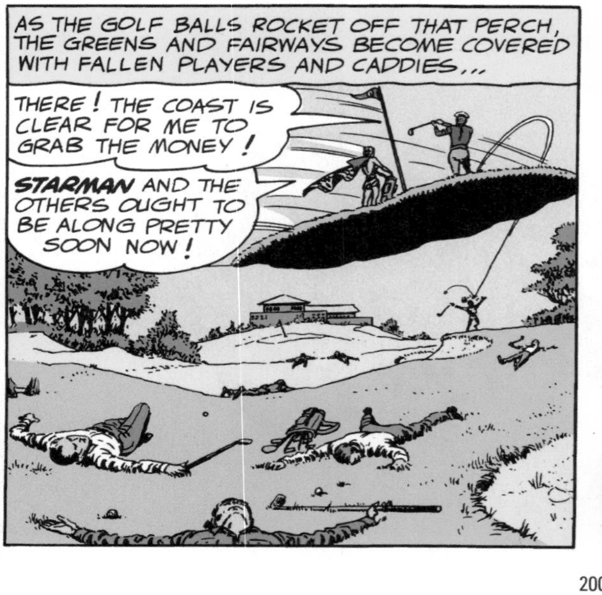
AS THE GOLF BALLS ROCKET OFF THAT PERCH, THE GREENS AND FAIRWAYS BECOME COVERED WITH FALLEN PLAYERS AND CADDIES...
THERE! THE COAST IS CLEAR FOR ME TO GRAB THE MONEY!
STARMAN AND THE OTHERS OUGHT TO BE ALONG PRETTY SOON NOW!

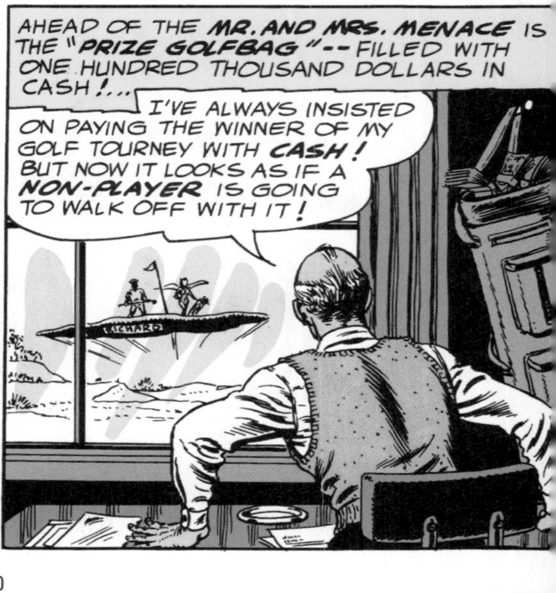
AHEAD OF THE MR. AND MRS. MENACE IS THE "PRIZE GOLFBAG"-- FILLED WITH ONE HUNDRED THOUSAND DOLLARS IN CASH!...
I'VE ALWAYS INSISTED ON PAYING THE WINNER OF MY GOLF TOURNEY WITH CASH! BUT NOW IT LOOKS AS IF A NON-PLAYER IS GOING TO WALK OFF WITH IT!

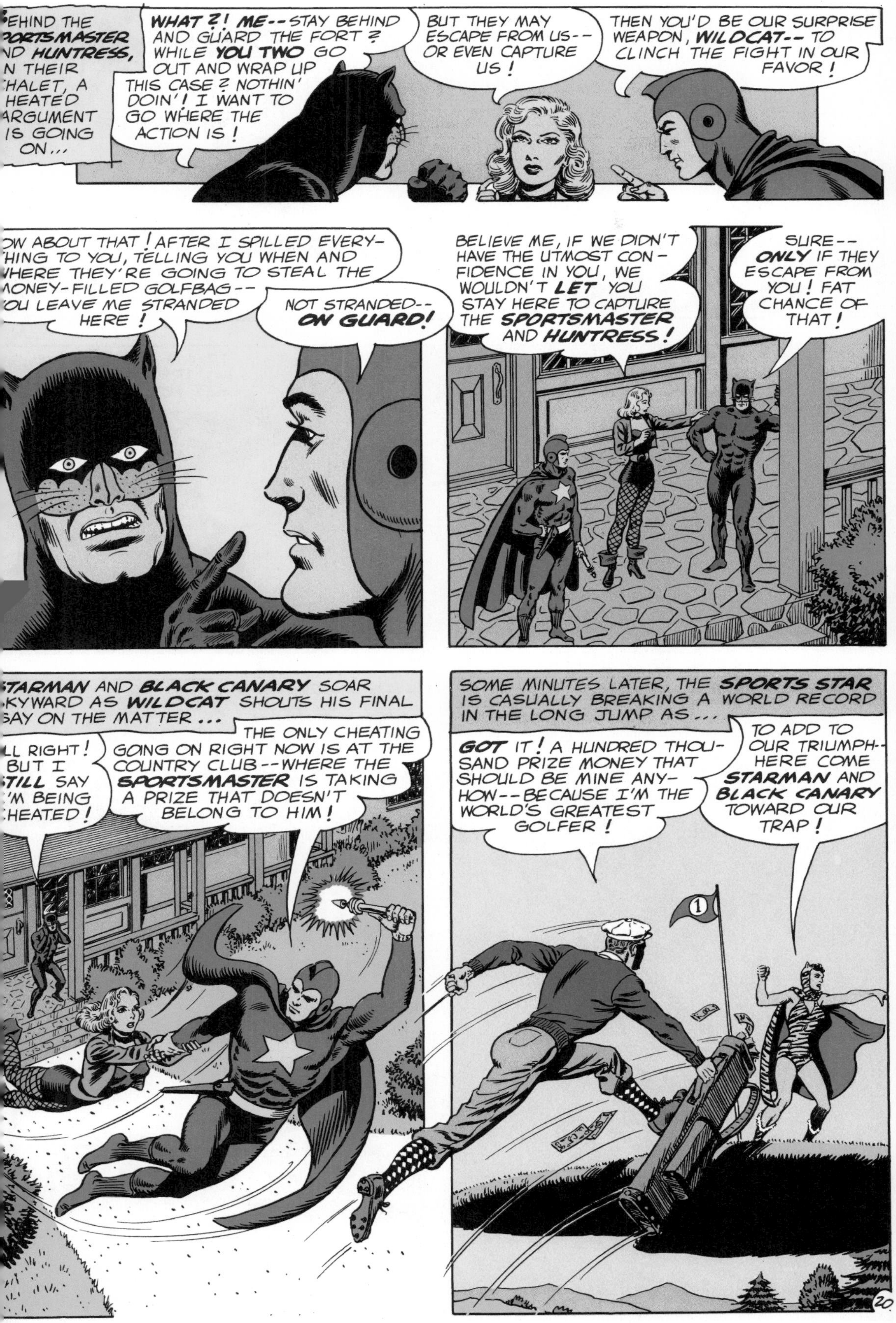

EHIND THE SPORTSMASTER ND HUNTRESS, N THEIR CHALET, A HEATED ARGUMENT IS GOING ON...
WHAT ?! ME--STAY BEHIND AND GUARD THE FORT ? WHILE YOU TWO GO OUT AND WRAP UP THIS CASE ? NOTHIN' DOIN'! I WANT TO GO WHERE THE ACTION IS!
BUT THEY MAY ESCAPE FROM US-- OR EVEN CAPTURE US!
THEN YOU'D BE OUR SURPRISE WEAPON, WILDCAT-- TO CLINCH THE FIGHT IN OUR FAVOR!
OW ABOUT THAT! AFTER I SPILLED EVERY-THING TO YOU, TELLING YOU WHEN AND WHERE THEY'RE GOING TO STEAL THE MONEY-FILLED GOLFBAG-- OU LEAVE ME STRANDED HERE!
NOT STRANDED-- ON GUARD!
BELIEVE ME, IF WE DIDN'T HAVE THE UTMOST CON-FIDENCE IN YOU, WE WOULDN'T LET YOU STAY HERE TO CAPTURE THE SPORTSMASTER AND HUNTRESS!
SURE-- ONLY IF THEY ESCAPE FROM YOU! FAT CHANCE OF THAT!
STARMAN AND BLACK CANARY SOAR SKYWARD AS WILDCAT SHOUTS HIS FINAL SAY ON THE MATTER...
LL RIGHT! BUT I STILL SAY 'M BEING CHEATED!
THE ONLY CHEATING GOING ON RIGHT NOW IS AT THE COUNTRY CLUB--WHERE THE SPORTSMASTER IS TAKING A PRIZE THAT DOESN'T BELONG TO HIM!
SOME MINUTES LATER, THE SPORTS STAR IS CASUALLY BREAKING A WORLD RECORD IN THE LONG JUMP AS...
GOT IT! A HUNDRED THOU-SAND PRIZE MONEY THAT SHOULD BE MINE ANY-HOW--BECAUSE I'M THE WORLD'S GREATEST GOLFER!
TO ADD TO OUR TRIUMPH-- HERE COME STARMAN AND BLACK CANARY TOWARD OUR TRAP!
1
20

THE FLYING PUTTING GREEN TAKES TO THE AIR AGAIN...

THEN WE ATTACK THEM AS PLANNED--STARTING WITH MY "BRASSIE BEANIE" AT STARMAN!

I'LL WRAP UP THE BLACK CANARY!

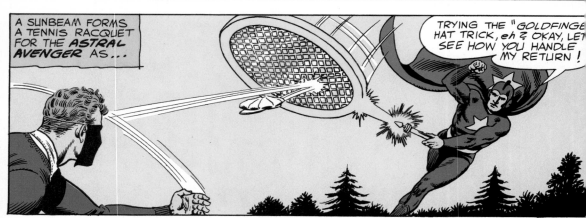

A SUNBEAM FORMS A TENNIS RACQUET FOR THE ASTRAL AVENGER AS...

TRYING THE "GOLDFINGER HAT TRICK, eh? OKAY, LET'S SEE HOW YOU HANDLE MY RETURN!

THE SPORTS ACE DUCKS JUST IN TIME TO AVOID AN OVERHEAD EXPLOSION...

NICE PLAY, STARMAN! BUT I'M SWITCHING GAMES--WITH THIS CUP-POLE!

WHAM!

1

HERE'S WHERE THIS DISGUISED GUIDED MISSILE MAKES A FALL GUY OUT OF STARMAN!

THE WAY SPORTSMASTER KEEPS BOMBARDING ME WITH HIS WEAPONS AS IF TRYING TO MANEUVER ME TOWARD BLACK CANARY!

200 YDS.

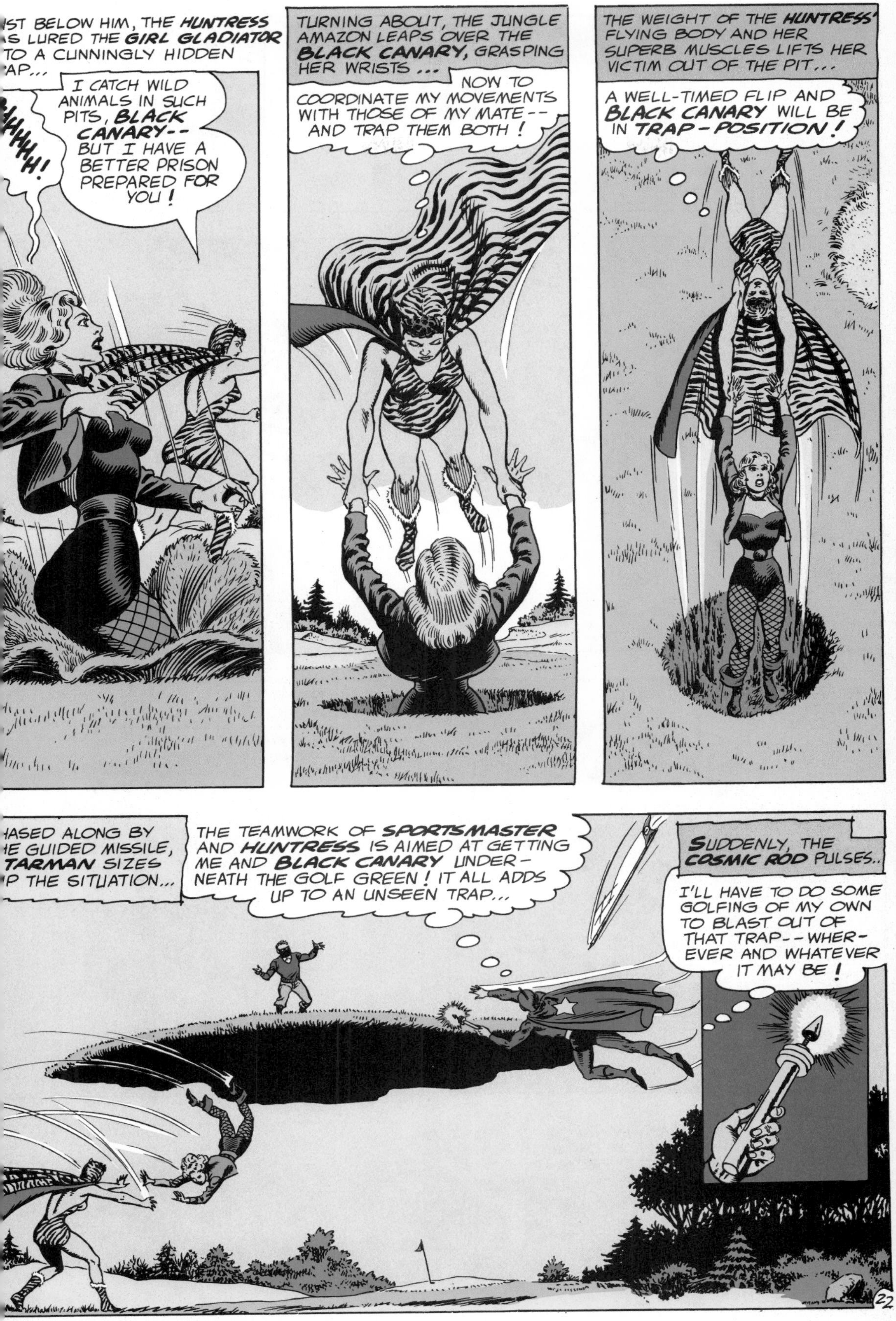
...ST BELOW HIM, THE HUNTRESS ...S LURED THE GIRL GLADIATOR TO A CUNNINGLY HIDDEN ...AP...
I CATCH WILD ANIMALS IN SUCH PITS, BLACK CANARY-- BUT I HAVE A BETTER PRISON PREPARED FOR YOU!
...HHHH!
TURNING ABOUT, THE JUNGLE AMAZON LEAPS OVER THE BLACK CANARY, GRASPING HER WRISTS...
NOW TO COORDINATE MY MOVEMENTS WITH THOSE OF MY MATE-- AND TRAP THEM BOTH!
THE WEIGHT OF THE HUNTRESS' FLYING BODY AND HER SUPERB MUSCLES LIFTS HER VICTIM OUT OF THE PIT...
A WELL-TIMED FLIP AND BLACK CANARY WILL BE IN TRAP-POSITION!
...HASED ALONG BY ...E GUIDED MISSILE, ...TARMAN SIZES ...P THE SITUATION...
THE TEAMWORK OF SPORTSMASTER AND HUNTRESS IS AIMED AT GETTING ME AND BLACK CANARY UNDERNEATH THE GOLF GREEN! IT ALL ADDS UP TO AN UNSEEN TRAP...
SUDDENLY, THE COSMIC ROD PULSES...
I'LL HAVE TO DO SOME GOLFING OF MY OWN TO BLAST OUT OF THAT TRAP--WHEREVER AND WHATEVER IT MAY BE!
22

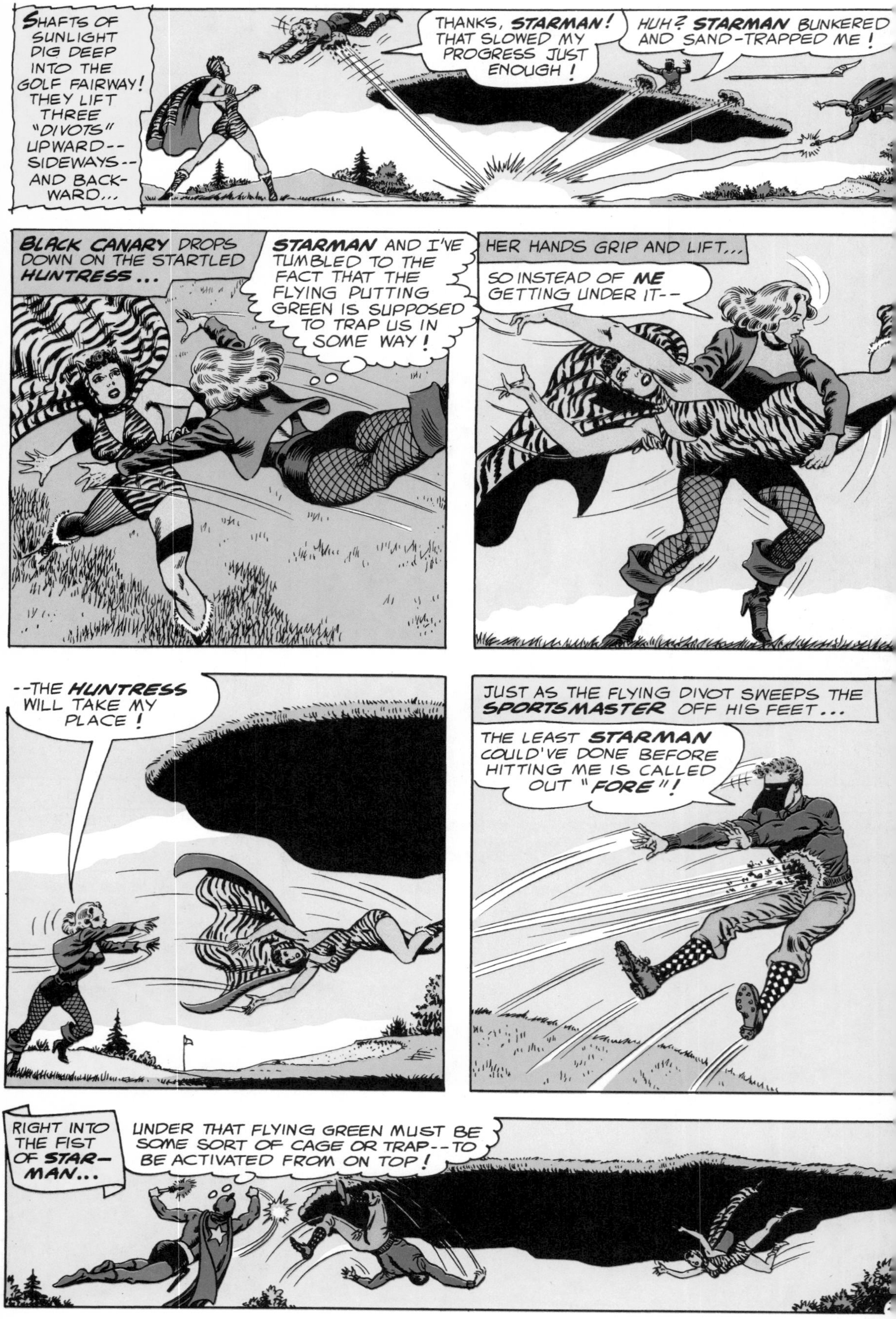
SHAFTS OF SUNLIGHT DIG DEEP INTO THE GOLF FAIRWAY! THEY LIFT THREE "DIVOTS" UPWARD--SIDEWAYS--AND BACKWARD...
THANKS, STARMAN! THAT SLOWED MY PROGRESS JUST ENOUGH!
HUH? STARMAN BUNKERED AND SAND-TRAPPED ME!
BLACK CANARY DROPS DOWN ON THE STARTLED HUNTRESS...
STARMAN AND I'VE TUMBLED TO THE FACT THAT THE FLYING PUTTING GREEN IS SUPPOSED TO TRAP US IN SOME WAY!
HER HANDS GRIP AND LIFT...
SO INSTEAD OF ME GETTING UNDER IT--
--THE HUNTRESS WILL TAKE MY PLACE!
JUST AS THE FLYING DIVOT SWEEPS THE SPORTSMASTER OFF HIS FEET...
THE LEAST STARMAN COULD'VE DONE BEFORE HITTING ME IS CALLED OUT "FORE"!
RIGHT INTO THE FIST OF STARMAN...
UNDER THAT FLYING GREEN MUST BE SOME SORT OF CAGE OR TRAP--TO BE ACTIVATED FROM ON TOP!

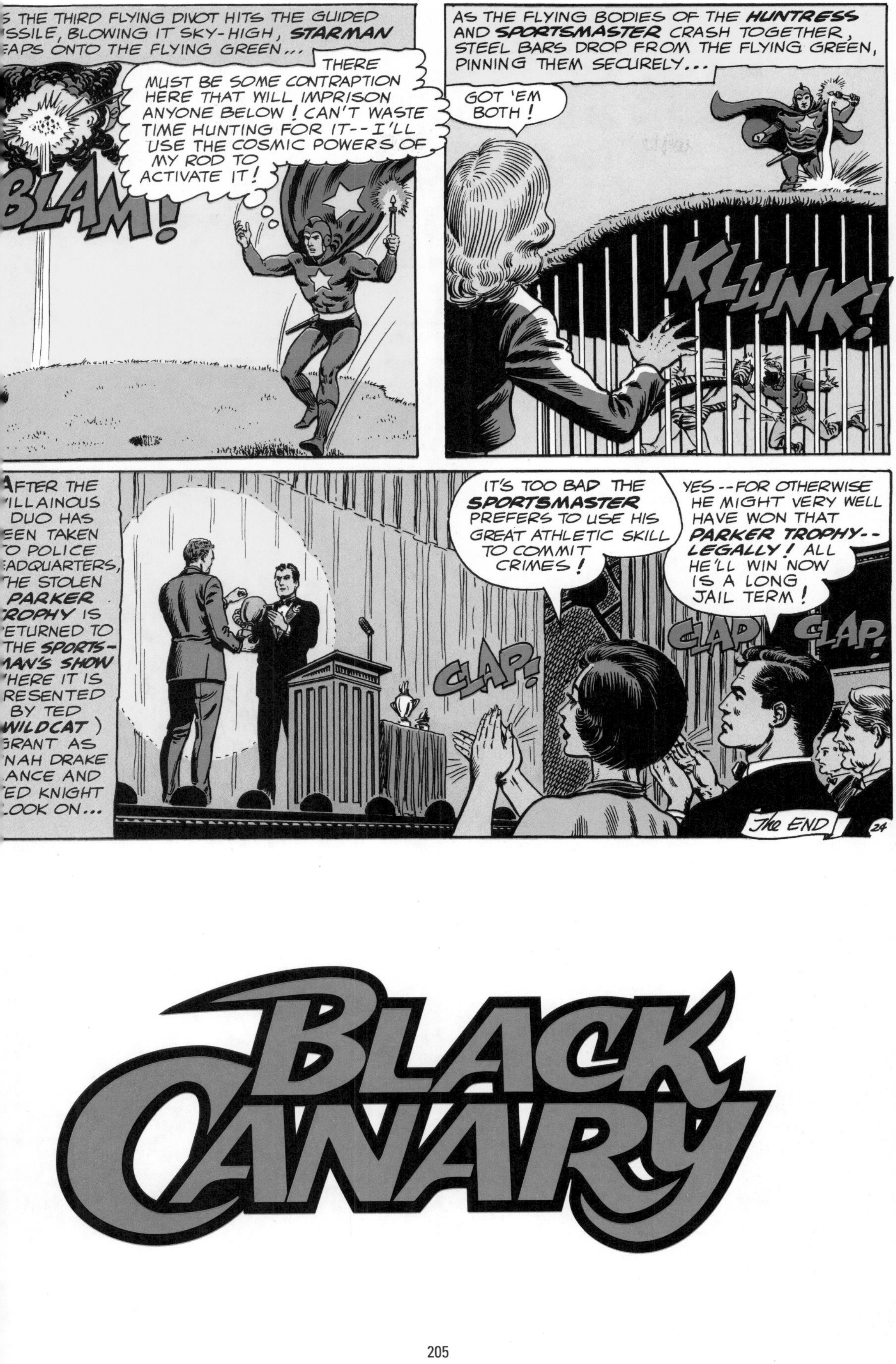
S THE THIRD FLYING DIVOT HITS THE GUIDED
ISSILE, BLOWING IT SKY-HIGH, STARMAN
EAPS ONTO THE FLYING GREEN...
THERE MUST BE SOME CONTRAPTION HERE THAT WILL IMPRISON ANYONE BELOW! CAN'T WASTE TIME HUNTING FOR IT--I'LL USE THE COSMIC POWERS OF MY ROD TO ACTIVATE IT!
BLAM!
AS THE FLYING BODIES OF THE HUNTRESS AND SPORTSMASTER CRASH TOGETHER, STEEL BARS DROP FROM THE FLYING GREEN, PINNING THEM SECURELY...
GOT 'EM BOTH!
KLUNK!
AFTER THE
ILLAINOUS
DUO HAS
EEN TAKEN
O POLICE
EADQUARTERS,
THE STOLEN
PARKER
ROPHY IS
ETURNED TO
THE SPORTS-
MAN'S SHOW
HERE IT IS
RESENTED
BY TED
WILDCAT)
GRANT AS
NAH DRAKE
ANCE AND
ED KNIGHT
LOOK ON...
IT'S TOO BAD THE SPORTSMASTER PREFERS TO USE HIS GREAT ATHLETIC SKILL TO COMMIT CRIMES!
YES--FOR OTHERWISE HE MIGHT VERY WELL HAVE WON THAT PARKER TROPHY--LEGALLY! ALL HE'LL WIN NOW IS A LONG JAIL TERM!
CLAP!
CLAP
CLAP!
The END
24

BLACK CANARY

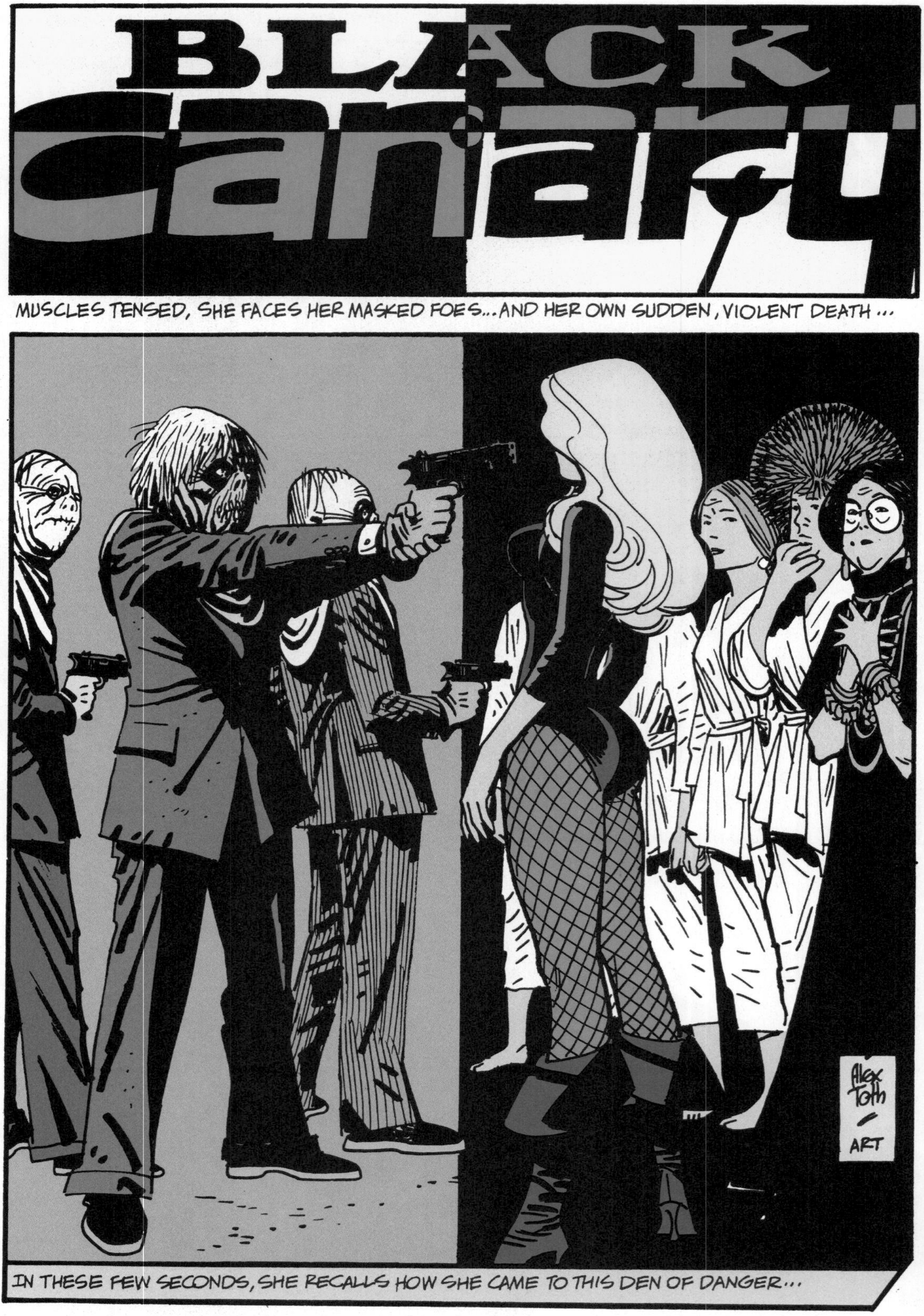
BLACK
CANARY
MUSCLES TENSED, SHE FACES HER MASKED FOES... AND HER OWN SUDDEN, VIOLENT DEATH ...
Alex Toth / ART
IN THESE FEW SECONDS, SHE RECALLS HOW SHE CAME TO THIS DEN OF DANGER...

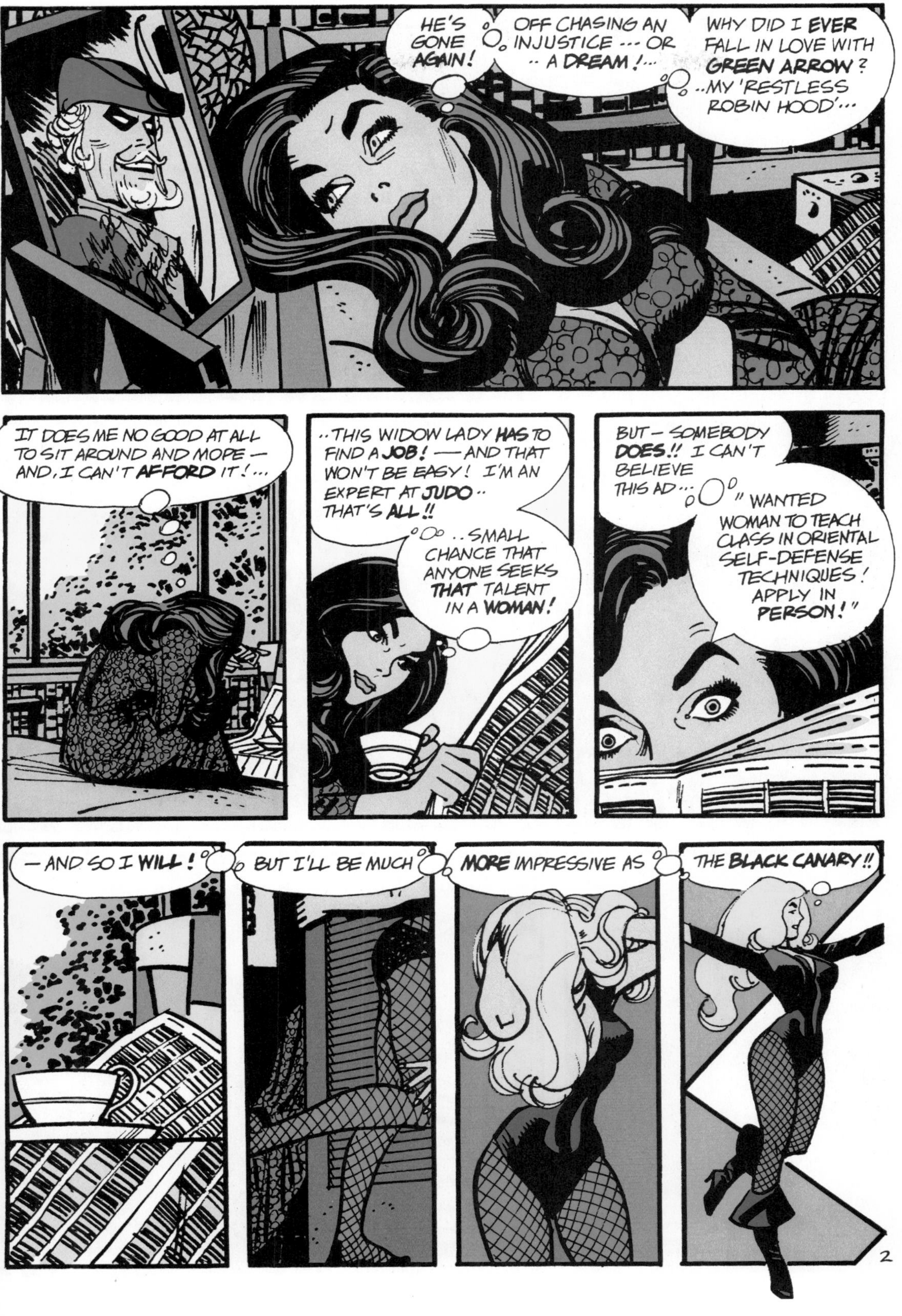
HE'S GONE AGAIN!
OFF CHASING AN INJUSTICE --- OR .. A DREAM! ...
WHY DID I EVER FALL IN LOVE WITH GREEN ARROW? ..MY 'RESTLESS ROBIN HOOD'...
IT DOES ME NO GOOD AT ALL TO SIT AROUND AND MOPE — AND, I CAN'T AFFORD IT! ...
..THIS WIDOW LADY HAS TO FIND A JOB! — AND THAT WON'T BE EASY! I'M AN EXPERT AT JUDO .. THAT'S ALL!!
..SMALL CHANCE THAT ANYONE SEEKS THAT TALENT IN A WOMAN!
BUT — SOMEBODY DOES!! I CAN'T BELIEVE THIS AD...
" WANTED WOMAN TO TEACH CLASS IN ORIENTAL SELF-DEFENSE TECHNIQUES! APPLY IN PERSON!"
— AND SO I WILL!
BUT I'LL BE MUCH
MORE IMPRESSIVE AS
THE BLACK CANARY!!
2

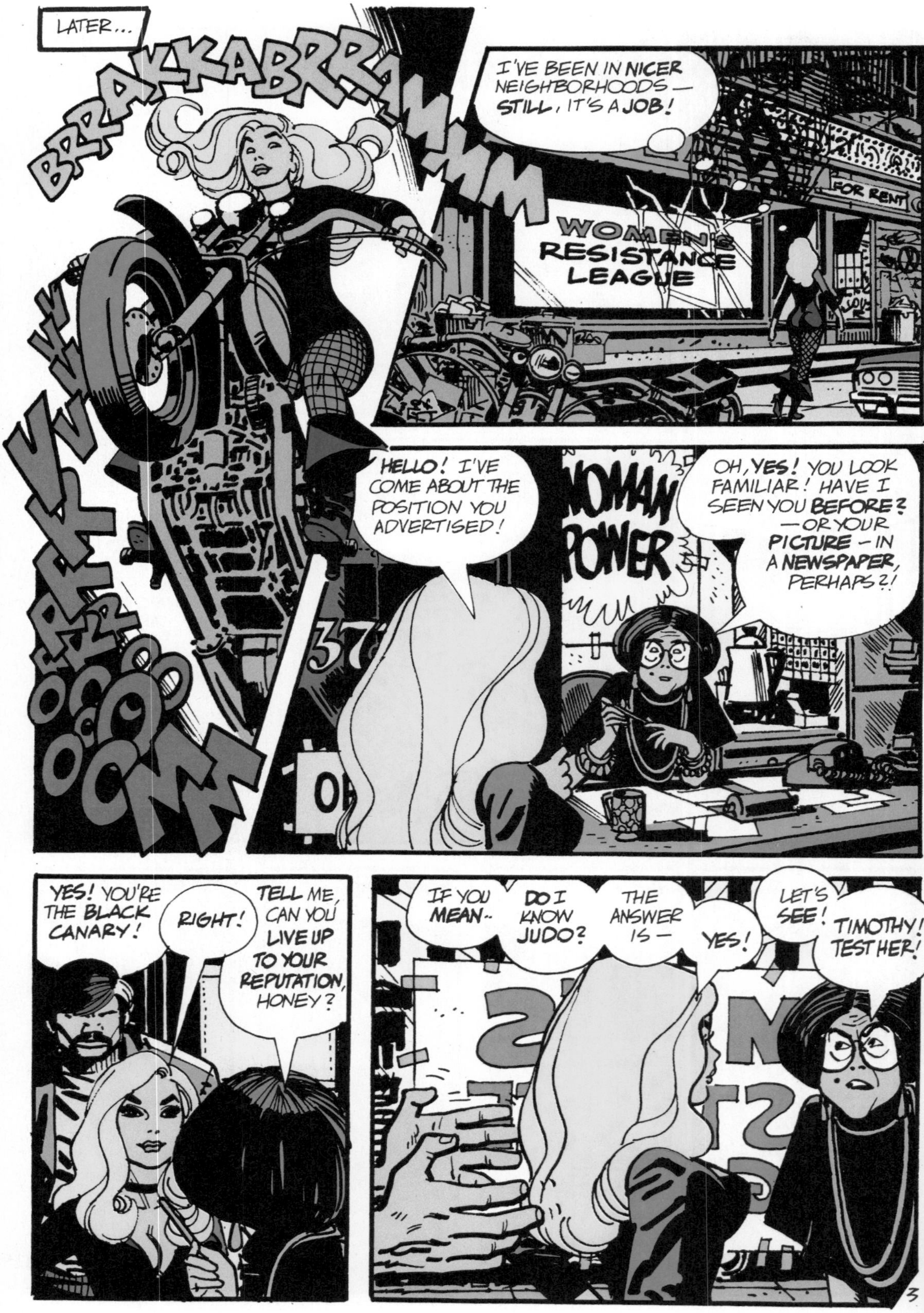
LATER...
BRRAKKABRRRAMMMM
I'VE BEEN IN NICER NEIGHBORHOODS — STILL, IT'S A JOB!
WOMEN'S RESISTANCE LEAGUE
FOR RENT
HELLO! I'VE COME ABOUT THE POSITION YOU ADVERTISED!
WOMAN POWER
OH, YES! YOU LOOK FAMILIAR! HAVE I SEEN YOU BEFORE? — OR YOUR PICTURE — IN A NEWSPAPER, PERHAPS?!
YES! YOU'RE THE BLACK CANARY!
RIGHT!
TELL ME, CAN YOU LIVE UP TO YOUR REPUTATION, HONEY?
IF YOU MEAN..
DO I KNOW JUDO?
THE ANSWER IS —
YES!
LET'S SEE!
TIMOTHY! TEST HER!
3

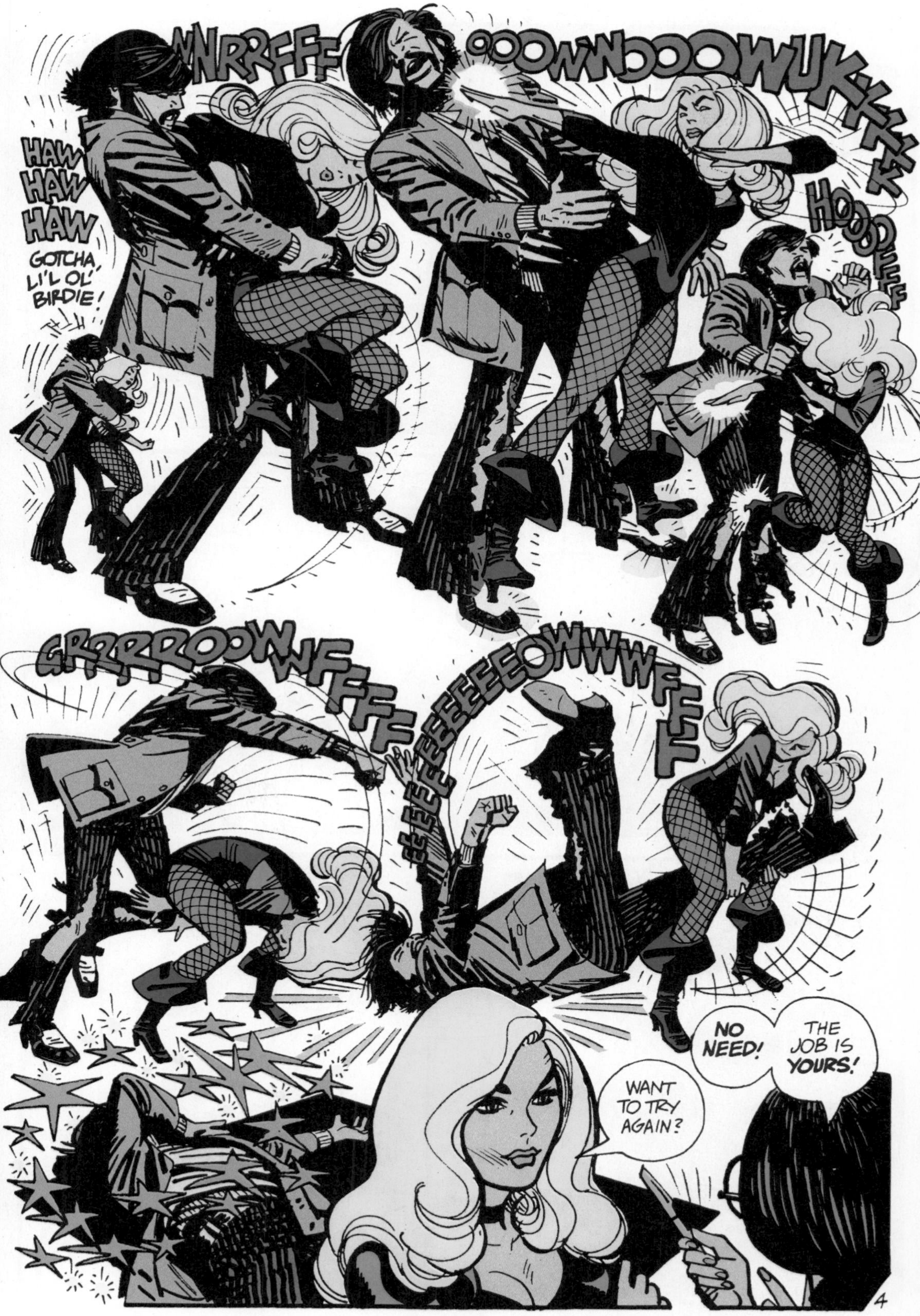
WNRRFFF
OOOWNOOOOWUK-K-K-K
HAW HAW HAW
GOTCHA, LI'L OL' BIRDIE!
HOOOFFF
GRRRROOOWNFFFFF
EEEEEEEEEEEOWWWWFFF
NO NEED!
THE JOB IS YOURS!
WANT TO TRY AGAIN?
4

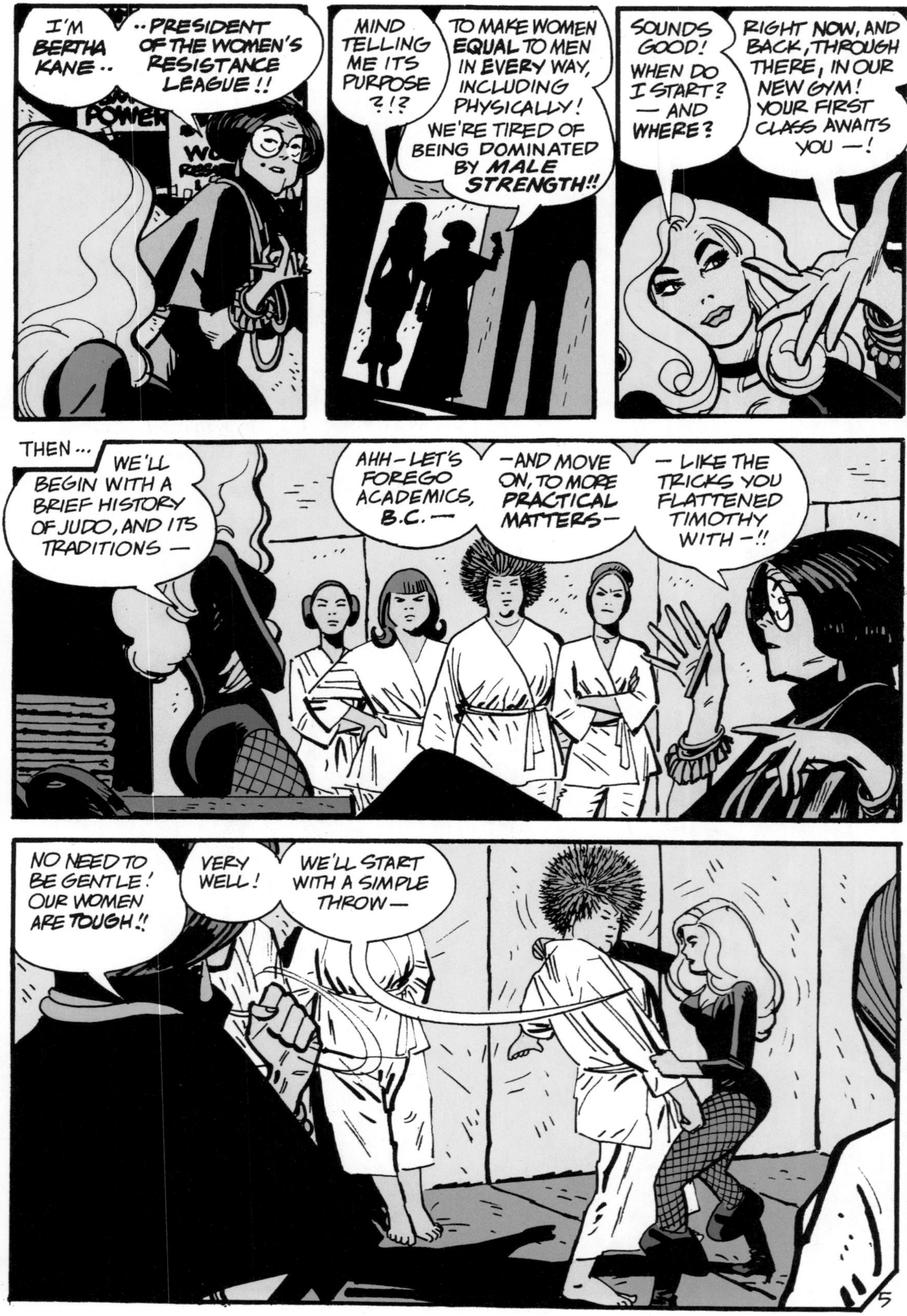
I'M BERTHA KANE..
..PRESIDENT OF THE WOMEN'S RESISTANCE LEAGUE !!
MIND TELLING ME ITS PURPOSE ?!?
TO MAKE WOMEN EQUAL TO MEN IN EVERY WAY, INCLUDING PHYSICALLY! WE'RE TIRED OF BEING DOMINATED BY MALE STRENGTH!!
SOUNDS GOOD! WHEN DO I START? — AND WHERE?
RIGHT NOW, AND BACK, THROUGH THERE, IN OUR NEW GYM! YOUR FIRST CLASS AWAITS YOU —!
THEN...
WE'LL BEGIN WITH A BRIEF HISTORY OF JUDO, AND ITS TRADITIONS —
AHH — LET'S FOREGO ACADEMICS, B.C. —
—AND MOVE ON, TO MORE PRACTICAL MATTERS—
— LIKE THE TRICKS YOU FLATTENED TIMOTHY WITH —!!
NO NEED TO BE GENTLE! OUR WOMEN ARE TOUGH!!
VERY WELL!
WE'LL START WITH A SIMPLE THROW —
5

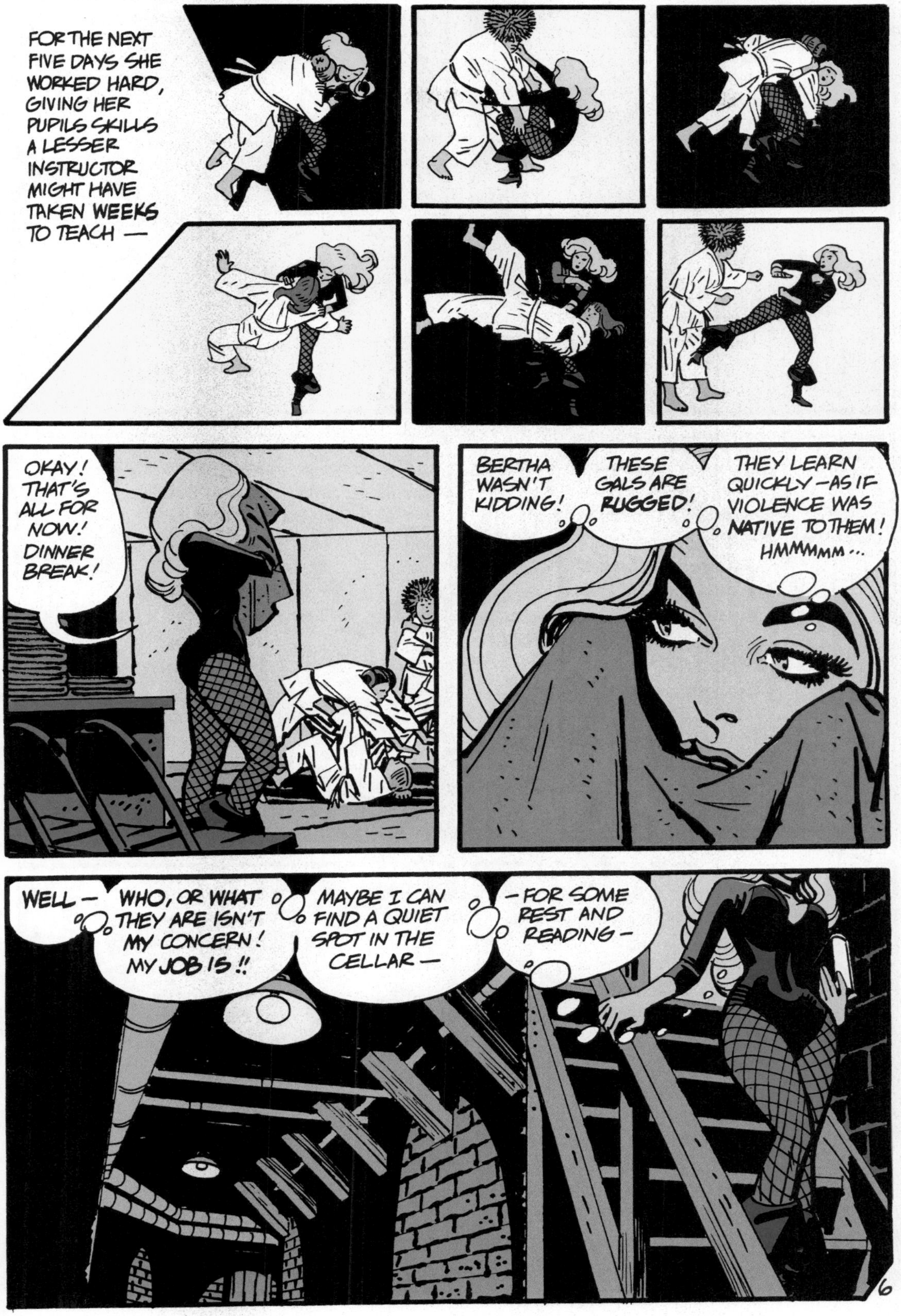
FOR THE NEXT FIVE DAYS SHE WORKED HARD, GIVING HER PUPILS SKILLS A LESSER INSTRUCTOR MIGHT HAVE TAKEN WEEKS TO TEACH —
OKAY! THAT'S ALL FOR NOW! DINNER BREAK!
BERTHA WASN'T KIDDING!
THESE GALS ARE RUGGED!
THEY LEARN QUICKLY — AS IF VIOLENCE WAS NATIVE TO THEM! HMMMMM...
WELL —
WHO, OR WHAT THEY ARE ISN'T MY CONCERN! MY JOB IS!!
MAYBE I CAN FIND A QUIET SPOT IN THE CELLAR —
— FOR SOME REST AND READING —
6

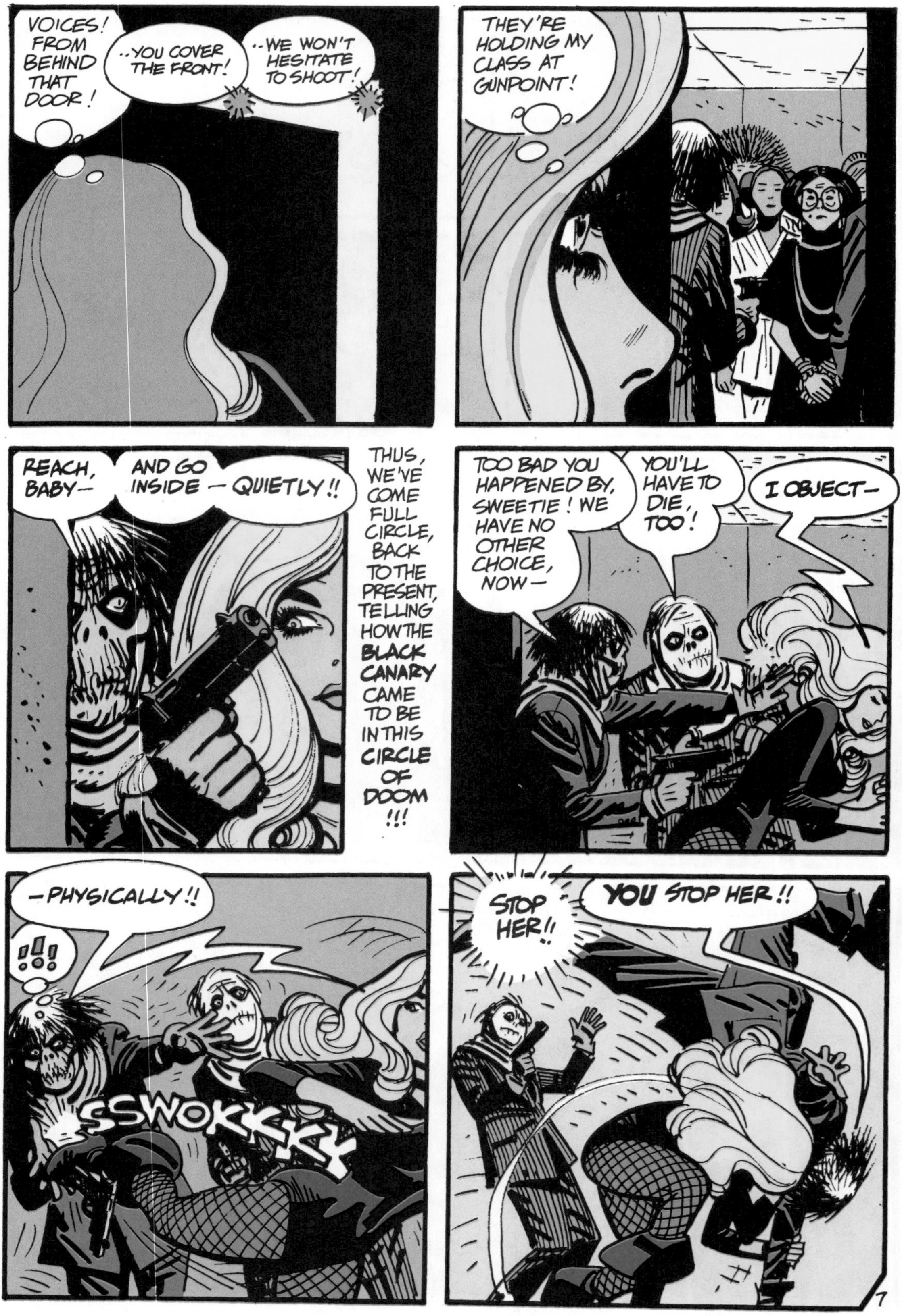
VOICES! FROM BEHIND THAT DOOR!
..YOU COVER THE FRONT!
..WE WON'T HESITATE TO SHOOT!
THEY'RE HOLDING MY CLASS AT GUNPOINT!
REACH, BABY—
AND GO INSIDE — QUIETLY!!
THUS, WE'VE COME FULL CIRCLE, BACK TO THE PRESENT, TELLING HOW THE BLACK CANARY CAME TO BE IN THIS CIRCLE OF DOOM!!!
TOO BAD YOU HAPPENED BY, SWEETIE! WE HAVE NO OTHER CHOICE, NOW—
YOU'LL HAVE TO DIE, TOO!
I OBJECT—
—PHYSICALLY!!
!!!
SSWOKKKY
STOP HER!!
YOU STOP HER!!
7

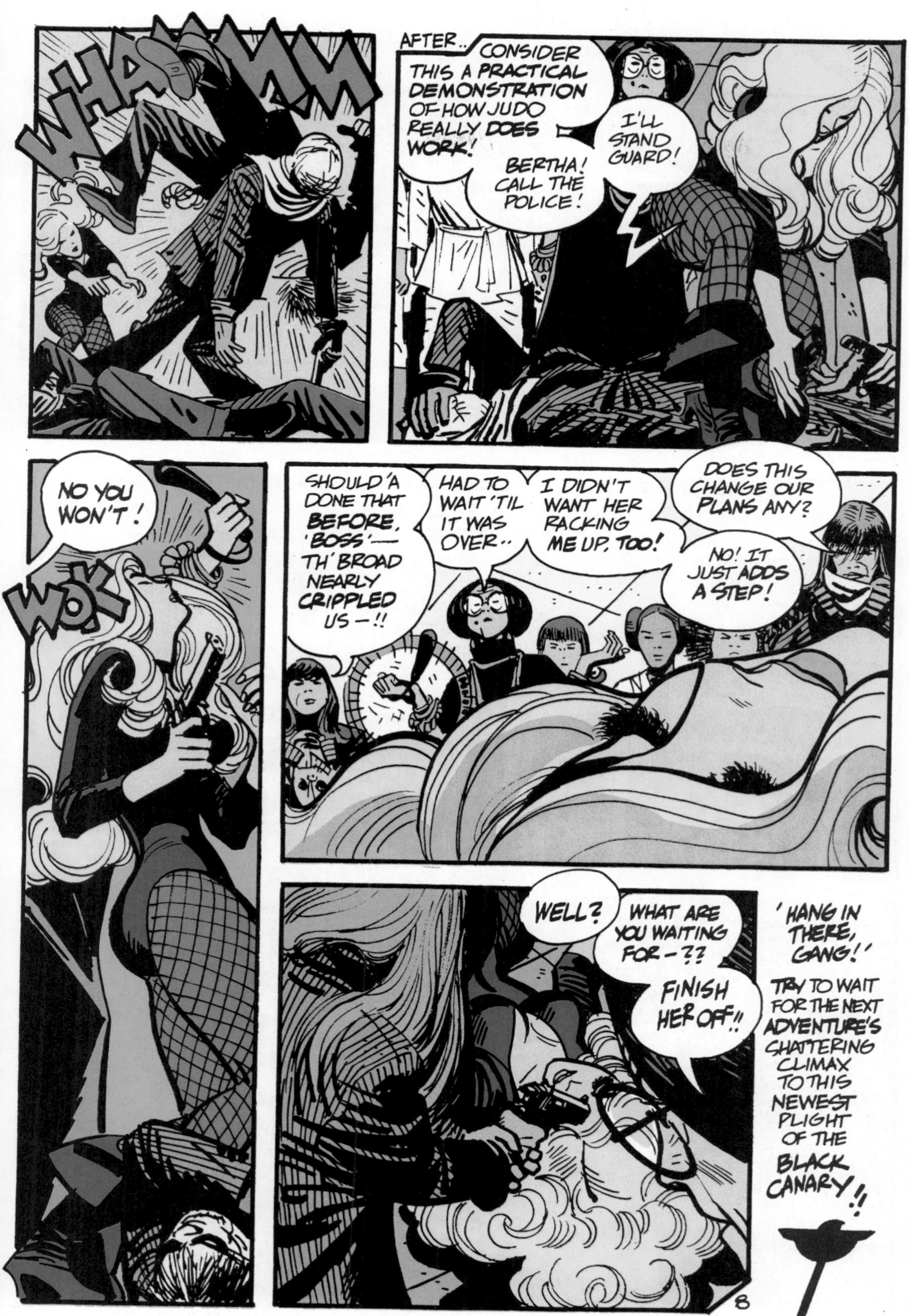
WHAMMM
AFTER..
CONSIDER THIS A PRACTICAL DEMONSTRATION OF HOW JUDO REALLY DOES WORK!
BERTHA! CALL THE POLICE!
I'LL STAND GUARD!
NO YOU WON'T!
WOK
SHOULD'A DONE THAT BEFORE, 'BOSS'— TH' BROAD NEARLY CRIPPLED US—!!
HAD TO WAIT 'TIL IT WAS OVER..
I DIDN'T WANT HER RACKING ME UP, TOO!
DOES THIS CHANGE OUR PLANS ANY?
NO! IT JUST ADDS A STEP!
WELL?
WHAT ARE YOU WAITING FOR—??
FINISH HER OFF!!
8
'HANG IN THERE, GANG!'
TRY TO WAIT FOR THE NEXT ADVENTURE'S SHATTERING CLIMAX TO THIS NEWEST PLIGHT OF THE BLACK CANARY!!

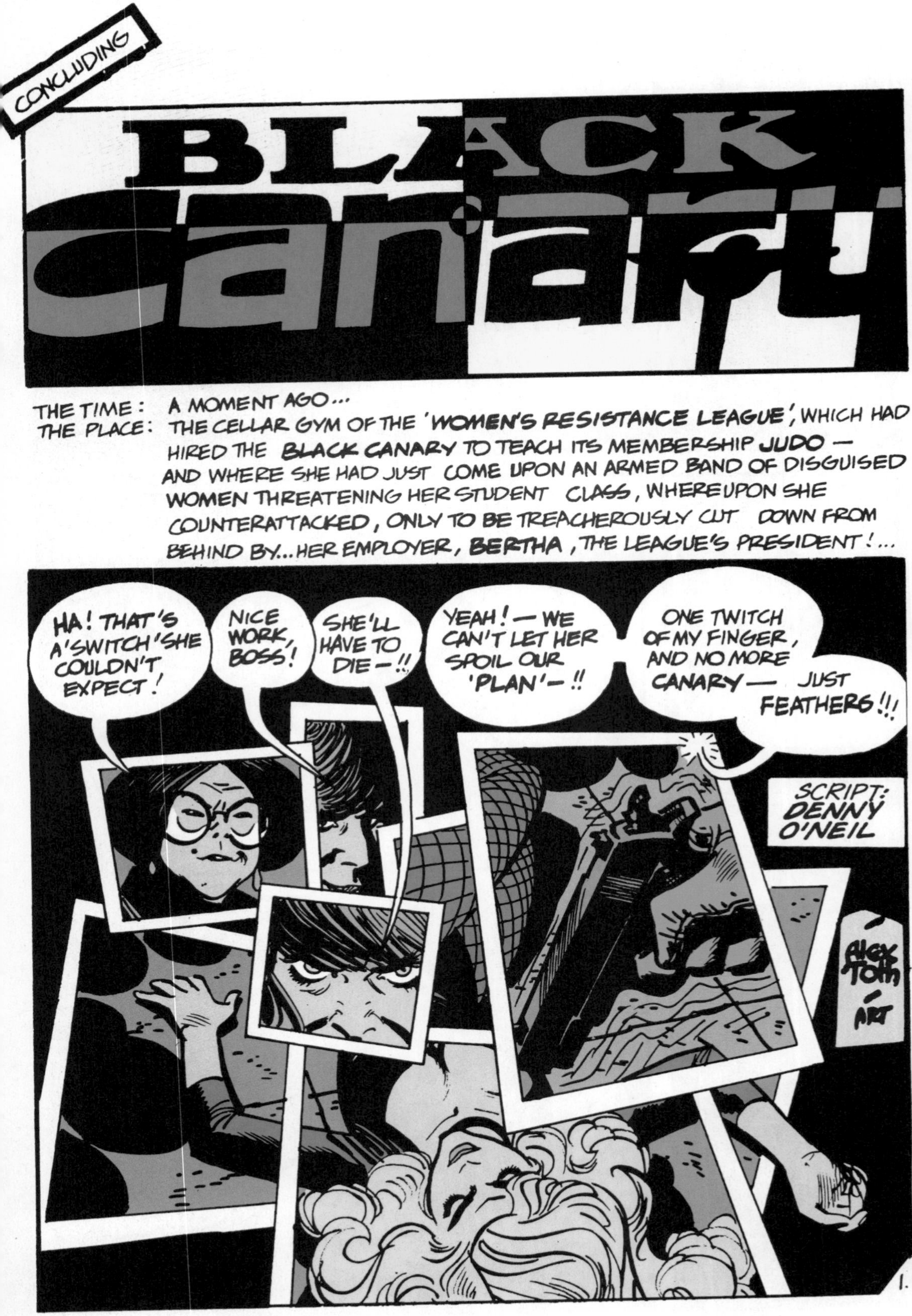
CONCLUDING
BLACK CANARY
THE TIME: A MOMENT AGO...
THE PLACE: THE CELLAR GYM OF THE 'WOMEN'S RESISTANCE LEAGUE', WHICH HAD HIRED THE BLACK CANARY TO TEACH ITS MEMBERSHIP JUDO — AND WHERE SHE HAD JUST COME UPON AN ARMED BAND OF DISGUISED WOMEN THREATENING HER STUDENT CLASS, WHEREUPON SHE COUNTERATTACKED, ONLY TO BE TREACHEROUSLY CUT DOWN FROM BEHIND BY... HER EMPLOYER, BERTHA, THE LEAGUE'S PRESIDENT!...
HA! THAT'S A 'SWITCH' SHE COULDN'T EXPECT!
NICE WORK, BOSS!
SHE'LL HAVE TO DIE—!!
YEAH! — WE CAN'T LET HER SPOIL OUR 'PLAN'—!!
ONE TWITCH OF MY FINGER, AND NO MORE CANARY — JUST FEATHERS!!!
SCRIPT: DENNY O'NEIL
ALEX TOTH — ART
1.

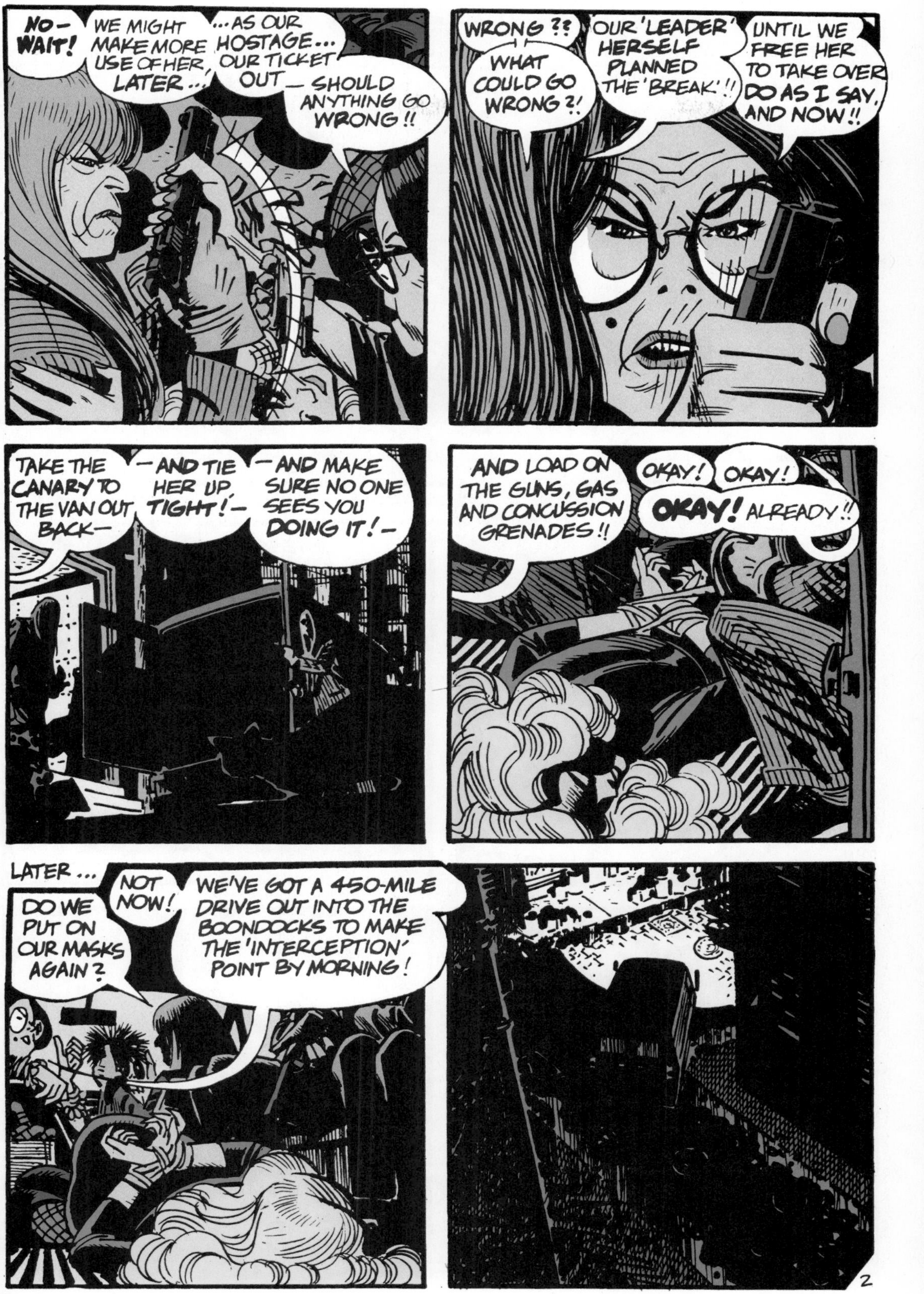
NO— WAIT!
WE MIGHT MAKE MORE USE OF HER, LATER...
...AS OUR HOSTAGE... OUR TICKET OUT
— SHOULD ANYTHING GO WRONG!!
WRONG ??
WHAT COULD GO WRONG?!
OUR 'LEADER' HERSELF PLANNED THE 'BREAK'!!
UNTIL WE FREE HER TO TAKE OVER DO AS I SAY, AND NOW!!
TAKE THE CANARY TO THE VAN OUT BACK—
—AND TIE HER UP, TIGHT!—
—AND MAKE SURE NO ONE SEES YOU DOING IT!—
AND LOAD ON THE GUNS, GAS AND CONCUSSION GRENADES!!
OKAY! OKAY!
OKAY! ALREADY!!
LATER...
DO WE PUT ON OUR MASKS AGAIN?
NOT NOW!
WE'VE GOT A 450-MILE DRIVE OUT INTO THE BOONDOCKS TO MAKE THE 'INTERCEPTION' POINT BY MORNING!
2

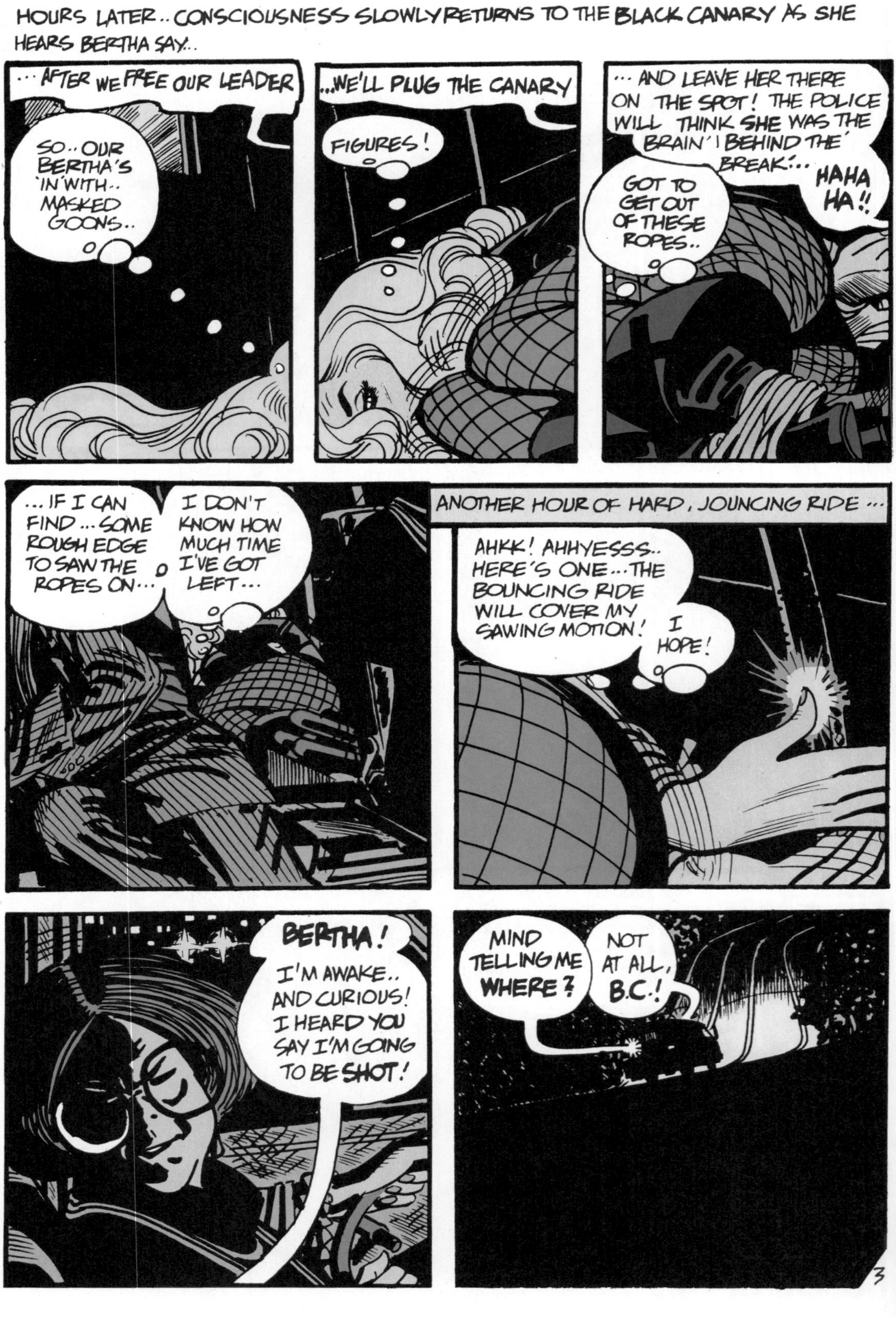
HOURS LATER.. CONSCIOUSNESS SLOWLY RETURNS TO THE BLACK CANARY AS SHE HEARS BERTHA SAY:..
... AFTER WE FREE OUR LEADER
SO.. OUR BERTHA'S 'IN' WITH.. MASKED GOONS..
...WE'LL PLUG THE CANARY
FIGURES!
... AND LEAVE HER THERE ON THE SPOT! THE POLICE WILL THINK SHE WAS THE 'BRAIN' BEHIND THE BREAK!..
HAHA HA!!
GOT TO GET OUT OF THESE ROPES..
... IF I CAN FIND ... SOME ROUGH EDGE TO SAW THE ROPES ON...
I DON'T KNOW HOW MUCH TIME I'VE GOT LEFT...
ANOTHER HOUR OF HARD, JOUNCING RIDE ...
AHKK! AHHYESSS.. HERE'S ONE... THE BOUNCING RIDE WILL COVER MY SAWING MOTION!
I HOPE!
BERTHA! I'M AWAKE.. AND CURIOUS! I HEARD YOU SAY I'M GOING TO BE SHOT!
MIND TELLING ME WHERE?
NOT AT ALL, B.C.!
3

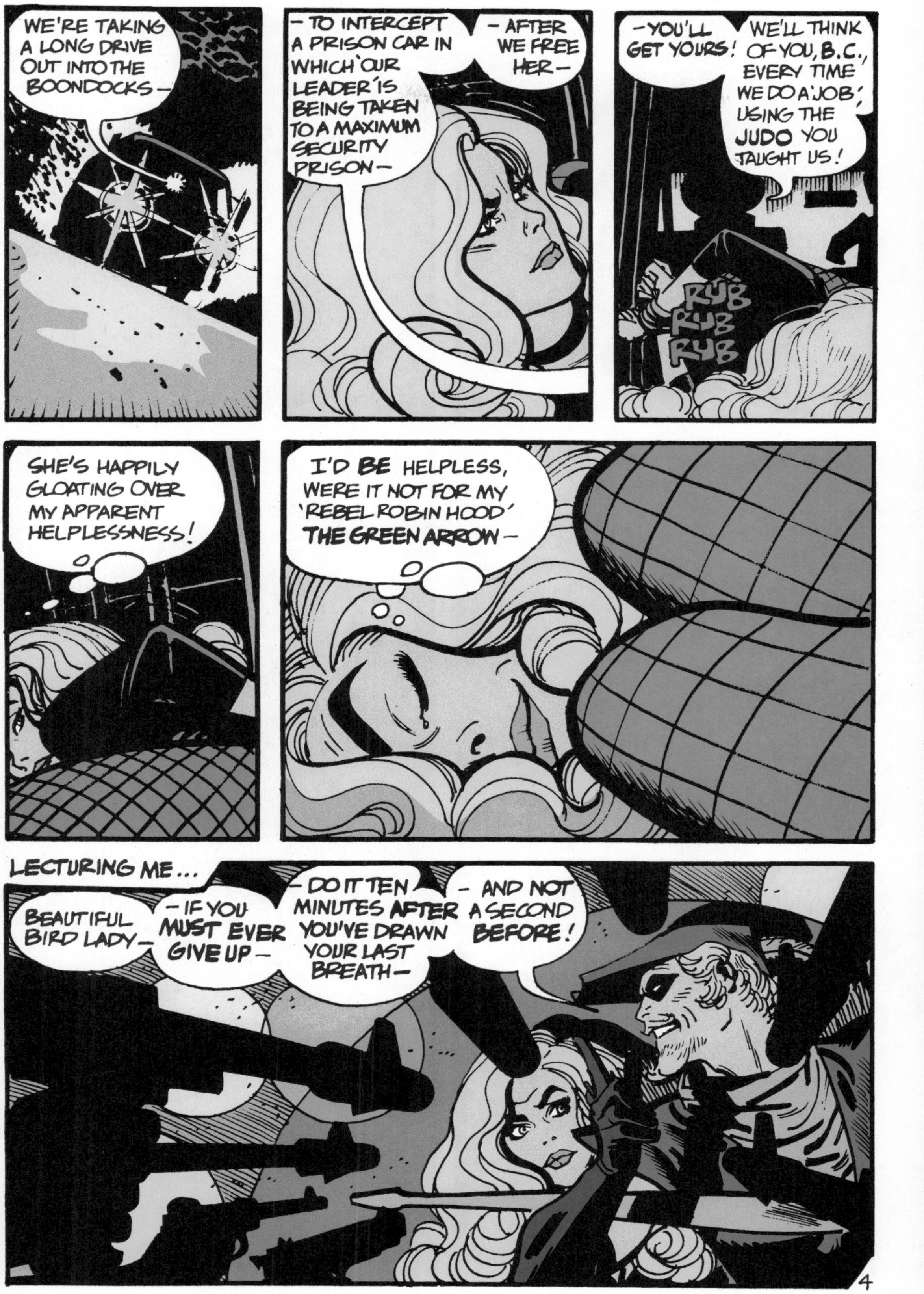
WE'RE TAKING A LONG DRIVE OUT INTO THE BOONDOCKS—
— TO INTERCEPT A PRISON CAR IN WHICH 'OUR LEADER' IS BEING TAKEN TO A MAXIMUM SECURITY PRISON—
— AFTER WE FREE HER—
— YOU'LL GET YOURS!
WE'LL THINK OF YOU, B.C., EVERY TIME WE DO A 'JOB', USING THE JUDO YOU TAUGHT US!
RUB RUB RUB
SHE'S HAPPILY GLOATING OVER MY APPARENT HELPLESSNESS!
I'D BE HELPLESS, WERE IT NOT FOR MY 'REBEL ROBIN HOOD' THE GREEN ARROW—
LECTURING ME...
BEAUTIFUL BIRD LADY—
— IF YOU MUST EVER GIVE UP—
— DO IT TEN MINUTES AFTER YOU'VE DRAWN YOUR LAST BREATH—
— AND NOT A SECOND BEFORE!
4

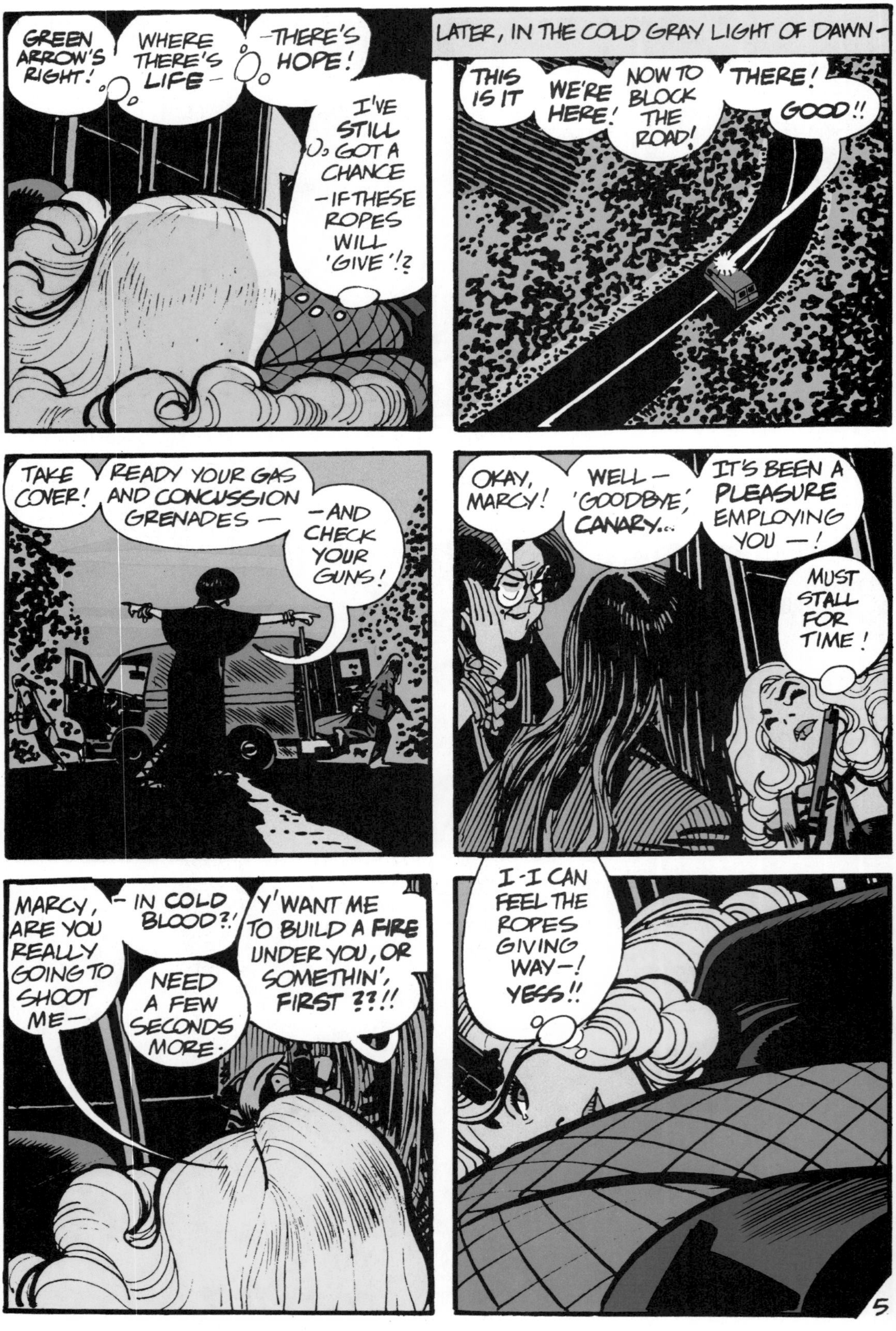
GREEN ARROW'S RIGHT!
WHERE THERE'S LIFE —
— THERE'S HOPE!
I'VE STILL GOT A CHANCE — IF THESE ROPES WILL 'GIVE'!?
LATER, IN THE COLD GRAY LIGHT OF DAWN —
THIS IS IT
WE'RE HERE!
NOW TO BLOCK THE ROAD!
THERE!
GOOD!!
TAKE COVER!
READY YOUR GAS AND CONCUSSION GRENADES —
— AND CHECK YOUR GUNS!
OKAY, MARCY!
WELL — 'GOODBYE,' CANARY...
IT'S BEEN A PLEASURE EMPLOYING YOU —!
MUST STALL FOR TIME!
MARCY, ARE YOU REALLY GOING TO SHOOT ME —
— IN COLD BLOOD?!
NEED A FEW SECONDS MORE.
Y'WANT ME TO BUILD A FIRE UNDER YOU, OR SOMETHIN', FIRST ??!!
I-I CAN FEEL THE ROPES GIVING WAY —! YESS!!
5

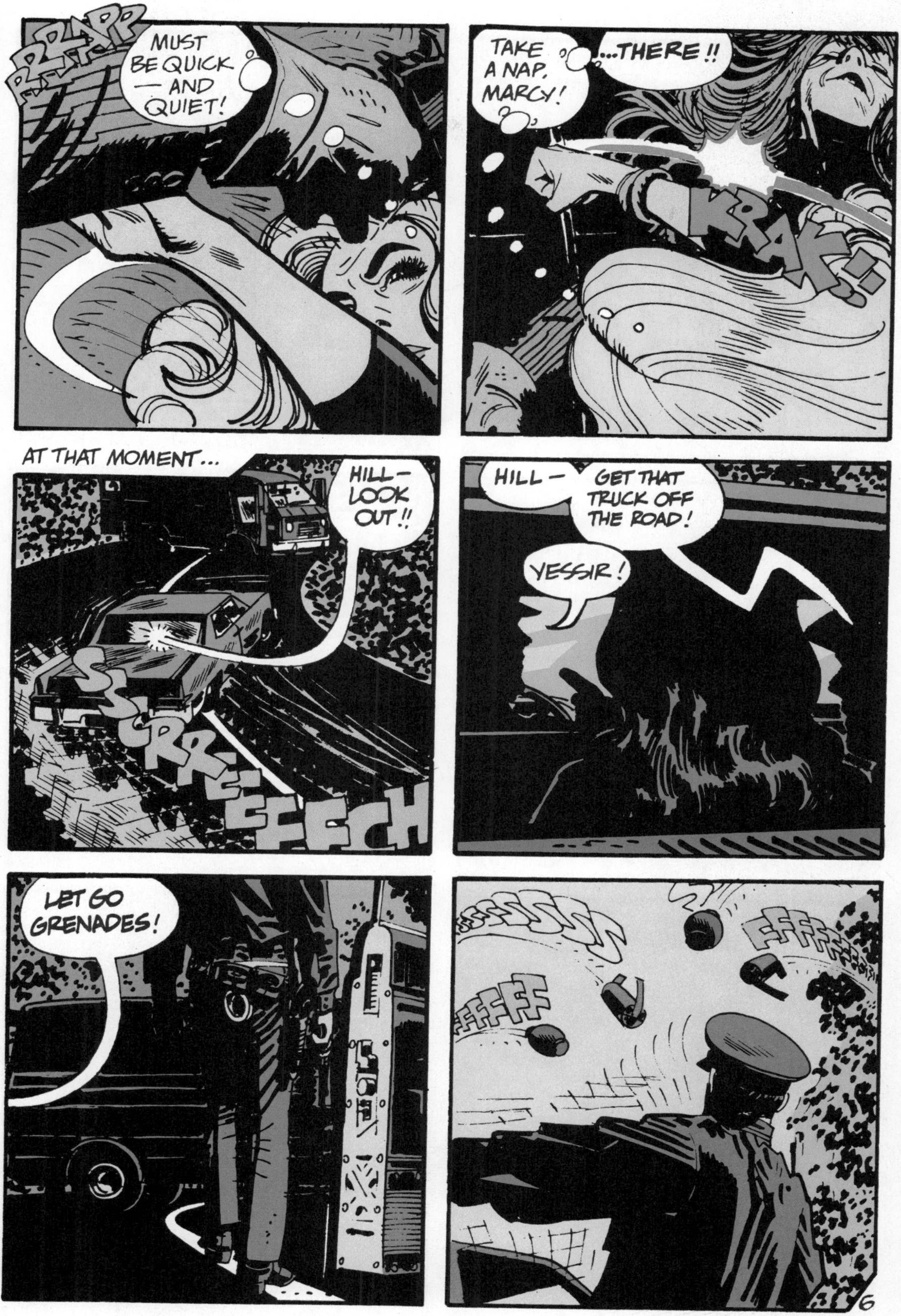
PRRAPP
MUST BE QUICK — AND QUIET!
TAKE A NAP, MARCY!
...THERE!!
KRAK!!
AT THAT MOMENT...
HILL— LOOK OUT!!
SSCRREEEECH
HILL—
GET THAT TRUCK OFF THE ROAD!
YESSIR!
LET GO GRENADES!
6

GAS AND CONCUSSION GRENADES ERUPT...

WSHUMPFF!

BERTHA'S BEGUN THE ATTACK!

SHE'LL PULL IT OFF, TOO —

— UNLESS —

— I SMASH UP HER AMBUSH PARTY —!!

VVNRRBOOMM!

NOW BACK TO BERTHA!

YIEEEEE RUN!!

RRIPPP

KRRAASHH

KKZTAKI!

SHE'S AT THE CAR —

GOT TO MOVE FAST AND HARD!

YOU, IN THE CAR! SEND OUT YOUR PRISONER, NOW, OR YOU'RE A CORPSE!

7

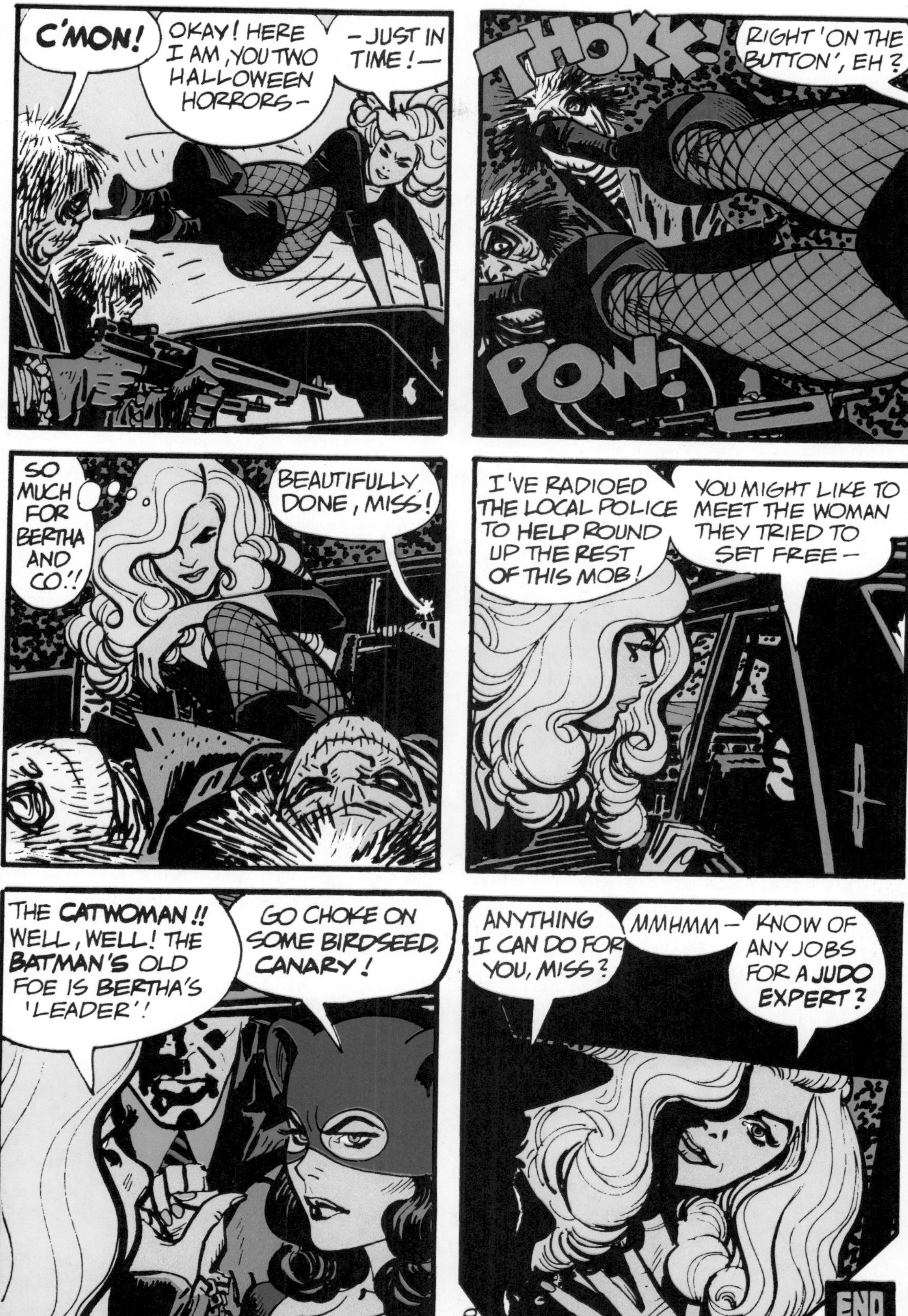
C'MON!
OKAY! HERE I AM, YOU TWO HALLOWEEN HORRORS -
- JUST IN TIME! -
THOKK!
RIGHT 'ON THE BUTTON', EH?
PON!
SO MUCH FOR BERTHA AND CO.!!
BEAUTIFULLY DONE, MISS!
I'VE RADIOED THE LOCAL POLICE TO HELP ROUND UP THE REST OF THIS MOB!
YOU MIGHT LIKE TO MEET THE WOMAN THEY TRIED TO SET FREE -
THE CATWOMAN!! WELL, WELL! THE BATMAN'S OLD FOE IS BERTHA'S 'LEADER'!
GO CHOKE ON SOME BIRDSEED, CANARY!
ANYTHING I CAN DO FOR YOU, MISS?
MMHMM -
KNOW OF ANY JOBS FOR A JUDO EXPERT?
END

ROBERT KANIGHER

Born on June 18, 1915, Robert Kanigher has long been recognized as one of the most prolific and innovative writers and editors in the comic book field. After writing for magazines, theater, and radio during the 1930s, he began his comics career at Fox Features Syndicate in 1940, working on such features as Blue Beetle, Samson, and the Bouncer. Hired as a scripter by DC Comics in 1946, Kanigher was quickly promoted to editor and given the responsibility of editing and scripting the iconic character Wonder Woman, whose creator and writer, William Moulton Marston, had recently died. More assignments followed, and over the next four decades Kanigher would eventually write stories for nearly every major DC character in addition to creating many new ones.

In 1952, Kanigher became the editor on DC's four main war titles (*Our Army at War*, *Our Fighting Forces*, *All-American Men of War*, and *Star Spangled War Stories*). His run on these books—which included the introduction of Sgt. Rock, Enemy Ace, the Unknown Soldier, and the Haunted Tank—would become legendary. Kanigher largely retired from editing in 1968, but over the next 20 years he continued to script Sgt. Rock, the Haunted Tank, and countless other features in nearly every genre of the medium, ensuring his legacy as one of the most productive comic book writers ever to work in the industry. He passed away on May 6, 2002.

GARDNER FOX

Born in 1911 in Brooklyn, New York, Gardner Fox was probably the single most imaginative and productive writer in the Golden Age of comics. In the 1940s, he created or co-created dozens of long-running features for DC Comics, including the Flash, Hawkman, the Sandman, and Doctor Fate, as well as penning most of the adventures of comics' first super-team, the Justice Society of America. He was also the second person to script Batman, beginning somewhere around the Dark Knight Detective's third story. For other companies over the years, Fox also wrote Skyman, the Face, Jet Powers, Dr. Strange, Doc Savage, and many others—including Crom the Barbarian, the first sword-and-sorcery series in comics. Following the revival in the late 1950s of the superhero genre, Fox assembled Earth's Mightiest Heroes once more and scripted an unbroken 65-issue run of *Justice League of America*. Though he produced thousands of other scripts and wrote over 100 books, it is perhaps this body of work for which he is best known. Fox passed away in 1986.

DENNIS O'NEIL

Dennis O'Neil began his career as a comic book writer in 1965 at Charlton, where then-editor Dick Giordano assigned him to several features. When Giordano moved to DC Comics, O'Neil soon followed. Once there, he scripted several series for Giordano and Julius Schwartz, quickly becoming one of the most respected writers in comics. O'Neil earned a reputation for being able to "revamp" such characters as Superman, Green Lantern, Captain Marvel—and Batman, whom O'Neil (with the help of Neal Adams and Giordano) brought back to his roots as a dark, mysterious, gothic avenger. Besides being the most important Batman writer of the 1970s, O'Neil also served as an editor at both Marvel and DC. After a long tenure as group editor for the Batman line of titles, he retired from editing in 2000 and returned to freelance writing. O'Neil passed away on June 11, 2020.

CARMINE INFANTINO

The man most closely associated with the Silver Age Flash, Carmine Infantino began working in comics in the mid-1940s as the artist on such characters as Green Lantern, Black Canary, Ghost Patrol...and the original Golden Age Flash. Infantino lent his unique style to a variety of superhero, supernatural, and Western features throughout the 1950s, until he was tapped to pencil the 1956 revival of the Flash. While continuing to pencil the Flash series, he also provided art for other strips, including Batman, the Elongated Man, and Adam Strange. Infantino became DC's editorial director in 1967 and, later, its publisher before he returned to freelancing in 1976. After that he pencilled and inked numerous features, including the *Batman* newspaper strip, *Green Lantern Corps*, and *Danger Trail*. Infantino passed away in 2013 at the age of 87.

MURPHY ANDERSON

Heavily influenced by artists Lou Fine and Will Eisner, Murphy Anderson entered the comics arena in 1944 as an artist for Fiction House. He took over the *Buck Rogers* comic strip for three years beginning in 1947, and in 1950 he began his lifelong association with DC Comics, pulling double duty as both a full illustrator (of the Atomic Knights and Hawkman) and an inker over other artists' pencil work (Adam Strange, Batman, Superman). Later in his career, Anderson ran Murphy Anderson Visual Concepts, a publishers' support service company. He passed away in 2015.

ALEX TOTH

Born in 1928, artist Alex Toth received his first professional assignment at the age of 15. He began working for DC Comics (drawing Dr. Mid-Nite, Green Lantern, Johnny Thunder, and assorted Western and science fiction tales) almost immediately after his graduation in 1947 from New York's High School of Industrial Art. Toth, whose style was highly influenced by newspaper strip illustrators such as Milton Caniff and Hal Foster, quickly established a reputation for excellence among his peers, and over the years his work earned him wide recognition as one of the greatest visual storytellers ever to work in the comics medium. In the course of his career he contributed work to a host of publishers, including Marvel, Standard, Dell, Whitman, Western, and Warren, and in 1964 he began a long association with the Hanna-Barbera animation studio, where he designed such cartoon characters as Space Ghost and the Super Friends. Though animation dominated the latter half of his career, Toth continued to create comics masterpieces throughout his life. He died at his drawing table on May 27, 2006.

JOE GIELLA

Joe Giella began his long career as a comic book artist in the 1940s, working for Hillman Publications and for Timely, the company that was later to become Marvel Comics. Giella came to DC in 1951 and over the next three decades worked predominantly as an inker, lending his clean, tight line to thousands of pencilled pages and to every major character the company published. During the 1960s, at the height of the TV-fueled "Batmania," Giella pencilled and inked the daily *Batman* newspaper strip. He illustrated the syndicated *Mary Worth* feature until his retirement in 2016.

FRANK GIACOIA

Born in Italy in 1925, Frank Giacoia came to the United States at the age of seven. Trained in the Chesler and Iger shops during the early 1940s, Giacoia went on to become one of comicdom's most prolific inkers, with a career spanning five decades. His inks have adorned stories of nearly every major comic book character from the Big Two publishers, including Batman, Superman, the Flash, Captain America, and the Fantastic Four. He passed away in 1989.

BERNARD SACHS

For nearly 20 years, Bernard Sachs was one of DC Comics' unsung heroes—a solid, dependable inker who tirelessly embellished the pencils of many of the artists in editor Julius Schwartz's stable, among them Mike Sekowsky, Gil Kane, and Carmine Infantino. Sachs began his comics career in the 1940s working for Quality and, later, for Hillman, where he pencilled and inked such features as Airboy and the Heap. Like Fox and Schwartz, Sachs could lay claim to having worked on both the Justice Society (1948-1951) and the Justice League (1960-1965) of America. In 1965 he left comics to work for Grey Advertising, where he drew storyboards and layouts for two decades before retiring in 1986. Sachs passed away in 1998.